Late Merovingian France

Manchester Medieval Sources Series

series adviser Janet L. Nelson

This series aims to meet a growing need amongst students and teachers of medieval history for translations of key sources that are directly useable in students' own work. It provides texts central to medieval studies courses and will focus upon the diverse cultural and social as well as political conditions that affected the functioning of all levels of medieval society. The basic premise of the new series is that translations must be accompanied by sufficient introductory and explanatory material, and each volume, therefore, includes a comprehensive guide to the sources' interpretation, including discussion of critical linguistic problems and an assessment of the most recent research on the topics being covered.

already published in the series

Janet L. Nelson *The Annals of St-Bertin: ninth-century histories, volume I*

Timothy Reuter *The Annals of Fulda: ninth-century histories, volume II*

Chris Given-Wilson *Chronicles of the Revolution, 1397–1400: the reign of Richard II*

R. N. Swanson *Catholic England: faith, religion and observance before the Reformation*

Rosemary Horrox *The Black Death*

John Edwards *The Jews in western Europe, 1400–1600*

Jennifer Ward *Women of the English nobility and gentry, 1066–1500*

P. J. Goldberg *Women in England, c. 1275–1525*

LATE MEROVINGIAN FRANCE

HISTORY AND HAGIOGRAPHY
640–720

by Paul Fouracre *and* Richard A. Gerberding

Manchester University Press
Manchester and New York

distributed exclusively in the USA and Canada by St. Martin's Press

Copyright © Paul Fouracre and Richard A. Gerberding 1996

Published by Manchester University Press
Oxford Road, Manchester M13 9NR, UK
and Room 400, 175 Fifth Avenue, New York, NY 10010, USA

Distributed exclusively in the USA and Canada
by St. Martin's Press, Inc., 175 Fifth Avenue, New York, NY 10010, USA

British Library Cataloguing-in-Publication Data
A catalogue record for this book is available from the British Library

Library of Congress Cataloging-in-Publication Data
Late Merovingian France : history and hagiography, 640-720 /
    by Paul Fouracre and Richard A. Gerberding.
             p. cm. — (Manchester medieval sources series)
    Includes bibliographical references.
    ISBN 0-7190-4790-0. — ISBN 0-7190-4791-9 (alk. paper)
        1. Merovingians—France—History. 2. France—History—To 987—Sources.
    3. Christian hagiography. 4. Church history—Middle Ages, 600-1500
    —Historiography. I. Fouracre, Paul. II. Gerberding, Richard A. III. Series
    DA64.7.L38   1996
    944'.013—dc20   95-21908

ISBN 0 7190 4790 0 *hardback*
ISBN 0 7190 4791 9 *paperback*

First published 1996

00 99 98 97 96   10 9 8 7 6 5 4 3 2 1

Typeset in Monotype Bell
by Koinonia Ltd, Manchester
Printed in Great Britain
by Bell & Bain Ltd, Glasgow

For our families: Nickie, George, Joanna, Jim, Dorothy and Louise

Contents

Foreword

Hagiography is a difficult genre for historians, but it is also the genre in most plentiful supply for the notoriously under-documented later Merovingian period. Both the genre and the period have recently been undergoing a revival of scholarly interest and Paul Fouracre and Richard Gerberding, connoisseurs of both, have been at the forefront of the revival. In *History and Hagiography* their skilled readings of the hagiographical evidence yield a plausible reconstruction of what has hitherto often been seen as a dauntingly repellant age of economic decline and political chaos. Later Merovingian Francia emerges here as a world with its own structures, values and rhythms of change – distinctively interesting, not just as a prelude to the Carolingians, but on its own terms. Fouracre and Gerberding, far from skirting the methodological problems of their material, tackle them with zest, and invite readers to share the effort and the rewards. Language and structure are explored with rare finesse. Since much of the material translated here is relatively little known and has seldom been used in teaching, this book will be indispensable to scholars as well as students, offering new approaches to an exceptionally interesting period.

Janet L. Nelson

Preface

Two teachers of medieval history, one on each side of the Atlantic, have planned and written this book in the hope that it will make their chosen field of study, Merovingian history, accessible to a wider audience. The aim has been to present the essential sources for the period in a way which will allow us to demonstrate how its history can be constructed. To this end we have translated eight narrative texts which cover the eighty-year period 640-720, a time in which Merovingian Francia is often said to have been in political and economic decline. We hope to show that there is rather more to the period than that. Seven of our sources are contemporary, but one, the *Annales Mettenses Priores*, was written some eighty-five years after the period. We have included it as a kind of postscript which shows how Merovingian history would be rewritten by later generations, starting with the Carolingian denigration of the reputation of their royal predecessors.

Our central concern has been with a kind of political history. Much of what we say is about the texts themselves and about the identity of the people who figure in them. We spend much effort simply trying to ascertain all that can be known about a given subject, not an easy task in most cases. Only then do we fit the pieces into a jigsaw of political history, and this we do not because we think that political history is generally the most important or the only way of looking at the past, but because it best serves the purpose of drawing the behaviour and actions of our particular subjects into a coherent pattern. This pattern we have always attempted to shape in accordance with the conceptions of contemporaries rather than with those of historians. And we can do so because our Merovingian writers were themselves very much concerned with the political behaviour and the political relationships of the leading members of their society. By politics we certainly do not mean simply a narrative of the deeds of queens, kings, warriors, monks and bishops, although we shall have many delicious things to say about all of these, but rather an investigation into the way in which this early medieval society organised itself for political ends.

We have tried to keep our translations literal and our discussions explicit in order to show how our material can be used by the historian. Since our sources are frequently difficult to interpret, the Merovingian period has often been subject to some fairly heavy-handed historical analysis, much of which seeks to confirm preconceived ideas about 'Dark Age' disorder. To counter this we have taken pains to comment on each of our sources at length and in a way which will allow the reader to engage with matters such as their originality and reliability, as well as to understand the various interpretations which may be placed upon them. The introduction, in fact, consists of substantial discussions, of the historical background, of the Latin of the texts, and of methodology, hagiography and historiography. These are intended to explain the issues which will be encountered later when each source is discussed. For it is our experience as teachers that when scholars assume too high a level of prior knowledge in this area they tend to choke off the interest of the uninitiated. Though in planning our book like this we had the student reader in mind, when actually working on our translations and interpretations we found time and again that we had to advance our own views on matters either not previously considered in the secondary literature or in need of re-examination in the light of recent research. In consequence the book contains much material which will be of interest to scholars as well as to students. We hope that we have succeeded in writing in a way which will stimulate both audiences.

The work has been our intermittent occupation for the last seven years. We are both immensely grateful to colleagues and friends who have helped and encouraged us. In particular we should like to thank Marie Adams and Rupert Segar, whose kindness made our work together possible. The University of Alabama in Huntsville, Research Institute and Humanities Center, provided travel expenses over the years. Rosamond McKitterick, Janet Nelson and Ian Wood kindly commented on drafts of various chapters and were typically generous with their advice. Janet Nelson also made essential improvements in the translation of the *Passio Praejecti*. David Ganz gave invaluable help with questions of manuscripts. David d'Avray, Peter Christian, Cyril Edwards, Andrew Louth and Anthony Pryer all cast light on matters liturgical, dramatical, theological and musical, which allowed us to cloak our ignorance. Our sincere thanks are also due to Gerard Velay of the University Library in Montpellier for kindly sending us a photocopy of ms. Montpellier, H 55, and to William. M. Daly for making available John Cox's translations of the *Vita Balthildis* and the *Vita S. Geretrudis*.

As with all long-term projects, this one has produced many joys and frustrations for us both. At the end of it we are still good friends and sign this preface in the hope that our work will make other good friends for the study of Europe in the early Middle Ages.

Richard Gerberding,
Huntsville, Alabama

Paul Fouracre, London

Abbreviations

AASS—*Acta Sanctorum*

ASSOB—*Acta Sanctorum ordinis S. Benedicti*

Archiv—*Archiv der Gesellschaft für ältere deutsche Geschichtskunde*

BEDC—*Bibliothèque de l'Ecole des Chartes*

ChLA—*Chartae Latinae Antiquiores*

CLA—*Codices Latini Antiquiores*

DA—*Deutsches Archiv für Erforschung des Mittelalters*

MGH, Dipl.—*Monumental Germaniae Historica, Diplomata Imperii*

MGH, Epistolae—*Monumenta Germaniae Historica, Epistolae*

MGH, Leges—*Monumenta Germaniae Historica, Leges*

MGH, SS—*Monumenta Germaniae Historica, Scriptores*

MGH, SSRG—*Monumenta Germaniae Historica, Scriptores Rerum Germanicarum in usum scholarum*

MGH, SSRM—*Monumenta Germaniae Historica, Scriptores Rerum Merovingicarum*

MGH SSRL—*Monumenta Germaniae Historica, Scriptores Rerum Langobardicum et Italicarum*

MIÖG—*Mitteilungen de Instituts für österreichische Geschichtsforschung*

NA—*Neues Archiv der Gesellschaft für ältere deutsche Geschichtskunde*

PL—*Patrologica Latina*

Settimane di Studio—*Settimane di Studio del Centro Italiano di Studi sull'alto Medioevo (Spoleto)*

Introduction

The seventh century in its historical context

Peter Brown has described the Roman Empire as an exquisite border of lace sewn to the sackcloth of the hinterland around the shores of the Mediterranean.[1] The Roman Empire was an urban phenomenon. Where the Romans conquered, they either took over existing cities or built new ones, and it was in the cities that their culture flourished. The hinterlands produced; the cities consumed. The hinterlands worked; the cities ruled. The cities taxed; the hinterlands paid. The hinterlands remained largely as they were; the cities became Roman. And although land was the economic base of Roman life, the political use of land was filtered through the medium of the cities. The cities through the use of money, among other things, ruled through permanent bureaucracies, paid troops and aristocratic magistrates who had vast rural estates but who lived in the cities and were the guiding force of the urban culture.

Medieval culture, on the other hand, is not urban but rural. Medieval Europe, to be sure, had its urban centres, but they were generally small by Roman standards. By the seventh century they no longer housed Europe's rulers and their culture was not foreign to the hinterlands round about them. For the most part, they did not contain the dominant aristocracy, a permanent bureaucracy or an organised taxing structure, nor did they sponsor paid armies. In other words, they were no longer the medium between the wealth the land produced and the use of that wealth for political ends. Europe's political structure had come to sit upon the land directly and nothing was more fundamental to its political history. It is in the seventh century, the period of our study, that we can first see many important facets of the new politics.

So far we have used the rather abstract phrase 'political ends'. Let us be more specific; our sources certainly were. Seventh-century chroniclers and hagiographers had no great love of the abstract; for them the

1 P. Brown, *The World of late Antiquity* (New York, 1980), p. 12.

purpose of political power was contained in one concrete and comprehensible word: peace. Peace could be broken in two ways: from without, i.e. by the invasion of foreigners, or from within, i.e. by internal disputes of all sorts, ranging from local vendettas to larger-scale civil wars. And here we have the two basic political responsibilities of their kings: to keep foreign peoples out, usually by conquering them, and to settle internal disputes, usually through a judicial system, but if need be also with armies. Thus the fundamental political problem the seventh century faced was: how would society now keep the peace, given that the urban or Roman system had disappeared or was dying? Our sources provide the answer, or, better, answers, in that they let us see, however dimly, the new political, religious, economic and judicial systems which developed to this end. Two things are significant here. One, these systems developed using resources coming directly from agriculture to finance them; there was no other significant source. Two, they seem to have been rather effective and well adapted to their rural European environment, for they lasted a very, very long time.[2]

By the year 500 every part of what had been the Roman Empire in the West was now governed by barbarian kings. In the sixth century, in what has become modern France, Luxembourg and parts of modern Belgium and Germany, that is, the area which the Franks ruled, three kingdoms developed: Neustria, centred on the Seine–Oise valley around Paris, Burgundy, along the Rhône, and Austrasia, with its heart in the eastern Champagne and the Meuse and Moselle lands. These three carved up the land south of the Loire into various appanages and thus came to rule a vast area of former Roman territory. We shall refer to them by the term 'Francia' because their rulers were Frankish. This is the first point about the new politics: political life now revolved around the courts of the Frankish kings.

Although the political system which developed in the Frankish lands revolved around the royal courts, political power was in the hands of a rural hereditary class, which modern analysts sometimes refer to as a nobility, sometimes as an aristocracy. The mechanism it used to organise and to exercise political power on a scale larger than the local one was the royal court, headed by a king, who was not, and obviously could not be, one of their number. Much fine scholarship has carefully

---

2 See below, pp. 52–8, for further comment on the nature of Merovingian political culture. For a survey of that culture across early medieval Europe see P. Fouracre, 'Cultural Conformity and Social Conservativism in Early Medieval Europe', *History Workshop Journal*, 33 (1992), 159.

explained the nature of early medieval kingship,[3] but we can content ourselves with a few important observations. First and foremost, the king was different from the nobility; there was an unbridgeable gap between them. We find what can appear at first to be a remarkable commitment by the Franks to exclusive rule by their hereditary Merovingian kings. But this state of affairs obviously served to dissuade non-royal aspirants from breaking the peace in attempts to gain the throne. Modern descriptions of early medieval kings emphasise their hereditary legitimacy. Legitimacy, however, is a misleading word. The Frankish sources do not use it to describe their kings, probably because the authors, writing in Latin, were very aware of its base in the word for 'law' (*lex, legis*). The Merovingians' status was based not at all in anything as changeable or open to interpretation as law, but in their bodies; they were born royal. Rather than talk about a king's legitimacy, the sources, following their preference for the concrete rather than the abstract, will list his father and perhaps his grandfather. Aristocracy and nobility, likewise, are words not found in our sources. We would not expect to find 'aristocracy', since it is Greek, and to express the idea of nobility the sources use the adjective *nobile* (famous or excellent) modifying the word *genus* (high birth). Modern discussions juxtaposing a nobility which enjoyed its privileged position because of its lineage (*Geburtsadel*) against one which did so because of the functions or service it performed (*Dienstadel*) offer refinements not found in our sources. In the contemporary view, the aristocracy and the king both enjoyed their position by the right of birth.

By the seventh century the Franks had long since been Catholic Christians. In a system such as the Roman, all the urban characteristics mentoned above, and especially the cities' concentration of movable wealth, acted as mediating and stabilising mechanisms between the land which produced wealth and the rulers who used it. Without a flourishing urban culture, however, early medieval society had need of other institutions to perform the mediating functions, and to a large extent it was the Church which did so. The Church began to collect land very early on, in fact, three-quarters of the land the Church was ever to own was already in its hands by the seventh

3 Cf. J. M. Wallace-Hadrill, *Early Germanic Kingship in England and on the Continent* (Oxford, 1971); P. H. Sawyer and I. N. Wood (eds), *Early Medieval Kingship* (Leeds, 1971); and T. Mayer (ed.), *Das Königtum. Seine geistigen und rechtlichen Grundlagen. Vorträge und Forschungen*, 3, (Lindau and Konstanz, 1956).

century.[4] If for no other reason, then certainly because of its landed wealth, the seventh-century Frankish Church had become a very important part of the political system.

The seventh century has left us many written 'deeds', or charters, recording land transactions. Most of these charters concern ecclesiastical land in some way, because it was the Church which kept or copied them throughout the centuries. Nonetheless, the facts that written deeds survive at all from a period when every other form of written culture in Francia was in steep decline, that we can clearly see the Church involved in important land transactions, and that many of the charters are royal instruments, all underscore how important the documents originally were, and this in turn emphasises the important new political role of land and the Church's involvement in it.[5]

For centuries the Christian bishops had been assuming more and more of what had been secular governmental functions in the cities in all parts of the Empire. In Gaul in the fifth and sixth centuries, most bishops had been members of the Gallo-Roman senatorial aristocracy, often proud and erudite men, very used to acting as local rulers and judges.[6] A bishop's assumption of the judicial authority especially put him in competition with the count, the Frankish king's local representative.[7] We have from one of them, the sixth-century bishop and historian Gregory of Tours, gruesome details of the type of bitter struggle that could arise between bishop and count.[8] By our period, the later seventh century, most of Francia's bishops had become Frankish, that is, they were strongly connected by family or factions with the Frankish royal court. This was true even in the south, where the local Gaulish senatorial aristocracy had long controlled the

4 E. Lesne, Histoire de la propriété ecclésiastique en France, vol. 1, (Lille, 1910), pp. 143–94 and 453–4.

5 See the discussion of Merovingian charters below, pp. 28–30.

6 K. Stroheker, Der senatorische Adel im spätantiken Gallien (Tübingen, 1948, reprint Darmstadt, 1970), pp. 72–4; D. Claude, 'Die Bestellung der Bischöfe im merowingischen Reiche', Zeitschrift der Savigny-Stiftung für Rechtsgeschichte, 80, Kanonistische Abteilung, 49 (1963), 18; and P. Riché, 'Centres of Culture in Frankish Gaul between the 6th and the 9th Centuries', in his Instruction et vie religieuse dans le Haut Moyen-âge, (London, 1981), p. 227.

7 M. Heinzelmann, Bischofsherrschaft in Gallien. Zur Kontinuität römischer Führungsschichten vom 4. bis zum 7. Jahrhundert. Soziale, prosopographische und bildungsgeschichtliche Aspekte, Beihefte der Francia, 5 (Zurich, 1976), p. 182.

8 Gregory, Decem Libri Historiarum, V, 48–9, eds. B. Krusch and W. Levison, MGH, SSRM, I ed. alt. (Hanover, 1951), pp. 257–63 et passim.

episcopate.[9] By this time, too, the selection of a bishop depended on royal appointment.[10] In other words, in addition to their spiritual functions, bishops had begun to play an important part in the larger political system based on the royal court. It is important to note, however, that a bishop's strong connection with the court does not necessarily mean that the 'central government' was using him to exert its influence over his diocese. It could work the other way as well, that is, the local diocese could benefit if its bishop had connections and influence at court.[11] As in most parts of the political system, so too with the bishops, the lines formed were reciprocal, and the personal element was more important than the institutional one.

An institution even more responsive to the changing political require-ments than the dioscesan Church was the monastic one. Sixth-century Gaulish monasteries were largely urban and not dedicated to missionary effort. The foundations of the mid to late seventh century, however, tended to be outside the cities, and those influenced by a startling new religious enthusiasm from the British Isles gave themselves whole-heartedly to missionary work, preaching and converting in the world. The monasteries too became land-rich, and, since their number was not fixed by extant diocesan boundaries, they could and did spring up anywhere. As we shall see, this rapid growth of institutions had marked effects upon the development of hagiography in our period. Although it will not be until the eighth century that the abbots in the councils of the king carry more political weight than the bishops, the number of monasteries and their growing wealth in our period bear testimony to their increasing importance. Of some 550 monasteries we know to have existed in Gaul by the year 700, far more than half, about 320, had been founded within the preceding 100 years,[12] placing the

9 K.-F.Werner, 'Bedeutende Adelsfamilien im Reich Karls des Grossen. Ein personengeschichtlicher Beitrag zum Verhältnis von Königtum und Adel im frühen Mittelalter', in W. Braunfels (ed.), *Karl der Grosse*, vol. I (Düsseldorf, 1965), pp. 83–142; trans. T. Reuter: 'Important families in the Kingdom of Charlemagne', in T. Reuter (ed. and trans.), *The Medieval Nobility* (Amsterdam, 1978), pp.137–202. The career of Aunemund, bishop of Lyons, provides a clear illustration of the links between the southern bishops and the royal court. See below, pp. 177–9.

10 Claude, 'Die Bestellung', 19–26.

11 Claude, 'Die Bestellung', 3, and see G. Scheibelreiter, *Der Bischof in merowingischer Zeit, Veröffentlichungen des Instituts für Österreichische Geschichtsforschung*, 27 (Vienna, 1983) for a full discussion of the relationship between bishops and the royal courts in the seventh century.

12 H. Atsma, 'Les monastères urbains du nord de la Gaule', *Revue d'Histoire de l'Eglise de France*, 62 (1976), 168.

bulk of another important development squarely in the seventh century.

In this political (peace-keeping) system, based on a rural hereditary nobility supported directly by landed wealth, movable wealth in the form of money, or what the sources call 'treasure', still had a political role to play. There certainly was gold and silver about; the sources love to mention them. Up to the later seventh century, Francia had many royal and episcopal mints striking gold coins. Some thirteen centuries later we are still finding their coins in buried treasure hoards. As might be expected, it is at the top of the political structure that we can see the political uses of gold: tribute payments, gifts between kings, royal dowries and, presumably, rewards for military commanders. These all are obviously important, but exceptional, events in Frankish political life. Silver coins, on the other hand, could be used for smaller, more basic and more normal transactions of a local and agricultural nature, as well as for rewarding the mass of soldiers.[13] It was in our period that gold coins stopped being produced all together and the currency became a monometalic silver one.[14] The shift was due in part to the shortage of gold in the Western economy, but it also indicates the increasingly rural nature of society. The use of silver eased commercial activity in the countryside, as it was more suited to transactions on a smaller scale. Cattle and slaves should also be included in the category of movable wealth. The desire to acquire movables remained a very important factor in political behaviour throughout our period, although it was land which provided the resources needed to hang on to power in the long term.[15]

The splendid cultural life so evident at the courts of Charlemagne (768–814) and his son, Louis the Pious (814–43), forms the central part of the cultural awakening historians like to call the Carolingian Renaissance. The phrase perhaps unduly centres attention on the Carolingians, for the revival was part of a general European movement whose boundaries both geographically and temporally extended beyond the Carolingians' direct sphere of influence. Its immediate causes

13 See below, p. 31–2, 242.

14 P. Grierson and M. Blackburn, *Medieval European Coinage. With a Catalogue of the Coins in the Fitzwilliam Museum, Cambridge*, vol. I: *The Early Middle Ages (5th–10th Centuries)* (Cambridge, 1996), pp. 93–5.

15 On the part played by plunder and tribute in the political economy of the Carolingian age see T. Reuter, 'Plunder and Tribute in the Carolingian Empire', *Transactions of the Royal Historical Society*, 5th series, 35 (1985), and T. Reuter, 'The end of Carolingian military expansion', in P. Godman and R. Collins (eds.), *Charlemagne's Heir* (Oxford, 1990).

were certainly such things as the increase in travel and the exchange of ideas across Europe, from Northumberland to southern Italy,[16] as well as the emphasis on study and contemplation in the monastic life. But the underlying cause lay in the fact that northern Europe's new political system was developing an intellectual life that reflected its values, and in the fact that the system itself had matured to the point where it could effectively gather the financial resources to support intellectual activity. Once again it is no coincidence that it is in the late seventh century that we see the first glimmer of this nascent cultural movement. For example, the first surviving dated manuscript from the monastery at Luxeuil comes from 669,[17] the famous scriptorium at Echternach began production shortly before 700, and the earliest surviving manscripts from Corbie indicate that production also began there sometime before 700.[18] It was the seventh century as well which was the century *par excellence* for the production of saints' lives.

Before the Merovingian period Europe's most important cultural and political centres were in the south, in the cities around the Mediterranean. By the Carolingian age we find them in the north. The Arab depredations in Spain and Provence played a role in this extremely significant geographical shift, but of far more consequence is the simple fact that the land of northern Europe began to produce more agricultural wealth than land in the south, and political power and cultural leadership will usually migrate to the areas which can best support them.[19] Francia in the seventh century saw two important steps in this long-term political development. By about the year 567 we see the existence of what Eugen Ewig has termed the *Teilreiche*, or separate kingdoms.[20] The great political divisions of Gaul in the sixth century had split the country into varying numbers of pieces, with a Merovingian king at the head of each. By the seventh century, the

16 Riché, 'Centres of Culture', p. 232.

17 Ms New York, Pierpoint Morgan M-334. E. A. Lowe, *Codices Latini Antiquiores*, XI (Oxford, 1966) no. 1659, p. 23.

18 D. Ganz, *Corbie in the Carolingian Renaissance* Beihefte der *Francia*, 20 (Sigmaringen, 1990), pp. 38–40 and 124–6.

19 See K. Werner, 'Le rôle de l'aristocratie dans la christianisation du nord-est de la Gaule', *Revue d'Histoire de l'Eglise de France*, 62 (1976), 67, for a list of the relevant secondary literature which points to the rise of the area in north-east Francia economically just before Martel's take-over.

20 E. Ewig, 'Die fränkische Teilreiche im 7. Jahrhundert (613–714)', *Trierer Zeitschrift*, 22 (1953), 85 reprinted in Ewig, *Spätantikes und fränkisches Gallien. Gesammelte Schriften (1952–1973)*, vol. I, Beihefte der *Francia*, 3 (Munich, 1976), p. 172.

number of pieces had settled at three, as the separate Merovingian kingdoms of Neustria, Burgundy and Austrasia became established political entities. In the course of the century the number dwindled to two, and eventually to one as all Francia united in reasonably permanent fashion under one court. The older system reflected a less developed political organisation, which by the seventh century had become more established and better able to govern a wider area permanently as a single unit. In the course of the seventh century the nobility in the north-eastern kingdom, Austrasia, developed a strong enough political basis to assert their independence of the nobility around the kings of Neustria, based near Paris and Soissons. On two important occasions the Austrasians demanded their own king and established their own court when accidents of royal death and Merovingian succession had placed them under the king of Neustria. The seventh century also saw their 'capital', if we can use the word, shift farther away from Paris. It moved from Rheims to Metz.

The end of the seventh century saw the second and even more significant shift of the cultural and political centres away from the Mediterranean. The Pippinids, soon to be known as the Carolingians, became politically the most powerful family in all Francia, beginnng their take-over of Neustria in the 680s and 690s and completing it in the 720s. They were based not on the Seine and Oise, as the dominant families had been until then, but on the Meuse, the Moselle and the Rhine.

Culturally we can observe the same shift northwards that we can see in the political life of Francia. One good indication of this geographical shift in culture comes from an analysis of the seventh century's 320 new monastic foundations we spoke of, since it was in the monasteries that the new cultural life began. Of the 320 founded in the seventh century, only ninety were founded in the south, whereas the north of Gaul established 230 new houses.[21]

To review: the Merovingian period saw the important centres of Europe's political life shift from the cities to the countryside and consequently from the Mediterranean areas to the northern part of the continent. In Francia it is in the seventh century that we discern many important aspects of this underlying development: members of the Frankish elite increasingly filled the high ecclesiastical offices, the first surviving written records of land transactions appeared, monasteries developed rapidly, the minting of gold coins was replaced by the

21 Atsma, 'Les monastères', 168.

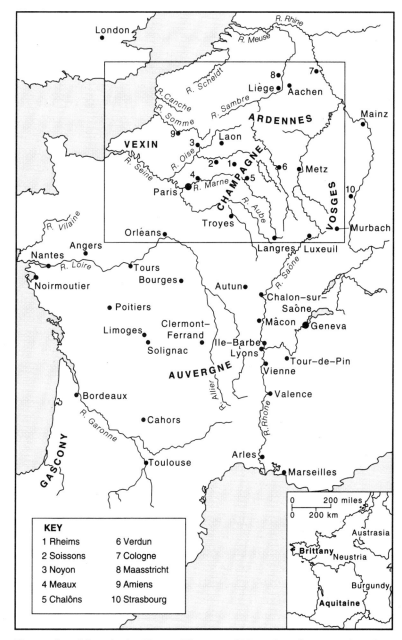

Figure 1 Late Merovingian France. The area of Neustria and western Austrasia within the 'box' is shown in greater detail in Figure 2.

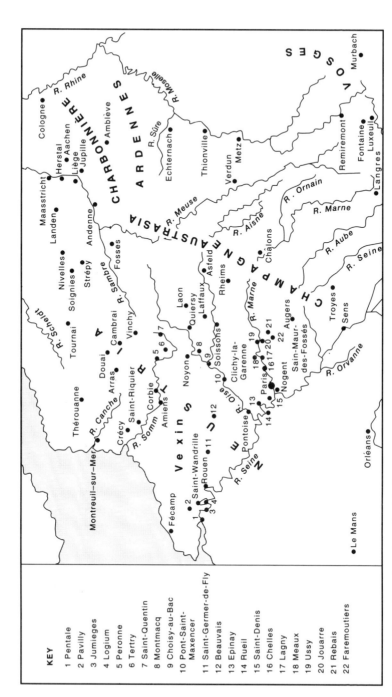

Figure 2 Neustria and western Austriasia

minting of silver ones, the cultural 'reawakening' began, the political system in the north-eastern realm matured and solidified, and, in the last decades of the century, that north-eastern area became the place in which Francia's most important political family was to be found. Having mentioned the foregoing general considerations in setting the seventh century in its broader context, let us turn to a brief overview of the events in Francia during the century itself.

The seventh century began with a political map that was anomalous and soon passed to another which was equally so. In the first years of the century the politics of faction and allegiance had left the Neustrian king, Clothar II (584–629), in control of only three districts (*civitates*) all tucked up against the English Channel. The rest of Francia had fallen to the control of two brothers: Theudebert II, king of Austrasia (595–612), and Theuderic II, king of Burgundy (595–613). According to the chronicler known as Fredegar, the royal politics were not really in the hands of the brothers but in those of their grandmother, the cunning dowager, Queen Brunhild, bitter enemy of the Neustrian royal line since the days of Clothar's father, King Chilperic II (561–84). In 612, so the story goes, Brunhild induced Theuderic to attack Theudebert by declaring that the Austrasian king was not really his brother. The Burgundians were successful, Theudebert was killed, and all Francia, except Clothar's small piece, was united under Theuderic and Brunhild.[22] Not satisfied, grandson and grandmother pushed to the west to attack Clothar as well. On the campaign Theuderic died of dysentery, but Brunhild, now with her infant great-grandson, Sigibert II, as king, pressed forward undaunted. But at this point the tide changed and the reasons are well worth noting because they reveal how the political system worked.

In 613 the strongest faction of the Burgundian nobility was led by Warnachar, the Burgundian mayor of the palace. The mayor of the palace (*maior domus*) played a vital role in the court system in each of the three kingdoms. It was he, as the Latin words of his title imply, who held a position more senior than the other nobles at the king's court. It was a position much sought after by the nobles and one from which a powerful lord could exert a great deal of authority because it controlled access to the king. Warnachar's faction in Burgundy, along

---

22 Fredegar, *Chronicarum quae dicuntur Fredegarii Scholastici Libri IV cum Continuationibus* (hereafter Fredegar, *Chron.*), IV, ch. 38, ed. B. Krusch, *MGH, SSRM*, II, (Hanover, 1888), pp. 139–40; and ed. and trans. J. M. Wallace-Hadrill, *The Fourth Book of the Chronicle of Fredegar with its Continuations*, (London, 1960), pp. 30–2.

with a faction of the Austrasian nobility headed by Pippin I and Arnulf, later bishop of Metz, invited Clothar to invade Burgundy and Austrasia and to rid them of Sigibert and Brunhild. The Neustrian king siezed the opportunity. Fredegar tells us that the infant Sigibert was killed and goes on to relate in gruesome detail how Clothar had Brunhild tortured to death. Although Clothar was now sole king of Francia, each of the three separate kingdoms retained its own identity and its own mayor of the palace. Warnachar retained the position in Burgundy, but in Austrasia it fell neither to Pippin nor to Arnulf but to Rado, leader of another faction with close ties to Neustria.[23]

In these events of 613 let us note three significant characteristics. First, the contemporary seventh-century chronicler Fredegar was aware that the nobility worked towards its political ends in factions; he uses the word.[24] Second, large-scale political and military action demanded co-operation between a born Merovingian king and a faction of the nobility. Neither could accomplish the objective without the other. Clothar was obviously dependent upon the Austrasian and Burgundian nobility, and without the rallying power of Clothar neither Arnulf's and Pippin's nor Warnachar's designs would have attracted enough followers to allow them to succeed. Third, the political system does not seem to have yet been capable of maintaining large areas as single political units. Clothar's sole rule was not such that it effaced the political identity of the three component parts and made them one realm, and even what unity his single royal authority provided was to last less than a decade before the Austrasian nobles demanded and recieved Clothar's son, Dagobert I, as their own king.[25] In other words, Frankish society had not yet developed mediating mechanisms capable of concentrating wealth and power from a large area. It would do so, however, in the course of the seventh century.

A significant early step towards this end seems to have come about in 613 or 614, shortly after Clothar's successful assumption of the eastern realms. The nobility and the king obviously needed to establish certain ground rules of how they were to govern in the new situation. We have a good written indication of what they decided in the form of a

---

23 A. Friese, *Studien sur Herrschaftsgeschichte des fränkischen Adels. Der mainländisch-thüringische Raum vom 7. bis 11. Jahrhundert Geschichte und Gesellschaft*, 18 (Stuttgart, 1979), p. 22.

24 *... factione Arnulfo et Pippino vel citeris proceribus Auster ingreditur.* Fredegar, *Chron.*, IV, ch. 4, p. 140.

25 Fredegar, *Chron.*, IV, ch. 47.

royal capitulary from 614 which has come to be known as the Edict of Paris.[26] Of its twenty-four chapters, two in particular, chapters twelve and nineteen, show how the nobility used the royal authority to organise and to control its rule. In chapter twelve the king decrees that his counts (*judices*) in the various regions must be residents of the locality and not from outside it. By requiring that the official should be one whose land was in the local area, this measure made the royal official more responsible, since abuses of his authority could be punished by sequestering his land. The measure also had the effect of preventing an ambitious faction based elsewhere from attempting to use the office of count to extend its authority into an area where its members did not live. Chapter nineteen stipulates the requirement of local residence for bishops, although, as we shall see, this provision was not often enforced.

From various sources which describe the royal court in the first half of the century, sources which we shall have occasion to explore in some detail when we examine the career of St Audoin,[27] we can see a little more of the nature of the Frankish political system. We are first introduced to many of its important characters as they served at court under Clothar II and then under his son, Dagobert I. As we have mentioned, Dagobert was sent to rule Austrasia in 622 or 623 while his father retained rule in Neustria. When Clothar died in 629, Dagobert acceeded to the throne in Neustria as well and moved his court out of Austrasia to the area around Paris. At the same time he created a kingdom south of the Loire for his half-brother, Charibert. The area south of the Loire had never been, nor would it ever be, very tightly bound to Merovingian rule. Charlemagne, too, would try the same method of establishing a separate royal court in the area in order to bind it more closely to Carolingian rule. Neither his nor this earlier attempt seems to have worked. When King Charibert died after only three years, Dagobert had his young son killed and the court was disestablished.

Dagobert's move to Paris, that is, the loss of a royal court in Austrasia, had predictable effects: the Austrasian noble factions began to vie and squabble with each other; foreign enemies took advantage and invaded. Pippin I, who had been close to Dagobert since the king had come to

---

26 *Clotharii Edictum*, in A. Boretius (ed.), *Capitularia Regum Francorum*, I, *MGH*, *Legum Sectio II*, pp. 20–3. For the argument that the legislation of 614 drew on Justinian's 'Pragmatic Sanction of 554', see A. Murray, 'Immunity, Nobility, and the Edict of Paris', *Speculum*, 69 (1994).

27 See below, pp. 137–52.

Austrasia, followed him to Paris, and Fredegar tells us that the Austrasians at home were so aroused against him for this that they sought to have him killed.[28] In the wake of the internal squabbling, the Wends, a Slavic people living east of Austrasia, pressed menacingly upon its borders.[29]

The solution to Austrasia's problems was obviously the re-establishment of its own royal court. This soon came about when, in 633, the Austrasian nobles demanded that Dagobert should send his three-year-old son, Sigibert, to rule over them. As Clothar had done with Dagobert, so Dagobert now did with Sigibert, and the Austrasian court was recreated in Metz with two powerful local magnates, Bishop Chunibert of Cologne and Duke Adalgisel from near Metz, as regents.[30]

At the same time, in Burgundy, unlike either Austrasia or the lands south of the Loire, the system seems to have to developed to the point where it could organise rule over a wider area. After King Theuderic's death in 613, Burgundy never again had its own king. As we saw, the royal court was kept alive under the mayor, Warnachar, but even that element of local organisation disappeared when Warnachar died in 626. In that year the Burgundian nobility asked Dagobert not to appoint a new mayor; from then on they would travel to the Neustrian court.[31] The Burgundians were thenceforth to do without their own court and without their own mayor, apart from a brief interlude in mid century about which we know little, since *The Chronicle of Fredegar*, which tells us about it, breaks off in mid story. The fact that Burgundy could do without a court of its own can only mean that its nobles were already part of the factions which made up the Neustrian court. There will be much that will show this to have been the case in the later part of the century, not least the fact that the religious movement most closely bound to the Neustrian court will be centred on the Burgundian monastery of Luxeuil and that one of that court's most powerful members, Leudegar, will be made bishop of the important Burgundian see of Autun. The disestablishment of the Burgundian court shows that the development of a single kingdom was well under way early on.

Dagobert I (623–38) is a hero among the later Merovingians. He is often held up as the last effective monarch before the reigns of the do-

---

28 Fredegar, *Chron.*, IV, ch. 61.
29 Fredegar, *Chron.*, IV, chs. 74 and 75.
30 Fredegar, *Chron.*, IV, ch. 75.
31 Fredegar, *Chron.*, IV, ch. 54.

nothing kings, the *rois fainéants*, under whose rule the dynasty continued until 751. Indeed, under Dagobert the Frankish political system seems to have worked very well, or, to express the same sentiment in more seventh-century sounding language, Dagobert was able to defeat foreign foes and keep the internal peace. To the east the Franks managed to organise other Germanic peoples – the Thuringians, Alamans and Bavarians – under Frankish dukes for defence against the Slavic Wends and the Asiatic Avars. The growing Lombard power in Italy was kept at bay, and Dagobert mounted armed interventions into Visigothic Spain. It is worth noting that the forces he used against the Visigoths were not from Aquitaine, which borders Spain, but from Burgundy.[32] This is a further indication that the Burgundians had accommodated themselves to the new political system whereas the lands south of the Loire had not. Dagobert's rule also had the Bretons, to the west, under some sort of Frankish overlordship. We know their king, Judicael, came to Dagobert's court in 636 to pay obeisance, but what the relationship was between the two peoples is not clear.[33] The Gascons, too, came to the Frankish court to submit to Dagobert about a year later.[34]

Dagobert is even more famous for keeping the internal peace than for his foreign exploits. Fredegar tells us that the very news of his coming 'struck terror' into the inhabitants of Burgundy when he made a tour dispensing justice there in 628 or 629. The next year he toured Austrasia doing the same. Dispensing justice, of course, means settling disputes, that is, keeping the internal peace, and for this it is important that the king should be known to have a terrible swift sword. By the seventh century, however, the process was not the sort of swift and ruthless royal judgement described by Gregory of Tours in his story about King Clovis and the vase of Soissons where the king arbitrarily killed a soldier to make a point about obedience. Surviving seventh-century charters show that the process was now conducted by the nobility at court through procedures defined both by ritual and by written texts and presided over by the king or his representative.[35]

32 Fredegar, *Chron.*, IV, ch. 78.

33 Fredegar, *Chron.*, IV, ch. 78. See J. M. H. Smith, *Province and Empire. Brittany and the Carolingians* (Cambridge,1992), p.19.

34 Fredegar, *Chron.*, IV, ch. 78.

35 See P. Fouracre, '"Placita" and the settlement of disputes in later Merovingian Francia', in W. Davies and P. Fouracre (eds.), *The Settlement of Disputes in Early Medieval Europe* (Cambridge, 1986).

Dagobert has had the reputation of an itinerant king vigorously enforcing his personal will throughout the realm. But in fact after 631 we have no record at all of his moving from the Paris basin. Fredegar scowls as he tells us that Dagobert became sedentary in Neustria, but this fact is yet another sign that the system was settling in. In other words, the Franks were beginning to be able keep foreign enemies out and to preserve domestic tranquillity from a permanently established court near Paris. The later do-nothing kings would be able to do nothing and yet maintain the borders and internal peace precisely because the system worked so well.

Dagobert died in 638 and Neustria passed to his five-year-old son, Clovis II (638–57), seemingly without a major breach of the peace. The dowager queen, Nanthild, continued as regent and the mayor, Aega, retained his position. Two years later, in 641, we hear of the episcopal ordination of Eligius and Audoin, who had been two of Dagobert's most important counsellors, and of the seemingly peaceful appoint-ment of Erchinoald as Neustrian mayor. In Austrasia, too, Dagobert's passing caused no great upheaval, although here matters became somewhat more agitated. Dagobert's other son, Sigibert III (633–51), also a small boy, had already been king in Austrasia for five years, and his mayor, Pippin I, continued in his position. Pippin, however, died only a year after Dagobert, in 639. At his death the office of Austrasian mayor fell not to his son, Grimoald, but to a certain Otto who was the tutor or supervisor (*baiolus*) of the eight-year-old Sigibert.[36] Otto seems to have led a group of Austrasian nobles who had strong connections with the Neustrian court; he was the son of Uro of Paris and enjoyed the support of Burgundofara, who came from a powerful Neustrian family.[37] By 643 Grimoald apparently felt his position strong enough to snatch the mayoralty. He had Otto killed by Leuthar, an Alamannian duke,[38] and reasserted the Pippinids' position as leaders of the Austrasian nobility. Thus in the decade when the sources which we have included below begin to illuminate Frankish history we can see that the families which were to play prominent political roles in these sources held the power in both kingdoms.

It is also with the 640s that we begin to perceive a clearer picture of the Church's political role. We have already commented briefly on the

36 Fredegar, *Chron.*, IV, ch. 86.

37 Fredegar, Chron., IV, chs. 86 and 87. Cf. Friese, *Studien*, pp. 22–3.

38 Fredegar, *Chron.*, IV, ch. 88.

important economic role the Church played in the political structure as an institution which permanently held and organised large areas of land. We have also mentioned that monasteries were particularly useful in doing this in the interest of powerful families or political factions (*Klosterpolitik*). But the Church had another major political role to play, less concrete perhaps, but no less important. It was the Christian Church that legitimised and expressed the norms of desirable political behaviour within the new system. The christianising of Frankish politics is easily discernible in the changing picture of the ideal Frankish king. For the full development of the ideal of a most Christian king we shall have to wait for the Carolingians, but the tendency is clearly in that direction already in the seventh century. Gregory of Tours's ideal of vigorous, heroic kings is softened, although not totally eliminated, in the rather conservative *Liber Historiae Francorum* (*The Book of the History of the Franks*), written in 727, part of which is translated below. Here the political virtues of loyalty and fairness receive the author's approval but he can also still give us a picture of a Frankish king who destroys his enemy in true barbarian fashion in heroic single combat.[39] In the Carolingian *Annales Mettenses Priores* (*The Earlier Annals of Metz*), also included in part below, a source written some seventy-eight years later, there is none of the latter. Its political heroes operate according to God's plan and are lauded for such behaviour as forgiveness and for tendering offers of peace to enemies, elements which, in turn, are missing in the earlier *LHF*. Although this christianisation of a political ideal is most obvious here at the top of society, when it concerns the king, it was of no less political importance in the way it affected all levels. In the political structure, based on the direct use of land and less and less on the use of mediating urban mechanisms, personal service and personal loyalty became the political virtues *par excellence*. From agricultural worker to mayor of the palace, all needed to share a common value system wherein such basics as the inviolability of service obligations and the high value of personal loyalty went largely unquestioned. In Frankish Gaul it was the Church that preached and taught such values; those values and the behaviour they produce are lauded as pious and deserving of divine reward in all the hagiographic sources included in this volume. It is no coincidence that it was in the second half of the seventh century – that is, when the political apparatus had become

39 *Liber Historiae Francorum* (hereafter *LHF*), ch. 41, ed. B. Krusch, *MGH, SSRM*, II (Hanover, 1888), pp. 310–14. We have translated chapters 43–53 below, pp. 87–96.

based in the countryside – that the Church in northern Gaul also spread out from the towns on to the land. The evidence for this is clear, the most important being the mushrooming growth of rural monasteries, which we have already mentioned.

The 640s seem to have been a decade of peace and stability in both kingdoms. In Austrasia Grimoald and the Pippinids held the upper hand among the factions under Sigibert III. The Austrasians had lost a war in which Radulf, duke of the Thuringians, rebelled against them in 639, but the victors did not separate themselves completely from their Merovingian overlords, existing rather in a semi-autonomous state.[40] In Neustria, Erchinoald managed Clovis II's court without major incident. Throughout Francia it was a decade of important monastic foundation and the spreading influence of monks and missionaries influenced by Irish ideas. This relatively tranquil picture would be given a jolt about the century's mid point in both kingdoms. In each the disruption occurred for different reasons and illustrates different points.

In the 650s the events in Austrasia are famous, controversial, and although they make a very good story in the telling they turned out to be less enduring than the less entertaining events in Neustria. When the Austrasian king Sigibert III died, his mayor, Grimoald, did not oversee the elevation of the king's son, Dagobert, to the throne but rather packed the young prince off in exile to a monastery in Ireland, where he was to remain for some twenty years. Grimoald proceeded to put his own son on the throne, giving him the royal Merovingian name Childebert. Grimoald seems to have maintained this rule in Austrasia for about four years. But a non-Merovingian on the throne, even one sporting a proper royal name, represented a dangerous political precedent not only for the Austrasians themselves but also for the Neustrians. Noble factions from both kingdoms combined to remove Grimoald and to bring him before the Neustrian king, Clovis II, for trial. In due course he and, possibly, his son 'Childebert' were put to death, although the boy is not mentioned expressly by our source.[41] Clovis himself then died (657) and was succeeded in Neustria

---

40 Fredegar, *Chron.*, IV, ch. 87.

41 *LHF*, ch. 43, below, pp. 87–8. A very plausible alternative explanation advanced by Ian Wood is that Childebert may have married Bilichild, daughter of Sigibert III and Queen Himnechild. With her daughter safely on the throne, Himnechild then abandoned Grimoald to the Neustrians and the adopted Childebert outlived his father. I. N. Wood, *The Merovingian Kingdoms 450–751* (London, 1994), p. 224.

by his son, Clothar III (657–73), with the new king's mother, Queen Balthild, as regent. In Austrasia, Dagobert was not brought back from Ireland and placed on his father's throne, perhaps because he was not the son of Sigibert's widow, Himnechild. Instead the Neustrian prince, Childeric, son of Clovis II and Balthild and brother of the reigning Neustrian king, Clothar III, was married to his Austrasian cousin, the Merovingian princess, Bilichild, daughter of King Sigibert III and Queen Himnechild, and sent to rule the Austrasians with his mother-in-law, Himnechild, as regent. The position of Austrasian mayor passed out of the hands of the Pippinids to Wulfoald, leader of another Austrasian faction.

This *coup* of Grimoald's has received much more attention than it probably deserves precisely because he was head of the family which would one day produce Charlemagne.[42] There are, however, some less romantic but more important points to be noted in these events. The fact that Grimoald could upset the court system at its core and maintain his non-royal son on the throne for four years shows that even that early in their history he and his family were very powerful indeed. What is surprising is not that his *coup* eventually failed but that it took place at all. The fact that the Neustrians, along with, presumably, Grimoald's enemies and Wulfoald's faction in Austrasia, dislodged him and restored actual Merovingian rule in the form of a boy king shows the Franks' deep commitment to the Merovingians and to the system of rule based on a properly established royal court. And last, the major royal characters in the restoration were women: the regents Balthild in Neustria and Himnechild in Austrasia. The most lasting effect of all this was itself only temporary in that the Pippinids lost the leadership of the Austrasian court for about twenty years. We shall find them back at the fore, however, led by Grimoald's nephew, Pippin II, in the late 670s.

Meanwhile the events in Neustria, although less flamboyant, were probably more significant. In the 640s and up to about 658 or 659 it was Erchinoald who was the Neustrian mayor. He was a man with familial connections both with the Merovingians and with the royal families of the Anglo-Saxons.[43] It was in fact he who provided King

---

42 E.g. see R. Gerberding, *The Rise of the Carolingians and the Liber Historiae Francorum* (Oxford, 1987), pp. 47–66 and J.-M. Picard, 'Church and politics in the seventh century: the Irish exile of King Dagobert II', in Picard (ed.), *Ireland and Northern France* (Dublin, 1991), pp. 27–52.

43 See below, p. 102–4.

Clovis II with his queen, Balthild, a woman who had been a slave in his household. His was a powerful family with connections extending far beyond the Seine–Oise valley into Burgundy. It was also he who established an important group of Irish missionaries first at Lagny and then at Peronne. He died shortly after King Clovis but, whereas the royal succession had been peaceful, the Neustrian nobility fought among themselves in a scramble to establish a new mayor. The position in the end was lost by Erchinoald's faction and passed not to his son, Leudesius, but to another group. The new mayor was Ebroin, whose origins and position at the time are largely hidden from us. Nonetheless, it was he who would become the most famous, or perhaps the most notorious, figure in seventh-century Neustrian politics and leader of what would be Neustria's most powerful faction.

Ebroin, along with Audoin, bishop of Rouen, Chrodobert, bishop of Paris, and other unnamed magnates, formed a council under the queen regent, Balthild, for the first years of the boy king, Clothar's, reign.[44] Once the controversy over the mayoral succession had ended, peace returned to Neustria and, it seems, also to Burgundy, where another feud between factions of the nobility had been raging. The Burgundian problem had grown up in the days of Queen Nantild's regency for the young Clovis II between two groups, one headed by Floachad, Nanthild's and Erchinoald's appointee to the temporarilily re-established position of Burgundian mayor, a group with presumably Neustrian leanings, and another group from south Burgundy, led by Willebad, a group presumably comprising the traditional Burgundian as opposed to Frankish nobility.[45] From what we can tell, the regency of Balthild and the council worked well, for it is credited with keeping the peace in Neustria[46] and with restoring it in Burgundy.[47]

During the regency Balthild and her councillors launched an important religious reform in the major cult centres of the realm and placed their nominees on the episcopal thrones of some of Neustria's and Burgundy's most important sees. We shall have much to say about the specifically political aspects of this religious policy later because it plays a major role in most of the hagiographical sources in this

---

44 *Vita Sanctae Balthildis*, ch. 5, ed. B. Krusch, *MGH, SSRM*, II (Hanover, 1888), p. 487. We have translated this *vita* below, pp. 118–32.

45 Fredegar, *Chron.*, IV, chs. 89 and 90.

46 ... *regno quidem Francorum in pace consistenti. Vita Balthildis*, ch. 5, below, p. 122.

47 *Burgundiones vero et Franci facti sunt uniti. Vita Balthildis*, ch. 5, below, p. 122.

volume. Suffice it here to remind ourselves of a perhaps obvious, but important, point: cult centres, bishops, queens, factions, local churches and mayors are interconnected in complex and ever-changing ways in the political sytem of seventh-century Francia, largely because, as we have seen and shall see in some detail, all the people involved move from one position to the other, changing their roles. We shall come to a less than clear understanding of this system if we assume that a position (a local bishop or a mayor) or an institution (the Church, the Crown or an 'Irish' monastery) defined the political interests of the people involved. Rather, it seems to have been the other way round – that is, personal rather than institutional or even local loyalty was the determining political factor.

About 664 young Clothar came of age and Queen Balthild ended her regency, retiring to her favourite monastery at Chelles, near Paris. Balthild's 'retirement' was not as straightforward an outcome as it may seem; behind it lay some bloody shuffling by the nobility which included the murder of Sigobrand, bishop of Paris. Because of our usual lack of information and in this case a strong bias in our major source about Ebroin, the *Passio Leudegarii* (*The Suffering of Leudegar*) we cannot see these events very clearly. It may have been that Ebroin was already beginning to excercise a degree of political control which overstepped the acceptable bounds. He certainly did so later. By the 670s he was preventing Burgundian magnates from coming to court unless they had his permission to do so and in 673, when Clothar III died, he tried to exclude certain nobles from the traditional assembly which would elevate the new king, Clothar's brother and Balthild's son, Theuderic.[48] These acts attacked the system at its core – exclusion from court meant exclusion from the political process – and were too much for the nobility to tolerate. They rose up against both Ebroin and Theuderic, tonsured them both – that is, deprived them of their military and political status – and packed the mayor off to exile in the Burgundian monastery of Luxeuil[49] and the king to the Neustrian monastery of Saint-Denis, near Paris.[50] In the resultant power vacuum, unresolvable internal dissension seems to have raged among the various factions. In the end they turned to Childeric, Balthild's son, who was king in Austrasia, and asked him to come and rule over them

---

48 *Passio Leudegarii Episcopi et Martyris Augustodunensis I*, ch. 5, ed. B. Krusch, *MGH, SSRM*, V (Hanover, 1910), p. 287. We have translated this *vita* below, pp. 215-53.

49 *LHF*, ch. 45, below, p. 89.

50 *Passio Leudegarii I*, ch. 6, below, p. 222-3.

as well. The solution did not work. Childeric arrived surrounded by Austrasian advisers and with his Austrasian mayor, Wulfoald. Soon our Neustrian and Burgundian sources are complaining of the king's heedless and oppressive behaviour,[51] meaning, of course, that the Neustrians were not being heard at court. The Neustrian leader was Leudegar, bishop of Autun, in Burgundy, but head of the faction of Neustrian nobility once led by Erchinoald. Tension mounted for about two years and then exploded at Easter 675, when Wulfoald exiled Leudegar to Luxeuil, where he sat imprisoned in the same institution as his old enemy, Ebroin. Within six months the Neustrians had risen in full-scale revolt, driven Wulfoald back to Austrasia and killed King Childeric, along with his pregnant wife, Bilichild.[52] Ebroin and Leudegar both burst out of Luxeuil and each made a bid for power. The system was in serious breakdown. In neither Austrasia nor Neustria was there a king and in neither was there anything resembling a consensus among the nobility.

In the crisis of 675, as opposed to that of the mid 650s, it is not without significance that it was Austrasia which rebuilt with less bloodshed and with more stable and lasting results. Neustria, on the other hand, was to experience a political trauma far beyond the limits of a palace *coup*; it was embroiled in civil war. Leudegar's side got the upper hand at first. They made Erchinoald's son, Leudesius, mayor, fetched Theuderic out of Saint-Denis and took control of the royal treasure. This left Ebroin down but certainly not out, for not all the Neustrians who mattered were in Leudegar's camp. There were powerful interests about who would support Ebroin against Leudegar and Leudesius, probably those which had supported him in his struggle against the same faction in the 650s after Erchinoald's death. Ebroin was no amatuer at the political game and he immediately made all the right moves. He straight away found a Merovingian claimant to the throne, a pretender he called Clovis, for he obviously needed a court. He secured the support of none other than Audoin, bishop of Rouen, long-time counsellor of kings and former fellow member of Balthild's regency council. There was no political figure in all Francia more influential. Ebroin then set forth on a military campaign stretching all the way from Luxeuil in Burgundy to Crécy near the English Channel, gathering support and influence as he went. He defeated and killed

51 *LHF*, ch. 45, below, p. 89; and *Passio Leudegarii I*, chs. 7 and 8, below, pp. 224 and 225–6.

52 *LHF*, ch. 45, below, p. 90.

Leudesius, snatched up Theuderic and the royal treasure, and, with a real Merovingian now in hand, abandoned his pretender. He turned south, attacked Autun, and his got his hands on Leudegar, whom he eventually had tortured and killed. He also eliminated Leudegar's brother, Gaerin, then count of Paris, and drove many of his enemies from their lands into exile.[53] He had done it. The old order seemed restored: a legitimate Merovingian was on the Neustrian throne, and Ebroin and Audoin's faction from the Seine–Oise valley, not Wulfoald's from Austrasia, had the leadership at the Neustrian court.

The crisis of 675 was no less jarring for Austrasia than it was for Neustria. With the murder of Childeric II, Austrasia, too, had lost its king, and its mayor, Wulfoald, had been dislodged and chased back to his own lands, probably around Wissembourg. In the aftermath, the eastern kingdom once again established its own court, but this would be the last time it did so. With Wulfoald's group defeated and out of the way, it was the Pippinids, under Martin and Pippin II, who once again assumed the Austrasian leadership, a position they had not enjoyed since Grimoald's fall some twenty years earlier. As king they recalled none other than Dagobert, the prince and son of Sigibert III, whom Grimoald had exiled to Ireland. In Austrasia, too, the situation now seemed to be political business as usual: a Merovingian on the throne and a leading local faction in charge at court. But there soon came a dramatic sign that there was tension in the system and that political life would not be as it had been. That sign was war.

At a date which is difficult to determine, probably shortly before September 679, the Austrasians attacked the Neustrians.[54] There had not been war between the two countries since the days of Queen Brunhild and Clothar II in the early years of the century. The clash came at Bois-du-Fays in the Ardennes and it was a major encounter, 'a great slaughter', says the *Liber Historiae Francorum*. The chronicle states that it was Pippin and Martin who had instigated the hostilities, but nonethless Ebroin and the Neustrians won the day. This war, after three generations of peace between the two Frankish nations, is an indication that the system was beginning to need adjustment. Another equally significant indication of long-term change came with Dagobert II's assassination shortly after the war, in 679. With his death the Austrasian court was dissolved. From that time forward the

53 *LHF*, ch. 45, below, pp. 90–1.
54 *LHF*, ch. 46, below, p. 91.

Neustrian court would be the only royal court in Francia, and the Austrasians, largely in the form of the Pippinids, would become an increasingly important part of it.

Ebroin was to rule for five years after regaining power until he too fell victim to assassination; significantly the assassins flew for protection to Pippin in the east. The new Neustrian mayor was Waratto, whose family lands were not in the Seine–Oise valley but on the lower Seine, near Rouen. For his position of leadership he probably owed a great deal to his ally, Audoin, bishop of Rouen and the most influential political figure of his day. Audoin, too, died shortly afterwards, some time in the early 680s. In many ways, with the deaths of Ebroin and Audoin, Neustria saw the death of an era. The political system we have described thus far continued to operate for another forty years, but throughout the rest of its life it would have to contend with the disrupting fact that the family which was increasingly becoming the most influential in Neustria was no longer Neustrian at all but from the ever more important north and east.

The 680s were not a quiet decade. Waratto seems to have been willing to keep the peace with the Austrasians but other Neustrian interests were not so disposed. They were led by Waratto's own son, Ghislemar, who actually displaced his father as mayor for a while. When Waratto died there was again disagreement in choosing a successor. Berchar, who married into Waratto's family, was the eventual choice, but he did not have strong support among the nobility and was unable to keep the peace. Once again war broke out between east and west, and this time it was the Pippinids who won. The famous battle of Tertry in 687, thanks largely to the action-packed description in the Carolingian *Annales Mettenses Priores*, has been seen since Charlemagne's day as Pippin's 'conquest' of Neustria.[55] But just as Ebroin's victory over Pippin at Bois-du-Fays did not mean Neustrian conquest of Austrasia, so too Pippin's victory now did not allow him to swallow up the western realm. The Pippinids would eventually rule Neustria as well as Austrasia, but their take-over would come in the slower, more permanent and more personal form of control over land and over those ecclesiastical and secular positions which mattered. Pippin's victory at Tertry obviously opened many doors to this end, but it would not be until the 720s, under Charles Martel, that the Pippinid take-over would be reasonably complete.

55 E.g. ... *la victoire définitive de Pepin II* ... A. Dierkens, *Abbayes et chapitres entre Sambre et Meuse (VII–XI siècles)*. Beihefte der *Francia* 14 (Sigmaringen, 1985), p. 307.

In the wake of Tertry, Berchar was killed by those wishing to ingratiate themselves with Pippin. Waratto's widow, Ansfled, was involved in the plot and soon Pippin's son, Drogo, married Ansfled's daughter, Anstrud. The marriage was extremely significant, for it gave Pippin's family a foothold on the lower Seine, and it was from there that they spread their influence throughout much of Neustria. The victory at Tertry gave Pippin the mayoralty and the royal treasure, but he did not remain at the Neustrian court. Instead he left a certain Norbert there to watch over his interests and returned to Autrasia. From careful examination of the charters issued by the Neustrian kings over the next three decades it is clear that at first very few of the nobles at court were Austrasians or people connected with Pippin's party;[56] he was obviously not going to make the mistake Wulfoald had made in the 670s. Thanks largely to ecclesiastical records (there are no others), we can see Pippin's supporters taking over episcopal sees and important monasteries in a great arc, starting on the lower Seine, moving up through modern Belgium and back southwards again through the Ardennes and out on to the Champagne, where he made his son, Drogo, duke. Significantly, the see of Paris and the lands and institutions in the Seine–Oise valley, the traditional Neustrian heartland, escaped Pippin's control.[57]

In 690, when King Theuderic III died and was succeeded by his young son, Clovis III (690–94), the Frankish realms were about to enjoy another twenty-five years of relative peace. We have reports of Pippin's foreign wars,[58] but they were foreign wars as foreign wars should be: on foreign soil. Francia's borders were secure and the internal peace was preserved. The system was working well, perhaps better than it ever had, and this in the very heart of the period of the 'do-nothing' kings. The real problem of the later Merovingians was not their supposed inactivity but their youth. The only reign of any length by an adult monarch was that of Childebert III (694–711) and in the eyes of his contemporaries he was anything but *fainéant*. We have some thirteen charters from his reign, most of them *placita*, or legal judgements. The earlier ones contain long lists of the high nobility who took part in the cases, including even the name of Antenor, the *patricius* (ruler) of far-away

---

56 P. Fouracre, 'Observations on the outgrowth of Pippinid influence in the "Regnum Francorum" after the battle of Tertry (687–715)', *Medieval Prosopography*, 5, pt 2 (1984), 6.

57 Gerberding, *Rise*, pp. 104–9.

58 *LHF*, ch. 49, below, p. 93; *Annales Mettenses Priores* for their years 709–12, below, pp. 363–4; and *Annales Sancti Amandi*, ed. G. Pertz, *MGH, SS*, I (Hanover, 1826), p. 6.

Provence. It may be significant that one of these charters records a case that went against the Pippinids and prevented them from taking some land from the important monastery at Saint-Denis.[59] The Franks were conducting their political business in the traditional way and there was peace in the land.

During these peaceful years, however, Pippin's influence in Neustria continued to grow, quietly and steadily. There is some indication that a natural resentment against him was building strength as well. After Childebert's death in 711 the court seems to have been less and less effective; fewer nobles took part and there are indications that those from the outlying areas ceased to attend altogether. Pippin's son, Grimoald, had been Childebert's mayor, and the withdrawal of support from the royal court may have represented anti-Pippinid feeling.

We know such feeling was deeply rooted in Neustria, for at Pippin's death in 714 it erupted in a full-scale war against the easterners. The Neustrians found a rather dubious Merovingian tucked away as a monk named Daniel in Saint-Denis. They let his hair grow and put him on the throne as Chilperic II (715–21), making one of their own number, Raganfred, his mayor. They then pressed their case militarily in a war lasting several years. This was their grand attempt to restore their old system, free of domination from the east.[60] It was, however, to be a short Indian Summer. By the early 720s Pippin's son, Charles Martel, had defeated the Neustrians and was ruling under Theuderic IV (721–37). The Neustrians' days were now over; the political future of Francia lay not with the old families of the Paris basin but with the family which controlled vast areas along the Meuse, the Moselle, the Rhine and beyond. We begin our translations with one Merovingian source, the *Liber Historiae Francorum*, which laments the passing of the old order and we end our collection with the Carolingian *Annales Mettenses Priores*, which celebrate its downfall.

Sources and historians: hagiography and history

The eight texts translated in this volume represent a selection from what is in fact a far wider range of written sources for Merovingian history. In order to show how our sources have been used to construct

---

59 *ChLA* no. 587.
60 *LHF*, ch. 52, below, p. 95.

that history we have chosen to concentrate on material which relates clearly to a conventional framework of narrative history. What we would term 'politics', the stuff of narrative history, was of genuine concern to most Merovingian writers, although they saw politics far differently from the way we do. One major narrative source is not translated and is rarely discussed here because it deals with the earlier rather than the later seventh century, and because it already exists in a good English translation and edition. This is the *Fourth Book of the Chronicle of Fredegar with its Continuations.*[61] Up to about the year AD 642 *Fredegar* (as the work is commonly called) provides a nearly contemporary and independent account of events from a Burgundian or (less often) Austrasian standpoint. From the late sixth century, when Gregory of Tours stopped writing, up to c. 650, the point at which the *Liber Historiae Francorum (LHF)* becomes more helpful in its coverage of events, *Fredegar* is often our sole source for political history, and without it there would simply be no intelligible narrative of events for early seventh-century Francia. It was of course this period that saw the childhood of the people who figure in the sources translated here, and most of them grew up in the milieu that *Fredegar* describes, although only two of them, Erchinoald and Audoin, actually appear in the chronicle. *Fredegar* ends abruptly in 642, but in the eighth century various authors added to it to bring its account up to AD 768. The first of these *Continuations*, completed in 736, is directly based on the *Liber Historiae Francorum* up to the year 721, when the *Liber's* account terminates. Although the author of the first *Continuation of the Chronicle of Fredegar* made very few alterations to the text of the *Liber Historiae Francorum*, the changes that he did make are nevertheless revealing. What they show is an early stage in the rewriting of Merovingian history from an Austrasian and (later) Carolingian viewpoint. One of the sources translated in this volume, the *Annales Mettenses Priores (The Earlier Annals of Metz)*, demonstrates how the rewriting of history in this way would develop and reach a highly polished form in the early ninth century.

We have included about half the hagiographic sources surviving from the later seventh century. We have concentrated on those saints' lives, or *vitae*, which illustrate the political history of this period. The sources we have not included are in other respects no less important than the ones we have, and we shall frequently refer to them. Many

61 *The Fourth Book of the Chronicle of Fredegar with its Continuations*, ed. and trans. J. M. Wallace-Hadrill (London, 1960).

more lives of Merovingian saints were in fact written in the
Carolingian period than in the Merovingian period itself. We should
always consider carefully the extent to which these later works can be
used to shed light on Merovingian history.[62] Information from
hagiographic sources, both Merovingian and Carolingian, has been
used above all to put flesh on the bare-boned narratives of the two
chronicles which cover the seventh century, namely the *Fourth Book of
the Chronicle of Fredegar with its Continuations* and the *Liber Historiae
Francorum*. The *vitae* lend themselves to this purpose quite easily for,
as we shall see, hagiography of the seventh century was generally
highly political, since its subjects (the 'Saints') were drawn from
among the political elite in Francia. For instance, one of the saints
studied here, Balthild, was a queen, and three others, Aunemund,
Audoin and Leudegar, were important political leaders. The subject
matter of the narrative sources of the period, both chronicles and
saints' lives, is therefore markedly 'regicentric', for even when it is not
directly concerned with was what was going on in the royal palaces it
is usually about people whose lives touched the palace circles.

Another important category of source material, charters, also reflects
this same political culture, and again provides evidence which increases
our understanding of the political history of the period. The historian
of later Merovingian Francia is fortunate in having available at her or
his disposal thirty-seven surviving original royal charters. These
originals are of exceptional value not only for the detailed information
they give but also for providing templates against which the other
eighty or so non-original surviving royal charters can be tested for
authenticity.[63] In addition, we also have the *Formulary of Marculf*.[64]
This work was most probably written in the late seventh century and

---

62 For an example of such debate, see chapter 4 below, where a case is made for using
   the tenth-century *Acta Aunemundi* as a source for seventh-century history. Failure
   to examine a later source with proper critical attention is likely to invalidate
   historical analysis, as seems to be the case, for instance, with the speculative political
   history which J.-P. Poly read into the *Vita Aigulphi*: J.-P. Poly, 'Agricola et eiusmodi
   similes: la noblesse romane et la fin des temps mérovingiens', in M. Sot (ed.), *Culture,
   Education et Société. Etudes offerts à Pierre Riché* (Editions Européennes Erasme,
   1990).

63 The surviving original charters are published with photostats in *Chartae Latinae
   Antiquiores*, ed. A. Bruckner and R. Marichal, vols. 13, 14, ed. H. Atsma, J. Vezin
   (Zurich, 1982). The edition of Merovingian charters of all types which is most
   widely available is *Diplomata, Chartae Epistolae, Leges, aliaque instrumenta ad res
   Galli-Francicas spectantia*, ed. J. Pardessus, 2 vols. (Paris, 1843, 1849) (reprinted,
   Aalen, 1969).

64 *Marculfi Formularum Libri Duo*, ed. and French trans., A. Uddholm (Uppsala, 1962).

was intended to provide models showing how all sorts of charters, both royal and private, should be drawn up. Some of these models are for types of charter of which no examples survive, but where we do have both models and charters they are very similar indeed. It seems reasonable to conclude that scribes consulted the *Formulary of Marculf,* or something very like it, when drawing up their documents. The result is that Frankish charters share a well defined set of stock phrases or *formulae,* and this not only allows the different types of charter to be clearly distinguished one from another, it also greatly helps in the task of identifying authentically Merovingian material in later collections. In fact the study of early medieval charter forms from the Frankish kingdoms is more straightforward than the study of charter forms from any other area once within the boundaries of the Roman Empire. Even though almost no charters survive from Frankish Gaul in the sixth century, the evidence of the seventh-century formularies suggests that the contemporary charters were the product of a bureaucratic tradition which stretched back to late Roman times, and which we can see continuing throughout the Carolingian period.[65] Other areas of Europe, of course, shared the same tradition, but only in Francia was there the long-term stability of political structures and personnel which allows us to see clearly the continuity in charter forms.

The overall pattern of continuity in charter forms suggests stability in political structures, and the contents of these documents indicate that the people who benefited from that stability were the kind of people who appear in our narrative sources. All the surviving original royal charters are connected with one monastery: Saint-Denis, a foundation so closely associated with the palace that it has even been referred to as the Merovingian 'chancery'.[66] Most of the other seventh-century

---

65 The essential surveys of the charter tradition in Western Europe are P. Classen, 'Kaiserreskript und Königsurkunde. Diplomatische Studien zum römisch–germanisch Kontinuitätsproblem', *Archiv für Diplomatik,* 2 (1956), and P. Classen, 'Fortleben und Wandel spätrömischen Urkundenwesens im frühen Mittelalter', in P. Classen (ed.), *Recht und Schrift im Mittelalter, Vorträge und Forschungen des Konstanzer Arbeitskreis für mittelalterliche Geschichte,* vol. 23 (Sigmaringen, 1977), pp. 13–54.

66 The term 'chancery' implies that there was formal machinery for charter production in this period, but the apparent function of the monastery of Saint-Denis as a writing office for the kings may simply result from the fact that the monastery was the beneficiary of the charters it preserved, and that these charters are almost the only originals to have survived. An alternative view, therefore, is that charters, even royal charters, were produced by those who received them: see D. Ganz, 'Bureaucratic shorthand and Merovingian learning', in P. Wormald (ed.), *Ideal and Reality in Frankish and Anglo-Saxon Society. Studies presented to J. M. Wallace-Hadrill* (Oxford, 1983).

charters, both royal and private, of which there are over two hundred
surviving in later copies, deal with the foundation of religious
establishments and with gifts to them. In our period it seems to have
been only the richest families who were involved in such transactions,
and so it is not surprising that the people we meet in these charters –
kings, queens, bishops, abbots, abbesses and high-ranking lay magnates – are often also known to us from narrative sources. Charters,
because they record the affairs of the political elite, are often important
in discussions of political history. They also tell us something about
the resources upon which political power was based by showing how
land ownership was organised and what income both the landowner and
the royal authority could draw upon. We can glean some information
about the countryside from the stock phrases used to describe aristocratic
estates in seventh-century charters, but for evidence of transactions at
a lower social level we must wait until the eighth century, when records
of grants to the Church from less well-off people begin to appear.
These slightly later records, especially from the monastery of Saint
Gall in Switzerland, testify to the surprisingly widespread use of
writing in society.[67] There are some indications that in the seventh
century too access to literacy was not just the privilege of the elite.
There are some hints of this in our hagiographic sources, and the wide
range of models in the *Formulary of Marculf* suggests that a great
variety of transactions were routinely recorded in writing.[68] Nevertheless, we have few letters from the period, although the one collection
we do have is invaluable in showing us how many of the most influential
people in the mid seventh century were, literally, old friends.[69]

Common to all these sources is fluency in the language of law and
evident familiarity with legal practice. In contrast to Italy, Spain and
southern England, however, Francia does not seem to have produced
any new collections of law in the later seventh century. The last
surviving example of royal legislation is from the year 614, although
there is reason to think that the issuing of royal edicts continued to be
a normal part of government thereafter. The Frankish Church, on the
other hand, certainly did legislate throughout the seventh century, and

---

67 On the St Gall charters and the use of writing, R. McKitterick, *The Carolingians and
the Written Word* (Cambridge, 1989), pp. 77–126.

68 For the place of writing in Merovingian society, I. Wood, 'Administration, law and
culture in Merovingian Gaul', in R. McKitterick (ed.), *The Uses of Literacy in Early
Medieval Europe* (Cambridge, 1990).

69 *Epistulae Sancti Desiderii*, ed. D. Norberg (Uppsala, 1961).

we have the records of ten Church councils.[70] Among other things, these records provide information which is vital for understanding our hagiographic sources, for they tell us about the organisation within which the careers of the saints unfolded. The lists of people attending the councils are also valuable, especially when compared with two other types of source: the witness lists of the charters, and the references in narrative sources. When we put all three types of material together we can often say more than a little about who was who in later Merovingian Francia.

The ecclesiastical legislation confirms the impression conveyed by other sources that the clergy were familiar with law and legal practice, for it records complaints about the frequent appearance of clerics in secular law cases. From these references to litigation, and from earlier laws and royal legislation, as well from what the charters, chronicles and saints' lives tell us about how people behaved towards each other, we can deduce the faint outlines of social structure and behaviour. We can, for instance, say a little about the operation of the courts at a local level, and we can just about see the basic legal distinctions between the different sorts of people in Frankish society. Hagiography may tell us something about social as well as religious attitudes, and miracle stories in particular have long been recognised as a source for social history.[71] Nevertheless, there is insuffcient source material to allow us to write social and economic history in any depth. One set of accounting documents from the monastery of St Martin's at Tours has been painstakingly pieced together, but its fragmentary nature and the lack of comparative data make it hard to assess the significance of the information it contains.[72]

Coinage does provides some evidence for the economy in seventh-century Francia. The gradual debasement of the gold coinage and its eventual replacement by a monometallic silver currency has attracted the attention of generations of scholars. There is great interest in the subject partly because it is seen as highly significant in relation to the

70 The records of the Merovingian church councils are in *Concilia Gallliae 511–694*, ed. C. de Clercq, *Corpus Christianorum, Series Latina*, vol. 148 A (Turnhout, 1963).

71 For an example of miracle stories used as source in this way, see D. Rollason, 'The Miracles of St Benedict: a Window on Early Medieval France', in H. Mayr-Harting and R. Moore (eds.), *Studies in Medieval History Presented to R. H. C. Davis* (London, 1985).

72 P. Gasnault, 'Documents comptables du VIIe siècle provenant de Saint-Martin de Tours', *Francia*, 2 (1974), 1–18.

transition from the ancient to the medieval world: the demise of the
gold coinage after decades of emaciation is taken to signify no less
than the death rattle of the ancient world's economy. By comparison,
the Merovingian economy has been seen as hopelessly weak, with a
low point in activity in the seventh century. This rather gloomy
assessment at one time cast its shadow over the whole of later
Merovingian history, picturing the period, as it were, as a dysfunctional interlude between the end of Antiquity and the rise of a
Carolingian civilisation which heralded the beginning of the Middle
Ages proper.[73] This view, as we shall see, is on the wane, among both
historians and archaeologists.

Traditionally archaeology and place-name studies on the Continent
have concentrated on what were seen as the Germanic aspects of
Frankish development, once again relating these to a transition from
the ancient to the medieval world, for this was a process in which the
Germanic invaders like the Franks were held to have been the motor
force. The evidence of warrior graves and of Frankish place names was
accordingly used to illuminate the spread of a mixed Romano-
Germanic culture which was seen as representing a new phase of
European development.[74] It is also generally true that, at a local level
in France, archaeologists have been more interested in finding Gallo-
Roman remains (and those of even earlier cultures) than in digging for
early medieval material. Recently more attention has been paid to all
aspects of Merovingian archaeology, and there have been challenges to
traditional interpretations of grave finds, which were based on the
assumption that there were distinct patterns of ethnicity to which

---

73 The chronology and causes of the decline of the economy of the ancient world have
   been the subjects of one of the classic debates of early medieval history, centred on
   argument around the so-called 'Pirenne thesis'. For a summary of positions in this
   debate, A. Havighurst (ed.), *The Pirenne Thesis* (Boston, 1976), and more recently
   (and based on the archaeological rather than historical evidence), R. Hodges and D.
   Whitehouse, *Mohammed, Charlemagne and the Origins of Europe* (London, 1983). For
   generally pessimistic assessments of the Merovingian economy, R. Latouche, *The
   Birth of the Western Economy* (London and New York, 1967), p. 139; R. Doehaerd,
   The Early Middle Ages in the West. Economy and Society (Oxford, 1978). More recent
   work has emphasised points of growth in the economy: W. Bleiber,
   *Naturalwirtschaft und Ware–Geld–Beziehungen zwischen Somme und Loire während des
   7. Jahrhunderts* (Berlin, 1981). See also I. Wood, *The Merovingian Kingdoms 450–751*
   (London, 1994), pp. 293–303, for the development of trade in the North Sea region.

74 E. James, 'Cemeteries and the problem of Frankish settlement in Gaul', in P. Sawyer
   (ed.), *Names, Words and Graves. Early Medieval Settlement* (Leeds, 1978), provides an
   excellent critique of traditional approaches.

material culture conformed.[75] We can now profit from several much more intensive investigations of rural settlements, as well as attempts to describe the development of various towns.[76] The early results of these studies serve to challenge some of the interpretations derived from our written sources. In particular the archaeologists' view of the low level of urban activity in this period conflicts with the language of many of our hagiographic sources, which speak of a vibrant urban culture. Likewise the excavation of rural communities suggests that even in the heart of Francia the spread of Christianity into the countryside was still limited in the seventh century.[77] Again, there is a contrast here with most of the written sources, which assume not only the Christianity of the population at large but also the ascendancy of religious over secular culture. Although we can often reconcile apparent contradictions between these two different kinds of evidence, archaeology is invaluable in reminding us that our written sources overwhelmingly represent only one cultural perspective.

The critical examination of the sources for Merovingian history began in earnest in the seventeenth century with the work of the Bollandists and the Maurists.[78] The Bollandists are a group of Jesuit scholars who, ever since the mid seventeenth century, have been engaged in the massive project of collecting and publishing the sources for the lives of the saints. Their scheme is to follow the liturgical calendar, dealing with each saint in the order that his or her festival is celebrated. Their work is known as the *Acta Sanctorum* and its first two volumes, covering the month of January, were published in 1643. The second

---

75 E. James develops his critique of cemetery archaeology in 'Burial and Status in the Early Medieval West', *Transactions of the Royal Historical Society*, fifth series, 39 (1989). G. Halsall, *Settlement and Social Organisation. The Merovingian Region of Metz* (Cambridge, forthcoming), chs. 3, 4, 8, 9, advances alternative interpretations of grave goods, based on age and gender rather than ethnicity and rank.

76 A path-breaking study of a single settlement was P. Demolon, *Le Village mérovingien de Brebières* (Arras, 1972), although James, 'Cemeteries', 57, was the first of several scholars to question the significance of the excavations at Brebières. On towns see for example the work of H. Galinié on Tours, the reports of which are published in the *Bulletin de la Société Archéologique de Touraine*, 39 (1978–81), 203–49, 607–49, 1041–84, and 40 (1982), 153–99.

77 This is the observation of C. Lorren, 'Le village de Saint-Martin de Trainecourt à Mondeville (Calvados), de l'Antiquité au Haut Moyen-âge', in H. Atsma (ed.), *La Neustrie. Les Pays au Nord de la Loire de 650 à 850*, vol. 2 (Sigmaringen, 1989).

78 D. Knowles, *Great Historical Enterprises* (London, 1963), pp. 1–62, gives a clear account of these movements.

January volume, in fact, contains material on the cults of St Balthild and St Praejectus, the subjects of two of the works discussed below. Even 350 years later, the dossiers on them in the *Acta Sanctorum* remain valuable. The Maurists were a group of Benedictine scholars interested in the sources for the history of monasticism. Their works were individual productions rather than a collective enterprise like that of the Bollandists. They are particularly useful because their material is edited according to a chronological rather than a liturgical arrangement, thus helping historians to reconstruct a continuous sequence of events. The work of one Maurist scholar, Dom Jean Mabillon (active from 1665 to 1707), stands out, for not only did he publish the first systematic collection of the materials for Merovingian history, he also made the first attempt to formulate principles of source criticism.[79]

The bulk of the Bollandists' programme was published in the eighteenth century, although it remains incomplete and work on it still continues today. The Maurists did not survive the upheavals of the Revolutionary period in France. Because both sets of scholars were working in the pre-Revolutionary period they preserved in copy and in print much material that would not otherwise have not survived the turmoil of the late eighteenth century. More settled times saw a fresh enterprise in publishing early medieval sources and one which would, as it were, industrialise the process. From 1826 onwards, early medieval texts, many of which had never been published before, were edited in a new series, the *Monumenta Germaniae Historica*. This enterprise, as the name of the series suggests, was dedicated to publishing the sources for German history, from the sixth century to the sixteenth. The definition of what constituted German history was very broad and included all Merovingian history, even when it was concerned with areas to the south of the river Loire. One sub-section of the *Monumenta* was devoted to Merovingian texts, and it is this series, the *Scriptores Rerum Merovingicarum*, which contains the editions of all but one of the Merovingian sources translated in this volume.[80] The work of the *Monumenta* editors has generally been in the best tradition of German scientific history, academic problems being formulated and 'solved' with all the confidence that this historical

79 J. Mabillon, *De Re Diplomatica Libri VI* (Paris, 1681–1704).

80 Knowles, *Enterprises*, pp. 63–97, describes the development of the *Monumenta*, with much interesting detail on the personal politics of the organisation. We do not, however, share Knowles's dissmissive attitude to the work of Bruno Krusch.

method inspired in its heyday. Much of the editing of the Merovingian texts in the late nineteenth and early twentieth centuries was outstanding, and the two scholars responsible for producing the *Scriptores Rerum Merovingicarum*, Bruno Krusch and his pupil, Wilhelm Levison, dominated the field of Merovingian history for over a generation. Although the criteria by which they selected works is not always clear, and despite the fact that some of their historical 'problem-solving' looks overly schematic today, it is hard to improve on their work as editors.[81] Not least this is because few moderns can match their fluency in Latin, or their command of classical, biblical and patristic sources. At the same time, Krusch and Levison's French and Belgian contemporaries were also producing excellent work on Merovingian texts, in particular on Merovingian charters. Several editions of these were published from the mid nineteenth century onwards, culminating in P. Lauer and C. Samaran's edition and transcription of the original royal charters, published in 1908 with photostats.[82] Finally, the first major catalogue of Mervovingian coins was published in 1896.[83]

The aim of these scholars was to establish a canon of sound texts, that is, texts containing authentically Merovingian material. To this end they were concerned to find the oldest version of each work, not an easy task because almost none of these works survived in manuscripts from the Merovingian period itself. By comparing later copies, and by using the evidence of the texts themselves, they tried to work out the date at which each work was composed. Research in this vein is still continuing, for some of the works which Krusch sometimes rather arbitrarily excluded from the *Monumenta* collection remain in need of critical examination, such as the *Acta Aunemundi*, which is included in this volume. New readings of manuscripts can also prove fruitful, and new collections of material can usefully be put together. In this way the corpus of Merovingian source material is always changing. Some works are added, but others are effectively removed when it can be

---

81 A classic example of problem-solving in this schematic way is the proposal that King Dagobert II ruled twice, which allowed Krusch to reconcile the contradictory chronological indications of the sources for the period 652–62. For more modern attempts to make sense of these sources, see chapter 1, below, p. 81.

82 P. Lauer and C. Samaran (eds.), *Les Diplômes Originaux des Mérovingiens* (Paris, 1908). The same original royal charters, with some original private charters, have now been re-edited, with new photostats, in *Chartae Latinae Antiquiores* vols. 13 and 14.

83 M. Prou, *Les Monnaies Mérovingiens* (Paris, 1896, reprinted Graz, 1969).

.hown that they were composed at a later date and are entirely derivative in content. For, impressive as the work of the late nineteenth and early twentieth-century scholars remains, their judgements as editors are not set in concrete.

As we have just seen, modern work on Merovingian texts began with questions about their age and provenance. Once it was established that a particular work had indeed been produced in the Merovingian period it could be quarried for historical information. The outlines of seventh and early eighth-century history had long been known through the narrative of the two chronicles which cover the period: *The Chronicle of Fredegar with its Continuations*, and the *Liber Historiae Francorum*. The latter work in particular had had a wide circulation since early medieval times, and had been incorporated into a host of later chronicles. As a far wider range of sources became available in print it became possible to fill out the narrative outline with a more detailed chronology and political history of the period. Texts were scanned and were valued according to how many 'useful facts' they contained.[84] By the mid twentieth century most of the straightforward 'facts' about Merovingian history as we now have them had been established, and the search for nominal data in these texts gave way to more subtle enquiries into their contents, structure and purpose.

It is now understood that our sources provide far more than the salient 'facts' of history. When each work is read as a whole, rather than as a series of extracts, it can yield more about the culture of the people who produced it than about the particular actions of the people who are its subject. Charters, for instance, are now used to shed light not just on the persons and institutions involved in the transactions they record, but also on wider issues such as the use of writing in society generally.[85] Their *formulae*, once dismissed as historically without value because these stock phrases were (by definition) unoriginal, being merely copied by scribes, are now seen as providing valuable information on the evolution of law, custom and belief in Frankish society.[86] The chronicles too

---

84 These values are clearly revealed in the essential guide to Merovingian sources: Wattenbach-Levison, *Deutschlands Geschichtsquellen im Mittelalter, Vorzeit und Karolinger*, part 1, *Die Vorzeit von den Anfängen bis zur Herrschaft der Karolinger* (Weimar, 1952), in which the assessment of sources is related to a framework of narrative history. On this period and on many of the sources translated in this volume, see pp. 127–31.

85 See, for example, McKitterick, *Carolingians and the Written Word*, pp. 77–126.

86 On the *formulae* in documentary records of court cases heard in the royal court, P. Fouracre, '"Placita" and the settlement of disputes in later Merovingian Francia', in

are now treated as sources which show how Merovingian and Carolingian people thought about themselves. Chroniclers, it is now accepted, selected information and shaped their accounts of the past to represent particular points of view and they were capable of advancing subtle arguments within their texts.[87] They were, in other words, not as naive as earlier scholars thought them. This we shall see clearly in the case of the *Annales Mettenses Priores*, one of the sources discussed in this volume. Underlying the reassessment of texts is a growing awareness of the complexity and sophistication of early medieval culture in general, and a growing interest in matters of belief and religious culture.[88] The latter had received short shrift at the hands of the *Monumenta* scholars. Krusch, for instance, was much irritated by the preference for conventional religious sentiment over sober reportage which he found in his material. This was most often the case with works of hagiography, a genre of writing strongly tied to the use of convention. It is in this field that modern re-evaluation of texts has made most progress, partly because there is a great deal of source material, and partly because the need to distinguish between convention and reality in saints' lives has great appeal to twentieth-century scholars. For this reason, and because hagiography accounts for such a large proportion of our material, let us look at the approaches to these texts in more detail.

Hagiography has long been a subject of interest because it is basic to the culture of sanctity in Western European society, and hagiography not only records but also constructs this socio-religious phenomenon. It was of interest too to secularist, positivist historians of the late nineteeenth and early twentieth centuries who, as we have seen, were

---

W. Davies and P. Fouracre (eds.), *The Settlement of Disputes in Early Medieval Europe* (Cambridge, 1986), and on the *formulae* in documents which granted immunity, P. Fouracre, 'Eternal light and earthly need: practical aspects of the development of Frankish immunities', in W. Davies and P. Fouracre (eds.), *Property and Power in the Early Middle Ages* (Cambridge, 1995).

87 In this volume, see the treatment of the *Liber Historiae Francorum* and of the *Annales Mettenses Priores*, and for a more detailed assessment of a chronicler's point of view, R. Gerberding, *The Rise of the Carolingians and the Liber Historiae Francorum* (Oxford, 1987).

88 The work of Peter Brown in particular has been instrumental in sowing renewed interest in the subject of sanctity. S. Wilson, 'Annotated Bibliography', in S. Wilson (ed.), *Saints and their Cults. Studies in Religious Sociology, Folklore and History* (Cambridge, 1983), provides a very useful survey of different kinds of work in this area. J. Smith, 'Early medieval hagiography in the late twentieth century, *Early Medieval Europe*, 1, pt. 1 (1992), examines recent trends in writing about the subject.

concerned to winkle information out of the saints' lives on matters other than the holy. Important here was the question of whether the author was contemporary with the events he or she described and could therefore provide independent and original information. Questions of originality also involved understanding the nature and content of each work, since it was crucial to distinguish between what was purely conventional in the writing, or even simply copied from elsewhere, and what was unique and could be added to the sum total of knowledge about the period. The Bollandists, from the beginning of their undertaking, have been interested in these matters, though their aim was to use the historical background to illuminate the cult of the saint, rather than the other way round. It is in fact a Bollandist, H. Delehaye, whose work on the nature and structure of hagiography has been seminal in this century.[89]

Delehaye identified and explained the use of the many conventions which were common in hagiography, and showed the great extent to which these conventions were employed. He demonstrated that some works were made up of nothing but well tried motifs and phrases, having no historical basis at all. Delehaye's work emphasised the importance of understanding the function and purpose of hagiography, and his insights have paid rich dividends when applied to Merovingian texts. In particular, work in the 1960s by F. Graus and F. Prinz broke new ground in relating the texts to their social and religious backgrounds. Along with P. Riché's survey of early medieval learning and education, the work of these scholars provided the basic terms of reference within which Merovingian hagiography is generally read and understood. What emerges from their studies is a picture of a socialised sanctity in which the conventional attributes of the saint were appropriated by leading members of the Frankish aristocracy. The saints' lives were both witness to and key agents in this process of 'aristocratic self-sanctification', and the conventional structure of the works had in this sense a definite social meaning.[90] Interpretations of Merovingian hagiography in this vein also fitted very well into the traditionally pessimistic view of the history of the period, that is, the

89 H. Delehaye, *The Legends of the Saints*, fourth edition, trans. D. Attwater (London, 1962); H. Delehaye, *Les Passions des Martyrs et les genres littéraires*, second edition (Brussels, 1966).

90 F. Graus, *Volk, Herrscher und Heiliger im Reich der Merowinger* (Prague, 1965); F. Prinz, *Frühes Mönchtum im Frankenreich* (Munich, 1965); P. Riché, *Education et Culture dans l'Occident Barbare Ve–VIIe siècle* (Paris, 1962). It was Prinz, *Frühes Mönchtum*, pp. 489–93, who formulated the idea of 'aristocratic self-sanctification'.

texts seem to point to the secularisation of the Church and to the secularisation, or debasement, of sanctity itself. Among historians the later Merovingian Church does indeed generally have a poor reputation, and the hagiography it produced is one source of that impression.[91] As we shall argue shortly, although this picture is generally helpful, it must in some respects be challenged, especially where there is a danger of circular argument, namely where hagiography supplies 'evidence' of a religious and social decline which then becomes the basis on which the hagiographical evidence is interpreted.

These insights have been produced by giving the whole text of each hagiographical work full consideration rather than simply chopping out of it the 'usable' historical information.[92] To privilege the text in this way invites us to go further and ask whether literary criticism might actually be more useful to us as a tool for analysing the texts than the traditional approach of the historian. The question is an important one, because one strain of post-modernist critical thought presents the view that, since we rely upon texts for our understanding of the past, we should admit that in effect 'the past' consists only of what we can read in the text.[93] This view calls for the critical examination of texts in terms of linguistic analysis in order to explore their meaning to the fullest possible extent. It further invites us to examine all kinds of texts and other sources of information on the basis that social being is constituted through language, and therefore all thought and social interaction, past and present, should be analysed in linguistic terms. To the historian this way of thinking constitutes a direct challenge, because historians have traditionally started from the assumption that the past existed outside and beyond the text and is capable of being

---

91 In J. M. Wallace-Hadrill, *The Frankish Church* (London, 1983), pp. 88–91, for instance, the later Merovingian Church is seen as not worth discussing in detail. See also G. Scheibelreiter, *Der Bischof in merowingischer Zeit* (Vienna, 1983), pp. 158–9.

92 Two important discussions about how to interpret hagiographical texts are M. Van Uytfanghe, 'Les avatars contemporains de l'hagiologie', *Francia*, 5 (1977), and F. Lotter, 'Methodisches zur Gewinnung historischer Erkentnisse aus hagiographischen Quellen', *Historische Zeitschrift*, 229 (1979).

93 The possibilities of applying the techniques of deconstruction to Merovingian texts are briefly explored by P. Fouracre, 'Merovingian History and Merovingian Hagiography', *Past and Present*, 127 (1990), 5–8. The issues are discussed in greater depth and in relation to the validity of traditional empiricist analysis by G. Spiegel, 'History, Historicism and the Social Logic of the Text in the Middle Ages', *Speculum*, 65 (1990). Spiegel's article sparked a debate about history and postmodernism in *Past and Present*, 133 (1991), and 135 (1992), with contributions by L. Stone, P. Joyce, C. Kelly and Spiegel herself.

analysed as a separate entity. Whereas, for the student of literature, the words of the text are a priority and constitute a certain reality, for the historian, writing comes after the event.

The promise inherent in a linguistic approach to the past is nevertheless great, in that the concentration upon language in theory allows one to dig deeper meanings out of texts. Meaning, in this view, is ultimately constituted not by the formal message of the writing but by its use of metaphor. The meanings it actually excludes in its use of language will be as important as the ones it includes at a formal level. By drawing attention to the excluded meanings, and to the difference between them and the overt message, the technique of 'deconstruction' aims to lay bare a 'sub-text' which reveals a more realistic level of social thought. Although post-modern critical approaches do therefore question the traditional notion of historical reality, they also offer even the traditional historian a valuable alternative based on working out a more realistic interpretation of language. Much in this way of thinking is cogent and should not be shouted down or ignored simply because it touches a raw nerve in questioning the wisdom of traditional empiricism. For it is indeed often the case that the historian's version of the past is to some extent his or her own literary and imaginative construction, and, as we have seen in relation to overviews of Merovingian history, that construction can be flawed by common misapprehensions or preconceptions about a society. For instance, even where more recent studies of hagiography have sought to identify the social, cultural and religious settings of the saints' lives, that background has often been placed in a preconceived scheme of history whose main focus is the decline of public authority in the early medieval world. It is that frame of thinking which has produced the pessimistic view of Merovingian history mentioned earlier in this chapter, and it is from this bind that post-modernist approaches to texts offer some prospect of escape. In practice, however, at least where the interpretation of Merovingian texts is concerned, the linguistic approach creates as many difficulties as it seems to solve, that is to say, subordinating the historical background, or context, of the text raises as many difficulties as does the traditional approach, which tends to use the general context as a basis for understanding the particular text.

On a purely practical level we may simply have too little information with which to attempt a proper deconstructionist analysis of our texts. Although a few Merovingian texts, such as the works of Gregory of

Tours, have been explored to the extent that they may be analysed in that way, with most other texts we are still generally at the stage where we are thinking about their provenance rather than their literary construction.[94] A dismissal of the traditional notion of historical context is also hardly appropriate for the early medievalist, for although the post-modernist approach seems to start with a naive view of the text – free, that is, of the historians' agenda – it does nevertheless assume a certain level of knowledge about the historical background. If post-modernism declares that it is possible to analyse a text without reference to the author, it is on the tacit understanding that it is at least known who the author was and when and where he or she lived. This information cannot be taken for granted in relation to many early medieval texts, and it is a major part of the early medieval historian's task to try to discover a text's background, something which is usually far more precisely known for works of later periods. In fact, we do not know who were the authors of any of the texts translated in this volume, and each of our commentaries necessarily involves speculation about the identity of the author. Likewise, our understanding of the language of many of our texts is at too rudimentary a stage to allow useful linguistic analysis. As we shall see in the next section, the nature of the language used in the later Merovingian period is a contentious subject. We may be able to reconstruct the original orthography, but we cannot say how it actually sounded. When we are not sure of meaning even at a purely lexical level, that is, if we are unsure of the range of meanings each word of the text may have, the technique of deconstruction cannot help us much, for if the intended literal meaning is unclear we cannot identify what has been excluded.[95]

Hagiography itself is a peculiar kind of literature in that its form is determined by its function rather than by aesthetic considerations, and genres within hagiography were imposed from without by religious needs rather than developed along artistic lines. The liturgical function of hagiography tends to disrupt the discursive speech mode normally used in communication and upon which socio-linguistic analysis is based. In other words, the language of hagiography is partly meant to elicit a ritual response and is open to interpretation in only a very limited sense. The readiness of each work to draw upon a

94 That establishing the provenance of texts is a task which must be undertaken before literary analysis can begin is one of Spiegel's points: 'Social Logic', 74–6.

95 Fouracre, 'History and Hagiography', 6–7.

common stock of conventions and to borrow wholesale from other texts, especially the Bible, also means that any sub-text will be hard to identify. We can indeed show how our authors used language metaphorically and employed opposing concepts to carry a hidden argument, but that does not reveal to us any meaningful sub-text, for the opposition between concepts serves merely to reinforce, rather than undermine, the overt message of the text. For instance, the *Passio Leudegarii* and the *Annales Mettenses Priores* both show authors using metaphors which opposed concepts of light and darknesss and appearence and reality in order to signify the differences between injustice and justice, or, more simply, wrong and right, in political contexts. However, the use of language here does not reveal any layer of social reality different from that formally expressed elsewhere in the texts. On the contrary, it reinforces conventional values by drawing political action into the metaphorical realm of the sacred. So strongly conventional is the written culture of this period that it is almost impossible to find within it any sub-text of opposition or dissent.

Although all texts belong to a single and self-reinforcing, and even colonising, culture, the hagiography of this period nevertheless shows great variety. Some saints' lives are indeed no more than composites of convention and copying, but others contain a great deal of original material within their conventional framework. Here the linguistic approach can help identify the unconventional, but it is not of use when we are faced with what is unique. Of more use in that case is an understanding of the conditions within which the text was produced, to which end we must try to imagine what lay beyond the text, even if this involves speculation, and even if our only source is the text in question. Let us now examine the conditions in which Merovingian hagiography was produced, and how these conditions affected writing about saints in the period. We shall then be in a position to consider the phenomenon of sanctity as portrayed in these works and to ask whether it really was of the inferior quality often ascribed to it.

An important characteristic of Merovingian saints' lives is that they were often written soon after the events they described. The basic reason for their temporal proximity to events lay in the spread of the Christian Church from its traditional urban bases into new areas in the sixth century and especially in the seventh. As the Church spread, so the demand for saints and the number of cults multiplied. It was the creation of new saints in the sixth and seventh centuries in the wake of this growth which led to the sanctification of growing numbers of the Frankish elite and which resulted, naturally, both in the writing of saints' lives about people who had lived in recent memory, and in the adaptation of hagiography to the needs of a new group of people.[96]

Hagiography is a highly conventional form of writing. Seventh-century hagiographers had a range of models and examples they could draw on in order to make their subjects appear the equals of earlier saints. Martyrs of the pre-Constantinian Church became the archetype of saints throughout the Christian world, and accounts of their sufferings, deaths and miracles were one of the main sources of hagiographical convention in later centuries. Another source of convention was the genre of writing about the career of the bishop in which the late Roman style of aristocratic epitaph became fused with concepts of ideal behaviour drawn from biblical and patristic models.[97] A third source was earlier hagiography itself, with a few widely circulated works acting in effect as templates for later authors. In Francia, chief among these early *vitae* were versions of the *Life of St Martin of Tours* which reconciled the office of bishop with the vocation of the monk and provided a hallowed example of a confessor figure, that is, of one whose ascetic practices meant that he endured hardship for his faith without actually dying for it as a martyr did. Another highly influential model in the mid seventh century was the *Life of St Columbanus*. Collectively, these templates and conventions could be applied to a variety of saints, from the aristocratic bishops and abbots, who in their official duties exemplified higher moral values, or who died or suffered for the faith, to the man or woman who ran the family monastery and may have founded it. Common to the Lives of all of these types were a host of conventional attributes, but above all what marked out the sanctity of those people was the ability to perform miracles after death. When the demand for saints' cults generated by new monastic foundations outstripped the supply of martyrs and notables of the early Church, new cults were created when miracles were observed at the tombs of contemporary spiritual leaders. Hagiographers helped to establish and

---

96 Fouracre, 'History and Hagiography', 9–13.

97 On the epitaphs, M. Heinzelmann, *Bischofsherrschaft in Gallien*, Beihefte der *Francia*, 5 (Munich, 1976), and on the fusion of aristocratic 'virtue' and Christian merit, Heinzelmann, 'Neue Aspekte der biographischen und hagiographischen Literatur in der lateinischen Welt (1.–6. Jahrhundert), *Francia*, 1 (1973), and Heinzelmann, '"Sanctitas" und "Tugendadel": zur Konzeptionen von "Heiligkeit" in 5. und 10. Jahrhundert', *Francia*, 5 (1977). On the influence of the Bible, M. van Uytfanghe, 'La Bible dans les vies de saints mérovingiens', *Revue d'Histoire de l'Eglise de France*, 62 (1976), 103–11, and *idem*, 'Le Culte des Saints', *Settimane di Studio*, 36 (1989), 172–88.

consolidate these cults by writing an account of the saint's life which showed that he or she had the conventional attributes of a saint and which recorded the miracles he or she performed. Older cult centres reacted to this invention of new cults by adding to their stock of saints, and the general result was that more new saints were created in the sixth and seventh centuries than in any other comparable period in the history of the post-Constantinian Church.[98]

The use of convention was fundamental to the way in which sanctity could be spread to new levels of society and to the way in which people whom we might regard as apparently mundane could be portrayed as meriting the extraordinary powers of the saint. Frequent analogy between such people and already established saints was another important element in the process of sanctification. Leudegar's biographer, for instance, drew analogies between his subject and St Lawrence and the prophet Elijah, and compared him above all with Christ himself. In fact the very language of these works places their subjects at the end of a hallowed tradition. Sometimes that tradition is explicitly stressed, as in the prologue to the *Passio Praejecti*. The message throughout, at all levels, is that the new saints were as holy as their illustrious predecessors had been.

The development of what amounts almost to a formula through which sanctity could be constructed allowed hagiographers to work unpromising material into an acceptable shape. What makes their output so very interesting to us is the way in which they blended a degree of circumstantial detail with the traditional and conventional elements.[99] Much of this detail has the ring of authenticity, for not only is it sometimes corroborated in other contemporary sources, but it also seems to serve no obvious purpose in building up the saintly credentials of the subject, and thus the author would have had no reason to invent it. Occasionally, indeed, it seems actually to complicate or even embarrass the case for the hero's sanctity. Merovingian hagiographers can thus appear to have been incompetent, or their subjects unsaintly, or both. We can, however, explain to some extent why these authors wrote in ways which at times seem to us to compromise their subjects' sanctity. First, we must remember that the

---

98 Fouracre, 'History and Hagiography', 9.

99 Merovingian hagiography was in this way also setting up conventions for later authors to follow. As Prinz has pointed out, what is novel and ingenious in works of this period often appears as commonplace in texts of the central medieval period: F. Prinz. 'Der Heilige und seine Lebenswelt', *Settimane di Studio*, 36 (1989), 298–9.

ultimate criterion of sanctity was the ability to work miracles after death, for it was a sign that God had accepted the saint into heaven, and miracles in turn drew attention to the intercessionary powers of the saint.[100] The hagiographers worked on the assumption that miracles had already demonstrated the holiness of their subjects, even if this quality became known only after death. The conventional structure of a saint's life leads up to this final demonstration of supernatural power, and every aspect of his or her earthly career is subordinated to the ultimate achievement. If, as the author of the *Passio Leudegarii* put it, people got the wrong impression about anything the saint had done on earth, then it was entirely the fault of their own lack of vision and faith. Faith, therefore, resolved all apparent contradictions, the truth being revealed from the grave. Authors were thus given a certain degree of freedom to be candid about the earthly careers of their subjects. That they felt the need to be candid is the second part of our explanation of the way in which they wrote. The chief factor here was the constraint which the living memory of the intended audience imposed upon the author.

The fact that there was a rapid expansion of cults at the time meant, as we have seen, that contemporary religious leaders were increasingly the subjects of saints' lives. Such figures were often involved in conflicts and, especially if they were bishops, were likely to have had bitter rivals. The saintly relatives of no less a figure than Gregory of Tours had been involved in some very unseemly wrangles in the sixth century.[101] The career of Praejectus of Clermont shows us that the infighting continued for at least another century in Gregory's native Auvergne. An additional hazard for religious leaders who were important political figures was involvement in the factional fighting which was integral to politics at the time. Living memory was thus likely to be strong where such persons were concerned, since most later Merovingian saints were powerful and active members of the political community. The works translated here, the Lives of Balthild, Audoin, Praejectus, Leudegar, Geretrud and Aunemund, and indeed many others, all make reference to political conflict in which their subjects took part. We must assume that the original audiences of

100 The performance of miracles was in imitation of Christ, who also exercised His supernatural power through God, and did not have direct control over it. See van Uytfanghe, 'Le Culte des Saints', 173.

101 R. Van Dam, *Saints and their Miracles in Late Antique Gaul* (Princeton, New Jersey, 1993), pp. 55–63, gives a good account of the family and its problems in the later sixth century.

these works already knew a lot about the people concerned and about the events in which they had been involved. In some cases the events were complex, authors could not ignore them, and the saint's role in them needed a great deal of explaining, hence the great quantity and high quality of detail.

As the saint's life was in effect a public document, to be read out with solemnity, and since it was predicated upon ideals of peace and forgiveness, it seems likely that where authors showed great concern to explain the course and outcome of conflicts in which the saint was involved, the written account may also have been intended to set out an agreed version of events which helped to re-establish peace in the community. The clearest case of peace-making like this in our collection is the *Passio Praejecti*, in which the author records both the repentance and the forgiveness of those responsible for the saint's death. The donations they made to his cult could be interpreted as the payment of compensation for his slaying.[102] The work also implies that Praejectus himself bore some responsibility for his fate. Another work of the later Merovingian period, the *Life of St Lambert*, illustrates the phenomenon perhaps even more clearly: Lambert was killed in an act of vengeance, and the author actually tells us that he was implicated in the original deaths which prompted the retaliation and that he recognised that wrong had been done.[103] His martyrdom is thus presented in the context of more or less justifiable revenge. In such cases, where the *vita* had a peace-making function, if the author appears somewhat equivocal in his or her attitude towards the subject, this apparently lukewarm attitude may, therefore, be the result of the need to paint a balanced picture rather than of lack of enthusiasm, or competence, for the task in hand. The *Passio Leudegarii* also has an overt peace-making element, although here the issue of who was on which side is much clouded by the complexity of the political narrative. In this work, and generally where conflict plays a significant part in a saint's career, the devil appears as a third-party protagonist and as the ultimate source of dissension. It is obvious that the use of a supernatural third-party scapegoat must have been a great aid to agreement between opposing

---

102 Compensation by means of establishing a martyr cult is more clearly demonstrable in Anglo-Saxon England, where the value of the endowment of the cult can be seen to be the equivalent of the murdered person's *wergild*, as Rollason has shown in the case of the cult of St Mildrith: D. Rollason, *The Mildrith Legend. A Study in Early Medieval Hagiography in England.* (Leicester, 1982), pp. 49–51.

103 *Vita Landiberti Episcopi Traeiectensis Vetustissima*, chs. 11–17, ed. B. Krusch, *MGH, SSRM*, VI (Hanover and Leipzig, 1913), pp. 364–70.

parties, but the increasing prominence of the devil in early medieval hagiography also reflects the unassailable position that the Catholic Church had achieved in many parts of Western Europe by the later seventh century.[104] As we have seen, the development of hagiography was highly influenced by the accounts of the martyrs in the early Church. Saints traditionally suffered because of the evil done to them by non-believers. In our period, however, there were in effect no non-believers. When Church leaders suffered it was at the hands of other Christians. Even Ebroin, for instance, the mayor of the palace, who came to enjoy a reputation as a dreadful villain after he had had Leudegar put to death, met his end on the way to early morning mass. Thus when hagiographers had to come to terms with conflict within the same religious community, and to explain how Christians could come to hate each other, it was necessary to invoke the devil. In fact the most common explanation was that hatred was the result of envy whipped up by the devil, and this is quite understandable when so many conflicts were the product of rivalry for what were obviously limited resources of power and wealth.[105]

The observation that the inclusion of a great deal of historical detail was characteristic of those Lives written within living memory of their subjects becomes clearer when we can see how the successive versions of a Life treated the same subject material. The first four versions of the *Passio Leudegarii*, which span the period from the late seventh to the mid tenth centuries, show this development clearly. As they will be the subject of discussion later in this volume, suffice it here to note that, as each version was futher removed from the events it described, detail faded and the subject matter became progressively more starkly conventional. Each later version had a special meaning for the time in which it was produced, but by the same token it simplified and transformed the events of the Merovingian world. The same process of simplification, or the cutting out of details no longer relevant or even comprehensible to later audiences, can also be seen in comparisons between early and later versions of the *Vita Audoini* and the *Passio Praejecti*. It is, finally, on the basis of these observations that we have argued that one of the works included in this volume, the *Acta*

---

104 Demons had always been prominent in hagiography, as F. Graus shows, 'Hagiographie und Dämonenglauben', *Settimane di Studio*, 36 (1989). In works of the later seventh century it is more often Satan himself who disturbs the peace of the whole community, rather than his helpers, the lesser demons, who troubled individuals in earlier times.

105 Fouracre, 'Hagiography and History', 32, 36–7.

Aunemundi, does contain genuine Merovingian material even though in its present form it dates from the tenth century. The argument is based on the complexity of its historical detail and upon the observation that some of that detail is basically unflattering to its hero. It is therefore a rather exceptional case in which a later author revised a Merovingian work with few alterations.

Now that we have seen how and why Merovingian hagiographers sometimes made their subjects appear worldly, it is natural to ask whether these saints really were inferior in holiness to those heroes of the early Church with whom comparison was so often drawn. In other words, had the multiplication of saints and the acculturation of a warrior elite to the tradition of Christian sanctity led to a debasement of holiness in society? As we hinted earlier, there is some consensus among scholars that it had. It is a consensus which conforms to a modern pessimistic view of Merovingian history, but which also derives from a very early critical view of the standards of the Merovingian Church. That criticism came from the Anglo-Saxon missionary Boniface, who was active in Hesse in Germany in the second quarter of the eighth century. Boniface felt that the Frankish episcopate was generally of a low standard. Many of the bishops he met he found worldly, boorish and unhelpful. In an article published in 1954 which took its title from the memorable opening of one of Boniface's tirades against such people, Eugen Ewig traced the problems of the Frankish Church back into seventh century and back to a structural change it had then experienced.[106] Change, according to Ewig, took place when the powers of the state declined and the bishops in outlying regions were forced to become the leaders of the areas in which they held office. In assuming political and military leadership in addition to their role as religious leaders they evolved into the type of warrior bishop which Boniface confronted. Ewig's model was subsequently elaborated by Prinz and later by R. Kaiser, and the notion of the independent bishop in his 'episcopal republic' has become a mainstay of thinking about the period.[107]

---

106 E. Ewig, 'Milo et eiusmodi similes', in *Sankt Bonifatius Gedenkgabe zum zwölf-hundertsten Geburtstag* (Fulda, 1954), reprinted in E. Ewig, *Spätantikes und Fränkisches Gallien*, vol. 2, Beihefte der *Francia*, 3 (Munich, 1979), pp. 189–219. The phrase quoted in the title of this article means: 'Milo and men of his ilk'.

107 F. Prinz, 'Bischöfliche Stadtherrschaft im Frankenreich vom 5. bis 7. Jahrhundert', *Historische Zeitschrift*, 217 (1974); R. Kaiser, *Bischofsherrschaft zwischen Königtum und Fürstenmacht. Studien zur bischöflichen Stadtherrschaft im westfränkisch-französischen Reich im frühen und hohen Mittelalter* (Bonn, 1981); R. Kaiser, 'Royauté et pouvoir episcopal au nord de la Gaule (VIIe–IXe siècles)', in Atsma (ed.), *La Neustrie*, vol. 1.

It bears upon our hagiographic material in two ways. First, it emphasises the growing influence of the Frankish elite upon the Church and places this in a context of developing aristocratic independence. As religious leaders the members of that elite would be well represented among the new saints of the seventh century, and so many leading families acquired a saint in their ranks that Prinz, as we have seen, felt able to talk of a general process of 'aristocratic self-sanctification' in which the super-natural was recruited to reinforce the family's power on earth. Second, it is in the hagiography of this period that scholars find evidence not only for the process of 'aristocratic self-sanctification', but also, from a reading of the kind of detail we were discussing earlier, for the impression that later Merovingian bishops were political animals of a contumacious or even violent disposition. Together, these observations concerning personnel and behaviour add up to a picture of sanctity gained by rank rather than earned by good conduct, and the implication is that the sanctity of the period was scarcely less debased than the coinage.

This verdict is arguably harsh on the Merovingian saints in a number of ways. A close association between aristocratic status and sanctity in fact anti-dates the Merovingian period, and as we have just noted, some of the conventional attributes of the Christian saint derived from late Roman notions of aristocratic 'virtue'.[108] The term *sanctus* was actually applied to bishops generally in the late fifth and early sixth centuries, so the convergence of holiness and high social status, or rank, we find in our saints' lives was already in the seventh century part of a long tradition. In that sense the phenomenon of 'aristocratic self-sanctification' was not new in our period; what had changed was that now the bene-ficiaries were people who were culturally Frankish rather than Gallo-Roman.[109] If we go back to the sixth century we can find Gallo-Roman aristocratic or 'senatorial' saints who were hardly less worldly, and certainly no less controversial, than their seventh-century counterparts.

At the other end of our period, Boniface's blistering critique of the Frankish Church may well not be as significant as Ewig thought. Some of the missionary's complaints were obviously well founded, such as the Franks' failure to hold Church councils, but the clash between Boniface and the bishops (for which, incidentally, we only have Boniface's side of the story) seems to have derived partly from unresolved cultural differences between the two. Frankish bishops in

108 Heinzelmann, '"Tugendadel"'.
109 Heinzelmann, *Bischofsherrschaft*, pp. 128–9.

their urban bases had always had more secular responsibilities than
their Anglo-Saxon counterparts, and that alone may have made them
look 'worldly' to Boniface. One could add that a more pronounced
secularisation of the Frankish episcopate took place at the very time at
which Boniface was active in the region, and that it took place in the
course of the wars through which Boniface's patron, Charles Martel,
rose to power. As Martel's sons moved to consolidate their family's
postion on his death in 741, they espoused the cause of Church reform
partly as a means of securing their control over the episcopate, and
partly as a means to building up the resources of power. Boniface's
critique provided them with the impetus to call the Frankish Church
together in council, and it was at one of these councils, that of Estinnes
in 743, that they demanded the right to use Church property for the
benefit of the whole Christian community which was 'surrounded by
enemies on all sides'.[110] It was at this point, and within this rhetoric of
reform, that the secularisation of Church property began in earnest,
with the granting of ecclesiastical lands to laymen in the form of leases
known as *precaria*.[111] There were, therefore, two things happening
roughly in order in the first half of the eighth century: the first was
what could be termed militarisation of the episcopate in conditions of
widespread warfare, the second was the granting of Church lands to
laymen. Both developments came after the period in which our saints
were active, and, although Ewig was justified in tracing the roots of
secularisation back to the seventh century, it is quite wrong to imply
that the Church then was in the parlous state that Boniface said it was
two generations later. As we shall see from the evidence provided by
three of the *vitae* of bishops discussed in this volume, the idea that
bishops in the later seventh century had taken power into their own
hands and ruled their dioceses as if they were 'episcopal republics' is
unsound. It is based on the false conviction that there was a natural
opposition between centre and periphery in the Frankish state. On the
contrary, it was the involvement of these provincial bishops in
'national' politics which led to the conflicts which resulted in their
deaths. Nevertheless, they did die in controversial circumstances, and

---

110 On the Frankish Church and the question of 'secularisation' in the time of Charles
    Martel, T. Reuter, '"Kirchenreform" und "Kirchenpolitik" im Zeitalter Karl Martells.
    Begriffe und Wirklichkeit', and H.-W. Goetz, 'Karl Martell und die Heiligen.
    Kirchenpolitik und Maiordomat im Spiegel der spätmerowingischen Hagio-
    graphie', both in J. Jarnut, U. Nonn and M. Richter (eds.), *Karl Martell in seiner Zeit*
    (Sigmaringen, 1994).

111 On the granting of *precaria* in this context, I. Wood, 'Teutsind, Witlaic and the
    History of Merovingian *precaria*', in Davies and Fouracre (eds.), *Property and Power*.

even if Boniface's critique has been misinterpreted, and even if we can understand why their biographers were sometimes less than flattering towards them, we are still left with the impression that these people only just scraped into the ranks of the saints.

A final thought on this issue of comparative sanctity may help to put the matter into a wider cultural perspective. As we have seen, it was above all the proximity of subject and audience which made the saint in Merovingian hagiography look somewhat worldly. It may be true that familiarity with the living saints sometimes bred an equivocal attitude towards their heavenly credentials, but we should remember that such familiarity also reflected the spread of sanctity into new areas and the need to find new saints among contemporary leaders. The multiplication of saints in the sixth and seventh centuries marked a massive advance of Christian culture in European society. From the mid eighth century onwards we meet with a rather different situation in which the advance of the previous centuries was consolidated. Fewer and fewer new saints were created as leaders, institutions and communities invested in existing cults which were now in plentiful supply. An additional element here was the increasingly organised control over cults which was exercised by leading families and, from the later eighth century, by rulers. This extension of control has already been alluded to with reference to the reform councils of the 740s, and it culminated with Charlemagne's order that no new saints should be created without his say-so.[112] Closer control over sanctity and over the process of sanctification had the effect of bringing convention even more strongly to the fore in hagiography, as the subjects it dealt with were people who had lived and died in what was now a remote past. Greater emphasis was also placed on the miracles wrought at the saint's tomb as institutions sought to conserve their attractiveness by promoting the powers of the saints they housed. As already noted, the amount of historical detail in the saints' lives decreased as the gap between subject and audience widened with the passage of time. The net effect was not just to strengthen the conventional element in hagiography but also to leave the saints looking much holier, and with a lot more miracles to their credit.

Comparative sanctity is therefore ultimately impossible to assess. Comparisons indeed may well be unfair, as the norms and conventions of sanctity which were established in new areas thanks to our Merovingian hagiographers were passed on to later generations. Then later, having

112 This order was given at the Synod of Frankfurt in 794: *MGH Capitularia*, I, ed. A. Boretius (Hanover 1883), no. 28, ch. 42.

been stripped of accompanying detail, these conventions conveyed an ideal type of sanctity against which the original Merovingian saints did not compare at all well. From the evidence provided in the Merovingian *vitae* themselves it is fair to be sceptical about the holiness of many of the figures who will appear in the pages of this volume. But, by the same token, one would have to question the entire tradition of sanctity in Western Europe in the period before the Gregorian reform. What makes these saints different from most of their predecessors and successors is that we know more about them. What we see here in more detail than elsewhere is consistent with what we know in general about sanctity in the early medieval period: that it developed only in ways which reinforced rather than challenged the groups which controlled the political and social structure. There may be grounds here for scepticism, but it would be anachronistic to imagine that medieval people were sceptical, for what made sanctity a mainstay of social consensus was precisely their willingness to believe in it, and their desire to enjoy its benefits.

We have now seen what sources there are for later Merovingian history and how the works translated in this volume fit into the general pattern of source material. We have looked at how historians have tried to assess the age, the originality and the veracity of the sources, and the general issues underlying the interpretation of early medieval texts. The focus has been largely upon hagiography, because that genre of writing not only forms the bulk of our material, it also requires us to think carefully about how we can attempt to deduce some sort of historical reality from texts of a highly conventional, yet sometimes controversial, nature.[113] We can now conclude this part of our introductory survey by looking at the different overviews of Merovingian history which have been constructed from our sources in the last century, and we will end with some thoughts of our own.

In the late nineteenth and early twentieth centuries historians tended to view the Merovingian period from the perspective of constitutional history (*Verfassungsgeschichte*), a perspective which derived from the view that societies were structured according to their laws.[114] This

---

113 Fouracre, 'History and Hagiography', addresses this question in relation to Merovingian texts; Prinz, 'Der Heilige und seine Lebenswelt', tackles it in much wider terms.

114 The two prime examples of this approach, which express different national points of view, are G. Waitz, *Deutsche Verfassungsgeschichte*, third edition (Kiel, 1882), and N. Fustel de Coulanges, *La Monarchie franque* (Paris, 1888).

legalistic approach also had an ethnic dimension, in that it perceived that in Francia there were two sources of law, Roman and Germanic, upon each of which was based a range of insitutions. In this view, change occurred when Germanic principles and institutions of a private and personal nature displaced Roman law and public institutions of Roman origin. This way of thinking has survived down to our own generation, for instance in the view that the battle of Tertry in 687, at which the ancestors of the Carolingians were victorious over the old Merovingian regime, marked the victory of Germanic over Roman systems of government.[115] A variation on this constitutionalist perspective comes from history written from a regional viewpoint, a tradition of writing which in France stretches back centuries to the Maurist school. In that tradition, historians have tried to read a regional point of view into the sources and thus to emphasise local variations in institutional development. In its most romantic form this approach has led to the anachronistic notion that regional identity was so strong that it was the basis of a political consciousness, and the general effect of regional studies been to encourage emphasis on the degree of regional difference in the Merovingian kingdom.[116] The regional viewpoint, therefore, has worked to reinforce the assumption that the Merovingian body politic was under constant strain, in this case with regional separatism pulling against central institutions.

Thinking on a more general level about society and culture in the Merovingian period has also been strongly influenced by the idea of a transition from a Roman to a Germanic culture, as we saw earlier in this introduction with reference to Merovingian archaeology. Attention here has focused on the character and behaviour of the aristocracy in the later Merovingian period, the assumption being that its behaviour changed once it had become culturally Frankish. This is what lies behind much of the discussion about warrior bishops and about the phenomenon of 'aristocratic self-sanctification'. In terms of the social and economic relations which such people had with those below them in society, again the general assumption has been that there was a blending of Roman and Germanic traditions. That there had been a

---

115 See, for instance, K.-F. Werner, 'Les principautés périphériques dans le monde franque du VIIe siècle', *Settimane di Studio*, 20 (1972), 493–4, reprinted in K.-F. Werner, *Structures politiques du monde franque (VIIe–XIIe siècles)*, (London, 1979), ch. 2.

116 An example with direct relevance to the sources discussed in this volume is M. Chaume, *Les Origines du duché de Bourgogne* (Dijon, 1926) which set the careers of both Aunemund and Leudegar in the context of a struggle for Burgundian 'separatism'. See below, pp. 176–7, 197–8.

synthesis between the two cultures, with Roman ideas of property being fused with Germanic social customs, was, of course, the cornerstone of Marx's theory of the 'feudal mode of production'. Although his comments upon this period were too general and too ill informed to have any immediate academic impact, Marx's general model of early medieval social development was highly influential in the first half of the twentieth century. His ideas were adapted and applied to the Merovingian period with great finesse, first by M. Bloch, and then by F. L. Ganshof.[117] What these scholars did was to take advantage of the increasingly sophisticated understanding of early medieval economic history which emerged in the inter-war period, and apply it to traditional notions of institutional and legal change. The result was a picture in which institutions of private power were seen to develop and then form the basis of an emergent state of a new type, a development which took place in tandem with concentration of the control of economic production in the hands of great landholders. So-called 'feudal' relationships allegedly evolved as political support and military service were rewarded with land tenure. These new relations of power were held to be both a cause and a consequence of the decline of the Merovingian state, which became critically short of land, income and loyalty. The Carolingians, by contrast, were said to have benefited from the new conditions, having much land at their disposal, and making sure that they got their loyalty's worth from it.

All these approaches to Merovingian history tended in practice to be schematic. In other words, their interpretation of the evidence narrows down to particular arguments which underpin their specific scheme of history. In our commentaries we will point out instances where a schematic approach has in this way had a distorting effect upon views of the period. The traditional approaches also had in common a pessimistic attitude, whether about the state of the Church, institutions of goverment, the performance of the economy, the quality of urban life or the character of the kings. The later seventh century has thus been interpreted as a low point for all these. Here the post-modernist critique we discussed earlier in relation to early medieval texts is in fact useful in revealing negative undertones in the language, not of our sources, but of modern historians. When talking about about this period they tended to focus on strongly opposed concepts, such as 'strength' and 'weakness' or 'separatism' and 'centralisation'. In

117 The two seminal works are M. Bloch, *Feudal Society*, trans. L. Manyon (London, 1965) and F. Ganshof, *Feudalism*, trans. P. Grierson (London, 1964).

the use of such concepts the negative term tends to refer to the Merovingian context, and the postive term to the Carolingian, with the latter term often posed as a solution to a problem. Ganshof, for instance, posed Carolingian 'feudalism' as a solution to Merovingian 'anarchy'. The disadvantage of thinking in such strong terms is that they exclude compromise, and compromise is actually very important in societies which have weak institutions.[118] The traditional discourse was also anchored to strong principles of change, whereas in fact early medieval society was in general remarkably unchanging.

Some recent work has sought to redress the balance by arguing for the survival of a much larger element of Roman culture in both Merovingian and Carolingian society, thus emphasising continuity rather than change. Walter Goffart, for instance, has consistently played down any Germanic element in early medieval culture, questioning the very use of the term 'Germanic' except to refer to the language group of that name.[119] Work on the economy, on law, literacy, government, the Church and, as we have just seen, on the culture of sanctity has sought to understand these subjects in their own terms rather than in relation to the long-term history of the European state.[120] There has also been growing interest in the history of women in this period, a subject which traditional scholarship largely ignored.[121] Recent overviews of the Merovingian period, such as that by Ian Wood,[122] have built upon this more enlightened research to present a picture of society in which cultural transformation was normal rather than dysfunctional and in which historical development did not revolve around a supposed clash between the private greed of magnates and the public authority of rulers. Let us close by examining the implications of these more nuanced views of Merovingian history.

By concentrating on the progressive decline of public authority as

118 Fouracre, 'History and Hagiography', 29–31.

119 This theme runs at various levels throughout Goffart's work (as it does too in the work of his former pupil, A. C. Murray). See, for example, its importance to the overall argument of Goffart, *The Narrators of Barbarian History* (Princeton, New Jersey, 1988).

120 No consolidated bibliography of Merovingian studies exists, but the list of works cited at the end of I. Wood, *The Merovingian Kingdoms*, gives some indication of the range of recent publications.

121 See, for instance, S. F. Wemple, *Women in Frankish Society. Marriage and the Cloister 500 to 900* (Philadelphia, 1981), and J. NcNamara and J. Halborg, eds. and trans., *Sainted Women of the Dark Ages* (London and Durham, 1992).

122 I. Wood, *The Merovingian Kingdoms*.

represented by the Roman state, historians used to imply that
Merovingian society was characteristically unstable. If, however, we
soften the sense of opposition between the public and the private and
also think of the transition from the Roman state to the medieval one
not as an interlude but as a lasting state of affairs in its own right, then
we get a rather different impression in which the Merovingian regime
was no different in essentials from its Carolingian successor, and thus
was a form of organised power which lasted for over 400 years. From
this point of view the onus upon us is to explain the stability and
durability of the Frankish polity rather than to concentrate upon its
perceived weaknesses. We must accept, of course, that in many ways
later Merovingian government was weak, and it is undeniable that
some of the later kings indeed justified description as *rois fainéants* ('do-
nothing' kings), if only because they were small children. But in
eschewing the negative approach we must think hard about why these
factors did not provoke collapse in what was a weak but nevertheless
massive kingdom, in fact, the largest in Western Europe. We must,
therefore, try to understand what factors made child kingship possible
here and nowhere else in Europe.

What emerges from the sources translated here is that in Merovingian
society (and in Carolingian society too) the 'state' held together largely of
its own accord. 'Consensus' is a word which will often be used in the
following pages in discussions about politics, and we feel free to use it
so frequently because it expresses the idea that important decisions
were properly made in consultation This idea was dear to the Franks
in our period. Emphasis on consensus also leads one to think that to
these people any notion of what constituted the 'state' was open to
interpretation, and the dividing line between what were public
institutions and what was seen as private prerogative was blurred.
Likewise the definition of law and custom remained elastic. What we
have in our sights is a kingdom which was massive in size and which
held together because its magnates – the dukes, bishops and counts,
the people who figure in the sources discussed here – were willing
participants in government either through the royal palace or in the
provinces. When significant numbers refused to participate the result
was near anarchy, as we see in the events of the crisis of 675–76, but
mostly they did work together. The reasons for their participation are
complex, but the overall impression remains that, in the last resort, it
was their way of securing their privileged position in society, that is,
of legitimising their power or of garnering the wealth to support their

high social status. In this way public authority was becoming less a fiscal and institutional arrangement than a cultural phenomenon as fiscal rights and control of institutions fell into the hands of magnates who used them both to bolster their private power and to maintain public order. Government was increasingly produced through an association of the powerful rather than by the direction of the ruler through a salaried bureaucracy, a development which took place not as a result of Roman giving way to Germanic systems of government but as the fiscal basis of bureaucratic government withered away.[123] We see the expression of this state of affairs in our sources in the form of intense interest in the politics of faction through which the rewards of government were distributed. Likewise our authors were all familiar with the language of power and were keenly aware of the role of law in limiting that arbitrary use of power which might threaten the strong as well as harm the weak. And, as we have seen at some length already, underpinning a sense of common identity and collective interest were a spreading Christian culture and ecclesiastical organisation which had the capacity to fill the spaces which were left when institutions inherited from the Roman world became moribund. It is against this background that we find the sense of opposition between concepts of 'public institutions' and 'private interests' unhelpful. Similarly, in this view, various Merovingian regimes may at times have been in crisis, but the polity as a whole worked relatively well, given its limited resources and meagre ambitions.

What we have outlined is a rough model, and in putting it forward we do not pretend that it is comprehensive. There are simply too many elements missing from our sources to allow us to understand Merovingian

---

123 The scholarly consensus that direct taxation withered away in Merovingian Gaul has been challenged in a series of articles by E. Magnou-Nortier in which she argues for a reinterpretation of the terminology of Frankish documents which deal with property and income, insisting that terms usually associated with private property have a fiscal significance: E. Magnou-Nortier, 'Etude sur le privilège d'immunité du IVe au IXe siècle', *Revue Mabillon*, 60 (1984); 'Les "Pagenses", notables et fermiers du fisc durant le haut Moyen-âge', *Revue Belge de Philologie et d'Histoire*, 65, vol. 2 (1987); 'La gestion publique en Neustrie: les moyens et les hommes (VIIe–IXe siècles)', in Atsma (ed.), *La Neustrie*, vol. 1. J. Durliat has surveyed the history of taxation throughout the early medieval period, and, basing his approach on Magnou-Nortier, has come to the conclusion that a system of direct taxation remained in force at the end of the ninth century, having survived in unbroken continuity from the later Roman Empire: J. Durliat, *Les Finances Publiques de Dioclétien aux Carolingiens (284–889)*, Beihefte der *Francia*, 21 (Sigmaringen, 1990). This view has found little support. For the basic objections to it see C. Wickham, 'La Chute de Rome n'aura pas lieu: à propos d'un livre récent', *Le Moyen Age*, 99 (1993).

society in greater depth. The dearth of information on economic matters has already been mentioned, and the vast mass of those who produced wealth in that society, female and male peasants and slaves, we meet only as the occasional stereotype in hagiography. It is therefore even more important to make the best sense we can of what information we do possess, and this is the strongest single reason for treating Merovingian Francia as a viable and normal rather than as a transitional state. In other words, we must try to some extent to share the perspectives of the people who appear in our sources if we are to understand why they behaved as they did. It is of course interesting, and in the wider frame important, to know what would later become of the world in which they lived, but that was no concern of theirs, and if we make it too much a concern of ours we shall not be able to understand them.

Merovingian Latin: the language of the sources

The surviving local and contemporary sources for the history of the Merovingian age were all written in Latin, every one. The vernacular languages in the Frankish areas did not find their way to a parchment we know about until half a century after the Carolingian take-over,[124] and the Greeks, Anglo-Saxons and others have left us precious little about matters Merovingian in their own tongues. To know the Merovingians is to read their Latin.

Our task in this section is to describe Merovingian Latin and to point out how and where the characteristics of the language itself either can be or should not be used as the basis of arguments helping us to understand the texts. To that end we shall begin with a very brief history of the Latin language from the time when the literary idiom was set in its 'Ciceronian' or classical form to the period of the Carolingian reforms. We shall then take up a description of 'Merovingian Latin', the Latin used in our texts. After commenting on the difficult problems linguists encounter when trying to analyse this Latin, we shall describe, as best we can, its vocabulary, grammar, spelling and style.

The Latin the Merovingians wrote is for the most part, with the exception of that written by the seventh-century chronicler known as Fredegar, thoroughly understandable to someone trained in the

---

124 J. Bostock, *A Handbook on Old High German Literature*, second edition, revised by K. C. King and D. R. McLintock, (Oxford, 1976), p. 74.

standard Ciceronian idiom. But Merovingian Latin is by no means Ciceronian; it varies from it greatly in its vocabulary, grammar and style. The study of Merovingian Latin is important for two reasons. First, the language occupies a crucial position in the history both of Latin itself and of the Romance vernaculars. Second, and more important for our purposes, the characteristics of the Latin often provide an important means by which we can assess whether or not a given text is indeed Merovingian. Although Merovingian Latin has been taken as evidence for the low educational level of the authors who used it and even of their surroundings, as we shall see, there are reasons to tread lightly here.

It is not only the written language of the Merovingian period but the spoken language as well which will demand our attention. The period saw great development in the spoken vernacular languages; in fact they seem to have come into being while the line of Clovis held the Frankish throne. But the famous question 'When did people stop speaking Latin?' has never found a satisfactory answer. For any period before the use of voice recording our only means of assessing a spoken language comes from written sources. Even when a written source contains a speech, a play, a sermon, alleged quotations from the spoken language, or appears to resemble what was spoken in some other way, we are beset with huge difficulties in trying to push past the written to hear the spoken. The language in which Cicero so elegantly harangued Cataline in the Senate in 63 BC was probably very close to that of the laboriously written version which he later published. But it was different from the spoken language which most people used, even those working in Rome itself on the very day he was speaking.

The Ciceronian form of Latin has endured unchanged because it is 'dead'. Cicero and the famous authors of the Augustan age established the norms of elegant written Latin and they have not changed. From the very beginning this Latin was erudite, rarified, and greatly affected by the literary language of the Greeks, whom the Latin authors often claimed to despise. In a sense this dead language was stillborn, since many of its admired qualities began as literary affectations. Even today as students bang away at memorising Latin paradigms, the example of 'good' Latin held out to them at the end of the lesson book will still be one of the Catalinarians or a passage from the *Aeneid.* Did the Merovingian authors 'learn' their Latin in that sense? If so, was their goal at the end of their studies the exquisite, erudite and dead language of the ancient Roman educated class or was it something else? Was it a

Christian Latin, taken from the, by then, long tradition of biblical, theological and liturgical texts? Or did they simply try to write what they themselves and their educated contemporaries spoke? Did they write what the uneducated masses could understand? Should we even consider what they wrote Latin at all, or was it the written version of an early form of the vernacular? What language did they think they were writing? Despite the flowing of much learned ink concerning these questions, the answers are not clear.

Cicero's world was pagan, the Merovingians' Christian; the difference was not only one of religion, but also one of language. From the very first, Christian authors, both Greek and Latin, tended to eschew the high literary language and to write in a simpler way. In Latin this simpler style contained many elements which must have been taken from the spoken language along with many religious words borrowed directly from Greek. There were some early Christian authors who clung to the ancient literary language (Minucius Felix, and to a lesser degree Lactantius and Ambrose), but after Tertullian (c. AD 160– c. AD 220) the high literary style tended to disappear in Christian texts. Eventually in the Christian tradition, instead of Cicero and the Augustan authors, it was Tertullian, Augustine and Jerome who set the standards. Their language took the earlier simple Christian Latin and made it capable of rich expression.[125] A good word to describe the result might be journalistic, that is, their Latin was on the one hand certainly neither elegantly turgid nor obviously literary, but on the other neither was it patronising nor irregular. It found dignity in clarity and beauty in directness. It was meant to communicate serious matters in a serious way, largely stripped of weighty allusion and periodic con-struction. This was the language Jerome used for the Vulgate, a somewhat unfortunate name since it sounds like 'vulgar Latin', the term used to describe the language spoken by the *vulgus*, the common people. The term 'vulgar Latin', too, can be misleading, because it may imply that the commonly spoken language had more unity to it than it did, or that it was spoken only by the uneducated.[126] Jerome's biblical Latin, although closer to the spoken than was the Ciceronian idiom, still varied greatly from vulgar Latin. Augustine wrote in many styles: a rather simpler one for his sermons, one tinted with mystic Neoplatonism

---

125 C. Mohrmann, 'Die Rolle des Lateins in der Kirche des Westens', in her *Etudes sur le latin des chrétiens*, vol 2, *Storia e Letteratura*, 87 (Rome, 1961), p. 39.

126 'The much-used term "Vulgar Latin" is multivalent and best avoided.' R. Wright, *Late Latin and early Romance in Spain and Carolingian France* (Liverpool, 1982), p. 52.

for the *Confessions*, and a more high-sounding one for the *City of God*. Alongside these developments in the written language, the spoken Latin, too, was changing. It was obviously the spoken language and not the written one which would evolve at various times and in varying degrees into the Romance vernaculars. Thus at the beginning of the period from which the Merovingian texts in this volume are drawn, that is, by the seventh century, there were at least three 'Latins' being used in Gaul. The ancient classical language was still taught in what remained of the Roman schools;[127] the biblical, patristic and liturgical Latin was used in the churches and in the monasteries; and the vulgar Latin, in whatever and in however many forms, was spoken by the people. All three influenced each other to a greater or lesser degree. Three there were, and yet none is the Latin of our texts.

As for the historian trying to see many of the other aspects of Merovingian history, so too the view of the period's written language is clouded by the 'cleansing' it underwent at the hands of Carolingian copyists. The reformed Carolingian written language is clearly a hybrid of the ancient Ciceronian and the patristic Christian forms. This fusion owes a great deal to Anglo-Saxon influence and especially to Alcuin, for the Latin written in the British Isles was closer to its 'purer' ancient form, probably because there the written language was clearly a different beast from the spoken one and thus open to far less influence from it. It is the Carolingians who are often accused of making Latin a dead language. Their reforms were far-reaching. Most immediately obvious to anyone reading their texts are the attempts to standardise the earlier orthography. They also 'corrected' grammatical usage and style. In reforming the Latin language, to a certain extent they mummified it by bringing it closer to its ancient standards and thus moving it further from the contemporary living language in either its written or its spoken version.[128] Parallel to this, it is assumed, the spoken language continued to change with time, as spoken languages

127 C. Mohrmann, 'Les formes du latin dit "vulgaire". Essai de chronologie et de systém-atisation: de l'époque augustéenne aux langues romanes', in her *Etudes sur le latin des chrétiens*, vol 2, p. 136. Reprinted from *Actes du premier Congrès d'études classiques*, Paris, 1951. Pierre Riché thinks that although the public lay schools shut in Gaul about the year 500, secular classical education went on with private tutors and in the ecclesiastical schools until about the year 700. P. Riché, 'L'instruction des laïcs en Gaule mérovingienne au viie siècle', in his *Instruction et vie religieuse dans le Haut Moyen-âge* (London, 1981), pp. 880–7, reprinted from *Settimane di Studio*, 5 (1957).

128 The strongest statement of this view comes from Roger Wright who says that the Carolingians did not just reform medieval Latin but invented it. Wright, *Late latin*. Despite disagreement from P. Godman, *Poetry of the Carolingian Renaissance* (London,

do, until it was no longer vulgar Latin but became a form of one of the early Romance vernaculars. This development, however, does not seem to have been a simple, separate and straightforward evolution from vulgar Latin to proto-Romance. Until the Carolingian reforms the spoken and written languages seem to have influenced each other as they travelled their separate tracks. It is a safe assumption that they were different, just as modern spoken English has many varieties, all differing from the standard written form. But how different the spoken language and the written language were is very much open to question. The Merovingian written texts appear to be Latin, but they may have been to a greater or lesser degree the written version of an early form of the vernacular. In other words, Merovingian scribes and authors may have used outdated Latin forms to record words which had a different contemporary pronunciation. This phenomenon exists in modern French and modern English, both of which contain words in every sentence whose written forms are so old that they have little relationship to way in which they are currently spoken. But even if such were the case with early medieval language, the development happened at some point in the Merovingian period, where we obviously cannot hear it, and unfortunately cannot see it very well in the surviving written texts. It is not until after the Carolingian reforms that we have evidence which may suggest that those writing in Gaul were aware that the spoken language was no longer Latin.[129]

When did people stop speaking Latin?[130] Or, in other words, when

---

1985), p. 146, and modification offered by R. McKitterick, *The Carolingians and the Written Word* (Cambridge, 1989), pp. 12–22, he stuck by his view ten years on. R. Wright, 'The conceptual distinction between Latin and Romance: invention or evolution?' in R. Wright (ed.), *Latin and the Romance Languages in the early Middle Ages* (London, 1991), p. 109.

129 The spoken language was referred to as *lingua rustica romana*, the phrase coming from the Council of Tours in the year 813. Cf. P. Riché, 'L'enseignement et la culture des laïcs dans l'Occident pré-carolingien', in his *Instruction et vie religieuse dans le Haut Moyen-âge* (London, 1981), p. 247, reprinted from *Settimane di Studio*, 19 (1972). McKitterick will postpone the development. Basing her conclusions on a careful analysis of Carolingian grammar books, she concludes that these books '… support the view that Latin was not learnt by the Franks in the ninth century as a foreign language but as the formal written form of the language they used every day.' R. McKitterick, 'Latin and Romance: an historian's perspective', in Wright (ed.), *Latin and the Romance Languages* (London, 1991), p. 132.

130 The classic treatment of the question is by Dag Norberg, who sees a long period of transition, with the years AD 600–800 as decisive. D. Norberg, 'A quelle époque a-t-on cessé de parler latin?', *Annales*, 21 (1966), 346–56. Marc Van Uytfanghe agrees. M. Van Uytfanghe, 'Le latin des hagiographes mérovingiens et la protohistoire du français', *Romanica gandensia*, 16 (1976), 81–2.

would a person without special training no longer have understood our texts? Recently an attempt has been made to make the question irrelevant by replying that most of Europe never did stop speaking Latin and still does speak it, in the form of the modern Romance languages.[131] Answering the question in that way is helpful because it reminds historians, addicts of written texts, that the main and natural line of development has been in the spoken, not the written, language, and that written Latin, at least since the Carolingian reforms, in many ways has had an artificial life of its own, at times closer to, at times further from, the classical norms. Obviously the Carolingian reforms did not mummify medieval Latin completely. The fact that several other 'reform' movements would follow the Carolingians' in the centuries to come shows that written medieval Latin once again became a living and changing medium with a life of its own.[132] With that in mind, historians should beware the alluring trap of judging the 'level' or quality of a medieval Latin text by the degree to which it varies from 'good Latin'.[133] The trap is alluring because the analysis is easy. In the antique written idioms, both patristic and Ciceronian, we have clear and known standards. Thus the degree to which a given medieval text varies from those standards is easily measurable and can be done in such a quantifiable way as to appear empirical.[134] Although in some cases such a comparison can yield valuable insight, the real quality of a text is more properly assessed by such criteria as how well it fulfilled its function and the degree to which its contemporaries saw in it the literary qualities they valued. As opposed to the measurement against classical usage, that sort of analysis is much more demanding precisely because there the standards of comparison are much more difficult to establish. They are difficult to establish because they must perforce arise from the very texts under scrutiny.

131 Roger Wright, in the introduction to his edited volume, *Latin and the Romance Languages*, p. 3. As Van Uytfanghe, 'Le Latin', 21, puts it: *Certes, il est devenu banal de dire ... que, somme toute, le français actuel est le latin du xxe siècle parlé dans la région qui est aujourd'hui la France.* Michel Banniard, however, disagrees: ... *quoique les langues romanes soint issues du latin, elles ne sont plus le latin, même au sens le plus large possible.* M. Banniard, *Viva Voce. Communication écrite et communication orale du ive au ixe siècle en Occident latin* (Paris, 1992), p. 15.

132 Mohrmann, 'Le latin médieval', in her *Etudes sur le latin des chrétiens*, vol. 2, p. 193. Reprinted from: *Cahiers de Civilization Médiévale*, I:3, (1958).

133 See Christine Mohrmann's elegant statement regarding the work of Taube and the earlier analysts of medieval Latin. Mohrmann, 'Le latin', pp. 184–5.

134 For example see M. Pei, *The Language of Eighth-Century Texts in Northern France*, (Ph.D. dissertation, Columbia University, New York, 1932).

What, then, caused the written Language to change over the centuries? Some consider the primary factor to have been influence from the spoken language.[135] Others see the changes arising from creative factors inherent within the language itself. Once the spoken and written were perceived as different languages, and not just different levels of formality of the same language, the Latin would be much less open to influence from the now vernacular tongue.[136] Latin authors would find inspiration for their creativity from within the world of Latin texts itself, and, so the argument runs, they would especially find it in the ancient texts, pagan as well as Christian.[137] Does the very fact that a Merovingian hagiographer wrote in Latin mean that in a very real sense he removed his intellectual life from his contemporary world and whatever it considered linguistically beautiful or intellectually valuable, and placed himself in a rather *Weltfremd* tradition which took its inspiration from the patristic age, if not from the classical pagans beyond? Or does it simply mean that Latin was the only written medium available?

Let us attempt to describe this Merovingian Latin as best we can. At the very beginning we are beset with a huge problem: we are all but lacking contemporary manuscripts. One manuscript of *The Chronicles of Fredegar* dates from the seventh century, but from the relatively full corpus of hagiographic material relating to the Merovingian period, a body of texts it took several large volumes of the *Monumenta Germaniae Historica* to edit, we have only two surviving manuscripts from the hand of scribe writing in the Merovingian era.[138] Some of these 'Merovingian' sources in the *Monumenta* were actually written in the Carolingian age and thus could not have been Merovingian manuscripts, but even for those truly contemporary late Merovingian narrative sources, all the surviving copies (except for the manuscripts

---

135 *Le Latin mérovingienne a surtout subi une influence profonde de la langue parlée.* D. Norberg, *Manuel pratique de latin médiéval* (Paris, 1968), p. 29.

136 Recently scholars have taken up meta-linguistic considerations, that is, questions concerning authors' (or speakers') perceptions of their own language, as opposed to characteristics of the language itself. See P. M. Lloyd, 'On the Names of Languages' in Wright (ed.), *Latin and the Romance Languages*, pp. 9–18, and the other articles in the same volume.

137 Mohrmann, 'Le latin', pp. 188–9.

138 Paris, BN Lat. 18315, which contains the *Vita Sancti Wandregiseli*, and Paris, BN no. 9550 (Suppl. lat. 839), which contains the *Passio Acanunensium martyrum.* Walter Berschin, however, accepts only BN 18315 as truly Merovingian. W. Berschin, *Biographie und Epochenstil im lateinischen Mittelalter, vol. 2: Merowingische Biographie. Italien, Spanien und die Inseln im Frühen Mittelalter, Quellen und Untersuchungen zur lateinischen Philologie des Mittelalters*, 9 (Stuttgart, 1988), facing p. ix.

mentioned above) were copied at a time when their scribes were open
to influences from the Carolingian reforms of the language. Alcuin's
De Orthographia was probably writtten to assist Carolingian scribes in
correcting the spelling when copying the older texts.[139] Does a con-
sciencious Carolingian scribe making a copy of an older work faithfully
copy what he has before him in his exemplar when he can see obvious
'misspellings' and 'mistakes' in the grammar? Or does he intentionally,
or for that matter inadvertently, change the Latin to reflect what he
has been taught is proper?[140] It seems some did change it and some did
not. Often the surviving manuscripts reflect two versions of a
Merovingian saint's life, one with rather standardised spelling and a
grammmar closer to classical norms and another one seemingly more
chaotic. We have chosen texts for this volume with an eye on their
ability to shed light on what appear to be differences between Latin
written during the Merovingian period and Latin written after the
Carolingian reforms. Comparing the *Liber Historiae Francorum*, our
first text and a Merovingian one, with the *Annales Mettenses Priores*,
our last text and Carolingian, has made many of the differences
obvious. In fact, the differences in the Latin are so striking that they
come through even in our English translations. The surviving manuscripts of the *Vita Balthildis*, our second text, fall into two groups, each
preserving a different version of the text. One appears to be Merovingian,
the other Carolingian, and thus this text too has provided us with a
fruitful basis for a comparison of the Latin.[141] Merovingian hagiography has been fortunate in having had extremely careful and skilful
modern editors, in Bruno Krusch and Wilhelm Levison. They rigor-
ously applied the methods of modern scholarship in order to reconstruct the Merovingian texts, and almost all the works now considered
to have first been written in the Merovingian period are contained in
the series *Scriptorum Rerum Merovingicarum* of the *Monumenta Germaniae
Historica*, which they edited.[142] But since, with the two exceptions, we

---

139 McKitterick, 'Latin and Romance', p. 132.

140 As Max Manitius thought. M. Manitius, *Geschichte der lateinischen Literatur des
Mittelalters*, vol. I (Munich,1911), p. 177.

141 For instance, in chapter 14 of the *Vita Balthildis* we find ... *et pios occulos ac sanctis
manibus ad caelum erectis* ... in the Merovingian version (A), and the more classical
reading ... *et pios occulos ac sanctas manus ad caelum elevans* ... in the Carolingian
version (B). See below, p. 129.

142 An important exception is the *Acta Sancti Aunemundi alias Dalfini episcopi*, not found
in the *MGH*, *SSRM*, but edited by P. Perrier, *AASS*, Septembris, vol. VII
(Antwerp, 1760), pp. 744–6. We have translated this text below, pp. 179–92.

have no manuscripts from before the Carolingian reforms, every edited text, even those with manuscripts seemingly less contaminated by the reformers, is a reconstruction based on manuscripts from some period after the advent of those reforms. The editors have usually put the authority of the manuscripts above all else, that is, they have rarely chosen a reading of a text which is not found in a manuscript. If, for instance, they were to find the phrase *vitae sinctorum* they would not change it to *vitae sanctorum* unless they found that reading in one of the text's manuscripts.[143] It is obviously wiser to use this method than to not do so, but it does nonetheless raise the suspicion that perhaps even sound editorial rules themselves present a Merovingian language to us that appears to have more variety in it than it actually did. On the other hand, even if modern editors do not 'clean up mistakes', perhaps the Carolingian scribes did, and in so doing present a Merovingian language to us that appears to have not more but less variety in it than it actually did. We have tried to translate the texts exactly as their skilled editors have given them to us, but on occasion we too have had to use a reading from a manuscript which varies from the edited text.[144] In addition to these general problems, the reconstruction of hagiographic texts for our period in particular, the late seventh and early eighth centuries, reminds us that this period is even 'darker' than the already dark earlier part of the Merovingian era. The older Frankish saints' lives, the ones from the fifth and sixth centuries, have survived in many more manuscripts. Whereas our texts are all anonymous, the earlier ones were often written by well known authors such as Fortunatus or Gregory of Tours,[145] more laymen seemed to have owned copies, and they were not as likely to have been limited solely to liturgical use.[146] By comparision, our texts have fewer surviving early manuscripts, something with makes their reconstruction even more difficult and consequently lays the attempt to describe the general characteristics of their language even more open to question. Nonetheless, fools rush in and we shall try.

143 There are exceptions. For example, in chapter 2 of the *Vita Geretrudis.* See *MGH, SSRM*, II, p. 457, n. c.

144 See the examples in the prologue and chapter 14 of the *Vita Audoini*, below, pp. 153, n. 125, and 162, n. 186.

145 Other examples of fifth and sixth-century authors are Paulinus, Possidius, Constantius, Ennodius and Ferrandus. See M. Heinzelmann, 'Neue Aspekte der biographischen und hagiographischen Literatur in der lateinischen Welt (1.–6. Jahrhundert)', *Francia*, I (1973), 42.

146 Heinzelmann, 'Neue Aspekte', 3.

A characteristic of language of great concern to the translator is obviously vocabulary. Most words have the same meaning in the Merovingian hagiographical sources as they do both in classical and in patristic Latin. There are, however, some notable exceptions, two of which lie at the very heart of a hagiographical text. The word *sanctus* in our texts has not lost its ancient meaning of 'holy' or 'sacred', but now when applied to a person it can simply indicate clerical status, as the words *venerabilis* or *dominus* often do in medieval and indeed modern usage.[147] In the late Empire *sanctus* was a title reserved for the emperor, but in the course of the fifth and sixth centuries it came to be applied to the bishops and the higher clergy and then eventually to all in the ecclesiastical hierarchy, including deacons and nuns.[148] In the Merovingian period the word had not yet taken on the more limited meaning of 'saint'. Even so, we shall not, for instance, translate *vitae sanctorum* for our period as 'lives of the churchmen', for, despite the fact that the word could be applied to any cleric, it is obvious that what interested hagiographers about their heroes was their sanctity and consequently we have used 'holy' or 'saint' in our translations. When opposed to *beatus*, *sanctus* can also mean 'deceased'.[149]

The word *virtus* is an extremely technical term in Merovingian hagiography and certainly as central to it as is *sanctus*. In our texts it has all but lost its ancient connection with the interior human qualities of manliness and virtue and become bound up much more closely with external and concrete manifestations of those qualities, that is, to laudable deeds. Since our authors were concerned with religious matters, it can almost always be translated by the modern word 'miracle' without falling too far short of the mark. It is a characteristic of hagiography in general to represent the internal and spiritual by the external and concrete, and although we have most often used the word 'miracle' to translate *virtus* it is with the clear realisation that the Latin word goes well beyond the visible. The heart of a saint's *virtutes* lies in the fact that they display his or her ability to effect God's power on earth. In Merovingian hagiography *virtus* means not only the miraculous deed itself but, more important, the supernatural power behind

---

147 F. Baix, 'L'hagiographie à Stavelot-Malmédy', *Revue Bénédictine*, 60 (1950), 136, n.1.

148 R. Aigrain, *L'Hagiographie: ses sources, ses méthodes, son histoire.* (Paris, 1953), p.111.

149 As it does in the *Additamentum Nivialense* where Foillan is *beatus* while living but *sanctus* once he has been killed. See A. Dierkens, *Abbayes et chapitres entre Sambre et Meuse (VII–XI siècle)* Beihefte der *Francia* 14, (Sigmaringen, 1985), p. 304, n. 147 and below, p. 328.

it.[150] It is important to note that *miraculum* and *virtus* are not synonymous, although they are close in meaning. *Virtus* is by far the more complex word, for it binds the wondrous element, the supernatural power, more closely to the saint than does *miraculum*, which concentrates on the deed itself. Although every *virtus* is a *miraculum*, a wondrous act of nature, for instance, would be a *miraculum* and not a *virtus* if no saint were involved in causing it. *Virtus* had a long secular history in the *fasti* and the ancient tradition of *laudatio funebris* where *virtutes* also came to mean 'exemplary deeds',[151] that is, concrete and visible manifestations of internal qualities. This complex word was the one most often chosen to describe the miraculous and wondrous elements in a saint's life, but it is also indicative of the age that its usage was often topographical, that is, certain *virtutes* became typical of people of certain social classes.[152]

Our understanding of the Merovingians' political world also derives in good measure from our understanding of the vocabulary they used to describe it. An important word we do not yet fully understand is *princeps*.[153] Sometimes the Merovingian sources use it to mean the king.[154] Very often it seems to be synonymous with *maior domus*, that is, with the mayor of the palace, although the *Liber Historiae Francorum* at one point draws a clear distinction between the two.[155] At other times authors seem to use it simply to mean 'leader'. For all its variety among the Merovingians, in the sources in this volume the word is even more elastic in the Carolingian source, *Annales Mettenses Priores*, where it is applied to the early Pippinids. As we shall see, the Carolingian author of that source uses *princeps*, along with *principatus*, an abstraction derived from it, in his attempt to explain the nature of Carolingian rule to his contemporaries. Obviously words must take on

150 J. Fontaine, 'Hagiographie et politique, de Sulpice Sévère à Venance Fortunant', *Revue d'Histoire de l'Eglise de France*, 62 (1976), 113 and 134; and Richard Collins, 'Beobachtungen zu Form, Sprache und Publikum der Prosabiographien des Venantius Fortunatus in der Hagiographie des römischen Gallien', *Zeitschrift für Kirchengeschichte*, 92 (1981), 16.

151 Heinzelmann, 'Neue Aspekte', 32 and 38–9.

152 M. Heinzelmann, *Bischofsherrschaft in Gallien. Zur Kontinuität römischer Führungs-schichten vom 4. bis zum 7. Jahrhundert. Soziale prosopographische und bildungsgeschichtliche Aspekte*. Beihefte der *Francia*, 5 (Zurich, 1976), pp. 38–9.

153 See H. Wolfram's doubts in his *Intitulatio I. Lateinische Königs- und Fürstentitel bis zum Ende des 8. Jahrhunderts*, MIÖG, *Ergänzungsband* 21 (Vienna, 1967), p. 27, n. 22a.

154 As in the *Vita Audoini*, ch. 2, below, p. 154, and the *Acta Aunemundi*, chs. 2 and 9 below, pp. 182 and 188.

standard definitions if they are to be useful at all, but this important word in particular reminds us of the danger of applying a definition seemingly obvious in one type of Merovingian source to its use in another. *Princeps* appears very frequently in the Merovingian diplomatic sources, where it always means the king, that is, it describes his royal dignity, echoing an ancient appellation of the Roman emperors. This conservatism is no surprise in diplomatic language, which then, as now, uses antiquated and high-sounding terminology.[156] But that is obviously not its meaning in the Merovingian hagiographic sources. Isidore of Seville declared that it could describe both an established *dignitas* as well as simply the position of being first.[157] We have translated it a number of ways, using our judgement according to the context.

The sources use a host of other words, some not obviously political which nonetheless carry political meaning. The word *Francus*, more often in the plural, *Franci*, can be very political. In the *LHF*, the *Vita Audoini* and the *Vita Balthildis* it does not mean the Franks in general, but is used for the Neustrians. *Matrona* carries considerable political weight. The word is reserved for women who exercise great authority in the political sphere.[158] We have translated the phrase *suo opere* as 'at his/her expense', but these two little words carry a great deal more meaning with them. The phrase is always used to designate contributions to the construction and equipping of a religious house. It does not mean providing the land, but rather paying for the construction of buildings, the liturgical apparatus and other furnishings.[159] It is used in both the diplomatic[160] and the hagiographic[161] sources with the same

155 *Grimoaldus maiorum domus ... egrotante Pippino principe ... LHF*, ch. 50, below, p. 94.

156 *... mots recherchés et des étymologies savants.* P. Riché, 'La formation des scribes dans le monde mérovingien et carolingien', in his *Instruction et vie religieuse dans le Haut Moyen-âge* (London, 1981), p. 76. Reprinted from W. Paravicini, and K-F. Werner (eds.), *Histoire comparée de l'administration (IVe–XVIIIe siècles)*, Beihefte der *Francia* 9 (Munich,1980).

157 *Princeps et dignitatis modo significatur et ordinis, sicut est illud Vergilianum (Aeneid, 9, 535): 'Princeps ardentem coniecit lampada Turnus' pro primus. Isidori Hispalensis episcopi Etymologiarum sive Originum Libri XX*, here IX, 3, 21, ed. W. M. Lindsay (Oxford, 1911), no page numbers given.

158 Plectrud: *LHF*, chs. 52 and 53, below, p. 95. Leutswinda: *Vita Balthildis*, ch. 3, below, p. 120.

159 M. Werner, *Der Lütticher Raum in frühkarolingischer Zeit* (Göttingen, 1980), pp. 360–1.

160 *MGH, Dipl.*, I, no. 22, p. 22 = J. Halkin and C. G. Roland (eds.), *Recueil des chartes de l'abbaye de Stavelot-Malmèdy* (Brussels, 1907), no. 2, p. 5.

161 *Vita Balthildis*, ch. 7, below. p. 124.

meaning. Another phrase found in both types of source is *vir inluster.*
We have translated it 'a man of illustrious standing', knowing full well
that the translation fails to convey the full political prestige of the
phrase. The words had a venerable history as an indication of high
noble rank among the senatorial aristocracy and may even have been
part of the Merovingian royal title.[162] The word *honor* is also one which
carries more meaning than any single English word can convey. In the
Merovingian sources it keeps its ancient meaning of 'public trust', that
is, a public position of great responsibility and prestige. But, much as
virtus is important because it reflects the divine power behind the
miracle worker, so too *honor* relects the secular power and trust,
usually the king's, which stand behind the office-holder. On the other
hand, the phrase *vir venerabilis* usually means simply 'monk'.

Some words simply belong to Merovingian hagiographic 'jargon'. For
instance, *nec immerito* simply means 'not wrongly'.[163] The words *datur
intellegi* are used to introduce the meaning of a story or event.[164] *Abbates*
does not have to mean abbots but can signify the senior clergy in urban
churches.[165] Such words and phrases help identify a text as Merovingian
and in the case of *datur intellegi* help to show the influence of Jonas's
Vita Columbani on other Merovingian hagiographical works.[166]

Whereas most of the words in a Merovingian text have a standard
Latin meaning, many sentences would be grammatically unacceptable
under ancient or Carolingian norms. It is usually assumed that the
grammatical characteristics of Merovingian Latin reflect the influence
of the spoken language, since many of those characteristics are evident
both in such sources as there are for the spoken language in the late
antique period and also in those of the Romance vernaculars when they
eventually become written. We should carefully note, however, that
this is the only basis for the assumption; not enough vulgar Latin
survives from either the antique or the early medieval periods to give
us a grammatical structure of the contemporary spoken language.
Scholars have gained valuable linguistic clues from the analysis of such

---

162 Wolfram, *Intitulatio I*, pp. 112 and 116–27.

163 As in *Jonas, Vita Columbani Abbatis Discipulorumque eius*, I, chs. 4 and 9, ed. B.
   Krusch, *MGH, SSRM*, IV (Hanover, 1902), pp. 67 and 75, and in the *Vita Audoini*,
   ch. 7, below, p. 158.

164 Jonas, *Vita Columbani*, I, 27, and the *Passio Praejecti*, ch. 4, below, p. 276.

165 *Passio Praejecti*, ch. 12, below. p. 280.

166 Berschin, *Biographie und Epochenstil*, p. 47.

things as contemporary inscriptions,[167] poetry, grammatical manuals, and texts such as ours, but in general what they present as vulgar Latin they have had to reconstruct synthetically by carefully working backward from the later vernaculars.[168] Keeping the *caveat* in mind that we should not form a judgement concerning the quality of Merovingian Latin on the basis of its variation from classical grammatical norms, nonetheless the clearest way to describe its grammar is to note how it varies from Ciceronian usage. The following are some of the non-classical grammatical structures which are found in the Merovingian texts in this volume with considerable frequency. There are many others, but these are some of the most striking.[169] We shall point them out only now and again in the notes on our translated texts. They appear far less frequently in our one Carolingian text, the *Annales Mettenses Priores*, a fact which shows at a glance the effect of the Carolingian reforms on the written language.

There is often a substitution of *suus* for *eius* and vice versa,[170] although the author of the *Vita Balthildis* uses them with their classical meanings. Deponents are often used with passive meaning.[171] A type of medial voice appears which uses certain verbs reflexively (*se simulare, se cernere, se ostendere*).[172] The uses and tenses of the subjunctive often differ from classical rules.[173] Infinitives are often used to express purpose.[174] Purpose can also be expressed by using the preposition

---

167 As has J. Herman, 'Spoken and written Latin in the last centuries of the Roman Empire: a contribution to the linguistic history of the western provinces', in Wright (ed.), *Latin and the Romance Languages*, pp. 39–40.

168 See Wright, *Late Latin*, pp. 45–103, esp. pp 48–50, for important modifications of the method.

169 See the refreshingly clear grammatical analysis of Venantius Fortunatus by Richard Collins in his two articles, one seemingly a translation of the other: R. Collins, 'Beobachtungen' (as above, n. 150), pp. 17–24, and 'Observations on the Form, Language, and Public of the Prose Biographies of Venantius Fortunatus in the Hagiography of Merovingian Gaul', in H. B. Clarke and M. Brennan (eds.), *Columbanus and Merovingian Monasticism, British Archaeological Reports, International Series*, 113 (1981), pp. 110–11. The standard syntactical analyses of early medieval Latin are still D. Norberg, *Syntaktische Forschung auf dem Gebiete des Spätlateins und des frühen Mittelalters, Upsala Universitets årsskrift*, 9 (1943), and his *Beiträge zur Spätlateinischen Syntax* (Uppsala, 1944).

170 E.g. *Vita Audoini*, ch. 4, below, p. 156.

171 E.g. *Additamentum Nivialense*, below, p. 328.

172 E.g. *Passio Leudegarii I*, ch. 16, below, p. 233, and *Vita Balthildis*, ch. 4, below, p. 121.

173 E.g. *Vita Balthildis*, ch. 13, below, p. 129, and *Vita Audoini*, prol., below, p. 153.

174 E.g. *Vita Geretrudis*, ch. 6, below, p. 324.

propter.[175] The passive is sometimes expressed with active forms.[176] Present participles are often used for finite verbs.[177] *Ut non* can be used to introduce a purpose clause.[178] Although rare, the perfect can be expressed with the auxiliary verb, *habere*.[179] We see what can only be described as an accusative absolute.[180] The accusative and ablative are often confused, especially in time and place expressions,[181] although the language does not, as has been claimed,[182] go so far as to distinguish only between an accusative and an inclusive 'oblique' case. The genitive relationship is often expressed by a preposition.[183] The preposition *in* with the ablative is used to express means, a usage already current in the biblical language.[184] Sometimes relative pronouns do not agree in number and gender with their antecedents.[185] *Quatenus* can express purpose,[186] and *ipse* replaces *is* and is often used as a kind of definite article.[187] *Vel* can lose its adversative nature and appears as a simple copulative.[188] *Igitur* and *itaque* are used for simple transitions, often temporal ones,[189] and *dum* can mean 'because'.[190]

175 E.g. *Vita Geretrudis*, ch. 7, below, p. 326, and *Additamentum Nivialense*, below, p. 327.

176 E.g. *Vita Balthildis*, chs. 9 and 10, below, pp. 125 and 126; *Passio Praejecti*, ch. 36, below, p. 297; and *LHF*, ch. 45, below, p. 91.

177 E.g. *Vita Balthildis*, ch. 17, below, p. 131; *Vita Audoini*, ch. 9, below, p. 159; and *Additamentum Nivialense*, below, p. 329.

178 E.g. *Vita Geretrudis*, ch. 2, below, p. 321.

179 E.g. *Vita Geretrudis*, ch. 7, below, p. 326.

180 E.g. *Vita Balthildis*, chs. 4 and 13, below, pp. 121 and 128; *Vita Audoini*, ch. 16, below, p. 194; *LHF*, ch. 46, below, p. 91; and *Acta Aunemundi*, ch. 2. In this last source the presence of the accusative absolute is one reason for thinking the *vita* has a Merovingian core. See below, p. 182.

181 E.g. *Vita Balthildis*, chs. 14 and 19, below, pp. 129 and 132; *Vita Audoini*, chs. 6 and 7, below, pp. 157 and 158; and *LHF*, ch. 53, below, p. 95.

182 P. Taylor, The Latinity of the Liber Historiae Francorum (New York, Ph.D dissertation, Columbia University,1924), pp. 13–14.

183 E.g. *LHF*, ch. 46, below, p. 91.

184 E.g. *in ore gladii*, *LHF*, ch. 2, *MGH*, *SSRM*, II, pp. 242–3.

185 E.g. below, p. 303.

186 E.g. *Vita Geretrudis*, ch. 4, below, p. 322.

187 E.g. *Vita Balthildis*, chs. 5 and 13, below, pp. 122 and 128.

188 E.g. *Vita Balthildis*, chs. 4 and 13, below, pp. 121 and 129; and *Vita Audoini*, ch. 7, below, p. 157.

189 E.g. *Vita Audoini*, ch. 16, below, p. 163.

190 E.g. *Vita Balthildis*, chs. 10 and 11, below, pp. 126 and 127.

Merovingian spelling is often inconsistent. Very frequently the same word will be spelled differently on the same folio of a manuscript.[191] Names of people and places are particularly prone to variation.[192] A new declension of proper names was developed with endings not known in classical Latin. Irish scribes and authors also had their own case endings for proper names in Latin. Among our texts these appear in the *Vita Geretrudis*.[193] The variation in spelling has been difficult not to regard as an indication that Merovingian scribes and authors were either careless, poorly educated, or both. The manuscript transmission, however, makes this assumption less secure. As we noted earlier, the manuscripts which survive are the work of Carolingian scribes, who, it is assumed, had the advantage of reformed instruction in Latin, if not access to such works as Alcuin's *De Orthographia*. Most of the variation in spelling occurs in the vowels, and that may simply indicate variations in pronunciation from place to place and in the course of time.

The style of the works is a simple one, something which is apparent even in our English translations. They are not, however, totally lacking in literary devices or, perhaps, literary pretensions. The prefaces to the lives are written in a far more elevated style than are the lives themselves. They can contain a simple type of homeoleuton.[194] Venantius Fortunatus and Gregory of Tours are the last Merovingian hagiographers to show evidence of familiarity with the classical pagan works apart from Virgil's *Aeneid*, and even Gregory's references to them are rare. In the later Merovingian texts, that is, the ones from which the texts in this volume have been taken, what classical allusion there is often comes indirectly, having been taken from Sulpicious Severus' *Vita Martini*, a work full of classical references which was both widely read and served

---

191 Norberg, *Manuel pratique*, pp. 29–30, explains many characteristics of Merovingian spelling as influences from the spoken language or the attempts of the scribes to avoid such influence and thus making mistakes in reverse: that is, to avoid using *-e* for the classical *-ae*, they would often replace an *-e* used correctly with an *-ae* where it did not belong.

192 See the comments on spelling in the introduction to the *Passio Praejecti*, below, p. 257.

193 See the comments in the introduction to the *Vita Geretrudis*, below, p. 307–8, n. 40.

194 The high point of the use of rhymed prose came in the eleventh and twelfth centuries, although there was also some use of it in the ninth and tenth. Our texts use very little, if any. Polheim called Merovingian efforts 'attempts' (*Proben*). The *Passio Praejecti* uses a very basic form (*Prädikatsreime*), which is usually simply the repetition of *est* at the end of a phrase. See K. Polheim, *Die lateinische Reimprosa*, second edition (Berlin, 1963), pp. ix, 331 and 376.

as a pattern for the genre of a saint's life.[195] In our texts almost all the citations and allusions are biblical rather than classical, but even then it is difficult to know exactly what the Merovingian hagiographers used as their source. Strong learned opinion emphasises the liturgy with all its biblically based components.[196] Older saints' lives also, especially *The Dialogues* of Gregory the Great and, once again, the *Vita Martini*, certainly could have served as sources of biblical material. On the other hand, the source could have been a direct reading of the Scriptures themselves. But scholars of the Merovingian period have not yet untangled the various versions of the Latin Bible which were used, their relationships to each other, and their zones of influence, nor do we have enough documents of the Gallican liturgy to identify positively many of the hagiographers' sources of biblical material.[197]

For all their allusion and attempts at other literary devices, the hagiographers employed a simple style. Once again it is difficult to say precisely what we should make of this. It is a reasonably safe assumption that they did so in order to have their works understood by a listening, rather by a than a reading, public. It is less certain who that public was or on what occasions the lives would have been read out. Once again the liturgy springs to mind; passages from the saint's *vita* were sometimes read as a part of the liturgy on the anniversary of his or her death;[198] we have evidence of this from as early as the time of Gregory of Tours.[199] Some may have been read to a strictly monastic audience at mealtimes. Although the earlier works may have been read aloud on specific occasions, they do not seem to have been written with that

---

195 J. Fontaine, *Sulpice Sévère, Vie de saint Martin*, vol. I, *Sources chrétiens* 133 (Paris, 1967), pp. 49–51 and 59–63. See below, p. 271.

196 J. Leclercq, 'L' Ecriture Sainte dans l'hagiographie monastique du Haut Moyen-âge', *Settimane di Studio*, 10 (1963), 126 *et passim*; and B. de Gaiffier, 'Hagiographie et historiographie: quelques aspects du problème', *Settimane di Studio*, 17 (1969), 155–6.

197 M. Van Uytfanghe, 'La Bible dans les vies de saints', *Revue d'Historie de l'Eglise de France*, 62 (1976), 109–10.

198 Riché, 'L' enseignement', p. 29; K. Heene, '*Audire, legere, vulgo:* an attempt to define public use and comprehensibiliity of Carolingian hagiography', in R. Wright (ed.), *Latin and the Romance Languages*, pp. 147–54; and B. de Gaiffier, 'La lecture des actes des martyrs dans la prière liturgique en occident', *Annalecta Bollandiana*, 72 (1954), 147–8.

199 Gregory of Tours, *De virtutibus S. Martini*, II, chs. 29 and 49, ed. B. Krusch, *MGH*, *SSRM*, I, pt. 2, pp. 170 and 176; *De virtutibus S. Juliani*, ch. 16, *MGH, SSRM*, I, pt. 2, p. 121; and *Liber in gloria martyrum*, ch. 85, *MGH, SSRM*, I, pt. 2, p. 95. Cf. Gaiffier, 'La lecture', 147.

purpose in mind. Writing for a listening rather than for a reading public seems to have been a particular characteristic of the later Merovingian period; hagiographic works written both before and after roughly the seventh century seem to have been written for readers, not listeners. Sulpicius Severus wrote his *Vita Martini* for the former *legentes*, and he uses the word in his text.[200] By the end of the sixth century, however, we find Gregory of Tours,[201] among others,[202] writing his *vitae* for *audientes*. In the Carolingian period the hagiographical works again were written largely for readers, not listeners. By then the liturgy was largely the Roman, not the Gallican, rite and had taken on a more sacral nature and as such was aimed more towards the clergy and less at the people. It seems the Carolingian hagiography followed suit.[203]

Does a simple style indicate a simple or an uneducated author? Obviously not necessarily. In the ancient *laudatio funebris* both Cicero and Quintilian used simple speech and thus it became part of the literary convention for recording the virtues of the dead.[204] Augustine, Gregory of Tours and Venantius Fortunatus were all exquisitely educated and yet used simple language in their hagiograhical works and sermons. Here obviously a simple style does not indicate a simplistic author at all. In the later Merovingian period, however, what the Latin itself indicates about the authors and their intellectual environment is much more difficult to assess. On the one hand, the injunction to use *simplicitas* in their works had episcopal authority behind it.[205] So too the very purpose of their works would by its nature

200 *legentibus*, Sulpicius Severus, *Vita S. Martini*, dedication; *legerit*, *ibid.*, ch. 27, 6 and 7, ed. Fontaine, *Suplice Sévère*, vol. I, pp. 248 and 316.

201 Gregory of Tours, *Liber Vitae Patrum*, prol., ed. B. Krusch, *MGH, SSRM*, I, pt. 2, p. 212.

202 *fidelibus auditoribus. Vita Caesarii Arelatensis*, II, ch. 1, ed. B. Krusch, *MGH, SSRM*, III (Hanover, 1896), p. 484 (*c.* AD 550); and *audientem*, *Vita Balthildis*, prologue, below, p. 119.

203 Heene, *'Audire'*, pp. 148–51.

204 Heinzelmann, 'Neue Aspekte', 40.

205 'Let the shepherd of a church preach in a fitting style to the people, tempering his skill so that neither a boorishness offend the learned nor an adorned wordiness become obscure for the unlearned. (... *pastor ecclesiae apertiori sermone populo praedicet, ita arte temperans, ut nec rusticitas sapientes offendat, nec onesta loquacitas obscura rusticis fiat*).' Germanus, Bishop of Paris, *Expositio brevis antiquae liturgiae gallicanae in duas epistolas digesta, ep. 1*, Migne, *PL*, 72, col. 92. Cf. Collins, 'Observations', p. 124, note 80. 'We do not want the eloquence of the world, even if it is available to us ... (*Non idigemus, vel si nobis suppeteret, eloquentia saeculari ...*)' *Vita Caesarii Arelatensis*, II, ch. 1, *MGH, SSRM*, III, p. 484. Cf. Collins, 'Observations', p. 108.

exclude the abstact and the learned. A saint's life is not theology, it is not an abstract and human analysis of a divine subject. It resembles far more a continuation of Scripture itself in that, through the saint and his or her *virtutes*, a *vita* concretely shows the real and historical action of God in the lives of local and contemporary people.[206] The author of the *Vita Eligius* tells us in his prologue that he intentionally adopted a simple style so as to be understood by the uneducated.[207] Gregory of Tours tells us that, at the reading of a passage from a *vita*, rustics worship the saints more fervently.[208] The Carolingian reformers realised that the simple Merovingian style was more suitable for reading aloud to a wider audience. At the end of the eighth century, when the monks of Saint-Riquer asked Alcuin to rewrite the *Vita Richarii*, they did not want the Merovingian language changed in those parts of the work which described the saint's miracles 'because the simple and less polished style better suits the brothers when they recite to the people'.[209] The Carolingian correctors were also eager to keep the style of the Merovingian language in their version of the *Vita Balthildis* because, as they admit in their prologue, its simple words rather than any elegance of their own would lead to the greater edification of the listeners.[210] The authors of the *Vita Trudonis*[211] and the *Vita Hucberti, I*,[212] however, while declaring that they are writing in a *sermo rusticus*, ask anyone who can improve it to do so.[213] In this volume, the authors of the *Passio Praejecti*, and the *Vita Balthildis* felt compelled to ask to be excused for their simple style, although this

206 Van Uytfanghe, 'La Bible', p. 105.

207 *Vita Eligii Episcopi Noviomagensis*, prologue, ed. B. Krusch, *MGH, SSRM*, IV (Hanover, 1902), p. 664.

208 *Mos namque erat hominum rusticorum ut sanctos Dei, quorum agones relegunt, attentius venerentur*. Gregory of Tours, *Liber in gloria martyrum*, ch. 63, *MGH, SSRM*, I, pt. 2, p. 81.

209 ... *cuius simplex et minus polita locutio quia fratribus ad recitandum in populo aptior vedebatur*. Alcuin, *Vita Richarii Confessoris Centulensis*, prologue, ed. B. Krusch, *MGH, SSRM*, IV, p. 389. Cf. M. Van Uytfanghe, 'A linguistic dichotomy in Carolingian Gaul', in Wright (ed.), *Latin and the Romance Languages*, p. 121.

210 ... *potius quam profana et falsa eloquentia ex proprio corde mendaciter fingentes. Vita Sanctae Balthildis*, B, prologue, ed. B. Krusch, *MGH, SSRM*, II, (Hanover, 1888), p. 482.

211 *Vita Tudonis Confessoris Hasbaniensis*, prologue, ed. W. Levison, *MGH, SSRM*, VI (Hanover,1913), p. 275.

212 *Vita Hugberti Episcopi Traiectensis*, I, prologue, ed. W. Levison, *MGH, SSRM*, VI, p. 482.

213 Heene, '*Audire*', p. 151.

seems a topos indicating a required humility on the part of the author.[214] The literal-minded and concrete style of the texts themselves does not necessarily indicate an unpolished or uneducated author, and it would be even more dangerous to use the Latin style of this genre of writing as an indication of the general intellectual level in the late Merovingian period. It is not the style of the text of the lives themselves which raises doubts about the sophistication of the authors but the clumsiness of their prologues which makes us uneasy. The more ambitious style of their prologues cannot but remind us of beginning students who use grand words and abstract terminology in order to sound learned. The prologues were not written to be read aloud; they contain neither miracles nor narrative. Often they were written to a bishop or some person of authority who had commissioned the saint's life, and in them their authors employed a style seemingly reflecting what they thought to be learned and commensurate with the dignity of the addressee. Even in our English translations, however, it will be obvious that their Latin was florid and awkward and no longer the capable linguistic instrument that it had been in the hands of Fortunatus and his contemporaries or would again be with Alcuin and the Carolingian writers. We do have, however, samples of a late Merovingian Latin other than that of the hagiographers which is reasonably narrative in character. They are found in a collection of letters which survives from the seventh century.[215] Here the style is more polished but still not without clumsiness.[216] Most of the correspondance comes from aristocratic bishops and most of these are from the southern and more Roman parts of Gaul. Pierre Riché sees a definite difference in educational level between northern Gaul and the lands south of the Loire during our period,[217] and to a certain degree the style of the Latin in our hagiographical texts could be taken as support for his thesis. The author of the *Passio Praejecti*, written in Clermont, probably in the 680s, makes more of an attempt to use an elevated style than do the other hagiographers in our volume and he refers to the 'barbarian language' used by those near Strasbourg, for

---

214 See below, pp. 272 and 118.

215 *MGH, Epistolae,* III; and D. Norberg (ed.), *Epistulae Sancti Desiderii* (Uppsala, 1961).

216 See Dag Norberg's careful analysis and masterly French translations of two of these letters. Norberg, *Manuel pratique,* pp. 105–22.

217 Riché, 'L'instruction', p. 877, who includes Paris, Trier and Koblenz as learned islands in the north.

him across the Voges to the north.[218] There are, on the other hand, considerations which argue against using hagiographic Latin to assess a possible geographical difference in general educational level. The degree to which the local spoken language varied from the written Latin may have had more influence on the style of the hagiographers than did their general educational level. As far as we can tell, the linguistic frontier between the Romance and Germanic languages was not yet fixed in the Merovingian period. The best that can be said is that the German tongue ruled beyond the Rhine and the Roman one south of the Loire and that between the two rivers there was a 'mixed zone'.[219] And even there our anonymous authors may not have been locals at all but foreigners, perhaps Irish or Anglo-Saxons.

In summary, we are forced to say that the prudent historian will pay close attention to the Latin of a Merovingian hagiographic work as good evidence of whether or not the work is indeed contemporary, but proceed with extreme caution when using the Latin of the seventh-century Frankish hagiographers to assess the intellectual climate of the era. In those parts of these works written to be heard and not to be read, that is, in their accounts of the lives and the miracles but not in their prologues, the Merovingian hagiographers used a Latin that was both clear and dignified. It recalled but did not duplicate the language of the Bible and probably that of the Gallican liturgy. Although not totally lacking in literary artifice, it was neither turgid nor literary, and its simplified grammar allowed the narrative to flow quickly and easily. In other words, the Merovingian hagiographers used a language admirably suited to their serious purposes.

---

218 See below, p. 269.

219 E. Ewig, 'Das merowingische Frankenreich (561–687)', in T. Schieder (ed.), *Europa im Wandel von der Antike zum Mittelalter*, (Stuttgart, 1976), p. 403.

I: *Liber Historiae Francorum* (The Book of the History of the Franks)

We begin this volume which examines mostly hagiographical sources with one which is not only not hagiographical but remarkable for its very lack of religious content. We do so for two reasons. First, the *Liber Historiae Francorum* (*LHF* for short) is our most valuable guide through the last half of the seventh century and the first two decades of the eighth. It is the framework, so to speak, which allows us to see how many of the people and events which appear in the hagiographical sources fit together. Without the help of the *LHF* the *vitae* would not yield very much historical insight, especially when their contents concern political matters. For instance, the important chapter 25 of the *Passio Leudegarii* would make no sense at all without the background provided by the *LHF*.[1] Second, and this is even more important, an understanding of a secularly-minded, contemporary Merovingian author provides us with an important point of reference in our attempt to understand the hagiographers. Although the work is anonymous, we can date and locate it with more certainty than we can the hagiographical ones. The *LHF* was written while a Merovingian king still ruled over the Franks and by someone geographically very close to the political centre of that realm. The fact that the *LHF* is a Merovingian and not a Carolingian production is its greatest asset. The following age would hold a very different view of the late Merovingian period from that of those authors who actually wrote their works before the Carolingian revisionists turned the seventh and eighth centuries to their own purposes. The author of the *LHF* leaves no impression at all that the Neustrian nobility served 'do-nothing' kings or that his age had no other purpose than to prepare the way for the sons of Pippin to replace the progeny of Merovech on the Frankish throne. Both these themes will appear in the coming Carolingian sources.

The last ten chapters of the *LHF*, the ones we have translated here, recount events from the death of King Dagobert I to the demise of Chilperic II, that is, from 638 to 721. It was a period of significant political and cultural change for the Franks. The long-established

---

1 See below, pp. 241-2.

Neustrian nobility centred on the Seine–Oise valley was forced from
its prominent political position by men and women from the Moselle
and the Meuse. Proud figures like Audoin, Ebroin, Erchinoald,
Leudesius, Warrato and Ansfled gave way to newcomers from the
east: Wulfoald, Pippin, Plectrud, and then finally Charles Martel. The
Frankish Church, too, changed and the cultural life of Francia took new
directions. Vast new areas lying at the back door of these easterners
were bound to Frankish *mores* and to the Frankish God by the work of
their missionaries. Although still the age of bishops and not yet a time
when abbots would surround the king, nonetheless the monasteries
greatly increased in number, in efficiency, and thus in political and
economic importance. This may have been due in great part to an
infusion of exciting new sanctity from the British Isles.[2] For the events
which made up these broad changes, it is the author of the *LHF* who
is our chronicler.

The chronology of these events is often very difficult to reconstruct,
in large part because the author of the *LHF* is so frustratingly
imprecise in his chronological information.[3] For part of the period the
Passio Leudegarii is of great help in adding to what can be gleaned from
the *LHF*. Although the two sources seemingly disagree on some
matters, it is clear from a reading of their accounts that both authors
held the same view of how the Merovingian political system worked.
The basic political dynamic of those years has usually been thought to
have resulted from a continuing conflict between the crown and the
court as a politically centralising force on the one hand, and on the
other a political force of local nobility seeking to stop royal Neustrian
encroachment and to protect local autonomy. Balthild and Ebroin have
been held up as champions of the former and Leudegar of Autun as the
champion of the latter. Yet for the author of the *LHF* it was not
conflict between nobility and Crown but co-operation between them
which was the basis of the political order. A properly functioning
system had a Merovingian on the throne reigning in concert with the
great of the realm. The mechanism which bound Crown and nobility
together was the *consilium*, the plan or advice. Kings acted properly

2 The influence of the Irish on the Frankish culture and ecclesiastical politics of the
  age is forcefully argued by Friedrich Prinz in his important work, *Frühes Mönchtum
  im Frankenreich* (Munich and Vienna,1965). See the discussion of both his work and
  the Irish question in our introduction to the *Vita Geretrudis*, below, p. 313.

3 See the discussion of the various interpretations of the chronology along with the
  often precarious bases for them in the sources in R. Gerberding, *The Rise of the
  Carolingians and the Liber Historiae Francorum* (Oxford,1987), pp. 67–84.

when they acted *cum consilio* of the Neustrian nobility and bad kings acted heedlessly. The nobility too should not act on its own without the consent of the Crown and certainly should not perform any act against the rightful ruler.

In the eyes of the author of the *LHF*, when King Dagobert I died in 638 the Merovingian political system was still largely as it had been and should be. The Neustrians mourned their departed monarch for many days and then placed his son, who would be known as Clovis II (638–57), over them as king. Dagobert's other son, Sigibert III, had been ruling the eastern kingdom, Austrasia, since 633. Sigibert's death caused a rather more tumultuous turn of events than his father's had done, but here too, according to the *LHF*, the eventual outcome was as it should have been. When Sigibert died, his mayor of the palace, the Pippinid, Grimoald, sent the Merovingian prince, Dagobert, off on a pilgrimage to Ireland and in his stead installed his own son on the throne, giving him the royal name Childebert. The Neustrian nobility, however, could tolerate neither a Frankish king who was not a Merovingian nor a mayor of the palace who had acted against his lord, and so they removed Grimoald by force and had him tried and executed by their king, Clovis. They sent Clovis's son, Childeric, to rule Austrasia with the powerful Austrasian nobleman, Wulfoald, as his mayor of the palace.[4] The Neustrians had a powerful precedent for their action: in 623 their king, Clothar II, had sent his son, Dagobert, to rule Austrasia, and in 633 Dagobert, now king in Neustria, had in turn sent the Austrasians his son, Sigibert, as their king. By their action the Neustrians had restored the proper order in Austrasia.

Shortly thereafter in Neustria itself, however, the author tells us, King Clovis's reign ended amid hard times for his kingdom because he had desecrated the relics of Saint-Denis.[5] Although after Clovis's death the Neustrians did peacefully manage to place his son, Clothar,[6] on the throne to rule along with his mother, Queen Balthild, they nonetheless

---

4 *LHF*, ch. 43. There is much disagreement concerning the dates of these events in Austrasia. Most scholars argue for Sigibert's death in 656 and Grimoald's removal in 661, e.g, J.-M. Picard, 'Church and politics in the seventh century: the Irish exile of King Dagobert II', in J.-M. Picard (ed.), *Ireland and Northern France* (Dublin, 1991), pp. 27–52. For another view placing Sigibert's death in 651 and Grimoald's fall in 656, see Gerberding, *Rise*, pp. 47–66.

5 *LHF*, ch. 44, below, p. 89.

6 Clothar III (657–73). He died between 10 March and 15 May 673. See B. Krusch, 'Chronologica Regum Francorum Stirpis Merovingicae', *MGH*, *SSRM*, VII (Hanover, 1920), p. 497.

fought among themselves when trying to establish a new mayor of the palace when the old mayor, Erchinoald, died.[7] Eventually it was Ebroin who won the position. His career was to be a long and stormy one, lasting from about 659 to about 680, and would involve many of the saints and characters who are the subjects and heroes of the *vitae* in this volume. In many ways Ebroin was the last powerful champion of the old order. Like Erchinoald before him, he represented the currently dominant faction of Neustrian nobility. But the Pippinids would prove too much for his successors, Waratto, Ghislemar, Berchar and Raganfred. After Ebroin, the Frankish political centre of gravity would gradually abandon the Seine–Oise valley for fresher lands to the east.

The *LHF* tells us little of the events of the reign of Clothar III, for which we turn largely to the *Vita Balthildis*.[8] When Clothar died in 673 the Neustrians installed his brother, Theuderic, on the throne. For reasons which the author of the *LHF* does not tell us, but the author of the *Passio Leudegarii* does, the Neustrians soon rose up against Ebroin and their new king and deposed them both.[9] From Leudegar's hagiographer we learn that Ebroin had prevented the nobility from coming together to perform their traditional oath-swearing at Theuderic's elevation,[10] – in other words, the mayor had interfered with an important traditional expression of co-operation between Crown and the nobility, apparently trying to isolate the new monarch from the nobility. The Neustrians tonsured them both, sending Theuderic to the monastery of Saint-Denis and Ebroin to Luxeuil. They called Theuderic's brother, Childeric II, from Austrasia to the Neustrian throne. Childeric arrived with his mayor, Wulfoald, from the east but he was to rule only two years. The *LHF* tells us that he acted heedlessly and violated the traditional rights of the nobility. Reaction was drastic. A group of hereditary Frankish nobility rose up and assassinated both the king and his pregnant queen, and Wulfoald was forced to flee whence he had come. This unleashed a bloody factional struggle, most likely a reprise of the one that had gone on at Ebroin's election in 657. Ebroin burst out of the monastery and, proclaiming a Merovingian pretender his king, made a grab for power. The *LHF* does not mention the pretender; we learn about him from

7 ... *defuncto Erchonoldo maiorum domo, Franci in incertum vacellantes....* *LHF*, ch. 45, below, p. 89.

8 See below, p. 107.

9 *LHF*, ch. 45, below, pp. 89–91.

10 *Passio Leudegarii*, ch. 5, below, p. 222.

the *Passio Leudegarii*.[11] The other side, however, Erchinoald's family,
now headed by Leudesius, his son, and Leudegar, bishop of Autun, had
already managed to secure the proper king, Theuderic, from Saint-
Denis and to get hold of the royal treasure. But they were no match for
Ebroin. In a bold march the old mayor captured Theuderic and the
royal treasure, discarded the pretender, who was no longer of use, and
had his enemies tortured and killed. He again took up the position of
mayor with Theuderic as king. It is remarkable that, unlike the author of
the *Passio Leudegarii*, to whom, as we shall see,[12] Ebroin is an unspeakable
villain, the author of the *LHF* recounts all this without passion. He
even adds a great deal of prestige to Ebroin's deeds by telling us that
the holy bishop Audoin of Rouen was party to them. We can learn two
things from this. First, the author either had not read or was not
influenced by the account in *Passio Leudegarii*, and second, the author
most likely approved of the rightful Theuderic being restored to his
throne and ruling with Ebroin, Audoin and the traditional Neustrian
nobility. The easterners had been packed off. In his next chapter he
recounts how they, now under Pippin II, tried to return but were
soundly defeated by Theuderic and Ebroin at Bois-du-Fay in the late
670s.[13] The author of the *Annales Mettenses Priores*, writing in the early
ninth century, when the Carolingians were firmly in power, will
conveniently ignore this military failure on the part of the Pippinids,
but the author of the *LHF* has no particular Carolingian axe to grind
and tells us that it was a major confrontation which the Neustrians
soundly won.

For about a decade, up to 687, there was peace between the two
Frankish kingdoms, but the factional squabbling among the Neustrian
nobility went on apace. Ebroin, himself, in the midst of this, fell victim
to it. He had planned to rid himself of a certain Ermenfred, but
Ermenfred acted first, killed the mayor and fled to Pippin in the east.
The Neustrians again had trouble agreeing on a new mayor. The
choice finally fell to Waratto, whose family was based on the lower
Seine. Waratto had an ambitious son named Ghilsemar who actually
displaced his father for a while, to the great disapproval of the author
of the *LHF*. So evil had been Ghislemar's action against his father that
he was struck down by God and Waratto assumed his former position.

11 *Passio Leudegarii*, ch. 19, below, p. 235–6.

12 Below, p. 201.

13 For this date see Gerberding, *Rise*, pp. 80–4.

When Waratto died about 686[14] the mayoralty remained in his family, falling to Berchar, who was related to Waratto by marriage.[15] The *LHF* author strongly disapproved of Berchar: he says the Neustrians made a mistake in choosing him and that he was a man small in stature, of low intelligence, and, what was far worse, harmful in *consilio*.[16] It soon came to another clash between east and west, and this time the easterners won. Berchar and Theuderic were defeated by Pippin II at Tertry in 687. In the wake of his defeat Berchar was assassinated, allowing Pippin officially to assume the mayoralty of the western kingdom. The new mayor, however, did not stay in Paris but returned to his Austrasian homelands leaving a trusted lieutenant with Theuderic at the Neustrian court.

As we noted in the introduction, pp. 24–5, this battle of Tertry in 687 has long been trumpeted as the Pippinid conquest of western Francia.[17] Indeed, as we shall see, it is certainly portrayed as such in the Carolingian sources.[18] But here in the Merovingian *LHF* it is passed over without fanfare; other conflicts between east and west both before and after Tertry arouse more interest with our author.

In the *LHF* the advent of the Pippinids into Neustria was a major political event. The author now begins to recount their history; we learn of their wars, their enemies both Frankish and foreign, their positions, and much about how they were related to each other. For their familial relationships before they had a direct effect on Neustria we must turn to the seventh source in this volume, the *Vita Geretrudis*. From the *LHF*, however, we learn a great deal of detail, beginning with Pippin II. We hear that he married Plectrud, that one of their sons, Drogo,

---

14 E. Ewig, 'Die fränkische Teilreiche im 7. Jahrhundert (613–714)', *Trierer Zeitschrift*, 22 (1953), 138. Reprint E. Ewig, *Spätantikes und fränkisches Gallien. Gesammelte Schriften (1952–1973)*, vol. I, Beihefte der *Francia*, 3 (Munich, 1976), p. 225.

15 The *LHF* is silent about Berchar's family, but from the information given by the following sources he would be Waratto's son-in-law: the first continuator of Fredegar, ch. 5, ed. J. M. Wallace-Hadrill, *The Fourth Book of the Chronicle of Fredegar with its Continuations* (London, 1960), pp 84–5 (hereafter Fredegar, *Chron.* for the Chronicle and Fredegar, *Cont.* for the Continuations); the *Annales Mettenses Priores* (for their year 693), below, p. 362; and the *Gesta Sanctorum Patrum Fontanellensis Coenobii*, IV, 1, eds. F. Lohier and J. Laporte, (Rouen, 1936), p. 39. A charter of Childebert III for Tussonval from 697, however, makes him the husband of Waratto's widow, Ansfled. *ChLA*, no. 581. Whatever his exact relationship to Waratto, it is clear he was of the same faction.

16 *LHF*, ch. 48, below, p. 92.

17 Above, pp. 24–5.

18 Below, pp. 339–40.

received the duchy of the Champagne, and that the other, Grimoald, became Neustrian mayor. Pippin had another wife, unnamed in the *LHF* but called Alpaida by the continuator of Fredegar.[19] From this union came a third son, named Charles, known to history as Charles Martel. Although the Pippinids dominate the *LHF* from chapter 49 to the end of the work, the author does not lose his Neustrian and Merovingian perpective. Kings – that is, hereditary Merovingian kings – were still very important to him even now in the reigns of the supposed 'do-nothings'. He is careful to note the succession of the Neustrian line, the length of the kings' reigns, their queens, their ages, their familial relationships one to another, and he always notes that the kings took part in the various battles he recounts. None of this will be important for the Carolingians as they retell the story of these years.

Charles Martel outlived both his half-brothers and at Pippin II's death in 714 was the only one of the three still alive. Nonetheless, his position was not a strong one, in fact it was the opposite. His powerful stepmother, Plectrud, had him in prison. It was she who controlled the family treasure and ruled the Neustrian goverment with the king and Theudoald, her grandson, as mayor.[20] But with Pippin gone, the traditional Neustrian nobility rose up in an attempt to rid themselves of the easterners and their partisans. According to the *LHF* the clash was a bloody one and took place in the very heart of Neustria, in the forest of Compiègne. The Pippinids lost the day and Theudoald had to turn tail and run. The Neustrians now elected one of their own, a certain Raganfred, mayor, formed an alliance with Radbod, duke of the Frisians, and with their king and army set out across the forest of Charbonnière, following up their victory as far as the Meuse.

The rest of the *LHF* belongs to Charles Martel. Although by no means one of the Neustrian nobility, he is nonetheless one of the author's heroes.[21] He not only managed to escape from Plectrud's custody in the wake of the Neustrian success, but did so 'with the help of the Lord'. When Dagobert III died in 715 the Neustrians found a supposed Merovingian, a monk called Daniel, and made him their king, calling him by the royal name Chilperic. The *LHF* author does not seem at all convinced by the legitimacy of this monarch,[22] and that

19 Fredegar, *Cont.*, ch. 6, ed. Wallace-Hadrill, p. 86.

20 *LHF*, ch. 51, below, p. 000.

21 ... *Carlo, virum elegantem egregius atque utilem....* *LHF*, ch. 49, below, p. 000.

22 *Franci nimirum Danielem quondam clericum, cesarie capitis crescente, eum in regnum stabilunt atque Chilpericum nuncupant: LHF*, ch. 52, below, p. 000.

may be one of the reasons why he so obviously supports Martel and his actions against the Neustrians and their king. Charles's rise to dominance was not without difficulties, and the *LHF* author does not shrink from recounting them. In the course of another incursion into Autrasia by the Neustrians, Charles was soundly defeated by their allies, the Frisians, under Duke Radbod.[23] But in 716, when they came a third time, attacking Plectrud in Cologne and taking much of the Pippinid treasure, Charles fell upon them at Amblève on their return and this time he won. Martel now had a force large enough to take the offensive, and this he did the following year, defeating Chilperic and Raganfred at Vinchy, near Cambrai. The author goes on to give us a good deal of detail about Martel's military and diplomatic activities, all of them successful, up to about 721, when Chilperic II died. For the period from 721 to 727, the year with which the chronicle ends, the author says nothing except to name the next Merovingian king, Theuderic IV, and to assure us that he was the rightful ruler by telling us he was the son of Dagobert III, which must be to say that he was not a son of the monk-cum-king, Chilperic.[24] The author makes absolutely no mention of any part played by Martel in the elevation of the new king, saying instead that it was once again the *Franci* – his word for the Neustrian nobility – who placed Theuderic on the throne. Thus the author ends his work in the way he began it, with his beloved Neustrians and their Merovingian kings.

We have in the *LHF* a view of the political climate of the late Merovingian period written by a reasonably knowledgeable contemporary close to the Merovingian court. It was not to be this contemporary view of the age, however, but one taken from Carolingian sources, which would dominate the way posterity saw the late seventh and the early eighth centuries. To point up the differences between between the two views and thus to help set the record straight, we have included as the last source in this volume the first part of the *Annales Mettenses Priores* (*Earlier Annals of Metz*). This is a source written in 805, when Carolingian rule was indeed firmly in place, and one whose view of our period was to be extremely influential in the years and centuries to come. We shall compare the two sources more fully below when we treat the *Annales*[25] but it will be of benefit in reading the *LHF* to anticipate that analysis briefly at this point.

23 *LHF*, ch. 52, below, p. 95.
24 *LHF*, ch. 53, below, p. 96.
25 See below, pp. 347–8.

The *LHF*, like most of the other Merovingian authors in thus volume, adopts a simple and direct style, without much classical allusion or a great deal of metaphor. The *Annales Mettenses Priores*, on the other hand, will clearly show the learned influence of the Carolingian reformers. For the *LHF*, even after the Pippinids had made their political weight felt in Neustria, the most important expression of proper rule is a hereditary Merovingian king, reigning *cum consilio* of the Frankish nobility. The *Annales Mettenses Priores* will disregard all this, pointing out only how the Pippinids controlled matters political and how it was divinely ordained that they should do so. In the *LHF* we see very little hagiographical influence; its heroes are not given patterned careers, divinely predestined; not so for *Annales Mettenses*. While the *LHF* author is disturbed whenever he sees action taken against a rightful lord, his work does not emphasise the problems of fidelity and infidelity, as do the *Annales*. In other words, in the *LHF* we see no crisis of loyalty; in the *Annales Mettenses*, we do. In the *LHF* the battle of Tertry is just one of many significant conflicts; it receives no special treatment. In the *Annales Mettenses* it is a decisive turning point. But the most enlightening difference is that in the *LHF*, as opposed to the *Annales*, the Pippinids rise to power just as others of the Frankish great had done, by the politics of family and faction, and the author takes great care to point out that they ruled *under* the Merovingian kings.

The last eleven chapters of
Liber Historiae Francorum
(The Book of the History of the Franks)

CHAPTER 43

After that, King Dagobert[27] was siezed by a powerful fever, and growing ill he died[28] at the villa of Epinay-sur-Seine in the district of the city

26 *Liber Historiae Francorum*, ed. B. Krusch, *MGH, SSRM*, II (Hanover, 1888), pp. 215–328.

27 Dagobert I, King of Austrasia (623–33) and of Neustria (629–38).

28 19 January 638, the date accepted by Courtois and Wallace-Hadrill. C. Courtois, 'L'avènement de Clovis II et les règles d'accession au trône chez les Mérovingiens', *Mélanges d'histoire de Moyen-âge dédiés à la mémoire de Louis Halphen* (Paris, 1951), p. 159; and Wallace-Hadrill, *Fredegar*, p. 67, n. 1. Krusch had placed his death in 639. *MGH, SSRM*, II, p. 315.

of Paris. He was buried in the basilica of blessed Denis the Martyr, and the Neustrians[29] mourned him for many days. He ruled forty-four years. The Neustrians placed his son, Clovis,[30] over them as their king and he took as his wife a girl from the Saxon nobility named Balthild.[31] She was beautiful and forceful in her slyness.[32] After this, however, when Pippin died,[33] Sigibert,[34] the king in Austrasia, established his [Pippin's] son, Grimoald, in the palace mayoralty. With the passing of time, however, King Sigibert died and Grimoald tonsured his [the king's] young son, named Dagobert,[35] and sent him to Bishop Dido of Poitiers[36] so that he might undertake a pilgrimage to Ireland and placed his own[37] son on the throne.[38] The Neustrians, however, enraged by this, prepared an ambush for Grimoald and removing him they brought him for judgement to Clovis, king of the Neustrians. In the city of Paris he was put in prison bound with painful chains[39] as one worthy of death because he had acted against his lord. His death came with terrible torture.

29 *Franci*, by which the author means the Neustrians.

30 Clovis II (638–57).

31 This is the same Balthild whose *vita* we have translated below, pp. 118–32.

32 *Omnique ingenio strenua*. This is a difficult phrase to translate. *Strenuitas* is a very masculine characteristic, usually applied to warriors, and *ingenium* usually means cleverness, but in political matters has the meaning of slyness. The author will call Ebroin *ingeniosus* in ch. 45. See H. Fichtenau, *Das Karolingische Imperium. Soziale und Geistige Problematik eines Grossreiches* (Zurich, 1949), p. 128; and J. L. Nelson, 'Queens as Jezabels: the Careers of Brunhild and Balthild in Merovingian History', *Studies in Church History*, Subsidia I (1978), 76.

33 639. Fredegar, *Chron.*, IV, ch. 85, says Pippin died about a year after Dagobert.

34 Sigibert III. Most, following Krusch, consider him to have ruled from 633 to 656. See the arguments presented to place his death in 651 in Gerberding, *Rise*, pp. 50–66.

35 He will eventually become Dagobert II (676–79).

36 According to the *Additamentum Nivialense de Fuilano (Nivelles Supplement to the Vita Fursey Concerning Foillan)*, Grimoald and Dido met at Nivelles at about this time. See below, p. 329.

37 *suus* and *eius* employed according to classical usage.

38 See the full treatment of this exile and the Irish evidence for it in Picard, 'Church and politics'.

39 There was an ancient proscription against binding a free man. See *Pactus Legis Salicae*, XXXII, ed. K. A. Eckhardt, *MGH, Legum*, sectio I, vol. IV, pt. 1 (Hanover, 1962), p. 122. The fact that Grimoald was bound shows the gravity of his offence.

CHAPTER 44

In that time Clovis cut off the arm of blessed Denis the Martyr at the instigation of the devil. And throughout the same period the kingdom of the Neustrians fell into disastrous circumstances. This Clovis was indeed given to every kind of filth, he was a fornicator, a delfiler of women and bloated by gluttony and drunkenness. His end and his death are not considered worthy of history. Indeed, the writers greatly condemn his end but, not knowing the extent of his evil, in their uncertainty about him they relate some things for others.[40] From his queen, Balthild, however, they say that he had three sons: Clothar, Childeric and Theuderic.[41] The above-mentioned King Clovis came to his end and he ruled sixteen years. The Neustrians placed Clothar, the eldest boy of the three, over them as king to rule with the queen, his mother.

CHAPTER 45

Some time later, when the mayor of the palace, Erchinoald,[42] died, the Neustrians, arguing back and forth in uncertainty, called the required council and established Ebroin in the high position of mayor of the palace at the king's court. In these days King Clothar, still a boy,[43] died, having ruled four years. His brother, Theuderic,[44] was brought up as king of the Neustrians and they sent Childeric,[45] his other brother, to take up rule in Austrasia along with Duke Wulfoald. Some time later the Neustrians formed a conspiracy against Ebroin and they rose up against Theuderic and deposed him from the throne. Dragging them off by force, they cut the hair of both. They gave Ebroin a tonsure and sent him to the monastery at Luxeuil in Burgundy. Sending into Austrasia for Childeric, they brought him to them and when he came with Duke Wulfoald they raised him to the throne of the Neustrians. But this Childeric was too frivolous; he conducted all the affairs so heedlessly that he grew to be a cause of offence and a great

40 This is not the view of him in the *Vita Balthildis*, ch. 4, where he is called pious. See below, p. 121.

41 All three of his sons will rule: Clothar III (Neustria 657–73); Childeric II (Austrasia 657–75, and Neustria 673–75); and Theuderic III (Neustria 673 and again 675–90).

42 Erchinoald played a major role both in Balthild's early life and in causing the Irishman, Foillan, to join Geretrud at Nivelles. See below, pp. 100–6 and 315–16.

43 Clothar III ruled from 657 to 673; he was not 'still a boy' when he died.

44 Theuderic III (673 and 675–90).

45 Childeric II (657–75 in Austrasia, and 673–5 in Neustria).

object of hatred among them as he greatly oppressed the Neustrians.
He ordered one of their number, a Neustrian named Bodilo, to be
stretched upon a stake and beaten illegally. Seeing these things, the
Neustrians were greatly enraged. Ingobert and Amalbert, along with
the other hereditary Neustrian nobility, entered into a plot against
Childeric. Bodilo, along with the others who were conspiring against
the king, rose up against him and killed him together with, I am sorry
to say, his pregnant queen. Wulfoald barely escaped by flight and
returned to Austrasia. The Neustrians then chose Leudesius, Erchinoald's
son, for the palace mayoralty. From Burgundy the blessed Leudegar,[46]
Bishop of Autun, and his brother, Gaerin, took part in this counsel and
they gave their consent. Ebroin, allowing his hair to grow, and
gathering a band of allies to aid him, left the monastery at Luxeuil
ready for battle and returned to Francia with an army. He sent off to
the blessed Audoin[47] so that he might give him [Ebroin] a plan. But
he [Audoin], through his messengers, sent only this in writing: 'Recall to
mind that [plan] of Fredegund's.'[48] And because he was sly[49] he understood. Rising up by night with his army assembled, he came to the
river Oise and, having killed the sentries, he crossed the Oise near
Pont-Sainte-Maxence, where he found some of those who had conspired against him and those he killed. Leudesius with King Theuderic
and many of their allies escaped by flight, but Ebroin pursued them.
Coming to Baisieux, he took the royal treasury.[50] From there after this,
coming to Crécy-en-Ponthieu, he captured the king. He requested
Leudesius to come to him, giving him a deceitful guarantee.[51] When
Leudesius did so, he killed him and quickly assumed the mayoralty
once again. He ordered the holy Leudegar, who had been smitten with

46 His *vita* is translated below, pp. 215–53.
47 His *vita* is translated below, pp. 152–65.
48 The plan is to rise up by night. In ch. 36 (not translated here) the author describes
   Fredegund's clever nocturnal march against the Austrasians using nearly the same
   words as he uses here: *De nocte consurgens ...*
49 *ingenuosus.*
50 This treasure, i.e. gold and silver, is not personal wealth but the means of rewarding
   warriors and thus a *sine qua non* for conducting large-scale military action. It recalls
   the golden ring giving in *Beowulf.* The author pays a great deal of attention to
   treasure and when it changes hands.
51 The breaking of this guarantee or 'given trust' (*data fide*) is a very serious matter
   which usually evokes a strong reaction from the author. His rather neutral language
   here in reporting Ebroin's treachery is remarkable and another indication that the
   author was not influenced by the *Passio Leudegarii* and its condemnation of the
   powerful mayor.

various punishments, to be killed[52] by the sword and he also condemned his brother, Gaerin, to harsh punishment. The rest of their
allies, indeed Neustrians, managed to escape by flight; some wandered
in exile, having been deprived of their possessions.

CHAPTER 46

In that time, Wulfoald of Austrasia having died and the kings having
died, Martin and the younger Pippin,[53] son of the late Ansegisel,
governed in Austrasia until finally it came to the point where these
dukes turned in hatred against Ebroin. Having gathered a large following
of Austrasians,[54] they sent the force against King Theuderic and
Ebroin. Theuderic and Ebroin came out against them with an army at
a place called Bois-du-Fays, and as soon as they joined battle they cut
each other down in a great slaughter. And there a great multitude of
the army fell. The Austrasians were defeated and turned their backs in
flight. Ebroin hunted them down with cruel slaughter and laid most of
that region to waste.[55] Martin, escaping by flight, entered Laon and
shut himself up there; Pippin, however, fled in the other direction.
Ebroin, therefore, having achieved his victory, returned. Coming with
his army to the villa of Asfeld, he sent envoys to Martin so that with
pledges having been given and with a guarantee he [Martin] might
come to King Theuderic. This they [the envoys] craftily and falsely
swore to him [Martin] on empty [relic] boxes. But he trusted them
and came to Asfeld, where he was killed along with his companions.

CHAPTER 47

Ebroin, indeed, cruelly oppressed the Neustrians more and more until
finally it came to the point where he secretly prepared an ambush for
the Neustrian, Ermenfred. He [Ermenfred] therefore rose up secretly
by night against the above-mentioned Ebroin, violently killed him, and
escaped, fleeing to Pippin in Austrasia. The Neustrians, then, conducting
careful deliberation[56] and by order of the king, established Waratto, a

52 *ferire.* Active verb used with passive meaning.
53 Pippin II (d. 714).
54 ... *excercitum plurimum Austrasiorum commotum* ... An accusative absolute.
55 ... *maxima parte ex illa regione* ... The genitive expressed by a preposition with the
ablative.
56 ... *consilio pertractantes* ...

man of illustrious standing, in his place as mayor of the palace. Waratto
received hostages during this period from the aforesaid Pippin and he
entered into a peace agreement with him. At that time Waratto had a
son named Ghislemar, a powerful and active man of untamed spirit and
harsh behaviour, and a plotter against his own father. And he forcibly
displaced him from his position of nobility. The blessed Audoin
forbade him to bring this evil upon his father, but he refused to listen.
Many arguments and internal clashes grew up between this Ghislemar
and Pippin. And he, because of the injuries he had brought upon his
father, and because of his other cruel sins, was struck down by God
and gave up his most evil ghost just as the holy Audoin had predicted
for him. Since he was now dead, Waratto again took up his former
position. It was during these days that the blessed Audoin, bishop of
Rouen, full of days and renowned for his miracles,[57] went to the Lord
while at the royal residence of Clichy in the environs of the city of
Paris. He was buried with great ceremony in the basilica of St Peter
the Apostle in the city of Rouen.

CHAPTER 48

In the following cycle of time the above-mentioned Waratto died; his
widow[58] was named Ansfled, a noble and cunning woman.[59] The Neustrians were split in various directions and could not decide. Eventually,
making a mistake, they installed the late Berchar, a man small in
stature, of low intelligence, and harmful in counsel, in the palace
mayoralty. The Neustrians fell out one with another. Pippin, rising up
from Austrasia, assembled a large army and directed the force against
King Theuderic and Berchar. They met for battle in a place called
Tertry, and when they had fought each other King Theuderic, together
with the mayor of the palace, Berchar, turned their backs in flight, and
Pippin emerged the victor. Some time having elapsed, Berchar himself
was killed by flatterers at the instigation of Ansfled.[60] After these
things, in the reign of King Theuderic, Pippin began to be the mayor of

---

57 *virtutibus preclarus.*

58 *matrona.*

59 *ingeniosa.*

60 This is the reading from the editor's B group of manuscripts. In version A the
   instigation of Ansfled applies to Pippin being made mayor of the palace, not to
   Berchar's murder. See *MGH, SSRM,* II, p. 323.

the palace at the royal[61] court. Having taken the treasury, and having left the late Norbert, one of his own followers, with the king, he himself returned to Austrasia. Prince[62] Pippin had a very noble and very wise wife named Plectrud. By her he had two sons: the name of the elder was Drogo and the name of the younger, Grimoald. Drogo received the duchy of the Champagne.

CHAPTER 49

Then King Theuderic died. He reigned for nineteen years. His son Clovis,[63] still a boy, offspring of Queen Chrodhild, assumed the royal throne. But not much later the boy king Clovis himself died; he ruled for two years. The celebrated Childebert,[64] his brother, was placed on the throne. Then indeed Norbert died. Prince[65] Pippin's younger son Grimoald was made mayor of the palace at King Childebert's court. Pippin also waged many wars against the gentile Radbod and other princes,[66] against the Suevi as well as many other peoples. Grimoald had a son named Theudoald by a concubine. About the same time Pippin's son Drogo died. By another wife the aforesaid Prince[67] Pippin had a son named Charles, a warrior who was uncommonly well educated[68] and effective in battle.

61 *principale.*

62 *principe.*

63 Clovis III (690–4).

64 Childebert III (694–711).

65 *principis.*

66 *principes.*

67 *princeps.*

68 … *nomine Carlo, virum elegantem egregius atque utilem.* Gregory of Tours used the same words to describe king Theudebert I. Gregory of Tours, *Gregorii Episcopi Turonensis Historiarum Libri X*, III,1, eds. B. Krusch and W. Levison, *MGH, SSRM*, I, ed. alt. (Hanover, 1951), p. 91. Pierre Riché notes that *elegans* often indictes intellectual qualities and lists, among other examples, the story reminiscent of one in Horace told by Gregory (*Hist*, IV, 9) about King Theudebert, whom Gregory terms *elegans*, and another one in Paul the Deacon, *Historia Langobardorum*, VI, ch. 17, ed. G. Waitz, *MGH, SSRL* (Hanover, 1878), p. 170, where Paul calls the cultivated Prince Cunnipert *vir elegans*. P. Riché, *Education et culture dans l' Occident barbare, VI⸱–VIII⸱ siècles* (Paris, 1962), p. 97, n. 39. See also C. DuCange, *Glossarium mediae et infirmae Latinitatis*, ed. nova, vol. V–2 (reprint Graz, 1954), coll. 334–5.

CHAPTER 50

Then the famous and just lord, King Childebert of good memory, passed away unto the Lord. He reigned seventeen years. He was buried at the monastery at Choisy-au-Bac in the basilica of St Stephen the first martyr. His son Dagobert,[69] a boy, reigned in his place. Grimoald indeed took a wife named Theudesinda, the daughter of the gentile Duke Radbod. And this mayor of the palace Grimoald was loyal, sober, cultured and just. But after a lapse of time Prince Pippin grew ill, and while he [Grimoald] was travelling to visit his father he was murdered without hesitation by the gentile Rantgar, a son of Belial,[70] in the basilica of St Lambert at Liège. Then by order of his grandfather they installed Theudoald in the office[71] and high position of his father at the court of the king.

CHAPTER 51

At that time Pippin died,[72] having been weakened by a strong fever. He held the governing position under the above-mentioned kings for twenty-seven and a half years. Then Plectrud along with her grandchildren and the king directed all the affairs of state under a separate government. During these times, at the instigation of the devil, Neustrians again attacked Neustrians and in the Forest of Compiègne they cut each other down in a most awful slaughter. Theudoald, however, was snatched up and he slipped away by flight. And there was at that time a terrible persecution. With Theudoald having flown, they therefore chose Raganfred for the governing position as mayor of the palace.[73] And together with an assembled army and the king they crossed the Forest of Charbonnière as far as the river Meuse, devastating and burning those lands. With Radbod, the gentile duke, they entered into an friendship treaty.[74] In these days Charles was held in custody by the lady Plectrud but with the help of the Lord he escaped with difficulty.

69 Dagobert III (711–15).

70 ... *filio Belial.* An extremely pejorative phrase also applied by the author of the *Passio Praejecti* (ch. 29) to a certain Agricius who acted as the devil's agent. See below, p. 292.

71 *honorem.*

72 714.

73 ... *in principatum maiorum palacii elegerunt.* The words used here are *maiorum palacii* instead of the usual *maiorem domus.*

74 *amicicias* [*amicitias*].

CHAPTER 52

In the following time King Dagobert took ill and died. He ruled for
five years. On the throne the Neustrians placed, in fact, Daniel, a
former cleric, having allowed the hair of his head to grow, and they
named him Chilperic.[75] In that time they once more gathered an army
and sent it to the river Meuse against Charles; from the other direction
the Frisians rose up with Duke Radbod. Charles, therefore, attacked
these Frisians and there he suffered a great loss of his followers, but,
taking to flight, he escaped. Time therefore having elapsed, with his
army assembled, Chilperic himself, along with Raganfred, entered the
forest of the Ardennes and came to the river Rhine and Cologne,
laying waste the land. Having taken a great amount of treasure from
the lady[76] Plectrud he turned back, but in a certain place [called]
Amblève Charles fell upon them and they suffered a very great loss.

CHAPTER 53

In that same period the above-mentioned warrior Charles, having
assembled an army, again rose up against Chilperic and Raganfred.[77]
They assembled a force, prepared for battle, and hastened out against
him. Charles, however, sued for peace. This they rejected and went out
to battle in the place called Vinchy at dawn on the twelfth day before
the Kalends of April, a Sunday in Lent.[78] Although they indeed fought
bravely, Chilperic and Raganfred turned their backs [in flight].
Charles emerged the victor. He laid those regions waste, took captives,
and with much booty returned to Austrasia, coming to Cologne, where
he caused an insurrection. He fought with the lady[79] Plectrud and
straightway took his father's treasure and established a king for
himself by the name of Clothar.[80] And then Chilperic and Raganfred
sought the help of Duke Eudo. And he [Eudo] assembled an army and
led it against Charles. He [Charles], however, was not afraid and
hastened steadfastly to meet him, but Eudo fled, fell back on Paris, and,
having snatched up Chilperic along with the royal treasure, retreated

75 Chilperic II (715–21).

76 *matrona*.

77 ... *Chilpericum vel Ragamfredo* ... Confusion of accusative and ablative.

78 21 March 717.

79 *matrona*.

80 Clothar IV (717–18).

across the Loire. Charles chased him but did not catch him. Clothar, indeed, the above-mentioned king, died that year. In the year following, Charles sent a delegation to Eudo and concluded a friendship treaty[81] with him. And he [Eudo] returned King Chilperic along with many gifts. But he [Chilperic] did not remain long on his throne. Indeed, he died after these events and was buried in Noyon. He ruled five and a half years. The Neustrians then placed Theuderic,[82] son of the younger Dagobert, who had been brought up in the monastery at Chelles, over them as their king, and he is now in the sixth year of his reign.

81 *amicitias.*
82 Theuderic IV (721–37).

II: *Vita Domnae Balthildis*[1]
(The Life of Lady Balthild, Queen of the Franks)

Almost every aspect of the life of Queen Balthild reminds us that, in trying to gain a clear picture of this fascinating woman, we are indeed dealing with ages dark to the historian's eyes. We do not know the date or place of her birth. We have no names for her family. We can only guess at when she married the king. We can be reasonably certain that she came to Neustria as a slave and that she later wielded great personal power as regent, but, again, why a woman with no basis in a powerful family of her own was able to become regent and to rule so forcefully in the political milieu of the mid seventh century can be answered only by conjecture. Balthild appears in several trustworthy contemporary souces, but it is the *Vita Balthildis* which gives us the most information about her.[2] For this we can either thank her hagiographer or curse him[3] for frustratingly whetting our appetite to know more.

Balthild's future husband, Clovis II, was born in the twelfth year of the reign of King Dagobert I,[4] that is, in 633, and it seems most likely that she too would have been born at some point near but after that year, since it was usual for a wife to be younger than her husband. She was a Saxon and brought as a slave 'from lands across the sea' to Neustria, where she was purchased by the mayor of the palace, Erchinoald, for a low price.[5] It seems most likely that those lands across the sea were in England, especially since we know the Franks to have had a healthy trade in Anglo-Saxon slaves.[6]

---

1 *Vita Sanctae Balthildis*, ed. B. Krusch, *MGH, SSRM*, II (Hanover, 1888) pp. 475–508.

2 See W. Levison, *England and the Continent in the Seventh Century* (Oxford, 1946), p. 9, n. 4, for a list of the sources which mention her.

3 See below, p. 000, for a discussion of whether the author was male or female.

4 Fredegar, ed. J. M. Wallace-Hadrill, *The Fourth Book of the Chronicle of Fredegar with its Continuations*, IV, ch. 76 (London, 1960), (hereafter Fredgar, *Chron*), p. 64.

5 *Vita Balthildis*, ch. 2, below, p. 000.

6 ... *cum navem ingrederentur utriusque sexus, ex diversis gentibus venientes, pariter liberabat [Eligius] Romanorum scilicet, Gallorum atque Brittanorum necnon et Maurorum, sed praecipue ex genere Saxonorum qui abunde eo tempore veluti greges a sedibus propriis evulsi in diversa distrahebantur. Vita Eligii Episcopi Noviomagnesis*, I, ch. 10, ed. B. Krusch, *MGH, SSRM*, IV (Hanover,1902), p. 677.

There can be little doubt that her hagiographer would have us believe that she was of low state: not only does he say that she cost her purchaser, Erchinoald, very little, but he quotes the Psalms to emphasise the point that she was raised from a low to a high status.[7] The Scriptural reference has been employed to reflect simply her elevation from slave to queen without necessarily indicating low status at birth. A low-born Balthild, too, would be in contradiction with the report of the *LHF*, which also tells us she came from the Saxon nobility.[8] Although the Merovingian kings did have a tradition of choosing low-born women not only for their concubines but also for their queens, only rarely did these women or their offspring come to exercise the sort of power and influence that Balthild and her progeny did.[9] The importance of family and faction in seventh-century Merovingian royal politics is a lesson learned from the *LHF*, the *Passio Leudegarii*, the *Vita Audoini* and other souces in this volume. We should err if were were to seek the key to Balthild's power in some abstract concept concerning the position of women detached from the importance of whatever family she represented. Balthild owed her later powerful position to her connections with an important family with whom the powerful Neustrians needed good relations. Her position was little different from that of other queens we know to have been born into important families. As we have seen, and shall see over and over again, the key to Merovingian high politics was co-operation between the Crown and some faction or factions of the powerful Frankish nobility. The 'slave' Balthild will play a key role in these politics.

In chapters 2 and 3 of her *vita* we find the story of how she came to marry the king. Stripped of its religious meaning, a meaning which the author points out expressly at every turn, the story runs like this. After she had been purchased by Erchinoald, her physical beauty caught his eye. He made her his cupbearer and close personal servant and then, when his wife died, declared his intention of marrying her. She, however, hid under a pile of rags in a distant corner of the house until Erchinoald

---

7 'He Who raises the poor man out of the dunghill and makes him to sit with the princes of His people.' *Vita Balthildis*, ch. 2, below, p. 119, = *I Kings* 2:8 and *Psalms* 112:7–8.

8 *de genere Saxonorum. Liber Historiae Francorum*, ch. 43, ed. B. Krusch, *MGH, SSRM*, II, p. 315.

9 For example: Theuderic II's wife, Bilichild, was an ex-slave (Fredegar, *Chron.*, IV, ch. 35); Sigibert III was the son of Dagobert's concubine (*quadam puella*), Ragnetrud (Fredegar, *Chron.*, IV, ch. 59); and most famous of all was King Chilperic's low-born queen, Fredegund.

had taken another woman as his wife. Then, we are told, she married the king. In its childlike and fairy-tale simplicity this story requires a great suspension of disbelief on the part of the reader. How does a chief servant hide under a heap of rags and thus avoid marriage with the lord of the house? For the author, these remarkable events happened by means of the divine intervention, which was the only conceivable instrument by which the slave girl, Balthild, could have persevered in her Christian virtues, avoided her master's bed when summoned, and come to marry the king. A political historian, however, might explain the slave girl's remarkable rise in another way. Providing a daughter as bride for the king was a valued and typical way for a powerful father to cement the relationship between his family and the Crown. Although not a daughter, Balthild was still a gift to Clovis from the dominant faction in his kingdom at the time. She was given away not by her father but by her owner, the Neustrian mayor, Erchinoald, and an examination of the nature of his position will go a long way to explain the nature of hers.

> After the death of Aega, Erchinoald, who was a relative of Dagobert's mother, was made mayor of the palace at Clovis's court. He was a patient man, full of goodness, and since he was patient and heedful, he responded with humility and goodwill to the bishops and to all patiently and kindly. He was not swollen with any pride, nor did he rage with covetousness. So greatly did he pursue peace in his time that it was pleasing to God. He was wise and especially sincere, moderately wealthy, and loved by all.[10]

Erchinoald was related to King Dagobert I through Dagobert's mother.[11] Thus Balthild's royal marriage did not mark the first time his family had provided the Merovingians with a queen. Piecing together scraps of information preserved in various surviving sources, we can see that although he owned land in the area near Saint-Wandrille and Jumièges on the lower Seine,[12] on the Marne at Lagny,[13] and at Peronne on the Somme,[14] his base was probably near Amiens.[15] If we can believe a late source which makes

10 Fredegar, *Chron.*, IV, ch. 84 (our translation).

11 Bertetrud, *Gesta Dagberti Regis*, ch. 2, ed. B. Krusch, *MGH, SSRM*, II, p. 401. There is controversy concerning who was Dagobert's mother. See I. N. Wood, *The Merovingian Kingdoms 450–751* (New York, 1994), p. 148, n. 50.

12 *Gesta Sanctorum Patrum Fontanellensis Coenobii*, eds. F. Lohier and J. Laporte (Rouen, 1936); (hereafter *Gesta Font.*) I, ch. 4, pp. 5–6, and I, ch. 7, p. 13.

13 *Virtutes Fursei Abbatis Latiniacensis*, ch. 11, ed. B. Krusch, *MGH, SSRM*, IV (Hanover, 1902), p. 444.

14 *Virtutes Fursei*, ch 12.

15 E. Ewig, 'Die fränkischen Teilreiche im 7. Jahrhundert (613–714)', *Trierer Zeitschrift*, 22 (1953), 91, n.14. (Reprinted in E. Ewig, *Spätantikes und fränkisches*

a certain Adalbald his brother, then we can probably find family land in the area around modern Douai as well.[16] In 641 he was made Neustrian mayor of the palace under Clovis II[17] and shortly thereafter helped the Irish missionary, Fursey, to establish the monastery at Lagny.[18] After Fursey's death his brother, Foillan, came as a fugitive from East Anglia to take over Fursey's leadership, something which most likely happened some time during 650 when the actions of Penda could have driven Foillan from Britain.[19] He was at first welcomed by Erchinoald but then, shortly thereafter, as the *Additamentum Nivialense* tells us, the mayor expelled the Irishman and his followers.[20] Erchinoald's relationship with Fursey's group of Irish had been long-standing and close; Fursey may even have baptised Erchinoald's son.[21] This rather startling about-face on the part of Balthild's master has troubled historians and has never been satisfactorily explained.[22] The fact that Erchinoald's change of heart toward the Irish at Peronne happened at about the same time as he gave Balthild in marriage to the king,[23] that is, some time shortly after

---

Gallien. Gesammelte Schriften (1952–1973), vol. I, Beihefte der *Francia*, 3 (Munich, 1976), p. 178, n. 14.)

16 An addition in an early thirteenth-century hand to the *Annales Marchianenses* for their year 664 makes Erchinoald and Adalbald brothers. *Annales Marchianenses*, ed. L. Bethmann, *MGH, SS*, XVI (Hanover, 1859), p. 611 In the *Vita Sanctae Richtrudis*, ch. 7, written in 907 by Hucbald of Saint-Amand, Adalbald is Richtrud's husband. This source mentions their land around Douai: ... *in pago Austrebatinse, ubi etiam pluribus locupletabatur possessionibus* ... *AASS*, Mai, III, p. 83.

17 Fredegar, *Chron.*, IV, ch. 84.

18 Bede, *Historia Ecclesiastica Gentis Anglorum*, III, ch. 19, ed. C. Plummer, *Venerabilis Baedae Opera Historica*, vol. I (Oxford, 1896)(hereafter, Bede, *HE*), p. 168, and *Vita Fursei*, ch. 9.

19 Bede, *HE*, III, ch. 18; *Additamentum Nivialense de Fuilano*, ed. B. Krusch, *MGH, SSRM*, IV (hereafter *Addit. Nivial.*), p. 449, and below, p. 327. See: A. Dierkens, *Abbayes et chapitres entre Sambre et Meuse (VII–XI siècles)*, Beihefte der *Francia*, 14 (Sigmaringen, 1985), p. 76; and C. Plummer, *Baedae Opera*, vol. II, pp. 173–4.

20 *Addit. Nivial.*, below, p. 327.

21 *Virtutes Fursei*, ch. 10.

22 Grosjean thinks Erchinoald simply politely asked the Irish to leave: *Plus or moins aimablement, mais sans ambages, il a invité ces pieux étrangers, après les avoir entretenus quelque temps, à se chercher d'autres protecteurs* ... P. Grosjean, 'Notes d'hagiographie celtique', *Annalecta Bollandiana*, 75 (1957), 389, n. 1. Prinz says it came to *Unstimmigkeiten* between the two and leaves it at that. F. Prinz, *Frühes Mönchtum im Frankenreich* (Munich, 1965), p. 128. Dierkens speculates that only Foillan and a few followers were thrown out, and that others of his party stayed at Peronne. He muses that Foillan may have wished more of a *peregrinatio* than Peronne could provide. Dierkens, *Abbayes*, pp. 306–7

23 *Vita Balthildis*, ch. 3, below, p. 121, and *LHF*, ch. 43, above, p. 88.

648, raises the question of whether his two actions could have been related by something other than temporal coincidence. Indeed, if we look
at what else we know to have been taking place between 648 and 651, we
may be able to put Erchinoald's relations with the Irish and his provision of a royal bride in their historical context. This is, however, admit-
tedly an especially risky analytical foray, even for Merovingian history,
since the period falls in the gap between the end of Fredegar's account
and the point at which the *LHF* begins to be more helpful.

In addition to the expulsion of the Irish and Balthild's royal marriage,
it was in the same period that Erchinoald himself remarried[24] and we
know the name of his new wife, Leutsinda.[25] It was then, too, that
Clovis II came of age.[26] It was in January 651 that Dido, Bishop of
Poitiers, and Grimoald, Austrasian mayor of the palace, met in the
Pippinid family monastery at Nivelles, probably to discuss Grimoald's
intended *coup* and Dido's help with the exile of the young Austrasian
royal prince, Dagobert.[27] On 1 March 649 Erchinoald sold a huge piece
of land to Godo, nephew of Wandregisel, for the founding of a
monastery which grew to be the important house of Saint-Wandrille,
near Rouen.[28] Some time too in the same period (649–53), at the behest
of Erchinoald, the Frankish bishops gathered in council at Chalon-sur-
Saône, where they reiterated their long-standing complaints against
secular officers encroaching on areas of episcopal jurisdiction.[29] This
council, however, added several provisions dealing with secular
encroachment specifically in rural areas. These new provisions would
have had special relevance to the north, where there were fewer cities

---

24 *Vita Balthildis*, ch. 3, below, p. 120.

25 *Virtutes Fursei*, chs. 20, 21, *et passim*.

26 E. Ewig, 'Studien zur merowingischen Dynastie', *Frühmittelalterliche Studien*, 8
(1974), 26.

27 *LHF*, ch. 43, above p. 88, and the *Addit. Nivial.*, below, p. 000. The date 651 is
proposed by R. Gerberding, *The Rise of the Carolingians and the Liber Historiae
Francorum* (Oxford, 1987), pp. 47–66. The more widely accepted date based on
Krusch's work is 656. B. Krusch, 'Chronologica Regum Francorum Stirpis
Merovingicae', *MGH, SSRM*, VII (Hanover, 1920), pp. 493–4. See also J.-M. Picard,
' Church and politics in the seventh century: the Irish exile of King Dagobert II',
in J.-M. Picard (ed.), *Ireland and Northern France* (Dublin, 1991), pp. 31–2.

28 *Gesta. Font.*, I, ch. 4 and I, ch. 7, eds. Lohier and Laport, pp. 5 and 13. See Lohier
and Laport's calculation of the date on p. 13, n. 26; and F. Lot, *Etudes critiques sur
l'abbaye de Saint-Wandrille, Bibliothèque de l'Ecole des hautes études*, 204 (Paris, 1913),
pp. 113–35 and 188–91.

29 'Concilium Cabilonense (647–653)', ed. C. de Clercq, *Concilia Galliae, 511–695,
Corpus Christianorum, Series Latina*, 148A (Turnhout, 1963), pp. 302–10. See O.
Pontal, *Die Synoden im Merowingerreich* (Munich, 1986), pp. 193–7.

and where churches were being established in the countryside.[30]

Can we make sense of these events and of Balthild's and Erchinoald's role in them? While mindful that the surviving evidence is slight, it nonetheless warrants the attempt. Since we are dealing with a royal marriage and with the mayor of the palace, we should not err too badly if we search the high politics for our answer.

Assuming that Balthild was a noble,[31] if not a royal,[32] Anglo-Saxon captive, then could not the same type of political change in England that forced Foillan out of East Anglia have made Balthild more valuable as a Neustrian king's wife and Foillan undesirable as abbot of an important Neustrian monastery? This does indeed seem very likely to have been the case. There are two reasons especially which lead us to suspect that events in England may have influenced Neustrian politics: first, we can see extensive contact between the Neustrian court and East Anglia in the mid seventh century and, second, Erchinoald himself seems to have been closely related to the Kentish royal house.

There was a great movement of very powerful people back and forth across the Channel. Probably some time before 616, King Sigberct of East Anglia, an English king with a very Merovingian-sounding name, fled to the Merovingians in fear of Redwald, his father or stepfather.[33] After his return home, it was Felix, a bishop from the Merovingian kingdom of Burgundy, who helped him to christianise East Anglia.[34] It may be no coincidence, either, that King Dagobert, the father of Balthild's husband, Clovis, also had a Saxon wife, Nanthild.[35] Dagobert exercised enough attraction even over the Northumbrians for the widow of their King Edwin (616–32) to send her two sons to Dagobert's court to be trained.[36] Faremoutiers-en-Brie had two East Anglian abbesses,

---

30 P. Fouracre, 'The Work of Audoenus of Rouen and Eligius of Noyon in extending Episcopal Influence from the Town to the Country in Seventh-century Neustria', *Studies in Church History*, 16 (1979), 78–9.

31 *LHF*, ch. 43.

32 ... *quae erat ex regali progeniae* ... . *Vita Balthildis (B)*, ch. 3, ed. B. Krusch, MGH, SSRM, II, p. 485.

33 Bede, *HE*, III, ch. 18.

34 Bede, *HE*, II, ch. 15, and III, ch. 18.

35 *LHF*, ch. 42. Nanthild may have been from Continental Saxony, but such is not the case with Balthild.

36 Bede, *HE*, II, ch. 20. See P. Riché, 'Les representations du palais dans les textes littéraires du Haut Moyen-âge', in his *Instruction et vie religieuse dans le Haut Moyen-âge* (London, 1981), pp. 161–2 Reprinted from *Francia*, 4 (1976).

Saethryd and Aethilberg, daughters of King Anna,[37] and Heresuid, mother of King Alduuld of East Anglia, came to the Merovingian kingdom to become a nun at Chelles.[38] The Frank, Agilbert, who took part in the Synod of Whitby (664) was bishop of the West Saxons about the year 650 and later became bishop of Paris.[39] As we have seen from the *LHF*, the location chosen by Grimoald and Dido of Poitiers for the exile of the Austrasian prince, Dagobert, was Ireland.[40] Scholars have noted parallels in the form of charters[41] from both sides of the Channel and a very probable Merovingian influence in King Aethelberht's legislation.[42] The magnificent seventh-century treasure buried at Sutton Hoo in East Anglia contains much that is Merovingian, probably offered as royal gifts and subsidies to further Merovingian interests.[43] The clear evidence of this marked contact, along with a difficult passage from Procopius,[44] has led one noted scholar to conclude that the Merovingians exercised overlordship over south-east England at least until the early seventh century.[45] Erchinoald's gift of the Anglo-Saxon Balthild to the Merovingian royal family certainly seems to add strength to his argument.

Erchinoald's connections with England were very close. When the East Anglian refugee, Fursey, first arrived along the Somme, Erchinoald

---

37 Bede, *HE*, III, ch. 8.

38 Bede, *HE*, IV, ch. 23. See: D. Whitelock, 'The Pre-Viking Age Church in East Anglia', *Anglo-Saxon England*, 1 (1972), 6; Plummer , *Bedae Opera*, vol. II, p. 173–4; and I. N. Wood, 'The Franks and Sutton Hoo', in I. N. Wood and N. Lund (eds.), *People and Places In Northern Europe 500–1600: Essays in Honour of Peter Sawyer* (Woodbridge, 1991), pp. 6–9.

39 Bede, *HE*, III chs. 7 and 28. Agilbert also sent his nephew, Lothar, to King Cenwalh of Wessex to be his bishop. Bede, *HE*, III, ch. 7.

40 *LHF*, ch. 43, above, p. 88. See Picard, 'Church and Politics'.

41 P. Wormald, 'Bede and the Conversion of England: the Charter Evidence', Jarrow Lecture (1984), pp. 9–10.

42 I. N. Wood, 'The Merovingian North Sea', *Occasional Papers on Medieval Topics*, I (Alingås, 1983), p. 13.

43 P. Grosjean, 'Notes d'hagiographie celtique', *Annalecta Bollandiana*, 78 (1960), 364–8, suggests that Sutton Hoo contains the money Erchinoald paid to Penda in about 650 to help Foillan ransom his monks. Dierkens, *Abbayes*, p. 71, disagrees, saying the burial ship dates from 624–5. Wood, *Merovingian Kingdoms*, p. 177, surmises that the collection of coins in the treasure was probably assembled in Francia, not in England, and may have been a subsidy paid to the East Anglian king, Sigbert, while he was in exile in Francia some time before 630. See also J. Campbell, *The Anglo-Saxons* (Ithaca, New York, 1982), pp. 32–3.

44 Procopius, *History of the Wars*, VIII, xx, 8–10, ed. and trans. H. B. Dewing, Loeb Classical Library, *Procopius*, vol. V (Cambridge, Massachusetts,1928), pp. 254–5.

45 Wood, 'Merovingian North Sea', pp. 12 and 17.

obviously recognised his importance, for he vied with a certrain Duke
Haymon in offering him land and money.[46] The Anglo-Saxons Wilfrid
and Benedict Biscop passed through the Frankish lands on Wilfrid's
first trip to Rome in 653, when Erchinoald was mayor.[47] Erchinoald has
a name part in common with several members of the Kentish royal
house; his name, rendered in the Saxon spelling, is Eorcenwald.
Erchinoald may well have been the father of Emma, wife of King
Eadbald of Kent (616–40).[48] If he did manage to provide the Kentish
king with a bride, it makes him the grandfather of King Eorcenberht
(640–64) and great grandfather of Eorcengota, who eventually entered
Faremoutiers as a nun.[49] It can also be no coincidence that Eorcenwald,
bishop of London from 675–93, bears the Neustrian mayor's name.

The foregoing is unfortunately as far as we can go. Even though we
can see close contact between the Franks and the English in general
during our period and Erchinoald's especially close relations with the
English in particular, we can say no more than that some English
reason for Balthild's elevation and Foillan's expulsion is highly probable.[50]
Balthild's hagiographer, of course, saw divine will as the reason for her
rise to the status of queen, but providence may well have had some
significant help from the contemporary politics of the British Isles.[51]

46 *Virtutes Fursei*, chs. 6 and 11.

47 Stephen of Ripon, *Vita Wilfridi I. Episcopi Eboracensis auctore Stephano*, ch. 3, ed. B.
   Colgrave, *The Life of Bishop Wilfrid by Eddius Stephanus* (Cambridge, 1927, reprint
   New York, 1985), pp. 8–9; and Bede, *HE*, III, ch. 7. See Plummer, *Baedae Opera*, vol.
   II, p. 316.

48 K.-F. Werner, 'Les rouages de l'administration', in P. Perin and L.-C. Feffer (eds.),
   La Neustrie (Rouen, 1985), p. 42, and Wood, 'Sutton Hoo', p. 7.

49 Bede, *HE*, III, ch. 8. See: J. Campbell,'The First Century of Christianity in England',
   in his *Essays in Anglo-Saxon History* (London, 1986), p. 56; F. M. Stenton, *Anglo-
   Saxon England*, third edition (Oxford,1971), p. 61; K.-F. Werner, 'Les rouages', p.
   42; and Wood, 'Sutton Hoo', p. 7.

50 It is extremely significant that when Erchinoald expelled Foillan, the Irishman fled
   not to Luxeuil or some other centre of Irish monasticism which had a close
   connection to the Neustrian royal court but northward to Nivelles and to the
   Pippinids, a family about to upset Merovingian rule in Austrasia. This is further
   evidence for Ian Wood's contention that we should not see the Irish on the
   Continent as one group: the Luxeuil Irish were different from Foillan's and Ultan's
   group. I. N. Wood, 'The *Vita Columbani* and Merovingian Hagiography', *Peritia*, I
   (1982), 68. We shall examine this more closely when we treat the *Vita Sanctae
   Geretrudis*, below, pp. 313–17.

51 King Cenwalh was restored to the throne of Wessex in 647 or 648. Bede, *HE*, III,
   ch. 7, and Plummer, *Baedae Opera*, vol. II, p. 144. Perhaps somewhere in these
   English political machinations lies our reason.

In addition to providing the king with a wife and expelling a potentially unwelcome political element from an important monastery he had helped to found, Erchinoald made other moves to consolidate his position. His marriage to Leutsinda probably bound him to another important family of the Neustrian nobility. If the school of history which lays great emphasis on the importance of Frankish naming practice as an indication of familial connections is correct, it would seem that Erchinoald's son Leudesius,[52] and Leudegar of Autun, since we know that these two were allies,[53] carry a name-part from her family. Erchinoald's marriage to Leutsinda may have been intended to strengthen his hand against the other dominant group headed by Audoin and later by Ebroin. On the other hand, Ebroin's own wife was called Leutrud, something which suggests that the Neustrian elite was widely interlinked through marriage ties and that alliances and enmities cut across family lines and across ties of spiritual kingship, for Ebroin and Leudesius were also said to be related as godparents. As we shall see when we examine the *Vita Audoini*,[54] Audoin's appointment as bishop of Rouen in 641 was an important step in extending the faction's influence into the area of the lower Seine. Erchinoald's land donation to Godo for the founding of Saint-Wandrille,[55] which seems to have taken place in 649,[56] that is, about the same time as Balthild married the king, can be seen as his side's effort to do the same in the area. Even the novel canons of the Council of Chalon may reflect the same factional division.[57] We know from the *Vita Eligii* that there was great animosity between Eligius (Audoin's group) and Erchinoald.[58] Those canons protesting at secular encroachment in rural areas could well reflect Audoin's and Eligius's attempts to thwart Erchinoald's expansion in the undeveloped areas around the monastery at Peronne. The fact that we know Audoin and Eligius to have been present at Chalon, the only council we know them to have attended, lends weight to the supposition. In such an atmosphere (we might add, a usual one for Merovingian politics) is it any wonder that Erchinoald would have

---

52 *LHF*, ch. 25.

53 *LHF*, ch. 45, above, p. 90.

54 Below, p. 151.

55 *Gesta Font.*, I, 5.

56 Vacandard's date, taken from the second *Vita Audoeni*, ch. 14. E. Vacandard, *Vie de Saint Ouen, évêque de Rouen (641–684)* (Paris, 1902), p. 165, n. 2.

57 'Concilium Cabilonense (647–653)', ch. 15, in de Clercq (ed.), *Concilia Galliae*, p. 306.

58 *Vita Eligii*, II, ch. 27.

found it quite a *coup* for his side to have provided the king with a wife, especially if that wife had somehow recently become a politically powerful Anglo-Saxon?[59]

Although some change in the status of her family in the British Isles and the political manoeuvrings of her master in Neustria probably catapulted the chamber slave to royal status, the security of that status for the future obviously demanded that she should produce royal heirs. According to a charming story in the *Vita Eligii*,[60] Balthild was well aware of her duty to produce the royal heir. Once pregnant, she confessed her worry to Eligius that if she were carrying a girl the kingdom would suffer. Her three sons were born quickly after her marriage to Clovis: Clothar between 649 and 652, Childeric in 653, and Theuderic in 654.[61] According to her hagiographer she began her acts of royal piety while her husband was still alive, although her great monastic foundations came later, in the period of her regency after both Clovis and Erchinoald had died. As queen, Balthild commanded a portion of the royal funds for alms and other pious purposes,[62] an indication of her growing personal importance.[63]

In the autumn of 657[64] Balthild's husband, Clovis II, met his death and was succeeded by his five-to-seven-year-old son, Clothar III, with Balthild as regent.[65] The nobility seem to have accepted her regency

---

59 *Erat autem saepedictus Erchinoaldus maior domus regiae insignis bonitate ac elemosinarum largissimus. Qui post transitum bonae recordationis saepefati Dagoberti regis, praefecturae ordinem ac curam maximam regni Francorum etiam cum filio eius Hlodoveo et Bathilde regina nobiliter amministravit. Gesta Font.* I, 5, p. 5. It seems these authors from the Carolingian period understood why Balthild became queen.

60 *Vita Eligii II*, ch. 32.

61 These are best guesses; the dates of the birth of Balthild's children cannot be fixed. The sources disagree about the order: *LHF* ch. 44 gives the order as Clothar, Childeric and Theuderic, whereas the *Passio Leudegarii*, ch. 5, below, p. 222, reverses Theuderic and Childeric. See: Ewig, 'Studien', 23; M.-J. Couturier, *Sainte Bathilde Reine des Francs. Histoire politique et religieuse* (Paris, 1909), p. 64; L. Levillain, 'Encore la succession d'Austrasie', *BEDC*, 106 (1945/46), 305, n. 1; and J. L. Nelson, 'Queens as Jezabels: the Careers of Brunhild and Balthild in Merovingian History', *Studies in Church History*, Subsidia I (1978), 47.

62 *Vita Balthildis*, ch. 4, below, pp. 121–2.

63 Nelson, 'Queens', 47.

64 The range for his death date has been firmly fixed by scholars, varying only by a few days. See: Ewig, 'Studien', 23; Nelson, 'Queens', 48; and C. Courtois, 'L'avènement de Clovis II et les règles d'accession au trône chez les Mérovingiens', *Mélanges d'histoire du Moyen-âge dédiés à la mémoire de Louis Halphen* (Paris, 1951), p. 160, who follows Krusch in *MGH, SSRM*, VII, pp. 495–7.

65 *LHF*, ch. 44, above p. 89.

without great objection; at least, we have no record of any upheaval. The transition may have been so smooth because Erchinoald retained his dominant position for the beginning of the regency. But some time before 659 he, too, seems to have died.[66] The passing of the old mayor and the selection of Ebroin to replace him indicate new political influences at court. We have seen from the *LHF* that the choice of Ebroin was anything but a matter of course.[67] When Balthild's hagiographer comments on these days and the conditions surrounding the rule of her son, the boy Clothar III, he makes no mention of her regency, saying that the young king ruled along with many magnates and listing three of them by name. Significantly, the three named are Chrodbert, bishop of Paris, Lord Audoin, and Ebroin.[68] Erchinoald's faction was out.

The years of Balthild's regency (657–63/4) were ones of relative peace, not only among the Merovingian kingdoms but also within them. Peace was a precious state of affairs, and Balthild herself may have played an important personal role in preserving it; at least, her hagiographer says she did. Her rule was firmer and more personal than her husband's had been; no source attributes any important act to him, whereas Balthild is seen as the author of many.[69] Since the fall in Austrasia of the Pippinid pretender, Childebert, her husband Clovis II had ruled both the Frankish kingdoms, and after Clovis's death her young son, Clothar III, did so as well under her regency. The Austrasians, however, preferred to have their own monarch and not to be subject directly to the Neustrian court at Paris. We recall that Clothar II had sent his son Dagobert I to rule in Austrasia in 622 or 623 and Dagobert, in turn, yielded to the Austrasians' demands and sent them his son, Sigibert III, in 633.[70] There was a living rightful Merovingian heir to the Austrasian throne, Prince Dagobert, son of Sigibert III. But he was in exile in Ireland and was not recalled at this point. Instead Balthild, probably after negotiation with Himnechild, Sigibert III's widow, arranged for her son Childeric II to marry Himnechild's daughter, Bilichild, and to assume the throne of Austrasia.[71]

---

66 *ChLA*, no. 557. A charter in which Erchinoald is called 'the late' (*quondam*).
67 See above, p. 82.
68 *Vita Balthildis*, ch. 5.
69 Couturier, *Sainte Bathilde*, p. 144.
70 Fredegar, *Chron.*, IV, ch. 66 (Dagobert); *ibid.*, IV, ch. 75 (Sigibert).
71 *Vita Balthildis*, ch. 5, below, p. 122; and *LHF*, ch. 45, above, p. 89.

Also in the internal Neustrian politics of family and faction, we have
good indications that Balthild knew how to build bridges between the
two major sides. Although she came from Erchinoald's household, it
was Audoin's partisan, Eligius, who had baptised her eldest son, Clothar
III,[72] and Bishop Aunemund, whom she would later replace with her
confidant, Genesius, who stood as godfather to him.[73] And although
most of her monastic and episcopal policies favoured partisans of Audoin's
circle, it was also Balthild who effected the appointment of Leudegar
to the important see of Autun in 663.[74] Her hagiographer, although
almost exclusively concerned with her pious acts, nonetheless shows us
that he was aware of the factionalism.[75] Peace-keeping required a person-
age of considerable standing, and in the eyes of her hagiographer that
it meant a person of considerable standing with God: 'And we believe
that with God guiding, and in accordance with the great faith of Lady
Balthild, these three kingdoms kept the harmony of peace among
themselves.'[76]

It is not surprising that, once Erchinoald had passed from the scene and
Ebroin had succeeded him, Balthild's actions should reflect the influence of Audoin's circle. The abbey closest to Balthild's heart was
Chelles. Chelles had been a Roman and then a royal Merovingian villa
where Clothild, Clovis I's wife, had founded a small oratory dedicated
to St George.[77] Balthild greatly enlarged the buildings and built a new
church to the Holy Cross. Although no charters survive, we have a
good indication that she endowed it heavily on two occasions: when she
first enlarged it[78] and when she retired to it.[79] In her choice of the first

72 *Vita Eligii*, II, ch. 32.

73 *Acta Aunemundi*, ch. 2, below, p. 192. Aunemund may also have officiated at the
baptism, see below, pp. 182, n. 48 and 187, n. 65.

74 *Passio Leudegarii*, I, ch. 2, below, p. 218. See Prinz, *Frühes Mönchtum*, p. 136.

75 See below, pp. 112–13.

76 *Et credimus, Deo gubernante, iuxta domnae Balthildis magnam fidem ipsa tria regna tunc
inter se tenebant pacis concordiam. Vita Balthildis*, ch. 5.

77 *Vita Balthildis*, ch. 18, below, p. 131. J.-P. Laporte, *Le Trésor des saints de Chelles*
(Chelles, 1988), p. 1.

78 *Vita Balthildis*, ch. 7, below, p. 123. According to the Carolingian version of her *vita*,
she and her sons left a royal charter testifying to her endowment of Chelles with
many rich *villae. Vita Balthildis* (B), ch. 7.

79 *Vita Bertilae Abbatissae Calensis*, ch. 7, ed. W. Levison, *MGH, SSRM*, VI (Hanover,
1913), p. 107. See R. Foltz, 'Tradition hagiographique et culte de sainte Bathilde,
reine des Francs', *Comptes Rendus de l'Académie des Inscriptions et Belles-lettres* (1975),
371–2; and K. H. Krüger, *Königsgrabkirchen der Franken Angelsachsen und
Langobarden bis zur Mitte des 8. Jahrhunderts, Münsterische Mittelalter-Schriften*, 4
(Munich, 1971), pp. 238–46.

abbess at Chelles we can again see Audoin's influence. The woman Balthild chose was Bertila, a member of a noble family from the area of Soissons and a nun since childhood at Jouarre,[80] an abbey founded by Ado, Audoin's brother.[81] From the *Vitae Bertilae* we know that Chelles prospered and soon became a double monastery.[82] Audoin's circle was also connected with Balthild's other great monastic foundation: the abbey of Corbie on the Somme. For Corbie's beginnings we have some charter evidence in addition to the report in chapter 7 of the *Vita Bathildis*.[83]

Queen Balthild not only founded monasteries, she devoted considerable wealth to sustaining them. Her hagiographer never tires of listing the houses to which she donated wealth and land, often from the royal fisc.[84] She saw to it that the foundations were provided with episcopal privilege and royal immunity.[85] She also sought to ensure that the

---

80 *Vita Balthildis*, chs. 7 and 8, below, pp. 124 and 125.

81 Jonas, *Vita Columbani Discipulorumque eius Libri Duo auctore Iona*, I, 26, ed. B. Krusch, *MGH, SSRM*, IV (Hanover, 1902), p. 100; and *Vita Sancti Agili Abbatis*, ch. 4, ed. J. Stiltingus, *AASS*. Aug, VI, (Antwerp. 1743) p. 582.

82 *Vita Bertilae*, ch. 6. See Foltz, 'Tradition hagiographique', 372.

83 A foundation charter was issued by Balthild and Clothar III some time between 657 and 661. L. Levillain, *Examen critique des chartes mérovingiennes et carolingiennes de l'abbaye de Corbie. Mémoires et documents publiés par la société de l'Ecole des Chartes* (Paris, 1902), pp. 213–18; a charter by Clothar III from 661 exempting Corbie from paying tolls (*ibid.*, pp. 218–20); and a charter by Bishop Bertfried of Amiens from 664 granting the episcopal privilege and free abbatial election, *ibid.*, pp. 220–6. This last was re-edited by B. Krusch, 'Die Urkunden von Corbie und Levillains letztes Wort', *NA*, 31 (1906), 367–75, where Krusch doubts the authenticity of Bertfried's privilege, or at least says it is heavily amended. See: Prinz, *Frühes Mönchtum*, pp. 173–4; Foltz, 'Tradition hagiographique', 372; Couturier, *Sainte Bathilde*, pp. 205, 208–10, 221–2 and 305–6; E. Ewig, 'Das Privileg des Bischofs Berthefrid von Amiens für Corbie von 664 und die Klosterpolitik der Königen Balthild', *Francia*, I (1973), 63–114 (reprint *Gallien*, vol. 2, pp. 538–83); and D. Ganz, *Corbie In the Carolingian Renaissance*, Beihefte der *Francia*, 20 (Sigmaringen, 1990), pp. 15–17.

84 *Vita Balthildis*, ch. 4, below, pp. 121–2; ch. 7, below, pp. 123–4; ch. 8, below, pp. 124–5; ch. 9, below, p. 126; and ch. 10, below, p. 126.

85 *Vita Balthildis*, ch. 9, below, p. 126. See Wood, *Merovingian Kingdoms*, pp. 197–200. The royal immunity was a guarantee from the Crown that royal officials would not enter the monastery. This was tantamount to exempting the monastery from certain royal taxes and other obligations. The episcopal privilege, on the other hand, resulted from the tendency of Merovingian bishops to violate certain traditional monastic rights. Their encroachments provoked the monasteries to seek guarantees from the bishops in the form of an episcopal privilege clearly delineating the bishop's rights over the monastery. See Couturier, *Sainte Bathilde*, pp. 57–61. Many such charters survive from the Merovingian era, the oldest being Bishop Burgundofaro's for Rebais. See: E. Ewig, 'Das Formular von Rebais und die Bischofsprivilegien der Merowingerzeit' in *Aus Reichsgeschichte und nordischer Geschichte. Festschrift für Karl Jordan, Kieler Historische Studien*, 16 (1972), pp. 11–42 (reprint *Gallien*, vol. 2, pp. 456–84).

monks would live according to a 'holy regular order'.[86] This last has been
taken to be a specific reference to the mixed Benedictine–Columbanan
monastic rule, a rule supposedly followed wherever Columbanan
monasticism had influence.[87] Although the *vita* leaves no doubt that
Balthild did try to foster monastic life according to a rule, recent
scholars have cautioned against assuming that the rule was a standardised code.[88] The *vita* singles out by name six eccclesiastical establishments which attracted her attention, calling them the *seniores basilicas
sanctorum*. These were the great holy places of the realm, sources of
supernatural power, and ones it was important to influence.[89]

In the seventh century the heads of monasteries did not yet hold the
secular political importance they would later gain;[90] it was the bishops
who were the ecclesiastical figures with the greater political weight.
The *Vita Wilfridi* tells us that Aunemund of Lyons was one of nine
bishops whom Balthild had killed, seemingly in order to replace them
with her own candidates.[91] We know the names of three and perhaps four
of her episcopal appointees: Genesius to the see at Lyons,[92] Erembert to
that at Toulouse,[93] Leudegar to Autun,[94] and perhaps Sigobrand to Paris
– at least we know that she was favourably disposed toward him.[95]

---

86 ... *sub sancto regulari ordine* .... *Vita Balthildis*, ch. 9.

87 Prinz, *Frühes Mönchtum*, p. 164 *et passim*; Foltz, 'Tradition hagiographique', 372–3;
    Gerberding, *Rise*, p. 68; and Nelson, 'Queens', 68.

88 G. Moyse, 'Monachisme et règlementation monastique en Gaule avant Benoît
    d'Aniane', *Hautes Etudes Médiévales et Modernes*, 47 (1982), 6–8; Dierkens, *Abbayes*,
    pp. 286–7; and Wood, *Merovingian Kingdoms*, p. 181.

89 Nelson, 'Queens', 70.

90 F. Felten, *Äbte und Laienäbte im Frankenreich*, *Monographen zur Geschichte des
    Mittelalters*, 20 (Stuttgart, 1980), pp. 129–35.

91 Stephen, *Vita Wilfridi*, ch. 6, and from it Bede, *HE*, V, ch. 19. Chapters 3–6 of the
    Acta Aunemundi, below, pp. 182–6, contain a report of Aunemund's death independ-
    ent of the one in the *Vita Wifridi*. Here Balthild is only indirectly responsible for his
    execution. It may be that, given Wilfrid's and Aunemund's great friendship,
    Wilfrid's biographer overstated the case against Balthild. See below, pp. 172–7, and
    Nelson, 'Queens', 63–4.

92 *Vita Balthildis*, ch. 4, below, p. 122.

93 *Vita Eremberti Episcopi Tolosani*, ch. 1, ed. W. Levison, *MGH, SSRM*, V (Hanover,
    1910), p. 654, where he is appointed *jussu regum* (Clothar and Balthild). Erembert
    was a Neustrian from the Chartres area and a monk at Saint-Wandrille. See
    Couturier, *Sainte Bathilde*, p. 171; Ewig, 'Teilreiche', 127 (reprint *Gallien*, vol. 1,
    p. 213); and Nelson, 'Queens', 62–4.

94 *Passio Leudegarii*, I, ch. 2, below, p. 218.

95 *Vita Balthildis*, ch. 10, below, p. 126. Sigobrand's predecessor, Bishop Chrodbert,
    signed a charter on 6 September 664, meaning that Chrodbert was still in office on

In addition to the founding of monasteries and richly endowing them, her *vita* emphasises three other particular acts of Balthild's Christian piety: she prohibited infanticide, often committed because the tax burden did not allow parents to provide for their children;[96] she attacked the practice of simony;[97] and she purchased and manumitted slaves, especially Saxon slaves, forbidding trade in Christian captives.[98] Once again it is noteworthy that two of these three practices are attacked in the acts of the council of Chalon-sur-Saône in language that is strikingly similar to that used by her hagiographer.[99]

The founding and endowing of monasteries, the support of Irish monasticism, appointing capable men to episcopal rank, and attacking the abuses of simony can all be seen as acts of the queen's piety. But they also lend themselves to a political interpretation. A long-standing view has it that Balthild skilfully used these and other means to expand the sphere of Neustrian royal interests at the expense of the nobility; her reform of the *seniores basilicas* has been used especially in support of this view.[100] But, as we have seen and shall see in our examination of the sources in this volume, the force which moved late

---

that date and that Sigobrand took over some time after it. Editions by: K. A. Pertz, *MGH, Dipl*, I (Hanover, 1872), no. 40, pp. 36–8; and Levillain, *Examen critique*, pp. 213–17. Balthild most likely retired some time between August 664 and August 665, see below, n. 102. Thus, if she did appoint Sigobrand, the appointment would have come in the last year of her regency. Since his murder happened before her retirement, his period of tenure as bishop was less than a year long.

96 *Vita Balthildis*, ch. 6, below, p. 123.

97 *Vita Balthildis*, ch. 6, below, p. 123.

98 *Vita Balthildis*, ch. 9, below, pp. 125–6.

99 Simony: 'Concilium Cabilonense (647–653)', ch. 16, ed. de Clercq, *Concilia Galliae*, p. 306. See Nelson, 'Queens', 61. Slavery: … *ut nullus mancipium extra finibus vel terminibus, qui ad regnum domni Choldovei regis pertinent, penitus non debeat venundare* … . 'Concilium Cabilonense (647–653)', ch. 9, p. 305 Compare the wording of *Vita Balthildis*, ch. 9: *Ut nullus in regno Francorum captivum hominem christianum penitus transmitteret. MGH, SSRM*, II, p. 494.

100 A widely accepted interpretation with many variations: H. Bonnell, *Die Anfänge des Karolingischen Hauses* (Berlin, 1866), p. 122 and *passim*; E. Ewig, 'Beobachtungen zu den Klosterprivilegien des 7. und frühen 8. Jahrhunderts', in J. Fleckenstein and K. Schmid (eds.), *Adel und Kirche* (Freiburg,1968), p. 62 (reprint *Gallien*, vol. 2, p. 422); I. Haselbach, 'Aufstieg und Herrschaft der Karolinger in der Darstellung der sogenannten Annalen Mettenses priores', *Historische Studien*, 412 (1970), 53; M. Rouche, L'Aquitaine des Wisigoths aux Arabes (418–781) (thesis, Université de Lille III, 1977), p. 394; G. Tessier, *Le Baptême de Clovis* (Paris, 1964), p. 235; Prinz, *Frühes Mönchtum*, pp. 140–1 and 173–6; and R. Sprandel, *Der merowingische Adel und die Gebiete östlich des Rheins, Forschungen zur oberrheinischen Landesgeschichte*, 5 (Freiburg, 1957), p. 49.

Merovingian politics was not tension between a centralising royal authority on the one hand and a decentralising nobility on the other, but rather co-operation between Crown and nobility set amid the manoeuvrings of the aristocratic factions. It is also possible to see her above-mentioned pious acts in a factional context. The monasteries Balthild founded and endowed were all closely associated with Audoin's circle and with the Irish monasticism emanating from Luxeuil. So too, it seems, were the bishops she appointed, except for Leudegar of Autun and perhaps Sigobrand of Paris, whose appointments, as we shall see presently, may have played a role in forcing her to retire. Even attacking the abuse of simony would serve to open bishoprics otherwise closed to her candidates by snatching the sees away from those who held the traditional right to purchase them.

Balthild's hagiographer, who presents her every important action as religiously motivated, still does not hide the factionalism which brought about her fall from political power:

It was, however, her holy vow that she ought to dwell in the monastery ... at Chelles .... But the Franks, for love of her, delayed in this especially, and neither would they have permitted it to come about had not an insurrection arisen because of the wretched Bishop Sigobrand, whose haughtiness among the Franks earned him mortal ruin. And from this a dispute arose because they killed him against her will. Fearing that the lady would hold it gravely against them and wish to vindicate his cause, they straightway permitted her to go into the monastery; ... it was not with a good heart that these princes then permitted this. But the lady considered it God's will that this was not so much their decision as a dispensation of God that her holy desire had been fulfilled .... And having been escorted by certain noblemen, she came to ... Chelles, and there ... she was honourably and very lovingly received into the holy congregation by the holy maidens. Then, however, she had a complaint of no mean size against those whom she had kindly nurtured because they had erroneously considered her suspect and even repaid evil to her for her good deeds.[101]

Some time between August 664 and August 665 Queen Balthild retired from the court.[102] By 663 or 664 her reigning son, Clothar III,

---

101 *Vita Balthildis*, ch. 10, below, pp. 126–7.

102 The date of Balthild's retirement has been calculated from surviving royal charters. The last one she signed was dated 6 September 664. Editions by Pertz, *MGH, Dipl.* I, no. 40, pp. 36–8; and Levillain, *Examen critique*, pp. 213–17. Beginning with a charter of Clothar III from August 665, her signature is lacking. *MGH, Dipl.* I, no. 42, pp. 39–40. Thus it seems she retired some time between the two dates. Neither of these charters survives in the original and neither is wholly authentic, although

had reached the age of majority.[103] If it were not for the above report in her *vita*, we might see Clothar's majority as reason enough for her retirement[104] to take up the life of a nun.[105] But it is very easy to set what the hagiographer tells us here in the context of factional politics. He lets us see that the immediate cause of her retirement was her friendship with Sigobrand, the bishop of Paris. Sigobrand's predecessor, Chrodobert, had been part of the dominant faction firmly in Ebroin's camp,[106] but the new pontiff was 'haughty among the Franks', as the hagiographer puts it. In other words, he did not listen to them, as Chrodobert had done, and so they killed him. It is also probably no coincidence that Balthild left the court for the monastery shortly after she had used her position to secure the see of Autun for Leudegar.[107] As we have seen from the *LHF*,[108] Leudegar would eventually ally with Erchinoald's son, Leudesius, in armed conflict against Ebroin's and Audoin's group, and his appointment to an important see also cannot have pleased them. To all appearances there was a growing rift between the queen and that group of Frankish nobles with whom she had ruled as regent and whose careers she had fostered. When the hagiographer tells us she carried a complaint against these men 'whom she had kindly nurtured', he gives us another indication that her retirement was caused by the factionalism which so governed the politics at court. Animosity towards anyone, even treacherous old friends, is by no means a trait worthy of a saint, and thus he quickly

parts of them appear to be. See: Krusch, *MGH, SSRM*, II, p. 476; Levillain, *Examen critique*, pp. 28 and 30; K. Stumpf, 'Über die Merovinger-Diplome', *Historische Beischrift*, 29 (1873), 368; H. Ebling, *Prosopographie der Amtsträger des Merowinger- reiches*. Beihefte der *Francia*, 2 (Munich, 1974), p. 215, n. 2; and P. Classen, 'Kaiserreskript und Königsurkunde', *Archiv für Diplomatik*, 2 (1956), 44, n. 207.

103 Ewig has calculated the age of majority of the Merovingian kings as fifteen. Ewig, 'Studien', 22–4. A passage in the *Lex Salica* may indicate that a boy of twelve had passed some legal dividing line: *Si quis puerum [ingenium] infra XII annos usque ad duodecimum occiderit ....* *Lex Salica* 65 title *(A)*, XIIII-1, ed. K. A. Eckhardt, *MGH, Legum*, sectio I, vol. IV, pt. 1 (Hanover, 1969), pp. 88–9. See Couturier, *Sainte Bathilde*, p 243; and P. Viollet, *Histoire du droit civil français*, second edition (Paris, 1893), pp. 511–12.

104 This is the view of the *Vita Bertilae*, ch. 4.

105 A 'phoney vocation'. Nelson, 'Queens', 52.

106 In addition to the mention of Chrodobert as Audoin's and Ebroin's colleague in ch. 5 of the *Vita Balthildis*, Audoin may have sent Chrodbert a copy of his *Vita Eligii* for correction. See Krusch, *MGH, SSRM*, V, pp. 651 and 741.

107 Leudegar was made Bishop of Autun some time between 662 and 664. See below, p. 218, n. 92.

108 *LHF*, ch. 45, above, p. 90.

adds that she patched up her differences, seeking their forgiveness for
the 'disturbance in her heart'.

We know little about Balthild's life during her retirement. Even
though her hagiographer turns almost exclusively to describing her
acts of piety and humility, he still lets us see that she tried from time
to time to exert her influence at court.[109] She would have been at
Chelles when her son, Clothar III, was buried there in 673,[110] and
during the troubles of 675 when Erchinoald's son, Leudesius, and
Bishop Leudegar made their abortive bid for power.[111] In this context
it is significant that the only specific miracle the *vita* contains concerns
a certain Bishop Leudegandus, who came to Balthild's tomb from the
Provence.[112] Leudegandus shares the name-part both with the two
rebels and with Leutsinda, Erchinoald's wife. Although we have no
contemporary textual evidence, a local tradition at Chelles makes it
seem that Balthild effected the translation of the body of her former
colleague, Bishop Genesius, there in 678 or 679,[113] and it is also at
Chelles that she probably died about 680.[114]

The *Vita Balthildis* is about as contemporary a Merovingian source as
has survived. The author claims to have been contemporary with the
events he describes[115] and there is little reason to doubt him. The only
terminus post quem we have for the composition of the *vita* is the date
of the death of the saint herself. The *terminus ante quem* can be set at

109 *[Balthildis] ... conferens sepe cum matre monasterii, ut et regem et reginam et proceres
    cum digno honore cum eulogias semper visitarent, ut erat consuetudo, ut ipsa domus Dei
    bonam famam, quam coeperat, non amitteret, sed amplius semper in affectu caritatis cum
    omnibus amicis atque validius in Dei nomine permaneret in dilectione, ut scriptum est:
    Oportet et testimonium habere bonum ab his qui foris sunt ... Vita Balthildis*, ch. 12,
    MGH, SSRM, II, p. 498.

110 The usually accepted date for Clothar III's death is between 10 March and 15 May
    673 (see Krusch, *MGH, SSRM*, VII, pp. 495–6), although the *LHF*, ch. 45, calls
    him *puer* at his death and says he ruled for only 4 years. For Clothar's burial at
    Chelles, see Krüger, *Königsgrabkirchen*, p. 243; and Laporte, *Le Trésor*, pp. 173–6,
    for the local tradition.

111 *LHF*, ch. 45, see above, p. 90.

112 *Vita Balthildis*, ch. 17, below, p. 131.

113 Laporte, *Le Trésor*, pp. 53–4.

114 Krusch in his introduction to the edition of her *vita* dated her death from the
    account in chapter 14, which says she was received into heaven by Genesius. *MGH,
    SSRM*, II, p. 476. He assumed Balthild died shortly after Genesius and listed his
    death as 1 November 679. B. Krusch, 'Zur Chronologie der merowingischen
    Könige', *Forschungen zur deutschen Geschichte*, 22 (1882), 485.

115 *... nostris peracta sunt temporibus eius multa bona, et que optime novivus ab ipsa gesta
    fuisse.' Vita Balthildis*, ch. 19, *MGH, SSRM*, II, p. 507.

690 if we assume that the author meant Balthild's children and not later descendants when he says in chapter 3 that her *progeniem* is still ruling. 690 is the usually accepted date for the death of her last surviving son, Theuderic III.[116] If, however, it is correct to assume that the author omitted any direct mention of Ebroin's complicity in Sigobrand's murder or in Balthild's retirement because the powerful mayor was still alive and in power when he wrote,[117] then the *terminus ante quem* for the *vita*'s composition would fall even earlier, in the early 680s, before Ebroin died. It would seem most natural to seek the author of a life of St Balthild among the nuns at her own monastery at Chelles.[118] The first line of the preface, however, expressly dedicates the work to the author's *dilectissimi fratres* and thus he was probably male. There is no other indication in the work of the sex of the author one way or the other. The author is pious, careful, and far more concerned with Balthild's saintliness, humility, and acts of generosity than he is with any miraculous powers. In fact, although the *vita* contains a vision[119] and a general assurance that wonders did happen at her grave,[120] it describes only one explicit miracle.[121] Balthild performed none while she was alive.

At the end of the eighth century, or the beginning of the ninth, this first version (A) of the *Vita Balthildis* was reworked into a new one (B).[122] The B version enriched the life with many Scriptural quotations and a heightened sense of the marvellous, but weakened its historical value. The chief value of the B version for our purposes is to compare it with A in order to underscore certain characteristics of the earlier work. Even though the spelling and vocabulary did not change very

---

116 Krusch, *MGH, SSRM*, VII, pp. 449–50.

117 L. Dupraz, *Contribution à l'histoire du Regnum Francorum pendant le troisième quart du VIIe siècle* (Fribourg-en-Suisse, 1948), p. 361, and Foltz, 'Tradition hagiographique', 364.

118 Thus Nelson, 'Queens', 46, n. 83; and W. Berschin, *Biographie und Epochenstil im lateinischen Mittelalter*, vol. 2: *Merowingische Biographie. Italien, Spanien und die Inseln im frühen Mittelalter, Quellen und Untersuchungen zur lateinischen Philologie des Mittelalters*, 9 (Stuttgart, 1988), p. 22.

119 *Vita Balthildis*, ch. 13, below, p. 128.

120 *Vita Balthildis*, ch. 16, below, p. 130.

121 *Vita Balthildis*, ch. 17, below, p. 131.

122 Krusch edited this later life as text B alongside the A version in double columns. Since B does not mention Balthild's translation on 17 March 833, we can assume it was written before that date. See G. Sanders, 'Le remaniement carolingien de la *Vita Balthildis* mérovingienne', *Analecta Bollandiana*, 100 (1982), 414.

much between the two versions, B is written in a heavier and more florid Latin. By the time the B author was writing, Balthild was the centre of a large cult, and the members of the supporting monastic establishment would have been well able to understand the dense style, if for no reason other than that they would have grown familiar with it through the cult's liturgy.[123] By comparison, the style of the earler version is simple and direct, as is typical of late Merovingian Latin.[124] The earlier version was probably directed at an audience wider than Balthild's devotees in the monastic life. Version B also wishes to be taken as having been written by a contemporary. In fact its author adds indications of his supposed status as a contemporary in places where A does not have them.[125] This is a powerful reminder that we should be wary of believing any hagiographical source's claim to be contemporary unless we see reasons beyond the simple claim. By the time the author of B wrote, he either did not understand or did not believe the political content of version A. He omitted any mention of Balthild's detractors from his prologue; in chapter 10 he changed the gender of the Latin words *quos* and *ipsos* from masculine to feminine and thereby turned A's report of a political conflict into a conflict among nuns within the monastery;[126] and in the same chapter he added a legal element so that those who had killed Sigobrand and forced Balthild to retire feared legal retribution, and Bathild's displeasure with them was for having broken the law. Thus author B erased the political factionalism in A's report.

If it is correct to assume that the author of A was not a nun at Chelles, and if the simplicity of the language indicates that his intended audience was not limited to members of Balthild's cult, for whom then did the author write? We suspect he tells us in his preface:

> But, though less skilful in learning, we wish to be the more eager to lay open for the edification of the many, who, like the wise bees, seek sweet nectar from the flowers: that is, the increase of truth from straightforward words, because truth edifies the hearer more than it puffs him up, so that it may openly show the store of her piety to those wishing to imitate it. Here, therefore, we show the truth which we can, not so much to her detractors, but rather to her faithful.

123 Sanders, 'La remaniement', 419.

124 See above, pp. 73–8.

125 Version B has Genesius appear to those standing at Balthild's deathbed (ch. 14). Version A says he knows (*novisimus*) her deeds, whereas B says he knows and has seen them (*novisimus et vidimus*, ch. 19). See Sanders, 'Le remaniement', 418–19.

126 Sanders, 'Le remaniement', 419.

In his last chapter he also says: 'Truly she reigns in glory with Christ in heaven in everlasting joy, not unmindful, we believe, of her own faithful friends.' Let us note two things.

First, the author's purpose in writing is to teach. The whole tone of the *vita* is didactic. Although there is a miraculous element, it is subdued. The work is not trying to attract worshippers to a miraculous cult centre or to enhance the value of a cult's relics. In simple language, and with much repetition, the author teaches that to imitate Balthild's virtuous way of life will lead to eternal salvation, and thus her memory should be preserved. In chapter 15 he makes it quite clear that there was an early effort to spread her commemoration:

> Then the Lady Abbess Bertila, taking care because of the eagerness of her piety, requested the holy priests that her holy memory might be preserved constantly throughout many churches in holy offerings [of the mass]. And throughout many places her worthy [memory] is still steadfastly celebrated.

Second, he knows there will be detractors who will not be anxious to commemorate her. His words sound very factional. Once again, the gender of 'detractors', 'faithful', and 'her own faithful friends' is masculine; he is talking not of nuns but of the wider world of politics. In fact we are not solely dependent upon him to know that she indeed had detractors: this queen so saintly here is called a Jezebel in chapter 6 of the *Vita Wilfridi* and for very political reasons.[127] By the time the *vita* was written, however, the allegiances which formed the factions in its chapter 10 described above may have shifted significantly, especially since, as we have seen, the Pippinids had most likely by then entered Neustrian court politics, upsetting many traditional loyalties.

A seventh-century hagiographical work whose author is concerned about 'friends' and 'detractors' of a saintly queen is a strong reminder of the period's intricate relationship between political power and Christian sanctity. In chapters 18 and 19 the author compares Balthild to the other Merovingian queens renowned for their Christian virtue. Loudly he proclaims Balthild their equal. It is significant that the three he lists were all foreign-born and that two are known to have been of royal ancestry.[128] Balthild, the former slave, amid such splendid company

---

127 *Vita Wilfridi*, ch. 6. See Nelson, 'Queens', 64–5; and below, pp. 172–3

128 Clothild, wife of Clovis I, was a Burgundian princess, Radegund, wife of Clothar I, was a Thuringian princess, and Ultrogoda, wife of Childebert I, was of unknown origin. See Ewig, 'Studien', 39–40.

is truly a Merovingian queen. He says that she gained the status because of her Christian piety[129] and that she used it both to preserve the political peace[130] and to benefit the many establishments of the Church.[131] This is a new element in Merovingian hagiography. The queens from earlier periods in Merovingian history performed their saintly acts after they had retired from their royal status, but Balthild used her royal position to perform her virtuous works.[132] As we have seen, her hagiographer tells us little about her years in retirement. In the saintly Queen Balthild we find, as we shall find again and again in the sources in this volume, that critical merger of power and sanctity which was such an important factor in attracting the support of those who mattered in the late Merovingian political structure.

Vita Domnae Balthildis
(The Life of Lady Balthild, Queen of the Franks)

CHAPTER 1

HERE BEGINS THE PROLOGUE TO THE LIFE OF THE LADY, QUEEN BALTHILD[133]

Indeed, most beloved brothers, I was commanded to accomplish this so fine and pious task, with Christ as my guide, even if my inexperience denies me the power of offering an arrangement of delicate narrative and learned words. But the strong influence of your most bountiful love commands us that the truth should be laid open and that it should not be puffed up with boastfulness. We know that the Lord Jesus Christ sought fruit rather than leaves in the fig tree.[134] Therefore, for the edification and profit of many, we have resolved to expose upon a candlestick and not to hide the fruit of truth. But, though less skilful in learning, we wish to be the more eager to lay open for the edification of the many, who, like the wise bees, seek sweet nectar from the

129 *Vita Balthildis*, ch. 3, below, p. 121.

130 *Vita Balthildis*, ch. 5, below, p. 122.

131 *Vita Balthildis*, ch. 7, below, pp. 123–4; ch. 8, below, pp. 124–5; and ch. 9, below, pp. 125–6.

132 Foltz, 'Tradition hagiographique', 369–70.

133 The proper title for the work is *Vita domnae Balthildis*, taken from this incipit, not *Vitae Sanctae Balthildis*, as Krusch has it in the *MGH* edition. The *vita* first calls Balthild *sancta* after her death. See Berschin, *Biographie und Epochenstil*, p. 22.

134 Matthew 21:18 and 19; Mark 11:12 and 14.

flowers: that is, the increase of truth from straightforward words, because truth edifies the hearer more than it puffs him up, so that it may openly show the store of her piety to those wishing to imitate it. Here, therefore, we show the truth which we can, not so much to her detractors, but rather to her faithful.

HERE ENDS THE PROLOGUE

CHAPTER 2

HERE BEGINS THE LIFE OF BLESSED QUEEN BALTHILD

Blessed be the Lord, *who wishes all men to be saved and to come to the recognition of truth*,[135] and *who causes them to will and to complete all in all*.[136] And therefore His praise must be deservedly sung first in the merits and miracles[137] of the saints, He *who makes great men out of those of low station, indeed, He who raises the poor man out of the dunghill and makes him to sit with the princes of His people*,[138] just as He has raised the present great and venerable woman, Lady Balthild, the queen. Divine providence called her from lands across the sea[139] and this precious and best pearl of God arrived here, having been sold at a low price. She was acquired by the late Erchinoald,[140] the leader[141] of the Franks and a man of illustrious standing,[142] in whose service she dwelt as an adolescent most honourably so that her admirable and pious religious way of life pleased both the leader and all his servants. She was indeed kind in her heart, *temperate and prudent*[143] in her whole character, and provident. She contrived evil against no one. She was neither frivolous in her fine expression nor presumptuous in speaking, but most honourable in all her acts. And although she was from the race of the Saxons,[144] the form

135 I Timothy 2:4.

136 This seems to be a combination of Philippians 2:13 and I Corinthians 12:6. See also Ephesians 1:23.

137 *virtutibus.*

138 I Kings 2:8; Psalms 112:7-8.

139 England. See above, p. 97.

140 Neustrian mayor from 641 to about 659. See above, pp. 99–104.

141 *princeps.* See above, pp. 68–9.

142 *vir inluster.* See above, p. 70.

143 I Timothy. 3:11.

144 *Et cum esset ex genere Saxonum....* This *cum* concessive clause can also be translated, 'And since she was from the race of the Saxons ...', a translation which would give the author insular inclinations.

of her body was pleasing, very slender, and beautiful to see. Her expression was cheerful and her gait dignified. And, since she was thus, *she was exceedingly pleasing to the prince*[145] *and she found favour in his eyes.*[146] He engaged her to serve him the goblets in his chamber, and as a most honourable cupbearer she stood quite often present in his service. Nonetheless, from the favour of her position she derived no haughtiness but, based in humility, was loving and obedient to all her equals. With fitting honour she so served her seniors that she removed the shoes from their feet and washed and dried them. She fetched water for washing and promptly prepared their clothes. And she performed this service for them without muttering and with a good and pious heart.

CHAPTER 3

And from her noble way of life, greatest praise and love among her companions accrued to her, and she earned such a favourable reputation that, when the wife of the above-mentioned prince Erchinoald died, he decided to join the most honourable virgin, Balthild, to himself in the matrimonial bed. And, having learned this thing, she secretly and earnestly withdrew herself from his sight. And when she was called to the bedchamber of the prince, she hid herself in an out-of-the way corner and threw cheap rags over herself so that no one would have thought anyone to be hiding there. Indeed, she was then still a shrewd[147] and prudent virgin fleeing empty high positions and seeking humility. She tried, as she was able, to avoid human marriage so that she might deserve to come to her spiritual and heavenly groom. But indeed, beyond doubt, it was accomplished by divine providence that the prince did not find her, whom he sought, and then joined another matron to himself in marriage.[148] And then the girl Balthild was finally found so that, by the true will of God who had shunned the nuptials

---

145 *princeps.*

146 Ester 7:3, 2:4 and 9, and 5:8. Ester was also a royal spouse of low origins. Van Uytfanghe sees Balthild's career in this *vita* presented as a conscious parallel to Ester's. M. Van Uytfanghe, *Stylisation biblique et condition humaine dans l'hagiographie mérovingienne (600-750), Verhandelingen van de Koninklijke Academie voor Wetenschappen, Letteren, en Schone Kunsten van België*, Klasse der Letteren 49, no. 120 (Brussels, 1987), pp. 209-10.

147 *astuta.* Berschin, *Biographie und Epochenstil*, p. 21, sees this attribute as a new virtue in the Merovingian hagiography. He translates it as *listig* or *gewitzt.*

148 Leutsinda. See *Virtutes Fursei*, chs. 20 and 21, and above, p. 101.

of the prince, she would later have Clovis,[149] son of the late King Dagobert,[150] in marriage so that He could thus raise her to a higher station through the merit of her humility. And in this station divine dispensation decided to honour her so that, seeing that she had refused a follower of the king, she might obtain union with the king and, from her, royal progeny might come forth.[151] And this has now come to pass, as it is obvious to everyone that the royal offspring reigning now is hers.[152]

CHAPTER 4

But as she had the grace of prudence conferred upon her by God,[153] with watchful eagerness she obeyed the king as her lord, and to the princes she showed herself a mother, to the priests as a daughter, and to the young and the adolescents as the best possible nurse.[154] And she was friendly to all, loving the priests as fathers, the monks as brothers, the poor as a faithful nurse does, and giving to each generous alms. She preserved the honour of the princes and kept their fitting counsel, always exhorting the young to religious studies and humbly and steadfastly petitioning the king for the churches and the poor. While still in secular dress, she desired to serve Christ; she prayed daily, tearfully commending herself to Christ, the heavenly king. And the pious king [Clovis],[155] taking care of her faith and devotion, gave his faithful servant, Abbot Genesius, to her as support, and through his hands she served the priests and the poor, fed the hungry, clothed the naked with garments, and conscientiously arranged the burial of the dead. Through him she sent most generous alms of gold and[156] silver

---

149 Clovis II, king of Neustria (638-57).

150 Dagobert I, king of Austrasia (623-33) and Neustria (629-38).

151 Cf. *LHF*, ch. 44: *Nam ex Balthilde ... 3 filios ... Chlotharium, Childericum, atque Theudericum. MGH, SSRM*, II, pp. 316-17. That is, Clothar III, king of Neustria (657-73); Childeric II, king of Austrasia (657-75) and Neustria (673-75); and Theuderic III, king of Neustria (673 and 675-90).

152 Version B at this point claims that she herself was of royal offspring: ... *quae erat ex regali progeniae ... MGH, SSRM*, II, p. 485.

153 ... *conlatam sibi a Deo prudentiae gratiam ...* Accusative absolute.

154 ... *ut mater ... ut filia ... optima nutrix se ostendebat.* Use of a reflexive verb as a kind of medial voice.

155 This is not the view the author of the *LHF* has of her husband, Clovis. See above, p. 89.

156 *vel* as simple copulative.

to the monasteries of men and women. And this servant of Christ, Lord Genesius, was later ordained bishop of Lyons at Christ's command. He was at that time regularly in the court of the Neustrians.[157] And through him, as we said, the lady Balthild, along with the authority of King Clovis and at the petition of this servant of God [Genesius], provided the generous alms of the king to all the poor throughout many places.

CHAPTER 5

What more is there to say? At God's command, her husband, King Clovis, went forth from his body, leaving a lineage of sons with their mother. In his place after him, his son, the late King Clothar,[158] took the throne of the Franks and then also with the excellent princes, Chrodbert, bishop of Paris, Lord Audoin,[159] and Ebroin, mayor of the palace, along with the other great magnates[160] and very many of the rest.[161] And, indeed, the kingdom of the Franks was maintained in peace. Then indeed, a little while ago, the Austrasians peacefully received her son Childeric[162] as king in Austrasia by the arrangement of Lady Balthild and, indeed, through the advice of the great magnates.[163] But the Burgundians and the Neustrians[164] were united.[165] And we believe that, with God guiding, and in accordance with the great faith of Lady Balthild, these[166] three kingdoms kept the harmony of peace among themselves.

157 *francorum.* This author uses the word *franci* to mean the Neustrians, as do the authors of the *LHF* and the *Vita Audoini.*

158 Clothar III, king of Neustria, 657–73.

159 Whose life is translated below, pp. 152–65.

160 *senioribus.*

161 Note how the author shows the broad base of the king's aristocratic support. This is the explanation for the peace in the realm.

162 Childeric II, king of Austrasia 657–75 and of Neustria 673–75.

163 ... *per consilium quidem seniorum* ...

164 *franci.*

165 *facti sunt uniti.* Probably 'were united in peace', referring to the fighting between the Frankish and Burgundian factions in Burgundy recorded by Fredegar, *Chron.* IV, ch. 90. See the strikingly parallel passage in the *Vita Audoini,* ch. 14, below, p. 162: '... the kingdoms were united in a peace for the peoples (*regna pace unita populis*). And so the unified peace between both countries lasted quite a little while.'

166 *ipsa* for *ea.*

CHAPTER 6

At that time it happened that the heresy of simony stained the Church
of God with its depraved practice in which they received the rank of
bishop by paying a price for it. By the will of God [acting] through
her, and at the urging of the good priests, the above-mentioned Lady
Balthild stopped this impious evil so that no one would set a price on
the taking of holy orders. Through her, the Lord also arranged for
another very evil and impious practice to cease, one in which many
men were more eager to kill their offspring than to provide for them
in order to avoid the royal exactions which were inflicted upon them by
custom, and from which they incurred a very heavy loss of property.
This the lady prohibited for her own salvation so that no one presumed
to do it. Because of this deed, truly a great reward awaits her.

CHAPTER 7

Who, then, is able to say how many and how great were the sources
of income, the entire farms and the large forests she gave up by
donating them to the establishments of religious men in order to
construct cells or monasteries? And she also built as God's own and
private houses a huge nunnery for women consecrated by God at
Chelles,[167] near Paris where she placed the religious handmaiden of
God, the girl Bertila, in the position of the first mother. And in this
place the venerable Lady Balthild in turn decided to dwell under the
pure rule of religion and to rest in peace. And in truth she fulfilled this
with a devoted will.

Nor must we pass over what pertains to the praise of God, whatever
God marvellously performs in his saints and elect, because as Scripture
says, *God is miraculous in His saints*,[168] and His spirit, the Paraclete,
works within through goodwill, as it is written: *God is the helper of each
willing good*.[169] And it is known that it was truly thus with this great
woman. As we said above, neither our tongue nor that of anyone, no
matter how erudite, I do think, is able to relate all her good deeds.
How many means of comfort and support did she give to the houses

167 According to ch. 18 below, it was Queen Clothild, wife of Clovis I (d. 511), who first
   built a church to St George at Chelles. It was version B's expansion of the report
   in ch. 18 which led to the idea that Clothild had founded Chelles. Cf. Laporte,
   Trésor, p. 1.

168 Psalms 67 (68):36.

169 Romans 8:28.

of God or to His poor for the love of Christ? And of what quality was the monastery called Corbie which she constructed at her own expense[170] in the parish of Amiens? And here the venerable man,[171] Lord Theudofred,[172] who is now a bishop but who was then abbot, had charge of a large flock of brothers which the above-mentioned Lady Balthild sought from Luxeuil, from the late most reverend Lord Abbot Waldebert,[173] and which she wonderfully directed to this monastery of brothers, and this is still known and praised.

CHAPTER 8

Indeed, what else? To the religious man, Lord Filibert,[174] at Jumièges, in order to build that monastery, she conceded both a large forest from the fisc where this monastery of brothers is located, and many gifts and pastures from the royal fisc.[175] Indeed, how many things, both a large villa and many talents of silver and gold, [did she concede] to Lord Laigobert for the monastery at Cobion?[176] Even her own royal belt, with which she was girded, she devotedly took from her holy loins and gave to the brothers in alms. All this she gave with a kind and joyous heart, for as Scripture says, *God loves the cheerful giver.*[177] Likewise, to both Saint-Wandrille[178] and Logium[179] she conceded much property. Indeed,

---

170 *suo opere.* See above, p. 69.

171 *venerabilis vir*, i.e. monk.

172 It is not known of what city he was bishop. See Krusch, *MGH, SSRM*, II, p. 491, n. 1.

173 Waldebert was made abbot in 629 and died in 670. See Krusch, *MGH, SSRM*, II, p. 491, n. 2.

174 See *Vita Filiberti*, ch. 6, ed. W. Levison, *MGH, SRM*, V, pp. 587-8, where both Clovis and Balthild are mentioned as providing Filibert with the land for founding the monastery at Jumièges. Filibert was another nobleman in Audoin's circle. He grew up at the court of Dagobert I and then took on his ecclesiastical career. In addition to Jumièges, he also founded Pavilly, Noirmoutier (*Vita Filiberti*, ch. 26) and Montivilliers (*ibid.*, ch. 31). He was not always in Audoin's and Ebroin's good graces and for a period he suffered an exile spent with Bishop Ansoald of Poitiers. See Prinz, *Frühes Mönchtum*, pp. 131-2, and below, p. 143.

175 The fisc was the great body of land the Merovingian kings inherited from their Roman predecessors or took by right of royal conquest. One of the reasons given for the weakening of the dynasty was the diminution of the fisc through concessions such as the one mentioned here to the point where the royal house lost its economic base.

176 Saint-Moutiers-au-Perbe (Orne).

177 II Corinthians 9:7.

178 Today, Saint-Wandrille-Rançon. Krusch, *MGH, SSRM*, II, p. 492, n. 2.

how many things, both many large entire villas and innumerable sums of
money, did she give to Luxeuil and to the other monasteries in Burgundy?
What [did she give] to the monastery at Jouarre, whence she summoned
the holy virgins with the above-mentioned Lady Bertila to her own
monastery at Chelles? How many gifts of fields and how much money
did she concede to that place? Likewise, she often gave large gifts to
the monastery of Faremoutier.[180] Near the city of Paris she conferred
many large villas to the basilicas of the saints and to the monasteries,
and she enriched them with many gifts. What more is there? As we
said, we are not able to relate every one, not even with difficulty the
half of them, and certainly all her good acts cannot be told by us.

CHAPTER 9

We certainly must not pass over [the fact] that throughout the senior basilicas[181] of Lord Denis,[182] Lord Germanus,[183] Lord Medard,[184] St Peter,[185]
Lord Anian,[186] and St Martin[187] or wherever her precept reached, she ordered the bishops and abbots, by persuading them for the zeal of Christ,
and sent them letters to this effect, that the monks dwelling in these
places ought to live under a holy regular order.[188] And in order that
they would freely acquiesce in this, she ordered a privilege to be confirmed[189] for them and she also conceded them immunities[190] so that she
might better entice them to exhort the clemency of Christ, the highest
king, for the king and for peace. And this must be called to mind, because it pertains to the increase of her reward, that she forbade Christian men to become captives, and she issued precepts[191] throughout

179 Logium was a monastery for women in that part of Neustria which is now
    Normandy. Krusch, *MGH, SSRM*, II, p. 492, n. 3.
180 Seine-et-Marne, near Nogent-sur-Seine.
181 These were the great holy places of the realm. See above, p. 110.
182 Paris.
183 Paris.
184 Soissons.
185 Sens.
186 Orleans.
187 Tours.
188 *sub sancto regulari ordine*, i.e. a monastic rule. See above, p. 110.
189 *fimare*. Active for passive.
190 These are the episcopal privilege and the royal immunity. See above, p. 109.
191 *datasque praeceptiones*. Accusative absolute.

each region [ordering] that absolutely no one ought to transfer a captive Christian in the kingdom of the Neustrians. And in addition she
paid the price and ordered many captives to be bought back and she released them as free. Others of them, especially from her own race,[192] men
and also many girls, she sent into the monasteries as her own charges.
However many she was able to attract, these she entrusted to the holy
monasteries, and she ordered them to pray for her. She even often sent
many generous gifts to Rome, to the basilicas of blessed Peter and Paul
and to the Roman poor.

CHAPTER 10

It was, however, her holy vow that she ought to dwell[193] in the
monastery of religious women which we mentioned above, that is, at
Chelles, which she herself built. But the Neustrians, for love of her,
delayed in this especially, nor would they have permitted it to come
about had not an insurrection arisen because of the wretched Bishop
Sigobrand,[194] whose haughtiness among the Franks earned him mortal
ruin.[195] And from this a dispute arose because they killed him against
her will. Fearing that the lady would hold it gravely against them and
wish to vindicate his cause, they straightway permitted her to go into
the monastery. And there is no probable doubt that it was not with a
good heart that these princes then permitted this. But the lady
considered it God's will that it was not so much their decision as a
dispensation of God that her holy desire had been fulfilled, through
whatever means, with Christ as her guide. And, having been escorted
by certain noblemen, she came to her above-mentioned monastery at
Chelles, and there, as is fitting, she was honourably and very lovingly
received into the holy congregation by the holy maidens. Then,
however, she had a complaint of no mean size against those whom she
had kindly nurtured,[196] because they had erroneously considered her

192 I.e. the Anglo-Saxons.

193 *conversare*. Active for passive form.

194 Bishop of Paris. See above, p. 110.

195 This is a very common reason for deserving death. The nobility does not tolerate
one of its own rising above his station.

196 *enutriverat*. Note the very political use of this verb in the *Annales Mettenses Priores*,
below, p. 351; and in Gregory of Tours: *comitibus, domesitciis, majoribus, atque
nutriciis vel omnibus qui ad exercendum servitium regale erant necessarii. Gregorii
Episcopi Turonensis Historiarum Libri X*, Bk. X, ch. 36, eds. B. Krusch and W.
Levison, *MGH, SSRM*, I, ed. alt. (Hanover, 1951), p. 391.

suspect and even repaid her with evil for her good deeds. But, discussing this quickly with the priests, she kindly forgave them everything and asked them to forgive her this disturbance of her heart. And thus, with the Lord as provider, peace was fully restored among them.

CHAPTER 11

Indeed, with a most pious affection she loved her sisters as her own daughters, she obeyed their holy[197] abbess as her mother, and rendered service to them as the lowest of handmaidens out of holy desire, just as [she had done] when she still ruled the royal palace and often visited her holy monastery. So strongly did she exhibit the example of great humility that she even served her sisters in the kitchen, and the lowest acts of cleaning, even the latrines, she herself did. All this she undertook with joy and a cheerful heart, in such humble service for Christ. For who would believe that the height of such power would serve in such lowly things if her most abundant and great love of Christ had not demanded it of her in every way? She remained incessantly in faithful prayer with tears and she very often attended divine reading; indeed, she occasioned constant consolation through her holy prayer and her frequent visitation of the infirm. For she grieved with the grieving through the eagerness of her love, she rejoiced with the joyful, and for the slaves[198] she very often humbly beseeched the lady abbess that they might be consoled. And she [the abbess], as her mother, lovingly granted all things to her petition because there was truly for them, in the manner of the Apostles, *one heart and one soul*[199] because[200] they loved each other tenderly and most fully in Christ.[201]

CHAPTER 12

The Lady Balthild began to weaken in body, and she suffered gravely from colic of the intestines, a most evil affliction of an illness, and, had the learning of doctors not come to her aid, indeed she would have died. But more than that, concerning her salvation, she always kept

197 *sanctae.*
198 We read *servis* for *sanis,* as Krusch suggests, *MGH, SSRM,* II, p. 497, n. i.
199 Acts 4:32.
200 *dum* meaning 'because'.
201 'in Christ' is Pauline language for 'spiritually'.

her trust in the heavenly healer. Indeed, in holy and pious conscience she did not cease to give thanks to God concerning her chastisement, to offer good and astute advice always, and to demonstrate the beauty of piety to her sisters, as an example of great humility from her servile activity. She often suggested to the mother of the monastery that they should constantly visit the king and queen and the palace nobles in befitting honour with gifts,[202] as was the custom, so that that house of God would not lose the good reputation with which it had begun, but would always remain more fully in the affection of love with all its friends and more strongly in the name of God in love, as it is written: *It is necessary to have a good report of them who are without,*[203] and for the love of Christ did the mother of the monastery, with a joyous and fleet spirit, fulfil all the holy teaching of salvation she had heard, especially to take care always of the poor and strangers with the greatest eagerness on account of mercy and love for them. But neither did she in turn in any way cease to fulfil these things for the increase of their common reward.

CHAPTER 13

But as her glorious death was nearing a famous vision was shown to her. It was as if a stairway was raised up, standing before the altar of St Mary, with its top reaching heaven, and with the angels of God accompanying her,[204] the[205] Lady Balthild ascended it. From this revelation it was clearly to be understood[206] that her lofty merits, patience and humility would quickly lead her as one to be exalted to the height of the Eternal King and to the crown of her reward. And when this vision had been revealed, the lady knew that she was about to go forth very soon from the body and to arrive there where she had already stored up the best treasure. But she admonished this to be kept silent from her sisters so that until her departure the vision would not be disclosed to the sisters or to the mother of the monastery on account of the sadness of grief. But rather, with a faithful and cheerful heart,

202 *eulogiae*, gifts presented in token of friendship or honour. See *Passio Praejecti*, ch. 18, below, p. 285.

203 I Timothy 3:7. An example of using Scripture to justify a saint's actions. See Van Uytfanghe, *Stylisation biblique*, p. 39.

204 ... *angelos Dei commitantes* ... Accusative absolute.

205 *ipsa* used as a kind of definite article.

206 *daretur intellegi*. See above, p. 70.

she admonished herself to press on more and more in holy prayer and to commend herself more intently with humble contrition of heart to her heavenly King, the Lord Jesus Christ. And with this hidden, she constantly urged and[207] comforted the Lady Bertila and the sisters, saying she was improving[208] a little from her infirmity, and she disguised the coming grief of her parting, which later and with great suddenness touched them.

CHAPTER 14

But when the lady sensed that her end was near, her holy heart was raised up toward heaven. And being informed of her great reward, of blessed repayment, she strongly prohibited those staying with her from notifying the other sisters or the lady abbess, who herself was gravely ill, lest she should also be endangered on account of the magnitude of her grief. There was at that time a certain child, her goddaughter, whom she wished to go with her, and she [the child] suddenly went out from her body and preceded her to the grave.[209] Then, making the sign of the cross in faith, and with her faithful eyes and holy hands raised toward heaven,[210] her holy soul was loosed from the chain of her body in peace. And suddenly a splendour from on high glistened most brightly in the little room. And without doubt this holy soul was gloriously received by a chorus of angels, and her very faithful friend, the late Lord Bishop Genesius, came out to meet her, as her great reward demanded.

CHAPTER 15

For a little while, those sisters ,with the sigh of grief as their companion, kept this hidden under silence, just as she had ordered, so that it was reported only to the priests who were to commend her most blessed soul to the Lord. And when the abbess and the whole congregation

---

207 *vel* as simple copulative.

208 *eo quod ... convalesceret ...* Imperfect subjunctive instead of the classical accusative-infinitive.

209 According to lectio 9 of the *Translatio S. Baltechildis*, ed. O. Holder-Egger, *MGH, SS*, XV, pt. 1 (Hanover, 1887), p. 285, a source written some time shortly after 856, the girl was seven years old and named Radegund. See Krusch, *MGH, SSRM*, II, p. 500, n. 1.

210 *... et pios oculos ac sanctis manibus ad caelum erectis ...* Accusative and ablative confused.

later learned of the matter, with great weeping they demanded how [it had happened] so suddenly and unexpectedly, as the hour of her depature was not known to them. It was as if this gem which everybody wanted had been snatched from them. All were stunned and likewise lay prostrate there on the ground. There was a great profusion of tears; weeping with an immense groan of grief, giving thanks to the faithful Lord, and praising Him together, they commended her holy soul to Christ, the faithful king, that He might guide it to St Mary in the chorus and company of the saints. Then, as was fitting for her, they buried her with great honour and much reverence. Then the Lady Abbess Bertila, taking care because of the eagerness of her piety, requested the holy priests that her holy memory should be preserved constantly throughout many churches in holy sacrifices. And throughout many places deservedly her [memory] is still steadfastly celebrated.

CHAPTER 16

To those following after her she left a holy example of humility and patience, an eagerness for gentleness and for the fullest love, a vigilance of boundless mercy and wise judgement, a confession of purity, and [the precept] that all was to be done by taking counsel[211] and nothing in any way without permission, but rather that every-thing should be made a matter of temperance and reason. She left a most holy example, this rule of piety, to her contemporaries, and on account of these holy virtues,[212] and greatly for her many holy merits, she received the crown of great reward already laid aside for her by the Lord. And now, among the angels in the presence of the Lord and her Groom with the white-clad flock of virgins, she enjoys what she had longed for: an immense and everlasting joy. Now, in order to make her sublime merit clear to the faithful, divine piety has accomplished many wonderful things at her holy sepulchre so that whoever comes there with faith, wasting with a fever, troubled by a demon, or weakened with pain of the teeth, goes forth from there healthy and whole with whatever vexation or illness having been straightway cast off through divine strength and through her holy intercession, as recently clearly happened with a certain boy.

---

211 ... *cuncta per consilium* ... *esset faciendum* ... See the discussion of *consilium* above, pp. 80–1.
212 *Viritutibus.* Here it does mean virtues, not miracles.

CHAPTER 17

There came[213] from the region of the Provence a certain venerable
man, Bishop Leudegandus, a friend and supporter of the monastery at
Chelles. A most savage demon had so possessed his boy[214] that he was
not able to be controlled by his associates unless they bound his hands
and feet because he would tear to pieces with exceeding ferocity those
whom he was able to touch. And when he had been borne by the hands
of friends to the place of the holy tomb, and had been thrown almost
half alive onto the pavement, the most savage demon, terrified by
divine fear, became stiff and silent, and, having been put to flight on
the spot, went out from him. The boy immediately raised himself up
and making the sign of the cross and, giving thanks to God, returned
to his people whole and sane.

CHAPTER 18

Indeed, we recall that other queens in the kingdom of the Franks have
been noble and worshippers of God: Clothild, queen of the late King
Clovis of old[215] and niece of King Gundobad,[216] who, by her holy
exhortations, led both her very brave and pagan husband and many of
the Frankish nobles to Christianity and brought them to the Catholic
faith. She also was the first to construct the churches in honour of St
Peter at Paris[217] and St George in the little monastery for virgins at
Chelles, and she founded many others in honour of the saints in order
to store up her reward, and she enriched them with many gifts. The
same is said of Ultrogoda, queen of the most Christian King
Childebert,[218] because she was a comforter of the poor and a helper of
the servants of God and of monks. And [it is said] also of Queen
Radegund, truly a most faithful handmaiden of God, queen of the late
elder King Clothar,[219] whom the grace of the Holy Spirit had so
inflamed that she left her husband while he was still alive and

213 *veniens.* Participle for finite verb.
214 *Puer.* A servant or bodyguard.
215 Clovis I (481-511).
216 King of the Burgundians.
217 See Gregory, *Hist.,* IV, 1, *MGH, SSRM,* I, ed. alt., p. 135; and *LHF,* ch. 17, *MGH,
    SSRM,* II, p. 267, and ch.19, *ibid.,* p. 273.
218 Childebert I (511-58).
219 Clothar I (511-61).

consecrated herself to the Lord Christ under the holy veil, and, with Christ as her spouse, accomplished many good things. These things are read in her Acts.[220]

CHAPTER 19

But it is pleasing, nevertheless, to consider this about her whom it here concerns: the Lady Balthild. Her many good deeds were accomplished in our times, and that these things were done by her herself we have learned in the best manner. Concerning these things, we have here commemorated a few out of the many, and we do not think her[221] to be the inferior in merits of those earlier [queens]; rather we know her to have outdone them in holy striving. After the many good things which she did before her evangelical perfection, she gave herself over to voluntary holy obedience and as a true nun she happily completed her blessed life under complete religious practice. Her holy death and her holy rites are celebrated on 30 January, and, having been interred, she rests in peace in her monastery at Chelles. Truly she reigns in glory with Christ in heaven in everlasting joy, not unmindful, we believe, of her own faithful friends.

And we, if not as we ought, then certainly as we were able, have taken care to fulfil your command out of eagerness for love. We beseech you to grant forgiveness for our awkwardness, and, out of love, to pray to the faithful Lord for the faults of our negligence.

The peace of the Lord be with you, to whom is glory for ever and ever Amen.

HERE ENDS THE LIFE OF SAINT BALTHILD, QUEEN

220 I.e. the *Vita Sanctae Radegundis* by Venantius Fortunatus.
221 *ea.* Confusion of accusative and ablative.

III: *Vita Audoini Episcopi Rotomagensis* (The Life of Audoin, Bishop of Rouen)

Audoin, powerful nobleman, bishop of Rouen, and saint, was the most influential and the most famous of the Frankish nobility in the mid seventh century. We know quite a bit about him and we owe a good deal of our gratitude for this knowledge to the author of his *vita*. The author, however, remains almost completely obscured from us. We assume he was a monk. We certainly do not know his name. From his own report that he knew Audoin's immediate disciples[1] we suspect that he was removed by about a generation from the events of Audoin's life. We can detect little else about him. He uses the word *Franci* to mean the Neustrians,[2] as do the authors of the *LHF* and of the *Vita Balthildis*, something which makes it very likely that he too was of Neustrian stock. We know nothing else.

Wilhelm Levison, Bruno Krusch's co-worker and successor as editor of the Merovingian narrative sources for the *Monumenta Germaniae Historica* and editor of the *Vita Audoini*, had a low opinon of its author. Levison lodged two major complaints against him: that he used a barbarous Latin style riddled with grammatical error, and that he cast his work using only few events and placing them in confusing order.[3] The style of this work, however, seems no less nor more barbarous than other Frankish works of the late seventh century, and, as we have seen, more recent philological thought has taught us to be more sympathetic in our assessment of Merovingian Latin.[4] A school older and less correct than Levison saw the hand of more than one author in the *Vita Audoini* as we now have it.[5] Although there are divisions in the work, none indicates the introduction of a new author. The prologue

---

1 … *quod a discipulis eius testes idoneos narrantes agnovi* … *Vita Audoini Episcopi Rotomagensis*, ch. 15, ed. W. Levison, *MGH, SSRM*, V (Hanover, 1910), p. 544.

2 … *inter gentem Francorum et Austrasiorum. Vita Audoini*, ch. 13, *MGH, SSRM*, V, p. 543.

3 *MGH, SSRM*, V, pp. 543–4. For an examination of this type of criticism of hagiographical sources, see above, chapter 2, pp. 36–7.

4 Above, p. 000.

5 E. Vacandard, *Vie de Saint Ouen, évêque de Rouen* (641–684) (Paris, 1902), p. xii.

is in a style obviously different from that used in the other chapters. But, as is often the case, the prologue is simply the author's purple patch in which he modestly professes his inability to undertake the literary task without God's help and does so ironically in a most laboured and florid Latin. Although Levison was disappointed with the author's style, certain medieval hagiographers certainly found his prologue rather to their liking and made heavy use of it.[6]

Important as the *Vita Audoini* is, we do not possess many manuscripts of it because a second and more extensive version of his life became more popular in the Carolingian age, and the older Merovingian work found few copyists.[7] The earliest manuscript we have postdates the work's composition by about a hundred years and it is only a fragment.[8] It was written at the turn of the eighth and ninth centuries and has preserved only as much as is contained in the first eighteen printed lines of the prologue in Levison's edition. To know the work, we are primarily dependent upon two late ninth-century manuscripts,[9] and neither gives us any further clue to the author's identity or the early distribution of his text.

Levison's other complaint, that the author included so few of the events of Audoin's life and then arranged them poorly, is understandable, coming from as it does an enquiring historian. We sense his frustration as he accuses the author of being in a position to know so much and yet of saying so little.[10] But the author did say a great deal about that aspect of Audoin which was important to him and to his age, that is, about Audoin's sanctity. In fact the events of Audoin's 'Life' upon which the author lavished the most attention were his death,[11] his burial[12] and the translation of his body.[13] The author's primary concern in writing the *vita* was to display the divine power (*virtus*) manifest in Audoin's acts of holy self-denial and especially evident in his deeds of wonder (*miracula*). It is now sometimes thought useful to catagorise

6 See Levison, *MGH, SSRM*, V, p. 544, for a list.

7 *Vita altera S. Dadonis vel Audoeni episcopi*, ed. J. Pinius, *AASS*, Aug, IV (Antwerp, 1739), pp. 810–19. Levison, in the notes to his edition of the first *vita*, also edited the portions of the second one which vary significantly from it.

8 Codex Montepessulanus H 55, saec. viii–ix.

9 Ms. Vienna n. 420 (Salib. 39), saec. ix–x; and ms. Sankt Gall, n. 563, saec. ix–x.

10 *MGH, SSRM*, V, p. 543.

11 *Vita Audoini*, ch. 15, below, p. 163.

12 *Vita Audoini*, chs. 16 and 17, below, pp. 163–4.

13 *Vita Audoini*, chs. 18 and 19, below, pp. 164–5.

miracles according to whether they display divine power in a tran-
scendental way or whether they express it thaumaturgically, that is, by
aiding the human condition of this world. Late Merovingian hagiography (post-650) tends to emphasise miracles which heal and eliminate
the maladies of this life,[14] and the *Vita Audoini* follows the pattern. The
author relates five miracles which happened during the saint's lifetime:
two are of the other-worldly type[15] and three are thaumaturgical.[16] Then,
as is usual in Merovingian hagiography, the author recounts many
miracles which the saint effected after death, and all these are of the
thaumaturgical variety.[17] The emphasis on miracles carries an obvious,
but nonetheless important, reminder for the historian: 'Miracles are
the whole point of the *vitae* ...'[18] We should not separate the wonder from
the man if we are to understand Audoin in context. Much as our own
age may wish to understand him by finding social, political or
economic reasons for his important position, we dare not demystify the
man himself. His own age saw him first as a holy man, and it was his
wondrous manifestations of power from the next world as well as his
birth and ability in this one which gave him his pre-eminence. We can
see this clearly in a report by the Burgundian chronicler, Fredegar, who
was not a hagiographer and was far more interested in things mundane:

> ... the Breton king, Judicael, went at once to Clichy with a quantity of gifts
> to ask pardon of King Dagobert ... However, he declined to eat or sit down
> at table with Dagobert, for he was religious and full of the fear of God.
> When Dagobert did sit down to table, Judicael left the palace and went to
> dine at the residence of the referendary, Dado, whom he knew to lead a
> religious life.[19]

The incident takes place about the year 636, when King Dagobert I

14 J.-L. Derouet, 'Les possibilités d'interpretation sémiologique des textes hagiographiques', *Revue d'Histoire de l'Église de France*, 62 (1976), 154–5.
15 They are his ability to converse with the saints departed and the holy light which
emanated from his head. *Vita Audoini*, ch. 8, below, p. 158.
16 They are: his prayers ending the drought in Spain, *Vita Audoini*, ch. 7, below, p. 158;
his healing of the miller's hand in Angers, *Vita Audoini*, ch. 9, below, pp. 159–60; and
his curing the mute in Cologne, *Vita Audoini*, ch. 13, below, p. 162.
17 *Vita Audoini*, chs. 17 and 19, below, pp. 164 and 165.
18 J. McNamara, 'A Legacy of Miracles: Hagiography and Nunneries in Merovingian
Gaul', in J. Kirshner and S. Wemple (eds.), *Women of the Medieval World. Essays in
Honour of John H. Mundy* (Oxford, 1985), p. 38.
19 *The Chronicle of Fredegar*, IV (hereafter Fredegar, *Chron.*), ch. 78, ed. and trans. J. M.
Wallace-Hadrill, *The fourth Book of the Chronicle of Fredegar, with its continuations*
(London, 1960), p. 66.

(623–38) was at the height of his power. Yet here Fredegar gives us this curious report of the client king of Brittany, Judicael, who, when he came cowering to Dagobert bearing gifts and promising whatever Dagobert demanded, nonetheless refused to dine with his great Frankish overlord. Instead he sought out the royal referendary, Dado, 'whom he knew to lead a religious life'. This Dado is none other than St Audoin,[20] and here, in a non-hagiographical source, written in the 640s when Audoin was still in the secular stage of his career,[21] we find him already known for his sanctity. This early and independent report of such holiness is unique among Merovingian sources. Audoin's obviously wide reputation for personal sanctity may explain why in the eyes of the author of his *vita* he was able to perform miracles while still alive, something which is also unusual, since most Merovingian saints effect the miraculous only after death.

We do not depend entirely on the *Vita Audoini* in order to get to know Audoin; we find him in many Frankish sources, some trustworthy, some not so. He appears in several royal and episcopal charters.[22] He signed the canons issued at the council of Chalon.[23] In addition to the above affirmation of his holiness by the rather secular Fredegar, we shall find him again mentioned by Fredegar's first continuator, who wrote some time after 736.[24] He exchanged letters with Bishop Desiderius of Cahors, some of which we still have.[25] As we have seen, the author of the *Liber Historiae Francorum* had a high regard for him.[26] But, as we might expect, Audoin plays an especially important role in the hagiographical literature. We find information about him and his family in Jonas of Bobbio's *Vita Columbani*, which was also written well

20 *Venerabilis ergo Audoinus cognomento Dado.... Vita Audoini*, ch. 1, *MGH, SSRM,* V, pp. 554–5.

21 See Wallace-Hadrill, *Fredegar*, pp. xiv–xxv, and W. Goffart, 'The Fredegar Problem Reconsidered', *Speculum*, 38 (1963), 207–9, for differing views about who Fredegar was and when he wrote.

22 *MGH, Dipl.* I, no.15, p. 17; J. M. Pardessus (ed.), *Diplomata, chartae, epistolae, leges aliaque instrumenta ad res Gallo-Francias spectantia*, vol. 2 (Paris, 1849), nos. 275, p. 19, and 254, p. 13.

23 'Concilium Cabilonense, a 647–653', ch. 15, ed. C. de Clercq, *Concilia Galliae* 511–695. *Corpus Christianorum, Series Latina*, 148A (Turnhout, 1963), p. 306.

24 *The Continuation of the Chronicle of Fredegar* (hereafter, Fredegar, *Cont.*), ch. 4, ed. Wallace-Hadrill, p. 84.

25 Desiderius of Cahors, *Epistulae Sancti Desiderii*, ed. D. Norberg (Uppsala, 1961), nos. I, 11, pp. 30–1, and II, 4, pp. 48–50. He also sent greetings in a letter from Eligius, bishop of Noyon, *ibid.*, no. II, 6, pp. 52–3.

26 See above, p. 92.

before Audoin died, some time between 639 and 643.[27] This is probably the earliest narrative source to survive which mentions him. For four decades he held the important see of Rouen as its bishop, and it is in the *vitae* emanating from the monastic centres in this area that he is treated with especial respect. Few of these sources, however, were written before the ninth century and consequently they must be treated with caution. Their authors were far removed from the events of Audoin's life and were greatly influenced by his reputation, which, as was so often the case, gained lustre in the years after his death.[28] Nonetheless, with careful use they can help to fill out the account of the man given to us in his oldest *vita*, the one we shall treat here, an account one noted scholar has rightly called extremely laconic.[29]

Audoin was born during the reign of Clothar II (584–629), near Soissons.[30] Soon the family moved to its villa, Vulciacum, modern Ussy on the Marne, near Meaux, where the members had extensive landed possessions.[31] The earliest source giving us the names of his relatives is the

27 Jonas of Bobbio, *Vita Columbani Abbatis Discipulorumque eius Libri Duo auctore Iona*, I, ch. 26, ed. B. Krusch, *MGH, SSRM*, IV (Hanover, 1902), p. 100. For date of composition, see Wattenbach-Levison, *Deutschlands Geschichtsquellen im Mittelalter. vol I, Vorzeit und Karolinger*, Pt. 1, *Die Vorzeit von den Anfängen bis zur Herrschaft der Karolinger* (Weimar, 1952), pp. 133–4, and I. N. Wood, 'The *Vita Columbani* and Merovingian Hagiography', *Peritia*, 1 (1982), 63.

28 This literature includes: *Vita Geremari Abbatis Flaviacensis*, ed. B. Krusch, *MGH, SSRM*, IV (ninth-century); the *Vita Amandi Episcopi I*, ed. B. Krusch, *MGH, SSRM*, V (mid eighth-century); *Vita Sancti Agili Abbatis*, ed. J. Stiltingus, *AASS*, Aug., VI (Antwerp, 1743) (ninth-century); *Vita Lantberti Abbatis Fontanellensis et Episcopi Lugdunensis*, ed. W. Levison, *MGH, SSRM*, V (c. 800); *Vita Filiberti Abbatis Gemeticensis et Heriensis*, ed. W. Levison, *MGH, SSRM*, V (late eighth-century); *Vita Sancti Waningi Confessoris*, ed. J. Mabillon, *ASSOB*, saec. III (Paris, 1669) (survives only in fragments dating from the Norman period); *Vita Sanctae Austrebertae Virginis et Abbatissae Pauliacensis in Caletis*, ed. J. Mabillon, *ASSOB*, saec. III–1 (Paris, 1672). See Wattenbach-Levison, *Geschichtsquellen*, pp. 138–9, and P. Fouracre, 'The Work of Audoenus of Rouen and Eligius of Noyen in Extending Episcopal Influence from the Town to the Country in Seventh-century Neustria', *Studies in Church History*, 16 (1979), 84.

29 L. Musset, 'De saint Victrice à saint Ouen: la christianisation de la province de Rouen d'après l'hagiographie', *Revue d'Histoire de l'Eglise de France*, 62 (1976), 141.

30 *Vita Audoini*, ch. 1, below, p. 153. A second life of Audoin, a redaction of the first written under Louis the Pious, purports to have more precise information. It tells us that Audoin was born in about the twentieth year of Clothar's reign (603/04) at Sancy. See Levison, *MGH, SSRM*, V, pp. 548–51 and 554, n. 1; and Vacandard, *Saint Ouen*, p. 349.

31 The *Vita Columbani I*, ch. 26, contains a report of Columbanus visiting the family at Ussy in 610 or 611. For a discussion of the chronological imprecision in Jonas, see F. Prinz, *Frühes Mönchtum im Frankenreich* (Munich and Vienna, 1965), p. 122, n. 2. See. also A. Friese, *Studien zur Herrschaftsgeschichte des fränkischen Adels der*

Vita Columbani by Jonas of Bobbio. According to Jonas, Columbanus set out from Meaux to Paris and en route came to Ussy, where he enjoyed the hospitality of the nobleman Autharius and his wife Aiga. Jonas talks of their two sons, Ado and Dado; a third son, Rado, is known to us from Audoin's *Vita* and from other contemporary evidence, although Jonas does not mention him.[32] All three brothers were to have brilliant careers. Ado held a high position at the court of Dagobert I but then left the royal service and founded the monastery of Jouarre in the Brie.[33] Audoin's younger brother, Rado, is a much more difficult figure to identify. The *Vita Audoini* tells us that Rado was made custodian of the royal treasury but neither gives us a date nor specifies under which king.[34] We know he assumed the position when his friend, Desiderius , relinquished it to become bishop of Cahors in 630. This would make the king Dagobert I.[35] The name Rado appears in various places in other sources, but which, if any, of these Rados is Audoin's brother is a matter of speculation. In 613, for instance, the year of Clothar II's conquest of Burgundy and Austrasia, we find a man named Rado in the very high position of Austrasian mayor of the palace,[36] but that Rado could hardly have been Audoin's younger brother, since in 613 he could have been at most nine years old. The Neustrian kings Clovis II (638–57) and

---

mainländisch-thuringische Raum vom 7. bis 11. Jahrhundert. Geschichte und Gessellschaft. Bochumer Historische Studien, 18 (Stuttgart, 1979), pp. 17–18. For treatments of this important family and its landed possessions near Soissons and Meaux, see: A. Bergengruen, *Adel und Grundherrschaft im Merowingerreich, Vierteljahrschrift für Sozial- und Wirtschaftsgeschichte*, Beihefte, 41 (Wiesbaden, 1958), pp. 66–80, and E. Zöllner, 'Die Herkunft der Agilulfinger', *MIÖG*, 59 (1951), 254.

32 *Vita Columbani I*, ch. 26; *MGH, Dipl.*, I, no. 16, p. 18; and *Vita Audoini*, ch. 1, below, pp. 153–4. The relationship between Columbanus and Audoin's family is treated by R. Sprandel, *Der merovingische Adel und die Gebiete östlich des Rheins, Forschungen zur oberrheinischen Landesgeschichte*, 5 (Freiburg, 1957), pp. 14–16.

33 *Vita Columbani I*, ch. 26. The *Vita Balthildis*, ch. 8, above, p. 125, calls Jouarre a nunnery. This leads to the supposition that it was a double monastery from a very early date. See Wattenbach-Levison, *Geschichtsquellen*, p. 138; Prinz, *Frühes Mönchtum*, p. 125; and Friese, *Studien*, pp. 20–1.

34 *Vita Audoini*, ch. 1, below, p. 154.

35 Rusticus, Desiderius' predecessor as bishop of Cahors, was killed ... *finiente anno VII regni Dagoberti et incipiente octavo* ... *Vita Desiderii Cadurcae Urbis Episcopi*, ch. 8, ed. B. Krusch, *MGH, SSRM*, IV, p. 568.

36 Fredegar, *Chron.*, IV, ch. 42. His name appears as late as 616 in the position. Pardessus, *Diplomata*, vol. I, no. 230, p. 211. In 617/18, however, a certain Chucus is mentioned together with the mayors of Burgundy and Neustria in a way that makes it probable that he and not Rado was then the Austrasian mayor. Fredegar, *Chron.*, IV, ch. 45.

Clothar III (657–73) had referendaries by the same name.[37] The *Vita Sancti Agili* claims that a Rado founded an important monastery on the Marne and named it Radilium (modern Rueil) after himself, something which historians are reluctant to believe.[38]

Working backwards from the charters of land donations, Alexander Bergengruen was able to show that either Audoin's mother or his father was related to Chagneric, another important nobleman from the area near Meaux and companion of Theuderic II (595–612).[39] Audoin's family was also connected with Bugundofaro, Chagnerich's son.[40] In view of all this information about his landed possessions and the careers of his brothers and other relatives, it is clear that Audoin stemmed from a wealthy and noble Frankish lineage; his family was part of that group of Frankish aristocracy, based in the upper Seine and Oise valleys, which surrounded the Neustrian king and held the most influential positions in the land.

Perhaps through the religious influence of Columbanus, or perhaps for reasons which escape us, Audoin was given a literary education, something which was becoming increasingly rare even among the high-ranking Merovingian nobility in the course of the seventh century.[41] In addition to his family's important position and his own obvious religious devotion, it could well have been his ability to read and write which caught the attention first of King Clothar II and then of his son, Dagobert I.[42] As a young man Audoin found himself at Clothar's court among other young noblemen destined for high civil and ecclesiastical office. Years later, Bishop Desiderius of Cahors recalled their salad

37 *ChLA*, no. 558; *MGH, Dipl.,* I, no. 33, p. 32; and *Gesta Sanctorum Patrum Fontanellensis Coenobii,* I–7, eds. F. Lohier and J. Laporte (Paris and Rouen, 1936) (hereafter, *Gesta Font.*) p. 12; See Levison, *MGH, SSRM,* V, p. 537, and H. Bresslau, *Handbuch der Urkundenlehre für Deutschland und Italien,* vol I, third edition (Berlin, 1958), p. 359.

38 *Vita Sancti Agili,* ch. 14. See Sprandel, *Merov. Adel,* p. 16; Levison, *MGH, SSRM,* V, p. 554, n. 8; and Prinz, *Frühes Mönchtum,* p. 125.

39 Bergengruen, *Adel und Grundherrschaft,* p. 77.

40 See *Vita Columbani, I,* ch. 26, and *II,* ch. 7, *MGH, SSRM,* IV, p. 120, where Burgundofaro's sister, Burgundofara, is called Chagneric's daughter.

41 *Vita Columbani I,* ch. 26; *Vita Audoini,* ch. 1, below, p. 154. For the state of education among the Frankish nobility see P. Riché, *Education et culture dans l'Occident barbare, VIe–VIIIe siècles* (Paris,1962), pp. 475–6.

42 *Vita Columbani I,* ch. 26: ... *qui* [*Dado and Rado*] *Clotharii regis primum ac deinceps Dagoberti gratissimi habiti.*

days together at court with great affection.[43] Under Clothar's son, Dagobert I, we find that Audoin, or Dado as he was still called, had become a royal referendary. Since Audoin was at the Neustrian court and held the position under Dagobert, we must assume that he became referendary some time after Clothar II's death in 628, when Dagobert came to rule Neustria as well as Austrasia. It is also from about this date that other evidence survives, although not as much as was once thought,[44] to confirm the *Vita Audoini's* report that he held the king's signet ring, that is, that he was made referendary.[45] Merovingian kings had more than one referendary simultaneously in their royal service, and it seems that one of Dado's colleagues was Burgundofaro, a friend and relative from his own home district and later bishop of Meaux.[46] The office of referendary was much like that of the later chancellor; its holder outranked the seneschals and other household officials, but was in turn outranked by the higher palace officials, the *duces, comites, patricii,* and of course by the mayor of the palace.[47] A referendary seems to have had about the same rank as a *domesticus,* a Merovingian official in charge of royal fiscal property. Many referendaries were rewarded with a bishopric as their careers advanced.[48] The refendaries often functioned as royal judges,[49] one is known to have commanded troops,[50] and they may also have controlled the tax rolls.[51] But their

---

43 Desiderius of Cahors, *Epistulae,* no. I, 11, pp. 30–1.

44 In Pertz's and Pardessus's editions of a royal charter from 632–33 Dado is listed as the referendary. Atsma and Vezin, however, state in comments to their edition that they can find no trace of the name of the referendary. Pertz, *MGH, Dipl.,* I, no. 14, p. 16. Pardessus, *Diplomata,* vol. 2, no. 279; P. Lauer and C. Samaran (eds.), *Les Diplômes originaux des Mérovingiens* (Paris, 1908), no. 3, pp.10–16. Atsma and Vezin, *ChLA,* no. 551.

45 *MGH, Dipl.,* I, no. 15, pp. 16–18, where Dado appears among the signatories and is named in the text of the charter as *referendarius noster;* ibid., no. 16, p. 18; *ChLA* no. 555 does not mention Dado but later copies of the charter do = *MGH, Dipl.,* I, no. 17, pp. 18–19; Fredegar, *Chron.,* IV, ch. 78; *Gesta Dagoberti I. Regis Francorum,* chs. 38 and 42, ed. B. Krusch, *MGH, SSRM,* II (Hanover, 1888), pp. 416 and 420.

46 *ChLA,* no. 554. See Prinz, *Frühes Mönchtum,* pp. 125–6, and Bresslau, *Handbuch,* p. 259.

47 *ChLA,* no. 576, a *placitum* of Clovis III from 692 or 693, where the referendaries are listed after the bishops, *optimates,* counts, and *domesticii,* but before the seneschals.

48 Just as the referendary Dado-Audoin became bishop of Rouen, so too Baudinus was enthroned at Tours, Flavius at Chalon-sur-Saône, Licerius at Arles, Charimeres at Verdun, and Bonitus at Clermont-Ferrand. See Bresslau, *Handbuch,* p. 360.

49 Marculf, *Marculfi Formularum Libri Duo,* I, ch. 25, ed. A. Uddholm (Uppsala, 1962), p. 103, and *ChLA* no. 562.

50 Fredegar, *Chron.,* IV, ch. 78.

most important function was exercised in the production of royal charters. As keepers of the signet ring they sealed the documents, and, although they seem not to have written them themselves, most likely they were the officials who proposed the outline of their contents.[52] If Audoin was at all typical as a referendary, he would have exercised great responsibility indeed.

Court life under the Merovingians is often painted in less than pleasing moral hues by the hagiographical authors in order to highlight the sanctity of their heroes who functioned in it. Life at court, however, does not seem necessarily to have been the devil's den on earth. We remember the nostalgia Bishop Desiderius expressed without vituperation for his days as a courtier under Clothar II.[53] Training, both military and literary, was given to the young noblemen at court, often under the direction of the mayor of the palace or perhaps the queen.[54] The attraction of the Merovingian court was in fact great enough to induce Ethelberga, the widow of Edwin, king of Northumbria, to send two of her children to be trained at the court of Dagobert.[55] The author of the *Vita Audoini*, although apparently critical of Dagobert himself, nonetheless does not rail at Audoin's life at his court, but seems to see it as a normal step towards the more important service of God as bishop.

In 635 Dado, along with his two brothers, founded the famous monastery of Rebais in the Brie. Although his act may have greatly forwarded the religious life of northern Gaul, it also created a seemingly impenetrable snarl-up for historians as they try to untangle and interpret the various accounts of the event. The founding of Rebais carries a weight for us far greater than just the establishment of another important monastery in the Irish monastic tradition on the

---

51 Gregory of Tours, *Gregorii Episcopi Turonensis Historiarum Libri X* (hereafter, Gregory, *Hist.*) V, chs. 28 and 34, ed. B. Krusch, *MGH, SSRM*, I, ed. alt. (Hanover, 1951), pp. 234 and 240.

52 Bresslau, *Handbuch*, pp. 361–2. Much of what we know about this important Merovingian office comes from Bresslau's work, especially in his reading of the Tironian notes in the documents. He provides a comprehensive list of Merovingian referendaries on p. 20.

53 Desiderius of Cahors, *Epistulae*, no. I, 11, ed. Norberg, pp. 30–1.

54 ... *quos ipsa [Balthildis] dulciter enutriverat.... Vita Sanctae Balthildis*, ch. 10, ed. B. Krusch, *MGH, SSRM*, II (Hanover, 1888), p. 496.

55 Bede, *Historia Ecclesiastica Gentis Anglorum*, II, ch. 20, ed. C. Plummer, *Venerabilis Baedae Opera Historica*, vol. I (Oxford,1896), p. 126. See P. Riché, 'Les representations du palais dans les textes littéraires du haut Moyen-âge', in his *Instruction et vie religieuse dans le Haut Moyen-âge* (London, 1981), pp. 161–2. Reprinted from *Francia*, 4 (1976).

continent. It has been termed a template for later monastic foundations,[56] and its legal position in relation to the Crown and to Audoin's
family is seen as a key to our understanding of the role of monasteries
in Merovingian politics (*Klosterpolitik*) and as affording an insight into
the relationship between king and nobleman. Although the original
document has not survived, we have a copy of Dagobert I's foundation
charter from the year 635, which reports all three brothers taking part
in the foundation of the monastery on royal land. Dagobert not only
provided the land but also partially endowed the institution.[57] This fact
has been seen to raise the important question of whether or not Rebais
may have been a royal monastery. Indeed, the episcopal privilege for
another monastery, the abbey at Saint-Colombe in Sens, from 660 lists
Rebais among the *regalia monasteria*.[58] On the other hand, other sources
lead us to suspect that Rebais was firmly under the control of Audoin's
family and that his family and not the king was able to treat the monastery
as private property. The *Vita Columbani* and the *Vita Filiberti* say the
founder was Audoin.[59] The *Vita Sancti Agili* names Rado as the founder,
although this information is not taken seriously.[60] The *Vita Filiberti*
says that Audoin established (*instituerat*) Agilus as Rebais's first abbot.[61]
Agilus was a member of that same group of Frankish aristocracy from
near Meaux and indeed was related to Audoin's family itself.[62] The
next abbot was Filibert, another of Audoin's protégés.[63] The question

---

56 *Musterkloster.* Prinz, *Frühes Mönchtum,* p. 125. See also Friese, *Studien,* p. 21, and
especially E. Ewig, 'Das Formular von Rebais und die Bishofsprivilegien der
Merowingerzeit', in *Aus Reichsgeschichte und nordischer Geschichte. Festschrift für Karl
Jordan, Kieler Historische Studien,* 16 (1972), 11–42. Reprinted in E. Ewig, *Spätantikes
und fränkisches Gallien. Gesammelte Schriften (1952–1973),* vol. 2, Beihefte der *Francia,*
3/2 (Munich, 1979), pp. 456–84; and his 'Beobachtungen zu den Bischofsprivilegien
für Saint-Maur-des-Fossés und Sainte-Colombe de Sens', *Geschichtliche Landeskunde,*
5/2 (1969), 1–24. Reprint *Gallien,* vol. 2, pp. 485–506.

57 *... super fiscum nostrum ... constructum atque ex parte ditatum. MGH, Dipl.,* I, no. 15, p. 17.

58 Pardessus, *Diplomata,* vol. 2, no. 333, p. 110. M. Werner, *Der Lütticher Raum in
frühkarolingischer Zeit, Veröffentlichungen des Max-Planck-Instituts für Geschichte,* 62
(Göttingen, 1980), p. 362, thinks the context of this charter does not indicate that
Rebais was a royal monastery.

59 *Vita Columbani* I, ch. 26; *Vita Filiberti,* ch. 2, p. 585.

60 *Vita Sancti Agili,* ch. 14. See Prinz, *Frühes Mönchtum,* p. 125.

61 *Vita Filiberti,* ch. 2; Pardessus, *Diplomata,* vol. 2, no. 275, pp. 39 ff.

62 Agilus was the son of Chagnoald and nephew of Chagneric of Meaux, whom we know
to have been Audoin's relatives. See above, p. 139, n. 39, and Zöllner, 'Herkunft', 254.

63 *Vita Filiberti,* ch. 4. For a defence of Audoin's position as '*Klosterherr*' of Rebais, see
J. Semmler, 'Episcopi potestas und karolingische Klosterpolitik', *Vorträge und
Forschungen,* 20 (1974), 388, n. 54.

of who, king or nobleman, controlled the monastery at Rebais is extremely important for those who assume that there was a basic antagonism between the Crown and the aristocracy. As we have seen, however, the age's politics were fuelled not by such antagonism but rather by co-operation.[64] Mathias Werner has perceptively concluded that Rebais, much like Solignac, is evidence that the king would give property to a leading figure of his circle to enable him to found a proprietary monastery and name its abbots. Although not royal foundations as such, these institutions remained in a close relationship with the king.[65] This manner of founding important monasteries is a further indication that the Merovingian kings ruled through, and not in opposition to, the great families of the realm. And one of the greatest of those families was Audoin's own.

Audoin was elected to the episcopal see of Rouen on the same day as his friend Eligius (French, Eloi) was elected bishop of Noyon.[66] Because neither of the friends had served the canonically required year in orders,[67] they were not ordained bishops until 13 May 641.[68] The *Vita Audoini*, chapter 7, contains two significant words at this point: it declares that Audoin was made bishop *iusso regali* (by royal command). The unnamed king would have been the boy Clovis II, aged eight.[69] Audoin's appointment was thus obviously made by the great nobles of the court, but their necessary agency was the king. As Audoin, the royal courtier and representative of a leading Frankish noble family, assumes the cathedral in a major see, we have landed once again at that juncture of power and sanctity which seems to characterise much of the politics of the age. A powerful element, perhaps the catalytic one, in this combination derived from what may seem at first glance a surprising source: Ireland.

---

64 See above, pp. 80–1.

65 Werner, *Lütticher Raum*, p. 362.

66 *Vita Eligii Episcopi Noviomagensis*, II, ch. 2, ed. B. Krusch, *MGH, SSRM*, IV (Hanover, 1902), p. 695.

67 'Conc. Arelatense, a 524', ch. 2, ed. C. de Clercq, *Concilia Galliae*,.p. 44; 'Conc. Aurelianense, a 538', ch. 6, *Concilia Galliae*, p.116; and 'Conc. Aurelianense, a 539', ch. 9, *Concilia Galliae*, p. 151. See Bresslau, *Handbuch*, vol. I, p. 264.

68 The *Vita Eligii*, II, ch. 2, says that two were ordained on the fourteenth day of the third month in the third year of young King Clovis's reign, that is, on 13 May 641. Both this source and the *Vita Audoini*, ch. 7, below, p. 158, declare that their elections preceded their ordinations by about a year.

69 Born 633. E. Ewig, 'Studien zur merowingischen Dynastie', *Frühmittelalterliche Studien*, 8 (1974), 13.

The spread of monasticism in northern Gaul and into those areas of
Germany the Franks would convert and rule was due in no small part
to Irish monks. Although, under the Merovingians, we do not find
abbots in the company of kings as we shall in the court circles of the
Carolingians,[70] nonetheless Merovingian monasteries were frequent
recipients of royal largesse both in land and in privileges. From the
days of Clovis I himself Merovingian kings had been very interested
in monasteries,[71] yet the advent of an Irish monastic missionary,
Columbanus, introduced a new element. A great deal of ink has been
expended in valuable description of early medieval Irish monasticism
on the continent,[72] but suffice it here to point out that this brand of
Christian monasticism, as indeed Irish Christianity in general, had on
the Continent a new and powerful attractive force. As is evident from
contemporary reactions, clerks and laity alike were enraptured by the
religious fervour of the Irish. Their asceticism horrified the ecclesiastical establishment, but their perpetual fasting, immersion in icy water,
and exhilarating way of praying with arms extended entranced the
people. It was their asceticism which made the Irish so popular. If it
came to a choice between a comfortable, traditional, Frankish cleric
and a wild ascetic 'mad for God', the choice fell upon the madman.[73]

There were, in fact, different groups of Irish who influenced the Frankish
establishment, but the one which most directly touched Audoin and his
circle was based on Columbanus' own foundation of Luxeuil in Burgundy.
Luxeuil was not a centre of learning as Lérins and many other foundations in the southern Gallic monastic tradition had been, but a home of a

---

70 F. Felten, *Äbte und Laienäbte im Frankenreich, Monographien zur Geschichte des
Mittelalters*, 20 (Stuttgart, 1980), pp. 129–35.

71 Fredegar, *Chron*, III, ch. 24, ed. B. Krusch, *MGH, SSRM*, II, pp. 102–3, and
Gregory, *Hist.*, II, ch. 37, *MGH, SSRM*, I, ed. alt., p. 88. See J. M. Wallace-Hadrill,
The Frankish Church (Oxford, 1983), pp. 55–62.

72 The most exhaustive study of the religious and political influence of Irish
monasticism on the Continent is Prinz's *Frühes Mönchtum*. See especially pp. 124–30.
A good English-language summary of the movement can be found in P. Riché,
'Centers of Culture in Frankish Gaul between the 6th and the 9th Centuries', in his
Instruction et vie religieuse dans le Haut Moyen-âge (London, 1981), pp. 230–2.
Reprinted from S. L. Thrupp (ed.), *Early Medieval Society* (New York, 1967), pp.
230–2. Basic too are the collections in both H. B. Clarke and M. Brennan (eds.),
Columbanus and Merovingian Monasticism. British Archeological Reports, International
Series, 113 (Oxford, 1981), and in H. Löwe (ed.), *Die Iren und Europa im frühen
Mittelalter*, vol. 2 (Stuttgart, 1982).

73 F. Prinz, 'Columbanus, the Frankish Nobility, and the Territories East of the
Rhine', in Clarke and Brennan (eds.), *Columbanus*, p. 67. See below, pp. 313–19, for
qualifications of Prinz's views.

fierce ascetic and spiritual life. It was the Bible which was studied here; other learned Christian works found little place. Luxeuil's daughter houses, Remiremont, Grandval, Rebais and Faremoutiers, became explosive exponents of the same tradition and from these centres the missionaries set out for the christianisation of northern Gaul. Columbanan monks became the bishops of Tournai, Vermand and Therouanne. In the second quarter of the century the 'Irishness' of the movement became tempered significantly by an admixture of the more sedate Benedictinism, and this new monasticism, especially under Luxeuil's abbot, Waldebert (629–70), became closely bound to the Merovingian royal court. Beginning with the very noblemen we have seen along with Audoin gathered around Clothar II and Dagobert I, its influence now spread not only across the northern sections of the Frankish realm but into the southern parts as well. The major proponents were royal officials who led a religious life at court and then went on to become bishops.[74] Even before receiving the mitre these highly placed noblemen often founded important monasteries in the Irish tradition.

The religious attractiveness of their type of Christianity is relatively easy to understand, but the political value of these figures may not be so readily apparent. The religious life of Merovingian Gaul had been relatively stable. Except for certain enclaves, it had long been christianised and had a well established ecclesiastical structure. By the mid seventh century the threat to it once posed by Arianism was now only a historical memory, and its political power, unlike that in its contemporary English kingdoms across the Channel, did not pass back and forth between Christian and pagan rulers. In this atmosphere of ecclesiatical stability, why did political leaders such as Erchinoald, Balthild and Ebroin seek out and foster these foreign enthusiasts, often at the expense of their own traditional churchmen?

A look at the episcopal privileges for the seventh-century Frankish monasteries will reveal one political advantage for the nobility in having Irish monasteries in their camp.[75] These privileges were often modelled on Bishop Burgundofaro's famous one for Rebais from 637,[76]

---

74 The list of these men is impressive: Audoin (Rouen), Ansbert (Rouen), Eligius (Noyon), Burgundofaro (Meaux), Chrodbert (Paris or Tours), Reolus (Rheims), Nivard (Rheims), Sulpicius (Bourges), Paulus (Verdun), Rusticus (Cahors) and Desiderius (Cahors). See Wattenbach-Levison, *Geschichtsquellen*, p. 126, and Prinz, *Frühes Mönchtum*, p. 124.

75 See above, p. 109, n. 85.

76 Pardessus, *Diplomata*, vol. 2, no. 275.

and the recipients were mostly monasteries connected with the Columbanan movement at Luxeuil. What is of interest to us is not the legal validity of these documents, but what they reveal about the attitudes of their recipients towards local episcopal authority. It seems the foreign missionaries brought attitudes with them from Ireland which reflected the way the Church was organised at home. In other words, as in Ireland, these Continental Irish monasteries expected to act as autonomous religious centres. Such a view seemed extreme to the Frankish Church, long organised on the episcopal model, in which the bishops were used to exerting strong local control over everything in their dioceses, including the monasteries. In the Frankish political system of family and faction a strong independent religious centre would be a juicy plum indeed for one side or the other. Such a monastery could, of course, work with the local bishop, but it could also work against him, depending on the factional allegiances involved.

Contemporary papal privileges for monasteries indicate the same yearning on the part of the Irish for independence from the diocesan bishop. From the time of Pope Gregory I (590–604) onwards we have records of papal privileges confirming the landed possessions and the right to free abbatial elections of various monasteries. It is significant, however, that the first such privilege we know of to specifically exempt a monastery from local episcopal authority was granted by Pope Honorius I in 628 to the Columbanan foundation at Bobbio.[77] There also survives a group of forged papal monastic privileges attributed to Pope John IV (640–42). These claim to have been granted by the Pope in response to petitions from King Clovis II, and once again the recipients were mostly monasteries connected with the Columbanan movement at Luxeuil.[78]

The economic structure of Irish monasticism shows another political advantage. The Irish monasteries were rural and seem to have been run

---

77 Ed. C. Cipolla, *Codice diplomatico del monasterio de S. Colombano di Bobbio, I Fonti per la storia d'Italia*, 52 (Rome, 1918), no. 10, pp. 100–3 as noted in H. Anton, *Studien zu den Klosterprivilegien der Päpste im frühen Mittelalter, Beiträge zur Geschichte und Quellenkunde des Mittelalters*, 4 (Berlin, 1975), p. 55, n. 49. See W. Levison, 'Die Iren und die Fränkische Kirche', in his *Aus Rheinischer und Fränkischer Frühzeit, Ausgewählte Aufsätze* (Dussseldorf, 1948), p. 256.

78 Editions: Pardessus, *Diplomata*, vol. 2, nos. 298, pp. 65–7, for Saint-Colombe; no. 299, pp. 67–9, for Luxeuil; no. 301, pp. 71–4, for Saint-Croix; no. 302, pp. 74–6, for Rebais; nos 303 and 304, pp. 76–80, for Remiremont; and one for an unknown S. Maria in Gaul, ed. K. Zeumer, *MGH, Formulae Merowingici et Karolini aevi*, 1886, pp. 498–500. See Anton, *Studien*, p. 59, n. 57. Wood sees these forgeries as possible evidence for the development of a royal monastic policy. Wood, 'Vita Columbani', 79.

on a sort of manorial system.[79] Whatever their system of agricultural exploitation was, they were expert in it. Columbanus found sixty monks working in a field at Fonataine, near Luxeuil.[80] Such mass labour may indicate large-scale rural production. Judging from the facts that Irish and Irish-inspired houses accumulated land quickly and that they built and endowed serveral churches on their sites, it seems they tended to be rich. Such an efficient and prosperous economic institution will not have escaped the notice of the politically ambitious.

The Irish monastic ideal was not only alluringly ascetic but also exuberantly missionary. Whereas the traditional Frankish monasteries cut themselves off from the world, the Irish invaded it. They preached, they converted, and they baptised. Their names are still associated with the Christian conversion of major areas of northern Europe: Columbanus (Burgundy), Gall (Alemannia), Eustasius (Bavaria) and Omer (Flanders and the lower Scheldt).[81] This characteristic will obviously hold less political advantage for someone trying to exert influence in the south or in some other stable area long within the Church. But to those building a political base in places which still had pagan elements, Irish monks were excellent allies. It is no coincidence, as we shall see, that our earliest sources treating the Pippinids, who lived nearer the pagan areas, are among those sometimes known as the 'Irish-influenced' works.[82]

Audoin's own role in the spread of this monastic movement was central, to say the least. He took part directly in the founding of four important monasteries: Rebais,[83] Saint-Wandrille (Rouen),[84] Fécamp (a nunnery),[85] and probably Saint-Germer-de-Fly.[86] Through his friend

---

79 Prinz, 'Columbanus', p. 76.

80 *Vita Columbani I*, ch. 17, p. 84.

81 Prinz, 'Columbanus', p. 65.

82 See below, pp. 318–19.

83 *MGH, Dipl.*, I, no. 15, p. 16; Pardessus, Diplomata, vol. 2, no. 275, pp. 39–40; *Vita Columbani I*, ch. 26. See Prinz, *Frühes Mönchtum*, p. 125.

84 *Gesta Font.*, I, 4; and *Vita Wandregiseli Abbatis Fontanellensis*, chs. 13 and 14, ed. B. Krusch, *MGH, SSRM*, V, pp. 20–1. See Prinz, *Frühes Mönchtum*, p. 127. Vacandard, *Saint Ouen*, p. 165, says it was founded on 1 March 649. He bases himself on the second *Vita Audoini*, ch. 14, and warns against accepting any other indication of the date.

85 *Vita Waningi*, chs. 4 and 5, *AASS* Jan., I, p. 591. See: Vacandard, *Saint Ouen*, pp. 34 and 206–7; Sprandel, *Merov. Adel*, pp. 53–4; and Prinz, *Frühes Mönchtum*, p. 127.

86 *Vita Geremari*, ch. 19. This *vita* reeks of Carolingian praise of Audoin. Krusch did not trust it. Krusch, *MGH, SSRM*, IV, p. 627.

Filibert he also probably had a hand in the founding of two more: Jumièges[87] and Pavilly.[88] Through his efforts and through those of Rouen's most important monastic house, Saint-Wandrille, the Irish influence spread to many other already extant abbeys.[89] But it would be prudent to guard against mistaking the new Irish component, even in its 'mixed' form, as a determinant in the whole structure of the Frankish Church and state.[90] Even by the 670s the majority of both the Frankish monasteries and the Frankish dioscesan churches show no evidence of Irish influence. And, as the careers of Leudesius, Ebroin, Waratto and Ghislemar show only too well, Frankish secular politics were still moved by mechanisms which had little to do with Irish monks.

It is not the Irish movement's supposed universality or even its longevity which makes it interesting for us, but rather its connection with the Neustrian court and with that group of nobility around the king whose influence it helped to spread. Audoin's central position was certainly not primarily dependent upon his fostering of Irish monasticism or even upon his position as bishop of the important see at Rouen. Audoin was not important because he was bishop; he was bishop because he was important. As early as 632 he witnessed an important land donation by his friend Eligius to the abbey at Solignac.[91] He signed the charter without a title, an indication that he was a man of note even before he assumed any royal or episcopal office. He and Eligius also appear as royal envoys sent to persuade Amandus to baptise Dagobert's son.[92] We find him judging an important land dispute under royal assign-

---

87 *Vita Balthildis*, ch. 8, above, p. 124.

88 *Vita Filiberti*, ch. 22. Prinz considered Audoin's role in the founding of these last two to have been a direct one. Prinz, *Frühes Mönchtum*, p. 127.

89 We suspect his influence in the older monastery of St Peter in Rouen. *Vita Audoini*, chs. 17 and 18, below, pp. 164–5. Audoin is buried there in what ch. 18 calls 'a place which he himself made' See Wattenbach-Levison, *Geschichtsquellen*, p. 128; and Vacandard, *Saint Ouen*, p. 172, n. 1. Saint-Wandrille's influence is also detected in Donzère (Dusera) on the Rhône, Indre (Antrum) and Montreuil-sur-Mer. Donzère: *Vita Ansberti episocopi Rotomagensis*, ch. 9, ed. W. Levison; *MGH, SSRM*, V, p. 625; Indre, *Vita Ansberti*, ch. 10, and Montreuil-sur-Mer, *Vita Wandregiseli II*, ch. 22, ed. J. Mabillon, *AASSOB*, saec II, p. 520. This list is considerably shorter than the one offered by Prinz in his *Frühes Mönchtum*, p. 127.

90 Sprandel disagrees: *Das Merowingerreich ist der Mitte des 7. Jahrhunderts ein Bischofs- und Mönchstaat. Sein Mittelpunkt ist nicht der Hof bei Paris sondern vielleicht der damals bedeutendeste Bischof im Reich, Audoin, und sein Hof an der Domkirche zu Rouen.* Sprandel, *Merov. Adel.*, p. 49.

91 Krusch edited the charter and argues convincingly for its authenticity against earlier objections. *MGH, SSRM*, V, pp. 743–9.

92 *Vita Amandi I*, ch 17.

ment,[93] and perhaps even intervening with his ally, Ebroin, in order to prevent Ragnebert from being executed.[94] Audoin stood at the centre of a network of aristocratic associates who in turn held some of Neustria's most influential positions. The following list of these magnates makes clear how pervasive his circle was:[95]

Eligius, goldsmith and minter for Clothar II, counsellor of Dagobert I, and later bishop of Noyon.[96]

Desiderius, royal treasurer for Dagobert I and later bishop of Cahors.[97]

Agilus, abbot of Rebais.[98]

Filibert, abbot of Rebais, Jumièges and Noirmoutier.[99]

Chrodobert, counsellor of Queen Balthild and bishop of Paris.[100]

Faro (or Burgundofaro), referendary for Dagobert I and later bishop of Meaux.[101]

Wandrille, counsellor for Dagobert I and later founder and first abbot of the monastery of Saint-Wandrille.[102]

Ansbert, referendary for Clothar III, later abbot of Saint-Wandrille and then Audoin's successor as bishop of Rouen.[103]

---

93 *Vita Lantberti*, ch. 4.

94 The report comes from the *Passio Ragneberti Martyris Bebronensis*, ch. 4, ed. B. Krusch, *MGH, SSRM*, V, p. 20. This source should be treated with caution. It is a ninth-century work and Audoin's place here in the story could be due more to his fame than to fact.

95 See R. Gerberding, *The Rise of the Carolingians and the Liber Historiae Francorum* (Oxford, 1987), pp. 85–7.

96 Eligius signed a letter to Desiderius with greetings both from himself and from Audoin: ed. Norberg, *Epistulae*, no. I, 11, p. 30; *Vita Amandi I*, ch. 17; *Vita Audoini*, ch. 4, below, p. 155; and *Vita Eligii*, I, ch. 12. It may have been Audoin himself who wrote a life of his friend Eligius which forms the basis of the eldest *Vita Eligii* to survive. See Wattenbach-Levison, *Geschichtsquellen*, p. 127; Sprandel, *Merov Adel.*, p. 50; and Fouracre, 'Work of Audoenus', 78.

97 His letter to Audoin, ed. Norberg, *Epistulae*, no. I, 11, p. 30.

98 *Vita Sancti Agili* , ch. 16.

99 *Vita Filiberti*, ch. 1. See Vacandard, *Saint Ouen*, p. 170; Prinz, *Frühes Mönchtum*, p. 131; and Sprandel, *Merov. Adel.*, p. 50.

100 *Vita Balthildis*, ch. 5, above, p. 122. Audoin may also have sent a copy of his *Vita Eligii* to Chrodbert. This is not certain because the Chrodbert mentioned here could also have been the contemporary bishop of Tours of the same name. See Krusch, *MGH, SSRM*, IV, pp. 650–1 and 741.

101 Pardessus, *Diplomata*, vol. 2, no. 275, p. 39.

102 *Vita Wandregiseli*, chs. 13 and 14.

103 *Vita Ansberti*, chs. 2 and 7. Ansbert wrote an acrostic poem in Audoin's honour, edition by Vacandard, *Saint Ouen*, p. 360.

Ebroin, counsellor of Queen Balthild, mayor of the palace for Clothar III and Theuderic III.[104]

Geremar, a nobleman with extensive land holdings in the Beauvais area, counsellor for Dagobert I, and founder and first abbot of Saint-Germer-de-Fly.[105]

Waratto, count (possibly in Rouen) and mayor of the palace for Theuderic III.[106]

Audomar, bishop of Therouanne.[107]

This list was compiled using stricter criteria than others have used and thus it comprises fewer names.[108] Even so, Audoin's contact with such men as these shows that his influence extended deep into Neustria's ruling circles.

104 *LHF*, ch. 45., above, p. 90; *Vita Balthildis*, ch. 5, above, p. 122; and *Passio Ragneberti*, ch. 4. It is significant that the first continuator of Fredegar, who was in the employ of the Pippinids and who copied the *LHF* for his account of these years, omitted the *LHF*'s account of Audoin's support for Ebroin. Apparently it was not prudent for him to report the lending of such prestige to Pippin II's formidable enemy. Fredegar, *Cont.*, ch. 2, ed. Wallace-Hadrill, p. 80–2.

105 *Vita Geremari*, chs. 6, 7. This *Vita* makes their relationship a close one. The author calls Audoin Geremar's *amicus* during their time at Dagobert I's court. Audoin received Geremar's son, Amalbert, from the baptismal font and later Geremar became abbot of Saint-Germer-de-Fly. Krusch, *MGH, SSRM*, IV, p. 627, places no trust in the *vita*. But even without the *vita*'s testimony, it is clear that any nobleman founding monasteries within the diocese of Rouen while Audoin was bishop would have needed his co-operation and support. See Prinz, *Frühes Mönchtum*, p. 131; Wattenbach-Levison, *Geschichtsquellen*, p. 139, n. 343; Vacandard, *Saint Ouen*, pp. 156–8; Sprandel, *Merov. Adel*, pp 50–1; and Fouracre, 'Work of Audoenus', 83–6.

106 *LHF*, ch. 47, above, p. 92, where Audoin warns Ghislemar not to supplant his father, Waratto; *Vita Condedi Anchoretae Belcinnacensis*, ch. 8, ed. W. Levison, *MGH, SSRM*, V, p. 650, where Waratto appears in a charter donating land to Saint-Wandrille, a monastery important to Audoin; *Vita Ansberti*, ch. 21, which says that, once Waratto was no longer in power in the Neustrian court, Audoin's close friend and successor, Ansbert, lost favour with Pippin II; and *Vita Audoini*, ch. 15, below, p. 163, which recounts Audoin's activities at court while Waratto was mayor.

107 *Vita Wandregiseli*, ch. 13, where Audomar consecrates Audoin's friend Wandregisel priest.

108 Vacandard presents a much longer list. In examining his sources, however, we note that he included people because they had served at Clothar II's court or were associated with the monastery of Saint-Wandrille. Both these criteria, while suggesting Audoin's influence, do not allow us to assume it with much confidence. Vacandard would add: Arnulf, bishop of Metz; Desiderius' brothers Rusticus, bishop of Cahors, and Syagrius, count in Albi and *patricius* of Marseilles; Paul, bishop of Verdun; Cyran, founder of Longrey; Romanus, bishop of Rouen; Romaricus, founder of Remiremont; Sulpicius, bishop of Bourges; Herbland, abbot of Indre in Nantes, and Erembert, bishop of Toulouse. Vacandard, *Saint Ouen*, pp. 38 and 190. Sprandel would also include the mayor, Erchinoald. Sprandel, *Merov. Adel*, p. 51. This last seems highly unlikely, given the antipathy between Audoin's partisan, Ebroin, and Erchinoald's son, Leudesius. *LHF*, ch. 45, above, p. 90.

If we examine certain episodes which occurred in his diocese during his period as bishop, we begin to suspect that the locals on the lower Seine did not always welcome the fact that their bishop was a powerful magnate from the distant Paris basin. When Audoin tried to set Geremar, a nobleman with extensive land holdings near Beauvais, over the monks at Penetale as their abbot, they drove him out.[109] It may be, too, that Audoin's hand-picked candidate to lead the house which would become Pavilly was rejected by the nuns.[110] Even the monks at Jumièges showed great reluctance to accept the man Audoin had chosen to succeed Abbot Filibert.[111] These examples of resistance to Audoin indicate that his hold over the monastic establishment at Rouen was not total. Here we can see the process of an important family encroaching on an area not yet securely in its sway, and as events turned out, Audoin's family would lose the area to Pippin's.

Audoin continued in the political limelight until his death. Even when the Neustrians temporarily dislodged Ebroin along with King Theuderic III from power in 673,[112] they did not deprive Audoin of his position. If the chronology derived from the second *Vita Audoini* is to be trusted, the magnificent royal welcome accorded Audoin upon his return from an extended trip to Rome falls in 675,[113] and this in turn makes Childeric II the king who proffered the bishop the display of such high royal regard. In 675, when the Neustrians revolted against Childeric II and his Austrasian mayor, Wulfoald, the king and his pregnant wife fell victim to the uprising.[114] The *Vita Lantberti* leads us to suspect that it was Audoin who stepped in to retrieve the royal bodies for burial.[115] In the bloody events which followed this regicide, events occasioned largely by Ebroin's explosive exit from Luxeuil and his lightning march towards the north-west on which he eliminated many of his political enemies, we see from the *LHF* that before he made his dramatic move he requested Audoin's *consilium*.[116] In 676 or 677 we find him again in high politics, acting as Ebroin's direct agent in condemning his old friend

---

109 *Vita Geremari*, chs. 8–11.

110 *Vita Sanctae Austrebertae*, ch. 12. This *vita* is not contemporary. See Fouracre, 'Work of Audoenus', 84.

111 *Vita Filiberti*, ch. 25.

112 *LHF*, ch. 45, above, p. 89.

113 *Vita Audoini II*, ch. 33.

114 *LHF*, ch. 45, above, p. 90.

115 *Vita Lantberti*, ch. 5, *MGH, SSRM*, V, p. 612. See Levison's n. 5.

116 *LHF*, ch. 45, above, p. 90.

Filibert.[117] Audoin's position outlasted Ebroin's death and he had close
relations with Ebroin's successor, Waratto. In fact, Waratto may well
have been Audoin's candidate for the mayoralty. We can suspect this
not only because Waratto's family came from near Rouen[118] and
because it was indeed Waratto who won the succession,[119] but also
because Audoin so firmly took the father's side in Waratto's dispute
with his son Ghislemar, as we have seen in the *LHF*.[120] Even as he
approached eighty years of age, his *vita* tells us, he was again sent on
a royal mission. It was Audoin whom the Neustrians chose to carry
their embassy of peace to the Austrasians.[121] Again if we can trust a
chronology derived from the second *Vita Audoini*, these would have
been the important negotiations between Waratto and Pippin with
which Waratto re-established peace with the Austrasians after the
wars conducted by his son Ghislemar.[122] Politics were Audoin's
concern to the end, for it was while conducting the king's business that
the venerable old bishop died at the royal villa of Clichy near Paris.[123]

Vita Audoini Episcopi Rotomagensis[124]
(The Life of Audoin, Bishop of Rouen)

IN THE NAME OF GOD THE HIGHEST, HERE BEGINS THE LIFE OF THE BLESSED BISHOP
AUDOIN

The life of a holy man, however glorious it may be in examples, very
often arises as difficult to relate. While the dull mind of man in no way
shines with prophecy, and in explaining remains sluggish und useless,
the faithful will urges on. Truly, its dedication draws forth the mind,
but slow sense weighs exceedingly upon the will's decision. It is then

---

117 *Vita Filiberti*, ch. 25.

118 The location of his landed base is evident from the donations of family land made
by his grandson, Bishop Hugo. *Gesta Font.*, IV, 2.

119 *LHF*, ch. 47, above, pp. 91–2.

120 *LHF*, ch. 47, above, p. 92. See Fredegar, *Cont.*, ch. 4, which contains a fuller
account.

121 *Vita Audoini*, chs. 13 and 14, below, p. 162.

122 *Vita Audoini II*, chs. 35 and 36.

123 *Vita Audoini*, ch. 15, below, p. 163. The date of Audoin's death is not certain; he died
at some point in the early 680s.

124 *Vita Audoini Episcopi Rotomagensis*, ed. W. Levison, *MGH*, *SSRM*, V (Hanover,
1910), pp. 536–67.

necessary to seek help from the Redeemer[125] who gives wisdom without reproach. He generously serves at the *tables of his heart*,[126] He who divided the baying of an ass into syllables.[127] May He vigorously strengthen our speech in order to relate the life of the venerable Audoin so that, from this, Christ may be praised among the peoples while the saints are venerated in their exceptional powers.[128] *The scent of a field which the Lord has blessed*[129] is redolent and it glistens among the many. Therefore Mother Church truly rejoices when some shine in glorious works, some gleam red as *the rose among thorns*,[130] some as lilies glisten white among the stems,[131] and others smell sweet as the violets among the groves; she holds nectar and aromatic balsam. And thus it happens that Almighty God delights his field with scents, feeds it with miracles,[132] glorifies it with works, and He is worshipped as Lord; it happens that he who delights the angelic heights in heaven in song, while undergoing human poverty, out of earthly things purchases heavenly ones; that the Church follows her head with her founder Christ so that He reigns without end through the ages. Therefore, with the Lord guiding, let me produce what I have proposed to relate.[133]

CHAPTER 1

In the time of glorious King[134] Clothar,[135] the son of King Chilperic,[136] in the province of Gaul, at the stronghold of Soissons, three venerable men were born, begotten as noble from one stock, and made famous by the grace of God from on high: Ado, Dado and Rado. Their father was

125 An example of our use of a manuscript variant. We have translated *a redemptore* from an early thirteenth-century manuscript (British Library, Harleian 2801) rather than the reading *ad redemptore* found in the edited text.

126 Proverbs 7:3.

127 Cf. Numbers 22:28.

128 *eximiis virtutibus.*

129 Genesis 27:27.

130 Song of Solomon 2:2.

131 These flowers refer to red and white martyrdom. Red martyrdom, actual death, and white martyrdom, death to the world through monastic renunciation.

132 *virtutibus.*

133 ... *quod proposui narrare edisseram.* Non-classical use of the pluperfect subjunctive.

134 *principis.*

135 Clothar II (584–628). *Vita* II adds that it was in the twentieth year of Clothar's reign, making it about 603–4.

136 Chilperic I (561–84).

Audecharius, their mother Aiga, each decorated with the height of Christianity. From the first stages of infancy, having been instructed in the subtlety of letters, they were beloved by the king himself and most well and most wisely educated by men of illustrious standing.[137] Their firstborn, Ado, flourished indeed in the monastic order, and, seeking the religious life, he scorned the malice of this world. Rado, on the other hand, was made custodian of the palace treasure, having attained high worldly office. Girded with the fear of the Lord and generous in alms, he faithfully guarded and served in high offices. The venerable Audoin, therefore, also named Dado, was elevated as bishop to the episcopal cathedra, having attained royal recognition.[138] And he performed his duties for a long time.

CHAPTER 2

Indeed, after Clothar's death, his son Dagobert,[139] a man clever to the limit, crafty in his slyness,[140] and fearsome in his authority, was made king[141] in the place of his father.[142] And he, holding the royal sceptre as a raging lion oppressing the necks of his servants,[143] bravely triumphed by containing the ferocity of [foreign] peoples.[144] Under the authority of his rule, the above-mentioned man of the Lord served militarily in the world, received the signet ring of the king[145] and, beloved by many, keenly guarded the position[146] entrusted to him. What more should I

---

137 *ab inlustribus viris.* See above, p. 70, for an explanation of this title. Its use here indicates that the author was familiar with the royal court and its politics.

138 *una cum honore regale adeptus. Honor* is always a difficult word to translate. Here it indicates that the episcopal position was a royal appointment. See above, p. 70.

139 Dagobert I (623–33 in Austrasia; 629–38 in Neustria).

140 *Ingenio.*

141 *princeps.*

142 This was in 629 and pertains only to Dagobert succeeding Clothar in Neustria. He had been ruling Austrasia since 622 or 623 when his father established him in the eastern realm. See Fredegar, *Chron.*, IV, ch. 47.

143 Ecclesiasticus 4:35. There is a feeling of antipathy towards Dagobert on the author's part here, for he recalls this passage in Ecclesiasticus which reads: *Noli esse sicut leo in domo tua, evertens domesticos tuos, et opprimens subjectos tibi.*

144 This sentence is a small *speculum regis;* the function of a Merovingian king was to keep the peace within his lands and to do battle with foreigners. The word used here for foreign peoples is *gentium.*

145 The keeper of the royal signet ring, the referendary. It was he who approved and presented charters to the king for signature. See above, pp. 140–1.

146 *honorem.*

add? Beloved by the king himself on account of his love of service, and
greatly trusted by the king among his other followers, he shone for his
wise prophecy in earthly matters.[147]

CHAPTER 3

Whereupon the servant of Christ, thinking little of the honour of this
world, strove most devotedly towards the heavenly realms. He often
fasted, spent the night in vigils, was constantly at prayer, was
generous in alms, keenly providing for the poor in the name of Christ,
and he was extremely ready for the commands of God. And commonly
indeed under his belt surrounded with the glint of gems, and beneath
his purple robe shining with gold, a rough hair shirt pressed against
the frame of his body for the ardour of faith.[148] And thus he was so
steadfast that he was a proper and strong recruit in the service of the
world while not veering from divine commandments, fulfilling the
precept of God, when He said: *Render unto Caesar the things that are
Caesar's and unto God the things that are God's.*[149] And thus the Lord
shaped his soldier so that he would serve in earthly high offices[150]
while not rejecting heavenly ones. Oh what great love, oh what great
zeal, he had for the religious and for those serving God. And he added
his own wealth to whatever Divine Grace conferred upon others.

CHAPTER 4

After this, in the love of the faith, he joined the blessed Eligius, Bishop
of Noyon, a man acknowledged for his miracles, and as *two* most
fruitful *olive trees and two* gleaming golden *candlesticks,*[151] as men

147 The pattern of Audion's career is a topos in which the saint has a successful
professional life at court and then later takes up the religious vocation. In this
volume it is true of saints Balthild and Audoin to whom we can add saints Eligius,
Arnulf and others.

148 The wearing of the hair shirt under earthly garb is a common hagiographical motif
to show that the saint was keeping to the spiritual life even in other vocations. St
Geretrud, too, wore a hair shirt. See *Vita Geretrudis*, ch. 7, below, p. 325.

149 Matthew 22:21; Mark 12:17; and Luke 20:25. This passage is an example of an
author using Scripture for the purpose of justifying. Here he justfies his hero
serving in a powerful worldly position. See M. Van Uytfanghe, *Stylisation biblique
et condition humaine dans l'hagiographie mérovingienne (600–750), Verhandelingen van
de Koninklijke Academie voor Wetenschappen, Letteren en Schone Kunsten van België*
(Brussels, 1987), p. 38.

150 *Fascibus terrenis.*

151 *Revelations* 11:4.

illuminated by the sun of justice, they both equally shone at the court of the palace.[152] And when the Lord saw that his soldier was pleasing and solicitous concerning his precepts, he placed him on the episcopal cathedra, the seat at Rouen,[153] having taken him from the earthly and shipwrecked realm. As an exemplary priest he performed his duty. For which reason, having been elected bishop by the Lord, and having been made an exemplary preacher, he shaped his lordly flock with his words as well as his deeds. Thus strengthened in the practice of his faith, with the Lord as protector, he turned the most savage ferocity of the Franks into gentleness, and from the holy font he so tempered them with the sweetness of honey, and so consecrated his parishes with the divine practice, that they abandoned the rite of the heathen and voluntarily placed themselves under the yoke of Christ and their necks under His[154] service.[155]

CHAPTER 5

If anyone should wish to learn clearly how many churches and how many monasteries for each sex were founded by him and under his pontificate, let him go throughout his parishes and see himself as an Egyptian marvelling at the battle lines of monks.[156] Accordingly, this man of God, by his words as well as by his deeds, protected the sheep of the Lord and the fold of the faithful from the biting of wolves. Who would ever be able to imitate his life and the straight and narrow path of the Redeemer along which he proceeded to the heavenly realms? Who would say that he [Audoin] ever had enough food or drink? And hunger had so weakened him in his body that his flesh was worn away and affected by pallor and emaciation, his cheeks were soaked with the flood of his tears, the circumference of his neck weighed down by a ring of iron, and likewise his arms along with the rest of his limbs were fettered by the mark of rings.

---

152 See the *Vita Amandi*, ch. 17, where these two are portrayed as Dagobert's willing envoys.

153 Levison dates his enthronement to 13 May 641. See *MGH, SSRM*, V, p. 556, n. 3.

154 *Sua* for *eius.*

155 For a discussion of Audoin's missionary work among the rural pagans see Fouracre, 'The Work of Audoenus'.

156 Egypt represented a holy land of armies of monks in the imagination of the early Middle Ages. This was due in large part to Evagrius' translation of Athanasius' *Life of St Antony* and Jerome's treatment of the same Egyptian saint in his *Lives of Famous Men.*

CHAPTER 6

The soldier of Christ, as if chained on account of the love of the Lord, had bound himself in such custody,[157] had condemned the desires of the world, and hastened to his heavenly homeland.[158] And just as the martyrs of Christ in the time of the persecution, having been condemned to incarceration in prison and sent into seclusion in the mines under the reigning tyrants, poured forth their precious blood in the name of Christ, so too this man, in a time of peace when the persecution had stopped, urged himself on as the fiery soldier and, being very famous for his faith, he earned the palm of a martyr by emulation. Furthermore, let us not be ashamed to relate what sort of bed he chose for himself and what sort of rest he served out to his body. This repose of his pallet was made not from the softness of feathers, but from a mass of wood, and, as if wasting away his body in prison, he rejected the flattering badges of worldly office, agreeing with the word of the Apostle when he said: *For the tribulations of this world are not to be compared with the future glory which is to be revealed to the saints.*[159] Oh power[160] of abstinence and mortification of the flesh, you who send the soldiers of Christ to heaven! Oh fervour of love, you who so burn in the heart that, having spurned fallen [earthly love], you enter into the kingdom of heaven. The Lord worked in God's servant Audoin and nobly exalted him and decorated him with His miracles in this life, and after such great suffering gave him rest.

CHAPTER 7

These few matters should be concluded briefly in a few words lest our crude phrasing be disagreeable. Let our account pass over to his miracles,[161] and[162] to what I learned from his pupils, whom I came to know to be proper witnesses as they recounted. I have taken care to include a few things from among many. So too, seeing that this holy man of God had by royal command occupied the episcopal position from a lay status, he feared in accordance with the sentiment of the

---

157 *custodiam*. Confusion of ablative and accusative.

158 *ad supra patria*. Confusion of accusative and ablative.

159 Romans 8:18.

160 *virtus*.

161 *miracula*.

162 *vel* as simple copulative.

Apostle where he forbids that a neophite be ordained lest he fall into the snare of the devil.[163] After taking up the authority, until a year should turn over in time, [he passed] as an exile from his homeland through the grades and orders rightly until he became a learned scribe in the Church.[164] Accordingly he went forth in the lands of Spain,[165] where the Lord performed a great miracle through him. Then nearly seven years were ending in which that region was suffering in drought; barrenness, famine, the disease of the pest, and death threatened on all sides. Finally merciful God, seeing the affliction of his people, took pity on the human sufferings, and, at the advent of his servant, Audoin, straightway yielded rain and tempered the thirsting land with a wonderful downpour. And from this a joyous feeling entered the lands of the Goths. Not wrongly[166] is the holy Audoin compared in his strengths to Elijah. For three years and six months heaven was closed against the Israelite people on account of their sins, whereupon [God], at Elijah's praying, infused the rough land with an abundance of rain.[167] So too our Lord Jesus Christ through his servant in renewed grace replenished Spain with water.[168]

CHAPTER 8

And thus the man of the Lord, having been greatly strengthened by this miracle, grew in the fervour of vigorous love; bristling at worldly impurity, he abandoned it and more earnestly sought the contemplative life. He gave his whole self and brought his whole self to the Lord. And thus protected by an angelic guard, and having obtained a certain state of servitude, he conversed quite often with the saints. And thus it is known that his disciples, who very often regarded him with their very eyes, discerned a very great light radiating from his bed. Benefiting, then, from the conversation of the saints, the servant of Christ exulted in the Lord. Whereupon the man of the Lord, in accordance with the

163 I Timothy 3:6.

164 The canonical requirement was that a new bishop must have spent at least a year in orders before his enthronement. See also *Vita Eligii II*, ch. 2, and the references above, p. 143, n. 67.

165 Here Spain probably means Gothic territory north of the Pyrenees. See Gregory, *Hist.*, IX, ch. 32, *MGH, SSRM*, I, ed. alt., p. 451.

166 *non immerito*. See above, p. 70.

167 3 Kings 17–18; Luke 4:25; and James 5:17 and 18. This is an example of Van Uytfanghe's *comparatio* in direct biblical references (*Stylisation biblique*, p. 19).

168 *aquas Spania*. Confusion of accusative and ablative.

Apostle, forgetting what lay behind and stretching himself for those things ahead,[169] purified the sanctuary of his heart, and, having been made *a temple of the Holy Spirit*,[170] he deserved to see the Lord, since it is written: *Blessed are the pure in heart, for they shall see God*.[171] Whereupon strength proceeded from his strength, purity from his pure heart, and the possession of [heavenly] things from his suffering. On account of his working of miracles[172] the servant of the Lord became great on earth, and he, with his work continuing, took up the heavenly kingdom. By making manifest his merit, almighty God glorified his servant among very many peoples and decorated him with apostolic signs.

CHAPTER 9

It happened at one point that he undertook a journey through the district of Angers. While a certain poor man made flour by working at a mill on Sunday, his hand became bound to the rod whence the millstone was turning such that his thumb went almost through the structure of the hand's nerves and veins.[173] Cold blood flowed out of the upper part and the guilty man paid[174] for his sin; he was never able to toss away the rod in his constricted hand. From this a fear and a very great amazement had spread through the people. And thus as the holy man travelled through the region, the poor man threw himself at his feet, and, admitting his guilt, said that he was thus afflicted because he had violated the day of the holy resurrection against the commandment of the Lord. When the man of the Lord saw him, he was moved

169 See Philippians 3:13.

170 I Corinthians 6:19.

171 Matthew 5:8.

172 *virtutum*.

173 Punishment for working on Sunday is a common theme; examples are found in: *Vita Hugberti Episcopi Traiectensis*, ch. 4, ed. W. Levison, *MGH, SSRM*, VI, p. 485, where a woman kneaded bread on Sunday and her hand was paralysed; Venantius Fortunatus, *Vita Germani Episcopi Parisiaci Auctore Venantio Fortunato*, ch. 51, ed. B. Krusch, *MGH, SSRM*, VII (Hanover, 1920), p. 404; Gregory of Tours, *Liber in gloria martyrum*, ch. 15, ed. B. Krusch, *MGH, SSRM*, I, pt. 2 (Hanover, 1885), p. 48; and in Gregory of Tours, *De virtutibus Sancti Juliani*, ch. 11, *ibid*, p. 119. See Richard Collins, 'Observations on the Form, Language, and Public of the Prose Biographies of Venantius Fortunatus in the Hagiography of Merovingian Gaul', in H. B. Clarke and M. Brennan (eds.), *Columbanus and Merovingian Monasticism British Archaeological Reports, International Series*, 113 (Oxford, 1981), p. 126, n. 99; and J.-L. Derouet, 'Les possibilités d'interprétation sémiologique des textes hagiographiques', *Revue d'Histoire de l'Eglise de France*, 42 (1976), 153.

174 Participle for finite verb.

by mercy, and, pressing the sign of the cross on to his withered hand, he recalled it to its original health. He warned him and gave him the salutary advice never to perform anything beyond a servile task on the Lord's day lest afterwards, on account of his contempt, things worse than the earlier ones[175] should happen to him. He said, given that the Jews from the commandment of the Lord observed the Sabbath, having been ordered to do so on account of the law, how much more ought the Christians, who had been redeemed by His blood, to venerate the Lord's day.

CHAPTER 10

And thus the holy man spread the seeds of his miracles and the sharpness of his words throughout the various parishes. For, since his heart always strove after heavenly matters on account of his love of the Holy Trinity, he burned with the desire that he might be able to hasten to worship the portals of the Apostles at Rome. And so he did, although he was worn down by old age, consumed by the length of abstinence of the body, and almost dissolved in the structure of his limbs. As a soldier desiring the loftiness of the Alps and the ridges of the Pyrenees,[176] made old in their snowy mass, he gave himself over to danger on acccount of his love of God and His disciples. He fulfilled his prayers, satisfied his desire, visited the monuments of the saints, and, having prostrated his body on their pavements, he affixed his kisses, devotedly fulfilling what he had long desired. And thus the man of God, supported by the approval of the saints, wandered all through the places of the saints seeking the benefit of their prayers. He took relics of many saints with him,[177] and, with the angel of the Lord as his companion, he returned to the regions of the Gauls. With his prayer answered, he ministered to the health of their souls and their bodies.

CHAPTER 11

And when he came to the borders of his own diocese, the citizens round about and the common people, rejoicing and at the same time weeping for joy, turned out in throngs to meet him. With crosses and

175 Matthew 12:45.

176 The author seems to have a poor idea of the location of the Pyrenees.

177 Rome was seen as an 'inexhaustble treasure house of relics'. P. Geary, *Furta Sacra: the Thefts of Relics in the Central Middle Ages* (Princeton, New Jersey 1978), p. 46.

lamps they came to meet their faithful shepherd, giving thanks to the Lord, who had returned their shepherd and bishop to them unharmed. Whereupon a happy messenger announced his coming at the royal court, and both the king[178] and the queen along with the nobles of the palace rejoiced, clapped their hands and blessesd Christ who had caused such a man and so great a shepherd to return to their realm. What shall I say concerning the priests and the multitudes of monks and many nuns, who, raising their hands to heaven, sang with one voice praising the Lord and saying, 'We give thanks to you, Jesus Christ, son of the living God, who has heard the voices of those crying out to you and who has returned to us the shepherd of our souls and the caretaker of our bodies'? Meanwhile the poor rejoiced, shouting that God had sent their provider back to them.

CHAPTER 12

Whereupon, although the blessed Audoin had returned in peace to his own lands, this peaceful man found that troubles had sprung up among the princes of the palace at the instigation of the devil, that sower of discord.[179] Then the man of the Lord, taking up *the weapons of righteousness,*[180] and remaining awake at night, exerted himself fiercely with vigils, excessive fasting, and constant prayers for harmony among them. It is not unknown to many how much and how heavy the perspiration flowed from his breast, and the many tribulations the blessed old man undertook both in order to render peaceful those men whose souls hatred had long defiled and in order that bloodshed and human calamity might not come about. Almost to the end of his life he piously and faithfully exerted himself, fulfilling the precept of the Gospel, the truth of the shepherd, freely *giving his own life for his sheep.*[181] Which of the miracles which the Lord deigned to perform in Spain, Italy, or in the parishes of the Gauls, shall I relate first? It would be extremely tedious to tell them all; the places where the miracles are are their witness. But I have caused a few from the many to be included in this work.

---

178 Although the author does not mention the name of the king, it was probably Childeric II. See Gerberding, *Rise*, p. 88.

179 *instigante diabulo.* The author uses strong language in describing the breach of the internal peace. See *LHF*, ch. 51, above, p. 94.

180 II Corinthians 6:7.

181 John 10:11.

CHAPTER 13

Therefore although the holy Audoin was always seen to fight for the harmony of peace, nonetheless, as time passed, conflicts arose between the people of the Neustrians[182] and the Austrasians.[183] And so the man of God continued, and taking up the holy plans, and, relying on God's help, he came as the son of peace to the city of Cologne.[184] He entered the city in order to examine the great number of martyrs. He visited the monuments and took away their relics, which he put up in his own city with the greatest honour.[185] In that city, however, there was a certain man who now for eleven years had not been able to utter a word, being mute the whole time. And the Lord reserved this miracle for the honour of his servant Audoin, that at his arrival he gave speech back to the mute, and the man's tongue, which had been stiff for a long time, sounded forth in praise. He, making the sign of the cross on his head, commanded the word that he should speak. And immediately the man began to speak, bearing praises unto the Lord.

CHAPTER 14

Whereupon, returning to Neustria with the agreements of peace confirmed, he came to the city of Verdun. As he entered the church, a certain woman who had an unclean spirit, which had begun to trouble her greatly, tried to rush at the man of God at a rapid pace. And so the bishop stretched out his hand upon her head, violently tossed out the demon, and returned her healthy to her relatives. Thereupon he came to the palace and showed that all the things, as he had performed them, were agreeable. And the true priest brought it about that the kingdoms were united in peace[186] for the peoples. And so the unified peace between both countries lasted quite a little while.

182 *inter gentem Francorum et Austrasiorum.* This use of *Franci* to mean *Neustrians* is also found in the *LHF* and the *Vita Balthildis.*

183 This is most likely a reference to the war which broke out between the Neustrian mayor, Ghislemar, and the Austrasian leader, Pippin II, in the early 680s. See *LHF*, ch. 47, above, p. 92.

184 Since Cologne was a Pippinid city, it was probably Pippin II who received him. See *LHF*, ch. 47, above, p. 92. Scheibelreiter emphasises that Audoin's willingness to undertake the trip at his advanced age shows how important the peace mission was. G. Scheibelreiter, *Der Bischof in merowingerischer Zeit.* (Vienna, 1983), p. 230.

185 See Geary's discussion of the justification for relic thefts in *Furta Sacra*, pp. 132–57.

186 The edition has *pax* but we have taken *pace* from St Gall manuscript no. 563 (ix–x

CHAPTER 15

And now, lest our uncultivated style arouse distaste, let it grow silent; to the death of the holy man let our speech tend. When he had come on the business of the king and the peoples, with the Lord protecting him, to the villa of Clichy-la-Garenne,[187] while Theuderic[188] was king, Chrodhild queen,[189] and Waratto was serving as *subregulus*,[190] the time arrived when by divine will the soul of the holy man should leave this world. A sickness of the body touched the holy man of God and he began to burn with fever. But the holy man beseeched the Lord more often that he should free him from the body, and the Lord, hearing the prayers of his servant, allowed the burden of the flesh to be laid aside and permitted him then to enjoy the fruit of paradise. And then, being a true Israel coming back from Egypt, his holy soul, carried off by angels, flew to the Lord. And a great wailing was made, all the royal entourage was shaken, all loftiness was brought low, all joy turned into sorrow, all laughter silenced, and the great sorrow grew greater. The royal house bewailed its most prudent adviser and the whole people rose openly in mourning because he [Audoin] always procured peace for the people and strongly exerted himself to prevent the shedding of human blood.

CHAPTER 16

Finally all were assembled outside the palace. Then[191] the king with the queen, the assembly of bishops, the mayor of the palace,[192] and the nobles of the palace, who had also come together, carried the holy man on the funeral bier and celebrated the holy obsequies with grief. Yet each rejoiced at the same time as he shared in the greatest mourning because he had been deemed worthy to carry the body of the holy man

---

sec.) in order to make the meaning clear. The phrase here also helps explain the puzzling passage in the *Vita Balthildis*, ch. 5: *Franci et Burgundiones facti sunt uniti.* In other words, they were united in peace. See above, p. 122.

187 Département. Seine, arrondissement. Saint-Denis.

188 Theuderic III (673–90).

189 Chrodhild, wife of Theuderic III and mother of Clovis III. See *LHF*, ch. 49, above, p. 93.

190 I.e. mayor of the palace. See *LHF*, ch. 47, above, pp. 91–2.

191 *Igitur* used temporally.

192 Waratto, who had regained the mayoralty after the death of his rebellious son, Ghislemar.

on his shoulders. And when they had come to Pontoise[193] with the greatest honour and the proper funereal sign of respect, both the king and the queen as well as all the people celebrated vigils[194] and spent the whole night in praises of the Lord. From there the royal entourage returned home with great sorrow.

CHAPTER 17

Then when a gathering of a great number of bishops, along with their abbots,[195] priests, and clerics was complete, and with a multitude of men of illustrious standing, and a crowd of the people, they entered the territory[196] of le Vexin. With great goodwill they came together and, carrying the blessed body on their shoulders, singing praises and hymns to God, they exhibited the bier of their shepherd with weeping. Through the various localities, as we have said, infused with sadness, they carried the blessed body, and in his own city of Rouen, in the basilica of Blessed Peter the Apostle, they buried him with great honour. And here, since Audoin's merits earned it, our Lord Jesus Christ deigned to perform many signs of divine power.[197] And not only in that place but throughout the various districts where the holy man lay in the body so great were the miracles which were shown forth powerfully that the blind were made to see there, lepers were cleansed, the lame were restored to walking, those beset with demons were cured, and various sufferers were healed. It would be tedious to relate the great miracles which there the Lord deigned to demonstrate through the merit of blessed Audoin. To have related a few from the many suffices. He who would wish to know this clearly, let him travel through Gaul, Aquitaine, Spain and Italy and he will discover that, as we recounted, we told the truth. He will never prove our words false.

CHAPTER 18

The blessed body lay in the place which he himself had made for about three years and nine months. After that, it seemed to the bishop, his

---

193 Département. Seine-et-Oise.

194 *celebratas vigilias.* Accusative absolute.

195 Note the subordinate role of the abbot to the bishop.

196 *opido.* Levison says, *Opidum aetate Merovingica saepe pagum, territorium significat.* Levison, *MGH, SSRM,* V, p. 564, n. 4.

197 *signa multa virtutum,* i.e. miracles.

successor,[198] that the blessed body should be translated to a higher position behind the altar of St Peter the Apostle. And thus, the bishop having called together an army of many monks, and when, on account of their love for Audoin, all the clergy of the church, the townspeople, and the ones from the province of that city arrived, they celebrated vigils throughout the whole night. When they had finished the praises of matins, they moved that holy body with great fear from the place where it had been buried and translated it to the place we mentioned above, on the day of the ascension of the Lord, the fortieth day after the glorious resurrection of the Lord, holy Easter, which Christian people celebrate with great honour.

CHAPTER 19

Therefore let us not shrink from relating the miracle which was performed on the very day they translated the holy body. For a strong illness of the body, which the people are said to call tertian fever, had affected the above-mentioned bishop. It shook him violently and, weakened as he was with the fever, death seemed near and threatened more acutely because of severe difficulty in his breathing. While mass was being celebrated by the priests, with the clergy and laymen in attendance, the bishop suddenly received his health; he was completely cleansed of the fever. Hale and healthy, he hastened off to his own quarters. And therefore with faith the bishop took away with his own hand the sudary, which was on the head of blessed Audoin as an offering for the relics and, through the largesse of the Lord, he earned health for himself and for many others from the same affliction. A joyous feast was held. On the blessed day of his translation the voices of the poor were united in one, praising the Lord and giving indescribable thanks especially for their shepherd, lord Audoin, as he had provided for them abundantly during his life and prepared such a great feast for them after his death.

HERE ENDS THE LIFE OF BLESSED BISHOP AUDOIN.

198 Ansbert.

IV: *Acta Aunemundi*
(The Deeds of Aunemund)

In the middle of the seventh century Aunemund held one of the most important positions in the Frankish Church: he was Bishop of Lyons. His brother was the secular ruler of Lyons, and it appears that Aunemund's family had a near monopoly of power in the area. Nevertheless, local rivals to the family and forces at the king's court were able to join forces in order to destroy that power, killing both Aunemund and his brother in the process. The fall of a powerful family can be most revealing to the historian. We can hope that it will show us how a political community operated, and from this we may learn more about the nature of that community. The story of Aunemund's fall thus deserves close attention. Let us begin with what little know about this powerful man and then turn to the textual history of the work which describes his life.

The first we can see of Aunemund, bishop of Lyons, is in a charter issued by Landeric, the bishop of Paris, in 653. The last sight we have of him is as a witness in two charters issued by Emmo, the bishop of Sens, in 660. His successor as bishop of Lyons, Genesius, is first attested in a charter issued by Bishop Berthefrid of Amiens in 664.[1] The scattered references in these charters provide a bare chronological framework within which we can place the events of Aunemund's life and death as they appear in the *Acta Aunemundi*.[2] According to the *Acta*, the bishop was from a leading family in Lyons. His father, Sigo, had been *praefectus* or secular ruler of Lyons and his brother also held

---

1 For Landeric's charter, see J. Tardif (ed.), *Archives de l'Empire – Inventaires et Documents. Monuments Historiques* (Paris, 1886), no. 10, p. 8. The authenticity of the body of this charter has been challenged, but, after Levillain, its witness list (which contains Aunemund's subscription) is accepted as genuine: see L. Levillain, 'Etudes sur l'abbaye de Saint-Denis à l'époque mérovingienne', *BEDC*, 87 (1926), 35–48. For the charters of Emmo and Berthefrid, J. Pardessus (ed.), *Diplomata, chartae, epistolae, leges, aliaque instrumenta ad res Gallo-Francicas spectantia*, vol. 2 (Paris, 1849), nos. 333, 335, 345; for further discussion of no. 333, see below, n. 24.

2 *Acta S. Aunemundi alias Dalfini episcopi*, ed. P. Perrier, *AASS*, Sept., vol. VII (Antwerp, 1760), pp. 744–6.

this position.[3] Aunemund too held secular power before becoming bishop. Although the *Acta* speak of the family as 'Roman', i.e. Gallo-Roman, we should note that both Aunemund and Sigo are distinctively Burgundian names.[4] Since we know other leading families in southern Gaul to have done so, it seems likely that Aunemund's family would have allied itself in marriage with others of similarly high status, and over time that meant joining with successive conquerors, first Burgundians, then Franks. The result of such intermarriage was the evolution of very powerful families of mixed race but of one political culture which was marked by the highly visible exercise of power.[5]

It seems to have been involvement in the world of politics beyond Lyons which led to the downfall not only of Aunemund but also of his brother. The bishop, the *Acta Aunemundi* tell us, had close connections with the kings of Francia. He had been brought up at the royal court and later as bishop he had baptised, or even stood as godfather to, Clothar III, the firstborn son of King Clovis II. His glorious career excited the envy of his local clergy, and they seem to have provided the basis for a charge of treason against Aunemund and his brother. The latter was accused, tried and executed at a meeting of the royal court. Aunemund too was called to answer the charge. When he delayed, an army was sent from the north to fetch him. In the meantime Aunemund called upon Waldebert, abbot of Luxeuil, to protect him.

---

3 The use of the term *praefectus* is unusual in the Merovingian context. When it is used in the *Vita Desiderii Cadurcae urbis episcopi*, ch. 7, ed. B. Krusch, *MGH, SSRM*, IV (Hanover, 1902), p. 568, and in *Vita Boniti*, ch. 3, ed. B. Krusch, *MGH, SSRM*, VI (Hanover, 1913), p.121, it is interchangeable with *patricius*, the more usual term for secular command in Burgundy and Provence. In the *Acta Aunemundi* it could be that a later hand exchanged *praefectus* for *patricius*, as the latter term went out of use in the mid eighth century, whereas the use of *praefectus* became more common in the Carolingian and later periods.

4 Both names appear among the counts listed as signatories to the *Liber Constitutionum*, the set of Burgundian laws issued at Lyons in the year 517. The name Aunemund appears twice, that of Sigo once: see *Liber Constitutionum*, ed. L. de Salis, *MGH, Legum, sectio* I, vol. 2, pt. 1 (Hanover, 1892), p. 34. For discussion of the significance of these names, see P. Amory, 'Names, ethnic identity and community in fifth- and sixth-century Burgundy', *Viator*, 25 (1994), 14–15.

5 On the development of a supra-regional elite of mixed-race families, see K.-F. Werner, 'Bedeutende Adelsfamilien im Reich Karls des Grossen. Ein personengeschichtlicher Beitrag zum Verhältnis von Königtum und Adel im frühen Mittelalter', in *Karl der Grosse*, ed. W. Braunfels, vol. 1 (Düsseldorf, 1965), translated in T. Reuter (ed. and trans.), *The Medieval Nobility* (North Holland, 1978). On the wide-ranging family contacts of Abbo, the last *patricius* in southern Gaul, see P. Geary, *Aristocracy in Provence. The Rhône basin at the dawn of the Carolingian Age* (Stuttgart, 1985), pp. 101–48.

When the royal army arrived, both Aunemund and Waldebert were taken away northwards. At the town of Mâcon Waldebert was ordered to leave the party. Then as the prisoner and his guards camped overnight at Chalon-sur-Saône, Aunemund was murdered in the dead of night. His body was later shipped back along the Saône and buried in the convent of St Peter's in his city of Lyons. His successor as bishop was an outsider, Genesius, who, according to the *Vita Balthildis*, had been one of the clergy at the royal court, and had been particularly close to the queen.[6]

Aunemund was subsequently venerated as a martyr and a lively cult developed around his tomb. By the eleventh century the cult had become widely known, and by the thirteenth the whereabouts of the bishop's tomb and remains had become the subject of a protracted dispute between the convent church of St Peter's and the church of St Nicetius, both in Lyons.[7] In the course of this dispute many documents concerning the martyr and his family were produced as each side tried to back up its claims with written evidence which appeared to come from the martyr's own time. A good example of this is a document which purported to be a will that Aunemund had made in favour of the convent of St Peter's.[8] The source of the authentic-looking detail contained in such documents was an early medieval account of the bishop's martyrdom and of the first miracles which established his sanctity, an account which obviously antedated the wrangling over his

---

6 *Vita Balthildis*, ch. 4, above, p. 000.

7 A. Coville's *Recherches sur l'histoire de Lyon du Vme siècle au IXme siècle (480–800)* (Paris, 1928) remains a valuable treatment of this whole subject. On the growth of the cult and the dispute see pp. 370–2 and 376–9; also see ch. 5 of P. Perrier's 'Commentarius Praevius' to his edition of the *Acta Aunemundi, AASS*, Sept. vol. VII, pp. 736–9. In sources other than narrative ones, Aunemund first appears as a saint in a Lyons-oriented martyrology dated before the year 806: Dom. H. Quentin, *Les Martyrologes historiques du Moyen-âge* (Paris. 1908). For the 'Martyrologe Lyonnais du ms. Latin 3879 de la Bibliothèque Nationale', pp. 132–221. For Aunemund, p. 205. For location and dating, pp. 219–21. References to Aunemund as saint in a letter from Leidrad, archbishop of Lyons, to the emperor Charlemagne are, as Coville argued, later medieval additions designed to lend spurious antiquity to the church of St Peter's claim to St Aunemund's cult: Coville, *Recherches*, pp. 274–7. In the early eleventh century the nuns of St Peters secured from Archbishop Burchard a sentence of excommunication on those *qui ... potestatem Sancti Aunemundi et Sancti Germani eius frangere voluerint*; see: M.-C. Guige (ed.), *Cartulaire Lyonnais*, vol. I (Lyons, 1885), no. 8, p. 14. Note that Coville, *Recherches*, p. 381, in what must be a misprint (IX for XI) dates this document to the early ninth century. On the reference to Aunemund's brother in this document, see below, n. 21.

8 'The Will of Aunemund' (*Testamentum Aunemundi*) is printed in full in Coville, *Recherches*, Appendix I, pp. 408–12.

relics. The *Acta Aunemundi* as printed in the *Acta Sanctorum* are based upon an early form of this account. What we must decide now is how much of the printed version we can trust.

Unlike the other works included in this volume, the *Acta Aunemundi* were not selected for edition in the *Monumenta Germaniae Historica* series. The editors of the *Monumenta* selected only those works which they thought had been written very close to the period with which they were concerned, and the best proof of early composition was for them the existence of a manuscript tradition stretching back to that period. The age of the *Acta Aunemundi* could not be demonstrated in this way, for their early manuscript tradition has not survived. They exist in an eighteenth-century printed edition which reproduces a seventeenth-century edition produced by the scholar Dom Chifflet. He drew upon the several manuscript versions of the life of the martyr he found in the Lyons area. Chifflet sensibly ignored those versions which showed an obvious interest in the dispute over Aunemund's grave and relics, for that effectively dated them after the twelfth century. He preferred instead a copy of a manuscript, now lost, said to be 'very ancient', and made in la Tour-de-Pin (about 56 km. south-east of Lyons) in 1571 by Jean Fournier, the curé of the church of St Chamond (St Aunemund), Lyons. This version from Tour-de-Pin seems to have provided the basic narrative upon which those rejected by Chifflet had drawn. These variants embellished the original narrative with detail and assumptions which favoured their own special interests. They also betrayed their later composition by misunderstanding the historical setting of the story of Aunemund. Nonetheless, Chifflet apparently incorporated into his edition two such points of later detail: an alternative name for Aunemund (Dalphinus) and the burial place of his brother.[9] So the text available to us in the seventh September volume of the *Acta Sanctorum* is basically that found in the manuscript described by Fournier in 1571 as 'very ancient' with what appear to be Chifflet's minor additions. Whether or not the *Acta* do conserve a genuine Merovingian tradition and thus allow access to Merovingian history cannot in these circumstances rely upon a manuscript tradition but must rest upon examination of the content and context of the *Acta* themselves.

9 For how the edition of the *Acta Aunemundi* in the *Acta Sanctorum* was assembled, see Perrier's 'Commentarius Praevius', ch. 2, pp. 724–7, and Coville, *Recherches*, pp. 372–5. Coville had the benefit of additional information on Chifflet's work provided by the Bollandist, Poncelet.

The *Acta Aunemundi* do display features strongly suggestive of
genuinely early composition. As Alfred Coville noted in his masterly
work on early medieval Lyons, the text speaks of events as if they were
recent and its prologue ends with a reference to a previous account of
Aunemund's life: 'I shall therefore once again tell of the life of Dalfinus
or St Aunemund and describe his martyrdom.'[10] Throughout the text
Aunemund is called simply 'bishop', whereas after the Merovingian
period the head of the church of Lyons was referred to by his proper
title of archbishop. Unlike later versions, the text's detail concerning
the Merovingian court and rulers in chapter 3 is not at all anachronistic. The author also uses appropriate terminology to describe the royal
assembly at Marolle at which Aunemund's brother was condemned.

Coville argued that the description of Aunemund as of 'Roman stock'
(chapter 2) was another indication of early composition, early because
it showed that there were still people around who saw themselves as
'Roman', a consciousness which scholars had thought to have hardly
stretched beyond the seventh century.[11] But this apparently strong
argument looks much weaker in the light of modern opinion, which
tends to see 'Roman' identity surviving as a form of political
consciousness well into the ninth century and even beyond.[12] Furthermore, the other ethnic designation found in the *Acta* may actually
indicate composition later than the Merovingian period. In chapter 14
there is a reference to 'a certain German'. The expression used –
Theuton – is not seen elsewhere before the ninth century.[13] There is
another feature too which suggests a later touch: in chapter 2 the name
of Aunemund's predecessor as bishop is given as Viventiolus in error

10 Coville, *Recherches*, p. 375 and n. 4.

11 Coville, *Recherches*, p. 375. The traditional view, held until recently, was that ethnic
   difference in the kingdom of the Franks had so receded by the end of the seventh
   century that the memory of the old identities was preserved only in the names given
   to the areas in which the different groups had once predominated. For example, the
   name Burgundy preserved the memory of the Burgundians. Thus E. Ewig,
   'Volkstum und Volksbewusstsein im Frankenreich des 7. Jahrhunderts', *Settimane di
   Studio*, 5 (1958) (reprinted in Ewig, *Spatantikes und fränkisches Gallien*, vol. I, Beihefte
   der *Francia*, 3 (Munich, 1976), pp. 231–73). See also Amory, 'Names'.

12 Either as an identity defining nobility itself by insisting on genealogical continuity
   with the late Roman nobility, thus J.-P. Poly and E. Bournazel, *La Mutation féodale
   X^e–XIIe siècles* (Paris, 1980), pp. 315–35, or as one of various available identities, to
   be emphasised when politically appropriate, but with ethnicity generally less
   significant than position in the class structure; thus Geary, *Aristocracy*, p. 111. See
   pp. 101–12 of Geary's work for an excellent discussion of the question of early
   medieval ethnicity. In relation to the *Acta Aunemundi* both views would allow the
   designation 'Roman' to be ninth century or later.

for Viventius. Viventiolus had indeed been a famous bishop of Lyons, but he had lived at the beginning of the sixth century.[14] This error suggests an author somewhat removed from the events of seventh-century Lyons. And, finally, in chapter 6 the author has Aunemund speak of having chosen King Clothar as his lord. A subject's ability to choose his lord is usually associated with the fragmentation of political authority from the late ninth century onwards. It looks distinctly odd in a Merovingian context. We have, therefore, features which suggest writing both at an early date, possibly as early as the seventh century, and at a later date, ninth-century or later. It thus looks as if we should accept the statement with which the author closes his prologue and regard the printed text as a ninth-century (or perhaps later) redaction of a Merovingian work.

We have other texts of more certain provenance and with a more certain line of development where we can see a similar process of redaction. In these we can observe the preservation of an original narrative outline which functioned as the framework for later embellishment and adaption.[15] In this volume the *Passio Leudegarii* provides the best example of a text which developed in this way. Its development shows us clearly how later generations stripped from the original narrative detail which no longer made sense to them, replacing it with more suitable material.[16] If we were to look at the *Acta Aunemundi* in this way, then it would be reasonable to suppose that the work's basic narrative is relatively unchanged from the original but that we should be wary of reported speeches, lengthy descriptive passages and posthumous miracles. In fact such elements are not dominant in the *Acta*, which is a relatively concise work. When we strip them away we are left with a narrative which does indeed look as if it were first composed in a period close to the events it describes.

13 The term *nationes Theotiscae* is first seen *c.* 830: H. Eggers, 'Nachlese zur Frühgeschichte des Wortes Deutsch', in H. Eggers (ed.), *Der Volksname Deutsch, Wege der Forschung,* 156 (Darmstadt, 1970), pp. 374–91. The form used here – *Theuton* – has origins in classical terminology, e.g. Caesar, *De Bellis Gallicis* 7, 7. The return to classical usage, like the introduction of the vernacular *Volksname,* is a development of the Carolingian period.

14 For the succession of bishops in Lyons, L. Duchesne, *Fastes épiscopaux de l'ancienne Gaule,* vol. 2 (Paris, 1910), pp. 157–61; on Viventiolus, Coville, *Recherches,* pp. 308–16, and on the confusion between Viventiolus and Viventius, *Recherches,* p. 387.

15 For a clear illustration of this process, see H. Delehaye, *The Legends of the Saints,* fourth edition, trans. D. Attwater (London, 1962), pp. 101–16

16 See below, pp. 206–9.

We have already mentioned the *Acta*'s detail describing the
Merovingian court. More generally, the story the *Acta* tell is perfectly
comprehensible in terms of what is known from other sources about
the political history of the period. Particularly striking is the theme of
local rivalry to Aunemund, rivalry which brings about his downfall:
'But whilst he thus stretched out his arm to feel the glory of his
achievement, it certainly seemed to the brethren [*fratres*] that he was
in company too elevated, and he fell back as everybody came to hate
him. Such people treacherously began to plot against him ...'. Again,
by analogy with the development of the *Passio Leudegarii*, and also
with the *Passio Praejecti*, it seems likely that a theme of local hostility
to the saint would be a feature of early composition, at a time when the
active memory of the intended audience would have forced any author
to include their common view of events.[17] Thus the outline of the story
of the bishop of Lyons, a magnate of the first order, who was a
prominent actor in royal politics and who met his end through a
combination of central and local political opposition, looks to be an
account we can trust.

Apart from the *Acta* and the four charters bearing Aunemund's name,
there is another source of information about him. This is the *Life of
Bishop Wilfrid*, written by one Stephanus, which we know to be a
contemporary work.[18] We must consider Stephanus's account in some
detail, because at first sight it appears to contradict the *Acta*. Wilfrid,
who lived from *c.* 633 to 709, was a Northumbrian bishop who in the
course of a stormy career had a great deal of contact with the
Continental Church. This contact began with a stay in Lyons in 653.
There, Stephanus tells us, he met Aunemund, who was so impressed
with the young Wilfrid that he tried to get him to stay in Lyons for
ever by offering him 'a good part of Gaul over which you shall be
permanent governor, and you shall have for your wife a maiden who
is my niece'. But Wilfrid was on his way to Rome and could not be
deflected from his vow to visit the Apostolic See.[19] On the return
journey, however, Wilfrid is said to have spent three years in Lyons

---

17 Suggestions of hostility to Leudegar: *Passio Leudegarii*, chs. 10, 12, 21 and 30,
   below, pp. 226–8, 229–30, 237–8 and 245–6. Note also the leniency with which
   Praejectus's biographer treats his subject's persecutors, who were still alive at the
   time he was writing: *Passio Praejecti*, chs. 31, 38 and 39, below, pp. 294–5, 298–9 and
   299–300.

18 *The Life of Bishop Wilfrid by Eddius Stephanus*, ed. and trans. B. Colgrave
   (Cambridge, 1927, reprinted New York, 1985).

19 *Life of Wilfrid*, ch. 4.

with Aunemund, being parted from him only by the latter's death, a fate he is said nearly to have shared. Aunemund's executioners refused at the last moment to harm him once it was discovered that Wilfrid was an Englishman.[20]

Stephanus's account of Aunemund and his death differs substantially from that given in the *Acta*: Stephanus refers to the bishop throughout as Dalphinus (in the *Acta* he is called only Aunemund); Dalphinus is killed on the orders of Queen Balthild in a purge in which eight other bishops are also killed (in the *Acta* only Aunemund and his unnamed brother are killed); Wilfrid is present at his death (he is never mentioned in the *Acta*); the killing takes place as a formal daytime execution (in the *Acta* it is a secret night-time assasination) and, finally, unlike in the *Acta*, in Stephanus's account there is no mention of the bishop's brother or of the abbot of Luxeuil, Waldebert.

Regarding Stephanus's first-hand knowledge of Wilfrid's career, scholars have traditionally tried to reconcile the two versions. This has meant incorporating the name Dalphinus into the *Acta* account, as Chifflet did. He saw that a later version of the *Acta* from the church of St Nicetius called the bishop both Aunemund and Dalphinus. So, presumably on the basis that the name Dalphinus is also found in the *Life of Wilfrid*, a source he knew clearly predated all surviving versions of the *Acta*, he added the name into the version of the text he had taken from the Tour-de-Pin copy. It seems, however, that it was the St Nicetius compiler himself who added the name to the *Acta*, having taken it from a reading of Bede's résumé of Stephanus's *Life of Wilfrid*.[21] Another solution was to assume that Dalphinus must have been the name of Aunemund's brother.[22] The brother is indeed called Dalphinus in the 'Will of Aunemund', but that source is a twelfth-century composition which looks as if it too has taken the name from an English source in order to be able to give a name to all the members of the martyr's family. Interestingly, the transfer of the name from

---

20 *Life of Wilfrid*, ch. 6.

21 For full discussion of the Aunemund/Dalphinus problem, see Coville, *Recherches*, pp. 381–5. Note also that as late as the early eleventh century Aunemund's brother was still nameless, though included in the martyr's cult (see the document quoted at n. 7 above). This may suggest that borrowing from the English sources took place after this time. Bede's résumé of the *Life of Wilfrid* is to be found in *Historia Ecclesiastica*, V, ch. 19, ed. C. Plummer, *Venerabilis Baedae Opera Historica* (Oxford, 1896), pp. 320–30.

22 So, for example, Colgrave in his notes to ch. 4 of the *Life of Wilfrid*, p. 153.

brother to bishop appears to be bound up with the dispute between St Peter's and St Nicetius, the latter first claiming the relics of the brother and then those of Aunemund himself. Indeed, the difference between the *Acta* and Stephanus over the name they call the bishop may well have been a factor in the origin of this dispute. In any case, both these name changes in the *Acta*'s tradition are based on very much later readings of versions of the Stephanus account.

Reconciliation of Stephanus and the *Acta* has also meant dating Aunemund's death to fit in with the known chronology of Wilfrid's movements.[23] But in the light of recent research this fit, which was always painfully tight, is no longer possible. We can be reasonably certain both that Wilfrid had returned to England by the end of 658 and that Aunemund signed a charter at the beginning of September 660.[24] It thus seems that Wilfrid had not been present at the martyrdom after all, and in the light of this observation confidence in the superiority of Stephanus's version collapses. On the difference in names we can say little, except to note, with Coville, that, about the time Wilfrid was in Lyons, Aunemund signed a charter in his own hand: *Aunemundus pecator consenciens subscripsi.* It was by the name Aunemund that the Bishop of Lyons was known to his contemporaries in the Frankish kingdom.[25]

In general terms it is surely anachronistic to think that in this kind of writing contemporaneity will of itself guarantee a greater degree of

---

23 Cf. C. Plummer's chronology of Wilfrid's *Life* in *Venerabilis Baedae Opera Historica*, vol. 2, pp. 316–20. This was the chronology Coville used, *Recherches*, p. 390.

24 Emmo's charter for Saint-Colombe-de-Sens (Pardessus, *Diplomata*, vol. 2, no. 333) was drawn up *anno tertio regnante domno Clothario glorioso rege* on 1 September 660. For discussion of the authenticity of text and witness list, see P. Deschamps, 'Critique de Privilège Episcopal accordé par Emmon de Sens à l'abbaye de Sainte-Colombe (660, 20 août)', *Le Moyen-âge*, second series, 16 (1912), but *caveat* Deschamps's August dating. More recently, see E. Ewig, 'Beobachtungen zu den Bischofsprivilegien für Saint-Maur-des-Fossés und Saint-Colombe-de-Sens', in *Festschrift Ludwig Petry, Geschichtliche Landeskunde*, vol. 5, pt. 2 (Wiesbaden, 1969), pp. 1–24 (reprinted *Gallien*, vol. 2, pp. 485–506). Coville, though citing Deschamps, who thought the charter basically sound, rejected its authenticity on the basis that, according to Plummer's chronology, Aunemund could not possibly have witnessed it: *Recherches*, pp. 389–90. Coville also ignored another Sens charter of much more obvious authenticity and also dated to the third year of Clothar III's reign: Pardessus, *Diplomata*, vol. 2, no. 335. This document alone serves to make a death date of 658 an impossibility. For the relationship between the two Sens charters, Deschamps, 'Critique', 144–6; Ewig, 'Saint-Maur und Saint-Colombe', pp. 4–5 and n. 10; p. 21.

25 The original of this charter has survived, preserving Aunemund's signature: *ChLA*, no. 558.

reliability. It may, if audience and author share common knowledge, but if they do not, the author can strain the bounds of credibility to build up the holy status of his or her subject. This pattern of variable restraint in writing is plainly visible in Stephanus's work. When writing about Wilfrid's career in England he is restrained to the point of being candid, because his English audience was likely to be familiar with the events described, but events on the Continent, beyond the horizons of his audience, are treated much more freely, even fantastically.[26] In associating Wilfrid with Aunemund's martyrdom Stephanus's aim, in Janet Nelson's words, was 'not factual reporting but the establishment of Wilfrid's saintly credentials at an early point in his *Vita*'.[27] One should add that Stephanus also reveals a hint of contemporary English criticism of Wilfrid's stay in Lyons.[28] His account of the martyrdom further serves to justify his hero's Continental dalliance.

If we take Wilfrid out of the martrydom scene, Stephanus's other references to Lyons, to Aunemund and to his death hardly conflict with the *Acta*. Indeed, the two sources could embody a single seventh-century tradition, for both emphasise the great material, as well as spiritual, power Aunemund and his family had in Lyons; both suggest that the decision to have the bishop killed originated in the royal court; they both tell of how Aunemund was ordered to appear before the court (or simply 'the dukes' in Stephanus's account), suggesting that he would be put to death on arrival, and, finally, both have the bishop accompanied by a holy man as he set out on the journey to his death. Abbot Waldebert's role in the *Acta* as confidant and spiritual comforter

---

26 For example, contrast Stephanus's coloured but revealing account of the Council of Austrefeld at which Wilfrid was condemned in 702 or 703, *Life of Wilfrid*, chs. 46–8, pp. 92–101, with his claim that the wicked Frankish leader Ebroin had tried to offer a barrelfull of gold for Wilfrid, dead or alive: ch. 27, pp. 52–5, and note that in the next chapter the same amount is offered to procure the death of someone else in a quite different context. For comment on Stephanus's purpose in telling this story in two contexts, see I. Wood, 'Pagans and Holy Men, 600–800', in P. Ní Chatáin and P. Richter (eds.), *Irland und die Christenheit* (Stuttgart, 1987), pp. 350–1.

27 J. L. Nelson, 'Queens as Jezabels: the Careers of Brunhild and Balthild in Merovingian History', in *Studies in Church History*, Subsidia, vol. 1 (1978), 66 (article reprinted in J. L. Nelson, *Politics and Ritual*, pp. 1–49).

28 It seems that Wilfrid and his mentor Benedict Biscop fell out over Wilfrid's delay in Lyons on the way to Rome. Stephanus himself compared the disagreement to that between St Paul and Barnabas (Acts 15:35–8): *Life of Wilfrid* ch. 3, p. 9. Biscop, the founder of Bede's own monastery, was an important figure in the early Anglo-Saxon Church. Any disapproval he may have voiced concerning Wilfrid's relationship with Aunemund would have been significant. Such disapproval may have contributed to Bede's somewhat cool attitude towards Wilfrid.

of Aunemund is rather like the role Stephanus gives to Wilfrid, and if this detail had appeared in the original Merovingian version of the text it could plausibly have influenced Stephanus's view of Wilfrid's relationship with Aunemund. The opposite case, that Stephanus's account could have been the basis of the tradition found in the *Acta*, seems impossible, given the weight of local detail which shapes the latter version but which is absent from the *Life of Wilfrid*.

We have already noted that the pattern of events in the *Acta Aunemundi* resembles that seen in other sources from this period. Let us now consider the story of the *Acta* in context. In later Merovingian Francia bishops, and even abbots, do not seem to have enjoyed much immunity from the violence of the high politics in which, as leading magnates, they were involved. Such involvement and its consequences are a main strand running through the works presented in this collection. We have also seen how traditional attempts to deduce clear patterns and 'policies' from the unfolding of events in the narrative sources have often led to too rigid an interpretation of the small store of information we have for this period.[29] No less than any of the other works presented here, the *Acta Aunemundi* have suffered their share of misinterpretation in this way. In conjunction with excerpts from the *Life of Wilfrid* they have been used to support complementary views of mid seventh-century Merovingian politics: namely that in this period there was a desire for political centralisation which, it is held, existed alongside and partly stimulated a separatist tendency, or at least a desire for local autonomy, in the outlying regions of the kingdom of the Franks. These opposing wants, it is said, gave rise to tension between centre and periphery in the kingdom. The unfortunate end of Aunemund is thus seen as the resolution of such tension in favour of the centre.[30]

---

29 See above, pp. 54–5.

30 This is how the *Acta Aunemundi* are interpreted in L. Dupraz, *Le Royaume des Francs. Contribution à l'histoire du Regnum Francorum pendant le troisième quart du VII* siècle* (Friboug-en-Suisse, 1948), pp. 342–4 and esp. pp. 353–4 for a particularly strong statement of the centralisation/separatism scheme; J. Fischer, Der Hausmeier Ebroin (dissertation, Bonn, 1954), pp. 90–8; M. Chaume, *Les Origines du duché du Bourgogne* (Dijon, 1926), p. 22; E. Ewig, 'Die Fränkischen Teilreiche im 7. Jahrhundert (613–714)', *Trierer Zeitschrift* 22, 1953, 122 (reprinted *Gallien*, vol. 1, pp.172–230). Both Chaume and Ewig made ethnic difference ('Burgundian' as opposed to 'Frank') a factor in Aunemund's separatism, but note that Ewig later changed his mind and had the bishop as a typical autonomist leading what he characterised as an 'episcopal republic': E. Ewig, 'Milo et eiusmodi similes', in *Sankt Bonifatius. Gedenkgaben zum zwölfhundertsten Todestag* (Fulda, 1954) (reprinted *Gallien*, vol. 2, pp. 189–219), pp. 432–3. F. Prinz, *Frühes Mönchtum im Frankenreich*

There are many objections to this schematic view of Merovingian history. Above all, it squeezes too much out of too little information, yet it also encourages one to read the sources selectively and simplistically. In this case the centralist/separatist argument ignores the emphasis the *Acta* give both to the bishop's closeness to the Merovingian court, and to the role of the clergy of Lyons in his downfall. Instead the argument chooses to concentrate on the prominence of the bishop's family in Lyons, on the charge of treason he faced, on the force sent to fetch him from Lyons and on the close relationship between Queen Balthild and Genesius, Aunemund's successor as bishop of Lyons. It is thus selecting from the source only those elements which fit the pattern of supposed growing provincial autonomy and of sharp central reaction to that growth. When we take into account all the elements in the outline of the story in the *Acta* our picture of events may be less tidy, but it remains one which more closely parallels what we know about the demise of other Church leaders in that society. In context, then, there is really no reason to seek a tidier or simpler interpretation, and what we see in the *Acta Aunemundi* is not to be taken merely as the clash of radically opposed local and central interests. All we can say with certainty is that we are looking at a man from a very powerful family who had enemies both in his home town and among the elite who made up the Merovingian court. In circumstances the exact nature of which are lost to us the two groups combined to bring the family crashing down. Let us now try to understand how such a combination succeeded, and how the whole episode relates to the more general context of Merovingian politics.

Aunemund certainly was one of the powerful elite who frequented the Merovingian courts. His power had two sources: his family's position in Lyons, and his own position within the Merovingian Church. In accord with his very high status he had been 'fostered and grew up' in the courts of the kings Dagobert I and Clovis II, and his future as bishop of Lyons was assured when, quite uncanonically, but possibly not unusually, he was consecrated bishop by his predecessor.[31] As

---

(Munich, 1965), p. 176, used the centralisation model but argued that resistance to the centre was directed at the court-backed Iro-Frankish monasticism which was rapidly expanding in this period. Given that Aunemund chose as his protector Waldebert, abbot of Luxeuil, the leading house of this monastic movement, such an interpretation seems quite inappropriate. For a more recent analysis of Aunemund's career in terms of the centralisation/separatism model, see also H. Müller, 'Die Kirche von Lyon im Karolingerreich', *Historisches Jahrbuch*, 107 (1987), 226–9.

31 See below, p. 181, n. 45.

bishop he is said to have baptised, or even to have stood as godfather to, Clovis II's firstborn son, Clothar III, and the charter evidence supports the *Acta* when they tell us that he was fully involved in the affairs of the realm, although it is reasonable to assume that they effectively exaggerate the pivotal nature of his position at court. From the information we have it is not possible to say exactly why Aunemund and his brother fell foul of the rest of the powerful. The detail that the clergy of Lyons provided the basis for an accusation of treason is one which looks too awkward to have been invented. That they should have disliked their bishop and were sensitive to any opportunity of getting rid of him seems unsurprising, as does their desire to involve outsiders with the power to bring him down by force.[32] Likewise a vigorous response from the centre, equally eager for opportunities to keep channels of patronage open and magnates in line, is in context quite normal.[33] But what opened up those opportunities is the key question. The *Acta* allow two suggestions: firstly that Aunemund planned to overthrow the regime – too standard and too general a charge to tell us much, as is the accusation that the bishop was greedy. Secondly, however, we learn that Aunemund was accused of secretly trying to bring in a foreign people, an *extranea gens*. This corresponds to an earlier statement that the bishop was so renowned that 'neighbouring peoples strove to please him from a distance with their gifts' (chapter 2). If these details have survived from the original Merovingian version of the work, then perhaps Aunemund really had been thinking of treason. 'Foreigners' in such circumstances could conceivably have been either the Visigoths or the Lombards. The emphasis on people in the plural makes it unlikely that the reference was to the outsider Wilfrid. There is no evidence to suggest that at that time the Visigoths were keen to push out from Septimania, the territory they held in southern Gaul, which was adjacent to Provence. In the year 673 they were active on the border with Frankish Provence, but they were plainly uncomfortable with the prospect of crossing over into Frankish territory.[34] There is, however, some evidence of clashes between Lombards and Franks in this period. Some time between 660 and 663 Franks from Provence invaded the Lombard kingdom, according to the historian of the Lombards, Paul

---

32 Both these factors figure too in the *Passio Praejecti* and the *Passio Leudegarii*.

33 For a description of this process as a 'circulation of power from the court to the provinces and back', Nelson, 'Brunhild and Balthild', 64 (*Politics and Ritual*, p. 35).

34 *Historia Wambae*, ch. 27, ed. W. Levison, *MGH, SSRM*, V, pp. 522–4.

the Deacon, writing in the late eighth century. He tells us that a Frankish army was defeated at Aosta in Italy.[35] It is possible that this invasion was in retaliation for Lombard support for Aunemund, support summoned at the bishop's bidding. Another possibility is that a later compiler added the detail about 'foreigners' because he was influenced by the story of the infamous Maurontus who as leader of Provence in the year 737 was said to have invited in the Saracens, in order to sustain a rebellion against Charles Martel.[36] The question of whether Aunemund really was involved with a 'foreign people' must remain open.

Overall we can be more positive in our contextual reading of the *Acta Aunemundi*. They show us that in the mid seventh century Lyons was to be counted as an integral part of the Neustro-Burgundian kingdom. The readiness of factions within the town to call upon central power also helps explain why Lyons was to remain open to intervention from the court for a very long time to come. The *Acta*, in short, make an important contribution to our understanding of how the kingdom held itself together in a framework of mutual self-interest. The collection of sources in this volume illustrates such a framework again and again. The particular value of this source is that it provides an example of the balance of power in an area which was not only distant from the centre but in which one family held both secular and ecclesiastical control during the reign of a child king. The story of the martyrdom of Bishop Aunemund thus provides us with a valuable lesson in Merovingian history.

Acta Aunemundi
(The Deeds of Aunemund)

CHAPTER 1

The miracles the martyrs of old once performed with divine help now light up the world, and their bodies, sown into the earth, shine like the starry bodies of the heavens. Those who have followed the path to martyrdom will likewise perform miracles. Heavenly Jerusalem, like a city, is always being built of living and chosen rock; nevertheless she

---

35 *Pauli Historia Langobardorum*, V, ch. 5, ed. G. Waitz, *MGH, SSRG* (Hanover, 1878), pp. 185–6.

36 The story of Maurontus is told in the *Continuations of the Chronicle of Fredegar*, chs. 20–1, ed. and trans. J. M. Wallace-Hadrill (London, 1960), pp. 93–6.

rejoices to be refurbished by the gathering, little by little, of holy souls. With scarcely less glory the earth has been made rich by martyrs' gore and now delights having been soaked in rosy redness. Thus effort must be made so that as their merits rise up to the heavens their limbs on earth are turned into salvation for men. Nor do we consider it idle to prize the faithful ones yonder whose miracles from on high stand out amongst the people.[37] I shall therefore once again tell of the life of Dalfinus, or St Aunemund, and describe his martyrdom.[38]

CHAPTER 2

He was the son of a man of most illustrious standing, Sigo, the *praefectus*,[39] and of Petronia[40] and he was fostered and grew up in the court of King Dagobert and his son, King Clovis, who ruled in his place.[41] He was, however, of Roman stock,[42] and, always endowed with authority, he was honoured with public office. For he was an excellent man, approachable and businesslike yet witty, brave yet humble, prudent and just, mild in his rebukes, the winner in public debates, just

37 In context the meaning here appears to be that the relics of miracle-working martyrs should be venerated, and that veneration will be rewarded by God. As this prologue shows, the purpose of the whole work is to encourage worship at an existing cult rather than the establishment of a new focus of worship. There is thus no need to argue at length for Aunemund's sanctity. This may indicate that there was an earlier hagiographic tradition which had set out Aunemund's saintly credentials at greater length.

38 The name Dalfinus is not found in sources from early medieval Lyons itself: see above, pp. 173–4 and n. 21. The term *rursus* ('again') is a further indication of a tradition older than the one presented here.

39 The term *praefectus* is unusual in the Merovingian context. More usual for a position of high secular command in southern Gaul would be the term *patricius*: see above, p. 167, n. 3.

40 The 'Will of Aunemund' spuriously names the whole family, giving the name Dalphinus to Aunemund's brother and inventing two sisters, Petronilla and Lucia, said to be nuns at the convent of St Peter's, and on whose behalf Aunemund donates property to St Peter's: see Coville, *Recherches*, Appendix I, p. 409.

41 Dagobert ruled 622–38 , Clovis 638–57. A feature of later versions of the *Acta* is that they reverse the order of these kings, thereby showing little understanding of the historical background. An upbringing in the royal court was conventional for young males of the highest nobility, cf. *Vita Audoini*, chs. 2–3, above, pp. 154–5, and for the queen as 'nurse' to them, *Vita Balthildis*, ch. 4, above, pp. 121–2. It is Aunemund's close connection with the Merovingian court which provides the stongest argument against the 'separatist' interpretation of these events discussed above, pp. 176–7.

42 A notion of 'Roman' identity persisted throughout the early Middle Ages in southern Gaul, see above, p. 170 and nn. 11, 12.

in giving judgement, unusually kind, devoted in his almsgiving and outstanding in his generosity, for he also had extensive property.[43] It came to pass that he was chosen to be Bishop of Lyons by Viventiolus,[44] who, whilst still occupying the position, consecrated him bishop by the grace of Christ.[45] In short, the Lord heaped such favour upon him that the people paid him respect to an unusual degree, and neighbouring peoples strove to please him from a distance with their

43 The content and style of this passage are reminiscent of the late Roman bishop's epitaph. Several epitaphs are recorded for bishops of Lyons who lived in the fifth and sixth centuries and who were buried in the church of St Nicetius at Lyons. In particular, the epitaph of Bishop Rusticus (d. 501) uses language similar to that seen here in the description of Aunemund's career before he became bishop: Rusticus was *fascibus emeritis et summo honore functus*; Aunemund was *semper ditionum honore praeditus, atque publicis fascibus honoratus*. Although the language is late Roman, it cannot be used to indicate that the passage was composed at a genuinely early date, for not only does this kind of writing survive into a much later period, but throughout the early Middle Ages these Lyons epitaphs were visible, and could be read, in the church of St Nicetius. Thus at any point in this period they could have served as a model for the description of the secular career of a bishop. On the epitaphs and the light they shed on the early episcopate, see M. Heinzelmann, *Bischofsherrschaft in Gallien*, Beihefte der *Francia*, 5 (Zurich, 1976), p. 103 for Rusticus.

44 In fact Viventius, not Viventiolus, had been Aunemund's predecessor, see above, p. 171, n. 14.

45 Ordination in this way was quite uncanonical: bishops could not choose and ordain their successors. That this did happen is suggested by the repeated legislation forbidding it. The Council of Paris in 614, for instance, decreed that: ... *nullus episcoporum se vivente alium in loco suo non elegat*, and this instruction was given royal backing in Clothar II's edict of the same year: *Ut nullus episcoporum se vivente eligat successorem*: C. de Clercq (ed.), *Concilia Gallia 511–695, Corpus Christianorum, Series Latina*, 148A (Turnhout, 1963), pp. 276 and 283. Ordination by predecessor was accepted practice among the Anglo-Saxons in this period: Boniface asked Pope Zachary if he himself might appoint his successor, and note how this was initially refused on canon law grounds: *S. Bonifatii et Lulli Epistolae*, ed. M. Tangl, *MGH, Epist. selectae*, I (Berlin, 1955), no. 51, pp. 86–92. However, failure to observe canon law in episcopal appointment was so common in Francia that it would be rash to argue that the English tradition must somehow have influenced this description of Aunemund's ordination. A more likely influence is Gregory of Tours' statement that his great-uncle Nicetius had been chosen bishop of Lyons by his predecessor, Sacerdos. It is more surprising to see the tradition of Aunemund's ordination by predecessor carried on into the later Middle Ages, into a period in which the admission of such a basic contravention of canon law would, one supposes, have been embarrassing. The 'Will of Aunemund' abbreviates the *Acta* account in a form which could almost echo the Merovingian legislation: *Viventiolus, eiusdem ecclesiae archiepiscopus, qui me praefate ecclesiae se vivente archiepiscopum ordinavit*. A possible explanation for the retention of this apparently awkward detail is that by being in obvious contrast with contemporary observance it could give the document the spurious appearance of antiquity.

gifts.[46] By the king and his followers[47] he was held in such esteem that whatever he asked for from them he got, and nobody was able to get anything for their own benefit unless he [Aunemund] won it by his own request from King Clothar III who had become his godson at the font of holy baptism.[48] But since, with arm extended,[49] he claimed the glory of his position, it certainly seemed to the brethren that he was in company too elevated and he fell back as everybody came to hate him. Such people treacherously began to plot against him, making the underhand accusation that he was machinating to overthrow the rule of that same Clothar who was king at that time.[50]

CHAPTER 3

Meanwhile there was an assembly convened at the king's command at the palace[51] called Marolle, which was built in a suburb near the town of Orléans. To this assembly came the king's followers, those nobles of high birth and dukes, along with the people, according to the usual custom,[52] and they believed that the blessed bishop and his brethren

46 Who these *finitimae gentes* were must remain a mystery, but the most likely possibility in a mid seventh-century context is that they were Lombards: see above, pp. 178–9.

47 The term *proceres* can mean both nobles in general and the nobles of the king's entourage in particular. The latter meaning is preferred here because the author is speaking about the royal palace, and because in the next chapter a distinction is drawn between the *proceres* and the more general *majores natu.*

48 Note that it says not that Aunemund baptised Clothar, but that he stood as godfather to him, although later, in ch. 8, the author does seem to be saying that he baptised him and does not refer to the godparenthood. This difference may signal that there was a tradition that Aunemund had been present at Clothar's baptism, but that the author was himself unsure whether it was as officiating priest or as godfather. According to the contemporary *Vita Eligii.* II, ch. 32, ed. B. Krusch, *MGH, SSRM,* IV, p. 717, the other godfather was Eligius, bishop of Noyon. Aunemund is not mentioned. If Clothar had indeed become *filiolus* to Aunemund, it would show that the latter really had been close to the Merovingian family. On spiritual kinship in general, see J. H. Lynch, *Godparents and Kinship in Early Medieval Europe* (Princeton, New Jersey, 1986).

49 *Brachium extentum* – this is the 'accusative absolute' construction, more typical of Merovingian than of Carolingian Latin.

50 This sentence strongly indicates that Aunemund's downfall was partly the result of rivalry within the church of Lyons, but also that it was necessary to call upon outside support to bring the powerful bishop down. On the conjunction of central and local interest here, see above, p. 178.

51 *Villa* is the word used here.

52 Stress on the customary nature of such assemblies was standard in both the Merovingian and the Carolingian periods. The meetings had both a political and a

would come too. But having been worn out by his recent hard work, he was still exhausted and could not come. Then they revealed the deceit they had planned for the holy bishop. His brother, who eminently discharged the office of prefect of Lyons (which is the head of Gaul and of other territories)[53] they falsely accused of treason, and the king and Balthild,[54] the queen, had his head cut off. His poor body having been carried away, the townspeople took it and handed it over for burial to the Church of the Apostles and the Forty-eight Martyrs.[55] It was via his brother's fate that the man of God learned that he would lose his own life too. But, though his spirit was ready, his flesh was always weak, and, having gone a little way from his town, he faltered and turned back.[56]

judicial function which drew strength from the backing of those present. The power of judgement of these court assemblies could be impressive: witness the fate of Aunemund's brother. For another Merovingian assembly in action, see *Passio Leudegarii*, chs. 5–6, below, pp. 222–3, and *Passio Praejecti*, chs. 24–5, below, pp. 289–91. For the political role of the assemblies, see P. Fouracre. 'Merovingians, Mayors of the Palace and the notion of a "low-born" Ebroin', *Bulletin of the Institute of Historical Research*, 57 (1984); for their judicial role, Fouracre, '"Placita" and the settlement of disputes'.

53 Lyons is described as *caput Galliae vel aliarum civitatum*. This is an unusual description. *Galliae* (pl.) usually refers to the former Roman provinces of the Gauls, but here the meaning appears to be restricted to the area around Lyons. *Gallia* (sing.) is used by Julian of Toledo in the later seventh century to describe Visigothic Septimania. The idea of a province of Gallia in the Lyons area could come from Gothic usage, but it more likely reflects the contemporary ecclesiastical organisation, in which Lyons was the premier diocese of the Church of Gaul. If this is so, then perhaps *civitates* should be translated as 'dioceses'.

54 The author does not condemn Balthild here, unlike Stephanus, who in the *Life of Bishop Wilfrid*, ch. 3, called her a second Jezebel and claimed that she had eight other bishops killed too: see above, p. 173. Elsewhere, of course, we see Balthild portrayed as a saint in the *Vita Balthildis*.

55 This was the church of St Nicetius in Lyons, the church which claimed to hold the relics of the executed brother. The detail was taken by Chifflet from a version of the *Acta* associated with the church of St Nicetius and added to the edition prepared largely from a copy of a manuscript from La-Tour-de-Pin.

56 It noteworthy that Aunemund should attempt to go to the assembly even though he knew what lay in store for him. This may not just be the hagiographer's wishful thinking: by charging others, often termed *fideiussores* (legal sureties or guarantors), with the responsibility of presenting the accused before the court, the Frankish judicial system could sometimes be very effective. The *Passio Praejecti*, chs. 23–4, below, pp. 288–90, provides an example of the system in operation. In Frankish procedure if the accused consistently failed to attend court, then they lost their case. Where the charge was treason, failure to attend would have rendered the accused immediately liable to capital punishment. That liability provides the context for what follows in the *Acta*. For a cogent discussion of suretyship in practice in a sub-Frankish context, see W. Davies, 'Suretyship in the *Cartulaire de Redon*', in T. Charles-Edwards, M. Owen and D. Walters (eds.), *Lawyers and Laymen* (Cardiff, 1986), pp. 72–91; on procedure in the Frankish courts, P. Fouracre '"Placita" and the settlement of disputes', pp. 34–7.

CHAPTER 4

Mindful of the prize, and wanting to be rewarded with martyrdom, he retraced his steps to his own town. At once he sent for the man of God, Waldebert, who ruled over the monks of Luxeuil as their abbot,[57] asking him to come as quickly as possible with just a few servants. Whereupon this man of God understood what idea lay behind such a request and without delay took himself to the walls of Lyons. The two men greeted each other with tears and, still weeping, exchanged pious kisses, then separated to remove themselves to a more remote place to mourn for others. And there his elder refreshed his purpose with fitting encouragement and congratulated him on the speed with which he had made up his mind.[58] Then, receiving his confession,[59] they spent the whole day and the night in saying prayers and keeping vigil. Nevertheless, three dukes had already been despatched with orders to convey the blessed Bishop Aunemund under sure guard to the king, or, if he resisted, to leave him behind as a corpse. And with ever quickening step they approached Lyons.

CHAPTER 5

Now as they hurried towards the aforesaid town to carry out what they had been ordered to do, God's servant [Aunemund] dreaded suffering and wanted to jump out of the way. Yet he turned back to the man of God [Waldebert] and said, 'It is better to undergo martyrdom as a result of this wickedly unfair charge than leave a bad example to others.' Thus he remained in the town which had been entrusted to his care, and so much did he exhaust himself in almsgiving, in fasting, in vigils and in continual prayer with his clergy, that, had he of late

---

57 Waldebert was abbot of Luxeuil 629–70. That he should have been summoned to protect Aunemund runs counter to F. Prinz's view that at the bottom of this whole affair lay tension between the long established monasticism of the Rhône valley, represented by the bishop of Lyons, and the more recent Iro-Frankish foundations modelled on Columbanus's house at Luxeuil: F. Prinz, *Frühes Mönchtum im Frankenreich*, p. 176. For further caution on exaggerating the distinction and tension between old and new in seventh-century Frankish monasticism, see I. Wood, 'A Prelude to Columbanus: the Monastic Achievement in the Burgundian Territories', in H. Clarke and M. Brennan (eds.), *Columbanus and Merovingian Monasticism*, British Archaeological Reports, International Series, 113 (Oxford, 1981). Note that Praejectus too associated himself with a holy man when under threat: *Passio Praejecti*, ch. 28, below, p. 292.

58 This is a loose translation of the difficult *de conventione suae celeritatis congratulans.*

59 Literally, 'his penitence having been received' (*accepta poenitentia*).

become guilty of anything through ignorance,[60] lamenting here he erased it through penitence. Then the town was surrounded by troops as they came to kill him, and they kindled fires here and there at the crossroads and destroyed everything in the forts. But when the servant of God had been told of these things, he at once celebrated the divine mysteries and, praying as if for a dead man, commended his spirit and soul to God. Then after he had received communion he spoke to those around him, saying, 'I beg you, my brethren, and I humbly entreat all you citizens that if in anything I have been unpleasant to you, or have taken anything by force, may you not consider me unworthy but in peace be forgiving.'

CHAPTER 6

But they all answered together, saying, 'Never, good Pastor, have you been unpleasant to us, nor have you seized anything from us by force. Indeed, from the least to the greatest of us we reckon that we have been uplifted and enriched by your gifts. Will you pardon our sins, so that whatever we have done against you in idleness we may, aided by your prayers, be able to correct?' Then the Holy Priest raised his eyes to heaven and said, 'Lord God Almighty, You who demanded the blood of Abel's destruction, who sacrificed Your son for all of us and pointed out the path of suffering to follow, whither He had gone before, and taught us to pray for our enemies, You who when St Stephen, your first martyr,[61] was trapped by a false accusation brought against him and beaten down by the blows of stones, swiftly hearkened to him when he prayed for his enemies and commended his spirit to You, I beseech You that You will not let me be cheated of this way of salvation, but that You will allow me to rejoice in the rest of those who have been unjustly persecuted and suffered. May You not account this sin to those who have forgotten their covenant with God and have violated their oath in the holy of holies. Almighty God, You discern my thought and the secrets of my heart are not hidden from You; [You know] if I have practised deception or wanted to destroy the king I chose to have as my earthly lord over me.[62] Because You repay to each

60 The suggestion is that he was capable of sinning only unintentionally.
61 The first martyr, Stephen, is the premier saint of the church of Lyons.
62 The notion of being able to choose one's lord looks out of place in a Merovingian context: it is more usually associated with later 'feudal' lordship. It is in areas of direct speech such as this that we should expect the work to have been most extensively re-written.

according to his own deeds, he who does not turn away from Your commandments You reward in the future with eternal bounty, and You give away far more even than You have promised.'

CHAPTER 7

And when he had finished praying, he fortified himself with the sign of the cross and bade farewell to them all, saying, 'To you I give my peace, and I shall carry the kiss of your love with me into eternity. Let not my disappearance upset you at all, for I am hurrying off to commend you to Christ. He has arranged that I alone should die and this is better than that He should need to have so many men horribly slaughtered on my account.[63] Then he left behind the mass of people who were following him, and with a picked band of comrades around him singing *Kyrie Eleison* and *Alleluia* he made his way as far as the commander of the soldiers. Then, having saluted them all, he said, 'Peace to you. I look upon you here standing with the crowd in an unaccustomed manner. If you have come here only for your salvation, today at my invitation and following my lead the Church will receive you as sons in peace. If, however, you wish to inflict some sort of punishment upon me, I shall neither turn away nor resist the words of your command.'

CHAPTER 8

Then spoke the commander, 'You may approach us today pretending to be meek, as if you have repented and are humble in heart, but you are not known as an innocent servant of God nor as a friend of the king.' To him the bishop replied, 'I had not thought that today I would hear this speech from your mouth, nor come to have known the one who publicly served the charge of high treason brought against me.[64] But hostile words do not cut down one who has no stain on his conscience. I have not become so wildly mad that I would envy the glory of the one whose name I took from the font, and of whose

---

63 In other words, he will not ask the citizens to resist on his behalf. A similar scenario is found in the *Passio Leudegarii*, chs. 21–2, below, pp. 237–9. In both cases it is hard not to conclude from the disinclination to resist that the bishop did not enjoy enough support to do so. Contrast the success of Genesius, Aunemund's successor as bishop of Lyons, in defending Lyons with the help of the citizens against another invading army in 675: *Passio Leudegarii*, ch. 26, below, pp. 242–3.

64 The meaning seems to be that Aunemund had not expected actually to meet his persecutors, not that he was already familiar with them.

Christianity I stand as witness,[65] and secretly try to bring in a foreign people.'[66] The deliverer of the charge said, 'It is not for us to argue with you over these or other things, or to wrangle with you over your superstitious words. Whilst you idled in this town, you were not as one in the priestly order, but you were here more like a tax collector.[67] Whereupon it is ordered that along with us you will be presented before the person of the king. And, to be sure, if you refuse, we will leave you here in this place, butchered.

CHAPTER 9

Then spoke the bishop, 'I will come with you unafraid, just as you have said.' With a smile on his face he was taken in hand by his enemies, and speaking bravely he demanded of their leaders that two priests and the same number of deacons and clergy should accompany him. On a different day, when they came to the town of Macon, the man of God wanted to visit and pray at the churches of the saints and to pay his due respects to Aganus,[68] bishop of that town, but he was prevented by

65 He is speaking of one *cuius nomen ego ex fonte paternum sumpsi cognomen, et testis Christianitatis existo.* This would seem to imply that Aunemund had actually baptised Clothar, rather than simply become his godfather as we learnt earlier, in ch. 2.

66 The *extranea gens* here is reminiscent of the *finitimae gentes* of ch. 2. Inviting in the foreign people seems here to be the basis of the charge of treason. It is a strange detail to invent, unless it echoes the memory of the eighth-century anti-Pippinid alliances between southern magnates and Saracen forces in Provence, for the term *gens* often means pagans. On the Saracens and the aristocracy of Provence, see P. Geary, *Aristocracy*, pp. 126–8. In the proper Merovingian context a more fitting interpretation of the phrase would be a possible alliance with the Lombards.

67 Dismissing Aunemund's speech as 'superstitious' looks odd in this context. The author is employing a convention which originated in the earliest accounts of the martyrs: on trial for his life, the martyr would make a profession of faith which the judge would dismiss as superstition. The proper context for this convention is the persecution of Christians in the Roman Empire: see H. Delehaye, *Les Passions des Martyrs et des genres littéraires* (second edition, Brussels, 1966), pp. 183–95. The second part of the charge against Aunemund seems to be that he abused his position as bishop for personal gain. This corresponds to the last sentence of ch. 5, where he begs forgiveness from the citizens: '... if in anything I have been unpleasant to you or have taken anything by force ...'. Again, it is reasonable to suppose that such non-complimentary detail is unlikely to have been invented, and it is interesting to note that, the second time it is made, the charge is not countered, so the detail is not here included simply to provide an opportunity to demonstrate the opposite view of Aunemund's episcopate. But here, as always, we should be wary of placing too much weight on passages which form part of speeches.

68 This is the only reference we have anywhere to a Bishop Aganus of Macon. There is, however, no reason to doubt the *Acta* on this point: the surviving list of bishops

the commander and his associates. Moreover, when the commander[69] saw that Abbot Waldebert, beloved of God, was constantly comforting him in Christ and carefully shielding him from the harm of his enemies, the dukes spoke to him in the following way, 'If you wish to accompany the bishop, that will be difficult for us and hinder our journey, for we have been ordered that he be led in and delivered up having been deprived by our effort of the comfort of priests and the conversation of friends.' But he [Waldebert] replied, 'My coming along does not hurt or hinder you at all. But I do see that chance to destroy him which you have made up your minds to seek.' All of them together said to him, 'This fate which you fear, let it befall us here or in the future if we fail to deliver him up into the presence of the king. So you leave today: at least let this be done – travel any other path along which you want to go.'[70]

CHAPTER 10

Thus the band of men hurried on into the diocese of Chalon and there, close by an estate of the town's church, they pitched their tents. Then a certain old priest of the neighbourhood, in order to encourage the man of God, hurried into the tent in which he was lying down and said, 'My lord, do not judge what is happening to you now as misfortune but reckon up the future benefits for the salvation of your soul. So endure your exile joyfully, undergo your martyrdom keenly, for those who have gone before you rewarded thus in such merit have likewise purchased rest in eternity by their gift. I beg you that out of love you will see fit to take a little bit of my meagre food ration and so refresh your body, which has been weakened by fasting'. Freely acceding to a request from the servant of God, he divided [the food] in two in the

---

of Macon is incomplete and often spurious for bishops before the ninth century, and there is nothing in any other source to preclude a Bishop Aganus at this time, for we know of no Bishop of Macon between 650 and 743: L. Duchesne, *Fastes Episcopaux*, vol. 2, pp. 196–9.

69 In consecutive sentences the author uses both *praeses* and *praefectus* to denote what, in context, must be the same person, the commander of the force. Presumably this commander was one of the three *duces*.

70 In other words, if Waldebert leaves, the dukes will find an opportunity to kill Aunemund. The author is here introducing a measure of dramatic tension, and whether the dukes really did mean to kill Aunemund after they had made this promise to Waldebert is left an open question. Such mystery is unusual in early medieval hagiography which normally prefers obvious villains who are demonstrably punished for the harm they do.

manner of worship and consumed the food offering with him. When eating was finished, they spoke of spiritual matters, then after a little while he bade a tearful farewell and departed to his own mean dwelling. The day had run its course and its neighbour, night, took its place. Then the man of God, Aunemund, having completed his singing of the psalms and worn out from his journey, got into bed and gave himself to sleep.

CHAPTER 11

It happened at that time, in the silence of the middle of the night, when all around were asleep, that he was secretly murdered by the sword by two men who had been despatched. When his happy soul was released from his body, immediately a fiery red rainbow appeared and stretched over the camps as the guards watched, and thus did many people learn that the just one had been unjustly killed. His clergy woke up forthwith and went over to ask the bishop to celebrate the morning service, for they had not yet seen that he was dead, but were thinking that he was deep in sleep. When they approached the bed and uncovered his face, they saw that he was all covered in blood, and said one to another, 'We have carelessly lost one whom we did not guard with proper care.'[71] Directly it was made known to the leaders of the army, who found his dead body when they came along at daybreak. And, mindful of the promise they had recently made to Waldebert, they left, upset.[72]

CHAPTER 12

After he had endured martyrdom[73] he was carried down to the stern [of a ship] by the few associates he had with him and he went by ship

---

71 *Solerti cura*, literally, 'expert care'.

72 They were *tristes*. Perrier, the editor of this text in the *Acta Sanctorum*, believed that the leaders must have been feigning distress and that with Waldebert gone they were carrying out their orders from Balthild: p. 747, n. r. This interpretation may have been based upon a reading of the *Life of Wilfrid*, ch. 3. An alternative view could be that the leaders had been seriously intent upon delivering up their charge for judgement and that the assassins had been sent without their knowledge. According to the *Passio Leudegarii*, ch. 20, above, pp. 236–7, at some time before 675 the bishop of Chalon was the notorious Diddo, henchman of Ebroin and the leader of an attack upon Lyons in 675. It may thus be significant that it was at Chalon that Aunemund met his end, but the actual circumstances of the killing must remain mysterious.

73 *Perpesso martyrio*. The deponent verb *perpetior*, used passively.

on the Saône back to Lyons. The next day,[74] after vespers, he landed
on the island called Barbe, where a column of watchful monks were
waiting for him.[75] As was proper, they washed him and honourably
wrapped him on a bier and put him back in the boat again to be carried
on to the city. In the morning his body was received by the clergy and
the people with the greatest of honour, everyone singing and saying,
'Glory be to You, Lord, we give thanks to You, because the one we
thought gone for ever, or at least destroyed, we have back full of
miracles.' After the customary mass had been said, his holy body was
taken off the bier and with a worthy funeral service they buried it in
the church of St Peter the Apostle, where he himself had recently
installed paupers to be fed from his own alms.[76]

CHAPTER 13

I think I must not omit to tell of the great miracles the Lord saw fit
to work through him. There was a vessel which was placed before his
tomb with oil for burning: it was never depleted, but very often
overflowed and provided light everlastingly. A certain blind man who
had by now been deprived of his sight for nearly fifteen years very
often stretched out before the tomb of the martyr, and there at last he
received his former sight. Once again a certain man who had been
paralysed, and who faithfully called upon his aid there, was given back
his old power to walk. Moreover, whosoever had a bit of the rod or
pastoral staff he carried in his hand, or a piece of the bed in which he

74 It is scarcely possible that they arrived so soon, even taking into consideration the
strong flow of the river Saône, for it is over a hundred kilometres from Chalon to
île-Barbe.

75 The monks were from the ancient monastery of Insula-Barbara (île-Barbe). For the
early history of the monastery, see Coville, *Recherches*, pp. 508–13, and Wood,
'Prelude to Columbanus', 11. Incidentally, later tradition made a connection
between île-Barbe and Ebroin, the villain of the *Passio Leudegarii*. According to the
ninth-century 'Chronicle of Ado', one resident of the île-Barbe was someone whom
Ebroin had blinded. Whilst sitting on the river bank he is comforted by the sound
of Ebroin being rowed to hell: *S. Adonis Chronicon*, ed. J.-P. Migne, *PL*, 123 (Paris,
1879), col. 117.

76 The reference to the church of St Peter is almost casual: there was not at this stage
any dispute over the cult of St Aunemund, and hence no need to stress at length the
saint's connections with the convent. Contrast later attempts to do this: in a late
twelfth- or early thirteenth-century addition to the letter of Bishop Leidrad to
Charlemagne, Aunemund is said to have founded the convent, Coville, *Recherches*,
p. 275. In the 'Will of Aunemund' the bishop is given sisters who are nuns at
St Peter's, Coville, *Recherches*, Appendix I, p. 409.

was struck down by the swordsman whilst sleeping, and placed it over their suffering limbs, they would get back the health they sought on the spot. If anyone had been seized by a demon, or beset by any other disease, when for love of the glorious martyr, Aunemund, they saw fit to visit the church of his grave, they left cured forthwith.[77]

CHAPTER 14

When the renown of the celebrated martyr Aunemund had filled nearly the whole world, it happened that a certain German,[78] blind from birth, dreamed that if he wanted to recover his sight he should go to the city of Lyons and there visit the tomb of St Aunemund, the martyr, in the church of St Peter the Apostle. Thus, setting off on the journey to the first among cities, he came at last to Lyons, exhausted by the long labour of his journey. Once inside the town walls he kept on saying, 'Aunemund, soldier of Christ, help me.' And when he got to the church of St Peter, wherein lay the body of the martyr and saint, he was received with honour and kindness by the nuns who served God there. When no sign of sight appeared on him (for his eye sockets were flush with the rest of his face), his fellow sufferers said to him, 'Brother, leaning on what support have you laboured on so long?' 'In order,' he replied, 'that the holy martyr Aunemund, whom the Lord has seen fit to reveal to me in a vision, may help me, one who has been blind from birth. So, I beg you, present me before him.'

CHAPTER 15

When they had done this, first mass was celebrated by the priest with ceremony and devotion. Now, as the deacon began to read the Gospels, the blind man's wife poked him in the side as he lay stretched out on the ground so that he would get up and stand to hear the Gospel. But he refused to – not at all his usual response – and his wife turned to him as he sighed and groaned in a strange way. Not long afterwards he who had been lying on the ground blind got up and, looking towards heaven with opened eyes, began to praise God, who had

---

77 Perrier, *AASS*, p. 737, noted that by the mid thirteenth century the relics of the saint were chiefly renowned for the curing of epilepsy, but there is no mention of this facility here.

78 *Quidam Theuton.* This is a classical term, not seen in the Merovingian period, see above p. 170, n. 13.

returned his sight to him through the merit of His martyr, Aunemund. You brides of Christ,[79] pray consider carefully with all your mental skills this miracle you have seen and pour out your prayers to the One who restored sight to mankind so that He may see fit to drive the shadows of unbelief from our hearts. And let your bodies be kept so pure that your heavenly bridegroom may flow into you and so arm you in this struggle that by fighting legitimately you may deserve to receive that crown of perpetual joy which is promised to us in the excellence of the Lord Jesus Christ, who with God the Father and the Holy Spirit lives and reigns for ever and ever.

---

79 It becomes clear only at this point that the work is addressed to an audience of nuns – the nuns of St Peter's, one must presume.

V: *Passio Leudegarii*
(The Suffering of St Leudegar)

The turbulent career of Leudegar, bishop of Autun from *c.* 662 to 676 is central to the history of later Merovingian Francia. This heroic figure achieved great fame in life, and even greater fame after his death, and the body of writing which has accumulated around him has become an invaluable source for the history of his time.[1] This material was mined as early as the first decades of the ninth century, as the authors of the *Annales Mettenses Priores* (*Earlier Annals of Metz*) used it in their work.[2] They presented their picture of an incorrigibly unjust Neustrian regime which in 687 had to be overturned by Pippin, Charlemagne's great-grandfather, largely by drawing upon a biography of Leudegar. And, as we have seen, the pessimistic view that the Carolingians took of their Merovingian predecessors has been very influential down to our own day.[3] But the tradition of Leudegar's life and death gives us far more than a gloomy foretaste of Neustria's eventual collapse. For although it shows in great detail the kind of factional fighting which could destroy any regime, it also allows us to see how people at the centre and in the provinces could make common cause, thus cementing together the different parts of the Frankish kingdoms. In this way the history of Leudegar complements those of Praejectus and of Aunemund, also discussed in this volume.[4] Leudegar, however, was to become much more famous than either of the latter two figures. As a consequence of the popularity and persistence of his cult, written accounts of his life and death would continue to be produced over the centuries. This body of material provides a quite fascinating illustration of the transformation of history into legend as writing about the bishop became more and more distant from the

1 Indicative of Leudegar's lasting fame is the fact that, when the saint's dossier was published in the *Acta Sanctorum* in 1765, no fewer than six ecclesiastical institutions claimed to be in possession of his head: *AASS*, Oct., I, pp. 457–60.

2 See below, p. 194, n. 8. For a brief statement of the popularity of and interest in Leudegar's biography, see F. Graus, *Volk, Herrscher und Heiliger im Reich der Merowinger* (Prague, 1965), pp. 377–9.

3 See above, p. 24.

4 Above, pp. 166–79, below, pp. 254–70.

events in which he took part. We shall look first at how the oldest text
of the *Passio Leudegarii* can be reconstructed and then turn to the
context of the work. This will allow us to appreciate the difficulties
faced by its author in presenting Leudegar's saintly credentials to an
audience which may have had good reason to doubt them. We can then
assess the value of the *Passio* as an historical source.

The edition translated here is that prepared by Krusch for the
Monumenta Germaniae Historica, and there is a strong consensus
among scholars that it represents the earliest version of the biography
of Leudegar.[5] Krusch reconstructed the text from two manuscripts
which were in fact younger than the first of those in which later
versions of the work appeared.[6] The oldest manuscript containing a
biography of Leudegar comes from the mid eighth century. In it is a
Passio Leudegarii written at Poitiers, home of the saint's cult from the
end of the seventh century onwards.[7] This Poitiers version Krusch
labelled 'B'. A later manuscript, ninth-century at the earliest, contained
a rather longer *Passio Leudegarii* written at Autun and dedicated to
Hermenar, Leudegar's successor as bishop of Autun. Krusch labelled
this work 'C'.[8] Finally, he found a third manuscript from the tenth
century which contained a sizeable fragment of the second half of
another *Passio Leudegarii*. This he called 'A'. Comparing A , B and C,

5 The text is *Passio Leudegarii I*, ed. B. Krusch, *MGH, SSRM*, V (Hanover, 1910), pp.
282–322.

6 For Krusch's reconstruction see his introduction to the edition, *MGH, SSRM*, V, pp.
243–59, and his 'Die Älteste Vita Leodegarii', *NA*, 16 (1891), 563–96. For a very
useful modern review of the dossier on Leudegar, see J.-C. Poulin, 'Saint Léger
d'Autun et ses premiers biographes (fin VIIᵉ–milieu IXᵉ siècle), *Bulletin de la Société
des Antiquaires de l'Ouest*, fourth series, 16 (1977).

7 Printed as *Passio Leudegarii II* in *MGH, SSRM*, V, pp. 323–56.

8 C is basically the text printed as the *Vita Leodegarii* in the *AASS*, Oct., I, pp. 463–
81. The *Passio Ragneberti*, ed. B. Krusch, *MGH, SSRM*, V, pp. 209–11, clearly draws
upon this C text. If Krusch was right to believe that the *Passio Ragneberti* was
written in the ninth century (see below, ch. 28, n. 200), then we may have evidence
that the C text, and therefore also the A text, were older than their oldest surviving
manuscripts. Another indication that the Autun (A and C) version of the *Passio* was
known early in the ninth century is its use in the *Annales Mettenses Priores*, where
there seems to be a reference to the pretender to the Merovingian throne, Clovis,
who is not mentioned in the Poitiers version (B). Similarly the *Annales Mettenses*'
reference to Ebroin's abandonment of his monastic vocation and his return to his
wife (*clericatum abiciens, uxore recepta, Annales Mettenses Priores* ed. B. von Simson,
MGH, SSRG, p. 5, and below, p. 353) echoes the C and A texts' *clericatum abiciens,
ad mulierem ut canis ad vomitum rediens* (*Passio Leudegarii*, ch. 18). This is a phrase
not found in B. Likewise the C text and the *Annales Mettenses* share the metaphor of
a poisonous serpent for Ebroin.

he found that in the later part of the biography, of which there were three versions, the longest version, C, was made up of A plus B. A clearly formed the main element of the C text, with only minor additions taken from B to enhance the miraculous element in the work.[9] Subtracting B from C for the later part of the work, Krusch got a text which corresponded very closely with the A fragment. He concluded that A represented a fragment of a later copy of the earliest biography and that C was based upon that version with only minor additions from the later B version. Subtracting B from C across the whole work, he was left with a coherent and internally consistent piece of writing which he concluded was the earliest version of the *Passio Leudegarii*.

There are many good reasons for believing that Krusch's reconstructed text does indeed represent the earliest version of the work. We shall cite but a few here. It seems obvious that, when the text from Autun is compared with the one from Poitiers, the latter can be shown to have been based upon a précis of the former.[10] The reconstituted text, moreover, was clearly written during the episcopate of Hermenar (whom we know to have been succeeded as bishop some time before 693). We can also see that it was written before Leudegar's cult was moved to Poitiers, probably in the early 680s. In part, the occasion of the work appears to have been Autun's bid for the saint's remains as they lay in their first resting place in the diocese of Beauvais. In fact, the B version tells of how this bid by Autun failed and of how Poitiers acquired the relics.[11] Furthermore, we suspect that the work was

9 B was used above all by the author of C to expand the section on Leudegar's posthumous miracles: compare *Vita Leodegarii*, chs. 55–76, with *Passio Leudegarii II*, chs. 23–32.

10 The précis formed the main body of the narrative of the Poitiers version. To this was added fresh detail on Leudegar's life in Poitiers (*Passio Leudegarii II*, chs. 2, 3), on Ansoald of Poitiers's acquisition of the saint's relics (see n. 11 below), and on the miracles.

11 *Passio Leudegarii II*, ch. 24. The competition over the relics was between Ansoald, bishop of Poitiers, Hermenar, bishop of Autun and Vindicianus, bishop of Arras, the diocese in which Leudegar had been executed. The three finally drew lots to see who should have the saint's body. After winning possession of the relics, Ansoald hastened to have them translated to Poitiers. The *Passio Leudegarii II*, ch. 23, implies that this all happened soon after the death of Ebroin (d. *c.* 680), who had effectively prevented official recognition of the cult. The same source, ch. 20, says that the saint's body lay in its first grave for two and a half years, although there is a slight contradiction here with the statement that Ebroin was killed almost three years after Leudegar's death (ch. 23). Given that Leudegar was put to death about two years after Ebroin's return to power, and allowing for some chronological

contemporary, or nearly so, because it is dedicated to Hermenar, Leudegar's successor as bishop of Autun. Two casual first-person eye-witness references to events, and the work's generally extraordinarily detailed treatment of affairs, both in Autun and at the centre of Frankish politics, also lead us to believe that the text was written, as it claims to have been, shortly after the events it described.[12] But perhaps the strongest suggestion that Krusch had indeed recon-structed a very early text is the whiff of controversy which surrounds the figure of Leudegar in that text.[13] That controversial element is quite absent in the Poitiers (B) version, and it seems inconceivable that doubt about a figure's saintly credentials would have been added, rather than removed, at a later stage in a cult's development.[14] Let us now look more closely at this controversial figure and at the tradition of his 'Life'.

According to his earliest biography (which we will now call the the Hermenar version) Leudegar was the nephew of Dido, bishop of Poitiers (c. 628–67). He was brought up in Poitiers and became archdeacon there before being appointed on Queen Balthild's orders to the bishopric of Autun in c. 662.[15] Autun had for nearly two years been racked by factional fighting over who should become bishop, and Leudegar's appointment may have been agreed as a way of settling this dispute. Leudegar may have been chosen for Autun partly because he had family connections with the region, but the evidence for such connections is too weak to allow us say much about them, and

---

confusion, we would get a date of 681–82 for the removal of Leudegar's body to Poitiers. The A and C version of the *Passio* dedicated to Hermenar would most likely have been composed before that date. More possible support for dating the translation of the relics to Poitiers to the early 680s may come from information that the church built to house them in the monastery of St Maxence was dedicated on 30 October. If that day was a Sunday it would have fallen in the year 684: see Krusch, *MGH, SSRM*, V, p. 255.

12 References to living eye witnesses: ch. 24, below, pp. 240–1; ch. 30, below, pp. 245–6.

13 See below, p. 203.

14 For how the traditions of a saint's life usually developed over time, H. Delehaye, *The Legends of the Saints*, fourth edition, trans. D. Attwater (London, 1962), esp. pp. 101–16. See above, pp. 47–8.

15 It is interesting to note that whereas Leudegar and his brother Gaerinus were prominent in the Neustrian palace, their uncle, Dido, Bishop of Poitiers, had Austrasian and Pippinid affiliations. According to the *Liber Historiae Francorum* (see above, p. 88), it was Dido arranged the exile of the young Dagobert II. Note too Dido's meeting with the Pippinid mayor Grimoald, reported in the *Additamentum Nivialense*, below, p. 329.

certainly not strong enough to encourage speculation that Leudegar's actions were determined by a local identity and interests. Evidence that his family did have interests in the Autun region rests primarily on the fact that Ansoald, bishop of Poitiers, to whom the B version of the *Passio Leudegarii* was dedicated, was said in that version to have been related to the saint.[16] Ansoald is elsewhere recorded as having had land in Burgundy near Chalon-sur-Saône (53k south-east of Autun), which he had inherited from his parents.[17] There also exists a will which purports to be that of Leudegar and which speaks of land near Autun that had belonged to the saint's mother, Sigrada.[18] In later tradition, Sigrada was also linked with the family of St Sadalberga, which was of Burgundian stock.[19] In his work on the origins of the duchy of Burgundy, published in 1928, Maurice Chaume drew all these threads together in order to present Leudegar as a champion of Burgundian interests in rather the same way that he imagined Aunemund to have been a fighter for Burgundian 'separatism'.[20] Leudegar's will is, however, almost certainly a later invention which drew on information from the *Passio Leudegarii* itself,[21] and the connection with Sadalberga's family is another later fiction. On the other hand, Ansoald may well have been related to Leudegar, for the earlier bishop of Poitiers, Dido, was said to have been the saint's uncle, and the document which refers to Ansoald's land in Burgundy looks authentic enough. Nevertheless, we cannot build a political identity or consciousness out of this one connection. It could equally be claimed

16 *Passio Leudegarii II*, ch. 24, p. 347, where Ansoald is reported to have claimed that *notum est [Leudegarium] meum esse parentem.*

17 J. Tardif, 'Les chartes mérovingiens de Noirmoutier', *Nouvelle Revue Historique de Droit Français et Etranger*, 22 (1899). The land, which had come to Ansoald, *a genitore vel a genetrice nostra*, was granted to the monastery of Noirmoutier. The charter's extensive reference to the *gesta municipalia* of Poitiers in connection with Ansoald's grant shows it to be genuinely Merovingian.

18 *Testamentum Leodegari*, in J. Pardessus, *Diplomata, chartae, epistolae, leges, aliaque instrumenta ad res Gallo-Francicas spectantia*, vol. 2, pp. 173–4.

19 See nn. 86 and 192, below.

20 M. Chaume, *Les Origines du duché de Bourgogne* (Dijon, 1928), pp. 22–3 and nn. 3–4.

21 See Krusch, *MGH, SSRM*, V, p. 254. Not only is the dating clause of the will non-Merovingian, the date for the king is impossible and his parentage wrong (Theuderic was not a son of Clothar, ruling in 653), but also it claims that all the land in question is being donated to the cathedral church in Autun to support the '*matricula* ... which we built in the porch of the church'. This looks as if it could have been inspired by ch. 2 of the *Passio Leudegarii*, below, p. 218, which tells of the bishop setting up such a *matricula* in the porch. It is thus unsatisfactory to lay emphasis on this will when thinking about Leudegar's connection with the locality of Autun.

that Leudegar was 'Neustrian' because his brother was count of Paris, and because his name had the same first element (Leud) as that of the son of Erchinoald, the Neustrian mayor of the palace (an element they both shared, incidentally, with Leutrude, the wife of their arch-enemy Ebroin). Leudegar's family background therefore made him a member of that supra-regional elite which had connections throughout the Merovingian kingdom, and whose vested interests lay in unity rather than in separatism. In this context, Leudegar's promotion to the see of Autun looks like an attempt by the royal palace to use the opportunity provided by local rivalry to push a powerful supporter into an important area, in the same way that Balthild managed to get her supporter Genesius made bishop of Lyons after the demise of Bishop Aunemund.[22] But, as we shall see, Lyons seems to have warmed to Genesius in a way that Autun did not to Leudegar.

Leudegar, we are told, restored order in Autun with some vigour, but it is clear that elements in the town opposed him, and, as was the case with Aunemund, such opponents seem to have lobbied against their bishop in the royal palace.[23] Once Queen Balthild had been removed, they made headway, and in 673 the mayor of the palace, Ebroin, was already manoeuvring against Leudegar when the death of King Clothar III threw the kingdom of Neustria and Burgundy into disarray. Leudegar, Gaerinus his brother, and other leading Franks threatened by Ebroin, seized the chance to overthrow the mayor and Theuderic, the new king, calling instead upon the latter's brother, Childeric II, ruler of Austrasia, to come and be their king too. Ebroin's life was spared at Leudegar's behest, but he was exiled to the monastery of Luxeuil, and Leudegar took over many of his functions in the palace.[24] Nevertheless, although he was now one of the most powerful non-royal figures in all Francia, the bishop still faced opposition in Autun itself and again his opponents seem to have looked for powerful supporters from outside.

At Easter 675 the royal court was held in Autun. Leudegar's enemies in the town fanned into action the existing hostility to the bishop, and when faced with accusations of treason, he fled. Arrested, he was exiled

---

22 On Balthild's use of patronage over the church, above, pp. 109–12, and J. L. Nelson, 'Queens as Jezebels: Brunhild and Balthild in Merovingian History', *Studies in Church History: Subsidia*, vol. 1 (1978), reprinted in J. L. Nelson, *Politics and Ritual*, pp. 1–48.

23 *Passio Leudegarii*, chs. 3–4, below, pp. 220–1.

24 *Passio Leudegarii*, chs. 5–6, below, pp. 222–3.

to Luxeuil to join his old enemy Ebroin. Hermenar then became bishop in his place.[25] But within six months the king, Childeric, had been assassinated and the two exiles returned. At first Leudegar's faction was able to exclude Ebroin from power and Leudegar recovered Autun from Hermenar. After a few months, however, Ebroin had built up enough support to be able to storm the palace and take over. Now he set about settling old scores and he sent an army to fetch Leudegar from Autun. Autun either could not, or would not, protect him, and he was given up to the army, in return for which the town was treated relatively leniently.[26] Leudegar was blinded by his captors and taken away to die, quietly and naturally, it was hoped, so that he could not be claimed as a martyr. In the end this plan failed, and despite his further mutilation Leudegar refused to die. Finally he was defrocked as bishop, formally condemned as an accessory to Childeric's murder and at last executed, some time between 677 and 679. Hermenar emerged once again as bishop of Autun. Despite Ebroin's best efforts, Leudegar was nonetheless hailed as a martyr and had, as we might say, the last laugh, for Ebroin was eventually struck down by someone else he was preparing to attack.[27]

Apart from the occasional detail, what we have just seen is a synopsis of the narrative of the Hermenar version of the *Passio Leudegarii* and it should at once indicate the exceptional value of this source as an historical document. It is in many ways closer to history than hagiography, for, throughout much of the narrative, historical detail appears to overwhelm hagiographical convention, and that detail in fact forms the basis of much of our understanding of the political history of the 670s.[28] The unusually large amount of history in this hagiographical work stems partly from the fact that Leudegar was involved in some very dramatic events, and in places the author seems to have risen to the challenge of capturing the drama. He paid particular attention to the events of 675–76, that is, to what happened after the death of Childeric and leading up to the despatch of the army

---

25 *Passio Leudegarii*, chs. 9–12, below, pp. 226–30.

26 *Passio Leudegarii*, chs. 15–24, below, pp. 231–41.

27 *Passio Leudegarii*, chs. 25–37, below, pp. 241–53. As G. Scheibelreiter has pointed out, the way in which people died was seen as a reflection upon their life. Sudden death, without the chance to confess sins, was a sign of God's judgement against an individual: G. Scheibelreiter, *Der Bischof in merowingischer Zeit* (Vienna, 1983), pp. 253–4.

28 See, for instance, E. Ewig, 'Die Fränkischen Teilreiche im 7. Jahrhundert (613–714)', *Trierer Zeitschrift*, 22 (1953), 127–30, reprinted *Gallien*, vol. 1, pp. 214–16.

to Autun.[29] Indeed, at one stage he seems to have been carried away
with the story of Ebroin's return to power, and, after three consecutive
chapters discussing this without reference to Leudegar, he had to
exhort himself to get on with the latter's story.[30] Another reason why
the author included so much historical detail likely lies in the controversial nature of his subject and its proximity to his intended audience.
That is to say, he was dealing with sensitive matters which needed a
great deal of explanation to people who knew much about them.

Leudegar, as we have seen, had opponents in his own town of Autun,
as well as enemies at the royal court. But, given the fact that the bishop
was hailed as a martyr very soon after his death, and the fact that there
were rival claims for possession of his body, the author's task was to
argue that the saint's proper resting place should be Autun.[31] This
meant showing that Leudegar had not really had enemies in the town,
or, if he had, that he had forgiven them, and they him. In particular he
seems to have been concerned to reconcile Leudegar and Hermenar,
who had been abbot of the author's own monastery of St Symphorian
and who succeeded Leudegar as bishop of Autun. His work was
dedicated to Hermenar, and as J.-C. Poulin has pointed out, the
author's request to Hermenar to check the work for errors before
anyone else saw it may not be simply rhetorical, and the same may be
true of his statement that Hermenar had frequently requested him to
write up the life of Leudegar.[32] In other words, Hermenar may have
wanted to publicise a version of events sympathetic to himself and his
town as soon as possible in order to attract the cult to Autun. That it
did in fact become associated with a place other than the town in which
the hero had held office is extremely unusual for a Frankish bishop
martyr, and it suggests that, despite Hermenar's efforts to convince
people otherwise, Autun was not regarded as a suitable place in which
to honour the saint's remains.[33]

29 *Passio Leudegarii*, chs. 15–20, below, pp. 231–7.

30 *Passio Leudegarii*, chs. 18–20, below, pp. 234–7. Chapter 20 ends with the words
   redeamus ad opum ceptum ('let us return to the task in hand').

31 Further support for the notion that the saint was hailed as a martyr soon after death
   (see n. 11, above) comes from another contemporary work, the *Passio Praejecti*, ch.
   26, below, p. 291, which speaks of Leudegar having '... grasped the palm of
   martyrdom, and now he is strong in the performance of holy miracles'.

32 Poulin, 'St Léger', 177.

33 Contrast the cults of Aunemund, Praejectus and Lambert, three other martyr
   bishops whose downfall was the result of local oppostion but who were all buried
   in their former see. For Aunemund and Praejectus, see above, p. 190, below, p. 296.
   For Lambert, *Vita Landiberti Vetustissima* ed. B. Krusch *MGH, SSRM*, VI (Hanover

The general plan of the Hermenar version of the *Passio Leudegarii* follows
established hagiographical convention. Leudegar's career is described
in anticipation of his martyrdom and consequent sanctification, and his
life is portrayed as a journey towards these ends. What drove him along
the path was his goodness and the reaction it elicited: '... goodwill is
always opposed by evil, and that age-old serpent envy always finds
those amongst whom it can sow strife'.[34] The real villain of the story
was the devil and in this context one can see why the notion of
diabolical envy was a favourite hagiographical device, for the devil
made a wonderful scapegoat.[35] Within the established hagiographical
framework the author's task was to explain how Leudegar came to be
drawn into politics – a sensitive point, since his political career nearly
led to the ruin of Autun. The principal means of explaining this was
to portray Leudegar's persecutor Ebroin as the devil's instrument, and
the *Passio Leudegarii* was in fact to establish for Ebroin an enduring
reputation as a particularly nasty ruler.[36] By describing political events
in some detail the author attempted to show that Leudegar's involvement was forced upon him and that he had to engage in political
struggle in order to combat evil. How the author portrayed the central
events of the work must also have been affected to a significant degree
by the constraint of common memory. He was certainly writing after
Ebroin's murder, i.e. after 680, and while Hermenar was still bishop of
Autun, i.e. before 693. In fact he probably wrote before 684, when
Leudegar's remains were finally housed in Poitiers. The author himself
had witnessed some of what had happened, for he gives a first-person
account of a visit made to comfort Leudegar shortly before his death,
and many of his intended audience must also have had first-hand
experience of events.[37] The constraint of living memory and the need
to reconcile different points of view are, as we have seen, two very

---

and Leipzig, 1913), pp. 353–84. Each of the three originated in the see in which he
held office. Lambert was buried next to his father, *Vita Landiberti*, ch. 18. Praejectus
was buried by a kinswoman, *Passio Praejecti*, ch. 32, below, p. 295. That Leudegar
was not eventually buried in his see may support the impression that he had no
powerful kindred in the Autun region who might have demanded his remains. On
the burial of bishops in general, Scheibelreiter, *Der Bischof*, pp. 245–6.

34 *Passio Leudegarii* ch. 3, below, p. 220.

35 In particular, the devil was associated with the misuse of power, 'tyranny', and thus
was prominent in conflicts between the saint figure and secular authority, cf. Graus,
Volk, Herrscher und Heiliger, p. 351 and n. 269. See also above, p. 47.

36 Note how in the *Annales Mettenses Priores* this reputation figures as the touchstone
of Neustrian injustice: below, pp. 353–4.

37 *Passio Leudegarii*, ch. 31, below, pp. 246–7.

important factors in limiting the use hagiographers could make of convention and in forcing them to take account of historical reality.[38] Both factors are visibly at work here. Let us look at the main areas in which they operate.

Even where Ebroin was concerned, the author seems not to have had the freedom to portray an entirely diabolical figure. He admitted that Ebroin began to move against Leudegar only after accusations about the bishop had been made to him and he showed that Ebroin was rarely alone in his actions – indeed, that he enjoyed considerable support.[39] Much more obvious is the extremely delicate way in which the author treated the overthrow of Ebroin's régime in 673, and in particular the care he took to explain how the rightful king, Theuderic III, was not only deposed but also had his hair forcibly cut. The latter act he portrayed as a kind of mistake committed by people trying to protect the king.[40] He even suggested that God disapproved of Theuderic's deposition and that his eventual restoration was divinely ordered.[41] Here the constraining factor could simply have been Theuderic himself, for he lived on as king until at least 690. Leudegar's leading role in the regime of Theuderic's replacement, Childeric II, also needed careful explanation, and this led the author into a detailed account of the reforms Childeric agreed to on becoming king of Neustria and Burgundy, portraying them as the benefits of Leudegar's influence. Here details of what was probably the standard confirmation by a new king of his predecessors' privileges was included in the argument.[42] Then, after some preliminary warnings about the envy boiling up again around Leudegar's goodness, we come to the most delicate description of all: the taking of Leudegar from Autun at Easter 675.[43]

---

38 Above, pp. 45–7.

39 *Passio Leudegarii*, ch. 4, below, pp. 220–1, '... the men of envy went to Ebroin and kindled in his heart a great fury against the man of God'; and when Ebroin returned to power, '... some people rejoiced with him': ch. 28, below, pp. 243–5.

40 *Passio Leudegarii*, ch. 6, below, pp. 222–3, '... certain men who were seen to be leaders in the kingdom and wished by flattery to persuade Childeric not to shed blood rashly ventured to order the cutting of their lord Theuderic's hair'.

41 *Passio Leudegarii*, ch. 6, below pp. 222–3, '... happily the God of Heaven whom he predicted he would have as his judge, afterwards let him rule.'.

42 *Passio Leudegarii*, ch.7, below, pp. 223–4. Childeric's 'legislation' parallels that of Clothar II in the Edict of Paris of 614, issued when Clothar, like Childeric, had become ruler of all three Frankish kingdoms and guaranteed the privileges of each of them: *Clotharii Edictum*, ed. A. Boretius, *Capitularia Regum Francorum*, vol. I, *MGH, Legum Sectio II* (Hanover, 1883), pp. 20–3, esp. ch. 12, p. 22.

43 *Passio Leudegarii*, chs. 9–12, below, pp. 226–30.

These events the author discussed as if they and the local people in them were well known to his audience. The impression that the events were controversial is confirmed by another of the sources translated here, the *Passio Praejecti* (*The Suffering of St Praejectus*), for Praejectus, bishop of Clermont, was also involved in them.[44]

According to the *Passio Leudegarii*, Leudegar took up the case of another magnate, Hector, ruler of Marseilles, and hoped to use his leading position at court to plead Hector's cause. This action by Leudegar the author of the *Passio Praejecti* called a *scandalum* ('stumbling block') on Leudegar's path to heaven. Hector, who was described as 'nobly born' and 'wise' in the *Passio Leudegarii*, but as 'a certain man of ill repute' in the *Passio Praejecti*, was in dispute with Praejectus and had forced him to attend a hearing of their case before the king.[45] Midway through the hearing, Hector and Leudegar became aware that they were about to be charged with treason, and fled the town. Hector was caught and killed along with his followers; Leudegar was also caught, but after some deliberation the king and court decided to exile him, making his exile particularly uncomfortable by sending him into confinement with his old enemy Ebroin.[46] In this sequence three problems faced Leudegar's hagiographer: first, the association between the hero and a secular figure involved in political intrigue; second, the fact that it was a monk of the author's own monastery of St Symphorian who accused Leudegar before the king; and third, the common belief that the then abbot of St Symphorian, none other than Hermenar, was 'the leader of Leudegar's accusers and that in this he was improving his chances of being allowed to hold the bishopric'.[47]

The author dealt with the first of these problems by advancing the rather disingenuous claim that Hector was, as it were, a martyr manqué. He claims that Hector would certainly have submitted himself to death had it not been Easter; his resistance to death was merely a (divinely approved) manifestation of virile instincts. That this had caused the death of others (who 'had gone to him for protection') was regrettable, but, since the manner of his death had purified him, he would be in a strong position to plead for their salvation.[48] The second

---

44 *Passio Praejecti*, chs. 23–7, below, pp. 288–92.

45 The dispute was over land. For a discussion of the case, see below, pp. 263–4.

46 The author adds that this was only an interim measure. The real intention was to have him killed in exile.

47 *Passio Leudegarii*, ch. 12, below, pp. 229–30.

48 *Passio Leudegarii*, ch. 11, below, pp. 228–9.

problem he dealt with by vilifying the monk in question, one Marcolinus.[49] But behind Marcolinus were the 'envious ones', and the biggest problem was to counter the belief that Hermenar was their leader. All the author could do was to place a different interpretation upon common observation: if after Leudegar's arrest Hermenar 'kept going into the king's lodgings' it was because he was frantically pleading for Leudegar's life, just as Leudegar himself had once pleaded for Ebroin's life, and it was only as a result of his efforts that the bishop was exiled rather than executed.[50] Although these passages show the author having to come to terms with an historical reality which determined the use he could make of hagiograghical convention, we should also remember that the overall structure of the work is conventional, and that it was written with the advantage and certainty of hindsight. So, despite any *scandalia* Leudegar may have encountered along the path to heaven, there was no doubt that he reached his journey's end. In that sense the end justified the means. Secondly we should note that, weak though the arguments may appear to us, they are nevertheless rich in a metaphorical language which rendered them holy. These metaphors revolved around the celebration of Easter. The actions of Leudegar and Hector were described in terms of wisdom, sacrifice, purity, peace, solemnity, heaven and salvation. Their opponents' behaviour evoked a sense of precipitate and ill-judged action, profanity, uproar and evil intention. Identifiable borrowings from the Bible were from the book of Wisdom and from Acts, and explicit comparisons were drawn between St Peter and Leudegar and between Herod and King Childeric. Thus the assertion that Hector would have been purified by persecution would not have been as hollow-sounding as we might judge. As ever, the events were put into the context of interaction between evil, envy and goodness, and so conform to the general pattern of the subject's career. And finally, running through the whole sequence is a skilfully worked tension between appearance and reality which comes to a climax at the end of the sequence around the denial of Hermenar's complicity in the affair. Any sense of fault is shifted to the accusers, those unable to see the reality of Hermenar's 'spiritual love' for Leudegar. The argument runs as follows. The accusations against Leudegar and Hector were made up, but Childeric

49 *Passio Leudegarii*, ch. 10, below, pp. 226–8. The passage reads as if Marcolinus were no longer a monk at St Symphorian and suggests that his dissolute way of life was well known. His infamy and death or departure from Autun made him a useful scapegoat.

50 *Passio Leudegarii*, ch. 12, below, p. 229–30.

believed them because he wanted to do harm to the pair; Marcolinus appeared as a holy man to the king, and again it suited him to believe he was. Conversely, when the king stumbled into 'real' light, he was dazzled and could see nothing; Hector appeared to be dodging martyrdom, but in reality he was restraining himself from polluting the Church with bloodshed on Good Friday. The king appeared to agree to send Leudegar into exile, but in reality he was intending to kill him. To counter these real intentions of the king, Hermenar frantically pleaded with him. It is thus ironic that people should doubt Hermenar's good intentions, and draw the wrong conclusion from appearances. The message, finally, is that those of good faith and intention can see through appearances to reach the truth.

Another section of narrative which must have caused difficulty for the author was the taking of Leudegar from Autun a second time.[51] Again the episode is given careful contextualisation in the world of politics, with evil forces engineering events beyond the bishop's control, and again what may appear to us as a series of unconvincing explanations was buttressed by holy metaphor. This time Leudegar was Christ-like as he refused to turn away from the impending agony.[52] The implicit comparison serves to explain why he did not leave the town at the approach of the army directed against him, despite the fact that 'his dependants and the clergy and his followers' were all keen that he should do so in order to save Autun. We are told that Leudegar immediately distributed his treasure to rally the citizens and then fortified the town. The army duly arrived, and for a day the townspeople fought against the invaders. Then after a certain Abbot Meroald had negotiated with the enemy leader, Leudegar 'of his own accord offered himself up to his enemies to save his city'. It is difficult not to believe that in reality Autun was unwilling to defend its bishop, unlike Lyons, which did defend its bishop, Genesius, from part of the same army.[53] But this time it was at least much easier for the author to blame outside forces for the suffering and to portray the hero as an innocent victim. This he did by giving details of the outrageous

51. *Passio Leudegarii*, chs. 21–4.

52 Poulin, 'St Léger', 188, notes comparison with Christ in the Garden of Gethsemane, a comparison which 'explains' why Leudegar could not flee the approaching danger. The comparison is made explicit when Leudegar shares bread and wine with his followers, '… entrusting the memory of his suffering to them, as Christ did to the disciples' (ch. 24, below, p. 241).

53 *Passio Leudegarii*, ch. 26, below, pp. 242–3. The unfavourable comparison between Autun and Lyons here was presumably inadvertent.

behaviour of Ebroin's party (so, incidentally, providing information found in no other source) and by having Leudegar reflect upon his fate and upon man's abuse of power in general.[54] He also chose this dramatic moment to show Leudegar asking for forgiveness from his flock, suggesting that some members of it had indeed been 'severely wounded' by their pastor 'in his ardent love of justice'. One cannot help wondering here whether on his return to Autun the bishop had taken revenge on those who had played a part in his earlier exile.

From this point onwards in the story the author was able to use a more conventional approach, since events took place at some distance from Autun and as Leudegar began to suffer horribly. He could thus make use of the motifs of suffering and heroic endurance which were standard in writing about martyrs.[55] Nevertheless, in order to strengthen the argument that Leudegar's troubles were largely of Ebroin's making, he continued to make reference to political events up to Ebroin's assassination, two years after Leudegar's execution.[56] Making continuing reference to Ebroin was also a way of conveying the growing power of the saint after death, as it is shown that the signs of sanctity were so strong that the mayor could not stamp out the cult. The author also made use of Leudegar's suffering to reconcile the hero with Hermenar. The latter was said to have visited the saint after he had been further mutilated, and after he himself had been made Bishop of Autun. Hermenar was thus able to acknowledge Leudegar as an imminent martyr, and whilst visiting him he 'earned not only forgiveness for things past, but also a blessing from him for what was yet to come'.[57] The episode was also a way of establishing Autun's prior claim to the cult, but the very need to include a final scene of reconciliation may help explain why Autun's bid to guard the saint's remains failed.

As we have already seen, it was Poitiers which eventually acquired Leudegar's relics and it was from Poitiers that the next version of his biography came, the version Krusch called B and which is printed as the *Passio Leudegarii II* in the *Monumenta* series. This was written by

54 It is, for instance, only from this source (chs. 19, 23, 28, below, pp. 235–6, 240, 243) that we know of Clovis, the pretender to the throne set up by Ebroin.

55 Cf. H. Delehaye, *Les Passions des Martyrs et les genres littéraires* (Brussels, 1921), pp. 273–87.

56 Again providing invaluable historical information, especially concerning how Ebroin brought the feuding to an end with some sort of legal settlement: *Passio Leudegarii*, ch. 28, below, pp. 243–5.

57 *Passio Leudegarii*, ch. 30, below, p. 246.

the monk Ursinus, probably around the middle of the eighth century, although it was dedicated to Ansoald, who was bishop of Poitiers 676– c. 696. The reason for disbelieving the author's claim that he was writing in the time of Ansoald is that he referred to Leudegar as 'mayor of the palace', a mistake unlikely in a genuinely seventh-century author, for the mayoralty was a purely secular office. Ursinus also 'corrected' the Latin of the Heremar version in ways which reflect the revival of learning in the early Carolingian period, and he seems to have drawn upon the *Continuation of the Chronicle of Fredegar*, a work of the mid eighth century.[58] On the other hand, it has been observed that a contemporary funerary inscription from the monastery of Ligugé near Poitiers bears the name Ursinus, and that an Ursinus is also referred to in a Poitevin text of this period, namely Defensor of Ligugé's *Liber Scintillarum*. But this information does not give us a seventh-century Ursinus, for the argument that both the inscription and the Defensor reference are from the late seventh century actually rests upon the 'evidence' that Ursinus's work was dedicated to the seventh-century bishop, Ansoald.[59]

58 See Krusch, *MGH, SSRM*, V, p. 258. Ursinus's idea that Leudegar's brother Gaerinus fled into Gascony could well have been inspired by the mid eighth-century *Continuation of the Chronicle of Fredegar*, ed. and trans. J. M. Wallace-Hadrill (London, 1960), ch. 2, p. 82.

59 M. Rochais, 'Le "Liber Scintillarum" attribué à Defensor de Ligugué', *Revue Bénédictine*, 58 (1948), 77–83, suggested that the *nutritor* Ursinus mentioned in this work was Ursinus author of the *Passio Leudegarii II*, and this encouraged J. Coquet, 'L'inscription tumulaire de Ligugé (fin du VIIᵉ siècle)', *Revue Mabillon*, 44 (1954), 97–104, to decipher the monogramme on the funerary inscription as Ursinus. Both Rochais and Coquet dated their material to the late seventh century, and this in turn led Poulin, 'St Léger', 178–9, to argue for a seventh-century Ursinus. Poulin also cited F. Prinz, *Frühes Mönchtum im Frankenreich* (Munich, 1965), p. 508, as another believer in an Ursinus contemporary with Ansoald. However, though Prinz cited Rochais's identification, he did not comment on the dating, and in *Frühes Mönchtum*, p. 295, he accepts Krusch's dating of the *Passio Leudegarii II*. Stonger support for Poulin has recently come from W. Berschin, *Biographie und Epochenstil im lateinischen Mittelalter*, vol. 2, *Merowingischen Biographie, Italien, Spanien und die Inseln im frühen Mittelalter* (Stuttgart, 1988), pp. 67, 69, nn. 177, 180, 181, and from M. Heinzelmann, 'Studia Sanctorum. éducation, milieux d'instruction et valeurs éducatives dans l'hagiographie en Gaule jusqu'à la fin de l'époque mérovingienne', in M. Sot (ed.), *Haut Moyen-âge. Culture, éducation et sociétés. Etudes offertes à Pierre Riché* (Paris, 1990), p. 115. The arguments of Rochais and Coquet, from which Berschin and Heinzelmann derived their support for Poulin, are in fact inescapably circular: both Rochais and Coquet reasoned that their material must be of the late seventh century because Ursinus figures in it and the dedication to the *Passio Leudegarii II* shows that he was contemporary with Ansoald. In addition, Coquet's reading of the monogramme is speculative, and the actual inscription which follows it is ninth-century in form. Their work may be able to shed some light on Ursinus, but it cannot tell us when he wrote.

What Ursinus did was to make a précis of the Hermenar version up to the point at which Leudegar's suffering began.[60] To this outline he added fresh detail about Leudegar's time in Poitiers, and an extremely interesting account of how it was decided that the saint's body should be translated to Poitiers.[61] Ursinus also seems to have been unable to resist embellishing promising scenes, as, for instance, Leudegar's meeting with Ebroin in Luxeuil.[62] Similarly, and with a licence time-honoured in the genre of hagiography, he greatly extended Leudegar's suffering, put a great deal more direct speech into the mouths of the principal actors and lingered over the moment of his death. The effect of Ursinus's extensive reworking of the biography was to strengthen both Leudegar's credentials as a saint and Poitiers's hold over his cult. In drastically reducing the narrative up to the point at which Leudegar was taken from Autun a second time, Ursinus cut out much of the detailed explanation through which the earlier author had justified the saint's actions and reconciled him to his opponents in Autun. Such detail would have made little sense to Ursinus's audience, and removing it had the added effect of weakening the association between the bishop and the town in which he had held office. Another result of the reworking was to simplify the story, which now became a straightforward struggle between good and evil, personified by Leudegar and Ebroin respectively. In that form the story would be understood and embroidered by successive generations.

Ursinus's work was the source for a mid ninth-century metric version of Leudegar's life, and also for a poem in the Romance language, the *Vie de Sanct Lethgier*, which survives in a manuscript of the the mid tenth century.[63] The tradition shows how the story of Leudegar's life would develop over time once the constraint of memory had been removed. The successive treatments of Leudegar's exile at Easter 675 will serve to

60 Ursinus condensed the first twenty-four chapters of the Hermenar version into eleven chapters of roughly comparable length.

61 See n. 11 above.

62 Compare *Passio Leudegarii II*, chs. 7–8, with *Passio Leudegarii*, ch. 13, below, p. 230.

63 *Vita Leudegarii metrica*, ed. L. Traube, *MGH, Poetae Latini aevi carolini*, III (Berlin, 1896), pp. 5–37; *Vie et Passio de Saint Léger*, ed J. Champollion-Figeac, *Documents inédits tirés des collections manuscrites de la Bibliothèque Nationale et des Archives ou des Bibliothèques des départements* (Paris, 1848), vol. IV, pp. 446–56. On the dating and provenance of the latter, see G. de Poek, 'Le ms. Clermont Ferrand 240 (Anc. 189), les Scriptoria d'Auvergne et les origines spirituelles de la Vie française de Saint Léger', *Scriptorium*, 18 (1964). It is interesting to note the strong possibility that the poem may have been written in Clermont, where Praejectus had been bishop, and where criticism of Leudegar developed in the seventh century.

illustrate this. Ursinus pruned the Hermenar version's delicate description of events by leaving Hector, Marcolinus and Hermenar out of the story. Leudegar, we are told, slipped away from Autun when he heard a false rumour that the king was angry with him, and he went only because he did not want to risk the king being stained with blood at such a holy time. The king was upset and ordered the bishop into Luxeuil only because Leudegar himself requested it.[64] The metric version added to this by putting a speech of tearful contrition into the king's mouth,[65] and the Romance poem added still more by having Leudegar beg to be allowed to enter a monastery because he could no longer bear the secular demands made upon him as a royal counsellor.[66] Thus each author tended to 'improve' the story to reflect more generously upon the hero. But, as the Easter episode also shows, the basic outline of the original story would remain in place: all four versions agree on the time and place of the events, on the name of the king involved and on the entry of Leudegar into Luxeuil. Nevertheless, the later versions are incapable of adding to our knowledge of the original events, though they are valuable historical documents in their own right as they brought the values and fashions of their own time to bear upon the story. The Romance poem, for instance, may be useful for what it can tell us about attitudes to lordship and kingship in tenth-century Aquitaine.[67] Ursinus's version, however, has often been regarded as providing genuinely fresh information about the seventh century, but apart from the pieces concerning Poitiers, the translation of the saint's relics, and the provision of a single name, all the historical information in the work can also be found in the Hermenar version. It is Ursinus's extensive reworking of the earlier work which sometimes makes it appear that he has drawn on material outside it, but in nearly every case it can be demonstrated that the Hermenar version was the source of his information. Occasionally, misplaced confidence in Ursinus has resulted in quite false impressions of the political history of the period.[68]

---

64 *Passio Leudegarii II*, ch. 7, p. 330.

65 *Vita Leudegarii metrica*, lines 234–65, pp. 12–13.

66 *Vie de Saint Léger*, verses 16–17, p. 450.

67 Kingship appears as a slightly remote, even exotic, institution: see for instance the comment on the anger of a king, verse 13, p. 449. Relationships between men and their lords are mentioned in terms of mutual obligation, in contrast to the Merovingian convention of obedience to the ruler.

68 Particularly unfortunate has been the speculative discussion proceeding from the belief that *Passio Leudegarii II*, ch. 8, p. 31, added 'new' information to the Hermenar version when it told how Ebroin allied with Austrasians, ... *quos habuerat aliquandos*

Comparison between the first and later versions of the *Passio Leudegarii* thus serves to emphasise the historical nature of the earliest version. How can we use the the the Hermenar version to improve our understanding of later Merovingian Francia? Obviously, we can use it as a narrative source for the political history of the period *c.* 670–80. It contains a great deal of information about people, places and events simply unavailable elsewhere. Above all, the quality of its narrative of the sequence of events from 673 to 676 is unmatched. Without it we would not know who, apart from Bishop Audoin, supported Ebroin, or of the existence of the pretender to the throne, Clovis, or of the military expeditions to Autun and Lyons. On the other hand, it would be wrong to believe that the *Passio Leudegarii* gives us anything more than a partial glimpse of matters which were selected for their direct relevance to the narrative of the hero's career. It does not tell us, for example, of Audoin's support for Ebroin, or that Bishop Praejectus was involved in the events of Easter 675 and was himself martyred soon after, information omitted no doubt because it would have been embarrassing. Other details, such as the fighting between the Austrasians and Neustrians, which the *Liber Historiae Francorum* tells us formed the backdrop to Ebroin's second tenure of the mayoralty, and the victory in that conflict which may have given Ebroin the confidence finally to dispose of Leudegar, seem to have been beyond the horizon of our author's interest.[69]

The only other source containing anything like the same detail about these events is the *Liber Historiae Francorum*.[70] We are extremely

---

adversarios. Much time has been spent trying to identify these *adversarii*, with some strange hypothetical alliances emerging as a result. In fact, Ursinus's wording seems to come from a misreading of the Hermenar version ch. 18, below, p. 234, where the *adversarii* were an assortment of Leuedegar's enemies. For more detailed discussion of this misreading and of the historiograhpy, see below, ch. 18, n. 163. For recent work, where Ursinus's rewording of the Hermenar version is treated simply as adding information to the latter, see Scheibelreiter, *Der Bischof*, pp. 122–3, on the *dux* Waimar.

69 On Audoin and his unimpeachable reputation, see above, pp. 135–7. It is also at first sight surprising that our author made no reference to the so-called 'Council of Autun' which figures in several collections of canons: 'Concilium Leudegarii Episcopi Augustudnensis', ed. C. de Clercq, *Concilia Galliae a 511–695, Corpus Christianorum, Series Latina*, 148A (Turnhout, 1963), pp. 319–20. We might have expected at least to hear that Leuedegar was especially interested in the welfare of monks and monasteries, since nearly all the canons were concerned with monastic matters. The fact that there is no reflection at all of the council in the *Passio Leudegarii* makes us suspect that it has been wrongly associated with Leudegar. Below, ch. 2, n. 96, for further discussion of this problem.

70 Above, pp. 89–91.

fortunate here that, whilst the two sources agree in a way that enhances each's credibility, they actually focus on slightly different aspects of the action so that they can be combined to give an unusually rich picture of events. The impression which they convey together is that the *coup* of 673, the failure of Childeric's regime, the establishment of a factional regime in 675 and Ebroin's violent return to power in 676 were indeed events which rocked the whole of the Frankish political community. It is an impression which is reinforced by two other sources translated here, the *Vita Audoini* and the *Passio Praejecti*. The turmoil, too, figures in at least three and most probably in six other works.[71] But of all the sources reporting these important events, the *Passio Leudegarii* is exceptional not only because it tells us what happened, but because the quality of its detail also allows us to see to some extent how and why it happened.

The manner in which the *Passio Leudegarii* depicts these events is strong support for a view of late seventh-century Frankish politics which sees that the affairs of the palace were the concern of magnates throughout the kingdom, and that the elite in Neustria and in Burgundy made up one political community. The kingdom was governed through a consensus within this community which was focused upon the palace and upon the figure of the king. Discord arose when that consensus was disrupted by one faction of magnates exerting exclusive influence over the king.[72] Ebroin, we are told, banned people from Burgundy from coming to the palace without his express permission, and this caused great alarm. He was overthrown when the chance death of the king led to a large assembly of magnates gathered to enthrone that king's successor. Here the description of the assembly and of its behaviour is particularly important: Ebroin tried to prevent the assembly gathering,

---

71 *Vita Audoini*, above, pp. 152–65, *Passio Praejecti*, below, pp. 271–300; the other sources are: *Vita Lantberti*, ed. W. Levison, *MGH, SSRM*, V, pp. 608–12, *Vita Filiberti*, ed. W. Levison, *MGH, SSRM* V, pp. 583–604, *Miracula Martialis*, ed. G. Holder-Egger, *MGH, SS*, XV, pt. 1, pp. 280–3. The events are most probably also reflected in the *Vita Eremberti*, ed. W. Levison, *MGH, SSRM*, V, pp. 653–6, the *Historia Wambae*, ed. W. Levison, *MGH, SSRM*, V, pp. 501–35 and the *Vita Germani Abbatis Grandivallensis*, ed. B. Krusch, *MGH, SSRM*, V, pp. 33–40. For a possible reflection of the events in the coinage, see P. Grierson and M. Blackburn, *Medieval European Coinage*, vol. 1, *The Early Middle Ages, 3rd–10th Centuries* (Cambridge, ⋅ 1986), pp. 93–5

72 On the tendency for factional fighting to break out at court in this period, R. Sprandel, 'Struktur und Geschichte des merowingischen Adels', *Historisches Zeitschrift*, 193 (1961), and for a qualification of Sprandel's view, P. Fouracre, 'Merovingians, Mayors of the Palace and the notion of a 'low-born' Ebroin', *Bulletin of the Institute of Historical Research*, 57 (1984).

and from this we may infer that he felt vulnerable to the collective force that it would represent.[73] For those outside his circle the assembly provided a chance to make sure that the new king would not be under the mayor's exclusive influence, 'because for as long as he kept the king, whom he ought to have raised up before the people to the glory of the fatherland, in the background and just used his name, Ebroin would be able to do harm to whomsoever he wished, with impunity'.[74] The result was that a collective decision was made to abandon King Theuderic, who was associated with Ebroin, and to call for his brother Childeric instead. With a new king came a new regime based upon Leudegar's faction in Neustria–Burgundy and upon the king's Austrasian followers. But, as our author shows us, there was significant resistance to the move: 'He who did not wish to accept this decision either escaped by flight or, menaced on all sides by the burning danger to his life, agreed but remained unwilling.'[75]

It is therefore clear that a consensus in the political community was not re-established by Ebroin's overthrow, and the consequence was a complex feud which threatened to destroy that community. First, there was growing animosity among different groups within the palace, probably with members of the Neustro-Burgundian community ('the great men of the palace') in conflict with Childeric's own Austrasian followers. Leudegar was the first casualty of this ill-feeling; Childeric was the second. After Childeric's death, the struggle between the two Neustro-Burgundian factions which had clashed in 673 broke out again, and the impression from our source is that people all over the kingdom were forced to take sides, with the result that there was general disorder. Our author makes it clear that in his opinion there was mayhem because there was no king.[76] He also tells us that whoever managed to re-establish the king and the palace would be able to take control, hence the dramatic race between Ebroin and Leudegar to be the first to reach Theuderic.

73 On the collective power of the magnates in making judgement, Fouracre, '"Placita"', p. 33.
74 *Passio Leudegarii*, ch. 5, below, p. 222. This passage, which clearly advances a concept of puppet kingship, is often cited as an important landmark in the progressive fainéance of the Merovingians. It also provides invaluable information on the ritual of Merovingian king-making: see J. L. Nelson, 'Inauguration rituals', in P. Sawyer and I. Wood (eds.), *Early Medieval Kingship* (Leeds, 1977), p. 53, reprinted Nelson, *Politics and Ritual*, pp. 283–304.
75 *Passio Leudegarii*, ch. 5, below, p. 222.
76 *Passio Leudegarii*, ch. 15, below, pp. 231–2. The terms used here may show some influence from the work of Isidore of Seville, below, p. 232, n. 147.

Again, we have the very strongly expressed idea that the wielding of power rested on control over the palace and that the palace could not exist without a king. The idea is further reinforced by Ebroin's behaviour when he was excluded from Theuderic's palace: he went off and made his own king, a pretender called Clovis, unattested in any other source. 'This,' we are told, 'allowed them to gather many people together to form an army,' since Ebroin convinced people that Theuderic was dead.[77] Then, having used the army to regain control of Theuderic's palace, Ebroin dropped this Clovis and once again assumed the post of mayor of the palace to Theuderic. The feud then came to an end, with the mayor crushing some enemies (like Leudegar) by force but also possibly by the arrangement of some sort of truce or legal settlement.[78]

The author clearly thought that power was formally constituted, lay in the hands of whoever controlled the palace, and had to be exercised in conjunction with the king. The *ius potestatis* ('right of power') thus had a legal quality and the ruler's orders had the force of law. The notion that power was properly executed only through legal channels is also expressed in the context of Autun itself. Leudegar gained control after his appointment as bishop through bringing unruly elememts to heel 'by the dire threat of justice'. As archdeacon in Poitiers 'in lay matters' he had also been 'a judge to be feared'.[79] The rights of power may have been perceived to lie in the subject's obligation to obey legally binding orders. Our source gives us the impression that in Frankish society power was formally structured and legally constituted, but it also shows us that the orders which the kings and mayors, even Ebroin, gave were the result of a process of collective decision-making. Collective agreement thus underpinned the obligation to obey. However, as our author makes clear, disagreement at the centre led to disorder, and then public power could quickly give way to private violence. On the other hand, the *Passio Leudegarii* suggests that when one faction was firmly in control and there was agreement at the centre, the power structure could indeed be very effective. The source gives a further insight into why this may have been so. It lies in the opposition which an established figure might face in his locality. When the rulers in the palace wished to control magnates in an outlying area

77 *Passio Leudegarii*, ch. 19, below, p. 236.

78 *Passio Leudegarii*, ch. 28, below, p. 244.

79 For the context of Leudegar's education in the field of law, see I. Wood, 'Administration, law and culture in Merovingian Gaul', in R. McKitterick (ed.), *The Uses of Literacy in early Medieval Europe* (Cambridge, 1990), pp. 67–8.

they could often form an alliance with local people who opposed a particular magnate. As we have seen, local elements in Autun combined with a palace faction to bring about Leudegar's downfall in 675, just as people in Lyons had involved the palace in Aunemund's demise a decade earlier.[80] Local rivalry could also provide an opportunity for outside intervention which could open up a distant area to palace patronage, as Leudegar's appointment itself shows. The source may thus be used both to show what held the political entity together and to show what could break it apart. It is therefore of direct relevance to the continuing debate among historians about the nature and extent of public authority in the early Middle Ages.

So far we have seen how the *Passio Leudegarii* may be used to provide a narrative of events and to explain why those events came about. In more general terms it has also allowed us to see something of the nature and structure of power in the late seventh century. Finally, we can draw from it observations about the developing Christian culture of that society. We have already noted how the author managed to smoothe out the awkward details of Leudegar's worldy career by dealing with them within the conventional hagiographical framework. The way in which he did this speaks firstly of his own ingenuity and skill. He did not use convention blindly, but adapted it to his own needs. Though the conventions of hagiography may themselves suggest that belief was growing to the point of credulity, the author's adaptations reveal a fairly pragmatic way of thinking. Such pragmatism seems appropriate to an age in which traditional beliefs were generally being adapted to new conditions.[81] As we saw in the introduction (pp. 1–78), traditionally, martyrs had been made by the pagan Roman state, or at least Catholics had suffered at the hands of heretics.[82] But here

---

80 On the background to alliances between local people and forces in the palace, P. Fouracre, 'Merovingian history and Merovingian hagiography', *Past and Present*, 127 (1990). On Aunemund, see above, pp. 177–9.

81 For strong *caveats* against presuming that medieval people were subject to blind faith, S. Reynolds, 'Social mentalities and the case of medieval scepticism', *Transactions of the Royal Historical Society*, sixth series, 1 (1991), and on the place of later Merovingian hagiography in the emergent Christian culture of the West, Fouracre, 'Merovingian history and Merovingian hagiography', 28–9. W. Goffart, *The Narrators of Barbarian History (A.D. 550–800)* (Princeton, New Jersey, 1988), is also illuminating on how authors adapted to changing conditions, especially in the case of Gregory of Tours, pp. 203–34

82 On the making of martyrs, Delehaye, *Les Passions*, pp. 236–315; on criteria for sanctity in the seventh century, E. Kemp, *Canonisation and Authority in the Western Church* (Oxford, 1947, repr. 1979), p. 35, and A. Vauchez, *La Sainteté en Occident aux derniers siècles du Moyen-âge* (Paris, 1981), pp. 15–22.

martyrdom was the result of conflict which emerged within a single community of Christians. In these circumstances, creating a credible martyr was a difficult job. But it was the success of authors such as this one which helped Christian culture to cope with conflict within the same religious community and with conflict between rulers and ruled. Bringing Frankish magnates into the ranks of the saints also helped to make possible a more general sanctification of power which complemented the clothing of power in law. Both power and sanctity were basic to a Christian concept of legitimate rule. That is what Leudegar as leader stood for. The same mentality is evident in all the works presented here. But no other work can match the *Passio Leudegarii* in showing a godly man in action in the world.

Passio Leudegarii
(The Suffering of St Leudegar)

THE LIFE AND MARTYRDOM OF ST LEUDEGARIUS BISHOP AND MARTYR

DEDICATED IN APOSTOLIC HONOUR TO LORD HERMENAR HOLY BISHOP OF AUTUN

At last I have set out to write the life of the blessed Leudegar, martyr and bishop, having frequently been requested by you to do so and having been driven on by the holy insistence of my spiritual brethren. I held back from obeying your command and entreaty for so long as I foresaw a twofold criticism raised against me: firstly I was afraid of my fog-like ignorance and unworthiness,[83] and secondly I dreaded being exposed to the derision of wise men. Thus in the first instance I beseech your Pious Devotion that you may pardon my rustic ways,[84] and, if it be pleasing to you, that at first you do no more than read this alone and in secret whilst either you improve with more refined language that which we set down at your orders, or so that what is left in place after you have read it may be the expression that has met with your approval, expression which will be judged irreproachably correct

---

83 *Caligo*, the term for fog, hence foggy vision, also appears in the prologue to the *Passio Praejecti*, below p. 279.

84 It is common in the prologues to Merovingian works for the authors to plead rusticity whilst attempting to write in as sophisticated a manner as possible: see above, pp. 76–7. The prologue to the *Passio Praejecti* provides a yet more obvious example of an author striving to show literary merit.

by other bishops too.[85] This I seek above all: that your strengths,
which my ignorance and inexperience deny me, your expertise and
enthusiasm for prayer, may persuade God to furnish the support
necessary to see this task through to the end.

END OF PROLOGUE

CHAPTER 1

Leudegar, renowned glorious bishop of Autun, has become a new
martyr of the Christian age. Just as the earth kindly brought him forth
of noble birth,[86] so until he grew from childhood to the strength of
manhood the grace of God was always with him, so that as he passed
through the various stages and orders, upright, he always stood out

85 This appeal is probably not just rhetorical. It may well relate to the part which
  Hermenar himself played in the following narrative and to the generally controversial nature of the events described. It reminds us that the work in effect furnished
  a public version of events.

86 No more is said about his origins. *Passio Leudegarii II*, ch. 1, p. 324, adds nothing
  more substantial, merely expanding the phrase *nobiliter exortus* to *ex progenie celsa
  Francorum ac nobilissima exortus*. A document which purports to be Leudegar's will
  refers to persons named Sigrada and Bodilo in conjunction with land in Burgundy
  said to be hereditary, see above, p. 197, n. 21. There is also a tenth-century copy of
  a letter which Leudegar is said to have to addressed to his mother, who is called
  Sigrada: *MGH, Epistolae*, III, ed. E. Dümmler (Berlin, 1882), pp. 464–7. We know,
  of course, of Leudegar's uncle, Dido, bishop of Poitiers, named in the text below, of
  his relation Ansoald, bishop of Poitiers, to whom the *Passio Leudegarii II* was
  addressed, and of his brother, Gaerinus, also named below, all three of whom are
  also firmly attested elsewhere. Finally, the name of a maternal aunt, Berswinda, is
  given in the late ninth- or tenth-century *Vita Odiliae*, ch. 2, ed. W. Levison, *MGH,
  SSRM*, VI, p. 38 (see also below, n. 192). It is quite likely that the Berswinda
  connection is fictional, intended to reinforce the association of Odilia's family with
  the cult of Leudegar. The names Sigrada and Bodilo could also be later inventions
  first intended to lend authentic-looking detail to the description of certain lands in
  Leudegar's will. The latter could then have been the source for the names, which
  were later used in other documents, such as the letter to Sigrada, or a later version
  of the *Vita Odiliae* in which Berswinda is made the sister of Sigrada. The invention
  of persons and the build-up of documents around the tradition of Aunemund's life
  is an analogous case: see above, p. 168, n. 7. It is interesting from an historio-
  graphical point of view to see that the more such names circulate in both medieval
  and modern works the more they are taken seriously and generate speculation on
  further connections and associations; see, for instance, how Ewig adds to the
  discussion of the name Bodilo, 'Teilreiche', 127, n. 6, and 128, n. 172 (*Gallien*, vol.
  1, pp. 213 and 215). In fact here the important point should be how little our source
  tells us about Leudegar's family, for in general saints' lives of this period stress the
  importance of lineage and name parents. Contrast, for instance, what the *Vita
  Audoini*, above, pp. 153–4, the *Acta Aunemundi*, above, p. 180, the *Passio Praejecti*,
  below, p. 272, and the *Vita Geretrudis*, below, p. 320, say about the origins and
  families of their respective heroes.

from the others. He was given an invigorating upbringing by his uncle, Dido, bishop of Poitiers, a man much renowned beyond his diocese for his wisdom and for his bountiful good works.[87] Fully accomplished in the various studies that lay noblemen are wont to pursue, he [Leudegar] shone in all the disciplines and was chosen to shoulder the task of being the archdeacon in Poitiers. As soon as he began his work as archdeacon his courage and wisdom shone forth so greatly that he was quite beyond comparison with his predecessors, especially when he came to know the severe judgement of the secular law, for in lay matters he was a judge to be feared.[88] When he had fully learned the doctrines of the Church he became an outstanding teacher of the clergy. Disciplined, he was also alert to the danger of fault: never did he seem to relax his guard against the sins of the flesh. In looking after the business of the churches he was wakeful and keen, in going to law he was vigorous,[89] as a counsellor he was wise and he glowed with eloquence.[90]

CHAPTER 2

Meanwhile events were making it ever more vital that they should ordain him bishop in the town of Autun. For recently a dispute over that see had broken out between two men, and their quarrelling had

87 Dido was bishop of Poitiers *c.* 628–67. He was certainly known beyond his diocese, being mentioned in the *Liber Historiae Francorum* and in the *Additamentum Nivialense*, see above, p. 88, and below, p. 329. The *Passio Leudegarii II*, ch. 1, p. 324, has it that as an infant Leudegar was sent to the court of King Clothar before being sent to Dido to be educated. King Clothar II died in 628. If Leudegar had indeed been sent to his court, this would mean that he was aged between forty and fifty when he became bishop, and between fifty-five and sixty-five when he died.

88 He was ... *saecularium terribilis iudex*. It is clear that in some areas officials of the Church had jurisdiction over lay persons.

89 He was *strinuus in ratiociniis*. Presumably this refers to Leudegar's advocacy of the rights of the church of Poitiers, but it could mean that he was generally active in pursuing legal disputes, cf, the contemporary Council of Bordeaux, ed. C. de Clercq, *Conciliae Galliae*, p. 312, which complained that the clergy were far too keen on going to law in general, with the effect that they had become indistinguishable from lay persons.

90 *Passio Leudegarii II*, chs. 2–3, gives more detail about Leudegar's time in Poitiers. It tells us that he was nearly twenty years old when made deacon, becoming archdeacon shortly afterwards. If it is correct that he attended the court of Clothar II, he would have been an archdeacon for at least fifteen years, after which he was made abbot of St Maxentius in Poitiers, ruling it for nearly six years before being called to the palace and appointed bishop of Autun.

become so fierce that there had been bloodshed.[91] Now, one of these
men had been laid low in death, and the other had been driven into
exile as the perpetrator of the crime. Then Queen Balthild, who with
Clothar her son ruled in the palace of the Franks, inspired by God's
advice, in our opinion, sent this vigorous man Leudegar to be bishop
in Autun in order that the church there, which now for almost two
years like a widow had stood alone in the turbulence of the world
around it, should be protected by his strength and guidance and be
thus defended from those who were violently attacking it.[92] What
more can I say? At his coming all the enemies of that church and city
as well as those who where struggling with each other in murderous
hatred were terrified, so much so that they did not want even to be
reminded of the scandalous behaviour that had gone before: for those
whom Leudegar could not bring to agreement by his preaching, he
forced by the dire threat of justice. Now bishop, and guided by the
Lord, he was so outstanding in the particular attention he paid to the
giving of alms to the poor that it would be tedious to tell of each
instance. But though we may remain silent, his works themselves will
bear witness: the table which he set up for the distribution of alms
remains near the church porch;[93] his beautiful treasure, sparkling with
gold, shines in the sacred vessels of the church;[94] there are as well the

91 For the occasion and historical setting of such disputes over bishoprics, see
   Fouracre, 'Merovingian history and Merovingian hagiography', 35–7. In the light
   of this passage, Leudegar's troubles in Autun could be seen partly as a continuation
   of the dispute over who should be its bishop. The narrative of the *Passio Praejecti*,
   below, pp. 280–3, could be interpreted in a similar way.

92 This provides a useful example of how a dispute over a bishopric could provide an
   opportunity for the palace to intervene and appoint its own candidate as bishop. It
   is not possible to give a firm date for Leudegar's appointment. His predecessor,
   Ragnobert, last appears in the year 660 as signatory to two charters of Emmo,
   bishop of Sens: Pardessus, *Diplomata*, nos. 333, 335, pp. 111, 114 (on the
   authenticity of these charters, see above, p. 174, n. 24). We are told that the
   appointment was made under Queen Balthild, and we know that the queen was
   forced out of power some time between autumn 664 and summer 665 (see above, p.
   112). If we take into account the interregnum in the church of Autun, which lasted
   'almost two years', we are left with the probability that Leudegar was made bishop
   some time in 662–64.

93 *Matricola* is the word used for this table. The term refers not just to the actual table
   but also to the institution of poor relief managed by the cathedral church. On
   matricularii and seventh-century bishops, with useful references, Scheibelreiter, *Der
   Bischof,* pp. 185–6.

94 It is interesting that silver is not mentioned here. This is consistent with the
   account later in the source of how Leudegar distributed his silver plate to the
   citizens of Autun when the town was under siege, ch. 21, below, pp. 237–8. In other
   words, there was none of his silver left in the church at the time of writing.

ornaments he caused to be made, with wonderful skill, in the baptistery. Though we may say nothing, the grave of the holy martyr St Symphorian and the glorious translation of his holy body there bear witness to how he loved and was devoted to the martyrs. Furthermore the church floor and the golden hangings, the building of a new churchyard, the rebuilding of the town's walls, the repair of houses, anything, indeed, that was worn with age was restored through him, and the visible remains indicating his industry are still there for those who look.[95] Let these few impressions suffice to remind us of the many other things.[96] Let us turn in our account to that time in which the champion of Christ took up the struggle against the devil.

95 In this period such industry was apparently typical of bishops, as they were responsible for the state of their cathedral towns. The provision of public services was one facet of this responsibility, another was the exercise of jurisdiction, referred to earlier in the chapter. See F. Prinz, 'Die bischöfliche Stadtherrschaft im Frankenreich vom 5. bis 7, Jahrhundert', *Historische Zeitschrift*, 217 (1974), and for an important argument that such responsibilities were exercised on behalf of, not in opposition to, central government, J. Durliat, 'Les attributions civiles des évêques mérovingiens: l'exemple de Didier évêque de Cahors (630–655)', *Annales du Midi*, 91 (1979). Note that Praejectus was also associated with building work: see below, p. 279.

96 It is surprising that there is no mention here of the church council said to have been held in Autun under Leudegar, or of the latter's special concern for the welfare of monks, which is the subject of nearly all the canons of the council. Canon 15 explicitly orders obedience to the rule of St Benedict, and, because of this, Leudegar is often said to have been the first to advocate exclusive use of the rule in Frankish monasteries. However, as A. Dierkens, *Abbayes et chapitres entre Sambre et Meuse (VIIᵉ – XIᵉ siècles)*, Beihefte der *Francia*, 14 (Sigmaringen, 1985), p. 287, has argued, reference to the rule at that date does not mean that it was followed in the way in which we understand for later centuries. The reference to the rule, moreover, is formulaic and general: ... *quicquid canonum ordo vel regula sancti Benedicti edocet, et implere et custodire in omnibus debeant.* The council is in *Concilia Galliae*, ed. C. de Clercq, pp. 319–20. On the date of the canonical collection in which it is attributed to Leudegar, G. Le Bras, 'Notes pour servir à l'histoire des collections canoniques: sur la date et la patrie de la collection dite d'Angers', *Revue Historique de Droit Français et Etranger*, fourth series, 8 (1929), 775–80. Although Le Bras seems right to have argued that the Angers collection containing the canons is from the Merovingian period, the association of Leudegar with the legislation is more questionable. It occurs only in the index of the collection and could have been made simply because of the saint's fame after his death rather than on the basis of his participation whilst alive. Le Bras himself could not resist associating the whole collection with Leudegar, imagining that it was *le résultat d'un réveil de l'église burgonde sous le pontificat de saint Léger.* Such conviction comes from taking the *Passio Leudegarii* at face value, without questioning why the source does not refer to any council held under Leudegar.

CHAPTER 3

In the time that the holy priest Leudegar so dwelled as bishop in
Autun he enjoyed success and peace. After he had restored what had
been destroyed he instructed the clergy in the divine offices, the people
he constantly taught by his heavenly preaching, and the poor he
nourished with the generosity of his almsgiving. In spirit so completely was he bound to observing the Lord's commands, and so
powerful was his will in all things, that whatever goal he decided to
tackle, God allowed him to achieve without difficulty. Nor did
Almighty God confer His grace on Leudegar undeservedly, because he
had already totally dedicated himself to keeping the Lord's command.
But goodwill is always opposed by evil, and that age-old serpent, envy,
always finds those among whom it can sow strife.[97] Thus there were
certain men of higher rank, ignorant of spiritual things, but holding
earthly power,[98] who, when they saw this man [Leudegar] stand out
as the unbending pinnacle of justice, began to squirm with malicious
envy and they decided to block his progress to further success.[99]

CHAPTER 4

At this time Ebroin was, as we say, mayor of the palace, and he ruled
the palace under King Clothar because the queen, of whom we have
spoken before, was living in the monastery which she had earlier
prepared for herself.[100] The aforementioned men of envy went to
Ebroin and kindled in his heart a great fury against the man of God
and, since they could find no real fault of which to accuse him, they
made up lying falsehoods, saying that, while everyone else obeyed
Ebroin's orders, Bishop Leudegar alone defied his commands. Now,
this Ebroin was so easily fired by the torch of greed, and so given to
the love of money, that in his presence only those who paid him the
greater sum had their case pronounced just. People had given over to

---

97 It was necessary to use the devil to explain why conflict arose between Christians.
    See above, p. 47.

98 The reading *potentiam secularem tenentes* is preferred here to *potentiam secularem
    timentes* (*MGH, SSRM*, V, p. 286).

99 Envy, inspired by the devil, was commonly used to describe opposition to a holy
    man.

100 King Cothar III, who ruled 657–73. On Balthild's withdrawal to her foundation at
    Chelles, see above, pp. 112–14; on the context of Ebroin's rise to power, Fouracre,
    'Merovingians, mayors of the palace'.

him a massive treasure of gold and silver, some because they were frightened of him, others as they paid to secure justice. The hearts of some of these people, however, were distressed by grief at his exploitation and they had already banded together against him, not only because he exercised his greed in his dealings, but also because for the slightest offence he was wont to shed the blood of many noblemen.[101] He thus began to be suspicious of Bishop Leudegar, as he could not win him over by argument, nor did Leudegar flatter him or acknowledge him as leader as others did, and Ebroin had seen that he always remained undaunted by all his threats.[102] Then he issued this unlawful edict: that no one from the region of Burgundy was to come to the palace unless he had ordered him to come.[103] Because of his fear now all the leading men were suspect, because he thought to increase his crime either by condemning certain people to death or by taking away their lands.[104]

100 The ninth-century *Passio Ragnoberti*, ed. B. Krusch, *MGH, SSRM*, V, pp. 209–11, may refer to here to the conspiracy alluded to here, for it tells of how Ebroin accused Ragnobert along with two other nobles, Bodo and Uniscand, of conspiring against him. However, this later work draws upon the *Passio Leudegarii* so heavily that it may be using the passage as source for an explanation of Ragnebert's downfall rather than corroborating it with independent information. The negative picture of Ebroin in this chapter actually agrees in some respects with the two more positive opinions we have of the ruler: in the *Miracula Martialis, ex Miracula Martialis,* II, ch. 3, ed. O. Holder-Egger, *MGH SS*, XV, pt. 1 (Hanover, 1887), p. 281, and in the *Passio Praejecti*, ch. 26, below, p. 291. All three sources agree that Ebroin was an exceptionally active and effective ruler. Note too the relatively neutral portrayal of Ebroin's character in the *Liber Historiae Francorum*, ch. 45. See Gerberding, *Rise*, pp. 73–4.

102 Ebroin and Leudegar may have enjoyed a happier relationship at an earlier time, for in 667 Leudegar signed a charter of Drauscius, bishop of Soissons, which guaranteed privileges for Ebroin's foundation, the convent of Notre Dame in Soissons: Pardessus, *Diplomata*, no. 355, p. 140.

103 The aim of such an order was to prevent access to the king and thus to deny the means to appeal against Ebroin's actions. The formula used here: *ut nullus ... praesumeret, nisi ...* , is seen in earlier Merovingian legislation, for example *Clotharii Edictum* ch. 4, ed. A. Boretius, *Capitularia Regum Francorum*, I, *MGH, Legum Sectio II*, p. 21.

104 It is not clear whose fear is meant here, but the translation is consistent with the later statement (ch. 28) that Ebroin persecuted people because he was in a state of fear.

CHAPTER 5

Meanwhile, whilst this business[105] remained unresolved, King Clothar was called by the Lord and left this world. Now, whereas Ebroin should have called together the leading men, and with due solemnity, as is the custom, raised up to the throne Clothar's full brother, Theuderic by name,[106] he became puffed up with arrogance and refused to call them together. Whereupon people began to be very frightened because as long as he kept the king, whom he ought to have raised up before the people to the glory of the royal fatherland, in the background and just used his name, Ebroin would be able to do harm to whomsoever he wished, with impunity.[107] When the crowd of nobles who were hurrying to meet the new king received Ebroin's order to break off their journey, they took counsel together and, abandoning Theuderic, they all demanded instead his younger brother Childeric who had been assigned the throne in Austrasia.[108] He who did not wish to accept this decision either escaped by flight or, menaced on all sides by the burning danger to his life, agreed but remained unwilling.[109]

CHAPTER 6

Now that because of the fear of Ebroin's unjust and oppressive rule everyone had established Childeric upon the throne of Neustria as well as upon that of Burgundy, the tyrant fled to the altar of the church, mindful of the great wrong he had done. His treasure was swiftly

105 The term for 'business' is *causa*, which can have the more precise meaning of 'law case'. If we take this latter meaning, it would suggest that Ebroin had already begun legal proceedings against Leudegar. This is what Ewig understood by the term *Teilreiche*, 127 (*Gallien*, vol. 1., p. 214).

106 *Sed cum Ebroinus eius fratrem geramanum nomen Theudericum, convocatis obtimatis, cum sollemniter, ut mos est, debuisset sublimare in regnum* .... The stress on custom and due process is strong here, suggesting that the author is providing authentic (and valuable) information on the process of king-making. The years of Theuderic's reign (673–91) were counted from the death of Clothar III, which suggests that Theuderic was actually raised to the throne before being deposed.

107 This is a clear statement of how mayors of the palace could wield great power if they could prevent other magnates having access to the king. One way in which Ebroin could make use of the king's name was to issue edicts such as the one referred to in the previous chapter. Only kings could issue edicts, and in Roman fashion they had the force of law.

108 Childeric had been made king of Austrasia in 662, see above, p. 19. He ruled over all three kingdoms 673–75.

109 It is interesting that the author should mention this element of coercion. It may suggest that such people were still alive and still influential at the time of writing.

broken down into many lots, and what the scoundrel had evilly gathered together over a long time was rightfully quickly scattered. Then at the intervention of certain bishops, and above all at the intervention of Bishop Leudegar, they did not kill him, but he was sent into exile to the monastery of Luxeuil,[110] that there by repenting he might wipe away the sins he had committed. But because he possessed eyes of his heart blinded by the dust of earthly greed, in his malevolent soul spiritual wisdom was of no benefit. Childeric now ordered his brother Theuderic, against whom he had come, having been called, to present himself, saying that he ought to speak to him. Then certain men, who were seen to be leaders in the kingdom and wished by flattery to persuade Childeric not to shed blood, rashly ventured to order the cutting of their lord Theuderic's hair and pushed to present him thus shaven to his brother.[111] But when Theuderic was asked by his brother what fate he preferred, he would say only this: that he had been unjustly cast down from the throne, and he declared that he was anticipating a swift judgement from God in his favour. It was then ordered that he should remain in the monastery of the martyr St Denis and be protected there until he grew his hair, which they had cut off. And happily the God of Heaven whom he had predicted he would have as his judge afterwards let him rule.

CHAPTER 7

Now that Childeric was king everyone demanded that he should issue the following edicts throughout the three kingdoms over which he had gained sway: that as of old the judges should maintain the law and custom of each kingdom and that rulers from one [province] should not intrude in the others lest one of them should, as Ebroin had done, take up oppressive and unlawful rule and after his example look down on his peers,[112] for, as they acknowledged that access to the highest

110 Later, in ch. 12, Hermenar would similarly plead for Leudegar himself to be exiled rather than killed. The analogy serves to strengthen the author's argument that Hermenar was Leudegar's saviour, not his chief accuser.

111 Long hair was, of course, the badge of Merovingian kingship, cf. *Gregorii Episcopi Turonensis, Libri Historiarum X*, III, ch. 18, ed. B. Krusch and W. Levison *MGH, SSRM*, I, pt. 1 (Hanover, 1951), pp. 118–19, where Gregory tells of how, when the kings Clothar and Childebert wished to exclude the sons of Chlodomer from the throne, cutting their hair was considered an alternative to killing them.

112 This legislation looks like the confirmation of regional privileges given out by King Clothar II when he too had become master of all three kingdoms: see above, pp. 12–13. Although the passage is cast in legal terminology and the measures are

position should be open to all, nobody was to presume to place himself before another.[113] Yet although he freely conceded what had been asked, Childeric was now corrupted by the advice he took from foolish and nearly pagan people. And, subject to the inconstancy of youth,[114] what he had confirmed through the counsel of wise men, suddenly he retracted.

CHAPTER 8

Childeric had astutely kept St Leudegar with him in the palace because he had seen that he was distinguished before all others by the light of his wisdom.[115] This was the reason why the envy of the wicked received new life and grew. Again they began to look for ways of accusing him so that whatever the king did, or whatever he gave out in judgement, just or unjust, they slanderously asserted that it was the work of Leudegar.[116] If the king had in fact complied with his advice, then he would have walked in God's commands. But because the judgement given from on high had now arrived, his heart was unable to comprehend the teaching of justice. So the judgement, which Theuderic declared he was waiting for the Lord to give, had to have its swift sentence carried out. The man of God, however, when he saw that the devil's envy was again boiling up against him, followed the apostle's example and, putting on the breastplate of faith and the helmet of salvation, and taking up the sword of the spirit, which is the word of God, he went out

---

termed *decreta*, it is not sensible to treat the sentences exhaustively as if they were actual decrees. This, for instance, is how J. Fischer treated them, seeing each statement as a precise reflection of what had been objectionable in Ebroin's regime: J. Fischer, Der Hausmeier Ebroin, dissertation, Bonn, 1954, pp. 122–8.

113 ... *dum mutua sibi successione culminis habere cognoscerent nullus se alio anteferre auderet.* The meaning is not clear here, as is shown by the variation in readings in the manuscript tradition (see *MGH, SSRM*, V, p. 289).

114 ... *ut erat iuvenile levitate praeventus,* cf. the *Liber Historiae Francorum*, ch. 45 on Childeric: *Erat enim ... levis nimis. The Continuation of the Fourth Book of the Chronicle of Fredegar,* ch. 2, adds the term *citatus* to the *Liber's* description. It is plain that Childeric's cardinal failing was judged to have been his inablity to follow good advice and his tendency to change his mind suddenly. In a political community which depended so heavily on consensus, these were critical faults.

115 In *Passio Leudegarii II,* ch. 5, p. 328, this is taken to mean that Childeric made Leudegar mayor of the palace. It is largely on the basis of this 'mistake' that Krusch thought that the author of the *Passio II* could not have been a contemporary, see above, p. 207.

116 This accusation appears again in ch. 15, below, p. 232. The following sentence serves to counter any suggestion that Leudegar was responsible for Childeric's behaviour and it prepares us to reject the accusation when it is made a second time.

alone to do combat with the age-old enemy.[117] Because the purity of the priest knows not how to fear a king's threats, so he began to upbraid Childeric.[118] Why, he asked him, did he so suddenly change the customs of the kingdoms when he had ordered them to be conserved?[119] Also, they say, he told him that the queen, his wife, was the daughter of his own uncle,[120] and unless he made amends for these and other unlawful abominations he would for sure very soon see that divine vengeance was close at hand. Although at first Childeric had begun to listen freely, later he was put off by the advice of his hangers-on and, whereas he ought to have applied his words to correcting his faults, he began to look for an opportunity to bring about his [Leudegar's] death. He was swayed in this by those who wanted to overturn justice, by those disorderly ones who wished to encourage the king in his youthful

117 The apostle was St Paul. The terms appear in Thessalonians 5: 8 and in Ephesians 6: 16, 17.

118 The source of the saying about the purity of the priest is unknown. The saying, termed a 'proverb', also appears along with the 'helmet of salvation' metaphor in the *Passio Praejecti*, ch. 24, below, p. 289. Although we could fairly characterise both the 'proverb' and the metaphor as clichés, their appearence in the two sources at the same point in their respective narrative sequences (just before the events at Easter 675) is unlikely to be mere coincidence. Krusch, in 'Die Älteste Vita Praejecti', *NA*, 18 (1893), stated on impressionstic grounds that he believed the *Passio Praejecti* to be the elder of the two works. Thus, in his view, the *Passio Leudegarii* borrowed from the *Passio Praejecti* at this point: 'Die Älteste Vita Praejecti', 632–33. Although it is impossible to say with certainty which of the two sources is the older. a plausible explanation of the borrowing could be that the author of the *Passio Leudegarii* had seen the other work and was aware of its critical attitude towards Leudegar. One way of pre-empting an unfavourable comparison between the two bishops would have been to describe Leudegar in the same terms as those used of Praejectus whilst excluding mention of the latter in the following events. Nevertheless it remains possible that the borrowing was the other way round. Whatever the case, it serves to emphasise that these events were highly controversial. Finally, it is curious that the two sources touch only on this point. Otherwise they appear quite independent of each other.

119 One can only speculate about how Childeric might have changed the customs. In the light of what follows, one possibility is that he had installed his Austrasian followers in Neustria and Burgundy.

120 She was Bilichild, daughter of Sigibert III, half-brother to Childeric's father Clovis II. An attack upon Bilichild and her mother Himmnechild could be seen as a Neustrian attempt to weaken Childeric's Austrasian following. The early ninth-century *Vita Lantberti*, ch. 3, ed. W. Levison, *MGH, SSRM*, V, p. 610, names the petitioners for a land grant to the monastery of St Wandrille and may afford us a glimpse of Childeric's chief followers. In addition to Bilichild, of the ten others named we can identify Leudegar and his brother Gaerinus, five Austrasians and the Neustrian count of the area with which the document was concerned. The two other petitioners are unidentifiable. If this impression is roughly correct, it would appear that Neustrians and Burgundians were in a minority among the king's closest advisers, hence Leudegar's attempt to weaken the Austrasian influence.

actions, and by those who had seduced him into destroying his own decree. For all these men, and those of the same feather who spent their time enjoying the sensual pleasures of the world, began to fear that the man of God would ruin their game. For they had already seen that it was no easy task to walk the narrow path of justice. Indeed, this old world weighed down with sin could not hold up the manliness of its holy citizen.[121]

CHAPTER 9

At this time there was a certain nobleman called Hector who ruled in Marseilles, holding the office of *patricius* there. Hector stood out from the crowd because he was nobly born of a famous line and in worldly affairs he was wise.[122] He came to see King Childeric in connection with a certain law case[123] and he hoped to obtain what he sought from the king through the intercession of the man of God. God's holy man thus welcomed Hector to his town and offered him his hospitality until, as he [Hector] had asked, he might intercede to commend him to the king, for he [Leudegar] had invited Childeric to come and celebrate Easter in his town's church. The envious ones found in this an opportunity to add even more to the wickedness which they had of late been pouring into the king's heart. Then they drew Wulfoald, the mayor of the palace, into their plan,[124] telling him lies about Leudegar and Hector, saying that they had bound themselves together to overturn the king's rule and to take for themselves the rights of power.

CHAPTER 10

There was in those days a certain monk of the monastery of St Symphorian the martyr[125] called Marcolinus. He had withdrawn from

---

121 In this section of the narrative the author could not use Ebroin's malevolence to explain Leudegar's difficulties. Instead he evoked the general sinfulness of mankind and thus invited analogy between Leudegar and Christ.

122 Contrast the *Passio Praejecti*, ch. 23, below, p. 288, on Hector: *erat quidam infamis vir Hector nomine.*

123 The law case was the result of Hector's charge that Praejectus as bishop of Clermont had wrongful possession of land which belonged to his spouse.

124 Wulfoald had been associated with Childeric since the latter had been made king in Austrasia in 662. After Ebroin's banishment he seems to have become mayor of the palace with authority over all three kingdoms, see H. Ebling, *Prosopographie der Amtsträger des Merowingerreiches*, Beihefte der *Francia*, 2 (Munich, 1974), pp. 241–3.

125 The author was himself a monk at the monastery of St Symphorian.

the world only in body, not in spirit; rather, as it became publicly known afterwards, he was too keen to seek the praises of men and honours under the false appearance of religion.[126] About his religious life,[127] since it is very obvious to everybody, I think it better to keep silent rather than talk of it. But the king, not knowing this man, regarded him almost as a prophet of God in all he said because he saw not that his accusations concerning the man of God were above all flattery which nurtured his own desire. So, that night on which the holy Easter vigils were being celebrated in the town,[128] the king, already suspicious of Leudegar, refused to attend and he and a few of his party called for the opinion of the above-mentioned hyocrites. Now whipping up his evil intent against the servant of God, when the moment of Easter came he was not afraid to receive the host there. But afterwards, whilst others were fasting and awaiting the holy celebration, the king got shamefully drunk on wine and he went into the church.[129] He was shouting and calling Leudegar by name, to flush him out in flight, as it were. At the same time he terrified would-be mediators by threatening to hit them with his sword. Shouting all the while, he then realised that Leudegar was in the baptistery and he went in there too. But so bright was the light there, and so strong the smell of the chrism that is used in the blessing of the baptised, that he was overwhelmed. Then when Leudegar answered his shouting, saying, 'I am here',[130] the king could not see him at all and walked on, coming to the bishop's mansion, which had been made ready for him

126 Perhaps some sort of public condemnation of Marcolinus is being alluded to here.

127 The term 'religious life' translates *conversatio.*

128 The night of Easter Saturday.

129 It is difficult to be sure of the precise meaning of this passage. In the context of the first part of the chapter, it looks as if the king received the host in the monastery of St Symphorian, got drunk, and then went into the cathedral church of St Nazaire, where Leudegar was leading the vigils. Such an interpretation is consistent with the *Passio Praejecti,* ch. 25, below, p. 290, which says that Praejectus led the prayers in the presence of the king. According to this view, there were two Easter celebrations going on at the same time, perhaps reflecting the factional division in the court. From what follows in the rest of the chapter, it seems likely that a midnight mass was celebrated in St Symphorian whereas in the cathedral church vigils were followed by the baptismal rites which could precede the first mass of Easter. Hence, when Childeric had received the host and had gone into the cathedral church to look for Leudegar, the latter was in the baptistery. On the tradition of Easter vigils and baptism, see J. Jungmann, *The Early Liturgy to the Time of Gregory the Great,* trans. F. Brunner (London 1959), p. 263.

130 The author is referring here to I Samuel 3:1–6.

and where he stayed.[131] The other bishops who had been holding the
prayers with the man of God returned to their lodgings, but Leudegar
continued with the holy rite until it was finished. Then, quite unafraid,
he went to see the angry king and with soothing words he asked of him
why he had not come before vigils and why during the solemnities of
that very holy night he doggedly remained full of anger. But the king,
confused by Leudegar's ineffable wisdom, could not answer, except to
say that he did have a certain reason to suspect him.

CHAPTER 11

Thereupon Leudegar, man of God, saw that the king had made up his
mind against him and that at the urging of his followers [satellites] he
had decided that Leudegar and Hector should be put to death. Now, in
this crisis Hector, as he was afraid, came to hate the king, not because
he himself was frightened to die, but rather because he was thinking
of the safety of those who had come to him for protection.[132] So he
decided to seek flight rather than court martyrdom and thereby
disrupt and bloody the Church at the time of the holy festival of Christ's
resurrection.[133] He also wanted to prevent those who had turned to
him from losing their lives arbitrarily. But is there no one who supposes
that he would not have dared to go through all to martyrdom? Well,
the day before, when he was at mass,[134] a certain monk, Berchar by
name, told him of the fate that had been decided for him. Nevertheless,
on the morrow, the day of our Lord's Passion, he went to the royal
palace and, pushing himself forward, he wanted to offer his blood to
Christ on the very day that Christ had poured out His own blood to

131 The layout of the buildings mentioned here can still be traced in Autun today. The
    baptistery, now under the parish church of St Jean-de-la-Grotte, lies to the east of
    St Nazaire, the former cathedral church, and between the latter and the bishops'
    palace. Hence, when the king 'walked on' from the baptistery, he came to the
    palace. See C. Sapin, 'Autun, archéologie d'un quartier épiscopal et canonial',
    Archéologia, 226 (1987), 30–5.

132 It is not clear who these people *qui ad eum causa tuitionis advenerant* were.
    Presumably they were the same ones as those mentioned below who *ad eum
    converterant* (who had turned to him). It sounds as if Hector had a significant
    following with him in Autun.

133 We are not told directly that Leudegar took flight too. This information is found
    in the *Passio Praejecti*, ch. 25. They took flight before dawn on Easter Sunday, and,
    we are told, the chief reason why Hector fled was that he had 'abused the
    confidence of the mayor of the palace, Wulfoald'.

134 The last mass before Easter is held on Maundy Thursday and commemorates the
    last supper, hence the term used here: *dominica caena*.

save the world. And the king, on that same day, wanted to cut Hector down with his own hand, but by the advice of certain wise nobles he was persuaded not to do so out of respect for the day. Without doubt it should be believed concerning this that he [Hector] was divinely saved in order that, if he had not led a blameless life, or if perchance some impurity had stuck to him, the fierce heat of a long persecution would have burned it off so that afterwards, like pure gold placed in the diadem of his heavenly king and like shining jewels, he would gleam in the power of his miracles. So it was that those who had been waiting for the outcome of this occasion set off after Hector at great speed and when they found him they killed him.[135] But because, God willing, he tried to defend himself like a man, he was attacked, along with some people who were with him, by a great crowd. Nor is it impossible to believe that through the merits of a holy martyr he [Hector] can obtain from God pardon for those souls who along with him innocently wished to fend off the storm of persecution.[136]

CHAPTER 12

Then they seized Leudegar, servant of God, and this feat was quickly made known to Childeric, for it was believed that whoever captured Leudegar would enjoy very great royal favour. Thereafter on the advice of the nobles and bishops it was ordered that he should be taken to the monastery of Luxeuil to stay there until all had taken counsel together to decide what should be done with a man of such great reputation. Since those who were seen to be leading men in the palace had been all won over by Childeric, they decided on what judgement to pass upon the man of God, and so they answered in one voice that if he did allow him to live he should order him to remain in Luxeuil in perpetual exile. This judicial decree was quickly confirmed, with some of the priests and bishops feeling that presently they would bring him back free from the king's anger. But King Childeric was seduced by the advice of wicked people and ordered him [Leudegar] to be led out of Luxeuil and handed over in mockery to his accusers, that they might

---

135 His speedy end contradicts the notion of a 'long persecution' a few lines above. The *Passio Praejecti*, ch. 26, below, p. 291, suggests that Hector was first captured and then executed by royal order.

136 It is quite clear that, whatever his merits, Hector himself could not be counted as a martyr. The use of the subjunctive mood in this passage suggests that he was worthy of being called one, although he did not actually have any miracles to his own credit.

do what they liked with him and bring about his death, just as Herod
had once handed Peter over to the Jews.[137] But at hand there was that
venerable man Hermenar, abbot of St Symphorian, the one into whose
care the king, by popular request, gave the town of Autun after the
man of God had departed. Again and again Hermenar threw himself at
the king's feet, imploring him to let Leudegar remain in Luxeuil and
not to order him to be led out to certain death according to the cruel
ones whom the devil had stirred up in rage against him. In the end he
was saved from death because of entreaties like this. Some people,
however, were thinking falsely that he [Hermenar] kept going into
the king's lodgings because he was the leader of Leudegar's accusers
and that in this he was improving his chances of being allowed to hold
the bishopric.[138] But it was quite different, and because one does not see
spiritual love with carnal eyes, his works were later his witnesses,
because as long as his [Leudegar's] life has lasted he [Hermenar]
served his needs as far as he was able with devoted charity.[139]

CHAPTER 13

At this time Ebroin was in Luxeuil, still an exile, tonsured, and living as
a monk.[140] He feigned friendship towards Leudegar, saying that since both
were (though for different reasons) under sentence of exile, they
should live a harmonious life. Meanwhile, these things having been so
done, God in His vengeance could no longer put off executing the
judgement He had declared against Childeric, for his dissolute way of
life was incensing all the great men of the palace. Finally one of them,
annoyed even more than the others, struck Childeric a death-dealing
blow whilst he was out hunting in the woods and thought himself safe.[141]

---

137 Acts 12:3–4, an apt parallel, as Peter was incarcerated just after Easter. The
   analogy also serves to stress the danger to Leudegar, which in turn helped the
   author to explain Hermenar's need to plead with the king. We are already familiar
   with such pleading because of the way in which Leudegar had earlier pleaded for
   Ebroin's life.

138 That he did in fact hold the bishopric during Leudegar's absence does suggest that
   this was precisely what he was doing.

139 I.e., he discharged his obligations. The sentence points forward to ch. 30, where
   Hermenar demonstrates his spiritual love for Leudegar by dressing his wounds,
   feeding him and clothing him, below, p. 246.

140 According to the *Liber Historiae Francorum*, ch. 45, above, p. 89, Ebroin had been
   tonsured at the time of his fall from power in 673.

141 The *Liber Historiae Francorum*, ch. 45 (above, p. 90), tells us that Childeric's wife
   Bilichild was killed too, despite (or because of) being pregnant. The source also
   names the assassin as Bodilo, saying that he had Amalbert and Ingobert and others

CHAPTER 14

Before this came about, the two dukes who had been ordered to take
Leudegar out of Luxeuil had remained close at hand throughout and
one of their underlings had conspired with them to kill Leudegar with
his sword if he saw the servant of God outside Luxeuil. But when he
came to do it an intolerable fear so filled his heart that not only did he
ask himself why he had thought of doing such harm to the servant of
God, he also confessed his fault out loud to all and still trembling,
threw himself at Leudegar's feet, beseeching pardon from him for such
villainy.[142]

CHAPTER 15

When Childeric's death was suddenly announced, those who had been
condemned to exile on his orders returned without fear, just as when
spring follows winter and poisonous snakes emerge from their
caverns.[143] A great storm arose in the fatherland[144] as they [the exiles]
raged with mad fury and things were so bad that it was openly believed
that the coming of the Antichrist was nigh. Those who should have
been the rulers of the provinces rose up against each other[145] – those
who should have banded together to keep the peace began to challenge
one another in hatred, and since no king sat firmly on the throne, each
saw as right whatever he himself wished to do, and that is how they
began to act, without the fear of discipline. Then, as we ourselves can
vouch, God's anger was shown so clearly that a star appeared in the

---

as his accomplices. The *Vita Lantberti*, ch. 5, p. 612, in addition names Lupus,
presumably Lupus, duke of Aquitaine. The event took place in late summer or
autumn 675. Ewig, 'Teilreiche', 127, n. 166 (*Gallien*, vol. 1, p. 213) wondered
whether Bodilo might have been related to Leudegar, for the name appears in later
documents associated with him. See above, n. 86.

142 This rather vague story may have been inserted to help substantiate the idea that
Leudegar's life had been in real danger and that only Hermenar's pleading had
saved him from swift assassination. The two dukes appear again in ch. 16, where
it is said that they have recently taken Leudegar out of Luxeuil. When they did so
is not clear.

143 The serpent and poison metaphor, which is sustained throughout the next chapter
too, was appropriate because of the devil's association with a serpent.

144 From the way in which the author uses the term 'fatherland' in ch. 5, above, p. 222,
it seems clear that he is referring here to the kingdom of Neustria Burgundy.

145 This particular observation may be intended as a contrast with the 'legislation'
described in ch. 7, above, p. 223, where in order to establish good government it
was decreed that 'rulers from one [province] should not intrude in others'.

heavens – the star astrologers call a comet:[146] when it rises, they say, the earth is convulsed with hunger, with the swift succession of kings, with the movement of peoples, and the clashing of swords threatens it.[147] And it is clearly known that all of these things happened then. But because, as it is written, the stupid are not corrected by words and very much less so by signs, these people returned from exile with evil intent. Whatever they had suffered on account of their crimes they now made the accusation that they had suffered those things at the hands of Leudegar's supporters.[148]

CHAPTER 16

At this time, for his own safety, the man of God was in the custody of the dukes we mentioned before – the ones who had recently taken him from Luxeuil.[149] Then, by heavenly grace, God bestowed this worthy honour upon His servant: not only the aforesaid dukes, but also their wives, their subordinates, all their dependants and even the general populace of those parts so united in love for him that they had no doubt that, if danger threatened, they would not hesitate to offer themselves up in his place.[150] When the dukes who were closely guarding the servant of God told the other leaders dwelling in the vicinity that they had recognised the sign of heavenly grace in God's servant, Leudegar, they now bound themselves together in Christian love to give him aid.[151] Agreeing among themselves, they decided that

146 This comet, which is attested in Chinese as well as in European sources, appeared in August 676. In this chapter the author is clearly generalising about events in the year following Childeric's death. The general picture established here gives a context for the particular problems Leudegar is seen to encounter in the following sequence.

147 The passage on comets clearly draws on Isidore of Seville: *Isidori Hispalensis Episcopi Etymologiarum sive Originum Libri XX*, III, ch. 71, 16, ed. W. Lindsay (Oxford, 1911).

148 We have already been forewarned about this false accusation in ch. 8, above, p. 224. 'Supporters' here translates the term *factiones*, which the author seems to use interchangeably with *factores*.

149 These dukes were mentioned in ch. 14, but there it was not clear that they had taken Leudegar out of Luxeuil.

150 This is the first of four occasions on which potentially hostile people were converted into supporters: see below, ch. 31 and 33, pp. 247, 248. In the sentence here, 'subordinates' and 'dependants' translate *ministri* and *familiae* respectively.

151 ... *religioso christianitatis amore, iam se eorum auxilio fuerunt sociati.* The author is suggesting here that Leudegar's faction had a quasi-religious basis, in contrast to Ebroin's, which was simply formed around a desire for revenge.

while disorder and disturbance had arisen, if before they could raise
Theuderic to the throne someone wished to injure saint Leudegar, he
would be protected by their aid. For in these same days out of Luxeuil
slid Ebroin, who, like Julian, lived the life of a monk in pretence only.[152]
Indeed, very soon a war band[153] of friends and servants gathered
tightly around him, and the aforementioned exiles, seeking his
following, made up their accusation [against Leudegar] and they
placed him [Ebroin] at their head[154] so that they might be able to
make use of his aid and counsel[155] and thereby take their revenge
together against the man of God. Thus Ebroin raised up his venomous
head and, like a viper renewing its poison, pretended (*simulans se*) at
this time that he was faithful to Theuderic, and on account of this he
and his allies hurried off to Theuderic as fast as they could go.[156]

CHAPTER 17

Now, the man of God hastened out on the same journey with the allies
we talked of earlier. They had travelled for less than a day when they
came up to the town of Autun.[157] There, Ebroin, urged on by his
supporters, forgot the friendship he had once promised and wanted to
capture Leudegar.[158] But he was prevented by Genesius, metropolitan
bishop of Lyons – either by his advice or through fear of the strong
force Genesius had with him. So once again Ebroin made a pretence of

152 The Roman emperor Julian (d. 363) was infamous as an apostate from Christianity,
but he had never been a monk.

153 'Warband' translates *comitatus*.

154 Here, as elsewhere, the author prefaces his description of Ebroin's diabolical
behaviour with the remark that the mayor was the instrument of other people's evil
intent.

155 It is interesting to see such an early use of the phrase *auxilium et consilium* ('aid and
counsel'), which is usually seen as a formula associated with lordship in so-called
'feudal' contexts from the ninth century onwards.

156 The suggestion here and earlier in this chapter is that whoever participated in
raising the king to the throne would enjoy power. Presumably we should interpret
this as meaning that the participants formed themselves into the group which
would govern the country through the palace.

157 The distance from Luxeuil to Autun is over 150 km. They could not possibly have
made the journey in less than a day.

158 There may have been more behind this notion of friendship than the necessary
truce the two agreed in prison in Luxeuil: Autun was not on the route from Luxeuil
to the Neustrian heartlands, and presumably Ebroin could have reached the king
first had he gone direct from Luxeuil to Neustria without this detour. Pperhaps at
this stage the two were in alliance, as the closing sentence of the chapter suggests.

friendship, and with their forces mingling together they entered the town at the same time. The church rejoiced at the return of its pastor, the streets were adorned with boughs,[159] the deacons prepared their candles, the clergy celebrated with singing, the whole town rejoiced at the coming of their bishop after the storm of persecution. Nor were the offices of praise they put on for him undeserved, for in the presence of the Lord he was hurrying towards a martyr's crown, and so they prepared delights to celebrate the arrival of the bishop, and they honoured his enemies too. The following day, however, they set out from there together so that they would reach Theuderic as one.

CHAPTER 18

Meanwhile, though they had begun their journey to reach the king, about half-way along the course the tyrant Ebroin deserted their company and went off back to his own people.[160] Throwing off the monk's garb, he rejoined his wife even though she had taken the veil,[161] just like the dog which returns to its vomit.[162] And he who was unable to fight for Christ's camp snatched up worldly arms along with Christ's enemies, and now that he had abandoned faith and God he showed himself to be the outright enemy of his earthly lord too.[163] For at that time Theuderic,

---

159 Implicit here is a comparison between Leudegar's entry into Autun and Christ's entry into Jerusalem on Palm Sunday.

160 Presumably this means that he returned to his homeland, which seems to have been the region of Soissons.

161 From the charter of Bishop Drauscius for the convent of Notre Dame de Soissons, Pardessus *Diplomata*, vol. 2, no. 355, p. 139, we learn Ebroin's wife was called Leutrude, and it seems likely that she had taken the veil in the family convent of Notre Dame.

162 This unsavoury quotation is from Proverbs 26:11.

163 *Et qui in castra Christi militare non potuit, cum adversariis secularem armam arripuit, et dum iam derelinquerat fidem et Deum, contra terrenum dominum etiam apertum se prodidit adversarium.* This sentence seems to have been misunderstood by Ursinus, the author of *Passio Leudegarii II.* In his précis of the passage, ch. 8, p. 331, Ursinus linked the *adversarii* with the *Austrasii*, who are mentioned slightly later. He thus tells us that *[Ebroin] cum Austrasiis, quos habuerat aliquando adversarios se sociavit ut amicos.* By this Ursinus understood that the *adversarii* were Austrasians and that they had once been Ebroin's own enemies rather than enemies of Leudegar and of Christ. This interpretation may have come from a reading of the *Liber Historiae Francorum*, ch. 46, above, p. 91, or *The Continuations of Fredegar*, ch. 3, p. 83, which tell of Ebroin's later struggles with an Austrasian enemy. Where it has been believed that Ursinus was providing extra information here it has led to tortuous speculations about Ebroin's shifting alliances and movements in 675. See, for instance, L. Dupraz, *Le Royaume des Francs. Contribution à l'histoire du Regnum*

having regained his throne, was staying unguarded at the villa of Nogent-les-Vierges when suddenly Ebroin and the Austrasians fell upon him.[164] Who could fully relate the plunder that then took place of the royal treasure and of the sacred vessels of the church which Catholic princes had formerly for the love of Christianity devotedly stored up in the sanctuary of the Lord? Or who could tell too of the killing of his mayor of the palace?[165]

CHAPTER 19

Ebroin acted in this evil way because he was being fuelled by the advice of men who were diabolically envious. For after Theuderic had been confirmed on the throne and the servant of God, Leudegar, had, with his permission, returned to live in his town, they saw that the whole people had faithfully shunned them and they began to lament that they had been rightly cast aside.[166] So again the envious ones began to squirm with spite because, whilst the just were standing upright, the depraved could not recover their strength. And as the devil had swayed them and stripped them of their faith, now blind, they could not find the counsel of truth. So through fabrication and falsehood they turned away to cause very great ruin. Through this they destroyed God's holy man and through this they brought great evil to the kingdom, butchering many in their ravaging and persecution. At last they took a certain lad, pretended that he had been a son

---

Francorum pendant le troisième quart du VIIe siècle (Fribourg-en-Suisse, 1948), p. 366, or J. Fischer, *Ebroin*, pp. 146–7 and 153.

164 Later, in ch. 25 and 26, we are given the names of two Austrasians: Waimar, duke of the Champagne, who had come with others 'from the borderlands of Austrasia', and Eticho, duke of Alsace, another Austrasian border area. These would seem to be the Austrasians the author is referring to. It is noteworthy that the diocese of Soissons, where Ebroin seems to have had his base, bordered the Austrasian Champagne.

165 The *Liber Historiae Francorum*, ch. 45, above, p. 90, does tell of this and beforehand says that the mayor was Leudesius, son of Erchinoald, Ebroin's predecessor as mayor. It says that Leudesius had been chosen mayor on the advice of Leudegar and his brother Gaerinus. *The Continuation of the Chronicle of Fredegar*, ch. 2, adds the detail that Leudesius was *conpater* (godfather) to, or perhaps with, Ebroin. This spiritual kinship made Ebroin's killing of Leudesius shameful. The author of the *Passio Leudegarii* omits these details, although later he does say more about how Ebroin fought his way back into the palace.

166 The author is jumping back in time, to a point before Ebroin's attack upon the palace.

of Clothar,[167] and this boy they raised to the throne in the regions of
Austrasia. This allowed them to gather together many people to form
an army[168] because it seemed to everyone that they were telling the truth.
So when by their ravaging they had put the fatherland under their
yoke, they gave orders to the judges in the name of their king,[169] the
pretender they had put up. They commanded that whoever wished to
refuse obedience to them should give up his right to hold power or, if
he did not take flight and go into hiding, he would be put to the sword.
Oh, just how many people did this scorching lie lead to believe that at
that time Theuderic was dead and this Clovis was the son of Clothar?[170]

CHAPTER 20

Now among the perpetrators of this falsehood were two leaders or, as
it were, rulers of the palace. One was Desideratus, known as Diddo,
who had once ruled the town of Chalon as bishop, the other, his
associate, was Bobo, who had once had control over the bishopric of
Valence.[171] Now these men were not worthy of the name bishop. They
guarded above all their earthly desires, the increase of their wealth

167 Clothar III was probably born in the year 649–50, and was therefore about twenty-
   three years of age when he died in 673. It was thus quite feasible that he should
   have had a son. See E. Ewig, 'Studien zur merowingischen Dynastie',
   Frühmittelalterliche Studien 8 (1974), 23.

168 This passage provides a clear indication of the importance of kings in the process
   of raising troops. The *Liber Historiae Francorum*, ch. 53, above, p. 95, tells of a
   similar situation in 717 when Charles Martel organised an army around a hitherto-
   unheard of Merovingian.

169 The suggestion here is that orders issued through a king would be legally
   compelling, *Praecepta*, the word used for 'orders', is the term also given to royal
   documents through which commands were issued and which had the force of law.

170 The pretender Clovis is not attested in any other source. Merovingians often
   named their first born sons after the infant's grandfather. As Clothar's father was
   Clovis II, Clovis was the obvious name to choose for a son of Clothar, real or
   invented (either by Ebroin's party or by our author). Interestingly, two years later,
   in 677, when Clothar's brother, Theuderic, had a son, he called him Clovis, which
   would suggest that the Clovis referred to here either did not exist or was not
   widely recognised as a grandson of his namesake.

171 In the privilege of Bishop of Landeric for Saint-Denis, issued in 654 (*ChLA*, no.
   558), an original document which bears the signatures of its witnesses, the names
   Desideratus and Bobo appear next to each other, both still apparently laymen.
   Among the other members of the palace elite who signed this document and who
   must have been relatively young in 654 were Ebroin and Gaerinus, Leudegar's
   brother. Those who became deadly enemies in the 670s had probably been on
   friendlier terms earlier in their careers, as Bishop Drauscius's privilege for Ebroin's
   own foundation of Notre Dame de Soissons also suggests for the mid 660s. In this

through worldly profits, whereas for the souls entrusted to them, and for the districts in which they were to see that justice was done,[172] they cared nothing. It was of the counsel of priests[173] like this and of nobles of the same kind that the tyrant Ebroin made use so that in this world, though blinded, he was raised up until such time as he was hurled into hellfire, still not repenting. But let us return to the task in hand.

CHAPTER 21

In these days events thus unfolded one by one. After Childeric was murdered, after the bishops and *patricii*[174] along with the nobles had gone away from Neustria, and away from Theuderic's side, back to the Burgundian lands, to their own property, and after Theuderic had been confirmed as king and they were residing in peace, then the envious ones raised an army against him, thinking above all of of those things he had done round about with King Childeric. These forces quickly reached the town of Autun, where the man of God, Leudegar, was living in order to take care of his people.[175] When he perceived that he was the target

document Bishop Desideratus is listed as a signatory along with Leudegar himself: Pardessus, *Diplomata*, vol. 2, p. 140. That the author chose to vilify Bobo and Desideratus is no doubt explained by the fact that an attack upon their conduct as bishops suggested a comparison in Leudegar's favour, and also by the fact that Bobo was later made interim bishop of Autun, with a brief to strip some of the assets of the church there (below, ch. 25. p. 242). Here the terms *principatum* and *dominium* are used to convey the impression that the two who ruled their sees more like secular lords than bishops. Unfortunately the passage has sometimes been quoted out of context to illustrate a supposed confusion between secular and ecclesiastical lordship in this period: see, for instance, R. Kaiser, *Bischofsherrschaft zwischen Königtum und Fürstenmacht, Pariser historische Studien*, 17 (Bonn, 1981), pp. 55, 58. The fact, however, that our author used the terms in this pejorative way suggests that he expected the distinctions between the two sorts of lordship to be quite clear in the minds of his audience.

172 There is probably a double meaning intended here In one sense it means the bishops' preparation for Judgement Day, and in another the actual jurisdiction in the hands of the bishop.

173 This is perhaps the closest the author comes to criticising Ebroin's chief political supporter, Audoin of Rouen, whose reputation seems to have been unassailable in the late seventh century: see above, pp. 136–7. The *Liber Historiae Francorum*, ch. 45, makes it clear that Ebroin turned to Audoin for advice before his storming of the palace in 675 or 676.

174 In southern Burgundy and Provence the title and office of *patricius* seem to have been equivalent to those of *dux* (duke) elsewhere in the kingdom.

175 The C text draws fom Ursinus here (cf. *Passio Leudegarii* II, ch. 10, p. 332), although Ursinus is at this point merely introducing the situation which led up to the siege of Autun, by making a précis of the older version of the *Passio*, as he usually does where events in Autun were concerned.

of the enemy forces, he did not allow himself to take the step of fleeing beyond their range, but undaunted he began to await God's judgement upon himself. Now although his dependants and the clergy and his followers were eager that he should carry off the treasures he had gathered together there and depart, so that when the enemy heard of this they might hold back from harrying and destroying the town, Leudegar would in no way agree to it.[176] Instead he immediately called them together in the treasury and marked off all that he had added to the store, saying this: 'All that you see here, brothers, this of earthly men I have faithfully gathered together to the best of my ability, in as much as the grace of God wished me to keep it for a long time for the common embellishment. But it is perhaps because the Lord sees fit to call us to heavenly grace that the men of this world are now angry with me. So why should I carry anything out of here when I cannot take it into heaven with me? Therefore, if it pleases you, my proposal is this: that I would rather give it to the poor to use than to wander hither and thither through this world with it as baggage weighing me down in shame. So let us be like St Lawrence: on account of what he distributed and gave to the poor his reputation for justice lives on from age to age and his glory is praised in music.'[177] At once he ordered the guards to throw outside the silver plates and as many of the other vessels as possible. He told the silversmiths to come with hammers, and they broke it all up into little pieces which at his order, under the management of his followers, were then paid out to the poor. But, out of this lot, the things which were suited to ecclesiastical use he added to the vessels of the church.[178] The monasteries and convents too, both in the town and in the vicinity, right well relieved a mass of poverty with this same silver. Were there any widows and orphans, or anyone from the multitude of the poor, who were there and did not receive comfort from his generosity?

CHAPTER 22.

The man of God, moreover, being filled with the spirit of wisdom, spoke these words to his clergy: 'Brethren, I have decided to reflect not one jot more on this world; I fear the sins of the spirit more than an earthly

176 The author does not disguise the fact that most people did not want Leudegar to try to defend himself in Autun. What follows looks like the saint's attempts to rally support among the mass of reluctant citizens.

177 St Lawrence (d. 258) was a famous Roman martyr whose suffering was celebrated in hymn by Prudentius: *AASS*, Aug., vol. II, pp. 512–16.

178 This suggests that most of the treasure was not suited to ecclesiastical use.

enemy. If God gives him the power, man on earth takes vengeance, he
seizes, he plunders, he burns, he kills. There is no way we can turn away
from these things and flee.[179] And if in the passing stream of such matters
we are handed over to punishment, let us not despair, but rejoice in the
pardon to come. Let us therefore at one and the same time valiantly fortify
our souls and the town's defences, lest either of the two kinds of enemy
find a gap through which they could bring in danger'. He thus mobilised
all the people of the town. They held a three-day fast, making the sign
of the cross and carrying the relics of saints around the circuit of the
walls,[180] stopping at the opening of each gate, where he bowed to the
earth and tearfully beseeched the Lord that, if he should be called to
suffering, God would not allow the people entrusted to him to be led
into captivity. And it has been proved that it came about thus.

CHAPTER 23

So, in fear of the enemy, the people from all around struggled to withdraw
into the town, to close up the gateways with strong barricades and to
fortify each position in turn. Then the man of God ordered everybody
to come into the church and he asked pardon of all of them together
so that if – as can happen – in his ardent love of justice he had rebuked
any of them or had wounded anyone by word, they might forgive
him.[181] For, as he had set out on the path of suffering, the man of God
knew that martyrdom would not be of benefit unless his heart had first
been wiped clean of spite so that it was spotless and unless [that path]
was lit with the torch of love. But no one there at that time, not even
if they had been severely wounded, had a breast so iron-hard[182] that they
would not have devotedly forgiven all malice of the heart. Not long

179 The author skilfully turns Leudegar's decision to stay in Autun into a moral
responsibility, and again he moves the bishop's particular problems into line with
the effects of man's sinful behaviour in general. Here he is drawing on Ephesians
6, which leads into the call to arms already seen in the 'helmet of salvation'
metaphor in ch. 8, above, p. 224.

180 There seems to be a further reference to St Lawrence's example here: he too spent
three days going round his town. Autun had been a large and important Roman
city, and the circuit of its original walls was massive. It is likely that in the later
seventh century the fortified area was restricted to the southern corner of the
Roman town in the area around the cathedral which was enclosed on three sides
by strong walls. For the topography of Autun at this time, C. Sapin, 'Autun'.

181 Again the author is revealing that Leudegar faced some degree of opposition in
Autun. It seems reasonable to suppose that on his return to the town he would
have taken measures against those who had conspired against him at Easter 675.

182 It is at this point that the fragment of the A text begins.

after this the town was besieged by the enemy army, and that day until
evening the people fought against it bravely. But then the forces of the
enemy surrounded the town with a powerful blockade, and day and
night they circled it, howling like dogs. The man of God considered
the danger threatening his town and, calming the conflict before the
walls,[183] he went to his people and with these words implored them: 'I
beg you, let us restrain ourselves from fighting these people. If they
have come here only to seek me, for my part I am prepared to grant
their wish and quiet their fury.[184] Lest, however, we seem to go out
without hearing what they want, let us send out one of the brothers to
them to ask why they have besieged the town'. Quickly they prepared
a way down through the bars of the wall for Abbot Meroald. Going up
to Diddo, he said to him: 'If we have committed any crime, recall, I beg
you, the sentence in the Gospels where the Lord said: "If ye forgive
men not their trespasses, neither will your heavenly Father forgive
your trespasses", and: "For with what judgement ye judge, ye shall be
judged,"'.[185] At the same time he beseeched Diddo to restrain the army
and to take what ransom he wanted. But because now a stony
insensitivity had hardened his heart (just as once happened to the
Egyptian king)[186] Diddo could not soften at all at the word of God and
he threatened that he would not withdraw from the attack upon the
town until he could take hold of Leudegar, nor could he slake the
raging desire of his fury until he had made Leudegar swear loyalty to
Clovis, whom they had falsely made king. Now, this deceit was his
chance, because everyone was swearing an oath that Theuderic was dead.

CHAPTER 24

The man of God heard these words and gave his answer to them thus:
'Let this be known to all of you, friends and brothers, foes and enemies
too, that, as long as God ordains that I should continue living, I shall
not be moved from that loyalty which before the Lord I promised to
reserve for Theuderic. I have decided that I would rather offer up my

---

183 'Before the walls' attempts to translate the difficult term *supermurale*.

184 Considering that Leudegar had just refortified the town in order to seek refuge
there, this claim looks rather disingenuous.

185 Matthew 6:5, 7:2.

186 Exodus 10:1, 'The Lord hardened Pharaoh's heart in order to show His signs
before him'.

187 Irony is here probably the author's intention: death was the usual penalty for
disloyalty, but Leudegar is facing death for refusing to be disloyal.

body to death than to expose my soul to disgraceful disloyalty'.[187] The enemy heard this, but they hurriedly pressed on with their attempt to break into the town on all sides, hurling darts and spreading fires. Leudegar, however, bade farewell to all the brethren, communing in the sharing of bread and wine, strengthening their doubting hearts, and entrusting the memory of his suffering to them, as Christ did to the disciples. Then without fear he made his way to the entrance of the gates. The gates were opened, and of his own accord he offered himself up to his enemies to save his city. Delighted, his adversaries seized him as their prey, just as if they were wolves and he a harmless sheep, and devising a most horrible plan of torture, they plucked the light of his eyes from his head. This blinding he was seen to bear with superhuman strength as the iron pierced him. Indeed, there are many illustrious men who were present there[188] and they witnessed that he did not allow his hands to be chained nor did even a groan pass his lips as his eyes were torn from his head. Instead, throughout he strove to glorify the Lord by singing the melody of the psalms.

CHAPTER 25

Amongst the other leaders there was a certain duke of the Champagne, Waimer by name, who along with Diddo had come from the borderlands of Austrasia to carry out this evil deed.[189] These two gave over the bishop's power in Autun to one Bobo, who had recently been anathematised and thrown out of the episcopacy of Valence.[190] Truer to say, they

---

188 *Testes enim sunt multi inlustri viri qui aderant in presente.* This is a clear reference to surviving eye witnesses. According to later local tradition, the blinding was supposed to have taken place at Couhard, just outside Autun. Couhard lies at the edge of the suburban Roman cemetry and is the site of a massive and curious Roman funerary monument. It may have been assumed wrongly that this structure was somehow connected with the event.

189 The *Passio Praejecti*, ch. 26, below, p. 291, names Waimer as the one who blinded Leudegar. This source adds that he went on to occupy the bishopric of Troyes and it is much more hostile towards Waimer than is our author. The latter's neutral attitude is to be explained by the fact that Waimer is later 'converted' by Leudegar, recognises his holy virtue and eventually returns to Autun the fine levied on the town following Leudegar's capture.

190 Bobo's deposition in not attested in any other source. Perhaps Bobo and Desideratus/Diddo, who were both supporters of Ebroin, had 'recently' been thrown out of their sees by King Childeric. If so, they could have been among the exiles who blamed Leudegar for what they had suffered under Childeric (ch. 15, above, pp. 232). It is not clear how long Autun was in Bobo's *dominium*, but it was probably for less than a year. He is not mentioned again, and in ch. 30, below, p. 246, Hermenar is said to have become bishop about two years before Leudegar's death.

handed over the town to be destroyed. Since they had lost their pastor, the hard-pressed citizens accepted this enemy, and through his order nearly all the movable wealth of the church was carried off. For now they had the chance, they seized from the church silver worth 5,000 *solidi*[191] as a ransom for the town in addition to despoiling the citizenry. But although the church suffered the loss of its possessions, God did not allow anyone to be led away in captivity.

CHAPTER 26

The enemy army thus gleefully divided up the loot and the man of God they handed over to the custody of the aforementioned Waimer. Waimer speedily returned to his homeland with Leudegar and with all his army. But Desideratus, known as Diddo, along with Bobo and Duke Chatalric, whom they wanted to be the *patricius* of Provence, pushed on to Lyons in order to bring the fatherland under their yoke.[192] From

191 It is interesting that Autun had such large reserves of silver. The Frankish coinage switched from gold to silver at precisely this time, and the first surviving silver *denarius* bears Ebroin's name: P. Grierson and M. Blackburn, *Medieval European Coinage*, vol. 1, pp. 93–5. The conflict of these years must have led to increased demand for coins to pay troops such as those Ebroin levied around the pretender Clovis, and at the same time it must also have increased the supply of silver via the kind of dethesaurisation and looting mentioned here.

192 Chatalric, Eticho or Adalric, as he was also known, was duke of Alsace and is attested in several other sources, among them the *Vita Germani Abbati Grandivallensis*, ed. B. Krusch, *MGH, SSRM*, V, pp. 33–40. In this work, which was composed at a date close to the events it describes, Eticho is the villain, as he was responsible for the murder of Abbot Germanus at about that time. Our author may have been ignorant of Germanus's murder. In the early eighth century Eticho's family became supporters of the cult of Leudegar, dedicating the monastery of Murbach to him. Later it was claimed that Berswinda, Eticho's wife, had been the sister of Sigrada, Leudegar's mother. The 'evidence' for this family link between the saint and his persecutor, Eticho, comes from the *Vita Odiliae*. This late ninth- or early tenth-century work says only that Odilia's mother, Berswinda, was generally known to have been related to Leudegar. The detail that she was Sigrada's sister comes from the even later *Chronicon Ebersheimense*, ch. 6, ed. L. Weiland, *MGH, SS*, XXIII (Hanover, 1874), p. 434, a work which leans heavily on the *Vita Odiliae* and which seems on this point to have elaborated it rather than drawn upon independent information. Both sources arguably deduced the relationship from the fact that the family supported the cult, whereas the connection with Leudegar may originally have been generated simply by Eticho's appearance in this passage in the *Passio Leudegarii*. For detailed discussion of early Etichonid history (and for a less sceptical view of the connection with Leudegar), see F. Vollmer, 'Die Etichonen', in G. Tellenbach (ed.), *Studien und Vorarbeiten zur Geschichte des grossfränkischen und frühdeutschen Adels, Forschungen zur Oberrheinischen Landesgeschichte*, 4 (Freiburg, 1957), pp. 141–3.

Lyons they would now have taken away Genesius, just as a little while before they had driven Leudegar from Autun. But the people from all sides gathered together, making up a strong force, so that with God protecting them they did not let them into this the greatest of towns.[193]

CHAPTER 27

When the people who were in charge of God's servant, Leudegar, informed Ebroin of what had happened, he ordered him [Waimer] to hide Leudegar secretly in the woods and to make up a lying falsehood, saying that he had died from drowning. And so whilst hungry starvation was slowly to consume him, he [Waimer] was to heap up his burial mound.[194] For he who can hear and see something believes it to be true. But the One who used a raven to feed Elijah in the wilderness did not desert His servant [Leudegar] there.[195] Indeed, after the martyr of God had suffered hungry starvation for a long time, Waimer, realising that the human frame could not endure like this unless the grace of Christ was sustaining it, ordered him to be brought into his house, and then his hard heart began to soften in piety. When Leudegar had become acccustomed to familiar conversation with him, in a little while he so drew him from his wild ways, and tamed him, and brought both him and his wife to fear God, that Waimer in affection offered him that church silver which he had recently taken as ransom for the town of Autun: he was to use it henceforth as he should decide. This silver the man of God accepted and sent back to the aforesaid town by a certain faithful abbot called Berto, and, dividing it, according to the Apostle, among the household of the faith, he [Berto] faithfully carried out his wish in this loving task.

CHAPTER 28

Now, since, as has been said, Ebroin could not hide his villainy any longer, he turned his scheming from the false king he had put up, in order that he might go back to the palace of Theuderic.[196] They formed

---

193 It is hard not to infer from this statement that Genesius enjoyed more support in Lyons than Leudegar had in Autun.

194 The point is that Ebroin was hoping to prevent Leudegar from being hailed as a martyr by showing that he had died of natural causes.

195 Cf. I Kings 17:6.

196 We are given no idea of what happened to the pretender, Clovis.

a faction of certain people and very soon he was again made mayor of the palace.[197] Some people rejoiced with him, others were fearful, but when they had raised him up to the supreme position, he immediately issued this edict: that if in the state of disorder that had existed anyone had inflicted loss on or had snatched booty from anyone else, let no one's claim for damages arise from it.[198] This was the pretext for not returning the spoils, because his agents had piled them up for him by robbing lots of people. Moreover, when his reawakened pride began to swell up, he feared and fretted that he might be opposed by some rival, someone to whose relatives he had done harm. Now he had obtained the rights of power, he doubled up his wickedness with envy.[199] At once, therefore, he began to persecute the more powerful nobles,[200] and whomever he was able to get his hands on he either put to the sword or drove them off to peoples beyond the realm, having seized their property.[201]

197 It is not clear who 'they' are here: *quorundam factionem suscoeperunt*. The use of the term *factio* reminds us that the conflict was between different groups within a single political community, of which the mayor of the palace was leader.

198 This 'edict' has strong echoes of late Roman legislation on claims generated in the aftermath of barbarian invasion: 'If during the disaster of barbarian devastation anything unworthy or odious has been done ... such deeds shall not be called to account by the cunning prosecution of litigants ...' *The Theodosian Code*, trans. C. Pharr (Princeton, New Jersey, 1952), XV, 14, p. 439. Our author may thus be misleading when he goes on to suggest that Ebroin was being devious in issuing such a commmand.

199 Ebroin's power, his *potestas*, was magnified once he had acquired the *ius*, the right, to issue legally compelling orders.

200 Ebroin's persecution of 'the more powerful nobles' (*potiores obtimates*) has been taken in conjunction with a suggestion from the ninth-century *Passio Ragneberti* that the mayor was 'low-born' (*ex infimo genere ortus*) to argue that he was an outsider, attacking the Frankish establishment, of which Leudegar was a leading figure. Recently Heinzelmann, 'Studia Sanctorum', p. 115, has described the *Passio Ragneberti* as a seventh-century text, citing Berschin. But Berschin, *Biographie und Epochenstil*, vol. 2, p. 78, merely stated that the events in the work took place in the seventh century, not that the work was composed then. Whatever the date of composition (and there seems to be no reason not to accept Krusch's arguments for the ninth century), it remains true that the *Passio Ragneberti* does not really provide independent supporting evidence for the argument that Ebroin was an 'outsider' of 'lowly origins', for its picture of Ebroin is derived from the *Passio Leudegarii* in general. In particular, this passage on the *potiores obtimates* seems to have provided the later author with the setting for Ebroin's attack on his or her hero Ragnebert, with the author deducing that Ebroin's malice was rooted in social envy. That Ebroin should have attacked certain *potiores obtimates* is, of course, neither surprising nor socially significant, for they were the ones with the power to oppose him. See further, Fouracre, 'Merovingians, mayors of the palace and the notion of a low-born Ebroin'.

201 *The Continuation of the Chronicle of Fredegar*, ch. 2, p. 82, adds the detail that these exiles fled south of the Loire all the way to the land of the Basques. It is probably

He even destroyed the convents of noble ladies, sending their spiritual leaders into exile. And since he had acquired the power to crush under foot the jewels of pearl, like the swine, without any feeling of remorse, he was not frightened to break into Christ's treasury.[202] And since he was unable to turn his attention to heaven, so his heart was stuck down in the mire of a worldy desire beyond measure.

CHAPTER 29

When Ebroin had exhausted his frenzy in the affairs mentioned above, he began again to search out the means whereby he might be able to conceal his blasphemous cruelty from human eyes. At this moment he pretended to be upset about Childeric's death (whereas before no one wished it to come about more than he), for that was the only way in which he dared publicly to persecute those whom he hated. He now therefore brought Leudegar back from his hidden exile and claimed that he, along with his brother, Gaerinus, had been the prime mover in Childeric's death, on account of which he cruelly ordered his lips and mouth to be cut with a knife and his tongue to be cut out as well. The aforesaid Gaerinus, however, he ordered to be pressed with stones, and the latter, encouraged by his holy brother, gave up the ghost whilst giving thanks to God.[203]

CHAPTER 30

And so in vengeance they continued to keep God's saint Leudegar alive and, disgracefully stripping him, they ordered him to be dragged through the dusty streets. And thus mutilated they handed him over for punishment to Waning so that being tortured under his more oppressive regime he would breathe his last.[204] Now, since his lodging

---

from this source that the Ursinus version of the *Passio Leudegarii* garnered the impression that Gaerinus, Leudegar's brother, had escaped to this region, from which he was, as we would say, extradited back to Francia on Ebroin's orders. If this mid eighth-century work was the source of Ursinus's information, then, of course, his version of the *Passio* must postdate it. See above, p. 207. The Hermenar version in fact says nothing more about Gaerinus at this stage.

202 Like the swine with pearls cast before them, Matthew 7:6.

203 Pressing with stones was presumably to force the accused to plead.

204 Waning appears as 'count of the palace' in a royal judgement issued some time between 658 and 679 (*ChLA*, no. 557). This officer was responsible for seeing that judgements were carried out, which is why Leudegar was given into his custody after trial.

was far away, they placed God's holy martyr on a cheap packhorse, and when he perceived that this was what had been done, he recollected this little verse from the psalms: 'I was a beast toward thee', it went. 'Nevertheless I am continually with thee'.[205] And although now he had neither lips nor tongue, in his love he could not keep from praising God, using the only voice he could, sounds made from the depths of his heart. And when everyone saw him so horribly injured they believed that on account of this he must give up the ghost. And so it was as one of our brethren, an abbot by the name of Winobert, followed after him from afar and came to the lodgings we spoke of. He begged the guards to let him secretly visit him, and when at last this was granted, he found him lying on straw covered with an old cloth from a tent, weakly panting out his breath. But whereas he [Winobert] believed he was going to expire there and then, he saw instead an inspired miracle. For among the bloody spittle and using a cut tongue without lips, his usual eloquence began to return. Although the amputation of his lips had bared the two rows of his teeth, clenched they brought forth the sound of words from his breath as he drew it in and out. Then the one who had come to him to lay him out in preparation for the funeral rites began to weep with joy and with hurried step he [went and] reported the event to Bishop Hermenar. The latter, indeed, came to Waning and demanded to be let in to see Leudegar, martyr of God. When this was allowed (in a pall of fear – for everyone feared the savage tyrant in his anger, as they would a lion) he made great and careful effort to tend his wounds and, with whatever skill he could, he refreshed him with food and drink and clothed him in garments better than those he had. For already he reverently bestowed honour upon him not as an earthly man but as a martyr carried to heaven. Because of this he earned not only forgiveness for things past, but also a blessing from him for what was yet to come.[206]

CHAPTER 31

Waning took Leudegar back to his own lands,[207] God's grace accompanying them, and then contrary to nature his lips and tongue began

205 Psalms 73:22–3.

206 This is a key passage in the argument that Hermenar and Leudegar were reconciled. It also serves to demonstrate that Hermenar, and Autun, were the first to recognise Leudegar as a martyr, even before he died.

207 These lands were in the 'Provincia Calciacensis', or the Pays-de-Caux in present-day Normandy, according to the much later *Vita Waningi*, ed. J. Mabillon, *AASSOB*, III (Paris, 1669), pp. 971–4.

to grow again at increasing pace. In fact, I saw words flow unceasingly from his mouth, even more than they had ever done.[208] When Waning recognised this miracle, he did not steel his heart to dole out evil as the tyrant had ordered him to do – it was quite the opposite, and now, seeing that he was a martyr of God, with much ado he made ready for him as lodging a convent which he had once built at God's instruction.[209] And there, for the fear of God, not only he but his wife and all those attached to it exhibited such venerable servitude that it was as if they deserved to see the Lord Christ Himself. As a result of his [Leudegar's] energetic preaching, he [Waning] lost all his savage pride and, aided by his prayers, he and his followers were made devout in their fear of the Lord, as if a lamb had been fashioned out of a wild beast. And since within the space of a few hours he had recovered the use of his face and tongue, and because he himself had already been given up to God, he was eager to offer the daily sacrifice.[210] But though spiritual light had filled him from within, nothing healed the eyes of his flesh.

CHAPTER 32

Thus, since he had suffered such a scourging (as befits a martyr), the faithful people exhibited venerable servitude to him, and, because his light could not be hidden under a bushel, so the Almighty revealed it openly to all. Whereupon his enemy began to seek vengeance. Leudegar had remained where he was praising the Lord for nearly two years and during this time they told him both of those who had been killed and of those who had been blamed for disloyalty and had fled to other kingdoms. For such people he wept with despair: he did not rejoice in [the thought of] revenge, because deathly destruction might catch them without penitence.[211]

208 The author here is the fourth person from Autun to have visited Leudegar since his arrest. This may suggest some kind of negotiated settlement over affairs in the town.

209 Ursinus here adds genuine detail: the convent was that of Fécamp and its abbess was called Childemarca. Though the founder, Waning, became the subject of a *Vita* in the Norman period (n. 207, above), the rulers of Fécamp were apparently not drawn from his family, and there seems to have been no cult arising directly out of the foundation.

210 In other words, he was keen to say mass. The author cleverly reinforces his point here by drawing upon the language of the mass: Leudegar received the *offitium* of his face and tongue, and he was already himself *oblatus* to God.

211 The meaning of this sentence is unclear, but the reference in the next chapter to Ebroin as 'one of them' reveals that the objects of Leudegar's despair here are the perpetrators of the outrages, not their victims.

CHAPTER 33

Now, one of them, Ebroin, that cunning craftsman who was to complete the crown of the blessed martyr, survived, and he had survived so that he should fulfil those things which remained for the glory of his [Leudegar's] passion. Again, then, that age-old serpent, envy, annoyed because it had been driven out of this place [Waning's convent] by his prayers, again began to goad Ebroin. He ordered Leudegar to be brought back to the palace so that he might be defrocked before a council of bishops, and thus would it be forbidden to him to carry on offering up the host.²¹² When he had been led into their midst, they sought from him some word whereby he might confess himself to have been a party to Childeric's murder. Recognising that by means of the devil's tricks a conflict again threatened him harm, as he did not deny that he had sinned on earth, at the same time he said that in no way had he counselled that crime, but he maintained that God rather than men knew it to be so. And since despite pressing him for a long time they could not get him to say anything else, they tore his tunic from his head.²¹³ Then the godless tyrant commanded him to be handed over to a certain man called Chrodbert who was at that time Count of the Palace, ordering that his life be taken from him at the blow of a sword.²¹⁴ Well, God's martyr was rejoicing in all his suffering because he began to feel the approach of the martyr's crown, his due reward from the Lord. And so the aforesaid man took him back to his own home and when he arrived he received a heavenly blessing in the following way: all the inhabitants there recognised him [as a martyr] and by confessing they abandoned their own sins and eagerly sought the healing refuge of his forgiveness. This indeed was how the Lord illustrated the grace of His servant. For wherever he had been passed on in his exile as they wickedly attempted to harm him, instead of hurting him people always became his devoted followers.²¹⁵

212 Leudegar's formal deposition may in fact have been one of several which took place at this time as Ebroin's faction moved against its opponents. A royal document of 677 refers to Chramnlinus, bishop of Embrun, having been deposed along with others *qui in infidilitate nostra fuerunt inventi: ChLA*, no. 565. Our author suggests that the defrocking was done in order to stop Leudegar functioning as a priest. It may, however, have been to prepare him for execution as a criminal.

213 The analogy here is with the Roman martyrs who could not be forced to deny their faith in public.

214 Decapitation by sword was the Roman penalty for treason, and the penalty which martyrs commonly suffered; see Delehaye, *Les Passions des Martyrs*, p. 274.

215 This was the last of the four occasions on which Leudegar converted his gaolers. The fact that each time the household of the officer concerned played an important role in recognising the saint's virtue may cast light on the domestic setting of public office at the time.

CHAPTER 34

At last came the day of his reward on which his persecution should come to an end. Then from the palace came a royal decree, the court's command: Leudegar must live no longer. But wicked Ebroin, fearing that the honour of martyrdom would be bestowed upon him by faithful Christians, ordered that a well should be found in a grove in the woods, therein to push his butchered corpse so that when the mouth of the well had been stopped up with earth and stones his grave would be unknown to men.[216] Meanwhile, a little before, that Chrodbert we mentioned earlier had begun to be converted by his preaching. So now he was quite unable to bear watching the death of the man of God. He thus told two of his servants that they must carry out the orders which had been given to him. Indeed, when news of the orders reached his household, his wife began to weep bitter tears, lamenting because her husband had been charged with the execution of such a disgraceful crime.

CHAPTER 35

Thus when the man of God saw that the end was at hand, he began to console the distraught woman, saying, 'Do not, I beg, weep on account of my going. In no way will my death lead to you being punished, but rather God will give you a heavenly blessing if in devotion you lay my poor body in a grave'. And when he had said this, urged on by the servants, he bade farewell and he was led off into the woods so that they might carry out the sentence of the order. First, therefore, they looked for the well in which they would hide his body just as they had been told to, but they could not discover it ahead of them at all. Looking for the well, they wandered about uselessly and as a result there was a delay before they struck him down. In the meantime God's martyr was allowed to stretch out in prayer and entrust himself to God for his journey. But, feeling his executioners come near, he began through the spirit of prophecy to speak to both of them of the things of the future. One of them, fired by the age-old enemy, was keen beyond measure to do his job. The other, however, had a gentle spirit and trembled as he prayed to him that he would not be punished for what he did to him. Yet Leudegar addressed both of them, saying,'You who are unwilling to carry out your orders, go at once to the priest to

---

216 The grave was where people might see those miracles which would establish the martyr's sanctity: with no grave, and no remains, it would be difficult for a cult to flourish.

confess your sins up to this point, and with repentance you will now be able to escape blame for this one too'. And to the other he said, 'If you do not do likewise, you will immediately have to be delivered up to God's swift punishment'. Then, again bending in prayer, with confidence he entrusted his soul to Christ, his Lord. And rising up he stretched out his neck and told the swordsman to carry through what he had been ordered to do. When the [keen] one we talked of earlier suddenly cut off his head, a chorus of angels led the spirit of the holy martyr, Leudegar, rejoicing towards the heavens, there to be brought before the Lord to reign with all the saints in the place that our Lord Jesus Christ is in the joyful company of the saints, Jesus who with the Father and the Holy Spirit lives and reigns for ever and ever. Amen.[217]

CHAPTER 36 ON THE WONDERS OF ST LEUDEGAR

God's holy martyr having been thus exalted by the pouring out of his blood, divine punishment soon struck down his executioner, just as he had predicted. For he was openly scorched by the flames of the spirit and on the fourth day he was torn bellowing from his body. Now, since they had been unable to find the well as the savage tyrant had ordered, they tried to hide the remains of the holy martyr in a grove in the

217 This account of Leudegar's death was, predictably, much embellished in later versions of the *Passio*. In the Ursinus version, for example, the two executioners have become four, three of whom begged for forgiveness, and the corpse remained standing headless for about an hour, despite being given a kick by the swordsman. We cannot date Leudegar's death with any accuracy, partly because it depends on the dates of Ebroin's return to power and eventual death, which are equally uncertain. According to Ursinus, *Passio Leudegarii II*, ch. 20, p. 343, Leudegar was buried on 2 October, the day after his execution. We know that he had been with Waning for nearly two years following Ebroin's return to power, but we cannot calculate the duration of the events following his capture and preceding his stay with Waning, nor do we know how long he spent with Chrodbert before his execution. Ursinus tells us that Ebroin was killed about three years after Leudegar's execution, but he also says that Leudegar lay in his first grave for about two and a half years before his relics were translated to Poitiers, something which happened after Ebroin's death. Krusch dated Ebroin's formal return to power to 677, the date at which he first appeared in a royal document (in fact, in the one dealing with Chramnlinus cited above, n. 212). Given that this is the only royal document in which Ebroin ever figured whilst in office, this dating appears unduly cautious. Nevertheless, if we take it as the latest possible date for Ebroin's return, and add two years for the stay with Waning, that gives us a date of *c.* 679 for Leudegar's execution, a date of *c.* 681 for Ebroin's death, and a date of 681–82 for Leudegar's translation to Poitiers. If we assume that Ebroin returned to power as swiftly as possible, then the earliest possible dates would be 677 for Leudegar's execution, 680 for Ebroin's death, and 680–81 for the translation.

woods so that they would lie invisible to men. But that excellent woman set out to find the body, to bury it with honour as she had vowed. When she found it she eagerly moved it to an oratorium, thus faithfully showing servitude to the martyr because she had seen that in truth he had devotedly desired to die in the name of Christ. Indeed, from that time the first signs of his powers began to gleam before men. Since Ebroin and his fellow thinkers did not wish to believe those signs, he ordered what had been heard and seen to be concealed lest he [Leudegar] should become even more famous to anybody. But in his hatred he erred concerning the faith of the masses, and then like the sun rising in the sky the signs began to grow bright and glowing to add to his glory. For at the place where the saint's body had formerly lain hidden, first a blind man received his sight again and a cripple walked. There the aforesaid woman worked to build an oratorium[218] with a congregation of monks charged with the perpetual chanting of psalms, and there wondrous signs of cures unceasingly shone out to the faithful. The sick were healed, the downtrodden were cared for, the fevered cooled, evil spirits were openly cast out, all the innumerable maladies by which the human frame is afflicted were cured. Whosoever came to those places deserved to find a cure for all things through the help of the holy martyr, with Jesus Christ, our Lord, reigning. To whom is the honour and the glory, for ever and ever.[219] Amen.

CHAPTER 37 ON THE WONDERS OF ST LEUDEGAR

The priest who served in the oratorium where they had transferred his holy body very often saw a strange and wondrous light at the entrance, and he swore fiercely that he had heard there such angelic singing that, trembling, he retreated lest he stay there unaccustomed to a spiritual vision. Ebroin, when he heard of this, did not believe it, so he sent one of his brethren to find out the truth. When the latter neared the grave of Leudegar the martyr, haughtily he asked where Leudegar lay and the blind man who had received his sight replied,

218 Ursinus, *Passio Leudegarii II*, ch. 20, p. 343, adds the detail that the oratorium was in a placed called Scarcingum, probably the present-day Saint-Léger, in the *département* of Pas-de-Calais.

219 The author seems not to have been interested in the details of these miracles of healing, perhaps because they were associated with the shrine at which they took place. Much more important for the author is the miracle of power which follows and which established the general truth of Leudegar's sanctity independent of his first resting place.

'Here in the miracles of God rests the holy man', and he added that he himself had had his sight returned and served him. The brother believed none of this, but he swelled up with arrogance and as he was leaving he tripped over the doorstep and he would not have got up again had he not been raised by the hands of his servants. And after he had been carried away to bed, that same night he breathed his last. And because when he had been high and mighty he had not believed, when he had been cast down he was forced to look upon the one he had looked down upon. But although the report of this remarkable affair brought joy to the faithful, when soon it was made known to Ebroin, too, he refused to make good the harm he had done, but with his heart still blind along with his followers he reinforced his disbelief. Indeed, by threatening he ordered them to conceal the miracle through which Christ, the Lord, showed forth the glory of His martyr and gave strength to those unable to believe His martyr whom He deemed worthy to shine forth to the faithful above the candlestick of the church. But although the tyrant hesitated and his thoughts wandered this way and that, he would not change to become more humble or to correct himself at all, for the devil made him more stiffnecked than ever in his arrogant and proud attitude towards everyone. So then was Solomon's proverb fulfilled against him: 'The heart of man is raised in haughtiness before he is brought down, and the spirit is haughty before it falls'.[220] And so that he should not escape unpunished after having committed such grave sins, he himself sought the moment of his own death, as if he were mad. For having found an opportunity he threatened a certain nobleman who was at that time in charge of the fiscal revenues and he robbed him until he took away all his chattels in punishment; worse, he threatened him with death.[221] This man realised that he was being threatened by death as well as by robbery, so he decided to seek remedy, and he watched near his doorway for Ebroin as he came out before daybreak on his way to matins. For it was indeed the Lord's day and he was thus about to set out to celebrate the morning service. As soon as he stepped out, lo! that man leapt forth

220 Proverbs 16:18.

221 'Nobleman' translates *optimas*. It is rare to see this term used in the singular. Another example is its use in this way in the *Passio Praejecti*, ch. 20, below, p. 286. The man is named as Ermenfred in the *Liber Historiae Francorum*, ch. 47, above, p. 91. This source agrees that Ebroin was preparing to move against Eremenfred, who struck first. It adds that he then took refuge with Pippin, Ebroin's rival in Austrasia. He later appears among the Franks of the Seine–Oise area in a document recording a royal judgement in 691 (*ChLA*, no. 575), presumably having returned to Neustria when Pippin established himself at the Neustrian palace in 688.

in inspiration and struck him on the head with his sword, and at a second blow he fell down dead. And thus his foul domination was taken away from the kingdom, just as once David removed disgrace from the sons of Israel when he laid low Goliath of the Philistines.

VI: *Passio Praejecti*
(The Suffering of Praejectus)

Praejectus was bishop of Clermont, in the Auvergne region of France, during the reign of King Childeric II (662–75), and he was killed in January 676.[1] Unlike Leudegar, Aunemund, Audoin, Geretrud or Balthild, the subjects of the other saints' *lives* studied in this volume, there is almost no record of Praejectus's existence apart from that provided by his biography. Whereas the other figures are attested in charters, or are mentioned in other narrative sources, we know of Praejectus's career only through the *Passio Praejecti*. Nevertheless, we can be sure that he really did exist, because we do have the information that his body was removed from the Auvergne in the mid eighth century.[2] There may be a basic explanation (apart from chance) for the relative silence concerning Praejectus: most of our sources come from, and focus on, northern Francia, that is, the sweep of territory between the rivers Meuse and Loire. Where figures from areas outside this territory do figure in more than one source, it is because, like Leudegar, or Aunemund, or Dido of Poitiers, they were members of that supra-regional elite which participated in politics based upon the palace. Compared with such powerful figures, Praejectus may have been something of a second-division player, not one of the political community which revolved around the king. It is, however, precisely these unusual circumstances which make the *Passio Praejecti* a text of exceptional historical interest.

1 Praejectus's martyrdom is celebrated on 26 January: see *AASS*, Jan., vol. II (Antwerp, 1643), pp. 628–30. That it took place in 676 is deduced from information contained in the *Vita Boniti episcopi Arverni*, ch. 4, ed. B. Krusch, *MGH, SSRM*, VI (Hanover and Leipzig, 1913), p.121, which says that Praejectus's successor had ruled Clermont for 'fifteen and a bit' years, dying whilst King Theuderic was still alive, hence before April 691. Given that Praejectus was killed after Easter 675, this must mean that his death took place in January 676.

2 In the year 755 Praejectus's body was taken from the monastery of Volvic to that of Flavigny in Burgundy, according to the chronicle composed by Hugh of Flavigny at the end of the eleventh century: *Hugonis Chronicon* I, ed. G. Pertz, *MGH, SS*, VIII (Hanover, 1848), p. 351. Flavigny, founded by Abbot Widerad, was already dedicated to Praejectus in 721, according to Widerad's will in Pardessus (ed.), *Diplomata*, vol. 2, no. 514, pp. 323–7. In Clermont itself there was a church dedicated to Praejectus: see A. Tardieu, *Histoire de la ville de Clermont-Ferrand*, vol. 1 (Moulins, 1879), p. 328.

The *Passio* itself suggests that Praejectus's family was not of the higher nobility, and that it was a clash with members of the so-called 'senatorial' aristocracy of the Auvergne which brought about his death.[3] Like Leudegar in Autun, or Aunemund in Lyons, Praejectus faced opposition in Clermont, and again like Leudegar, his successor as bishop seems to have played a part in his downfall. The result was again a text which was composed very close to the events with which it is concerned, and which aimed to reconcile the saint with his enemies. Yet Praejectus's biographer was even more candid about the problems his or her hero faced than was Leudegar's. Whereas the author of the *Passio Leudegarii* could show from his local standpoint that outsiders like Ebroin, Childeric, Bobbo and Diddo were to blame for Leudegar's demise, Praejectus's problems clearly began and ended in his native community. The frank details of the *Passio Praejecti*, therefore, afford us a unique glimpse into the workings and tensions of that community. At the same time, the *Passio* provides further information on the relationship between the politics of the locality and the politics of the centre, for, as we have already seen, a land dispute between Praejectus and Hector, the ruler of Marseilles, was heard at the royal court at Autun at Easter 675.[4] Praejectus had a brief moment of glory in Autun as he became the touchstone of the *coup* against Leudegar, a *coup* in which Hector was the first casualty. For his part in Hector's downfall Praejectus would eventually pay with his life, when Hector's 'senatorial' allies in the Auvergne later took their revenge upon him. These points we shall explore further, both to suggest that the text may in part have been intended to demonstrate some sort of public reconciliation between Praejectus's family and his killers, and to see what the detailed account of the bishop's career may tell us in general about later seventh-century Clermont. First, however, we must look at the edition of the text translated here, and try to understand its plainly rather awkward structure. We must then ask who could have written it.

In 1893 Krusch discovered in Rouen a tenth- or eleventh-century manuscript containing the version of the *Passio Praejecti* which he later published in the *Monumenta* series, and which is translated here.[5] Krusch was rather pleased with his discovery, for it allowed him to

---

3 *Passio Praejecti*, ch. 1, below, p. 272.

4 *Passio Leudegarii*, ch. 9, above, p. 226.

5 The text is in *MGH, SSRM*, V, pp. 225–48. Krusch first discussed the work in 'Die älteste *Vita Praejecti*'. *Neues Archiv*, 18 (1893), 629–39.

solve what had been regarded as something of a mystery. Earlier scholars had seen, and published, two versions of the *Passio* contained in various manuscripts dating from between the eleventh and fifteenth centuries. One version told of Praejectus's career from the time he became bishop until his death; the other related his whole life, and in addition that version had a stylish prologue, evidently from the Merovingian period. It also contained a series of posthumous miracles. Nevertheless, despite its early prologue, the longer version seemed generally to be later than the version of the *Passio* which dealt merely with Praejectus's career from the time he became bishop. For when the two versions were compared at those points at which they both covered the same events, the text which had the prologue was plainly a précis of the shorter text which began with Praejectus's election as bishop and ended with his death. Given that this shorter text seemed to be the source of some parts of the longer version, the problem was to identify the source of the remainder of the longer version, that is, the prologue, the information on Praejectus before he became bishop, and the account of the miracles which occurred after his death. This source was what Krusch discovered in his Rouen manuscript, where he found the missing parts in a version of the *Passio Praejecti* with a prologue, a section on the early career of Praejectus, a central section which matched that found in the shorter versions, and posthumous miracles, all of which together formed a text which was plainly the source of those complete, but abbreviated, versions which earlier scholars had seen. Krusch concluded that he had before him the earliest complete version of the *Passio Praejecti.* Having established the earliest text, surprisingly he did not offer further comment on its plainly unusual stucture.

What is odd about the earliest version of the *Passio Praejecti* is that it could almost be two works rolled into one, for the central section (chapters 14–31 in the *Monumenta* edition) has a kind of prologue of its own and can stand separately as an account of Praejectus's career as bishop and of his death. This, presumably, is why the central section had a separate manuscript tradition. The work as a whole (as in the *Monumenta* edition) reads awkwardly, for it stops and starts again right in the middle of the account of how Praejectus became bishop. This awkwardness is avoided in the abbreviated version which omits the new beginning in chapter 14 and makes the account of Praejectus's appointment easier to follow by leaving out much of the detail. Indeed, the desire to clarify could be one reason why the text was rewritten in précis, another aim possibly being to remove passages critical of the behaviour of the secular clergy in Clermont. A further complication in the earliest version is the mention in chapter 5 of a Bishop Genesius who was Praejectus's patron in his youth. Later, however (in chapter 14), we hear of a Count Genesius who was chosen as bishop but declined the honour, leaving it to Praejectus. This Count Genesius then became a benefactor to the church of Clermont, giving his own land for the foundation of a convent over which one Evodius was put in charge. Yet in another invaluable contemporary work from Clermont, the *Vita Boniti*, the life of Bonitus, bishop of Clermont in the generation after Praejectus, we hear that Bishop Genesius founded a monastery on his own land, and that Evodius became its abbot.[6] How might we explain this awkwardness and apparent contradiction?

First, it must be stressed that the *Passio Praejecti* was composed soon after its hero's death, for it contains convincing detail about contemporary events, and gives two clear eye-witness references.[7] Although the central section appears as if it could have been a separate work, there are in fact indications that the same author composed the whole piece. For instance, in chapter 32, in the context of Praejectus's burial and thus outside the central section, a certain Gundila is referred to as 'aforementioned'. Gundila (or 'Gundilana') was first mentioned in the central section (chapter 15), so whoever wrote chapter 32 must at least have seen the earlier reference. There is a less explicit cross-reference too between the saint's martyrdom in chapter 30 and his birth in the first chapter, for the description of his death fulfils almost to the letter the forecast his mother made shortly before his birth. The author's idiosyncratic spelling of the names of persons and places is also spread fairly evenly throughout the whole text, and so are the results of his or her attempts to emulate the style of classical authors. This classicising tendency may in fact be partly responsible for the disjointed appearance of the text. The author clearly rose to the challenge of opening the work in grand style in the first prologue, and may have seen in the elevation of Praejectus to the bishopric a suitable place to return to that style, emulating Caesar in an excursus in which the Auvergne and its position in Gaul were surveyed in panorama. What looks like a new beginning may therefore be the result of a badly

6 Compare *Passio Praejecti*, ch. 15, below, pp. 283–4 with *Vita Boniti*, ch. 16.

7 Eye-witness references are in chs. 5 and 31, below, pp. 276, 294.

managed classical literary device.[8] The uneven quality of the text, however, comes chiefly from the way in which the beginning and end are focused on Praejectus's family, whereas the central section is a more distanced account of his career as bishop. It looks as if the author was dealing with information from different, possibly conflicting, sources and did not make a very neat job of synthesis.

What appear to be contradictions in the work may be accurate reflections of the complexity of clerical politics in Clermont, as we shall see in the tortuous sequence telling how Praejectus became bishop. The author also makes it more difficult to follow events by failing on several ocasions to comment when he or she mentions people of the same name more than once. In the case of Genesius, for instance, Bishop Genesius may well have been the father or grandfather or uncle of Count Genesius, with our author failing to tell us this. It would not, in fact, have been unusual for one family to have supplied a region's count and its bishop, and to have expected to retain the bishopric, much as Aunemund's family did in Lyons.[9] Likewise a family might well found monastic establishments in successive generations and be linked in both generations with the same abbot, here Evodius.

The question of who wrote the *Passio Praejecti* is an open one. Krusch was convinced that the author was a monk, because the work is slightly critical of the life style of the secular clergy in Clermont. He also thought that the author could not be a local person, first because he or she believed that the river Loire flowed near Clermont, whereas the nearest river is in fact the Allier, and second because on four occasions the spelling of the names of local people and places is idiosyncratic.[10] In particular, he noted that the name 'Garivald' was Lombard in form, as opposed to the Frankish 'Charivald'. This hint of a Lombard connection he followed up in the prologue's praise of the work of Jonas of Bobbio, and Krusch reasoned that the author could have been an Italian pupil of Jonas, drafted in specially to write the work. Against this argument we must consider the local knowledge which is undisputedly displayed in the work, not least in the impression that

8 On the literary style of the second prologue, see W. Berschin, *Biographie und Epochenstil im lateinischen Mittelalter* vol. 2, *Merowingische Biographie, Italien, Spanien und die Inseln im frühen Mittelalter* (Stuttgart, 1988), pp. 74–5.

9 See above, pp. 166–7.

10 A fifth example of unusual spelling is 'Ugimer' for 'Waimer', the duke of Champagne, attested in several sources, one of them the *Passio Leudegarii*, ch. 25, above, p. 241. For his discussion of authorship, Krusch, 'Die älteste *Vita Praejecti*', 638–9.

Praejectus was known personally to the author.[11] Moreover, there is not really a 'mistake' about the course of the Loire, for the Allier is a tributary of the Loire, and the reference is made in the context of the panorama of Gaul, which starts with the Auvergne and sweeps along the course of the river round Aquitaine to the Atlantic Ocean: in these terms the Loire does flow near Clermont. As for the 'spelling mistakes', spelling is too variable in this period for anyone to be sure of their significance. Praise of Jonas's work also may not have the significance Krusch attributed to it, for the prologue lists in chronological order the eight most famous authors whose works are worthy of imitation. That this list should end with Jonas, the most widely read hagiographer of the first half of the seventh century, is natural.

It is, as we have seen, sensible to think that the *Passio Praejecti* had a single author, even if the disjointed nature of the work may suggest that the author was required to to represent different views of Praejectus and his career. There are, as we shall see shortly, several moments at which the point of view of Praejectus's oppponents may be represented, but on balance, the greater input into the work seems to have come from the hero's family. The author may therefore have been a member of that family, or a monk of Volvic, the monastery which housed Praejectus's relics and was controlled by his family, or possibly some neutral figure.[12] Another possibility, hitherto not considered but as likely as any other, and arguably more so, is that the work could have been written by a nun of Chamalières, the convent founded by Genesius at Praejectus's urging. The author singles out the abbess of Chamalières, Gundilana. for special praise, notes the arrangement by which Evodius was to oversee the convent, tells of the rules it was to follow, relates the foundation of another convent and adds that until Praejectus's time there were hardly any convents in the area.[13] The work's faint hostility towards the secular clergy, which Krusch observed, would fit the view of a nun quite as well as that of a monk. We are also told that it was Gundilana who recovered and washed

---

11 *Passio Praejecti*, ch. 5, below, p. 276.

12 P. Riché, *Education et culture dans l'Occident barbare VIe–VIIe siècles* (Paris, 1962), p. 413, assumed that the author was a monk of Volvic. I. Wood has suggested that the author may have been a monk of the monastery of St Amarin in the Vosges, that is, someone connected with Amarinus who was killed alongside Praejectus: I. Wood, 'The Ecclesiastical Politics of Merovingian Clermont', in P. Wormald (ed.), *Ideal and Reality in Frankish and Anglo-Saxon Society. Studies presented to J. M. Wallace-Hadrill* (Oxford, 1983), p. 35, n. 2.

13 *Passio Praejecti*, chs. 15, 16, below, pp. 283–4.

Praejectus's body and she would seem to have been the initiator of his cult.[14] From her name Gundilana was almost certainly a member of Praejectus's family and it is reasonable to think that, even if one of her nuns, or she herself, were not the author of this piece, she must have been a major influence upon it, not least in supplying the information on the saint's early life.[15] Scenes from childhood are, in fact, given a prominence unusual in the hagiography of this period. In the two references the author makes to herself or himself and and to her or his peers, the way in which the Latin pronouns are used does not reveal the gender of the person. In linguistic terms a female author is therefore a distinct possibility. There is, finally, no reason why a woman in the seventh-century Auvergne should not have had the education in classical literature and patristic works which the author of the *Passio Praejecti* displays.[16] Let us now turn to what the author, whoever she or he was, actually tells us about the life and death of Praejectus.

The *Passio Praejecti* stresses the Christianity, rather than the nobility, of the saint's ancestors, and, though nowhere is it made explicit, we may assume that Praejectus's family were not of the higher nobility.[17] That he would climb to the position of bishop and martyr is indicated by a miracle, which shows both that his success was preordained by God and that it was unexpected in human terms. Praejectus's uncle was an 'archipresbyter' and he too seems to have been schooled for a career in the Church from an early age, unlike Leudegar, who had some elements at least of a layman's education, or Audoin, who had a career at court before entering the Church.[18] Unlike these figures of

14 *Passio Praejecti*, ch. 32, below, p. 295.

15 *Passio Praejecti*, ch. 2, below, p. 273. Praejectus's father was called Gundolenus, which is the masculine form of the name.

16 As P. Riché pointed out, *Education et culture*, p. 235, Herchenfreda the mother of Desiderius of Cahors (d. *c.* 655) was educated in the Auvergne, presumably at the end of the sixth or the beginning of the seventh century. Her letters to her son show the high standard of her education.

17 G. Scheibelreiter, *Der Bischof in merowingischer Zeit* (Vienna, 1983), p. 31, remarks that in this context stress on the Christianity of the saint's family was conventional when the family was not from the highest noblity. Another example is the opening of the *Vita Eligii*, ed. B. Krusch, *MGH, SSRM*, IV (Hanover, 1902), p. 670. Contrast the statements about the origins of the saints in the other *Vitae* discussed in this volume.

18 On information about education in the saints' lives of this period, see M. Heinzelmann, 'Studia Sanctorum, éducation, milieux d'instruction et valeurs éducatives dans l'hagiographie en Gaule jusqu'à la fin de l'époque mérovingienne', in M. Sot (ed.), *Haut Moyen-âge. Culture, éducation et société. Etudes offerts à Pierre Riché* (Paris, 1990).

magnate stature, Praejectus was educated not at court but in the household of Genesius, who was first an archdeacon and then bishop of Clermont. It seems to have been due to Genesius's favour that Praejectus rose up through the ranks of the clergy at a rate which excited envy among his peers, who tried, and failed, to upset his progress. Genesius put him in charge of the important church of Issoire,[19] then later, under Bishop Felix, he became 'senior abbot' of the monastery of Chantoin, and was to be counted among the five most senior clergy of Clermont. On Felix's death Praejectus challenged for the position of bishop. The *Passio* tells us that he publicised the miracle which had forecast his greatness, but the response was that he was not rich enough to be bishop. Moreover, in attempting to become bishop, Praejectus was upsetting an agreed arrangement that the position should go to an archdeacon named Garivald.

In terms which may reflect the views of those who had opposed Praejectus, the *Passio* tells us that Garivald believed that he should succeed Felix as bishop because it was the custom in Clermont that the senior archdeacon should normally become the next bishop.[20] In order to secure the succession, Garivald and four of the other senior clergy, including Praejectus, drew up a legally binding agreement, thus publicly stating that Garivald should be the next bishop. When Praejectus broke this agreement by telling of his miracle, Garivald formally displayed the document which recorded their pact. The author then goes on to say that Garivald paid the laity to back his claim, and with their help forcibly suppressed the clergy and became bishop. His appointment could thus be portrayed as manifestly 'unjust'. This description may, however, also imply that Garivald drew upon the force of law to defend his legitimate claim based upon the earlier agreement. In the event, Garivald did not enjoy his office for long, dying after forty days. The *Passio* then breaks, moving to the 'new beginning' we discussed earlier, and it reopens the narrative with what appears to be a separate account of how Praejectus became bishop, stating simply that the Auvergne lacked a bishop. It then tells us that one Genesius was count of Clermont, and places the Auvergne in a panorama of Gaul, before going to describe how Genesius was chosen as bishop because the clergy could not agree on which of their number should be appointed. Genesius then stood down, 'lest he be acting

---

19 Scheibelreiter, *Der Bischof,* p. 107 suggested that Praejectus would have been made a deacon on his appointment to Issoire.

20 *Passio Praejecti,* ch. 13, below, pp. 280–1.

against canon law'. Praejectus was chosen to replace him.[21]

Because the work has a single author, we should treat the passages on Praejectus's appointment as a continuous sequence, and not as two separate and conflicting accounts. We should probably understand, therefore, that Praejectus became bishop only at the third attempt. His first attempt was effectively declared illegal, his second (if indeed he did make another bid upon Garivald's death) did not receive sufficient support from the clergy, and his third succeeded presumably because he had the support of Genesius, whose earlier namesake had been his patron. Conflict over the appointment of bishops was, of course, not uncommon. As we know from the *Passio Leudegarii*, for instance, Autun experienced almost two years of such conflict before Leudegar was sent in to restore order, and Gregory of Tours shows us that disputes over the bishopric of Clermont had a long history.[22] As we see from the *Acta Aunemundi*, even when the bishop was drawn from a family which dominated the town, he could still face dangerous opposition from rivals who might enlist support from outside. In Praejectus's case, the circumstances of his appointment, his rise at the expense of other members of the clergy, and his apparently meagre personal wealth, meant that he was a particularly vulnerable figure. We cannot, however, say that opposition to him was motivated simply by differences in social class. Once he became bishop, his two principal supporters were Genesius, who had been count of Clermont, and was presumably related to that Genesius who earlier had been bishop, and Evodius, whose name suggests that he was a member of the Hortensi family, and thus definitely to be counted among the 'senatorial' aristocracy. As we have already noted, Evodius was the abbot of a monastery founded by Bishop Genesius, and had charge of a convent founded by Count Genesius. In AD 571 Evodius's ancestor, named Euphronius, had been a rival of Avitus, a member of another great Auvergne family. At issue had been the post of bishop, which Avitus obtained.[23] Just over a century later, another Avitus would become

---

21 *Passio Praejecti*, ch. 14, below, pp. 282–3.

22 *Passio Leudegarii*, ch. 2, above, pp. 217–18. Wood, 'Ecclesiastical Politics', for the history of disputes over the bishopric of Clermont.

23 Gregory of Tours, *Gregorii Episcopi Turonensis Historiarum Libri X* (hereafter Gregory, *Hist.*), IV, ch. 35, ed. B. Krusch and W. Levison, *MGH, SSRM*, I (Hanover, 1951), pp. 167–8. Euphronius was the son of Evodius, who was of 'senatorial family' and descended from Hortensius. On Gregory's personal involvement in the dispute of 571, see R. Van Dam, *Saints and their Miracles in Late Antique Gaul* (Princeton, New Jersey, 1993), pp. 59–60.

bishop after Praejectus's murder, and it is tempting to wonder whether the ancient rivalry between the Hortensi and Aviti families was a continuing factor in the politics of later seventh-century Clermont, with Praejectus, and Genesius, lining up on the side of the Hortensi.

Whether as a client of others, or acting independently, Praejectus certainly did antagonise elements of the 'senatorial aristocracy'. The *Passio* gives us some insight into why this happened, although the author is never explicit about why the 'senators' had their bishop killed. First, Praejectus may have given offence by trying to take control of the cults of the saints Cassius, Victorinus and Antholianus. Having earlier written a 'little book' about these saints, Praejectus as bishop attempted to discover their relics and to establish a monastery in which to house them. 'Obstacles' prevented him, however, and it was left to his successor, Avitus, to accomplish the unearthing and translation of the relics.[24] It may be that the saints were regarded as having a particular association with Avitus's family, and, in the case of Antholianus, a connection with the family can indeed be traced back to the late fifth century.[25] It is a fair guess that the 'obstacles' which prevented Praejectus getting hold of the relics were put there by members of Avitus's family. There is a parallel here with Leudegar, who translated the relics of St Symphorian, thus no doubt antagonising their former guardian, his rival and successor, Hermenar.[26] The second area in which Praejectus offended 'senatorial' interests was in the acquisition of land for the church of Clermont. When the childless Count Genesius made the church his heir, this was done presumably without difficulty, but when Praejectus was bequeathed land by the widow Claudia, her daughter's spouse, Hector, ruler of Marseilles, raised a legal objection to the bequest. As we know, Hector forced Praejectus to court over the issue, and the two met in Autun at Easter 675. From the frank account in the *Passio Praejecti* it seems that the bishop would probably have lost the case had not Hector been forced to flee mid-way through the proceedings.[27]

The author makes it clear that Hector's downfall was the result not of this case but of higher-level political factors: he had 'abused the trust' of Wulfoald, the mayor of the palace. Nevertheless, Praejectus was

24 *Passio Praejecti*, ch. 17, below, pp. 284–5.
25 Wood, 'Ecclesiastical Politics', p. 39.
26 Above, p. 219.
27 *Passio Praejecti*, chs. 23–6, below, pp. 288–91.

drawn into high politics by virtue of having called upon the protection of Queen Himnechild at the moment at which the power of Himnechild's adversary Leudegar was being challenged. He was invited to celebrate the Easter vigils with the royal party, presumably in the monastery of St Symphorian, because we know from the *Passio Leudegarii* that the king did not join Leudegar in the celebration at the cathedral in Autun.[28] This preference for Praejectus may have been the signal that Leudegar's influence was at an end, and both he and Hector fled from Autun in the middle of the night. Helping the king in this way, Praejectus may have been seen as partly responsible for Hector's death, or at the very least as an enemy. He would thus have been regarded as a fair target for vengeance. After he had won his case, Praejectus returned to Clermont and was there joined by Abbot Amarinus, the leader of an ascetic community in the Vosges mountains. The author fails to mention that, not long after Praejectus's triumph, King Childeric had been murdered and the power of Wulfoald and Himnechild had collapsed. This left the bishop to face his enemies alone, and having Amarinus as a constant companion may have been intended as some sort of safeguard, rather as Aunemund had had Abbot Waldebert as a protector when he was in grave danger.[29]

Praejectus was killed, along with Amarinus and Gundolenus, a relative of the saint, in January 676.[30] The author is vague about the events leading up to the killing, perhaps because they were well known, or perhaps it was discreet not to dwell on such matters, for we know that the author drew upon the witness of some of those who were involved. That the killings were at least in part revenge for Hector's death has generally been assumed, from as far back as the end of the eleventh century.[31] The connection is understood from the narrative sequence, that is, that Praejectus was killed after returning from Autun, and it is also assumed that Hector was close to the 'senators' who are said to have been responsible for the murder. The aftermath of Childeric's murder was a time of great upheaval. We see from the *Passio Leudegarii* that an

---

28 *Passio Leudegarii*, ch. 10, above, p. 227.

29 *Acta Aunemundi*, ch. 4, above, p. 184.

30 It is to be assumed that Gundolenus was related to Praejectus because the saint's father was also called Gundolenus.

31 At the end of the eleventh century the chronicler Sigibert of Gembloux wrote that Praejectus 'was martyred by the leading men of the town in revenge for Hector *patricius* of Marseilles, executed by Childeric king of the Franks for the wrongs he had done to the church of the Auvergne'. *Sigiberti Chronicon*, ed. C. Bethmann, *MGH, SS*, VI (Hanover, 1844), *sub anno* 670, p. 326.

army moved south to take Leudegar from Autun, and that Eticho attacked Lyons in a bid to become ruler of Provence and thus occupy Hector's position. It is interesting to note that it was Avitus's brother, Bonitus, who seems to have ended up holding Marseilles.[32] Perhaps the struggle for Marseilles was another factor in the killing of Praejectus and the avenging of Hector. Here again, however, we must be content with speculation and resist the temptation to build too firm a political history out of these events.

When describing Praejectus's death the author made use of the conventional idea that the martyr actively sought death. This was also a way of saying that Praejectus chose to die, and we are left in no doubt that he could have avoided his fate: in a decidedly bathetic scene, the murderers broke into the saint's villa at Volvic, where Praejectus and Amarinus had taken refuge, but mistaking Amarinus for Praejectus they killed him instead.[33] Praejectus had then to call back the departing assassins and identify himself to them. That this treatment is sensitive to the saint's enemies is made clearer in the next passage, where two bystanders, the 'senators' Bodo and Placidus, said to have been among the authors of the crime, are immediately associated with the cult of the saint by witnesssing the ascent of his and his companions' souls to heaven.[34] This witness began a process of repentance, with the author suggesting by analogy with the fabled Longinus that they fully deserved to be forgiven. In contrast, the person who actually delivered the death blow, a Saxon named Radbert, soon suffered the agonising death with which the killers of saints were usually punished. Both Bodo and Placidus were alive at the time the *Passio Praejecti* was composed, as was Ursio, another of the conspirators, who became the subject of two of the five miracles which took place after Praejectus's death.[35] The saint was thus demonstrating favour towards Ursio by

32 *Vita Boniti*, ch. 3, Bonitus was chosen *praefectus* of Marseilles at a time when King Sigibert III's nephew was on the throne. This could refer either to Childeric II (662–75) or to Theuderic III (673–91). *Vita Boniti*, ch. 4, p. 121, says that while Bonitus was in charge of Marseilles, Avitus was bishop of Clermont, which means that Bonitus must have been *praefectus* some time in 676–90. He does not, however, figure in an original royal document of the year 677 (*ChLA* no. 565) in which two other rulers of Provence are mentioned. This may suggest that in 677 Bonitus was ruler of Marseilles, but that Marseilles was not yet under the control of the Neustro-Burgundian regime which issued the document that year.

33 *Passio Praejecti*, ch. 30, below, pp. 293–4.

34 *Passio Praejecti*, ch. 31, below, p. 294.

35 *Passio Praejecti*, ch. 31, below, pp. 294–5: Bodo and Placidus 'still assert today' that they saw Praejectus's soul rise to heaven. On Ursio, chs. 38 and 39, below, pp. 298–9.

answering his prayers. In return for the saint's help, Ursio gave silver to his tomb, and we are told that upon hearing this the others involved in the murder donated gold and other riches. Unlike the outsider Radbert, a Saxon, these men were part of the established elite of the Auvergne. Their donations can be seen in the light of both personal atonement and public peace-making.

Throughout early medieval Europe it was a common legal principle and established custom that those who had killed someone could come to terms with the slain person's kindred by agreeing to compensate for the life lost. By donating to Praejectus's cult, Ursio and the others may have been coming to terms with Praejectus's kindred. It seems that, as well as Praejectus, other members of his family were attacked at this time, possibly to forestall any attempts at retribution or revenge. One family member, Gundolenus, who had the same name as Praejectus's father, was killed whilst protecting the saint; another, Eligius (who had the masculine form of his mother's name), was killed in unspecified circumstances, and a third, Godo, fled the Auvergne at the time of the murder. It was left to a female relative, Gundilana (again we see a variant of the family name), the abbess of Chamalières, to recover Praejectus's body and to prepare it for burial. According to the *Passio* it was the growing popularity of the saint's cult which eventually forced Praejectus's successor Avitus to recognise the sanctity of his predecessor.[36] The terms in which he did so suggest that he too was making his peace with the saint's family. After some hesitation Avitus proceeded by negotiating with Godo. Godo returned from his refuge in the monastery of Agaune and it was agreed with Avitus that together they should set up a monastery at Volvic, the site of the murder. Avitus would endow the foundation and Godo become its abbot. This was done and later a document was drawn up which formally listed all the property which Avitus had given over to Volvic. This document was a public statement of the gifts to the monastery, and the public and binding nature of the transaction may have been an important part of any peace-making process. We may perhaps view the *Passio Praejecti* as a whole in this light. The work is, in effect, a public record of Praejectus's life and death, and one which represents the viewpoints of both the saint's family and their enemies. As we saw earlier, it is the juxtaposition of views required to achieve this effect which lends the work an uneven quality. The very process of composing the work could itself have been part of the peace-making if

36 *Passio Praejecti*, ch. 34, below, p. 296.

that meant negotiating a public version of events, in which the saint was not entirely blameless, nor his enemies wholly bad, and in which his persecutors could be seen properly to have atoned for their crime and accordingly to have been forgiven by the saint. In this text it is naturally Praejectus's sanctity which brings the opposing parties together. Whether in reality some kind of third party was involved in the settlement it is impossible to tell.

Documenting the endowment of Praejectus's cult was a way of demonstrating the public acknowledgement of his sanctity. That our author should have been as much at ease with the material as with the spiritual side of her or his hero's sanctity is quite normal for a hagiographer, for the success of a cult was measured by the gifts it attracted. It is also generally true that in early medieval cultures the languages of law and religion often intermingled, and the meanings of terms such as 'right', 'wrong', 'justice' and 'punishment' drew upon both. The clearest examples of this we have seen were in the language of the *Passio Leudegarii*, in which the struggle between Good and Evil was expressed in terms of a political struggle, with power being understood as the right to issue legally binding orders, and with the quality of justice being a prime indicator of a regime's morality.[37] The author of the *Passio Praejecti* was similarly well versed in the language of law, and for the same reasons: in that society much of the important business of the day was done within the framework of legal agreements, and the Church also used its spiritual sanction to endorse and defend property rights.[38] Our text reveals some of the documents produced as a consequence of the legal activity in which Praejectus was involved. The author refers, for instance, to the written agreement that Garivald should follow Felix as bishop; there are two references to royal documents, one to a privilege for the church of Clermont, the other to the judgement in Praejectus's favour against Hector; and as we have seen, the author describes the drawing up of an inventory of Volvic's property. The *Passio Praejecti* thus provides important evidence for the widespead use of documents in the later seventh century.[39] The concern with legal activity also casts light more generally on the

37 See above, pp. 213–14.

38 For a discussion of the relationship between property, power and spiritual sanction, see 'Conclusion: Cultural Aspects of Power', in W. Davies and P. Fouracre (eds.), *Property and Power in Early Medieval Europe* (Cambridge, 1995).

39 For discussion of the extent of literacy in the seventh century, see I. Wood, 'Administration, law and culture in Merovingian Gaul', in R. McKitterick (ed.), *The Uses of Literacy in Early Medieval Europe* (Cambridge, 1990).

organisation of Clermont, on the Auvergne and on the region's links with the wider world. It is to these issues that we now turn.

Throughout the seventh century the Auvergne preserved a largely Roman culture, as we can see at once from our author's use of the term 'senators' for the region's elite. We must assume that it was Roman law which was in use there, for not only does the *Passio Praejecti* say that Praejectus used Roman law in his defence at Autun in 675, but the *Vita Boniti* also tells of how Bonitus (who was Avitus's brother) studied the Theodosian Code, the essential collection of later Roman law.[40] The *Passio Praejecti* refers too to the use of canon law. Finally, as we saw earlier, there is a reference to the use of custom in the context of Garivald's succession, namely, that it was the custom that the senior archdeacon should become the next bishop. Our source mentions a count, Genesius, who presumably had responsibility for the enforcement of law, and the 'senators' who could mobilise their own armed force or *satellites*, but apart from this the author is concerned only with the affairs of the clergy. This clerical community is shown as a hierarchy bound together by the bishop's command, by custom, and by canon law. Within it there was clearly great rivalry for promotion, and possibly tension as people progressed at different rates though a well defined career structure. Twice Praejectus's progress excited opposition, first as a youth when he was favoured by Bishop Genesius, and later when he tried to push past Garivald to become bishop.[41] It is easy to see why these conditions might produce rivalry, for the top position, bishop, was well worth fighting for, and Praejectus's career suggests that it was sometimes possible for someone without massive wealth to get to the top. Consequently there would often be fierce competition for the post of bishop.

Given the emphasis that sources such as the *Passio Praejecti* place upon the importance of bishops in their communities, it easy to imagine that in many areas bishops were, *de facto*, the rulers. It has often been supposed that the towns farther away from the centres of royal power in northern Francia would have been particularly likely to become subject to 'episcopal self-government'. However, as we saw in the cases of Autun and Lyons, even distant towns were prone to intervention from outside, largely because elements within each town sought help from the palace. The *Passio Praejecti* provides another example of the

---

40 *Vita Boniti*, ch. 2.
41 *Passio Praejecti*, chs. 4 and 13, below, pp. 275, 280–2.

ways in which a remote town with a strong sense of identity might be linked to the political community based upon the palace. As the family names of the 'senatorial' aristocracy of the Auvergne suggest, this community had a long history and a long memory. As a centre of Roman culture, both remote and economically separate from northern Francia, the Auvergne might be expected to have been precisely the kind of region in which an 'episcopal republic' would have developed. The evidence, however, shows that the leaders from this area actively sought contact with the rulers of the north, despite the fact that those rulers were usually kings in Austrasia, which meant both that they were difficult to reach and that they inhabited lands where people spoke a language different from that of the Auvergne. The *Passio Praejecti* tells how on one visit to King Childeric, presumably at Strasbourg, the bishop had to cross the Vosges mountains. Interestingly, the author alludes to the 'barbarian language' of the inhabitants of the area as well as stressing how difficult it was to travel through the mountains.[42]

Praejectus made this journey to court in order to get a *privilegium* for the church of Clermont, by which we should understand that he received a document granting or confirming the rights of his church. The great effort required to go and get this document suggests that it was highly valued, and that royal authority was indeed felt in the Auvergne. The author also tells us that those who wanted to install Count Genesius as bishop got 'royal edicts' to that end, which may indicate that the palace had some influence over the appointment of the bishop in Clermont, as it certainly did over the choice of bishops for Autun, Rouen and Lyons, the other appointments we have looked at in this volume.[43] The clearest sign that the ruler did have some authority in the region is in fact the episode of Praejectus's second visit to the royal court. Hector had made accusations there against Praejectus, and the bishop was summoned to answer the charges. The author implies that he did not wish to go to court but was forced to do so by the use of sureties.[44] Here the conduit for outside intervention was the operation of law, through which local rivalry was played out at the highest court.

42 *Passio Praejecti*, chs. 20–2. It was on this trip that Praejectus made contact with Amarinus, who was in charge of an ascetic community in the Vosges mountains. The Austrasian royal palace of Strasbourg was adjacent to the Vosges. From Clermont to Strasbourg is a distance of well over 500 km.

43 Palace influence on the choice of bishops for Clermont can be demonstrated from the early sixth century through to the early eighth: see Wood, 'Ecclesiastical Politics'.

44 *Passio Praejecti*, ch. 23, below, p. 288.

Praejectus's earlier contact with the court had also had a legal dimension as he sought royal protection for his church. Royal authority was valued because in this context it was useful.

More intimate contact between the royal court and the Auvergne is revealed in the *Vita Boniti* which tells of Bonitus's career at the courts of Sigibert III and Childeric II.[45] One wonders whether Avitus, Bonitus's brother, also spent time at court. Certainly, their probable associate Hector was a magnate who was a member of the supra-regional political community, and close to Leudegar. The Auvergne obviously did not stand outside that community, and though it is correct to stress its Roman culture, it was open to other influences. Members of Praejectus's own family had names of Frankish origin, and it was, remember, a Saxon who killed him. As we have seen, the background to the killing lay in a local dispute which had got caught up in the feuding at the royal court in 675. The evidence of the *Passio Praejecti* therefore strengthens the impression which we get from the *Passio Leudegarii*, namely that the effects of this feuding were widespread, and that following the murder of King Childeric there was indeed serious disorder in the provinces. What the *Passio Leudegarii* shows so well is the capacity of this political community to repair itself at the centre, where Ebroin was eventually able to return to government through the palace. The fascination of the *Passio Praejecti* is that it shows us peace being re-established at a local level, with those behind the bishop's murder becoming patrons of a cult which celebrated his status as a martyr. It was this ability to make peace at both local and 'national' level which enabled the Frankish political community to survive its periodic bouts of feuding. The *Passio Praejecti* is a source of immense value in providing us with clues about what may have motivated such flexibility, and why a remote community such as that based on Clermont did not decline into disorder or reject the authority of its distant overlord.

---

45 *Vita Boniti*, ch. 2, Bonitus was sent to court as an adolescent. He later became a royal steward and then *referendarius*, the same position Audoin had held at the court of Dagobert I.

Passio Praejecti
(The Suffering of Praejectus)

HERE BEGINS THE PROLOGUE TO THE STORY OF THE MARTYRDOM OF SAINT
PRAEJECTUS, BISHOP AND MARTYR

Guided in their effort by the wisdom of Christ (without whom no good
is done), the most learned men of old were keen to set forth in writing
the miracles of those whom they saw to be strong with holy acts, for
'by imitating the good deeds of predecessors and by entrusting them
to memory will posterity have a glorious future'.[46] Indeed, Eusebius of
Caesarea, a man powerful with fluent eloquence, followed the examples
set by his seniors and described the suffering of countless martyrs, and,
imitating him, Rufinus continued the account up into the consulship of
the emperor Theodosius.[47] The blessed Athanasius, bishop of Alexan-
dria, edited the acts of Antony, and Jerome, most holy and erudite in all
things, edited the acts of Paul and Hilary and others whom he showed
praiseworthy for the good life they led; as a result I may come to the holy
anchorites and confessors. Moreover, Posthumianus, Severus and Gallus
set down in their pages the life of the exemplary Martin. The most blessed
Gregory too, the bishop of the church of Rome, to whom the secrets of
heaven lay open, inserted the suffering of the saints in his book called
the *Dialogues* in which he wrote about their sweet deeds. In living memory
too the eloquent Jonas produced his very splendid life of St Columbanus
and his disciples Athalus, Eustasius and Bertulf.[48] In comparison with
these writers I reckon myself a worth-less buffoon, but be ye mindful of
the command of our Lord and Saviour: 'Ask and it shall be given to you,
seek and ye shall find, knock and it shall be opened unto you,' and that
little prayer of the psalm writer: 'Open thy mouth wide and I shall fill it.'
Satisfying your orders although rashly, but nonetheless not falsely or

---

46 This sentence is quoted from the *Vita Columbani* I, ch. 1, ed. B. Krusch, *MGH,
SSRM*, IV (Hanover, 1902), p. 65.

47 It is probably correct to assume that the author would not have been able to read
Eusebius, who wrote in Greek, but that she or he knew of Eusebius's work through
Rufinus's Latin epitome. But as W. Berschin points out in *Biographie und Epochenstil*
vol. 2, p. 73, the author is wrong in saying that Rufinus continued the account up
into the consulship of the emperor Theodosius, for Rufinus did in fact go up to
Theodosius's death. The error raises the question of whether the author knew of
these works but had not actually read them. The following list nevertheless
provides positive evidence for the models available to a hagiographer in the late
seventh century.

48 Ionas's work was completed *c.* 642. As our author was writing in the time of Bishop
Avitus (676–90), 642 would indeed have been within living memory.

with a striving for presumption, I shall set out to weave these deeds
and to discover that which I have found out concerning the high bishop
Praejectus by means of an investigating pen as well as by the report of
many people.⁴⁹ Whereupon I beg the reader – should anyone, seized by
love for the bishop, decide to read this, they should not look here for
the eloquence of a Tully or for the fluency of an orator, nor for the
adornment of a philosopher nor for the various declarations of the
historians, but only for the simple purity of the holy Church.⁵⁰ For when
the eagle spreads its wings it does not always fly up to the upper air but
more often it slackens its wings and heads for the fields, and even among
the feasts fit for a king lowly fruits and rustic lettuces can also be
reckoned the best. We must pray to God the Father that He may remove
the clouds of a very dense understanding and of a dull sense. And we
must pray to our Lord Saviour Jesus Christ that He may see fit to blow
the breeze of the Holy Spirit to disperse the fog of my heart and give me
the gift of speech so that I may be able to discuss the deeds of Bishop
Praejectus, who always burned with the love of Christ.⁵¹ Thus should
his example and the power of his wise mind be transmitted to posterity.
May the everlasting sower of [men's] affairs who makes even the language of little children clear be aided by your prayer to grant this. Amen.

Here begins the story of the Martyrdom of St Praejectus, Bishop and
Martyr.

CHAPTER 1

St Praejectus, then, was born in the province of the Auvergne, and he
shone out in his family of Roman stock. His father was called
Gundolenus, his mother Eligia, and they traced their lineage through
a long line of Catholic men most worthy of their Christian faith,
through whom the Lord has manifested many miracles.⁵² But it is not

49 Since the work has no dedication (unlike the *Passio Leudegarii*, above, p. 215), we
can only guess at who may have ordered it to be composed, just as we cannot know
who the author was.
50 Whilst protesting his or her 'holy simplicity' the author shows familiarity with, and
strives to imitate, the classical literary tradition to which that simplicity was in
theory opposed. See above, pp. 257–8, for general discussion of our author's use of
Latin.
51 The author of the *Passio Leudegarii* used the same image of foggy vision: see above,
p. 215.
52 Note the emphasis on the Christianity rather than the nobility of the family, which
suggests that Praejectus was not a member of the 'senatorial' aristocracy of the
Auvergne.

to be omitted how when his mother was about to bring him into the world, in the manner of those who are born on earth, a few days before, she said she saw a vision in which, to her amazement, her son emerged from her side, followed closely by a soaking surge of blood.[53] Restless and shaken by the vision, she began to move hither and thither, wailing. What, she wanted to discover, did these portents hold in store for her? It happened that whilst she was thinking of these things along came Peladius the archypresbyter, a most holy man, her brother, who began to search in detail for the reason why she was shaking in such an unaccustomed way.[54] Forthwith she related her vision and the holy man of God told her everything: that she would bring forth a child who would in his time be a great man among his fellows in the world and who would tread the path all the way to martyrdom.[55] His mother rejoiced to hear such words so that, as I reckon, she stood there beseeching the Lord; at one in faith with the priest's prediction, she heartily desired that it would turn out thus for her son.

CHAPTER 2

The boy was born, in his cradle he squalled, and he was nourished by milk. What more should I say? He grew, as human beings do, and when the time came for him to acquire the skills of letters he was handed over to be taught by the schoolmaster at the church of Issoire. Oh truly how the Lord filled out His boy. So quickly was he brimming with the mysteries of learning that to all who were there he appeared no longer to be a youngster; indeed, he was ahead of his age group in the sounds of grammar and in chanting the liturgy.[56] Mighty is the

---

53 In the *Vita Columbani* I, ch. 2, the mother of Columbanus is described as having had a similar vision, with light radiating out of her belly. The similarity between the two stories goes no further, for the author of the *Passio Praejecti* then turns to purely local detail to set the events in context.

54 The term 'archipresbyter' probably means priest of a baptismal Church: it was used in this sense in an Auvergne context by Gregory of Tours.

55 The vision and its interpretation are used later to explain Praejectus's ambitions, which supports the impression that his family did not belong to the social elite from which the Bishops of Clermont were usually drawn.

56 The reference to the saint's secular as well as religious education follows the tradition established by the *Vita Columbani* I, ch. 3, in which Columbanus was also said to have studied grammar. The *Passio Leudegarii*, ch. 1, above, p. 217, similarly mentions Leudegar's secular education. On what the saints' lives of this period tell us about the education of their subjects, see Heinzelmann, 'Studia Sanctorum'. For comment on the type of school Praejectus may have attended at Issoire, Riché, *Education et culture*, p. 325.

One who brought this about, the One who points out to all the prophet among the gatherers of the sycomore fruit.[57]

CHAPTER 3

After this Peladius, whom we mentioned before and who was related to Praejectus, was invited to a meal by a man called Babo who was a deacon, and he motioned the boy to come along with him. The lad followed his uncle and they arrived at the house of their host. But that Babo, as is usual with wicked men, sought out disgrace rather than what would be of use to his soul's needs, and he kept those animals which are wont to give comfort to men and to terrify by their wild ferocity, [that is] dogs, chained up to keep guard outside the gates of his house. Their fierceness was such that they did not hesitate to bite human flesh. But in order that God's grace would now be made manifest in our boy Praejectus, he decided to go up to the gates. As the wretched dogs saw him, they burst their chains asunder and they barked loudly at the boy, wanting to tear him to pieces. But God wondrously saved him, he who thereafter was to belong to the faithful, and the fierce dogs did the boy no harm. As the others came up the dogs returned to their savage fury and they bit the unfortunate people so that it might be granted to be understood that they had not dared to lacerate with bites the one God loved, he who had armed his brow with the protection of the Lord's cross.[58]

CHAPTER 4

After these events Praejectus was given by his parents into the household of Genesius, who was then archdeacon and who not long after was raised up to the high dignity of bishop.[59] Genesius took the

---

57 The reference is to the Prophet Amos, who claimed to be a mere gatherer of the sycamore fruit: Amos 7:14.

58 This seems to be a low-key miracle story, even by early medieval standards. The distaste for guard dogs may echo late sixth-century conciliar legislation which forbade the keeping of guard dogs at the bishop's mansion in case they should bite the poor who had come there looking for help: 'Concilium Matisconense a 585', ch. 13, in C. de Clercq (ed.), *Concilia Galliae a 511–695, Corpus Christianorum, Series Latina*, 148A (Turnhout, 1963), p. 245.

59 Bishop Genesius is also attested in the *Vita Boniti*, ch. 16, where it is said that he founded the monastery of Manglieu on his own property and made Evodius its abbot. For discussion of the possible relationship between Bishop Genesius, Count Genesius and Evodius, see above, pp. 262–3. There is no way of telling when Genesius was bishop, except that it was before 660, when a Bishop Gyroindus

boy with fatherly affection and he brought him up and educated him
with great care and when he was made a bishop he had him as an
intimate counsellor and made him as well the distributor of the money
given over to the poor. He so esteemed him in his love, so tested him
in his training, so educated him in all things to do with letters as [far
as] his age could manage that many people reacted to all this by filling
their gullets with envy.[60] And, as is the way of the clergy to crush in
an overbearing fashion the knowledge of many, they wish, because
they cannot fill their own store rooms with wisdom, to pour evil
hatred over those others dedicated to wisdom. The poisons of the
clerics urged into envy against Praejectus a certain Martin who was
responsible for giving the tone in the varied kinds of prayers to the
various holy churches, [suggesting] that he should make the boy
amongst the others give the note of a certain tone of which he had no
experience,[61] a tone which he could hardly have produced even after a
long time and, so to speak, with a well drilled mouth, but one which
for a long time now his rivals were [i.e. had been] singing with their
voices.[62] The boy was ordered to perform what he learned nothing
about. But the lad set his brow, steeled his chest, sought patience and
called upon St Julian the martyr to come to his aid.[63] And so that he
might not detract from the authority of the master, so that he might
break the anger and lay to rest the ill intent of his other rivals, the
Lord filled His boy so that the tone which he had not memorised
before now he sang with the voice of a master. Thus were his rivals

---

signed the privilege of Emmo of Sens in Clermont's place in the order of episcopal
signatories. (On this document, see above, p. 174, n. 24) Genesius was formally
recognised as a saint in the year 1230. As Tardieu pointed out, *Histoire de Clermont-
Ferrand*, vol. 1, p. 182, he was the only one of the early bishop-saints of Clermont
to be canonised rather than simply acclaimed a saint.

60 The Latin construction of this sentence makes it clear that the envy was the result
of the personal attention Praejectus received from Genesius.

61 This attempts to translate: *fatiat puerum inter ceteros meditum cuiusdam soni*. It is not
possible to be sure what is meant by the term *meditum*, whether the author meant
to convey the sense of tone, or musical note. At this period there seems to have been
no established technical vocabulary for singing.

62 Again the Latin is difficult: *vix tandem, ut ita dicam, puncto ore meditum personasse,
quem sui aemuli longo iam evo sonitum vocibus decantabant*. What the author may be
trying to convey is the notion of a certain fluid vocal sound which is wordless,
perhaps something similar to what St Augustine called the *iubilum*. The general
sense, however, is clear: Praejectus was asked to sing something difficult which was
new to him but which the others had been practising for some time.

63 The cult of St Julian of Brioude was one of the most popular in the Auvergne; see
R. Van Dam, *Saints and their Miracles*, pp. 41–8.

wrenched in their own malice, for whilst they had wished to punish the boy they ended up praising him. Thereafter it was usual for Praejectus to be preferred to his fellows, and this memory of him was forgotten, so much so that it could never have been brought up again. How else can this be understood (*datur intelligi*) except in terms of the One whose grace was all-powerful within him, surrounding him with His protection.

CHAPTER 5

Not long after this the blessed Genesius expressed the wish that he should make over the church of Issoire to St Praejectus to control.[64] We must not remain silent about how and how much he then tried to make himself an example of steadfastness in his office; how frequently he fasted, how ready he was to say the daily prayers, how vigorously he rejoiced in the mysteries of reading the Scriptures: there are witnesses who tell of having seen all this. On fast days he was accustomed to make his lodging in the store room under the monastery building:[65] save that he had contact with the servants of the faithful, he avoided meeting lay people. What more should we dwell upon? In this office through God's grace he showed himself as humble as he could so that already then he appeared to us and to his followers as a most kind-hearted teacher.[66]

CHAPTER 6

Finally, as his wealth increased he began to spread in Christ's fields – that is, the bosom of the poor – quite a lot of coins. For at that time, since he had given to a certain Gundobert, a relative of his, a little money to be kept for alms, poor people came importunately beating at the gates.[67] It oppressed Praejectus to see how little there was to distribute among so many, because he had no more than two coins.

---

64 Scheibelreiter, *Der Bischof,* p. 107, thought that the posting to Issoire meant that Praejectus was made a deacon, in charge of other clergy. He was certainly a deacon by the time of the events referred to in ch. 9, below p. 278.

65 *Cella* is here translated as 'store room'.

66 The strong implication here is that the author was a contemporary of Praejectus. It is not possible to tell to whom the author was referring in the terms 'us' (*nobis*) and 'followers' (*suis*), which can be either masculine or feminine in gender. If the author were a nun (see above, pp. 259–60) she might thus be referring to her sisters.

67 Note that the name Gundobert has the same first element as that of Praejectus's father, Gundolenus, which suggests that Gundobert was a relative on his father's side.

When the soldier [i.e. Praejectus] returned to the usual comforters of his hands, he prayed to God who is the giver of all gifts that he might bestow upon him something to pay out in alms to the rest. He called Gundobert and ordered him to give out the few coins, but when he mentioned how few there were, this wondrously miraculous thing happened: the Lord there showered down as many coins as there were poor people standing in the crowd before the gates.[68]

CHAPTER 7

We must speak too of the miracle that happened when guests arrived. For, since in his usual holy way he called for food to be charitably provided for them, he asked his servant if he had any fish for a meal. The table servant replied that he had none or at most a morsel. He ordered the lad to to go down to the river to fetch water. As water flowed into the vessel he caught a fish sufficient to provide a meal to comfort the guests in their hunger. Strong is the hand of the Lord who spontaneously provides anything at all for His own, the Lord who as He wished created all things at His own order.

CHAPTER 8

As is customary among those in charge of parishes, at Easter time they go to meet the bishop, so as usual several of the priests went to the town and present among them was the blessed Praejectus. After he had paid his respects Praejectus went to his own house in that same town and prepared a feast, and as he was accustomed to confer with his fellows on such days he ordered a meal to be laid out for him on the gallery. Quite a crowd of diners arrived, among whom there were three who were in a state of penance. These were their names: God's servant Venerianus, who honoured his name with his work, Christ's witness Gosoaldus and the monk Marialdus. They reclined at table as is usual[69] and the dishes were offered round but their fellow diners rebuked the penitents and mocked them with rude laughter and silly

68 This miracle provides important evidence of the way in which alms were distributed, and of the use of coin among the poor. Compare the *Passio Leudegarii*, ch. 2, above, p. 218, where Leudegar is said to have set up alms distribution for the poor, but no detail is given.
69 That they should recline to eat is suggestive of Roman fashion.

jests, in no small way belittling their penitence.[70] The blessed Praejectus, by contrast, as was usually his way, tried to persuade them that it behoved them to put up with such things rather than to belittle them. But they would not stop mocking the servants of God; indeed, they reached a new pitch with their jokes amid gales of laughter. But the One who judges and who arranges and controls everything with faithful guidance, and who offers strong succour to His own, was there to help Praejectus in no small way. The beams of the gallery sprang apart and collapsed in pieces on the ground floor; the rivals, the disparaging ones, fell all the way to the bottom. Blessed Praejectus and his colleagues the penitents remained sitting at the table, triumphant, so that thereby it might be understood that He is powerful, just as the psalm singer says: 'I will reprove thee and set them in order before thine eyes.' He saved those worthy of Him and curbed those who spoke ill; but by the grace of God they were rescued and, pulled from the depths of the house, they returned to their own dwellings. Thus, oh thus, did the mess-mates learn to accept the Lord's bridle and not to dare threaten His servants when they were in a state of penance.

CHAPTER 9

What a large and good library had the Lord founded in the store chest of his heart, and we must marvel at how when still carrying out his duties as deacon he began, as it were, to go into the affairs of his predecessors as, inspired from heaven through every good gift of the holy martyrs, that is, Cassius, Victorianus and Antholianus and the others their comrades, he brought forth a little book [of] how they fought against the worship of idols, and how with Christ's support they made their way to a refuge in heaven. With wonderful talent in night-work most worthy and sharp he dedicated these tales to God's people. At that time too he crafted in fitting language the deeds of the martyr, St Austremonius, whose grave lies outside the church of Issoire over which he himself presided.[71] But the guardian of humility

70 The state of penance in this form, i.e. abstinence, may have been a relatively recent introduction in Francia, hence the amusement it occasioned. The interest in penance here also follows the direction of the *Vita Columbani*, see I. Wood, *The Merovingian Kingdoms 450–751* (London, 1994), p. 191.

71 If he did compose these works, no trace of them has survived. In ch. 17, below, pp. 284–5, we are told that Praejectus also tried to locate, and intended to translate, the bodies of Cassius, Victorinus and Antholianus but was prevented from doing so. Perhaps this writing about them was the first step in atttempts to bring these cults, which were already well established, under his control. Gregory of Tours mentioned

was ever present so that after such works he stopped lest by chance the flattery of his peers should be brought to his ears and lead him away from the blessing of his Creator.

CHAPTER 10

After this he took up the abbacy of the monastery of Chantoin, being ordered to shoulder the burden by the bishop of the time, one called Felix.[72] This was because he was always wont to demand for himself such agreeable service in order to have the ministry of holy souls, and he alone harvested the crop and cared for the clergy no less than a shepherd. Oh, how he always made himself walk in Christ's way and set an example so that the inhabitants of that place brought forth praises.

CHAPTER 11

It would be tedious to go in turn through all the miracles God deigned to show through him whilst he held this office. But let me touch upon a few of the best:[73] like when he decided to repair an old house in a district of the town and it happened that in that place the builders set up a treadmill in their usual way so that they could build up higher the fabric that was now old and so make it sound.[74] The bishop was there in person and the machine was nearly forty feet up from the ground. It happened that as the builders were running through the treadmill a wall collapsed, a countless number of stones falling to the ground and crushing a bystander. So great was the pile of rocks that it was reckoned that he would be found dead or, at the very least, all broken. St Praejectus with anguished cries went into the church which was in

the martyrs in *Hist.* I, ch. 33, and referred to Antholianus in *Liber in Gloria Martyrum*, ch. 64, ed. B. Krusch, *MGH*, *SSRM*, I (Hanover 1885, new edition 1969), pp. 51–2. The latter reference makes clear the connection of the Avitus family with the cult.

72 Bishop Felix is unattested elsewhere. His episcopate must have been after that of Gyroindus, who was attested in the year 660, for it was Felix whom Praejectus eventually succeeded as bishop some time in the reign of Childeric II (662–75). The posting to Chantoin seems to have been further promotion for Praejectus, as it made him one of the five leading clergy of the diocese.

73 The author promises to tell of *pauca*, 'a few' miracles, but goes on to relate only one.

74 In *Passio Leudegarii*, ch. 2, above, p. 219, Leudegar too was said to have repaired old houses in Autun. It was, however, Desiderius, bishop of Cahors, who was the most celebrated builder of the seventh century: see R. Rey, 'Un Grand Bâtisseur au temps du Roi Dagobert: S. Didier Evêque de Cahors, *Annales du Midi*, 65 (1953). But no other source provides as much detail on building methods and on the height of buildings.

the neighbourhood, the church of St Adiutor, and he cried out that he was responsible for this death, that he had killed the man. Pouring out his tears in a shower, he prayed to the God of Saboath, and at the same time he asked for the mass of stones covering the man to be thrown aside so that at least they might drag his body out. Those carrying out his orders found the one they were thinking dead alive and unharmed. Who could have arranged it thus, unless it was the most merciful grace of almighty God who directed Praejectus to perform this miracle?

CHAPTER 12

A few days later, when the Lord had several times seen fit to show signs through His servant, the bishop named Felix who at that time discharged the episcopal duty in the aforesaid town of Clermont came to the end of his days. The aforesaid Praejectus, after he had buried him with much grief, returned with sadness to the memory of the vision he had learnt of in times past as handed down by his uncle and his mother.[75] He thought it fitting to reveal it openly to the people at large, but he got only this reaction from them all: did he know how much in the metals of gold and silver he would have to have to be able to take on that job? By contrast he gave this answer: that if God wished him to serve Him in that way he believed he would not have to offer any money, just as the law of the Church stated.[76] And afterwards events proved him right in this.

CHAPTER 13

In the time of Bishop Felix, who had now died, one Garivald then ministered as deacon and he became archdeacon. It came about that five of the senior clergy got together in a group.[77] They were: the aforesaid Garivald of holy memory; Praejectus of whom we have spoken before; Arivald, a leading priest of great faith; Aginus the priest, and the fifth was Stephen the deacon. Because they held the authority over

---

75 See ch. 1, above, p. 273. The vision revealed that it was his destiny to be a great man.

76 The prohibition of simony was repeated often by church councils, which suggests that the buying of Church office was indeed common practice. Here, Praejectus was in effect using canon law to contest the status of Garivald's document, which is described in the next chapter.

77 *Seniores abbates* is the phrase used to mean 'senior clergy'. The term *abbas* could mean leader of the secular clergy as well as the head of a monastery.

the clergy in the aforesaid town, they drew up a document[78] [to show]
that these five were then in agreement that after the death of the aforementioned Bishop Felix he [Garivald] should, God willing, become
shepherd of the flock. And this business of the aforesaid archdeacon
had been made binding in law[79] because he believed that he should be
the next bishop, for the custom[80] of succession among his predecessors
had been that the person serving in that deacon's post took over the
pastoral care if the opportunity offered itself. When the aforesaid
Garivald saw that the blessed Praejectus was telling of the vision that
he had learnt about from his kin, in opposition he displayed the
document openly in the church to be read out to everybody.[81]
However, the above-mentioned men who had corroborated the document with their own hands[82] now changed their minds to support the
election of blessed Praejectus. But Garivald. since he saw that he was
pressed on all sides, and that whereas he used to believe [that he
would have] support from the side of the clergy he was suffering its
loss, and having lost them and having been abandoned by the rest of
the clerical brotherhood, he sought the support of the laity, nourishing

78 The term for document here is *epistola*. What follows is an interesting example of
   a voluntary agreement drawn up in writing and given force by public witness.
   Though such documents could be drawn up outside the process of the judicial
   courts, they could subsequently be used as evidence in court. The evidence for these
   types of agreements suggests that the use of written documents was widespread,
   and it has been argued that the number of private agreements probably greatly
   exceeded the number of formal court records, which are more prominent only
   because they have been better preserved. See P. Geary, 'Extrajudicial means of
   Conflict Resolution', *Settimana di Studio* , 42 (1995).

79 Literally, 'this document of the aforesaid archdeacon was made for the pursuing of
   his right and to be binding'.

80 The term for custom here is *ritus*, which also carries a sense of religious observance,
   thus lending solemnity to Garivald's claim.

81 The phrase *ostendit releganda* ('displayed to be read out') is also seen in charters and
   formularies, where it refers to the presentation of written documents in court, as,
   for instance, in the mid eighth-century *Formulae Senonenses Recentiores*, ed. K.
   Zeumer, *MGH, Legum*, sectio V (Hanover, 1886), no. 6, p. 214. The use of a phrase
   with strong overtones of legal terminology may suggest that Garivald presented a
   formal legal case against Praejcetus. As our author presents the case, Garivald was
   technically clearly in the right.

82 The phrase *manu propria roboraverant* ('they had corroborated it with their own
   hands') again has legal resonance. The author may have seen the document in
   question, and here could be quoting from it. That Praejectus put his own hand to
   an agreement, and then broke it, is a strong hint that he was acting unjustly in his
   bid for the episcopate. That the author should include such detail suggests that the
   facts were well known at the time of writing, and/or there was pressure on the
   author to include them in the public record of events which this work provides.

it with the application of gold and silver.[83] The laity indeed took the money and by force they suppressed all the clergy and they raised up the aforesaid Garivald to the position of bishop. But not long after – though four tenths [forty days] had been completed – this Garivald ended his days and the bishopric he had undeservedly acquired he left to a better candidate.

So far: what happened before he became bishop; now the sequence of his deeds [as bishop].

CHAPTER 14

In the reign of King Childeric of blessed memory, who held sway over Germany,[84] the church of the people of the Auvergne was afflicted because it lacked a bishop. And at that time one Genesius, a man shining with diligence and generosity and well endowed with wealth, held the post of count in the aforementioned town.[85] That town, once savage and supreme, now much richer from the blood of martyrs, [is] in a delightful area (except that it suffers rather often from westerly winds and thunderbolts) near by which flows the river Loire[86] as it descends in its headlong course, flowing round the' province of Aquitaine and after many twists and turns extending across a great stretch of land enters the wide sea, the Atlantic Ocean. But let us turn to what we had begun. When the views of the different companies of clergy were canvassed (which is usual in such matters), it lay unresolved and each one tried to put forward another and they were in dispute among themselves. But then when a majority arranged with the greatest effort, that is, by royal edicts, to raise up the aforesaid Genesius to the bishopric,[87] the latter was struck with fear lest he be acting against canon law and he addressed the people, saying that he

83 This statement, to be taken in conjunction with the reference to canon law strictures against simony in the previous chapter, allows the author to close the passage with points in Praejectus's favour

84 The author is using the Roman term for the region, which became part of Austrasia.

85 This Genesius must be distinguished from Bishop Genesius, Praejectus's patron in ch. 4, above, p. 274.

86 The nearest river is in fact the Allier, a tributary of the Loire. The author is, however, using poetic licence here in a panorama of Gaul which may imitate the opening of Caesar's *Gallic Wars*, I, ch. 1.

87 There was a long history of royal involvement in the appointment of bishops of Clermont, as in the other bishoprics discussed in this volume. On Clermont, Wood, 'Ecclesiastical Politics'.

was unworthy to become bishop.[88] But the citizens called out for the election of Praejectus, who at that time held the office of priest in the town. When their agreed choice reached the ears of the ordinary people, all the men of the clergy and the laity declared in one voice that Praejectus was worthy to become bishop. What more [is there to tell]? By the Lord's will he was ordained bishop, and he was indeed a most devout man and unusually agreeable, of cheerful countenance, softly spoken, unmatched in his almsgiving and fasting, strong in his virginity, handsome in frame, full of love, manifestly humble, famous for his knowledge and eloquence, excellent in his manners. Thus beneath his human form you would see him living an angelic life.[89]

CHAPTER 15

In those days he had as his ally Evodius, a man extremely well endowed with holy wisdom and conspicuous in his saintliness: many of the people of Clermont and neighbouring towns who had been ensnared by the poison of the age-old serpent Evodius called back to the bosom of the Catholic Church, using as an antidote health-giving penance.[90] When he had already for a long time been strong in these good things, with Christ (without whom nothing good is done) as his guide, he [Praejectus] energetically began to offer to the aforesaid Count Genesius this wholesome advice: that as he had no descendant to make his legal heir, he should adopt the stainless, unmarked Church. It did not take this illustrious man long to accept the advice. He arose to build with unsparing effort and endeavour a monastery of holy virgins in a suburb of the aforesaid town in a place called Chamalières, and the monastery followed the rule of all the holy men, that is, St Benedict, St Cesarius and St Columbanus.[91] With the greatest eagerness, of that

---

88 It was clearly against canon law for a layman to be elected bishop. See the *Vita Audoini*, ch. 7, above, pp. 157–8, for an example of how a layman could be prepared for the episcopate without breaking canon law.

89 There is no echo here of the first thirteen chapters of the work. In contrast to the previous detail about Praejectus's early life, this reference to his character is generalised and highly conventional.

90 Evodius appears in the *Vita Boniti*, ch. 17, as abbot of the monastery of Manglieu, founded by Bishop Genesius: see above, p. 257.

91 A combination of rules like this was normal. For another example, see the privilege of Bishop Drauscius for the convent of Notre Dame in Soissons in the year 666, Pardessus *Diplomata*, vol. 2, no. 355, pp. 138–40, and for useful general comment, Wood, *The Merovingian Kingdoms*, pp. 188–9. Quite how the rules were combined in practice is unknown.

monastery he put in charge the aforementioned Evodius to exercise the norms of faith and religion and the keeping of mortification, and he made over for their need there some of his goods obtained by law. Moreover the holy bishop Praejectus also instituted there as abbess a certain woman of distinguished family called Gundilena who since adolescence had delighted in putting all her energies to Christian use.[92]

CHAPTER 16

The God-filled man, seeing Christ's following spring up all around him, ordered another monastery to be built in a suburb of the town on a piece of land which had once belonged to a woman called Cesaria and he consecrated it by filling it with girls dedicated to God.[93] Actually, before that time it was difficult to find a convent of girls in those parts. He also had built a hospital in the eastern manner, on his own property in a place called Columbarius. He arranged for energetic healers to do the work of nursing there so that there were always twenty sick people being healed and receiving food rations, then after they had recovered they gave over their allocation of care to others.

CHAPTER 17

But because the lengthy treatment of matters, as Orosius says, generally results in both a desire to know more and obscurity, so I will hold forth in but a few words and not so much lay out his life, but his death will be drawn out to weave an account of the events of his suffering. It is thought – rightly – that in this same town there lies buried a whole legion of saints who in the days of pagan princes poured out their own holy blood in the name of Christ. Ancient history shows that the leaders of this legion were Cassius, Victorinus and Antholianus. He [Praejectus] had vowed to build a monastery for them but obstacles on this earth prevented him, so he began the work but it was left unfinished.[94] However, he made up his mind that if he found any of the above-mentioned comrades he should move them to honourable settings. Accordingly at the places of the saints he had night vigils held by abbots and clergy so that from their relics he

92 Note that Gundilana shares the first name element with Praejectus's father, Gundolenus. The 'distinguished family' is therefore probably the saint's own.

93 No more is known about this convent.

94 Above, p. 263, for discussion of why Praejectus may have failed in this task, leaving it to his successor Avitus to complete it.

might quickly find out the truth of the matter. When he himself had snatched up the iron [spade?] and ordered them to open the ground in which the holy bodies had been buried, there, at God's will, a certain poor man who had been disabled for nearly twelve years received back his health. And so that it might not seem unbelievable to anyone that this miracle had been St Praejectus's – for the Lord sees fit to reward the saints thus on this earth when they deserve it, when they crucify their own wills on His behalf – it was revealed in such truth that he who saw these things himself expressed them in words. The bodies of the saints, moreover, were wondrously translated by Praejectus's successor as bishop, Bishop Avitus.

CHAPTER 18

Because he was powerful in the performance of these and other miracles, the bishop of Tours, Chrodbert, hearing of this, sent his deacon with eulogies [i.e. gifts] to visit him [Praejectus].[95] The latter gave him a keen welcome and had him recline with him at table. But, when this deacon took a drink, a violent frenzy he was prone to took hold of him and finally he was worn out by an epileptic attack. The venerable bishop examined him in his frenzied madness, his teeth gnashing, and with gentle effort he began to comfort him, calling upon divine help so that no more would this harmful element inhabit a body dedicated to Christ. Soon, in a wondrous manner, he was returned to health and never again was he exhausted by such a fury.

CHAPTER 19

Another time, on the most holy Sunday the day of the Resurrection when he held the feast of Easter, one of his servants who customarily brought him food furtively stole a silver vessel which he was meant to be looking after, and having buried it in the countryside he attempted to conceal it. Since the other servants began to ask among themselves what, pray, would happen to the criminal's silver, the crime came secretly to the ears of the bishop. He therefore ordered all who served him in that capacity to present themselves before his close gaze, and he began to advise them with a fatherly word, saying that the evil theft could bring forth good out of harm through a confession. If not, he

---

95 Chrodbert was bishop of Tours some time in 654–84 and figures in contemporary letters: see Krusch, *MGH, SSRM*, IV, p. 651.

said, he would pray through the dark of the night for the Lord's help
that he might uncover the crime that had been committed and the
offence that had been done, that through his piety he might protect the
innocent and bring the guilty to light. Having completed his vigil, the
man of God gave himself fully to sleep and then in his sleep he saw a
man clad in shining white raiment like the Angel of Peace who opened
the ground to show him where the aforesaid vessel had been hidden.
Waking from his sleep, the blessed Praejectus ordered all the staff who
served in that position to come to him. When he asked all of them in
turn what they had found out about the theft, with all of them denying
it, they proclaimed that they knew nothing about this. Then the man
of God motioned with his hand, and with his finger pointing out the
thief by name, he said in addition: 'You and you, go to this place and
you will solve the hidden crime.' When the servants came to the place
that had been named, the vessel they had lost on a earlier day they
brought to the aforementioned bishop. Though exposing the thief in
front of everyone he gave him his forgiveness, exhorting him to do
such penance as befitted him.

CHAPTER 20

At about the same time it happened that the man of God went to the
palace of King Childeric on business concerning his church. Along the
way his route went through the great wilderness called the Vosges,
and, struggling through the hills, across the ridges of mountains and
valleys, he came at last to a place which the barbarians call in their
gentile tongue Doroangus.[96] Not far from there is a little monastery
which the venerable Amarinus, of blessed memory, had built with the
greatest of effort, leave and help being given by the great noble
Warnachar.[97] It is clearly evident that at that time he had novices there
of such poverty for God that they would take but a morsel of bread and
a drink of water at table and in their poverty they served Christ the
Lord according to that precept of the Gospels which says: 'Blessed are
the poor in spirit, for theirs is the kingdom of heaven.'[98]

96 Today called Saint Amarin, in Haut-Rhin, France. The terrain is indeed mountain-
   ous.
97 The term for noble here, *optimas*, is rarely seen in the singular. Another example is
   to be found in the *Passio Leudegarii*, ch. 37, above, p. 252. Warnachar was 'mayor
   of the palace' of Burgundy, and he died in *c.* 627. As Krusch pointed out (*MGH,
   SSRM*, V, p. 238), Amarinus must have been a very old man by the time he met
   Praejectus.
98 Matthew 5:3.

CHAPTER 21

But we must not remain silent about the miracle the Lord showed forth through His venerable bishop Praejectus in this place. For the aforesaid Amarinus had been stricken by the recurrence of an old fever, so badly that he could not move a step nor keep down any food except liquids. When this came to the ears of the blessed Praejectus, being brought to his attention by the monks, he poured out his prayers as usual and went to the cell where the venerable abbot lay sick. Arming himself with the shield of faith,[99] he entered the mean dwelling, gave the sign of the cross, transmitted healing, and the fever left the body. Taking him by his hand, he led him into the refectory building, and, it is wondrous to tell, he led him whole again. The monks congratulated the father on getting back his former health. Oh, what rejoicing was there there, that through a miracle such as this, performed through His servant Praejectus, in the midst of the desert a sick man had suddenly received back his health.

CHAPTER 22

But after [exchanging] holy and salutary words the man of God gave himself up to sleep, spending the night in prayers and vigils until the dawn of day, when the reddening sun made its most welcome return to the earth, and then with the blessing of the monks he took up again the journey he had already begun and he arrived before the king in peace. The Lord provided for him such favour with the mayor of the palace that what he asked for he obtained with the greatest honour.[100] The king and his court, his entourage and nobles, rejoiced and he was wholeheartedly received by the bishops of the Lord. His church's privilege,[101] moreover, was strengthened by royal authority, and with Christ's protection he returned to his homeland.

99 The phrase is taken from Ephesians 6:16.

100 The friendly mayor of the palace must have been Wulfoald, who appears later as an opponent of Leudegar.

101 The term 'privilege' (*privilegium*) is likely to refer to a document. The word for 'strengthened' is *roborata*, which in surviving documents refers to the king's signing of the privilege. What the king actually granted to Praejectus we cannot tell, but according to surviving examples the privilege probably conveyed a degree of judicial and fiscal immunity for the church of Clermont. As the *Vita Balthildis*, ch. 9, above, p. 125 shows, the major churches in Neustria–Burgundy were also receiving privileges at this time.

CHAPTER 23

In those days there was in the aforementioned region of the Auvergne
a certain lady called Claudia who was dedicated to God and used to come
to him to hear sermons. She gave over to the aforesaid bishop and the
poor he had charge of part of her property, but not long afterwards she
ended her days and was buried with full honour [*cum summo honore*]
by the blessed Praejectus. These things having happened thus, there was
a certain man of ill repute called Hector who had obtained the public
position of *patricius* of Marseilles.[102] Hector had siezed the daughter of
this Claudia and wickedly joined himself to her and then, having subjected
her to the misery of concubinage,[103] he went to King Childeric, who was
ruling at that time, having taken over both kingdoms, and he joined with
another in his crime, one called Leudegarius.[104] Afterwards this
became a kind of stumbling block in the latter's achievement of
martyrdom.[105] He accused the bishop of claiming Claudia's lands for
himself,[106] and, drawing up charges before the king, he got him to
despatch long-distance agents who were to send for him by means of
legal sureties and cause him to be presented at the king's court.[107]

102 Contrast the *Passio Leudegarii*, ch. 9, above, p. 226, which presents Hector in a
positive light.

103 Since Hector went to court to defend the rights of Claudia's daughter, it seems
likely that she was his wife rather than concubine.

104 Childeric ruled both kingdoms 673–75. Leudegar was a chief adviser to the king
and thus an appropriate person for Hector to lobby in support of his case.

105 The Latin is *Quod postea in eiusdem martyrium perficiende fomis scandali fuit*. Such a
critical attitude towards a martyr is unique in Merovingian hagiography. It
reinforces the impression that Leudegar was a controversial figure, and helps
explain the extraordinary delicacy with which this episode is treated in the *Passio
Leudegarii*. The remark also tells us that the *Passio Praejecti* was written after
Leudegar's death (*c.* 678). In the *Passio Leudegarii* there is no mention at all of
Praejectus: Hector's business at court is not specified.

106 It was not uncommon for relatives to challenge donations to the Church after the
donor had died. The challenge here underlines the difficulties women in particular
had in bequeathing land outside their family. For discussion of this issue, J. L.
Nelson, 'The Wary Widow', in Davies and Fouracre (eds.), *Property and Power*.

107 This information on how people could be summoned to court is invaluable: agents
were sent from the palace and they organised sureties (*fideiussores*), that is,
guarantors who were responsible for delivering the accused to court or suffering
some sort of penalty. The *Acta Aunemundi*, above, p. 184, suggest what might
happen if someone refused to attend court to answer a serious charge: force could
be used to escort them to the king. On what is known about suretyship from the
Cartulary of Redon, a source which has a relatively large amount of ninth-century
material relating to the subject, W. Davies, 'Suretyship in the *Cartulaire de Redon*',
in T. Charles-Edwards, M. Owen and D. Walters (eds.), *Lawyers and Lawmen*
(Cardiff, 1986).

CHAPTER 24

When he had been informed about this case and came to give his answer he was smitten with great grief because the holy day of Easter was approaching and he would be prevented from solemnly celebrating the holiest night of Easter in his own town.[108] But as a true saying has it, 'The priest in his purity fears not the attack of a king.' So, having armed himself with faith and put on the helmet of salvation, like Paul the outstanding preacher, he hurried off to the palace.[109] There, as is the custom in the king's court, he went into the place where cases are heard so that he could have legal proceedings with Hector over the business mentioned earlier. Praejectus began to refuse [to plead?] and to reply with true argument according to the statutes of the canons and the law that is called Roman: because the Saturday on which the vigil of holy Easter was always kept was an important day, he could in no way give his answer in this law case.[110] But, as is the way among disputants, everyone began to press him, saying that he should not delay to give an answer for such a reason.[111] When the man of God saw that on all sides they were gathering together against him, driven by necessity, he answered in this way: he said that he had entrusted the legal affairs of his church to Queen Himnechild.[112] When

108 It is clear that Praejectus faced formal court proceedings, in which he had to appear in court by a certain time, otherwise he would have lost the case. On procedures in the royal court, P. Fouracre, '"Placita" and the Settlement of Disputes in later Merovingian Francia', in W. Davies and P. Fouracre (eds.), *The Settlement of Disputes in Early Medieval Europe* (Cambridge, 1986).

109 Again the author quotes from Ephesians 6:16. In ch. 8 of the *Passio Leudegarii*, there is a quote from the same passage and the same saying about the fearless priest. This may suggest that at least one author had seen the work of the other: see above, p. 225.

110 According to the *Theodosian Code* II, 8: 19, trans. C. Pharr, p. 44, no cases should be heard for seven days before or after Easter.

111 It is interesting to note that this Roman law argument was seen as invalid. There was a strongly pragmatic element in legal discussions, and here we can see how it operated to deal with a mixture of Roman law, canon law and Frankish procedure. Decision-making was collective, and it seems to have been the general opinion that Praejectus was 'playing for time'. Presumably the assembly was keen to get the matter settled before Easter celebrations began.

112 Queen Himnechild was a natural ally because Leudegar was her opponent, having tried to separate King Childeric from his wife, Bilichild, who was her daughter: see above, p. 225. It is not clear when Praejectus had entrusted his affairs to Himnechild, nor is it obvious why this statement should have interrupted the proceedings, but it is plain that he was in a very weak position before he made this move. Since there is no other example of a queen mother being called upon as a legal protector, a role which normally had strong masculine associations, we cannot see what was involved here, although in the Formulary of Marculf there are

they recognised this claim, the business then remained uncompleted. At last blessed Praejectus then explained about the hardship of his journey and told how he had come having been summoned through legal sureties. Well, the king and queen were struck with fear and in front of everyone they begged a pardon from Bishop Praejectus and they felt grief at the hardship he had undergone.[113]

CHAPTER 25

Helping Hector at that time was Bishop Leudegar. Since now the sun had gone through the noon quarter and was sinking towards its setting, it was the usual hour at which it could be thought that it was now late enough to allow the solemn vigil of holy Easter to be kept.[114] With the agreement of the king and the nobles, the bishops and the priests who had gathered together in the town of Autun on account of the king's power, they asked – nay, rather, with great longing they implored – the blessed Praejectus to celebrate mass before God that same night for the well-being of the king and the peace of the Church.[115] Since Hector had seen how great this reverence [for Praejectus] was, and especially because he had abused the trust of Wulfoald, the mayor of the palace, both of them fled in the dead of night, [though] with St Leudegar having been evilly punished.[116] This turn-around could fit the saying in the Life of St Silvester, where it is

---

two models for the granting of the right to legal protection: *Marculfi Formularum Libri Duo*, ed. and French trans. A. Uddholm (Uppsala, 1962), nos. 24 and 36, pp. 98–100, 138–4.

113 The king's remorse conflicts with the statement in the previous chapter that the order for Praejectus to be presented through sureties had been issued through the king. The distance from Clermont to Autun is over 150 km and perhaps the deadline for Praejectus's appearence in court had been tight.

114 This was the Saturday night vigil which was to be kept until the morning of Easter Sunday.

115 The phrase 'for the well-being of the king and the peace of the church' (*pro statum regis vel pacem ecclesie*) is common in the liturgy and also echoes the language of royal charters, which often made grants *pro stabilitatem regni*, and of Church councils, which made their decisions *pro statu ecclesiae vel stabilitatem regni*, as for instance in the 'Concilium Burdegalense' (Bordeaux), held *c.* 674, ed. de Clercq, p. 312. Praejectus most probably celebrated mass in the monastery of St Symphorian outside Autun, for we know from the *Passio Leudegarii*, ch. 10, above, p. 227, that the king did not attend the vigils and mass in the cathedral church in Autun, thus signalling his hostility to Leudegar.

116 The author here admits that Praejectus played only a minor part in Hector's downfall.

written concerning Perpenna Tarquinius that, at the same hour at which he had said that the blessed Silvester should appear before him in court, he was cast out of his house and carried to his grave on a bier.

CHAPTER 26

But when dawn brought a new day and the bright light of the sun lit the earth,[117] the king found out through his nobles that Hector had run away, and then more and more they began to busy themselves to honour the bishop. However, when Hector was captured he was put to death by royal command.[118] But Leudegar, having been led back in repentance, was exiled to Luxeuil. Later he was taken from Luxeuil and, close by his own town, he had his eyes torne out by Waimer, a faithless and wicked man who later oppressed the town of Troyes.[119] Then not much later he was put to death very wickedly by Ebroin, count of the palace, a man at other times energetic but too cruel in his killing of priests,[120] and so he grasped the palm of martyrdom and now he is strong in the performance of holy miracles.[121]

---

117 This poetic description of sunrise is taken from Virgil's *Aeneid*, as Riché noted in *Education et Culture*, p. 233.

118 The *Passio Leudegarii*, ch. 11, above, pp. 228–9, gives more details concerning Hector's death.

119 This has been taken to mean that Waimer became bishop of Troyes, although in the *Passio Leudegarii*, ch. 25, above, p. 241, he is named as the 'duke of Champagne': see L. Duchesne, *Fastes Episcopaux de l'Ancienne Gaule*, vol. 2 (Paris, 1910), p. 455.

120 *Strenuus*, the term for 'energetic', does have positive connotations in Merovingian writing. It was, for instance, applied to Balthild as a term of approval in the *Liber Historiae Francorum* ch. 43, above, p. 88. The *Passio Praejecti* was thus neutral in its attitude towards Ebroin. This viewpoint may have been widely shared before Ebroin's portrayal in the *Passio Leudegarii* as an evil figure became the chief source of his reputation. Interestingly, the probably late seventh-century section of the *Miracula Martialis*, another source which was not influenced by this evil reputation and which contained a most flattering reference to Ebroin, also referred to him as 'count of the palace': *Ex Miracula Martialis*, ed. O. Holder-Egger, *MGH, SS*, XV, part 1 (Hanover, 1887), ch. 3, p. 281.

121 This statement supports the view that Leudegar was swiftly recognised as a martyr and that his miracles were proclaimed rapidly and widely. Without this confirmation, one would be tempted to assume that when the author of the *Passio Leudegarii* made the same points he was simply writing in conventionally exaggerated terms.

CHAPTER 27

So, by royal order and by the generosity of the king, as he had decided,[122] the blessed Praejectus obtained judgement concerning the property which Hector was trying to get hold of: his church was to hold it as of right for all time.[123] Bidding farewell to the king and to his nobles, and wondrously honoured, he returned to his homeland.

CHAPTER 28

When the aforesaid Abbot Amarinus heard that everything had gone well with the man of God he followed after him to the town of Clermont, a place where he would find food to nourish his brethren in the poverty and harsh endurance they practised for Christ in the desert.[124] The aforesaid bishop gave him his help and support. When the remarkable man saw this, he accepted it as a divine gift; then day and night he had him as companion in what later events showed was a journey to heaven.

CHAPTER 29

But since, with Christ as their leader, they were occupied with such good works, this was beyond the endurance of the enemy of mankind, for he envied one of them for the love he gave, the other for how he received it. So he of whom it is written, 'He has a thousand clever ways of doing harm,' approached a certain wicked man, a son of Belial. He was to use one Agricius to hurry off to the more prominent people of the Auvergne and, using any means he could, to whip them up to shed the blood of the men of God.[125] As Agricius had at that time taken the advice of the wicked ones, at this he at once rushed off, like a wild beast

122 The choice of words in the phrase 'as he had decided' (*ut sibi placuerat*) may have been influenced by the fact that the term *placitum* was normally used to refer to a court case and to the formal record of judgement.

123 Again the wording here may have been influenced by the terms of the formal record of judgement, which in cases of dispute usually confirmed the winning party's eternal right to the property in question.

124 This statement is rather curious: Clermont was a very long way for Amarinus to go to secure supplies for his monastery. It seems more likely that Amarinus was there because Praejectus knew that he was in danger and required the protection of a holy man, much as Aunemund had called for the help of Abbot Waldebert of Luxeuil, see above, p. 184.

125 The author here seems actively to avoid giving any reason for Praejectus's murder.

126 Volvic lies 11 km to the north of Clermont. It is well known today as a source of mineral water.

unchecked, like, as it were, the age-old serpent straining with poison, and with a crowd of his followers gathered around him he came upon the man of God at the villa of Volvic.[126] At about a mile from the aforesaid villa they sounded a war horn from the forest, just like when ravenous wolves howl outside a sheepfold. When the blessed Praejectus and Amarinus heard the sound of the war horn, they both prayed, waiting to receive from the Lord the crown which does not fade. However, all the retinue who had accompanied the aforesaid bishop were stricken with fear when they heard the braying of the war trumpets, and having thrown off their tunics and cast aside their weapons,[127] they fled off through the woodland thickets of thorn bushes. When the wicked men had reached the entrance of the house and wanted to get in, then, it is said, the doorkeeper of the house, called Gundolenus,[128] put up a fight for the man of God, for he chose to bare his neck to the sword rather than make his peace after the death of the man of God.

CHAPTER 30

But then when about twenty armed associates and followers of the wicked people got into the house, Amarinus, it is said, spoke to Praejectus, man of God, saying: 'My lord, do you think it would be wise[129] to abandon this place to these screeching, wicked men; for it may be that God in his boundless love sees fit that we should escape the snares of the wicked ones?' To this the man of God answered: 'No more, brother, no more, for if you were thus to deny yourself this crown, you might never ever get it back again.' At these words Amarinus fell silent, but blessed Praejectus poured out a great stream of prayers to the Lord and began to entrust himself to the Holy Spirit. After the prayer had ended, the evil ones came in and, coming first upon God's servant Amarinus in a corner of the house, they butchered him in place of the blessed Praejectus. But whilst the man of God lay on his bed and wetted his couch with his tears,[130] these executioners

---

127 The Latin is *armis expoliati.*

128 Gundolenus had the same name as Praejectus's father, and is therefore likely to have been a close relative of the saint.

129 The Latin here is difficult to translate: *si tui consilii aderat.*

130 Tears during prayer were a sign that a person was in direct communication with God. Private (as opposed to public) anguish, signified here by the wetting of his couch with tears, was a sign of special religious devotion. Crying features relatively often in saints' lives. For the range of its significance, see the entry for *larmes* in F. Cabrol and H. Leclercq, *Dictionnaire d'Archéologie Chrétienne et de Liturgie* (15 vols., Paris, 1907–53), vol. 8, pt. 1, pp. 1394–402.

turned back whence they had come and left the blessed Praejectus unharmed. When the man of God saw that he might thus be denied his martyr's crown, he offered himself again to his persecutors, saying: 'Here I am, the one you are after; carry out what you have been ordered to do.'[131] And as he said this one of the war band who was more brazen in this foul work, a man of Saxon race called Radbert, siezed a dagger and struck the blessed Praejectus in the chest.[132] A surge of holy blood thus poured out of the man of God,[133] but, not being able to look at the point of the dagger, he placed his fingers over his eyes. Then his executioner quivered his sword into his skull and drove out his brains. Thus was that holy soul loosed from its fleshly bonds and flew off to the Lord.

CHAPTER 31

Bodo and Placidus, two of the senators who had joined in the conspiracy to make a martyr of him, were standing nearby when they saw three stars, one shining brighter than the others, pass over the house where God's holy men lay slaughtered, and proceed towards heaven. These men still assert today that they saw such a vision. This miracle, we believe, both shows forth their glory and serves to call such men back to repentance.[134] For there is no one in this life who if they wish to be converted need despair of pardon. For we even read that the soldier Longinus who pierced the side of the Lord with a lance was afterwards converted and deservedly earned the crown of martyrdom.[135] But the followers who carried out this crime with bloodied

131 The clear implication is that Praejectus could have escaped death had he chosen to.

132 Radbert was presumably a Saxon mercenary. Saxon mercenaries in Septimania at this time are also mentioned in Julian of Toledo's *Historia Wambae Regis*, ch. 25, ed. W. Levison, *MGH, SSRM*, V, p. 521. Their use may therefore have been widespread.

133 The surge of blood, *sanguine unda [perfusus]* fulfils the prophecy made in chapter 1, where Praejectus's mother had a vision of an *unda sanguinis* pouring out of her belly, which showed that he would become a martyr. The implicit cross-reference between chs. 1 and 30 is evidence of the integrity of the whole *Passio*, as is the explicit cross-reference between chs. 32 and 15, below.

134 Bodo and Placidus were thus the first to proclaim Praejectus's sanctity, and in return they were forgiven.

135 Longinus was a purely legendary saint, invented by attaching a name and career to the soldier mentioned in the Bible. This reference suggests that accounts of his life may have been widespread by the later seventh century. For the Longinus tradition, see *AASS*, March, vol. 2 (Antwerp, 1668), pp. 376–90.

hands dragged the body of the blessed Praejectus outside into the view of his persecutors to show that they had finished their wicked task. Moreover that Radbert who had stretched out his hand to kill a priest of God was struck down by divine vengeance: he was eaten up by worms and so he finished an unworthy life with a fitting death.

CHAPTER 32

Gundila, mother to the nuns, whom we mentioned before,[136] heard the news through messengers and then, somewhat upset, she got up and began to search everywhere among the clergy for people she could send to go and wash the bodies of the saints – which was then done. Moreover the bishop, successor to the man of God, sent out members of the clergy with orders to bury their bodies in a manner worthy of them.[137]

CHAPTER 33

At that time there were two men, Godo and Eligius, equally related to the aforementioned bishop, whom he used constantly to keep with him in his innermost counsels.[138] Truly, as in the event it turned out, he very often learnt from them in their talks of what sort of death these two hoped for him. But he would answer them, saying: 'I am not worthy to receive the crown of martyrdom as you say I am. For I believe I have been both born in sin and afterwards in this world to have contracted sin. So the only way I believe I would earn the crown is if the pouring out of my blood washed away my sin.' What more can I say? One of the aforesaid men [himself] became a martyr, the other, Godo, rushed off to the region of Agaune.[139]

---

136 Gundila was mentioned in ch. 15, where she was called Gundilana. Both names are related to that of Praejectus's father, Gundolenus. See above, p. 259–60, for the suggestion that she might have been connected with the composition of the *Passio Praejecti*. The cross-reference between chs. 32 and 15 is important evidence of the integrity of the whole work.

137 It is curious that Praejectus's successor Avitus seems to have been in control of the clergy so soon after the saint's death. The author may have been referring to him in retrospective terms as 'bishop' (*presul*), in which case Avitus could have been in control of the clergy as archdeacon, or he may have been acting as bishop even before Praejectus's death.

138 Eligius had the masculine form of the name of Praejectus's mother. 'In his innermost councils' translates *in conventicula*.

139 Whether or not Eligius died in connection with Praejectus we cannot tell, but the context of the statement that he was martyred, plus the information that Godo

CHAPTER 34

Now, since God in his mercy revealed several miracles at the house where the saints were, and lots of people were with the greatest zeal making haste to visit these places of the saints, the man of God's successor Bishop Avitus was made more and more aware of this and he began to debate with himself and ask the help of God – that, if he ought to build something on the site, God should give him some sign of this. Then a few days later through Rago, a monk of the aforesaid monastery [of Agaune], he got Abbot Godo to come back to his homeland. So the aforesaid bishop began to make a plan with Godo that they should build a monastery of monks at the aforesaid site in Volvic. And when a regular community of monks had been gathered together at the place this task was accomplished. And out of reverence for these saints he conferred many gifts there.[140]

CHAPTER 35

Not far from the aforesaid place Volvic there was a parish called Riom, and in that neighbourhood there was a certain sick man who was exhausted by the suffering of a fever. Since he was undergoing his usual suffering for many days, he began in the fullest piety to vow that if he should recover his health through the intercession of the saints, as far as he was able he would forthwith hasten to prepare thank offerings for Christ's poor who were living there. When he appeared promptly cured, as he had promised of his own free will he loaded some of his provisions on to his own shoulders and, moreover, took up a small wine vessel for his own shoulder,[141] and he set off on the journey to the holy place decided on beforehand. He made his way with difficulty and came to the foot of the mountain which leads to that holy place. There he left off and began to think to himself of what he should do concerning the aforesaid vow in order to go back to his home. Looking into the distance, he saw a crowd of poor people, and he made

---

fled, make it seem likely that the two deaths were connected. In the next chapter it is made clear that Godo fled to the monastery of St Maurice at Agaune, Switzerland.

140 The sense of this chapter is that Avitus was reconciled with Godo on the basis that he recognised Praejectus's sanctity and endowed the new monastery of Volvic. In ch. 37 Godo is referred to as abbot of Volvic. It is likely that Avitus's gift here was a form of compensation for the killing of Praejectus.

141 The sense is that he took the wine vessel for his own use.

over to them what he had brought by his vow. He, indeed, having entered the house of the saints to pray, left the small vessel before the gates of the church, and when he returned from his prayer he found what he had left full.[142] This became known to everyone.

CHAPTER 36

But enough of these things so done; let us turn to our account of another miracle. There was in the aforesaid town a bench on which the aforesaid bishop had been accustomed to lie. Thence it had been carried away by clowns and given over to the playing of actors.[143] But when some miracle had been revealed at this bench it was snatched up[144] and taken into the church of St Symphorian, and there the Lord saw fit to show forth many miracles. There was a man of venerable life called Venerianus, surnamed Sanctus, whose life was made equal to his name.[145] This man had learnt by the telling of many people that many miracles were revealed through the aforesaid bench. When very early he came to look upon this piece of work, when the brilliant sun had already risen and was lighting the world, when he had prostrated himself in prayer he saw that all the lamps had been extinguished. Wetting the ground with his tears, looking up he saw that by the Lord's command the lamps had been lit and were shining. This miracle was made known to both the bishop of that place and to all the other servants of God.

---

142 It was presumably empty when he left it, but the author does not tell us this.

143 This is one of the earliest medieval references to the humourous entertainment of *mimmi*, 'mimics' or 'actors', although it was not picked up in the useful survey of the subject by J. Ogilvy, '*Mimmi, Scurrae, Histriones*: Entertainers of the early Middle Ages', *Speculum*, 38 (1963). It is important as a reference to secular actors, for most histories of the medieval stage seek the origins of medieval theatre only in the Church liturgy of the early Middle Ages: see R. Vince, *Ancient and Medieval Theatre* (Westport and London, 1984), pp. 23–31. As Ogilvy observed, entertainment of this type was generally condemned by ecclesiastical authorities. It is therefore interesting to note that the author of the *Passio Praejecti* mentions the *mimmi* without adverse comment. .

144 The verb 'snatched' (*arripuit*) is in fact in the active, but it is translated as a passive, as it has no obvious subject.

145 Venerianus figured in an earlier miracle (ch. 8), where there was a similar reference to the way in which he lived up to his name. It is therefore curious that it does not say here that he was mentioned earlier in the work.

CHAPTER 37

Later, indeed, Bishop Avitus made over to Abbot Godo whatever he had of his own free will procured for the house of the saints. The aforesaid abbot began to urge the aforesaid Venerianus that he should give him an inventory for this community.[146] The latter, however, because he had charge of the seal ring in place of the bishop, began to hesitate whenever it was time to draw up the aforesaid document. But thereafter happily it was done thus by Christ the High Priest. The aforementioned Godo began to have within himself an anxiety about how he should carry out this task. However, he decided in his heart that on a certain day, having dropped other concerns,[147] wherever he might be able to find him, he should go to the above-mentioned Venerianus about this business. That same night the Lord appeared to Venerianus himself in a vision, telling him how the aforementioned abbot had a plan. Getting up very early, and taking with him notaries, with all haste he drafted the aforesaid inventory. Moreover, he gave orders for a meal to be prepared and for everyone to be given notice that that same day he would have Abbot Godo to take food with him. When this was known to all, the aforesaid abbot appeared at his gates. He himself got up and received him with a welcoming and he imparted and showed everything that had been ordered to him in the vision and he revealed openly in words both to him [Godo] and to everyone [else] how he had had divine help concerning both his own arrival and the aforesaid document.

CHAPTER 38

One day, one of the originators of his murder, Ursio by name, whilst seated on his horse and going very fast hunting in the woodland, slipped and was thrown down onto the ground and, his right arm having been broken and other limbs disabled, he was carried crippled

---

146 The term for inventory is *descriptio.* It may refer to the drawing up of a document which listed the monastery's resources according to peasant households. Such assessments preserved elements of Roman taxation and prefigured the Carolingian estate surveys later known as 'polyptychs': see W. Goffart, 'From Roman Taxation to Medieval Seigneurie: Three Notes. Part II', *Speculum,* 47 (1972), 373–5. Despite the endowment of Volvic and the documentation of its rights, the monastery may not have survived for long after Godo's abbacy. By AD 755 Praejectus's body had been removed from Volvic. See above, p. 254, n. 2.

147 The word for 'concerns' is *conditiones.* The same word was used earlier in the passage to refer the document in question.

into his own house. There, when several doctors and other rivals had gathered for the purpose of healing, to make him better, by no effort of the doctors nor of the sayers of charms could he be cured.[148] Having been left alone, he began to speak urgently to his wife that she might send to the tomb of the blessed Praejectus and that having taken oil from his lamp it should be brought back to him. Wonderful to say, when he was anointed with the oil, he won back his old health. When he saw that he had regained his sound health, he sent a silver vessel weighing ten pounds to adorn that tomb. When the others who had been at hand in that persecution heard of this, they each began to donate gold or other riches to adorn the tomb.[149]

CHAPTER 38

Another time, indeed, the aforesaid Ursio, moved by devotion, came to a place called Vesedon to give thanks by prayer for his conversion. There the aforesaid martyr had had from infancy what was known to be his own property where he had been both mostly brought up and had had his zealous conversion.[150] In his chamber where he had always been accustomed to sleep, the Lord saw fit to reveal so many miracles that the human understanding can scarcely explain them. When, as said, the aforementioned Ursio kept vigil there, he asked one of the servants to bring down a vessel with a little oil with which to adjust the lights. As he himself positively swore afterwards, it held no more than a pound or two [of oil], but went as far as to affirm that it had filled up as many lamps as he had there, and he found the vessel brought back fuller. Furthermore, indeed, he tells of how in the other churches which he had founded in his honour it also filled twenty or

148 This reference to healing by incantation is derived from the *Life of Sylvester*, but presumably the author would not have quoted it if the practice had been unfamiliar. On the continuation of pagan healing practices in a Christian culture, see V. Flint, *The Rise of Magic in Early Medieval Europe* (Oxford, 1991), esp. pp. 240–52. For argument that these practices were more peripheral and culturally less significant than Flint allows, A. Murray, 'Missionaries and Magic in Dark Age Europe', *Past and Present*, 136 (1992).

148 This gift-giving is another illustration of the process of reconciliation between Praejectus and his enemies. The saint communicated his forgiveness by performing miracles which honoured these people.

150 Apart from the *villa* at Volvic, this is the only indication of where Praejectus's family held land. 'Brought up' translates *edocatus*, which is preferred to 'educated' (as Heinzelmann reads it, 'Studia Sanctorum', pp. 114–15), because we were told in ch. 2 that Praejectus was handed over to be taught by the schoolmaster at the church of Issoire.

thirty lamps and still he always found more in that vessel and thence he liberally sent it to other holy places.[151]

Enough has been said of the past; hereafter let us save future things for future people.[152]

THE END. AMEN.

---

151 The miracle emphasises the precious nature of lamp oil. For the cultural, liturgical and economic contexts of these 'lighting miracles', see P. Fouracre, 'Eternal light and earthly needs: practical aspects of the development of Frankish immunities', in Davies and Fouracre (eds.), *Property and Power.*

152 'People' is preferred to 'men' here as the Latin *futuris* is not gender-specific.

VII: *Vita Sanctae Geretrudis*[1]
(The Life of Saint Geretrud)
and the *Additamentum Nivialense de Fuilano*
(the Nivelles supplement to the *Vita Fursei* concerning Foillan)

To grasp the importance of the *Vita Sanctae Geretrudis* for historians, we need only try to imagine the Frankish seventh century without its help. It is a particularly valuable source because it concentrates not on Neustria or Burgundy, as do most other surviving contemporary texts, but on Austrasia, the eastern Merovingian kingdom, and on its most important family, the Pippinids, soon to be called the Carolingians. It is the oldest surviving narrative source to do so. Much of what we know about the Pippinids' seventh-century doings in Austrasia depends exclusively on this source and on two other works dealing with St Geretrud, the *Virtutes Sanctae Geretrudis* and the *Additamentum Nivialense de Fuilano*. It is from this small corpus that we have learned how many of the members of the family were related to each other, the geographical location of their first known landed possessions, and much about their political and religious life in what is now southern Belgium.

Compared with the other holy heroes whose *vitae* are discussed in this volume, Geretrud is presented to us, politically at least, as a *sainte fainéante*. She was born about 621 to Pippin I and his wife, Itta. After the death of her father, her widowed mother, Itta, founded the monastery at Nivelles and placed her at its head as abbess. Her *vita* explains that she could take on such a responsibility because she was mature beyond her years, for she was only about twenty-six at the time.[2] Here she stayed, leading the quiet life of the devout Christian ascetic, until her death in 653.[3] We do not hear that she ever moved

---

1 *Vita Sanctae Geretrudis*, ed. B. Krusch, *MGH, SSRM*, II (Hanover, 1888), pp. 447–74. See Krusch's additions and corrections to his edition in *MGH, SSRM*, VII (Hanover, 1920), pp. 791–7.

2 *Vita Geretrudis*, ch. 2, below, p. 321.

3 The exact dates of Geretrud's life are difficult to determine.

beyond the monastery to participate in the high politics or even in the local disputes which raged about her.

Although her life seems to have been quiet and steady, her *vita* on the other hand had a stormy career when it came under academic scrutiny. Heinrich Bonnell, who was a pioneer in delivering the history of Charlemagne's ancestors from the realm of late medieval fancy and basing it on more trustworthy contemporary sources, misjudged the *Vita Sanctae Geretrudis*. He put forward a very convincing argument for considering it to have been written in the eleventh century in the course of a local Brabantine political dispute.[4] Denying historical authority to Geretrud's *vita* also meant erasing any basis upon which the middle Meuse in Brabant could claim to have been the area of the family's origins. Without the authority of the *Vita Sanctae Geretrudis* the 'cradle of the Carolingians', as it was called, was thought to have been along the middle Moselle in Luxembourg.[5] It was there, as we shall see, that the second Pippin and his wife Plectrud controlled vast landed estates.[6] Bonnell's views, however, met convincing counter-arguments first based on the text's orthography[7] and then came crashing to their death with the discovery of an eighth-century manuscript of the text, which, of course, proved the work was far older than Bonnell had thought.[8] When Bruno Krusch edited the life, he put forward arguments showing that it is indeed a work nearly contemporary with the events it describes.[9] With its authority restored, not only could Geretrud, Itta and Begga resume their rightful place in the Carolingian family tree, but southern Belgium too could once again boast its role as the Carolingian cradle. By such thin strands does our view of the seventh century hang.

---

4 H. Bonnell, *Die Anfänge des karolingischen Hauses* (Berlin, 1866), pp. 68 and 149–53.

5 Bonnell, *Anfänge*, pp. 52–133.

6 Below, p. 311.

7 J. Friedrich, 'Excurs über das Alter der Vita Geretrudis Nivellensis und die Genealogie des karolingischen Hauses', in his *Kirchengeschichte Deutschlands*, vol. 2, pt. 1 (Bamberg, 1869), pp. 667–70. See Wattenbach-Levison, *Deutschlands Geschichtsquellen im Mittelalter, Vorzeit und Karolinger*, pt. 1, *Die Vorzeit von den Anfängen bis zur Herrschaft der Karolinger* (Weimar, 1952), pp. 122–3.

8 Ms. Montpellier H55. See: Krusch, *MGH, SSRM*, II, p. 449; G. Waitz, 'Handschriften der Universitätsbibliothek zu Montpellier', *NA*, 7 (1839), 197 (who does not seem to have recognised the *Vita Geretrudis*); and L. van der Essen, *Etude critique et littéraire sur les vitae des saints mérovingiens de l'ancienne Belgique* (Paris and Louvain, 1907), p. 4.

9 *MGH, SSRM*, II, p. 448.

The controversies surrounding the *vita* and its author were by no means laid to rest by Krusch's work, although it must be said that for our present purposes, that is, for viewing Merovingian history through Merovingian eyes, the scholarly disagreements since Krusch's edition have been more a matter of fine tuning than a fundamental change in our picture. The *vita* is now considered by most to have been written before about 670.[10] There are indeed good reasons for accepting 670 as the *terminus ante quem*: the existence of the eighth-century Montpellier manuscript; the fact that, as we shall see, a work appended to the *vita* in its earliest manuscripts called the *De Virtutibus quae Facta*[11] *sunt post Dicessum Beatae Geretrudis Abbatissae* must itself have been written in the 690s;[12] and the fact that the style of the Latin also indicates composition in the mid seventh century.[13] But the strongest reason comes from the fact that this author, as opposed to those who make false claims, presents himself so convincingly as an eye witness of much of what he relates.[14] The *terminus post quem* is determined by the mention in chapter 6 of Abbess Wulfetrud's death, which occurred in 663.

We can make several rather solid deductions about the author of the *Vita Sanctae Geretrudis*. Much of how we know him comes about because he speaks about himself in his text. We know he was a monk: 'I and another brother …'[15] Most assume he was Irish, one of the Irish brothers we know were attached to the nunnery at Nivelles.[16] There is,

10 Wattenbach-Levison, *Geschichtsquellen*, p. 127. M. Van Uytfanghe, *Stylisation biblique et condition humaine dans l'hagiographie mérovingienne (600–750)* (Brussels, 1987), p. 9, places it a little after 670.

11 See the comments about Merovingian Latin, above, p. 72.

12 Edited by Krusch, *MGH, SSRM*, II, pp. 464–71, following his edition of the *vita*. For the date of composition of the *Virtutes* see: Krusch's comments in his introduction (*ibid.*, pp. 448–9); J. J. Hoebanx, *L'Abbaye de Nivelles des origines au XIVᵉ siècle* (Brussels, 1942), pp. 33–4; and Wattenbach-Levison, *Geschichtsquellen*, p. 127, n. 303.

13 Krusch pointed out that the author's use of *gignarus* for *gnarus* (ch. 2) would have hardly been understood after the middle of the eighth century. Krusch, *MGH, SSRM*, II, p. 448. Hoebanx, *L'Abbaye de Nivelles*, pp. 27–8, notes the use of forms of proper names which are Merovingian.

14 … *juxta quod vidimus* … *(prologue)*; … *quod ipsa Dei famula* … *nobis narravit* (ch. 4); *Certe quod audivi et vidi nobis testor* … (ch. 5); and *Dum ibidem ego et alius frater Rinchinus nomine fuissemus evocati propter sororum consolationem* … (ch. 7).

15 *Vita Geretrudis*, ch. 7, below, p. 326.

16 F. Rousseau, *Le Meuse et le pays mosan en Belgique. Leur importance historique avant le XIIIᵉ siècle* (Namur, 1930), p. 54; Van der Essen, *Etude*, p. 3; and W. Berschin, *Biographie und Epochenstil im lateinischen Mittelalter, vol. 2: Merowingische Biographie. Italien, Spanien und die Inseln im frühen Mittelalter* (Stuttgart, 1988), p. 20.

however, no compelling reason why he could not have been a Frank;
certainly the 'other brother' had a Frankish name.[17] It is remarkable
that an Irishman should make no mention in his work of the arrival of
the Irish monk Foillan and his companions at Nivelles, an event we
know occurred while Geretrud was abbess. He also says nothing,
either, about how Geretrud's mother, Itta, helped Foillan to found the
important Irish monastery at Fosses or anything about Geretrud
sponsoring the search for Foillan's body after his murder. For all these
things we must turn to the *Additamentum Nivialense de Fuilano*,
something which we shall do presently. Whether Frankish or Irish, his
work nonetheless shows Irish influence, especially in the appearance of
St Patrick in chapter 7. He also seems to have been of some standing
in the community, since he was sent to Britain on the monastery's
business[19] and since it was he who was called to console the sisters at
St Geretrud's death.[20]

In the group of manuscripts which Krusch called B, a version of the
oldest *vita* appears with its syntax and vocabulary retouched. Krusch
edited this B version in columns parallel to the orignial A. Since the
contents of the retouched version do not vary from the earlier one, we
can date it no more precisely than to say it follows on after some
years.[21] For our purposes we can largely ignore it.[22]

Later centuries, too, continued to revise the contemporary *vita*. The
oldest versions (A and B) seem to have sufficed medieval readers until
the eleventh century, a period of a broad flourishing in writing new

17 Hoebanx, *L'Abbaye de Nivelles*, p. 29.

18 P. Riché calls it one of the corpus of Irish-inspired lives. P. Riché, 'Columbanus, his
followers and the Merovingian Church', in H. B. Clarke and M. Brennan (eds.),
Columbanus and Merovingian Monasticism. British Archaeological Reports, International series, 113 (Oxford, 1981), p. 69.

19 *Vita Geretrudis*, ch. 5, below, p. 323.

20 *Vita Geretrudis*, ch. 7, below, p. 326.

21 See: Krusch *MGH, SSRM*, II, pp. 450–1; Hoebanx, *L'Abbaye de Nivelles*, p. 40; and
Van der Essen, *Etude*, p. 3.

22 Recently an English translation of the B version has appeared in print. The
translators chose B because they thought the *MGH* editor, Bruno Krusch, preferred
it. J. McNamara and J. Halborg, *Sainted Women of the Dark Ages* (London, 1992),
p. 220. We disagree. Version A is the elder and preferable and Krusch clearly says
so in his introduction: *Editionem A vetustiorem eamque praestantiorem esse quam B,
paucis probabo*. Krusch, *MGH, SSRM*, II, p. 451. The translator also seems to have
misread Krusch's date for the *vita*'s composition, placing it after Begga's death in
the 690s, which is where Krusch placed the composition of the *Virtutes S. Geretrudis*,
not the *vita*. Krusch, *ibid.*, pp. 448–9.

saints' lives and rewriting old ones. Here we find two more versions of the *Life of St Geretrud.* The first has been named the *Vita Tertia.*[23] It is based directly on the contemporary life with an expanded genealogy taken from the *Annales Mettenses.* The second eleventh-century version is called the *Vita Sanctae Geretrudis Tripartita* and is a far more expansive work, full of legendary material.[24] Neither of these later versions will concern us.

In those manuscripts of the *vita* which Krusch placed in the A group on his stemma, we come across the second of our corpus of contemporary sources concerning St Geretrud. Here the contemporary *vita* is followed by the *De Virtitutibus ... Beatae Geretrudis* mentioned above. We have chosen not to include a translation of the *Virtutes* in this collection, but rather to content ourselves with a brief discussion of them.[25] Their date of composition falls at some point near 700. Most scholars have followed Krusch in thinking this author to have been different from the author of the *vita,* for two reasons. First, if our dates of composition are correct, there is a space of over twenty years between the two works, and second, in chapter 3 of the *Virtutes,* when the author describes the fire that broke out ten years after Geretrud's death, he does not present himself as an eye witness,[26] whereas, as we have seen, the author of the *vita* saw the events he relates. Krusch's case, however, is not final, and if we come to another view of the authorship of the *Virtutes* it will also affect our view of the early history of the abbey at Nivelles.

It is pertinent to note that it is only the episode of the fire which the author of the *Virtutes* tells us he heard from others; in all the other miracles and events he relates he makes no mention of hearsay. Could it not have been that he was physically rather than temporally absent from the abbey during the blaze? The suggestion gains weight by the fact that he tells us that he himself travelled. He does assert his status as an eye witness: '... I call God as my witness, that I saw with my own

23 So named by S. Balau, *Etude critique des sources de l'historie du pays de Liège au Moyen-âge* (Brussels, 1902–03), pp. 243–4. The text of the *Vita Tertia* was edited by J. Gheldolf de Ryckel, *Historia S. Geretrudis* (Brussels, 1637), albeit with the prologue from the older version. Cf. Van der Essen, *Etude,* p.12–13, n. 6.

24 This is the version contained in the manuscripts Krusch called C in his edition of the contemporay life. See *MGH, SSRM,* II, pp. 450–1. Its only edition is a poor one by J. Gheldolf de Ryckel in his *Vitae Sanctae Geretrudis abbatisse Nivellensis* (Louvain, 1632). Cf. Van der Essen, *Etude,* pp. 5–12.

25 An English translation can be found in McNamara and Halborg, *Sainted Women,* pp. 229–34.

eyes or heard through trustworthy witnesses that which I have written,'[27] although such assertions by authors are often not true. In his first chapter he also expressly says that it was he who wrote Geretrud's life from the first stage of her youth. In order to make two authors out of one, Krusch would like to interpret the author's verb 'wrote' (*conscripsimus*) as 'copied' (*descripsimus*),[28] but there is no textual basis for this editorial change.[29] Krusch also thought that the author of the *Virtutes* was not very familiar with the early history of the abbey at Nivelles because matters which the *Vita* in chapter 6 tells us pertained to Abbess Wulfetrud the *Virtutes* in chapter 4 ascribe to an Abbess Dominica.[30] There is, however, more than a little reason to question the existence of this Abbess Dominica. If we were to read the word *dominica* as an adjective, meaning 'Lordly', that is, 'of the Lord', rather than as a proper name, this confusion in chapter 4 of the *Virtutes* clears up. We then realise that the niece of Geretrud 'who governed the monastery at Nivelles after her' was not 'Dominica' but Wulfetrud, whose succession is attested by chapter 6 of the *Vita* and described there in the same language used here in chapter 4 of the *Virtutes*. Removing 'Dominica' also eliminates any need to follow Krusch in his assumption that the author of the *Virtutes* erred in his picture of the succession of Nivelle's first abbesses.[31] The adjective *dominica* also occurs in the prologue to the *Vita* in connection with the abbess who commissioned the work. Here Krusch lists the spelling in his edition as *Dominicane*.[32] But in checking his primary manuscript (A1), a manuscript he himself did not see because he relied upon a collation made by F. Braunschvig,[33] we find not *Dominicane* but *dñica*, which expands to the same adjective.[34] If our date for the composition of the

---

26 ... *ignem exortum fuisse adserunt* ... and *In tantum autem, ut dicunt, erupuit flamma* ... *Virtutes*, ch. 6, *MGH, SSRM*, II, p. 467. Cf. Krusch, *ibid.*, p. 448.
27 *Virtutes B. Geretrudis*, ch. 11, *MGH, SSRM*, II, p. 471.
28 Krusch, *MGH, SSRM*, II, p. 448.
29 Hoebanx, *L'Abbaye de Nivelles*, p. 32.
30 *Vita Geretrudis*, ch. 6, *MGH, SSRM*, II, p. 460, and *Virtutes B. Geretrudis*, ch. 4, *MGH, SSRM*, p. 466.
31 Krusch, *MGH, SSRM*, II, p. 467, n. 2. Both Hoebanx, *L'Abbaye de Nivelles*, pp. 33–5, and Henschenius, *AASS*, Mart. I, vol. II, p. 149, n. b, and 157–8, n. f, doubt the existence of an 'Abbess Dominica' at Nivelles.
32 *MGH, SSRM*, II, p. 453.
33 *MGH, SSRM*, II, p. 449.
34 Our thanks to M. Gerard Velay of the University Library in Montpellier for a photocopy of the manuscript.

Vita (c. 670) is correct, then it would not have been an 'Abbess Dominica' who commissioned it, but Abbess Agnes, who we also know commissioned a church in honour of St Geretrud at Nivelles.[35]

About 783 someone at Nivelles added a continuation to the *Virtutes*, found now in the group of manuscripts Krusch called A3. It contains only two miracles, and these centre on Geretrud's tomb.[36] We have also not included a translation of this continuation and it will not concern us.

The third contemporary source concerning St Geretrud's monastery at Nivelles is a short one and was named the *Additamentum Nivialense de Fuilano* by Bruno Kursch, who edited it for the *Monumenta Germaniae Historica*.[37] It was written as a complement to the *Vita Fursei* and could actually be slightly older than the *Vita Sanctae Geretrudis* and its continuations. Since it speaks of Foillan's murder and the discovery of his body, we know it was written some time after these gruesome events, that is, some time after 650. Most scholars have also assumed that the text's *terminus ante quem* falls before the death of Geretrud's brother, Grimoald I, since the author calls him 'most reverend *patricius*' and makes no mention of his violent downfall and execution.[38] Since we know Grimoald was executed by King Clovis II of Neustria,[39] who died in 657, we can conclude that Grimoald was also dead by that date and so too that the *Additamentum* was probably written by then. Although, like all arguments from silence, this one is not particularly strong, for stylistic reasons we do know at least that the text is from the seventh century.[40] The author was most likely a

---

35 *Virtutes B. Geretrudis*, ch. 6, *MGH, SSRM*, II, p. 467.

36 See Krusch's comments in *MGH, SSRM*, II, p. 449 and his edition, *ibid.*, pp. 471–4.

37 *MGH, SSRM*, IV, pp. 449–51. Krusch admits that his manuscripts were both much emended and contained many omissions (*ibid.*, p. 431). The *Monumenta* discovered a ninth-century manuscript of the work after Krusch's edition was published, and they later published its variants from the printed text in *MGH, SSRM*, VII, pp. 837–42. Even though Krusch worked without this better manuscript, most of his critical choices in the edition seem correct. See P. Grosjean, 'Notes d'hagiographie celtique', *Annalecta Bollandiana*,75 (1957), 380–1, who adds other early manuscripts.

38 Thus A. Dierkens, *Abbayes et chapitres entre Sambre et Meuse (VII–XI siècles)*, Beihefte der *Francia* 14 (1985), p. 304, n. 147; Hoebanx, *L'Abbaye de Nivelles*, p. 39; Grosjean, 'Notes 1957', 382; Van der Essen, *Etude*, p. 153; and Wattenbach-Levison, *Geschichtsquellen*, p. 127, n. 303.

39 *LHF*, ch. 43. See above, p. 88.

40 The text preserves the spelling *Foilnanus*, whereas the *ln* dies out in Ireland between 780 and 832 and is replaced by *ll* (*Foillanus*). Cf. T. O'Maille, *The Language*

monk at Nivelles, and, whether Irish[41] or simply heavily influenced by
the Irish,[42] he was contemporary with the events he describes. The
work has been translated several times into modern European languages, including a masterly English version by Ludwig Bieler.[43]

It is only from this group of three sources that we can piece together
the familial relationships of Charlemagne's ancestors in the generations before Pippin II (d. 714). Using hagiographical sources to
determine who the members of an early medieval family were and how
they were related to each other can be a very hazardous enterprise. It
was important for politically powerful families to have saints in their
family trees. As we have seen over and over again, the relationship
between power and sanctity is an important and reciprocal one in all
its aspects. When we come to examine this relationship within the
families of the seventh-century Frankish nobility, rather than within
the long-established Merovingian royal line or within the families of
the Gallo-Roman aristocracy already ensconced for centuries in the
cities south of the Loire, we may find a special need to be able to boast
saintly relatives. Families such as Pippin's were by no means Johnnies-
come-lately to the reins of political power, but as they changed over
the centuries from a pagan warrior aristocracy to a landed and
Christian nobility they needed new justification of their privileged
position.[44] Long-haired heroic warriors with vague connections with
far-off, and now discredited, pagan gods would have seemed far less
valuable ancestors than ones who could prove concretely through
their *virtutes*, duly witnessed and recorded, the favour of the Christian
God towards the family. Charlemagne himself, son of a usurper, saw
the Lombard author, Paul the Deacon, reach back over 150 years to
include Arnulf, the holy man of Metz, in the Carolingian royal family

of the Annals of Ulster (Manchester, 1910), p. 103. The forms *maiorum domus, Annani*
(*Anna* in the genitive) and *Itane* (*Itta* in the ablative) are Merovingian and thus also
bespeak an early date. See Friedrich, 'Excurs', 668–9, and Grosjean, 'Notes 1957',
383.

41 Krusch, *MGH, SSRM*, IV, p. 428, and L. Montford, Civilization in Seventh-century
Gaul as Reflected in Saints' Vitae Composed in the Period (Ph.D. dissertation, St
Louis University, 1973), p. 173.

42 Grosjean, 'Notes 1957', 381–4.

43 L. Bieler, *Ireland: Harbinger of the Middle Ages* (London, 1963), pp. 99–100.

44 F. Prinz, *Frühes Mönchtum im Frankenreich* (Munich, 1965), pp. 492–5; and K. Bosl,
'Die germanische Kontinuität im deutschen Mittelalter (Adel-König-Kirche)', in his
Frühformen der Gesellschaft im mittelalterlichen Europa (Munich, 1964), p. 102. See
also above, p. 38.

tree.[45] How then can we be certain that places in the family for the holy women, Geretrud, Itta, Wulfetrud and Begga were not similarly invented? The answer is that we cannot, but the danger is greatly diminished by the simple but crucial consideration that our group of three sources attesting to their familial membership seems to be contemporary or nearly so. As opposed to authors and audiences removed by time, those who wrote these three sources and those who read them, especially those readers at Nivelles itself, would have known who was related to whom and how. Even if an author had consciously sought to invent, the thought that his audience was knowledgeable would have prevented him.[46] Here we have information we can probably believe.

Apart from telling us that Geretrud's mother was Itta and her father was Pippin, the author of the *Vita Geretrudis* says nothing about her further familial origins because all 'living in Europe' know the loftiness of her lineage.[47] The Pippinids were not in power in the early 670s, the period in which we assume the author wrote; it was the mayor Wulfoald's faction who held the reins in Austrasia.[48] The fact that Geretrud's powerful family had been dislodged politically may have been one of the reasons why the author is so coy here. To wish to add lustre to a family presently in need of it may also have been an important factor in motivating him to write Geretrud's *vita*. Although it would have been marvellous to learn some names of either Pippin's or Itta's ancestors, we are happy at least to learn that Itta was Pippin's wife and Geretrud their daughter. The *Vita Geretrudis* is our oldest and most reliable source for this information.

---

45 Paul the Deacon, *Gesta Episcoporum Mettensium*, ed. G. Pertz, *MGH, SS*, II (Hanover, 1828), p. 264. M. Werner, *Der Lütticher Raum in frühkarolingischer Zeit, Veröffentlichungen des Max-Planck-Instituts für Geschichte*, 62 (Göttingen, 1980), pp. 396–7, n. 2, also has doubts about Arnulf's supposed position as *Stammvater*, as does B. Krusch,'Der Staatsstreich des fränkischen Hausmeiers Grimoald I', in *Festgabe für Karl Zeumer* (Weimar, 1910), p. 414, n. 5. On the other hand, E. Hlawitschka, 'Die Vorfahren Karls des Grossen', in W. Braunfels (ed.), *Karl der Grosse*, vol. I (Düsseldorf, 1965), p. 74, n. 7, and I. Haselbach, 'Aufstieg und Herrschaft der Karolinger in der Darstellung der sogenannten *Annalen Mettenses priores*', *Historische Studien*, 412 (1970), 45, n. 25, do not question it.

46 See above, p. 45.

47 *Vita Geretrudis*, prologue, below, p. 320.

48 *LHF*, ch. 45, above, p. 89. See R. Gerberding, *The Rise of the Carolingians and the Liber Historiae Francorum* (Oxford, 1987), pp. 80–4, for a discussion of when Pippin II came to power in Austrasia.

Chapter six of the *Vita Geretrudis* seems almost like a short independent *vita* of another female member of the Pippinid family inserted into the author's account of the life of Geretrud. The author strays for only one chapter, catching himself by the beginning of chapter 7 and saying, 'But let us return whence we digressed.' Chapter 6 is the story of Wulfetrud, whom Geretrud appointed her successor as abbess when she felt her death approaching. Once again, it is the only contemporary source allowing us to include this important person in the Pippinid family tree. We learn that Wulfetrud is Geretrud's niece, '... born of the same ancient and famous family of the Franks as she herself [Geretrud] was'; nothing more is stated expressly. The author goes on to tell us that, because of hatred for her father, the kings, queens and even the priests tried to dislodge her from her position. By deduction, then, Wulfetrud's father must have been Grimoald I, whose brazen attempt to dislodge the Merovingians the *Liber Historiae Francorum* has already recounted.[49] Again, it is useful to note that here too a piece of Merovingian history hangs by another thread. An important part of Pippinid family history dangles from the two words *odio paterno* here in this one source, words which were intended to state the motivation of Wulfetrud's enemies, but which actually allow us to assign her a specific place in the family. Without them we would know only that she was Geretrud's niece. But even more than knowledge of her place in the family has been hung upon these words. They have been taken to suggest that Grimoald was still alive when she took over the monastery and experienced the trouble with the politically powerful trying to dislodge her. Grimoald, however, certainly could have been dead by this point; hatred was often vented upon the original perpetrator's descendants.[50] When Wulfetrud died on 23 November 663 her successor by unanimous choice was Agnes.[51] We have no evidence which would allow us to make a Pippinid out of her, although she must have had very close connections with the family to have been chosen to lead its monastery.

It is chapter 10 of the *Virtutes* which allows us to add the third holy woman to the family. This is Begga, full sister of Geretrud (*sue germane*). Begga came to Nivelles in the thirty-third year after her sister's death to seek the necessary relics and aids to found a monastery of her own.

---

49 *LHF*, ch. 43, above, p. 88.

50 See Gerberding, *Rise*, pp. 57–9, for a detailed discussion of *odio paterno*.

51 *Virtutes B. Geretrudis*, ch. 6, *MGH, SSRM*, II, p. 467.

The author of the *Virtutes* calls her *christianissima matrona* and, as we have seen, *matrona* is a word which the sources use to describe a woman with considerable political power.[52] Indeed, by this point Begga had had a full life. We know from other sources that she was married to the powerful Ansegisel, and that it was from their union that the Pippinid line was continued through their son Pippin II.[53] It is once again the *Virtutes Sanctae Geretrudis* which allow us to place her exactly.

With Itta, Geretrud, Wulfetrud and Begga safely added to the family, we can gain a good indication of where the early familial land holdings were located. If the *vita* were once again to be considered unreliable, then historians would also be again forced to turn to other sources to determine where the Pippinids came from. St Arnulf has generally been considered Ansegisel's father and thus Arnulf's large holdings between Metz and Verdun could reflect the family's landed origins.[54] The familial connection between Ansegisel and Arnulf, however, seems to have been the result of later Carolingian desire to have Arnulf as the family's holy patriarch, and although much land around Metz did come under Pippinid control, this seems to have happened after the 670s, when the Pippinids returned to power. The string of surviving Pippinid land donation charters begins in 697/98 with the gift of Echternach and other properties to Willibrord by Pippin II's wife, Plectrud, and her mother, Irmina.[55] These charters reveal that the family held many estates in the middle Moselle region. This land, however, was not Pippinid but first came into the family's possession with Pippin II's marriage to Plectrud some time around 670.[56] The familial connections revealed by

52 See, for example, its use in the *LHF* to refer to Ansfled (ch. 48, above, p. 92) and to Plectrud (chs. 52 and 53, above, p. 95).

53 *Annales Mettenses Priores*, below, p. 351; Hlawitschka, 'Vorfahren', 74, n. 8; and M. Werner, *Lütticher Raum*, pp. 396–7.

54 See the list of charters donating family land to the church in Metz in I. Heidrich, 'Titular und Urkunden der arnulfingishchen Hausmeier', *Archiv für Diplomatik*, 11/12 (1956/57), 248–54.

55 C. Wampach, *Geschichte der Grundherrschaft Echternach im Frühmittelalter, I–2 Quellenband* (Luxembourg, 1930), nos. 3 and 4, pp. 17–23; and *MGH, Dipl.*, nos. 55 and 56, pp. 173–5;.

56 M. Werner gives a good account of the landed holdings the Pippinids gained by Pippin II's marriage to Plectrud. M. Werner, *Adelsfamilien im Umkreis der frühen Karolinger* (Sigmaringen, 1982), p. 31. Determining the date of the marriage offers another object lesson in the swamp of Merovingian chronology and shows what little firm ground we have when we try to date events. The *LHF* in ch. 48 tells us that their son Drogo was made *Dux Campaniae* after Berchar's death (688) and before Theuderic III died (March–May 690). If we assume that he would have been at least twenty years old at this point, then his parents must have married at least

our group of hagiographical sources concerning St Geretrud, however, show us the Pippinids' landed home at least two generations earlier than these charters do and allow us to place it neither on the middle Moselle in modern Luxembourg (Plectrud's land) nor in modern France between Metz and Verdun (the lands of Adalgisel, whom historians have confused with Begga's husband, Ansegisel),[57] but rather in modern Belgium around Nivelles, Fosses[58] and Andenne.[59]

Our group of sources does even more for us than name Pippin II's maternal relatives in the preceding generation and tell us where they came from. The three works also give us a valuable insight into the political and religious life of the family in the mid seventh century. Even though contemporaries would have had little reason to foresee that Pippin I's offspring would some day become the kings of the Franks, none of the works in question shrinks from revealing the family, even at this very early stage, as one of Francia's most powerful. The words in chapter 1 of the *vita* claiming that all in Europe know the lustre of Geretrud's family, although hyperbole, are nonetheless a loud witness to the family's early renown. The same chapter gives us another and more concrete indication of the high political position of Pippin and Itta when it relates the visit to their home of the long-reigning and powerful king of Austrasia, Dagobert I. There was another politically powerful guest at that 'lordly meal' whom we know only as the 'son of the/a duke of the Austrasians'.[60] The author expressly tells us that the young nobleman sought Geretrud's hand in

---

twenty years earlier. That puts the date of their marriage between 668 and 670. Thus M. Werner, *Adelsfamilien*, p. 30, n. 79. E. Hlawitschka, 'Merowingerblut bei den Karolingern?', in J. Fleckenstein and K. Schmidt (eds.), *Adel und Kirche* (Freiburg, 1968), p. 85, puts the marriage in 675.

57 E.g. the standard reference work by J. F. Böhmer and E. Mühlbacher, *Regesta Imperii. Die Regesten des Kaiserreichs unter den Karolingern, 751–918*, second edition (Innsbruck, 1908), p. 2, equate the two. See E. Hlawitschka, 'Zur landschaftlichen Herkunft der Karolinger', *Rheinische Vierteljahrsblätter*, 27 (1962), 16, who separates them.

58 The monastery at Fosses was probably on the site of a former Roman villa, traces of which were found around the church of St Foillan in 1952. This villa may have been the centre of the Pippinid domain of Bebrona. In 1975 remains of walls which could have come from the seventh-century monastery were discovered on the site. See Dierkens, *Abbayes*, p. 75.

59 The exact early land holdings of Itta's family, with the exception of Nivelles and Fosses themselves, are difficult to determine. See Hoebanx, *L'Abbaye de Nivelles*, pp. 86–95 and his map between pp. 226 and 227; and Rousseau, *La Meuse*, p. 222.

60 A. Friese, *Studien zur Herrschaftsgeschichte des fränkischen Adels des mainländisch-thüringischen Raum vom 7. bis 11. Jahrhundert, Geschichte und Gesellschaft*, 18 (Stuttgart,

marriage 'for the sake of worldly ambition and mutual alliance'. Let us note two things. First, this nobleman sought permission not just from Geretrud's father, Pippin, but also from the king. Alliances among the powerful nobility seem to have been a direct concern of the Crown. And, second, Geretrud did not marry him. It seems the family, even at this early stage, was strong enough to resist the royal will.

In chapter 6 of the *vita* we have a third direct reflection of the family's early political position. We can see that who led the family monastery at Nivelles was a matter of royal concern. When Wulfetrud succeeded Geretrud the Crown tried to eject the Pippinids forcibly from Nivelles. The attempt must have come about in the wake of Grimoald I's failed *coup d'état*. The fact that the royal party did not dislodge the Pippinids is significant. As we have seen from the *LHF*, the family were particularly strong in the area around Nivelles and, even in the aftermath of their failure in the national politics, the forces gathered around the kings could not remove them from an important holding in Itta's homeland.

The most important revelation, however, about the political and religious position of the early Pippinids provided by this group of sources is what they show us about the family's relationship with the Irish. In our investigation of Audoin and the men who surrounded him we have already seen what an important role Irish religious figures and their Continental supporters played both in the religious life of seventh-century Gaul and in the politics of those circles which mattered.[61] The Pippinids too were to have a long and significant connection with the British Isles, a connection which appears here at the beginning, so to speak, as an important part of these, the earliest, sources treating the family. It is important, however, to differentiate 'Pippin's Irish' from 'Audoin's', that is to say, the figures of the Columbanan movement so closely allied to the Neustrian court circle were not those whom we find surrounding the Pippinids.[62] The *Vita Sanctae Geretrudis* makes no mention at all of Columbanus and his

---

1979), p. 22, n. 41, would like this suitor to be the son of Adalgisel. He arrives at this conclusion through a process of elimination, and, while it is possible, it is far from certain.

61 See above, p. 144–8.

62 Here, following the perceptive work of I. N. Wood, *The Merovingian Kingdoms 450–751* (London, 1994), p. 190, we disagree with Prinz, 'Columbanus', p. 80; and with *Frühes Mönchtum*, pp. 278–9; and with Hoebanx, *L'Abbaye de Nivelles*, p. 58, who see Nivelles as part of Columbanan monasticism.

mission among the Franks, a strange omission if the Irish were all one group. There were at least two distinct groups of Irish: those emanating from Luxeuil and those centred on Nivelles and Fosses. The differences between them are significant. The Pippinid group looked to St Patrick as 'the apostle of the Irish', whereas the followers of Columbanus probably looked to Palladius.[63] The two groups may have used different monastic rules and practices, although the question of who used what rule is now known to be far more complex than was once thought.[64] But the most important difference between the two groups is one of politics and patronage. Although the Patrician group also found its first Continental foothold under the patronage of the Neustrian court at the monasteries of Lagny and Peronne,[65] it soon experienced a sharp break with its former patrons and, for a time at least, landed squarely in the midst of the Pippinids.

The founding of the family monastery at Nivelles took place as part of a second wave of evangelisation in northern Francia, a wave which would all but eradicate paganism from the area. A good indication that there were indeed still pagans in the area during the mid seventh century comes from chapter 5 of the *Vita Sanctae Geretrudis*, where the sailors on the author's sea voyage call to their pagan gods. It was the Irish who led this missionary effort and, as was their national wont, they used monasteries as missionary bases. Although the Irish played a major role at Nivelles from its early days, it was actually the

63 I. N. Wood, 'The *Vita Columbani* and Merovingian Hagiography', *Peritia*, 1 (1982), 69–70.

64 It was once thought that the only two widely used monastic rules in seventh-century Gaul were the Benedictine and the 'Mixed Columbanan–Benedictine', with the latter achieving the dominant position under the influence of Luxeuil and Remiremont. Thus, for instance, L. Levillain, 'Etude sur l'abbaye de Saint-Denis à l'époque mérovingienne, II: Les origines de St-Denis', *BEDC*, 86 (1925), 77; Prinz, *Frühes Mönchtum*, pp. 163–4 and 268–93; and Hoebanx, *L'Abbaye de Nivelles*, p. 76. More recent scholarship, however, has shown that this view has oversimplified the situation. There was great diversity of monastic practice before the eventual triumph of the Benedictine Rule. See Wood, 'Vita Columbani', 65–7, and *Merovingian Kingdoms*, pp. 188–9; Dierkens, *Abbayes*, pp. 286–7; G. Moyse, 'Monachisme et règlementation monastique en Gaule avante Benoît d'Aniane', *Hautes Etudes Médiévales et Modernes*, 47 (1982), 6–12; and R. McKitterick, *The Frankish Kingdoms under the Carolingians, 751–987* (London, 1983), ch. 5.

65 The earliest reference to St Patrick on the Continent other than from the group at Fosses and Nivelles seems to come from Peronne in an inscription in a chapel dedicated to him and built at some point under Abbot Cellán (675–706). It is preserved on foll. 61–2 of ms. Florence, Laurenziana, Cod. Lat. plut. LXVI 40 and begins: *Istam Patricius sanctus sibi vindicat aulam* ... K. Meyer, 'Verses from a chapel dedicated to St Patrick at Péronne', *Ériu*, 5 (1911), 110.

Aquitanian Amandus who had encouraged Itta to found the house. At some point between 647 and 650 Amandus began a three-year tenure as the diocesan bishop of Maastricht,[66] and it was during these years that he persuaded Itta to found the monastery at Nivelles. The foundation therefore seems to have taken place some time between 647 and 650, that is, after Amandus had become diocesan bishop and before Itta died.[67] Amandus, although a maverick with a brilliant and very independent career, had a long and deep connection with Columbanan monasticism and consequently with the Neustrian court circle.[68] It is therefore some time after its founding that Nivelles seems to have begun to go its own way politically and in religious matters. The break had everything to do with Pippinid family politics and, as we have seen in our study of the life of Queen Balthild, with the less obvious figure of the current Neustrian mayor of the palace, Erchinoald.

Erchinoald first welcomed Fursey from East Anglia some time between 641 and 644,[69] vying with a certain Duke Haymon to persuade the Irishman to settle under his protection.[70] Erchinoald won the contest and established the monastery at Lagny for Fursey and he became its first abbot.[71] He died there 'not much later', as both Bede and Fursey's *vita* report.[72] His body was buried by Erchinoald in the

66 M. Werner, *Lütticher Raum*, p. 233.

67 *Vita Geretrudis*, ch. 2, below, p. 321.

68 Jonas of Bobbio, *Vita Columbani abbatis discipulorumque eius*, I, *Epistola*, ed. B. Krusch, *MGH, SSRM*, IV (Hanover, 1902), p. 62. Prinz, *Frühes Mönchtum*, p. 186.

69 C. Plummer, *Venerabilis Baedae Opera Historica*, vol. II (Oxford, 1896), p. 173.

70 *Virtutes Fursei Abbatis Latiniacensis*, chs. 6 and 11, ed. B. Krusch, *MGH, SSRM*, IV (Hanover, 1902), pp. 442 and 444.

71 *Vita Fursei Abbatis Latiniacensis*, ch. 9, ed. B. Krusch, *MGH, SSRM*, IV (Hanover, 1902), pp. 438–9; and Bede, *Historia Ecclesiastica* (hereafter, *HE*), III, ch. 19, ed. C. Plummer, *Venerabilis Bedae Opera Historica*, vol. I, p. 168.

72 ... *non multo post* ... Bede, *HE*, III, ch. 19, p. 168; and *Vita Fursei*, ch. 9, pp. 438–9. The date of Fursey's death is difficult to determine. Plummer says, 'The chronology of Fursa's life can only be fixed within rather vague limits.' Plummer, *Bedae Opera*, II, p. 173. He lists Fursey's death in 649 with a question mark. *Ibid.*, p. xviii. The *Vita Fursei* is no help in dating and Bede little more. The Irish annals, which are of a later date and not accurate with chronological information, have the date of his death variously. *The Annals of Inisfallen*, ed. S. MacAirt (Dublin, 1951), p. 92, have it in 649; the *Chronicum Scotorum*, ed. W. Hennessey (London, 1866), p. 91, in 646; *The Annals of Clonmacnoise*, ed. D Murphy (Dublin, 1896), p. 105, in 646; *The Annals of Ulster*, ed. W. Hennessey (Dublin, 1887), vol. I, pp. 109 and 117, list his death in three different years: 647, 648 and 660. Picard, following *The Annals of Ulster*, prefers 649. J.-M. Picard, 'Church and politics in the seventh century: the Irish exile of King Dagobert II', in J.-M. Picard (ed.), *Ireland and Northern France* (Dublin, 1991), p. 32.

church at Peronne and four years later he translated it to a chapel within the same church.[73] The translation was most likely the occasion for the establishment of the famous Irish monastery at Peronne.[74] Fursey's death preceded the arrival of his brothers, Foillan and Ultan.[75] These two were also received by Erchinoald, but 'not much later', as the *Additamentum Nivialense* tells us, the mayor expelled the pilgrims. They hastened north and 'were honourably received by the most religious handmaiden of God, Iduberga, also named Itta, and her daughter, the sacred virgin of Christ, Geretrud'. The *Additamentum* goes on to recount that Grimoald took the Irishmen under his protection and made arrangements for the construction of their new monastery at Fosses. Even if the Irish on the Continent were of one group previously, here is the break. From this very early point in the known history of the Pippinid family, with these actions of Erchinoald and Grimoald, we can see the two groups and their very different politics. A body of religious Irish was as important to the Pippinids as it was to the powerful at the Neustrian court, but perhaps for slightly different reasons.

The areas in which the Pippinids had their original family lands, that is, along the Sambre in what is now southern Belgium, bordered the areas which were still pagan in the mid seventh century, and indeed there were even still enclaves of paganism very near their lands. Thus they could profit politically more than could the Neustrians from Irish missionary zeal.[76] From the account of the author's own sea voyage 'on monastery business' in chapter 5 of the *Vita Geretrudis*, and from the account in the *Additamentum Nivialense* of Foillan's proposed grand journey by land, it seems that both Nivelles and Fosses were quickly becoming institutions of some scope, with business and interests far afield. In these less settled and more rural parts of the Frankish realm where the possibility of expansion was greater than in the more densly settled parts, the Pippinids would have found the Irish trait of good economic management of their monasteries very valuable indeed.

73 Bede, *HE*, III, ch. 19; *Addit. Nivial.*, below, p. 327; *Vita Fursei*, ch. 10; and *Virtutes Fursei*, ch. 22.

74 J. Fuhrmann, Irish Medieval Monasteries on the Continent, dissertation, Catholic University of America, (Washington, D.C., 1927), p. 25.

75 *Addit. Nivial.*, below p. 327.

76 *Qu'on le veuille ou non, le christianisation était en même temps la structuration politique et économique de ce pays destiné à un grand avenir.* K. F. Werner, 'Le rôle de l'aristocratie dans la christianisation du nord-est de la Gaule', *Revue d'Histoire de l'Eglise de France*, 62 (1976), 72–3.

There is one other possible characteristic of the Irish houses which would have made them particularly valuable allies to a rising political power such as the Pippinids: the institution of the 'monastic bishop'. A monastic bishop was one who lived within a monastery as a monk subject to its abbot. The institution is particularly Irish, we do not find it anywhere else in the Western Church, and it appears on the Continent only after the Irish arrive.[77] If a monastery has its own bishop, it can become almost totally independent of the local dioscesan bishop, since it has little need of him, even to perform the usual episcopal spiritual duties. Thus a monastic bishop becomes useful politically in drawing power away from the established diocesan structure, something the Pippinids were very interested in doing. We know the Church in Ireland had monastic bishops and we also know that the Irish houses in the Pippinid areas had them in the eighth century. Once again, we have evidence from before and after our period, but a direct witness for them in the mid seventh century is lacking.[78] The Pippinids began to use them at some point to such a degree that they have been seen as the keystone of Pippinid monastic politics in the regions of the Sambre and Meuse.[79]

And, last, there seems to have been an immediate political reason for the Pippinids throwing their arms open to Foillan and the Irish in the early 650s. The *Additamentum Nivialense* tells us that Grimoald was holding a meeting with Bishop Dido of Poitiers in the monastery at Nivelles at the time of Foillan's gruesome murder (650). Dido may seem a rather odd conferee for the Austrasian mayor until we remember from the *LHF* that it was Dido who acted as Grimoald's agent in the exile of the young Austrasian prince, Dagobert, son of Sigibert III. The exile would take place shortly after this meeting between the two plotters, and the place to which the young Merovingian would be sent was none other than Ireland.[80]

---

77 H. Frank, *Die Klosterbischöfe des Frankenreiches, Beitragen zur Geschichte des alten Mönchtums und des Benedictinerordens,* 17 (Münster, 1932), pp. 5–6; and K. Hughes, *The Church in Early Irish Society* (Ithaca, New York, 1966), pp. 63 and 83.

78 Krusch thought that the phrase ... *a quocumque spirituali pontifice* ... in Burgundofaro's privilege for Rebais, Pardessus, *Diplomata,* vol. 2, no. 275, pp. 39–41, from 638 or 639, meant that monastic bishops had the right at Rebais to exercise the episcopal spiritual duties, the *pontificalia.* Krusch, *MGH, SSRM,* IV, p. 29.

79 Dierkens, *Abbayes,* pp. 298–9.

80 See Picard's thorough treatment of the subject. Picard, 'Church and Politics'.

We shall end our discussion of these three sources with a parenthetical comment, concerning the nature of the miraculous element found in them. It has been postulated that one characteristic of Irish hagiography is its tendency to eschew thaumaturlogical miracles, that is, those which alleviate human suffering: exorcism, healing, raising from the dead, release from prison, etc.[81] Rather than these, it has been said, in Continental Irish hagiography the miracles are more likely to be transcendent ones: visions, journeys to paradise, discussions with angels and the like.[82] Our three sources seem to contradict these obvervations. Although there certainly are a number of transcendent miracles in them, the majority are of the other type, helping to alleviate human suffering. For instance, we find Geretrud saving lives at sea,[83] stopping a fire at the monastery,[84] curing a blind girl,[85] helping a boy to escape kidnappers,[86] rescuing a man from chains,[87] resuscitating a servant boy[88] and many others. This raises the question of just how distinctive the so-called Irish monasticism on the Continent really was. In our three sources, for instance, we see that Irish holy men enjoyed prestigious positions in Frankish monasteries, but the written sources from which we learn this fact do not appear to be very Irish at all. They are, on the contrary, very much in the main stream of the Frankish hagiographic tradition and are quite different from the writing about saints by seventh-century Irish authors in Ireland.[89] The group of Irishmen who figure in this group of three sources are

81 Also termed evangelical miracles by J. Fontaine, *Sulpice Sévère, Vie de saint Martin*, vol. III, *Sources chrétiens*, 135 (Paris,1969), p. 988, n. 1.

82 Riché, 'Columbanus', pp. 69–70; J.-L. Derouet, 'Les possibilités sémiologiques des textes hagiographiques', *Revue d'Histoire de l'Eglise de France*, 62 (1976), 15–55; and J.-M. Picard, 'The Marvellous in Irish and Continental Saints' Lives of the Merovingian Period', in Clarke and Brennan (eds.), *Columbanus and Merovingian Monasticism*, British Archaeological Reports, International series, 113 (1981), 92.

83 *Vita Geretrudis*, ch. 5, below, p. 323.

84 *Virtutes B. Geretrudis*, ch. 3, *MGH, SSRM*, II, p. 466.

85 *Virtutes B. Geretrudis*, ch. 5, *MGH, SSRM*, II, pp. 466–7.

86 *Virtutes B. Geretrudis*, ch. 8, *MGH, SSRM*, II, p. 468.

87 *Virtutes B. Geretrudis*, ch. 9, *MGH, SSRM*, II, pp. 468–9.

88 *Virtutes B. Geretrudis*, ch. 11, *MGH, SSRM*, II, pp. 470–1.

89 For a good summary of the relevant portions of the Irish tradition in Ireland see R. Sharpe, *Medieval Irish Saints' Lives. An Introduction to Vitae Sanctorum Hiberniae* (Oxford, 1991), pp. 8–14. According to the criteria laid down by J. M. H. Smith, 'Oral and written: saints, miracles and relics in Brittany, c. 850–1250', *Speculum*, 65 (1990), 309–43, the Irishmen who are portrayed as saints in seventh-century Frankish sources are much closer to the norm for Frankish than for Celtic holy men.

considered to be more characteristically Irish than the group based at Luxeuil,[90] but their monasteries, as portrayed in our sources, seem little different from monasteries of other types. The Irish holy men themselves were obviously highly valued by the politically powerful in Francia, but it does not seem that they had much influence on the Frankish hagiographic tradition or that they left much of an enduring Irish imprint on the monasteries which they led. Once again it seems the personal rather than the institutional relationship was the more significant.

Vita Sanctae Geretrudis (The Life of St Geretrud)

IN THE NAME OF OUR LORD JESUS CHRIST, HERE BEGINS THE LIFE OF SAINT GERETRUD, VIRGIN

With holy and inseparable love bestowing, we believe and hold in inviolate and lasting faith that it is possible to aid those desiring to keep the path to their heavenly home and abandon totally earthly profits in order to obtain heavenly rewards, if I endeavour to teach by writing or preaching truthfully for the edification and advantage of our neighbours certain things, however few, about the life and monastic life of the saints and the holy virgins of Christ. [I do this] in order that the examples of the holy men and holy virgins who have gone before may be able to illuminate the shadows of our heart with the flame of love and the fire of holy remorse. Therefore, with the Holy Spirit, the artisan of all men, assisting, and because the holy daughter, the Lord's Abbess, and the holy congregation at the monastery in Nivelles, where the holy virgin [Geretrud] was in charge, have beseeched me, I shall try by writing to Your Charity[91] to expound concerning the example and monastic life of Geretrud (most blessed virgin and mother of the family of Christ, who lived under the axis of the heavens, following God and the teaching of the monastic rule) according to that which we saw or, Christ helping, heard through worthy witnesses. But it would be tedious to insert in this account in

90 A. Dierkens, 'Prolégomène à une histoire des relations culturelles entre les îsles britanniques et le continent pendant le haut Moyen-âge', in H. Atsma (ed.), *La Neustrie. Les pays au nord de la Loire de 650 à 850*. Beihefte der *Francia*, 16–2 (Sigmaringen,1989), pp. 386–7.

91 Abbess Agnes. See above, p. 306–7.

what line of earthly origin she was descended. For who living in Europe does not know the loftiness, the names, and the localities of her lineage?

CHAPTER 1

When, therefore, Geretrud, the holy daughter of God, was in the house of her parents, at the feet of her mother, Itta,[92] of blessed memory, she grew dear to God by day and night in word and wisdom, beloved by men beyond her contemporaries. At the very beginning her choice was the service of Christ, as I have learned through a just and truthful man who was present. When her father Pippin[93] had invited King Dagobert[94] to his house for a lordly meal, the son of a duke of the Austrasians arrived, a noxious character, and he had entreated the king and the parents of the girl that this girl be promised to him in matrimony according to the custom of the world for the sake of his worldly ambition and a mutual alliance. This pleased the king and he persuaded the father of the girl to call her with her mother into his presence. They, however, did not know why the king had summoned the child. Between courses, she was asked by the king whether she would like to have that boy dressed in silks and decorated with gold as her bridegroom.[95] But she, as if filled with rage, refused him with an oath and said she wanted to have neither him nor any other earthly man as her groom, but rather Christ the Lord. The king and his palace nobles marvelled greatly at these things which had been spoken by a small girl at God's command. The boy, however, departed confused and full of anger. The holy girl turned back to her mother and from that day forth her parents knew by what sort of king she had been loved.

CHAPTER 2

After fourteen years, when her father Pippin had gone from this light, she followed her mother in mourning, and chastely and soberly served her in obedience and in God's commands. And when the above-

---

92 Itta (c. 591–650).

93 Pippin I (d. 639), sometimes called Pippin of Landen.

94 Dagobert I, king of Austrasia (623–33) and of Neustria (629–38). This royal visit probably occurred before Dagobert gave Austrasia to his son Sigibert III in 633.

95 The B version says she was asked by her father. Here is a clear example of royal brokerage of marriages among the powerful nobility. It is also noteworthy that Pippin's family, even at this early date, is already strong enough to thwart the royal will.

mentioned *materfamilias*, Itta, was pondering daily what was to be done concerning herself and her orphaned daughter, a man of God, Bishop Amandus,[96] came to her house preaching God's word, and from the Lord's command he requested that she should build a monastery for herself, for her daughter Geretrud, maidservant of God, and for a family of Christ. As she quickly understood the significance of the stranger to pertain to the salvation of souls, she took up the holy veil and gave herself and all she possessed to God. But at the instigation of the enemy of the human race, who from the beginning has been envious of good works and has hardened the hearts of evil men to resist so that from those who ought to help her do the will of God, she sustained no small trial.[97] If they were listed singly, it would be tedious to record the nature of the injuries, insults and deprivations that the above-mentioned servant of Christ, together with her daughter, suffered in the name of Christ. But they possessed in themselves a divine longing and devotion equal to their suffering. In order that profaners of souls should not[98] carry off her daughter by force to the seductive pleasures of this world, she took shears and cut the hair of the holy girl into the form of a crown. But Geretrud, the holy servant of Christ, rejoiced, giving thanks to God because in this short life she had deserved receiving a crown on her head for Christ so that in the next she would be worthy to have an eternal crown of the body and purity of the soul. Whereupon merciful God, our helper in tribulations, called those adversaries to the harmony of peace. They ceased their quarrels and the devil's side was defeated.[99] The *materfamilias*, Itta, handed over her daughter, Geretrud, chosen of God, to the priests of the Lord so that she might take up the holy veil with her comrades and at Christ's command she placed her in charge of the holy flock of nuns, for in the temperance of her character, the sobriety of her heart and the moderation of her words she anticipated maturity.[100] She was indeed

---

96 Bishop of Maastricht, 647–53.

97 The troubles, related here, which Itta experienced at her husband Pippin's death would have come about in connection with the successful bid by the faction headed by Otto to replace the Pippinids in the circles closest to the Austrasian king, Sigibert III: *The Fourth Book of Fredegar with its Continuations*, (hereafter Fred., *Chron.*), ed. and trans. J. M. Wallace-Hadrill (London, 1980), chs. 86 and 88.

98 *ut non* as purpose clause.

99 Fredegar, *Chron.*, IV, ch. 88, records that Otto was slain at the instigation of Pippin's son, Grimoald. This act assured Grimoald of the position of Austrasian mayor.

100 In 647 Geretrud would have been only about twenty-six years old.

endowed with love, beautiful of visage, but more beautiful still in her heart, unblemished in her chastity, generous in alms, devoted to fasting and prayer, caring in looking after paupers and pilgrims, loyal to the infirm and old, but vigorous in the training of the young. With the greatest eagerness she exercised pastoral care towards the implements of ecclesiastical study, and with God's inspiration she deservedly obtained through her envoys, men of good reputation, relics of the saints and holy books from Rome, and from the regions across the sea,[101] experienced men for the teaching of divine law and to practise the chants for herself and her people.

CHAPTER 3

Having appointed all these things according to divine order, full of days and her life complete, leaving an example of good works for posterity, seeing her children and, from them, her grandchildren,[102] Itta of blessed memory in about the sixtieth year of her life, in the twelfth year after the death of her husband, the very famous Pippin, commending her spirit to God and the angels, departed unto the Lord.[103] She was placed with due ceremony in the sepulchre in the house of blessed Peter the Apostle in the monastery at Nivelles. Therefore after her mother's death Geretrud, the blessed maidservant of God, took the whole burden of governing upon herself alone; within herself she thought about that heavenly contemplation without the din of the world which she had chosen for herself. Outside she assigned the familial care to good and faithful administrators from the brothers, but within the enclosure of the monastery she gave it to her spiritual sisters so that[104] day and night, by means of vigils in holy combat, prayers, holy readings, and fasts, she would be able to fight against spiritual wickedness. The outcome of the matter happened thus: she put in her memory almost every book of divine law,[105] and, as the Holy Spirit revealed them, she openly disclosed the hidden mysteries of allegory to her listeners.[106] Likewise, she constructed churches of the saints and

---

101 Britain or Ireland. Note the religious importance of Rome to the Franks in the pre-Bonifatian period. This we see also in the *Vita Audoini*, ch. 10, above, p. 160.

102 Itta's children: Grimoald I, Geretrud and Begga (see *Virtutes*, ch. 10); grandchildren (i.e. Grimoald's offspring): Childebertus *adoptivus* and Wulfetrud, future abbess of Nivelles.

103 'in the twelfth year' is eleven years after Pippin's death, i.e. in 650.

104 *quatenus* to express purpose.

105 I.e. the Bible.

other special buildings from the ground up, and with all generosity she furnished daily alms to orphans, widows, captives and pilgrims.

CHAPTER 4

We must not leave out, I think, what this servant of God herself, terrified almost to shaking, told us. When she stood in prayer at the altar of St Sixtus the martyr,[107] she saw descending above her a flaming pellucid sphere such that the whole basilica was illuminated by its brightness for about half an hour, and gradually it receded whence it had come. And later it again appeared to other sisters above them in the same manner. What does the appearance of that light indicate if not a visitation of the True Light which does not cease to illuminate every holy person praying for himself and for all?

CHAPTER 5

On a certain day, the invocation of the same Geretrud of blessed memory saved our lives at the right moment as we were in danger on the sea. As we were peacefully sailing over the sea on the monastery's business, there appeared in the distance something like a ship of wondrous size; it came from abeam. As, however, it drew near, a huge storm arose and churned up the sea with mighty waves. And behold! A great and terrible monster appeared to us as if tossed up from the deep. We only saw it partially, not the whole thing, just its back. The sailors trembled and, having no hope for their lives, they turned to their idols. We, however, invoking the name of the Lord, hoped for that final hour. But one of us, who is still alive, cried out and said three times, 'Geretrud, help us, as you promised.' Indeed, what I saw and heard I bear witness to you. At the third repetition of that phrase the monster sought the depths, and in joy and with peace we reached port that very night. Thus, through the prayer of His maidservant, Christ deigned to free His poor creatures from death.

106 Van Uytfanghe, *Stylisation biblique*, p. 43, thinks that this phrase, ... *et obscura allegoriae misteria, Spiritu sancto revelante, aperte auditoribus apperuit*, indicates that Geretrud had knowledge of exegetical works.

107 Sixtus was a Roman martyr whose relics appear to have been under the control of the papacy. Pope Gregory I, in fact, sent some of them to Kent. Sixtus' relics may have been among those brought back from Rome which the author talks about in ch. 2 above. See M. Deansly and P. Grosjean,'The Canterbury Edition of the Answers of Pope Gregory I to Saint Augustine', *Journal of Ecclesiastical History*, 10 (1959), 28–32.

CHAPTER 6

Then after some years, because of too much abstinence and keeping of vigils, so that her body was sorrily exhausted with serious illness, she saw through divine revelation that her departure from this light was nearing. With the advice of the male servants and handmaidens of God, on account of the love of Christ, she completely relinquished every office and official title and every responsibility which she physically exercised for her flock, keeping only her spiritual functions. In her place, to govern the assembled flock of God and to care[108] for the poor, she established her niece named Wulfetrud who had been imbued and nurtured at her feet from the cradle with sacred writings according to the holy rule. At that time this consecrated girl, Wulfetrud, had completed the twentieth year of her life; she was born of the same ancient and famous family of the Franks as she herself [Geretrud] was.[109] She had a bright countenance, was dear to the household, kind to her subordinates, firm with the proud, generous to the poor, faithful to her relatives, agreeable in her speech, and, with love towards God and her neighbour, she remained pure in chastity. It happened, however, out of hatred of her father that kings, queens, and even priests, through envy of the devil, wished to drag her from her place, first by persuasion and later by force, so that they might evilly possess the property of God, which the blessed girl oversaw. But since she was protected from all her adversaries by the mercy of the Lord and the prayers of the holy men, Christ, to whom she had devoted herself as His handmaiden, restored it in a wondrous manner. And God so conferred his grace upon her that those who formerly through greed had been her abductors and accusers were later, with generosity and gifts,[110] her defenders.

With all things having been well ordered and repaired for the church of Christ, in the eleventh year[111] from when she had undertaken governing the flock entrusted to her, beset by weakness, she kept to her bed for more than fifty days. In her usual way, she distributed generous alms to the poor and destitute, to all she forgave their debts according to the Gospel, and from all she received peace and blessing. Among [her fellow] spiritual maidservants of God, confidently trusting with faith and hope in Christ, in the thirtieth year of her life, death took her spirit

108 *regere* and *ministrare*, infinitives used to express purpose.
109 That is, she was the daughter of Geretrud's brother, Grimoald.
110 *beneficiis.*
111 663.

on 23 November. With the greatest care she was covered with a marble tomb in the nave of the basilica of the blessed apostle Peter; there she awaits the day of the resurrection of all the saints.

CHAPTER 7

But let us return whence we digressed. The blessed servant of God, Geretrud, for a period of almost three months after she slackened the chain of office from her conscience, did not cease to speak in constant praying, in exhorting herself, and in preaching the word of God to her people. Rejoicing in hope, bearing up in tribulation, devoted in her heart, and calm in her appearance, she longed for her last day to be present, the day of her [heavenly] journey. Out of prison into power, out of darkness into light, out of death she hastened into life. And since she was here in body only, in spirit she journeyed daily to eternal matters in the strength of constant prayer in the pain of extraordinary abstinence. In addition she even secretly dressed her poor body with a rough hair shirt[112] so that she would not have any pleasantness of comfort in this life unless it be where the saints *will shine as the sun in the kingdom of their Father.*[113] And when she came to her last day, she decreed that in that place of her sepulchre they should lay no woollen nor linen clothing over her except one very cheap cloth (which a certain pilgrim nun several days earlier had sent her to cover her head in return for a blessing) and that hair shirt. In the tomb, where she rests in peace, she is covered by no other cloth, except these two: the hair shirt in which she was dressed and the old head cloth with which the hair shirt was covered. Indeed, she used to say that excess property is able to provide aid neither to the dying nor to the living, and this wise men witness to be true. Then when the day of the assumption of her soul approached, she called one of the brothers and ordered him, saying, 'Go quickly to that pilgrim who is remote [from the world] in the monastery which is called Fosses[114] and say to him: "Geretrud, the virgin of Christ, sent me to you to ask you which day she will depart from this light because she says that she greatly fears and likewise she greatly rejoices." And he will tell you what you must report. Go and

112 See *Vita Audoini*, ch. 3, above, p. 155.

113 Matthew 13:43.

114 This hermit is usually considered to be Ultan, Foillan's brother. The *vita* does not name him and certainly does not call him abbot of Fosses. See Grosjean, 'Notes 1957', p. 397; Dierkens, *Abbayes*, p. 295, and K. Hughes, review of Grosjean, 'Notes de hagiographie celtique', *Irish Historical Studies*, 12 (1960–61), 64.

do not hesitate.' Shortly her order was carried out, that which had been entrusted to him was asked, and that servant of God gave him an answer and said, 'Today is 16 March, tomorrow during solemn mass the maidservant of God and virgin of Christ, Geretrud, will go forth from her body. And say this to her, let her neither fear nor be alarmed concerning her death, but may she pass on joyously because blessed Bishop Patrick with the chosen angels of God and with great glory are prepared to receive her. Go now quickly.' The brother who had been sent asked him whether he had seen this by divine revelation, so that he might in turn tell her. In response, he said, 'Go my brother, hurry. May you know this: it is tomorrow; why do you ask me more?' When he returned, he reported to the maidservant of Christ what had been said to him. But she, as if waking from a sleep, responded with a happy countenance because of her joy, giving thanks to God because he had seen fit to comfort his handmaiden through his servant. From this promise her joy remained so strong that she, along with her sisters, kept the vigil throughout the whole night in psalms, hymns and prayer. Then on the next day, a Sunday, just before the sixth hour, according to the pronouncement of the man of God, she received the most holy provision of the body and blood of Christ, and when the priest had finished[115] the Secret[116] for Sunday, in the thirty-third year of her life, on 17 March, she gave thanks to her creator, who deigned to call her without blemish to his kingdom. When she had said these things, she gave up her spirit to God who wished for it. While I and another brother, Rinchinus by name, had been called to that place for[117] the comforting of the sisters, the servant of God, Rinchinus, called me by name and said, 'Do you notice anything?' And I answered, 'I see nothing but the sisters in great sadness.' When I had said these things, there came a most pleasant odour, as if a burning mixture of scents, and it perfumed that little cell where the holy body lay. And we, having gone out from there, still sensed the sweetness of that wonderful scent in our nostrils. When all matters which concern the most blessed body along with the offices had been completed in her underground tomb, which she had formerly prepared for herself, the body of the most blessed virgin of Christ, Geretrud, was put into the sepulchre with divine praises by the priests and the maidservants of God, and daily in that place blessings of prayer[118] are manifested.

HERE ENDETH THE LIFE

115 *habuit finitam.* Perfect expressed with the auxiliary verb *habere.*
116 *secretam sententiam,* usually called the *oratio secreta.*
117 *propter* used to express purpose.
118 I.e. miracles.

Additamentum Nivialense de Fuilano[119]
(The Nivelles Supplement to the *Vita Fursei* concerning Foillan)

After the departure of the blessed man Fursey, there was violence, which he had foreseen in spirit as he was serving [God] in lands overseas. For after the most Christian king, Anna, had been expelled, the monastery which he had built there was looted by an invasion of pagans of all its possessions and its monks were carried off. Abbot Foillan, himself, uterine brother of the above-mentioned man, would have been[120] led off into custody to die if the Divine Right Arm had not saved him for[121] the profit of many, the pagans having been terrified by the reported arrival of the above-mentioned King Anna. With the monks redeemed from captivity, the holy relics found, with the holy implements of the altar and books having been loaded on a ship, they then sought the lands of the Franks and in the same place where blessed Fursey was buried,[122] they were received by the above-mentioned[123] *patricius*,[124] Erchinoald. Not much later than this they were expelled by the *patricius*, who despised the pilgrims, but they were honourably received by the most religious handmaiden of God, Iduberga, also named Itta, and her daughter, the sacred virgin of Christ, Geretrud. With Grimoald himself pleased, protecting the same holy men, and making the arrangements, he[125] built a monastery of religious monks in a villa which is named Bebrona[126] from the river

119 *Additamentum Nivialense de Fuilano*, ed. B. Krusch, *MGH, SSRM*, IV (Hanover, 1902), pp. 449–51. The *Monumenta* later discovered an important early manuscript and published its variants in *MGH, SSRM*, VII (Hanover, 1920), pp. 837–42. For still other manuscripts of this text, see Grosjean, 'Notes 1957', 379–420.

120 Correct use of the pluperfect subjunctive.

121 *propter* used to express purpose.

122 In Peronne. See *Vita Fursei*, ch. 10, *MGH, SSRM*, IV, p. 439.

123 'Above-mentioned' here means in the *Vita Fursei*, not in this supplement.

124 As in the *Passio Leudegarii*, ch. 26, above, p. 242, the word *patricius* is usually used to describe the Merovingian governor of Provence and Marseilles, not the mayor of the palace as here.

125 The Latin is ambiguous, making it difficult to decide who is the subject of the sentence. If it is Grimoald, the ablative absolute is not autonomous, as would be called for in classical grammar; on the other hand, the position in the passage of Foillan, who was obviously the leader of the group, is too distant to be the clear subject of the verb.

126 Below the author also names the place Fosses. Today it is called Fosses-la-Ville in southern Belgium. The river is now called the Biesme.

flowing [through it], with the above-mentioned handmaiden of God
providing all the necessary things. It happened here, that after the
above-mentioned handmaiden of God,[127] departed for the realms
above, having dispensed many fruits of alms throughout many places,
having comforted[128] many paupers, having received many pilgrims
with every kindness, feeding the hungry, clothing the cold, offering a
roof to guests, providing much money for the sacred [altar] vessels,
and strengthening the army of holy virgins with the above-mentioned
noble lady in the Lord,[129] Foillan, the man of the Lord, concerning
whom we have made mention above, undertook a journey for the
benefit of the flock entrusted to him. He sang the solemnities of mass
on the day of the vigils of the most holy martyr Quintin in the church
at Nivelles, beseeching the older brothers that his body, if he should
happen to die anywhere on the way, should be sought out by the
brothers who constantly labour with that contemplation of charity,
and, taking leave of all, he set forth. On the same night, having been
led off the path by a certain evil man, and entering a small dwelling of
evil men near a certain small villa,[130] they were received with false
kindness. But the companions of the blessed[131] man, being suspicious
of the inhabitants, remained awake throughout the night. With matins
completed, having spoken kindly to the locals, when, after prayer, he
had given himself to sleep, telling his own men not to suspect any evil
of any of them, the diabolical men, rising up along with others who had
been added to them from elsewhere, killed the holy man; his comrades
also they likewise killed. But the holy man exclaimed the grace of God.
Lest his voice should be heard any longer, they amputated his
venerable head and in the next building, where a herd of swine were
feeding, having made a ditch, they impiously buried the four nude and
lacerated bodies together. And the matter lay thus hidden for many
days because they sent abroad their clothes, horses and whatever they
had and sold them to the inhabitants far away. But when they did not

---

127 I.e. Itta.
128 *consolatis*, deponent verb used passively ('many paupers having been comforted').
129 I.e. Geretrud.
130 Strépy, arr. Soignes, cant. Roeulx. Krusch, *MGH, SSRM*, IV, p. 450, n. 2.
131 Foillan is called blessed (*beatus*) while living, but holy (*sanctus*) once he has been
    killed.

arrive at the aforesaid *placitum*,[132] the brothers were moved by the
worry of love and, calling for him everywhere, they sought him. But
the above-mentioned virgin of Christ, Geretrud, beseeching the Lord
with fasting and prayer, having sent envoys everywhere throughout
the neighbouring localities, drew the business of darkness into bright
light. And thus on the seventy-seventh day of their death the sacred
bodies were discovered. This mystic number is noted[133] in many places
in Divine Scripture. They were found on the very day when blessed
Fursey, his brother, migrated from the body unto the Lord. The bodies
were taken up and, with candles and the light of torches and with
spiritual antiphones and canticles, were carried with honour by the
clergy and the people on their shoulders through the whole night to
the monastery at Nivelles. And there the venerable man, Dido, Bishop
of Poitiers, and the mayor of the palace, Grimoald, a man of illustrious
standing, arrived that very day in order to visit the holy places, and
each of them was informed of the arriving bodies by the Lord. For the
bishop, resting after matins, was asked in a dream what he was doing
and was immediately ordered to hasten to meet blessed Elijah. And he,
arising instantly and asking a servant what was happening, heard from
him that the venerable bodies were present. And straightway the
venerable man went forth to meet them, pouring out many tears and
raising up the praise of the Lord in full prayer, along with the above-
mentioned most reverend *patricius*; taking up the burden of the
venerable body, they carried it on their own shoulders. And having
been received into the monastery of the holy virgins, with relics taken
from it, he was carried reverently with psalms and canticles to his own
monastery. And when noble men had flocked from all sides to meet
him and carried him on their own shoulders, he was established with
every honour in the most famous place called Fosses by another name,
where the blessings of prayer[134] are performed, our Lord Jesus Christ
aiding. Who with the Father and the Holy Spirit lives and reigns as
God for ever and ever, amen.

---

132 A *placitum* is a court where disputes, usually having to do with land ownership, are
  settled by officials of some authority, usually the king. The author has not made
  previous mention of any *placitum*. Perhaps he means the meeting of Grimoald and
  Bishop Dido of Poitiers to plan the exile of Prince Dagobert to Ireland. An Irish
  leader would certainly have been an important part of such a meeting.
133 *adnotante*. Present participle used for finite verb.
134 I.e. miracles.

VIII: *Annales Mettenses Priores*
(The Earlier Annals of Metz)

The *Annales Mettenses Priores* are in many ways a misfit among the company they keep in this volume. Their language is of a different style, they are a different type of source, but, most important for us, they come from a different era. Although in their early pages they treat many of the political events of the late Merovingian age in engaging detail, they were actually written more than half a century after the Carolingians had ursurped the Merovingian throne. It is precisely because they were written under the new regime that we have included them here. As we have often mentioned above, succeeding centuries have usually seen the late Merovingian age through Carolingian eyes, and that vision has produced a warped view. Here in the *Annales Mettenses Priores* we have one of the most influential Carolingian sources treating our period, and consequently a comparison between it and the more contemporary Merovingian works will help to clear up much of the distortion. Of our sources, the *Annales* most closely resemble the *Liber Historiae Francorum* and we shall find ourselves making comparisons most often with that source. Even here, however, the two sources differ enough in their form that the comparisons will not always be able to be drawn in perfect parallel.

As their title announces, the *Annales Mettenses* are annals and they are the only source of this type we have included in this collection. The *LHF* is called a chronicle, that is, a source which gives a largely chronological account of events without much attempt at synthesis or profound analysis. Nevertheless, the author of a chronicle can treat themes or events which span several years, as we have seen the *LHF* do. Annals, on the other hand, are organised year by year. They list all one year's events together in a single entry. The annal as a form for recording history grew from notational additions made to the Easter tables. Since Easter is a movable feast, its date must be calculated anew for each year. It was not until the eighth century that our current system of numbering the years consecutively from the birth of Christ gained currency. Once this Dionysian system – so-called after its inventor, the sixth-century monk, Dionysius – was adopted, it was possible to draw up tables listing the date of Easter for many years to come. The earliest Easter tables tended to list nineteen years per page, with each year on a separate line. The line would begin with the Dionysian year and list the other, older ways of identifying it (its place in the indiction or in the lunar cycles, for example) and then give the date of Easter. Later users of these tables began to record a few important events 'as they happened', as it were, between the lines after the pertinent year.[1] It was from this practice of noting events in the Easter tables that the type of source called annals developed. Since the Dionysian system was not widely used during the Merovingian era, it was not until the Carolingian period that annals appeared. What began as a contemporary record year by year in the Easter tables soon became a form for writing history, both of the present and of the past. In fact we have only one surviving manuscript of one set of annals where the scribal hand changes with each year's entry, indicating that the events were recorded year by year.[2] We cannot prove that any of the many other surviving Carolingian annals were written exclusively as the events occurred. In other words, the writing of annals no longer meant solely noting important contemporary events, but became a new method of recording the past. This was certainly the case with the *Annales Mettenses Priores*; they recorded both the history of their own Carolingian times and that of the late Merovingian era. In fact, as we shall see, despite their name, in many sections their form is hardly annalistic at all.

The *Annals of Metz* are a textually difficult source. The historiography of their study is both fascinating and famous. André Duchesne published what he called the *Annales Francorum Mettenses* in 1626.[3] Since these annals contained such great praise of St Arnulf, and since their only surviving manuscript came from St Arnulf's monastery at Metz,[4] Duchesne assumed they had been written there. Their account extended to 904 and drew on many known sources. In 1826 George Pertz edited the work for the *Monumenta Germaniae Historica*.[5] These annals are now known as *Annales Mettenses Posteriores* (*The Later Annals of Metz*) to distinguish them from the earlier version we have

---

1 For a discussion of annals and their origins see R. McKitterick, *The Frankish Kingdoms under the Carolingians, 751–987* (London, 1983), pp. 2–6.

2 The Vienna manuscript of the *Lorsch Annals* beginning in 794. See McKitterick, *Frankish Kingdoms*, p. 4.

3 *Annales Francorum Mettenses*, ed. A. Duchesne, *Historia Francorum Scriptores coaetanei*, vol. III (Paris, 1641), pp. 262–333.

4 Now ms. Berlin, Meerman 114, saec. xi/xii.

5 *MGH, SS*, I (Hanover, 1826), pp. 314–36.

translated here. Although many of the works these annals drew upon could be easily identified, scholars suspected there to have been a 'lost source' which provided the information for the work's earlier sections. Indeed, there were fragments to be found of an earlier work which could have been part of this lost source.[6] The fragments disagreed in places with the *Annals of Metz* as then published and may have contained much earlier material, but most scholars in the nineteenth century distrusted them, assuming that they had been written in the late tenth century.[7] Then it happened. While on a research journey for the *MGH* in the cathedral library in Durham in December 1895, Karl Hempe discovered not fragments but a complete text of annals for the years 687–830 in an early twelfth-century manuscript.[8] This manuscript would become the basis of the published version of the *Annales Mettenses Priores* as we know them.

The most recent edition of the work was produced by Bernard von Simson for the *Monumenta Germaniae Historica* in 1905.[9] Von Simson used as his basis the then newly discovered Durham manuscript. Since that manuscript is a late copy from the first part of the twelfth century, he also took into account readings from the *Later Annals of Metz*,[10] which would have used the earlier annals in places, and he also drew on the texts of the sources which the author had used. In addition, he used some of those fragments we spoke of which antedate the Durham manuscript.[11]

The *Earlier Annals of Metz* divide themselves into three sections: (I) 687–805, the early years, compiled by one author in 805 or 806;[12] (II) 806–29, a very close transcription of the *Annales regni Francorum* for

6 G. Waitz published some of the fragments: *Annalium veterum fragmenta partim ex Mettensibus desumpta*, in *MGH, SS*, XIII (Hanover, 1881), pp. 26–33. See B. von Simson's comments in his introduction to his edition of the *Annales Mettenses Priores, MGH, SSRG* (Hanover, 1905), pp. vi–viii.

7 For example, H. Bonnell, *Die Anfänge des Karolingischen Hauses* (Berlin, 1866), pp. 157–81, and E. Mühlbacher, *Deutsche Geschichte unter den Karolingern* (Stuttgart, 1896), p. 32.

8 Codex Dunelmensis, C. IV. 15 (Durham) foll. 2–28v. See. K. Hempe, 'Reise nach England vom Juli 1895 bis Februar 1896', III, *NA*, 22 (1897), 694–6; B. von Simson, 'Die wiederaufgefundene Vorlage der *Annales Mettenses*', *NA*, 24 (1899), 399–424; and von Simson's 'Nachtrag', *NA*, 25 (1900), 177–83.

9 *MGH, SSRG* (Hanover, 1905).

10 His manuscripts B1 and B2.

11 His manuscripts A2, A3, A4 and A4* (von Simson, *Praef.*, pp. v–viii).

12 The case for single authorship of the first part was convincingly put by H. Hoffmann, *Untersuchung zur Karolingischen Annalistik, Bonner Forschungen*, 10 (1958), pp. 10 and 53, and has since become the reigning opinion. Thus I. Haselbach, 'Aufstieg und

the same years, and (III) 830, a later addition which does not itself give an indication of the year but which fits the year 830. Since it is the first part which treats the late Merovingian era, it is that section and its author which will concern us. We have provided a translation of it up to 727, the year in which the *LHF* ends its account.

Although the first section was compiled by a single author, it is by no means a homogeneous account and not always in the form of annals. The author made heavy use of his sources, most often by lengthy direct transcription. From the beginning up to 742 he used the Continuators of Fredegar. This source is in the form of a chronicle, not annals, and making it fit into the annalistic form was a difficult task. Consequently the indications of the Dionysian years given here are often wrong. It is difficult to determine the origin of many of these indications of the years, since the manuscripts often disagree and the Durham manuscript sometimes leaves the years out. From 742 to 768 our author used both the Continuators of Fredegar and the *Annales regni Francorum*. Throughout we can also find traces of the *Annales Petaviani*. The account of the last few years, beginning in 803 and extending to 805, shows far less use of known sources. Some of the parts for which we cannot identify any source undoubtedly came from ones now lost, but much is obviously the author's own material.

In the use of sources he (less likely, she) did not always remove the overlapping portions, and thus his work contains repetitions. Some of these irregularities in von Simson's edition are only apparent, since they were not part of the original text but additions which crept in during the centuries of manuscript transmission. Wilhelm Levison questioned the inclusion of the Dionysian years in the earlier part, where they are obviously wrong and repetitious,[13] and Hartmut Hoffmann was able to argue successfully for the elimination of some of the passages taken from the *Annales regni Francorum* included in the entry for 804/05. He persuasively stated that these must have been added later, since their inclusion gives the work a degree of repetition and confusion not found in its other parts.[14] Irene Haselbach, too, has

---

Herrschaft der Karolinger in der Darstellung der sogenannten *Annalen Mettenses priores*', *Historische Studien*, 12 (1970), 9; and Wattenbach-Levison, *Deutschlands Geschichtsquellen im Mittelalter, Vorzeit und Karolinger*, pt. 1, *Die Vorzeit von den Anfängen bis zur Herrschaft der Karolinger* (Weimar, 1952), pp. 261–3.

13 W. Levison, 'Zu den *Annales Mettenses*', in his *Aus rheinischer und Fränkischer Frühzeit* (Dusseldorf, 1948), pp. 475–6.

14 Hoffmann, *Untersuchung*, p. 51. Haselbach, 'Aufstieg', 15, agrees.

argued that certain sections included in the edition were not part of the original work but added later by scribes who copied marginal notes into the body of the text. On the whole her arguments are not compelling, and we have kept her disputed passages in our translation with the exception of the one which von Simson himself calls into question in a footnote to his edition.[15]

The *Annales Mettenses Priores* open with an account of Pippin II. Even though he was a secular figure, their treatment of him often resembles the way in which hagiographers portrayed their saintly subjects.[16] Pippin's youth, much like that of a saint, contains an early revelation of his special election: 'While still in the flower of youth ... Pippin's power and victory were made known to the people far and wide.'[17] As with many hagiographical subjects, Pippin is heir to the special piety of his parents and ancestors: 'Strengthened, therefore, by the teachings and most holy exhortations of these, as I would say, holy relatives, he

---

15 For stylistic reasons, Haselbach, 'Aufstieg', 35, claims that three passages in the portion of the annals which treat Pippin II were added later and thus do not belong to the original text (ed. von Simson, p. 4, line 20, to p. 5, line 6; p. 12, line 24, to p. 13, line 6; and p. 13, lines 9–11). We disagree and have included all three in the translation as von Simson included them in the edition. The second of these three passages is a report of Pippin II's success against the *gentes* achieved after the battle of Tertry. In this context it is helpful to recall the words of the *LHF*, ch. 49 (above, p. 93), for the same period: 'Pippin waged many wars against the gentile Radbod and other princes, against the Suevi as well as other peoples.' See also von Simson, edition, p. 16, n. 5; and Levison, 'Zu den Annalen', p. 475, n. 3. In the section which treats Charles Martel, she argues unconvincingly for two other passages to be considered later additions. The first (ed. von Simson, p. 21, lines 3–7) does include an episode out of proper chronological order, as she says, but the author is careful to point out that he is going backwards. The second (ed. von Simson, p. 25, lines 9–10) is an extract from the Fredegar *Continuations*, ch. 10, which relates Martel's taking of Pippin's treasure from Plectrud. This does not seem a later addition either, for two reasons. First, the author's naming Martel as Pippin's heir in the same sentence would make little sense in this situation without the report of this obtaining his father's treasure. Second, the extract is in the correct place, both according to the Fredegar Continuator in *The Fourth Book of Fredegar with its Continuations* (hereafter Fredegar, *Contin.*), ed. Wallace-Hadrill (London, 1960), p. 89, and *LHF*, ch. 53, above, p. 95.

16 The presence of hagiographical tone and style is noted in passing by L. Halphen, *Etudes critiques sur l'histoire de Charlemagne* (Paris,1921), p. 50. Haselbach,'Aufstieg', 38, sees the parallels with the first chapter of the *Passo Leudegarii* (above, pp. 216–17) as the most striking. She also notices a loose dependence (*lose Anlehnung*) on Seutonius. Be that as it may, the hagiographical parallels are clearly stronger. We also have noted several with the *Passio Leudegarii*, above, p. 000.

17 Below, pp. 350–1.

progressed along the pathways of justice to the guidance of the realm
without stumbling.[18] Pippin too exhibits noticeably early maturity and
high morality as a lad: 'For the strength of his justice, the unconquerable solidity of his bravery, and the guidance of his moderation freely
acquired such a place in the heart of this youth ...'[19]

After treating Pippin's youth, the author moves on to relate his glorious
military success over foreign peoples (the *gentes*). In fact the report is
over-enthusiastic, claiming success for Pippin which he never
achieved.[20] After the divinely ordained victories over foreigners, Pippin,
with God's help and again in accordance with the divine plan, returned
all Francia to a blessed state of internal peace. This pacific condition
was brought about by a momentous clash between good (Pippin) and
evil (King Theuderic III and his mayor, Berchar) at the battle of
Tertry. The battle is recounted in the most heroic style, complete with
Virgilian idiom, a pervading metaphor of light and darkness, and
hortatory speeches reminiscent of Livy and Thucydides. The peace
was short-lived, however, and within two years Pippin was forced to
deal with many rebellions on the part of the subjugated peoples. Here
Pippin's most noted campaign was his conquest of the Frisians
through the defeat of their leader, Radbod. After that, secure in his
position and with his realm again at peace, Pippin received envoys and
other signs of respect and recognition from the foreign peoples round
about: Greeks (i.e. Byzantines), Romans, Lombards, Huns, Slavs and
Saracens. There follow accounts of him establishing Merovingian
kings on the throne at the occasion of royal deaths and disposing of
various high offices to members of his own family. In all this, Pippin
and his power are described with the most royal, if not imperial,
vocabulary (*regnavit, a Pippino ordinatur, rexit, regnum,* and *imperium*).

So far the account has taken us to about the year 697 and has been
largely rendered in the author's own words. He recounts the rest of
Pippin's life, however, with much heavier reliance on the wording of
his sources, largely the *Continuator of Fredegar.* He returns to his own
words for 714 in order to give us his version of the beginning of
Charles Martel's rule. Although he begins these entries with
Dionysian years, they can hardly be called annalistic; we are confronted with the full account of a chronicler. All in all, his account of

18 Below, p. 352.
19 Below, p. 351.
20 See below, n. 120.

Pippin II seems like a biography forced, often with unhappy results, to fit the format of annals.[21]

Charles Martel's early life is given a remarkably similar treatment to that given Pippin's youth, a treatment, however with an important difference. The early revelation of Martel's elevated status appears in a nearly blinding simile: 'Then just as the eclipsed sun gradually unveils its bright rays to the whole world, so Charles, the most worthy heir of Pippin, began to shine forth as a mighty defender before a people suffering and almost despairing of hope.'[22] Just as we have been told that Pippin was heir to the family's virtues, so now we are forcefully reminded that Martel was Pippin's legitimate heir: 'But Charles, whom his father had left behind as the only surviving heir worthy of such great power …; … legitimate governance of his father's authority'; and especially '… it was as if their ruler Pippin had come to life for their comfort'.[23] Martel's virtues are listed; we find him called *precellentissimus*, *invictus*, *providus* and using *prudentissima meditatione*. The forms may be parallel to those used for Pippin and perhaps here also reminiscent of hagiographical patterns, but we are immediately struck by the shocking absence of Christian piety and virtue. Although Charles Martel's early life, and indeed his whole career, are expressly guided by God's will, nowhere is he adorned with the most Christian virtues that Pippin and his holy ancestors had sported. Martel's good points are strictly those tried and proven virtues which brought success in Frankish political and military spheres.

Next we are given a detailed account, although not always an accurate one, of how Martel gained the leadership of the Austrasians. It is significant that the author shows us that he did this largely through battles with external enemies. Conquering the *gentes*, as we remember, was also presented as the first important task undertaken by his father, Pippin. In the first year after Pippin's death, Austrasia suffered attacks from the Frisians, the Saxons and the Neustrians. The author leaves little doubt that he considered Neustrians foreigners. Not only does he recount the military operations of the Neustrian king, Chilperic II, and his mayor, Raganfred, as invasions, but he calls the Neustrians *gens illa*, inserting the phrase in his own words into an account he is

---

21 Haselbach, 'Aufstieg', 34, thinks that there may have been an original text, a chronicle, which was later forced into the annalistic form.

22 Below, p. 366.

23 Below, pp. 365–6.

copying from the Fredegar continuator. From 717 onwards, that is, for the years of Martel's rule, the author returns to a truer annalistic format and includes less and less of his own original material. The result is that for Charles Martel we have less of a biography than we had for Pippin II.

The years Pippin III led the Frankish realm (741–68) are recounted in purely annalistic style. The material is mostly original, or at least we see less and less use of known sources. Pippin III, like Martel before him, is not brushed with the glitter of Christian virtue as Pippin II had been, and the historical information here is more sober and more accurate. The themes remain much the same: conquest of foreigners and maintenance of the internal peace. Internal peace for the realm has now become largely a matter of settling the succession problems within the Carolingian family. The author is surprisingly sparing in relating the events of 751 and the assumption of the throne by Pippin. For him the deciding event in the Pippinids' rise was not Pippin III's royal assumption in 751 but Pippin II's victory at Tertry in 687.

With that period of Charlemagne's rule which the first part of the *Annales Mettenses Priores* treats, that is, from 768 to 805, the author never departs from the annalistic form. He no longer makes use of the *Continuators of Fredegar*, relying almost exclusively on the *Annales regni Francorum*. He now rarely changes any of his source material, being content to add to it from time to time. From 793 to 798 he does not make any additions at all. From 803 to 805 he again writes original material.[24]

There is little disagreement that the first section of the *Annales Mettenses Priores* was written by a single author in or shortly after the year 805.[25] We know little about him; we cannot even be certain where he wrote. The manuscipt tradition is of no help in locating him. There are few manuscripts, and even the earliest known fragment is removed from his time of writing by nearly a century.[26] From his own words, and especially from his account of the period from 803 to 805, it is obvious that he was concerned with and knowledgeable about the

---

24 Haselbach, 'Aufstieg', 29–30.

25 The argument is Hoffmann's, *Untersuchung*, p. 41, who, once he had eliminated certain repetitions as later additions, clearly revealed the work's stylistic unity. Haselbach, 'Aufstieg', 22–3, agrees. See Wattenbach-Levison, *Geschichtsquellen*, pp. 261–4.

26 Ms British Library, Arundel 375, IX/X saec.

affairs of Charlemagne's court.[27] As we have mentioned, it is also likely that his calling the Neustrians foreigners means that he was Austrasian. But since during Charlemagne's rule an Austrasian could find himself anywhere in the Frankish realms, most scholars have placed him either in the monastery at Saint-Denis or in the double monastery at Chelles. A third possibility, however, is that the *Annals of Metz* were actually written in Metz.

Pückert and Kurze noticed that the surviving royal charters of Saint-Denis from Pippin II's time were issued at Montmacq, a place which the *Annales Mettenses* call the seat of Merovingian power. The author adds his own report of the burial of Queen Bertrada at Saint-Denis in 783, and he had good information about places where the monastery of Saint-Denis had landed possessions: Tertry, Vincy and Swabia, especially Cannstat.[28] On the other hand, he twice mentions Chelles: once when Martel's concubine, Sonihild, was banished there and also when Charlemagne visited his dying sister, Gisela, there in 804. If the *Annals* were written at Chelles, the fact that it was indeed Charlemagne's sister who was the abbess there at about the time of their composition might go a long way toward explaining their obvious intimacy with his court. Hartmut Hoffmann has opted for Chelles.[29]

The suggestion that the annals were written at Chelles brings up the question of whether the author was a woman. It seems unlikely, or at least, if the author were a woman, she would have been a misogynistic one. The author obviously cannot favour Pippin II's wife, Plectrud, who opposed his hero, Charles Martel, but the invective he uses to describe her hardly indicates female authorship: '... and she [Plectrud] in a womanly plan presumed to control the reign of so great a kingdom. Because she had decided to rule with feminine cunning more cruelly than was necessary ...' These are the author's own words inserted into

---

27 Cf. W. Schlessinger, 'Kaisertum und Reichsteilung. Zur *Divisio regnorum* von 806', in R. Dietrich and G. Oestreich (eds.), *Forschung zu Staat und Verfassung. Festgabe für Fritz Hartung* (Berlin, 1958), p. 39, reprinted in W. Schlessinger, *Beiträge zur deutschen Verfassungsgeschichte des Mittelalters*, vol. I, Göttingen, 1963, 193–232, with Nachtrag, 345; and Levison, 'Annales Mettenses', 475.

28 F. Kurze, 'Ueber die Karolingischen Reichsannalen von 741–829 und ihre Ueberarbeitung. III Die zweite Hälfte und die Ueberarbeitung', *NA*, 21 (1896), 31.

29 Hoffmann, *Untersuchung*, pp. 53–61. Also for Chelles: H. Beumann, 'Nomen Imperatoris. Studien zur Kaiseridee Karls des Grossen', *Historische Zeitschrift*, 185 (1958), 529. Haselbach, 'Aufstieg', 24, concludes that it could have been either Saint-Denis or Chelles.

the less passionate report of the Fredegar continuator which he was copying.[30]

As we have seen, this work has been called the *Annales Mettenses* for the wrong reason, but the wrong reason may have nonetheless produced the correct answer. The high regard in which the author held Bishop Arnulf of Metz may have been, as Haselbach argues,[31] because of Arnulf's supposed position as father of Charlemagne's dynasty, but it may also have been because the author belonged to St Arnulf's monastery at Metz. It is significant that the author shies away from calling Arnulf Pippin II's grandfather, referring to him instead as a 'close relative'.[32] Although the author will not make Arnulf Pippin's physical ancestor, he certainly is very eager to include the bishop of Metz as one of his spiritual ones. He has Arnulf, along with St Geretrud and Begga from the Pippinid side of the family, act as a direct spiritual mentor for the young Pippin. Metz is mentioned as often as is either Saint-Denis or Chelles, and, as is becoming increasingly noted, the city and its prelates enjoyed a close, if not central, role in the operation of Charlemagne's court.[33] Nonetheless, the evidence is too slight to allow us to decide for certain.

Wherever our author wrote, he did so with considerable style and learning. A comparison of the *LHF* and the *Annales Mettenses Priores* quickly reveals that the Carolingian renaissance has made itself felt in the second. Gone is the clipped and unpolished directness of the *LHF*; instead we find simile, metaphor, and even Virgilian, Horatian and Caesarian turns of phrase. It was the Bible, of course, which exercised the greatest stylistic influence on both works, be it directly or indirectly.[34] The author of the annals uses his vocabulary, from whatever source, not merely to describe but also to paint verbal pictures. Compare the two authors relating the battle of Tertry: the *LHF* in three sober lines, the *Annales* in five pages where we not only see military tactics and

30 See below, p. 365.

31 Haselbach, 'Aufstieg', 23, is correct to reject von Simson's contention that the similarity in Drogo's title found in forged charters for Metz and in the *Annales Mettenses* is an indication of the annals' origin at Metz.

32 *agnatione propinquus.*

33 W. Goffart, 'Paul the Deacon's *Gesta Episcoporum Mettensium* and the Early Design of Charlemagne's Succession', *Traditio*, 42 (1986); and O. Oexle, 'Die Karolinger und die Stadt des heiligen Arnulf', *Frühmittelalterliche Studien*, 1 (1967).

34 For a perceptive discussion of the uses of the Bible by early medieval authors, see M. Van Uytfanghe, *Stylisation biblique et condition humaine dans l'hagiographie mérovingienne (600–750)* (Brussels, 1987).

hear speeches but come to know what the author sees as the essential elements of the major players' personalities.[35] Is it any wonder that the Carolingian version won the field in convincing readers?

A more important question for our purposes than either where the author lived or what style he used, is why he wrote. The answer could yield important insight into the *Ideenwelt*, the *mentalité*, of the court in about 805. This is important information for a Carolingian enquiry, but it has a direct bearing on our Merovingian study as well. An appreciation of why the author of the first section of the *Annales Mettenses Priores* wrote will enable us to make better use of his work as a source for Merovingian history.

The question is by no means a new one and several answers have been put forward. We shall consider in some detail four of the most significant and then suggest our own. First, the *Annales* are riddled with royal and imperial language describing the Carolingian family before it obtained either the Frankish crown in 751 or the imperial title in 800. The author has also been careful to make God's hand clearly visible in the family's rise to power. These factors have suggested that the *Annales* were written to justify the royal and imperial power the Carolingians exercised by 805.[36] Second, others have contended that they were written to show Carolingian superiority over Rome in imperial–papal relations.[37] Third, the existence again of an emperor in the West and the questions which that raised in his dealings with Byzantium may also have caused the author to write. Or, fourth, perhaps the *Annals* were written to provide guidance in planning for the eventual division of the Empire and for the royal and imperial succession at Charlemagne's death.

Reflections of imperial thinking and royal thinking appear often in the *Annales Mettenses Priores*, where they are complex and sometimes quite subtle. Although the *Annales* begin their account with Pippin II, they do make passing reference to his grandfather, Pippin I (d. 639): '... the late most excellent leader, Pippin, who with just laws governed the population living in the vast areas between the Forest of Charbonnière and the river Meuse up to the borders of the Frisians.' Although the words describe the elder Pippin, whose actual status was anything but

---

35 *LHF*, ch. 48, above, p. 92. *Annales Mettenses Priores* for their year 690, below, p. 355–9.

36 Schlessinger, 'Kaisertum', 38–41; Hoffmann, *Untersuchung*, pp. 61–3; and Haselbach, 'Augstieg', p. 10.

37 Schlessinger, 'Kaisertum', p. 42.

royal, they are nonetheless thick with royal inuendo. The adjective 'most excellent' (*praecellentissimus*) used here to describe Pippin belonged to the language of formal, royal, predicates used for the Germanic kings since the sixth century.[38] Other words, too, with which the author described his various Carolingian heroes from the period before the family achieved either its royal or its imperial status reflected those statuses in the official parlance of the age. *Invictissimus* had been part of the late antique imperial cult, and was applied to Charlemagne by Popes Stephen II and Hadrian I.[39] *Nobilissimus* was originally a title of the Caesars and was also applied to the royal Carolingians.[40] *Gloriosus* also comes from the language of royal predicates of rank, and *serenissimus* was reserved for the Byzantine emperor from about the year 600.[41] All such vocabulary which the author of the *Annales* applies to the early Pippinids is missing in the *LHF*'s accounts of them.

The use of such words by our author is subtle. Although it is obvious that they carry royal and/or imperial connotations, he also applied them in places where they cannot be regal or imperial in a technical sense.[42] This makes his use of them to describe the early Pippinids seem a much less blatant misuse and allows him to derive advantage from their connotations without seeming to be purely fabulous. Perhaps the most striking example of this is his use of the very word *imperium*. A court dominated by Alcuin would have known the word in Bede's sense, that is, simpy rule over several kingdoms without the slightest whiff of Roman imperial majesty. The word could also carry a simple geographical meaning, that is, denoting an area of rule, as it does in the *Divisio regnorum* of 806. This document, roughly contemoprary with the composition of the first section of the *Annales Mettenses*, does not use *imperium* but *dominatu imperiali* when it speaks of imperial power.[43] Although our author used *imperium* where it meant no more than

38 E. Ewig, 'Zum christlichen Königsgedanken', in T. Mayer (ed.), *Das Königtum. Seine geistigen und rechtlichen Grundlangen. Vorträge und Forschungen*, 3 (1956),17, n. 46. (Reprint, *Gallien*, vol. 1, 13, n. 46.)

39 Foltz, *Coronation*, p. 79.

40 Ewig, 'Zum christlichen Königsgedanken', 49. (Reprint, *Gallien*, vol. 1, 47.)

41 Ewig, 'Zum christlichen Königsgedanken', 17. (Reprint, *Gallien*, vol. 1, 13); Foltz, *Coronation*, p. 99.

42 E.g. ... *nobilissimus et cognatus sanguis Francorum* ... Below, p. 357.

43 *Divisio regnorum*, ed. A. Boretius, *Capitularia Regum Francorum*, vol. I, *MGH, Legum Sectio II* (Hanover, 1883), *imperium* used geographically, pp. 126–7, *dominatu imperiali*, p. 130. See F. Ganshof, trans. B. and M. Lyon, *Frankish Institutions under Charlemagne* (Providence, Rhode Island, 1968), p. 112, n. 91.

'command' or 'authority',[44] he also used it in places where he wanted its imperial nature to colour his heroes.[45]

Princeps is an imperial word as old as the Empire itself. Once again, the author uses it both in a general and in an imperial sense. He does not use it exclusively to mean mayor of the palace,[46] and in the plural (*principes*) he does not limit its use to the Pippinids.[47] He often uses both it and its abstraction, *principatus*, to mean simply 'leader' and 'leadership' or the geographical extent of authority.[48] Nonetheless, the way in which he uses it to describe the ancestors of Charlemagne leaves no doubt that he was painting them in imperial colours: Pippin I: ... *pippini precellentissimi quondam principis* ...;[49] Ansegisel: *nobilissimi quondam Francorum principis* ...;[50] Pippin II: ... *invicti principis pippini* ...;[51] and Charles Martel: ... *serenissimus princeps carolus* ...[52]

What may seem a simple literary allusion can also carry imperial freight. At the very beginning of his work the author compares Pippin II's slaying of Gundoin to David's triumph over Goliath. Late antique imperial ideology linked the emperor with David, and the title 'New David' became another of the imperial predicates.[53] Alcuin, Paul the Deacon

---

44 *Ad solidandum quoque ipsius* [Pippin II's] *imperii fundamentum erat ei ... Arnulfus ... episcopus.* Below, p. 352; ... *Francorum summo obtemperabant imperio.* Below, p. 353; [Theuderic III] *Francorum suscepisset imperium* ... Below, p. 353; and '*Caroli autem regis* [Charlemagne] *et principum eius qui cum eo erant imperio usus, totus ille exercitus* ...' Ed. von Simpson, p. 94, line 12 (not translated here).

45 ... *de utilitate imperii* ... for Pippin II, below, p. 361; and ... *ad orientales partes sui imperii* ... , below, p. 369.

46 ... *Ansegisili nobilissimi quondam Francorum principis* .... Ansegisel was never mayor, see below, p. 350. He uses both *princeps* and *maior domus* in the same account: *Carolus princeps* ... *exercitum commovit* ... *Quo conperto, Hilpericus cum Raganfrido maiore domus* ... , below, p. 368. He even has a substantive for mayoralty: ... *honorem iterum maiorisdomatus arripuit* [Ebroin], below, p. 353.

47 E.g. ... *principum qui cum eo exstiterant* ... , below, p. 365, and ... *per desidiam precedentium principum* ... where the *principes* may refer to the Merovingian kings and/or other leaders. See I. Heidrich, 'Titulatur und Urkunden der arnulfingischen Hausmeier', *Archiv für Diplomatik*, 11/12 (1955/56), 78–86, for a discussion of the Merovingian use of the term.

48 E.g. ... *de principatu Francorum* ... , below, p. 350; and ... *fines principatus eius crebris irruptionibus vexabat* ... , below, p. 363.

49 Below, p. 351.

50 Below, p. 350.

51 Below, p. 366.

52 Below, p. 368.

53 Foltz, *Coronation*, p. 75; H. Fichtenau, 'Byzanz und die Pfalz zu Aachen', in: *MIÖG*, 59 (1951); Ewig, 'Zum christlichen Königsgedanken', 11, 46 and 52; and Schlesinger, 'Kaisertum', 39.

and others at the Carolingian court used it increasingly for Charlemagne. The implications of the comparison would not have been missed. On the other hand, the author can abandon all pretension to subtlety, as when he says that Charles Martel 'ascended the throne of his father'.[54]

A second possible motive for the author was to show Carolingian superiority over Rome. The relationship between Charlemagne and the papacy was in a critical stage at about the time the author of the first section of the *Annales Mettenses Priores* composed his work. Charlemagne was becoming increasingly dependent upon the Church as the lay mechanisms which had held the realm together were becoming increasingly unreliable. To put it more concretely, there was a crisis of loyalty. Since the Frankish monarchy did not have a moneyed system of civil servants as did the Byzantines and the Moslems, the ties which traditionally bound the Frankish upper classes to their king were considerably weakened when he no longer had a large supply of land, positions or booty to hand out in reward for loyalty. Religious and ecclesiastical loyalty, however, could go a long way towards filling the vacuum, and thinking at court increasingly saw the realm as an *imperium Christianorum* with Charlemagne at its head.[55] One view has it that the *Annales* were written to thwart the worldly claims of the papacy, which now in trying to dampen royal encroachment took a particularly encroaching stance of its own *vis-à-vis* the monarchy with the publication of the *Donation of Constantine*.[56] It is most probable that this bogus document was brought to the Frankish court by Pope Leo III himself on his visit in 804.[57]

Indeed, there is much in our text which may indicate that the author wrote with the problems of loyalty and of papal relations on his mind. He is much occupied with loyalty, disloyalty, and the taking and breaking of oaths. One of his favourite words for the foreign enemies of the Carolingians is *perfidus*.[58] With the last decade of Charles Martel's

---

54 ... *solium patris conscenderat* ... , below, p. 366.

55 Foltz, *Coronation*, p. 48.

56 Schlessinger, 'Kaisertum', 42.

57 Schlessinger, 'Kaisertum', 44.

58 ... *gentem perfidam Sarracenorum* ... (ed. von Simson, p. 27, line 7); *Perfida gens Frisionum* ... (ed. von Simson, p. 28, line 10); ... *Sarracenos in suae perfidiae presidium adsciverat* ... (ed. von Simson, p. 30, line 14); *Hunaldi perfidi ducis* ... (ed. von Simson, p. 35, line 26); *Theodericum perfidum ducem illorum* [Saxons] ... (ed. von Simson, p. 36, line 6); ... *perfidum Theodricum* ... (ed. von Simson, p. 41. line 10); and ... *perfidus rex* [Aistulf] ... (ed. von Simson, p. 48, line 5). These sections are not translated below.

rule he begins to pepper his accounts with the taking of oaths and then the breaking of them.[59] Followers, too, are often called *fideles* and enter into a superior's *fidem*, 'faith' or 'protection'.[60] It is again significant that this vocabulary and this concern with loyalty and disloyalty do not play the same role in the *LHF*.

There is no doubt that the author was careful to portray the Popes as subservient to the Carolingians. Beginning with Charles Martel, the author usually adds an expanded account in his own words to that of his source when an event deals with a Pope. In 743 he added the report of false papal legates to what he took from the Fedegar continuator.[61] In 754 we find Pope Stephen coming to seek Pippin III's help against the Lombards, and then, in one of the longest accounts given in his own words in the whole work, he recounts Pippin's campaign against Aistulf, king of the Lombards. Here the Pope even prostrates himself and will not rise again until Pippin promises help.[62] The author continues in the same vein with Charlemagne. For 773 the author inserts a description in his own words of Charlemagne's position *vis-à-vis* the Pope into an account taken from the *Annales regni Francorum*:

> ... [Peter, Pope Hadrian's envoy] begged him [Charlemagne] with apostolic entreaties to go forth to defend the Roman Church so that he would free the Roman people and the holy Church from the hands of the haughty King Desiderius, adding that he [Charlemagne] was the legitimate protector and defender of that people ...[63]

'Protector' and 'defender' are words from the vocabulary of lordship

59 E.g. 734, the Frisians break their promise to Charles Martel (ed. von Simson, p. 28); 742, Hunowald takes an oath to Martel and his sons then break it (ed. von Simson, p. 33); 747, King Aistulf promises to pay tribute to Pippin III and give back papal lands but then goes back on his word (ed. von Simson, pp. 47–8); 757, Pippin makes Tassilo and the Bavarian nobles swear loyalty at Compiègne (ed. von Simson, p. 49); 758, the Saxons promise to fulfil Pippin III's will (ed. von Simson, p. 50); 760–61, Waifair's treachery in attacking part of Burgundy is explained as the breaking of an oath (ed. von Simson, pp. 50–1); and 763, Tassilo breaks an oath (ed. von Simson, p. 52). These passages are not translated below.

60 ... *suis fidelibus* ... (ed. von Simson, p. 2, line 4. Below, p. 350); *ad nostram fidem* [protection] ... (ed. von Simson, p. 8, line 21. Below, p. 356); ... *suorum pectora roboavit fidelium* [Pippin II's] ... (ed. von Simson, p. 11, line 2. Below, p. 358); ... *suis fidelibus* [Pippin II's] ... (ed. von Simson, p. 12, line 2, and p. 14, line 3. Below, pp. 359 and 360); and ... *ex suis fidelibus* [Martel's] ... (ed. von Simson, p. 31, line 31, not translated below).

61 Ed. von Simson, p. 34.

62 Ed. von Simson, pp. 44–5.

63 Ed. von Simson, p. 59, lines 15–23. Our translation.

and clearly show the relationshlp between emperor and Pope. In 804, in a revealing use of a verb, the author has Charlemagne 'permit' the Pope to return home.[64]

The Carolingian relationship with Byzantium may also have caused the author to write. The culmination of the ruling position of the Carolingians came in 800 when Charlemagne was crowned Roman Emperor. This imperial coronation is in one view '... one of the least understood and most complex events in the whole history of the west'.[65] The Frankish court no longer regarded the Byzantine Empire as holding valid claims to universality; instead it was now termed 'the Empire of the Greeks'.[66] Our author goes to some trouble to show that the re-established imperial dignity in the West was the equal of Byzantium's. To the rather sparse account in the *Annales regni Francorum* of the meeting between Greek and Frankish legations in 803 he adds many colourful details which clearly depict the Greeks holding the lower status. It was the Greeks who asked for the peace treaty. Their patriarch himself was part of the delegation, the author lists the magnificent gifts he had brought for Charlemagne, and he has Charlemagne discharge the Byzantines *cum honore imperiali*.[67]

Problems concerning the royal succession and the division of the Empire also could have been the author's motivating factor. At about the same time as the author was writing the first section of the *Annales Mettenses Priores*, the court produced one of the most mystifying and controversial documents from Charlemagne's whole reign: the *Divisio regnorum* of 806.[68] Chapters 1–5 record the arrangements for Charlemagne's succession made by the emperor and the great of the realm at an assembly held in February 806 at Aachen. Chapters 6–20 appear to be measures concerned with maintaining internal peace presented in the form of a usual capitulary, and these two sections were combined into one edict during the summer assembly at Thionville.[69] What is so striking here is the seeming absence of any provision for the passing on of the title of emperor or the preservation of the unity of the

---

64 Ed. von Simson, p. 93, line 6.

65 R. Folz, trans. J. E. Anderson, *The Coronation of Charlemagne* (London, 1974), p. xi.

66 The phrase used in the *Libri Carolini*. Foltz, *Coronation*, p. 92.

67 Ed. von Simson, p. 90, line 4.

68 *Capitularia*, I, *MGH, Legum Sectio II*, no. 45, pp. 126–30. Schlessinger's 'Kaisertum' is still basic to an understanding of the *Divisio*. See also Goffart, 'Paul the Deacon's *Gesta Episcoporum Mettensium*'.

69 Folz, *Coronation*, p. 167.

Empire. This absence could be only apparent, with the Empire alive and well in the imperial *formulae* used in the document's vocabulary.[70] A perhaps over-subtle argument has also been put forth claiming that the division of the realm into three parts actually maintained in the contemporary mind the Empire's essential unity in the way the contemporary controversies over the Trinity maintained the unity of the Christian godhead.[71] Others have taken the absence as real and see in the *divisio* a reflection that ideas of rule had changed since the coronation of 800. In this view, imperial considerations were now taking a decided back seat to the traditional Frankish means of succession, that is, rather than preserving the unity of the Empire, the document made a real division among all the legitimate royal heirs.[72]

These questions of how and whether the Empire should be divided do indeed seem to have been on the mind of the author of the first section of the *Annales Mettenses Priores*. A careful modern analysis of Paul the Deacon's *Gesta Episcoporum Mettensium*, a work written about 784, has suggested that Paul showed in ways the contemporary audience would have understood, but which we may miss, that Charlemagne's rule was to be passed on undivided to his eldest son, Charles.[73] In much the same way, our author, in those passages which he added to his sources, associates the son, Charles, with his father in rule and military valour and has him take on increasingly important roles. For instance, the author added the report, which is most likely true, that Charlemagne gave Charles the important duchy of Le Mans as early as 789.[74] On the occasion of Charlemagne's coronation as emperor in 800, he has young Charles also crowned king. All the other Frankish annals, including the *Annales regni Francorum*, our author's source, passed over young

70 P. Classen, 'Karl der Grosse und die Thronfolge im Frankenreich', in: *Festschrift für Hermann Keimpel*, III (Göttingen, 1972).

71 H. Mitteis, who points out that Alcuin himself had recently written his *De trinitate*, an important treatise on the mystery of the trinity in 802. H. Mitteis, 'Der Vertrag von Verdun im Rahmen der karolingischen Verfassungspolitik', in his *Die Rechtsidee in der Geschichte* (Weimar, 1957), pp. 429–30.

72 McKitterick, *Frankish Kingdoms*, p. 72. Ganshof, although conceding that the Frankish practice prevailed, nonetheless sees the obligation to protect the Church as a unifying factor and '... therefore ... the imperial idea was not wholly absent from the regulation'. Ganshof, *Frankish Institutions*, p. 17. See also Beumann, 'Nomen imperatoris', 540–9; Schlessinger, 'Kaisertum', *passim*; and D. Bullough, *The Age of Charlemagne* (London, 1965), p. 197.

73 Goffart, 'Paul the Deacon's *Gesta Episcoporum Mettensium*', 89–91.

74 Ed. von Simson, p. 78. The *Annales S. Amandi* for their year 789 (*MGH, SS*, I, p. 12) call it a *regnum ultra Segona*.

Charles's coronation in silence,[75] yet the *Annales Mettenses Priores* include the report and give him the title of king from this point forward.[76]

Be that as it may, the first section of the *Annales Mettenses Priores* is clearly far more of an historical justification for the traditional and Frankish system of succession by division than for any idea of united empire. The author is much occupied by the idea of division. At Pippin II's death in 714, he emphasised, the succession was to fall to Martel, not to Plectrud's grandson, Theudoald, because Pippin's other sons, Drogo and Grimoald, were already dead and because Pippin had ordained it that way.[77] For the division at Martel's death in 741, he adds in his own words that it was done 'fairly and equally between his sons'.[78] He then launches into a long original account of how the pretensions of Sonihild, whom he twice calls a concubine, and her thus illegitimate son by Martel, Grifo, violated the proper arrangements made for Carlomann and Pippin III, whom he calls the legitimate heirs.[79] Grifo appears over and over again, breaking the internal peace and disrupting the governance of the realm until his death in 753. It is very clear that the author did not like the fact that Martel was persuaded to include the illegitimate Grifo in the succession. This is the only error the author attributed to this otherwise perfect hero. The fact heightens the effect of his lesson that, when the succession is not effected legitimately, disastrous disruption of the internal peace follows. For Pippin III's death, he copied the report of the division between Carolmann and Charlemagne from the Continuator of Fredegar, adding significantly in two important original words that Pippin made the division *iure paterno*.[80]

Why then did our author write? It has been obvious to all the careful scholars who have studied these annals that they presented serious historical justification of the ruling position of the Carolingian family. The author's account shows each successive family leader as fulfilling a stage in God's plan, a plan which culminated in Charlemagne's glorious rule. A comparison with the *LHF* brings this into sharper

75 We know of it from a letter of Alcuin, ed. E. Dümmler, *MGH, Epistolae*, IV (Berlin, 1895), no. 217, p. 30, and from the *Liber Pontificalis*, ed. L. Duchesne, *Le Liber Pontificalis* (Paris, 1892), p. 7.

76 Classen, 'Karl der Grosse', 111.

77 Below, p. 365.

78 ... *inter filios suos aequa lance divisit* ... , ed. von Simson, p. 31, line 17.

79 Ed. von Simson, pp. 32–3.

80 Ed. von Simson, p. 55, line 24.

focus. The *Annales Mettenses Priores* are quite clear that it was not the family's early leading political position which put it on the path to imperial power but its place in the divine plan, buttressed by the Christian virtues of the family members. In the *LHF* Pippin II comes to power through the politics of family and faction. We have already mentioned the royal and imperial language the author of the *Annals of Metz* applied to the Carolingians in places where it does not rightfully belong; in the *LHF* there is none of this. As we have seen, the *LHF* was careful to point out that the Pippinids ruled under the Merovingian kings.[81] This author, on the other hand, has the Merovingians rule under the Pippinids. Immediately after the battle of Tertry, he shows us what the relationship between the kings and the family was: 'And when it [Paris] had been brought back by subjection to his [Pippin's] authority, taking [King] Theuderic as well, with unimaginable faithfulness he reserved the name of king for him lest he [Pippin] should seem to exercise tyranny or cruelty. But he retained the governance of the whole kingdom, the royal treasure, the ordering in law of private property, and the command of all the army.'[82] The author has Theuderic III rule three years under Pippin II;[83] and King Childebert, upon whom the author of the *LHF* heaped high praise,[84] dies 'with Pippin governing'.[85] The same is true for Charles Martel: 'When Charles, however, took the king [Chilperic II], he acted mercifully towards him and conceded his royal throne to him under his own [Martel's] authority.'[86]

It would, of course, be misguided for us to take the author's account of the Carolingians' rise at face value. In his ambition to glorify his heroes he is prone to factual error. For example, he has Pippin I govern a much larger area than he actually did.[87] Not only does he omit any account of the disastrous *coup* of Grimoald I, but he actually denies that this powerful Pippinid prince ever existed.[88] And he has

---

81 Above, p. 87.

82 Below, p. 359.

83 Below, p. 361.

84 '*vir inclytus*' (*LHF*, ch. 49, above, p. 93). '*bonae memoriae gloriosus*' (*LHF*, ch. 50, above, p. 94).

85 … *gubernante Pippino* … , ed. von Simson, p. 18, line 14., and below, p. 000.

86 Below, p. 370.

87 See below, p. 351, n. 103.

88 See below, p. 351, n. 104.

Pippin II conquer the Bavarians, something which Pippin never did.[89] It would be equally misguided to assume that the author's intentions were to falsely imbue the Pippinids with the new Roman idea of *imperium* or *regnum* when it had not belonged to them, in the hope that his contemporaries would believe him. The Carolingian learned world was well aware of who had been and who had not been a king or an emperor and was not likely to be fooled. Rather than impose a rule where it did not apply, the author set out to define for his readers what the nature of *regnum* and *imperium* was in the Frankish historical terms they understood. The theocratic nature of rule is always in the forefront for him; obviously rulers here as in all our sources must enjoy and court divine favour. But the co-operative nature of Frankish rule is as present in his work as is the divine plan. Although the nobility and the mechanism of *consilium* do not play here as close to centre stage as we have seem them do in the *LHF*, nonetheless this Carolingian author rarely lets the account of a year go by without mentioning that the king met in council with the great of the realm. His Pippinids do all the things that kings do: they consult, receive ambassadors, dispense justice, keep the internal peace and defeat foreign foes. For this author our modern distiction between traditional Frankish rule and Roman imperial rule would seem false. As he shows us on every page, *imperium* and *regnum* did not reflect new means which the family had recently acquired either in 768 or in 800, but represented the way this very Frankish family had always ruled. Einhard's worry about the importance of having the 'name' of king does not seem to trouble him.[90] In fact, his narration shows that the Merovingians had the royal title by the grace of the Pippinids and he uses this fact to list his heroes' virtues of faithfulness and humility in allowing them to retain it. Modern worries about the lack of the imperial title and a unified succession for the Empire in the *Divisio regnorum* would seem strange to him. For this author, writing in 805, with his close connections with Charlemagne's court, *consilium*, *regnum*, *imperium* and all the honorific adjectives used by the Romans represented the very Frankish way the Pippinids had always ruled from the days of Pippin I. His record of their deeds proved it.

89 See below, p. 353, n. 120.
90 Einhard, *Vita Karoli*, ch. 1., ed. L. Halphin, *Eginhard, Vie de Charlemagne* (Paris, 1967), p. 8.

The first section of *Annales Metteses Priores*[91] (The Earlier Annals of Metz)

In the six hundred and eighty-eighth year[92] from the incarnation of our Lord Jesus Christ, Pippin, son of the late most noble leader of the Franks, Ansegisel, happily succeeding his glorious father, took up the leadership[93] of the eastern Franks after many battles and triumphs given to him by God. And the commentaries on his memorable deeds, which he accomplished before his rule[94] or during it, shine forth, having been made known to all the people of the Franks. The leadership, however, stands as the crown of his famous victory and lasting praise because while still in the flower of youth and in inestimable good fortune he avenged the unjust death of his glorious father with the aid of divine power.[95] He brought low the perpetrator of this unspeakable crime, a man awash with foreign pleasures, killing him in a surprise attack by his youthful hand, yet with heroic ferocity.[96] This is not unlike what is read concerning David, who, with the Lord guiding him and with his youthful blow, deprived the immense Goliath of his life and head with his [Goliath's] own sword. When this most cruel tyrant named Gundoin[97] along with his followers had been killed, and when his riches had been given to his own faithful,[98] Pippin's power[99]

---

91 *Annales Mettenses Priores,* ed. B. von Simson, *MGH, SSRG* (Hanover and Leipzig, 1905).

92 The battle of Tertry happened in 687. The years given in the *Annales Mettenses* often do not correspond with the ones modern scholars prefer. See above, p. 333.

93 *principatum.* As far as we know, Ansegisel was never mayor of the palace. The word *principatum* here refers to the family's position of leadership, not the specific office of mayor.

94 *principatum*

95 *virtutis.* See above, pp. 67–8.

96 Paul the Deacon tells of how Pippin crossed the Rhine with only one follower and then surprised and killed a certain enemy (*adversarium quendam*) in his bedroom. Paul the Deacon, *Historia Langobardorum,* VI, ch. 37, eds. L. Bethmann and G. Waitz, *MGH, SSRL* (Hanover, 1878), pp. 177–8.

97 This is our earliest source for the name of Ansegisel's murderer. We know of a Gundoin who lived at about the same time and came from the middle Moselle. The two Gundoins may have been the same person. See Ebling, *Prosopographie,* p. 168; Ewig, *Trier im Merowingerreich. Civitas, Stadt, Bistum* (Trier, 1954), p. 137, n. 152; and *MGH, Dipl.* I, no. 29, p. 28.

98 Note the use of movable wealth for military and political purposes.

99 *virtus.* The word can also mean 'miracle'. Its double meaning may have been used to suggest that Pippin's power was God-given.

and victory were made known to the people far and wide. Then too when the leaders and the magnates of the Franks, whom his glorious father had fostered[100] and formerly elevated with highly honoured positions, heard of the death of the most evil tyrant, they were filled with great joy, hastened to Pippin, and gave themselves over to his authority along with all those whom they governed. As support, however, in the administration of such a large state, the Lord providing, he had his glorious mother, Begga by name, worthy of all praise.[101] She was the daughter of the late most excellent Pippin,[102] who with just laws governed the population living in the vast territories between the Forest of Charbonnière and the river Meuse up to the borders of the Frisians.[103] Doubtless, because offspring of the masculine sex was lacking to him,[104] he left his name along with his leadership to his surviving grandson,[105] Pippin.[106] The above-mentioned lady[107] Begga, filled with every good sense, daily instructed her son Pippin with the salutary exhortation that, with the Lord helping, he should keep himself in his coming rule[108] among the the teachings of his youth without the contagion of iniquity. But he, endowed with divine grace, surpassed all the salutary teachings of his mother in his energetic character. He shone with so great a light of prudence that he aroused the greatest admiration in the aged and higher-born people subject to him. For the strength of his justice, the unconquerable solidity of his bravery and the guidance of his moderation freely acquired such a place in the heart of this youth that the sources of these virtues[109] were believed without any doubt by all the people whom he

100 *nutriverat.* The same verb is used by the author of the *Vita Balthildis.* See above, p. 126.

101 This is the only mention of Begga's political regency; the Merovingian authors treat her religious life.

102 Pippin I (d. 639), often called Pippin of Landen.

103 The author has exaggerated the extent of Pippin's rule. The family's position seems to have been west of Namur and to have touched the Meuse only slightly, if at all. See Gerberding, *Rise,* p. 121 and the literature listed there.

104 This account is not true. Grimoald I, who staged a short-lived *coup* against the Austrasian royal house, was his son. See *LHF,* ch. 43, above, p. 88. Grimoald's failure would not fit this author's vision of divinely ordained success for the Pippinid family. See above, p. 348.

105 Classical use of *nepos,* 'grandson', not 'nephew'.

106 Pippin II (d. 714), often called Pippin of Herstal.

107 *Matrona.* See above, p. 69.

108 *regno.* The term is usually used for royal rule.

109 *virtutum.*

governed[110] to lie open to him not only from natural instillation (because he had possessed them from the unconquerable lineage of his parents) but also from divine inspiration.[111] As the founding basis of his rule[112] he had a close relative on his father's side, a certain man full of powers,[113] Arnulf by name, the bishop of Metz.[114] He of all the Franks is held before God and men to be a special patron. He nonetheless very often strengthened him [Pippin] with sacred admonitions and divine and human learning so that he would be strengthened for more important matters. He, indeed, being no slow listener, happily employed himself in all the Lord's commandments and works. In addition, his maternal aunt, named Geretrud,[115] a virgin consecrated to God, who, filled with the grace of God from the cradle of her infancy, gave herself over to the service of the immortal Lord, along with her mother, Itta,[116] having constructed a monastery in the place which is called Nivelles on her own inherited property, with a great band of virgins, repaid worthy service to the Lord. She therefore, with her fruitful stream of heavenly teaching, watered the young man's spirit as it exulted among the joys of fresh strength. Strengthened, therefore, by the teachings and most holy exhortations of these, as I would say,[117] holy relatives, he progressed along the pathways of justice to the governance of the realm[118] without stumbling. All the nobles of all the eastern Franks streamed to his court, and he became for them their defender against all rivals and their most just ruler in setting right their character.

110 *regebat.* Again royal.

111 This is far better in the Latin. From his parents the virtues came by *insertione,* a putting into, that is, the physical component. But from God they came by *inspiratione,* a breathing into, the spiritual component. Haselbach, 'Aufstieg', 49, uses this passage to claim that the author saw a Germanic holy lineage (*Sippenheil*) in Pippin's family. If so, this would be very important for the usurpers of the Merovingian throne, but the author makes no reference to any such sacred blood elsewhere.

112 *imperii.* Imperial vocabulary.

113 *virtutibus.*

114 Note that Arnulf is not called Pippin II's paternal grandfather, but simply a close relative. Von Simson thinks that the author does not want to admit that the Carolingian line came from a priest. On the other hand, the evidence for Arnulf as actual ancestor is very thin. See above, p. 309.

115 This is St Geretrud, whose *vita* is translated above, pp. 319–26.

116 Here called Itaberga, wife of Pippin I.

117 *ut ita dixerim.* The verb in the singular is strong evidence for single authorship.

118 *regni.*

In the six hundred and eighty-eighth year[119] from the incarnation of our Lord Jesus Christ, Pippin, in a favourable succession, took up the leadership of the eastern Franks, whom in their own language they call *Osterliudos.* Hereupon he brought under the yoke of his authority the Swabians, Bavarians,[120] and Saxons, worn down by repeated attacks and frequent battles. Indeed, these peoples and several others, acquired with many labours, submitted to the highest authority[121] of the Franks. But on account of the do-nothingness of the kings,[122] domestic disagreements, and civil wars, which had fallen upon many areas of the divided realm, they, one by one in their own land and deserting the lawful authority, attempted to defend their freedom with arms. But the unconquerable[123] leader Pippin, with the Lord's help, held this stubbornness in check by frequent expeditions, very effective military strategy, and frequent devastation. And, with divine power accompanying him, he brought the most savage nations under his own domination.

In the same period, Theuderic,[124] king of the western Franks, whom they call Neustrians, ruled the Empire,[125] having a mayor of the palace, Ebroin by name, a cruel man and prone to several vices.[126] At one point he, forced by certain circumstances, joined the monastery which is called Luxeuil, and there, the hair of his head having been cut, he, with a vow, took up the habit of the monastic life. But with the passing years, when another king[127] who had been friendly to him took up the rule of the Franks, he, leaving the monastery behind and keeping the habit only so far as the tonsure,[128] abandoned the monastic habit, took a wife, and again snatched up the position of mayor of the palace. But compared with the irregular and illicit way he succeeded to the management of the office, he exercised his rule even more perversely

119 This is 687, the same year as above.

120 As von Simson points out, Pippin II certainly did not conquer the Bavarians.

121 *imperio.*

122 Note the very different view of late Merovingian kings here from that in the *LHF.*

123 *invictus.* This regal adjective is commonly applied by the author to Pippin.

124 Theuderic III (673–90).

125 *imperium,* meaning land under a king's authority.

126 Neustrian mayor of the palace (*c.* 657–*c.* 680). This negative view of Ebroin is typical, probably because of the influence of the *Passio Leudegarii.* Compare the rather neutral view of him in the *LHF* above, pp. 89–91.

127 This was not another king but the same Theuderic III who was put back on the throne in 675. See *LHF,* ch. 45, above, p. 90.

128 *LHF,* ch. 45, says he let his hair grow. See above, p. 90.

and wickedly. For he so persecuted those who were seen as his adversaries in the loss of his first rule that he deprived some of their life, many of their freedom, and more of their private property.[129] And in this furore even Leudegar,[130] a bishop of exceptional holiness, was crowned with martyrdom because he alone tried to expose his insanity. At that time many of the noble Franks, because of the savageness of the aforesaid tyrant, abandoned Neustria, fled into Austrasia to Pippin, and begged his clemency, asking him to snatch them from the hands of their most cruel enemy. And he, moved by the effect of his usual faithfulness, mercifully received them. Truly, when almighty God had decreed an end to his monstrous power, Ebroin was slain by the nobleman Ermenfred, who, with the mighty tyrant prostrate, fled to Pippin.[131] And since the cause of the homicide which he had perpetrated was understood, he was received by him [Pippin] with his usual faithfulness, and by the law of humanity he was honourably joined to the other refugees. Since Ebroin had died, King Theuderic established Waratto,[132] an energetic man of illustrious standing, as mayor of the palace. This same Waratto, however, had a son named Ghislemar, a slippery and exceedingly sly man, who, gripped by the lust for power, deposed his father from his position and wickedly snatched up the power. There were many disagreements[133] between him and the unconquerable leader Pippin which the deservedly early death of Ghislemar ended. When Ghislemar died, his father was honoured with his original position. And he too departed from this life a short time later.[134]

Therefore in the year of the incarnation of our Lord 689, Waratto having died, his son-in-law,[135] Berchar, was was set up as mayor of the

129 See Fredegar, *Contin.*, chs. 2–4, and *LHF*, ch. 45, above, p. 91.

130 Bishop of Autun, whose *vita* is translated above, pp. 215–51.

131 *LHF*, ch. 47, above, p. 91.

132 A leading nobleman from the lower Seine near Rouen. Pippin will gain entry into Neustrian ruling circles by marrying his son, Drogo, to Waratto's daughter, Anstrud. Waratto's importance is indicated by his appearance in many sources: *Gesta Sanctorum Patrum Fontanellensis Coenobii*, IV, 1 (hereafter, *Gesta Font.*), eds. Lohier and Laporte (Rouen, 1936), p. 39; *Vita Condedi anachoretae Belcinnacenses*, ch. 8, ed. W. Levison, *MGH, SSRM*, V, p. 650; *Vita Filiberti Abbatis Gemeticensis et Heriensis*, ch. 31, ed. W. Levison, *MGH, SSRM*, V, p. 600; *LHF*, ch. 47, above, pp. 91–2; and Fredegar, *Contin.*, ch. 4, p. 84, where the story of Waratto and his son, Ghislemar, is the same but expressed in different words.

133 The *LHF* and Fredegar's continuator express these disagreements in military terms: *bella civilia et multae discordiae*.

134 Waratto died about 686. Cf. Ewig, 'Teilreiche', 138.

135 The exact relationships within this family cannot be determined with certainty.

palace by King Theuderic.[136] Berchar did not vary from the character
of the impious Ghislemar, [acting] outside the intelligence of mind
and the wisdom of earthly advice. Therefore the refugees,[137] whom
Pippin in his mercy had taken up, approached him [Pippin] with
frequent complaints, beseeching him to avenge their wrongs out of
divine love. But Pippin with a calm spirit peacefully sent ambassadors
to Theuderic requesting him to order that the refugees, whom Ebroin
out of his greed had expelled from their land and had despoiled of their
goods, should be returned and called back to their own homes by royal
justice, with their patrimonies restored which had been unjustly
carried off, and that the rules of fairness should be preserved. At
Berchar's entreaty, Theuderic received this legation haughtily and
promised that he at any moment would seek his runaway servants,
whom Pippin had taken up contrary to justice and the law. The legates
returned, bore Theuderic's response to Pippin, pointed out the
haughtiness of the king, reported the threats which he had poured out,
and made clear Berchar's shallowness and inconstancy. Pippin, with
the nobles agreeing, brought the matter into the open and in turn
exposed the response of the haughty king, exhibited the tears and
wretched supplications of the refugees who had entrusted themselves
to his protection, and recalled to mind the threats of the wicked
prince.[138] He also explained the danger which, because of the reception
of the exiles, threatened his homeland unless it could be wisely averted
before it arrived and he sought to learn what was to be done by him
concerning them.

In the year of the incarnation of our Lord 690[139] all Pippin's leaders
decided wholeheartedly to take up arms, to fight for the robbed and

---

The first continuator of Fredegar (ch. 5) tells us that Berchar was Ansfled's son-
in-law but does not tell us which daughter he married. Here the *Annales Mettenses*
name the daughter Anstrud. This is the version most scholars have accepted.
Lohier and Laporte, however, in their edition of the *Gesta Font.*, p. 37, n. 94, claim
instead that Berchar was married to Ansfled and that Anstrud was his daughter,
not Waratto's. This version derives from a charter of King Childebert III, *ChLA*,
no. 581, which names Anstrud as Drogo's wife and Berchar as his father-in-law.
See Gerberding, *Rise*, p. 92, n. 1; Ebling, *Prosopographie*, pp. 234–5; Ewig,
'Teilreiche', 140–1, n. 217; and Krusch, *SSRM, II*, p. 323.

136 Berchar was probably made mayor in 686 and certainly before the battle of Tertry
    in 687. The date given here is again incorrect.
137 Fredegar, *Contin.*, ch. 5, is more specific: ... *Audoramnus, Reolus, et alii multi,
    relinquentes Bercharium, ad Pippinum per obsides coniungunt* ...
138 *improbi principis. Princeps* used for the king (Theuderic).
139 687. See Krusch, *SSRM, II*, p. 322, n. 5.

wretched who had safely sought his protection and defence, and to
defend the fatherland not from a plundering [i.e. invading] enemy but
by a deterrent foray into their [the enemy's] haunts. When he
received from the magistracy[140] the plan which it was considering,
Pippin was filled with great joy and he gathered the army with which
he would prevent the boasting of the stubborn king. When the army
had been assembled, Pippin came to the Forest of Charbonnière, the
boundary which had divided both kingdoms. When his nobles, or
rather his whole army, had been called together, he made known his
intention in a brief address. 'Oh, most brave men, our faithful of God,'
he said, 'lest any one of you think that I wish to exercise tyranny or
cruelty in such a journey and not that I have been forced by a triple
necessity to call you forth to such a battle, briefly listen to me as I
speak, and hear what forces me to this. I am incited especially by the
complaints of the priests and the servants of God who have very often
approached me to help them, on account of love of the Lord, to
intervene, or even to fight, for the possessions of their churches,
illegally taken. Very frequently through ambassadors I humbly
besought Theuderic for them, whence I managed to receive nothing
but a pompous response full of pride. The second cause which
provokes me to such an undertaking is the tears and lamentations of
the noble Franks fleeing to our protection, who, oppressed by the
torments of so many losses, unceasingly think us able to obtain divine
help. Third, because it will help us to obviate the intentions of the most
haughty king so that we may rather, with the Lord helping, turn the
devastation of our fatherland, which he unjustly threatens, into his
own destruction, and that we, who will submit to the judgement of the
Lord, may force him to expropriate in his own haunts, [leaving] our
land unharmed. For the love of the Lord and his saints, we endure
struggles of this type.' When these things were said, the whole people
were strengthened and at the same time with their voices and clashing
of arms they confirmed the sentiments of their leader. Then, having
unanimously invoked the help of God, they crossed the above-
mentioned Forest of Charbonnière, militarily devastating everything,
bravely came to the interior sections of that kingdom, and pitched
their camp not far from Saint-Quentin en Vermandois, near a villa
whose name is Tertry. When Theuderic, therefore, had heard that an
enemy was dwelling in the interior of his kingdom, he gathered an
army, drew up a battle line against Pippin, and pitched his camp on

140 *a magistratu.* A term unknown in the Merovingian sources.

another side of the said villa. Between them flowed a stream, small
indeed but difficult to cross, which is called the Omignon by the locals.
Pippin, therefore, had camped to the north of this stream, Theuderic
to the south. Pippin, therefore, *sent legates* to Theuderic. *Offering conditions
of peace,*[141] he indicated the causes of his coming, that is, that he
[Pippin] should intercede with him on behalf of the churches of God,
in order that what evil tyrants had taken away from them he
[Theuderic] should replace in their common alms for the refugees
who had sought his [Pippin's] protection, that he [Theuderic] order
justice to be done concerning their expropriated possessions. He also
promised to donate many pounds of gold and silver if [Theuderic]
would acquiesce to his requests and choose to make peace with him
rather than war, lest, when he refused, a civil war should come about
in which most noble[142] and kindred blood[143] of the Franks would be
poured forth in the fickle attack of battle. When the messengers of the
legation performed their duty, Theuderic addresses[144] his counsellors
and asks what is to be done about these matters. Berchar, in his usual
manner, with evil advice, casts aside the peace offered by Pippin, urges
that the enemy should be driven from the homeland by arms so that
they would atone with their blood for the damage which they had
perpetrated on this campaign. Theuderic, therefore, declares war and,
shamelessly addressing the legates of Pippin, orders them to return to
their own [places], and rejects *the conditions of peace.*[145] The legates
inform Pippin concerning all these things. And he quickly makes these
things known to his nobles and finds nothing else remaining but to
vanquish with Christ's help the grasping fury of the proud [enemy].
Then that whole day both sides deliberated concerning the beginning
of the battle – not, however, with equal plans. For Theuderic with
lifeless words was boasting in the magnitude of his innumerable people
rather than in the counsel of prudence, confident that Pippin together
with his whole army had already been handed over to him. And he
affirmed that Pippin had sought peace for no reason other than that,

141 Luke 14:32.

142 *nobilissimus.* The word is used here without imperial connotations. See the
discussion above, p. 341.

143 *cognatus sanguis.* This author, like the author of the *LHF*, has grave concern for the
spilling of Frankish blood by Franks. See also below at the battle of Vinchy , p. 000.

144 The author, here as elsewhere, shifts into the historic present tense to add
vividness to his account.

145 Luke 14:32.

146 *dulcibus alloquiis,* Horace, *Epodes,* XIII, line 18.

terrified with trembling, he did not dare to join battle with him. Pippin, on the other hand, warned his nobles with *sweet encouragement*[146] to commend themselves with prayers and offerings, as ones to be defended, to the omnipotence of God, who gives honour and victory *to all who fear him and keep his precepts.*[147] He [Pippin] did not hesitate to set himself against such great dangers, not because of any greed for rule but on account of the complaints of the oppressed who had sought his protection, having invoked the name of the Lord. In good faith, then, he declared himself about to go out to battle, which he waged for the love of Him who has the power *to save those trusting in Him*[148] and who examines both the desires of all and the intentions of the heart in the inescapable light of His knowledge. With these and like encouragements, he so *strengthened the hearts*[149] of his faithful that they intoned thanks to the almighty Lord with a *glad heart*[150] as if the victory were already won from on high. Therefore, with one mind, they girded themselves for battle. Pippin, therefore, from a certain rather high hill, with his very wise forethought, selected the place for the battle and pointed out with careful observation where it must be approached. The leader Pippin therefore spent that day with the night *on a great sea of cares.*[151] At the break of day, he led his troops from the camp, crossed the river Omignon in complete silence, and on the east side of Theuderic's camp, as he had decided on the day before, he stationed his battle line. He handed over each legion to its leader and, as they patiently awaited the sunrise, announced that, with God's help, the eye of the enemy would reel under the reverberating rays of the sun, but for him and his men the light infused with comfort would help fighting the enemy. When the sun had already risen, Theuderic's men informed him that Pippin's camp had been deserted and destroyed by fire. Hearing these things, he led his troops from the camp to pursue the enemy; but leader Pippin attacked him, being courageous and superior in both plan and arms. When they had engaged this extremely fierce battle, *Theuderic, along with his counsellor Berchar, having turned to flight,*[152] left behind all his nobles *killed by the sword.*[153] He did not end

147 Psalms 118 (119):63.
148 Psalms 16 (17):7.
149 *pectora roborant*, Horace, *Carmen* IV, 4, line 34.
150 III (I) Kings 8:66.
151 *Aeneid* VIII, 19.
152 *LHF*, ch. 48, above, p. 92.

the course of the flight he had undertaken until he had crossed the flowing waters of the river Seine. Berchar, also, driven and wandering, stricken with fear, and hiding in various places, was at last killed by his own people not tolerating his foolishness. And Pippin, the victor, invading the enemy's camp and returning thanks to God, shares the ample spoils with his faithful. Many, however, having slipped away by flight from the battle, entrusted themselves for protection to churches and monasteries. Of these the greatest crowd sought refuge at the portals of blessed Quentin the martyr,[154] and some at the monastery of the Irish at Péronne, in which blessed Furseus rests in the body.[155] As the abbots of those places intervened on their behalf, the most gentle leader Pippin spared the life and inheritance of them all, taking only vows from them. Setting out from there, he pursued the fleeing Theuderic and arrived at the city of Paris. And when it [Paris] had been brought back by subjection to his authority, taking Theuderic as well, with unimaginable faithfulness he reserved the name of king for him lest he [Pippin] should seem to exercise tyranny or cruelty. But he retained the ordering of private property in law,[156] the governance of the whole kingdom, the royal treasure, and the command of all the army.

Therefore in the year of the incarnation of our Lord Jesus Christ 691,[157] Pippin took over sole leadership of the Franks, and, having set right all the confiscations which in those regions had come about over many years through the greed and injustice of the leaders, he returned the whole fatherland to a most peaceful state, flourishing in the service of Christ. Therefore from that time, He [Christ] no longer pressed a struggle on the invincible leader for the leadership of the Franks but for the acquisition of the various peoples who had once been subjected to the Franks, that is, [a struggle] against the Saxons, Frisians, Alemans, Bavarians, Aquitainians, Gascons and Britons. For the leaders of those peoples, having turned into stubbornness, withdrew themselves in evil presumption from the rule of the Franks because of the idleness of the [Franks'] former leaders. The most excellent leader

---

153 *in ore gladii.* A common biblical expression, e.g. I Samuel 15:8.

154 This is probably Saint-Quentin to the south-east of Tertry and not the abbey of Mont-Saint-Quentin, north of Péronne. See Dierkens, *Abbayes,* p. 308.

155 See the *Addit. Nivial.,* above, p. 327.

156 *propriae facultatis iure disponenda.* Perhaps meaning the *placita,* the formal law cases heard in the royal court.

157 687.

Pippin[158] had already subjugated certain of these, those who had emerged as rebels for a short time. Having wisely arranged all things in the guidance of the western realm, he returned with the highest glory and exultation to the seat of his own eastern rule.[159] And there, with Christ providing, in favourable circumstances, giving thanks to God his protector, he happily completed the remaining time of that year's cycle.

Whereupon, in the year of the Lord's incarnation 692,[160] Pippin ordered the whole army of the Franks to unite. With plans for the well-being of the realm having been drawn up, he went out to oppose the pride of Radbod, leader of the Frisians, who was so enveloped by a fog of stupidity that he presumed to prepare for battle against the unconquerable leader Pippin. Defeated, however, and put to flight in [the battle], he lost the greater part of his army. Led by a belated repentance, he sent legates to Pippin, sued for peace, and placed himself along with those whom he ruled under his authority. With hostages also being given, he becomes a tributary of Pippin. When these things were completed, he [Pippin] ordered a synod to convene, and when the well-being of the churches, orphans and widows had been considered at it,[161] he stationed himself with his followers in the richest[162] seats of his realm for winter quarters. But each year on the kalends of March he held a general council with all the Franks, according to the custom of the ancients.[163] In which, on account of his [Pippin's] respect for the name of king, he ordered him [the king], whom he had placed before himself because of the magnitude of his [Pippin's] humility and clemency, to preside while offerings were received from all the nobles of the Franks, pledges made for peace and for the defence of the churches of God, orphans and widows, the rape

158 The author may mean Pippin I, whom he describes with the same phrase above (*precellentissimus princeps Pippinus*) when describing his rule between the Carbonnaria and the Meuse.

159 *imperii*.

160 689. See *LHF*, ch. 49, above, p. 93; Fredegar, *Contin.*, ch. 6; and Bede, *HE*, V, ch. 10.

161 See the *Vita Dagoberti III*, ch. 8, ed. B. Krusch, *MGH, SSRM*, II, p. 516, where the wording is almost identical to that used here. Widows and orphans were under royal protection. Having Pippin provide for them is another way to show the royal nature of the Pippinids' position.

162 The edited text has *opinatissimis*, which makes no sense. We have used *opulentissimis* from ms. A2.

163 The Merovingians often held this great gathering, which served military, judicial and royal purposes, at Compiègne. See Ewig, 'Teilreich', 89–90, n. 6.

of women and arson forbidden with a stern decree, and an order was also given to the army that, on whatsoever day it should be determined, they must be prepared to set out for a region which he [Pippin] had chosen. With these things concluded, he sent the king to the royal villa[164] at Montmacq to be kept in custody with honour and respect.[165] He, then, girded in strength, with divine help as his companion, governed the kingdom of the Franks internally with justice and peace and externally with most prudent policies and the unconquerable protection of arms, with the Lord helping. Delegations, however, of the nations living round about, that is, the Greeks, Romans, Lombards, Huns, Slavs and Saracens, poured in to him. *And the fame of* his victory and triumphs so *went out among all peoples*[166] that, deservedly on account of his virtue and prudence, all the nations round about sought his friendship[167] with great gifts and rewards. And, receiving them kindly, he rewarded them with even greater gifts and sent them home. And he, with no less speed, sending his own legates through the various regions at the right moment for the well-being of his realm,[168] obtained peace and friendship from the surrounding peoples with the greatest goodwill.

In the six hundred and ninety-third year[169] of the incarnation of our Lord Jesus Christ, in the third year of the single leadership of Pippin, Theuderic, who ruled fourteen years before he was conquered by Pippin and three years under him, died.[170] And following him, on account of the effect of his [Pippin's] above-mentioned loyalty, his young son named Clovis was appointed king by Pippin.[171] And he, when he had completed his fourth year on the throne, ended his

164 *villam publicam.* The ususal term for a royal residence.

165 This is a great distortion and disagrees greatly with the view of the late Merovingians held by the author of the *LHF.* See above, p. 348.

166 Matthew 9:26.

167 *Amicitia.* A treaty concluded by exchanging gifts and oaths.

168 *imperii sui.*

169 690.

170 The *LHF*, ch. 49, says he ruled nineteen years, Fredegar, *Contin.,* ch. 6, the source for the annals, says seventeen. Note that the Latin uses ordinal numbers for the incarnation and for Pippin, and cardinal numbers for Theuderic's regnal indication. Most have followed Krusch in placing Theuderic III's death in 691. Wallace-Hadrill, *Fredegar,* p. 85, says 690–91.

171 Fredegar, *Contin.,* ch. 6. See *LHF,* ch. 49, above, p. 93. Neither of these sources makes mention of Pippin supposedly appointing (*a Pippino ordinatur*) the new king. He is known as Clovis III (691–94).

innocent life.[172] But Pippin nonetheless established Childebert,[173] his
brother, as king in his place. Indeed, giving to these men the name of
kings, he kept the reins of the whole realm and governed with the
highest glory and honour. Therefore as the yearly cycles slipped away
and the neighbouring peoples were subjected and tamed, Pippin
organised his rule of the Franks with wonderful order. He made his
firstborn son, Drogo, leader of the Burgundians, of Rheims, Sens, and
of the other cities belonging to his duchy,[174] giving him Anstrud as his
wife, the daughter of the late mayor of the palace, Waratto, and widow
of Berchar,[175] who, as we have related above, had fled from the battle
at Tertry and perished, having been killed by his own people. This
woman bore Drogo a son, whom she named Hugo.[176] And his devoted
and energetic grandmother, the Lady[177] Ansfled, that is, Waratto's
widow, took him in order to bring him up.[178] This woman, therefore,
filled with the spirit of wisdom and thoughtful diligence, is said to have
so strengthened the mind of the boy with daily teachings that he gave
himself over, along with all that he had, to the service of God. Whence
it came about that, imbued with eagerness for sacred writings, he
excelled all his fellows in wisdom and devotion, and, following the
suggestion of his outstanding provider [Ansfled], he began to despise
all worldly things and to strive eagerly for the heavenly realms. *His*
[*Pippin's*] *younger son, Grimoald by name, he set up as mayor of the palace
with King Childebert.*[179] *This Grimoald was an extremely mild man, full of
every goodness and gentleness.*[180] And, as he had learned from his father,
he ruled the Franks with the highest vigilance and piety.

---

172 Fredegar, *Contin.*, ch. 6. The *LHF*, ch. 49, says he ruled two years.

173 Childebert III (694–711). Again the *LHF* and the Fredegar Continuator make no
mention of Pippin's role in the succession.

174 The *LHF*, ch. 48, above, p. 93, says he received the duchy of Champagne. Part of
this sentence was falsely placed in the mansucripts. We have moved it here as von
Simson suggests in his edition, p. 16, n. 5.

175 There is conflicting evidence concerning Berchar's familial relationship. See above,
p. 354, n. 135.

176 He later became archbishop of Rouen, bishop of both Paris and Bayeux, and the
abbot of Saint-Wandrille and Jumièges.

177 *matrona*.

178 The fact that Hugo was brought up not by the Pippinids but by his maternal
grandmother has important implications for the political struggles which followed
Pippin II's death in 714. See Gerberding, *Rise*, p. 138.

179 Childebert III (694–711).

180 Fredegar, *Contin.*, ch. 6. See *LHF*, chs. 49 and 50, above, pp. 93–4.

In the six hundred and ninety-seventh year from the incarnation of Our Lord, the leader *Pippin* led an army *against* the Frisians and *Radbod*, their savage and pagan *leader*,[181] who had often defied the orders of the leader Pippin and was troubling the borderlands of his territory[182] with frequent invasions. Therefore, with his army assembled, he pitched camp[183] near the stronghold called Durstede. And Radbod went out against him with a strong and haughty band, and, drawing up their lines against each other, they joined in a mighty battle where the Frisians were struck down in a great defeat. *Since their leader Radbod fled, Pippin emerged the victor. Having taken many spoils, the victor returned*[184] to his own [lands]. From that time on each year Pippin bravely defeats the peoples round about and subjected them to his authority.

Several years had slipped by *since these events* when, in the seven hundred and eighth year from the incarnation of the Lord, *Pippin's son, Drogo, died and was buried near the city of Metz in the basilica of blessed Arnulf, the confessor.*[185] And since his father Pippin arranged it, his brother Grimoald succeeded him in leadership.

In the seven hundred and ninth year from the incarnation of the Lord Pippin led an army against the Alemans, triumphed magnificently over them, and conquered all that region.

In the seven hundred and tenth year, Pippin again led an army against the rebellious Alemans. And with the same region aflame, and with having taken many captives and spoils, he returns the victor to this own [lands]. In the same year the waters overflowed in force.[186]

In the seven hundred and eleventh year from the incarnation of the Lord King Childebert died.[187] *He was buried in Choisy-au-Bac*[188] *in the basilica of St Stephen the Martyr. He had reigned*, with Pippin governing,

---

181 689. See *LHF*, ch. 49, and Fredegar, *Contin.*, ch. 6. Bede, *HE*, V, ch. 10, ed. Plummer, vol. I, p. 299: ... *quia* [*Pippinus dux Francorum*] *nuper citeriorem Fresiam, expulso inde Rathbodo rege, ceperat.*

182 *Principatum* used geographically.

183 The phrase *castra metatus est* is common in these annals and is also a favourite of Caesar's.

184 Fredegar, *Contin.*, ch. 6.

185 Fredegar, *Contin.*, ch. 6. Cf. *LHF*, ch. 49, above, p. 93. The *LHF* does not mention Metz or the basilica of St Arnulf.

186 711. The information about the flood comes from the *Annales Petaviani* for their year 711, ed. G. Pertz, *MGH, SS*, I (Hanover, 1826), p. 7.

187 Childebert III (694–711).

188 Seine-et-Oise.

for sixteen years.[189] After his death, Pippin, in his usual faithfulness, appointed his [Childebert's] son, Dagobert, king. At that time *Grimoald took the daughter of Radbod, leader of the Frisians, as his wife.*[190]

In the seven hundred and twelfth year Pippin again, moved by the stubbornness of the Alemans, crossed the Rhine with a mighty band, overturned that whole region, and brought it under his authority.

In the seven hundred and thirteenth year the leader Pippin arranged *the conditions of peace*[191] within the confines of his authority and in that year he led an army into no region.

In the seven hundred and fourteenth year from the incarnation of the Lord, *when Pippin grew ill in* the royal villa of *Jupille, which is located on the river Meuse,* his son *Grimoald hastened to visit him and, as he proceeded to prayer in the basilica of St Lambert the Martyr,* and as he persisted a long while lying face down in his prayer, he was run through with a sword *by a most evil man named Rantgar*[192] and he died. But out of just retribution, leader Pippin, recovering from his illness, killed all those who had been part of the plot.[193] *And in Grimoald's place as mayor of the palace with King Dagobert he appointed his little boy named Theudoald, born of a concubine.*[194] In the same year the leader *Pippin,* having reduced all

189 Fredegar, *Contin.,* ch. 7. Cf. *LHF,* ch. 50, above, p. 94, which more correctly says he reigned seventeen years.

190 Fredegar, *Contin.,* ch. 7. Cf. *LHF,* ch. 50, above, p. 94, which gives us her name, Theudesinda.

191 Luke 14:32.

192 Fredegar, *Contin.,* ch. 7. Cf. *LHF,* ch. 50, above, p. 94. According to the *Annales Sancti Amandi,* ed. G. Pertz, *MGH, SS,* I (Hanover, 1826), p. 6, for their year 714, Grimoald died in the month of April and his father, Pippin, in December.

193 Note that this sentence is one in the author's own words is wedged between two that he took from the continuator of Fredegar.

194 Fredegar, *Contin.,* ch. 7. The *LHF,* ch. 50, also mentions his birth by a concubine. Theudoald was probably born about 708. This date is based upon the account in *LHF,* which reports his birth at the time Drogo died. This would make him only six years old in 714 and would explain the use of *filium parvulum,* both by the author of the *Annales Mettenses* and by Fredegar's continuator, who in turn was his source. Not all modern scholars agree. J. Semmler, 'Zur Pippinidisch-Karolingischen Suzessionskrise', *Deutsches Archiv,* 33 (1977), 3, offers doubts; Bonnell, *Anfänge,* p. 130, n. 9, thinks he was born in 691. In 715 we find him urging King Dagobert III to issue a confirmation for Saint-Denis in *Gesta Font.,* III, 4, p. 29. The question of Theudoald's age is far from moot, for if he were only six at the time he became mayor, and only nine when he took part in the important legal matters reflected in King Dagobert's charter, he would obviously have performed his functions in name only, indicating that the Pippinids controlled those functions by a right of succession. This would, however, not necessarily have been the case if he were already an adult.

the neighbouring peoples to the domination of the Franks, again *weakened by bodily illness, died* in peace on 16 December.[195] *He had ruled*[196] *the people of the Franks for twenty-seven years and six months. He left a surviving son named Charles.*[197] When Pippin died, the greatest disorder grew up among the people of the Franks. For his elder sons, Drogo and Grimoald, had departed from this life while he was still living. Theudoald, Grimoald's son by a concubine,[198] was still a boy. And although he had succeeded his father in the leadership, he was hardly able to direct the head of so great an affair. But Charles, whom his father had left behind as the only surviving heir worthy of such great power, was gravely suffering the plots of his stepmother. Because Grimoald's mother, Plectrud, desired to promote her grandson, Theudoald, she was keeping Charles from the legitimate governance of his father's authority[199] and she herself, with the infant, in a womanly plan, presumed to control the reins of so great a kingdom. Because she had decided to rule with feminine cunning more cruelly than was necessary, she quickly turned the wrath of the Neustrian Franks to the destruction of her grandson and the leaders who were with him. And they, rushing upon them in a surprise attack in the Forest of Compiègne, butchered them in a very great slaughter.[200] Theudoald along with a few escaped with difficulty, but at a time not much later he ended his innocent life.[201] And in his place they appointed Raganfred as mayor of the palace under King Dagobert.[202]

---

195 714.

196 *rexit*, again royal language.

197 Fredegar, *Contin.*, ch. 8. The *LHF* in ch. 51, above, p. 94, makes the same report but with significant differences in vocabulary: *obtenuitque principatum sub suprascriptos reges annis 27 et dimidos.* Note that in the *LHF* Pippin held the *principatum*, he did not reign (*rexit*), and that he held it under (*sub*) the Merovingian kings. The *LHF* makes no mention here of Charles Martel.

198 The author is emphasising Theudoald's illegitimate birth.

199 *Imperii.*

200 This is known as the battle of Compiègne (715), also reported by *LHF*, ch. 51, above, p. 94, and Fredegar, *Contin.*, ch. 8.

201 The author may be in error concerning Theudoald's death date. The *Annales Laureshamenses./Alamannici./Nazariani., MGH, SS,* I, pp. 26–7, relate the death of a Theudoald in 741 who may have been this mayor. For a discussion of the *Annales Mettenses'* motive for claiming that Theudoald died as a child, see Roger Collins, 'Deception and Misrepresentation in Early Eighth-century Frankish Historiography: Two Case Studies', in J. Jarnut, U. Nonn, and M. Richter (eds.), *Karl Martell in seiner Zeit*, Beihefte der *Francia*, 37 (Sigmaringen, 1994), pp. 230–5.

202 Dagobert III (711–15).

Then that people [the Neustrians], forgetful of all the benefits of the invincible leader Pippin,²⁰³ *hastened* with full force into Austrasia *up to the river Meuse and laid waste that whole region. They also concluded a pact with Radbod, leader²⁰⁴* of the Frisians, against the Pippinids.²⁰⁵ But the Lord, who giveth and upbraideth not, rescuing Charles from the plots of his stepmother, brought him openly before the trembling peoples. Then just as the eclipsed sun gradually unveils its bright rays to the whole world, so Charles, the most worthy heir of Pippin, began to shine forth as a mighty defender before a people suffering and almost despairing of hope. As, however, he appeared to the hesitating people, he was received with such favour and rejoicing by everyone it was as if their ruler Pippin had come to life for their comfort.

In the second year after the death of his father, Pippin, Charles obtained the leadership of the Austrasians. For in the first year after the death of Pippin, Raganfred *devastated* the Austrasians *up to the river Meuse and entered into a pact with Radbod.*²⁰⁶ The Saxons, too, devastated the land of the Attuarii.²⁰⁷

*At the same time King Dagobert died; he had ruled five years,*²⁰⁸ and Chilperic²⁰⁹ succeeded him. When, therefore, this same Chilperic along with Raganfred heard that Charles in great part had already ascended the throne of his father, out of envy, or indeed fear, they assembled an army against him. Charles, however, the most excellent leader, having learned of the coming of Radbod, went out against him. They engaged in battle and a great slaughter resulted on both sides. *When night disrupted the slaughter,*²¹⁰ each host retreated to its own.²¹¹ Charles, however, decided to increase his forces in order to resist the enemy. Going out from there, sending legates hither and yon, he ordered an army to

203 *invicti principis pippini.* Imperial language, see above, p. 342.

204 Fredegar, *Contin.,* ch. 8. Cf. *LHF,* ch. 51, above, p. 94.

205 *Pipinios.*

206 Fredegar, *Contin.,* ch. 8. Cf. *LHF,* ch. 51, above, p. 94.

207 *Annales. S. Amandi, Tiliani, Petaviani* for their year 715, *MGH, SS,* I, p. 7.

208 Fredegar, *Contin.,* ch. 9; *LHF,* ch. 52, above, p. 95; *Annales Petaviani, MGH, SS,* I, p. 7. Dagobert III died between 26 September 715 and 29 February 716. E. Ewig, 'Studien zur merowingischen Dynastie', *Frühmittelalterliche Studien,* 8 (1974), 27.

209 Chilperic II (715–21), formerly known as the monk, Daniel. See *LHF,* ch. 52, above, p. 95.

210 *Dirimente nocte cedem.* A very classical phrase used by Caesar, Virgil, Livy and Ovid.

211 In direct opposition to the version of this battle given here, the *LHF,* ch. 52, above, p. 95, tells us that Charles was soundly defeated by Radbod and forced to flee.

assemble to defend the homeland so that it might attack the invading army at the proper moment. While these things were being done, a messenger arrived and made it known that Chilperic with Raganfred had crossed the forest of the Ardennes with a large army. Then the far-seeing leader Charles divided his army into many parts, and placed them among hilly positions in order to ambush the enemy in both directions. He, with nearly five hundred men, by climbing, gains the forest of the Ardennes and the villa of Amblève, and, viewing the enemy's camp from the top of a hill, he considered in most prudent thought what defeat he would be able to inflict upon them. For their army was exceedingly large, covering the whole plain in which the royal villa of Amblève was situated. It was, however, the hour of the noon meal, and, as the summer weather[212] recommended, Chilperic's forces were refreshing their bodies under tents and sunshades. And as the unconquerable leader was viewing everything[213] from the top of the overhanging hill, one of the soldiers came to him asking that he might be permitted to disrupt the enemy's lines with a single attack. And when he finally with difficulty obtained this through his entreaties, he took up his course with haste and attacked the centre of the line of the reclining men. Also, at a distance, he took up his shield, drew his sword and, changing his course from the midst to the flanks, he slew all those whomsoever he came upon, proclaiming to them in a loud voice that Charles was about to appear. Therefore they rush upon him from all sides and press forward to cut down the shouting[214] enemy. But he hastened by the swiftest course to reach the safe headquarters of his lord. Charles, however, seeing his soldier in great danger of his life, did not allow him thus positioned to perish, but quickly orders his comrades to take up arms and as the brave rescuer he rushes to his endangered servant. Snatching him [to safety], he drives off the enemy and turns an innumerable multitude of the adversaries to flight. Many of them fled for safety to the church which was located in that villa of Amblève. And when a certain one in the haste of his flight hurried to enter it, one of the pursuers with his sword quickly cut off

---

212 The usual date for this battle is April 716. April is a month which does not have summer weather in Belgium. This detail raises the suspicion that the author is giving us a fictitious account of the battle.

213 The Latin of the edition makes no sense at this point. We have used a manuscript variant (ed. von Simson, p. 22, n. g) which has *omnia* instead of *lumine.* In so doing we disagree with von Simson who would change *imminenti lumine* to *imminentem hostem.*

214 *bachantem.*

his trailing foot which was outside the threshold of the church. And when his comrades, in a pious state of mind, asked him accusingly why he had violated the enclosure of the church, he is said to have responded that he had been careful not to touch what the church contained; what, however, in the speed of the chase, he had found outside the walls he asserted to have amputated legally. The most serene leader Charles, however, spared the life of those who had fled to the church for refuge, and he permitted them to depart unharmed after Chilperic, who was fleeing to the plain. But he, having taken spoils from the enemy, remained for a time in his own lands.[215] But Chilperic with his wounded army continued to the city of Cologne.[216] But since he was attempting to take it and persevering in a doubtful outcome of the battle, and since the advent of Charles frightened him day and night, he took money from the townsmen and, with what speed he could muster, entered the safety of his own kingdom, not as a victor but as a fugitive.

In the seven hundred and seventeenth year from the incarnation of our Lord, leader Charles, not unmindful of the injustices of Chilperic, gathered an army from the east, crossed the Forest of Charbonnière and in part laid Chilperic's kingdom waste.[217] When Chilperic discovered this, he likewise, along with Raganfred, his mayor of the palace,[218] hastened out to meet him in order to defend their fatherland. Each army, however, encamped not very distant from the other in the area of Cambrai near the villa of Vinchy. The leader Charles, however, in the manner of his ancestors, *sends his legates* to Chilperic, *requesting conditions of peace.*[219] And lest the blood of the noble Franks be poured out among them,[220] he urges that the leadership of his father be restored to him. He says that it is known to all that his father Pippin had once governed the western Franks with justice and piety and that he demanded nothing

---

215 Further evidence that Martel's landed base was near Amblève on the middle Meuse. See Gerberding, *Rise,* pp. 119–26.

216 Both the *LHF,* ch. 52, above, p. 95, and Fredegar, *Contin.,* ch. 9, report that the battle of Amblève happened not on Chilperic's way to, but on his return from, Cologne.

217 See the accounts in *LHF,* ch. 53, above, p. 95, and Fredegar, *Contin.,* ch. 10, which describe the same battle in different words.

218 Here we have Martel called *princeps* and Raganfred called *Maior domus.* Obviously the words do not always mean the same thing.

219 Luke 14:32.

220 There is the same concern here as there is in the *LHF* for the spilling of Frankish blood by Franks.

other than that he should be in charge of those whom his father had once governed by rightful authority. And when Chilperic and Raganfred heard this, they were filled with great indignation. Not only did they deny him this authority,[221] but they threatened to deprive him of that which he had inherited from his father's rule. And they warned him that he should prepare for battle on the following day, that he would there undergo the judgement of divine justice, and that divine authority would declare who ought in turn to rule the kingdom of the Franks. When the leader Charles had heard this, he made known the answer of the haughty king to his dukes and nobles;[222] indeed, they, with the help of God, did not hesitate to join with a vigorous spirit the war which the king had declared. Therefore, on the following day,[223] when the sun shone brightly over the earth, each army, equal [to the other] neither in size nor in bravery, stood prepared for battle each with its line joined. For Chilperic awaited the arrival of Charles with a huge army, but one indeed mixed with the common people; the leader Charles, on the other hand, indeed with a lesser host but with men very well tested for battle, sent his line against the enemy. On that day the fiercest battle was joined. And for a long time it was contested on each side with the prospect of victory uncertain. Finally, with divine mercy aiding Charles, *King Chilperic along with his men was put to flight; Raganfred also, having slipped away in flight,*[224] abandoned his allies to be killed in the bloody massacre.[225] But the leader Charles, having obtained the victory with divine help and having distributed the many spoils to his men, began to make the journey to pursue King Chilperic and Raganfred. *And he pursued them as far as Paris.*[226] When the whole region was conquered, he returned in great joy and good fortune to the eastern parts of his realm. And having entered the city of Cologne and having taken his father's treasure from Plectrud, his stepmother, he, as the most worthy heir, settled down on the throne of his kingdom.[227]

---

221 *imperium.*

222 *ducibus et optimatibus.*

223 '21 March, a Sunday in Lent'. *LHF,* ch. 53, above, p. 95.

224 Fredegar, *Contin.,* ch. 10.

225 The *LHF*'s account of this battle in chapter 53, above, p. 95, is much shorter, lacking the invective and partisanship.

226 The report that Martel pursued Chilperic and Raganfred as far as Paris is doubtful. It is related by Fredegar's continuator, ch. 10, but is not a part of the *LHF*'s account. See Gerberding, *Rise,* p. 140.

227 *in solio regni sui ... resedit.* Both Fredegar, *Contin.,* ch. 10, and the *LHF,* ch. 53, above, p. 95, avoid this very royal language in their accounts.

Chilperic and Raganfred sent a delegation to Eudo, duke of the Aquitanians,
requested his help that he should, with them, resist Charles, and enticed him
with great rewards.[228]

In the seven hundred and eighteenth year[229] from the incarnation of the
Lord, Eudo, duke of the Aquitanians, having raised an army of Gascons,
together with Chilperic and Raganfred, took up arms against the leader
Charles. Charles hastened bravely against them. But when Eudo heard
that Charles was on the march and prepared to repel the haughty
enemy from the lands of his kingdom, he was frightened and fled, and,
snatching the royal treasures, he took King Chilperic along with him.
But Charles pursued him to the city of Orleans. There he pitched
camp, sent legates to Eudo, and demanded that he should not refuse to
send him the king with the treasures he had carried away. He [Eudo],
however, struck with terror, not daring to despise the words of the
leader Charles, straightway sent him King Chilperic with the treasures.
Once he had received the king, Charles acted mercifully towards him and
conceded the royal seat to him under his his own [Charles's] authority.

In the same year the leader Charles laid Saxony waste in a great strike
and pushed through to the river Weser. Having subdued the whole
region, he returned as the victor to his own [lands].

In the seven hundred and nineteenth year[230] from the incarnation of
the Lord, Charles, having gathered an army, crossed the Rhine,
surveyed Alemannia, and pushed through to the Danube. And when he
had crossed it, he occupied the lands of the Bavarians. Having
conquered that people, he returned to his own haunts, with the Lord
helping, as the victor with much treasure and a certain lady, Pilitrud
by name, and her niece, Sunnichild.

In the seven hundred and twenty-fifth year[231] from the incarnation of
the Lord, after the cycles of nearly five years had passed, the former
mayor of the palace, Raganfred, tried to rise up against Charles. And
Charles led an army against him and shut him up in the city of Angers.
Taking his son as hostage, he [Charles], with his usual faithfulness,
conceded that he [Raganfred] should have that county for himself as
long as he lived.

228 Fredegar, *Contin.*, ch. 10. Cf. *LHF*, ch. 53, above, p. 95. Fredegar's continuator tells
   us what those great rewards were: *regnum et munera tradunt.*
229 Here the author seems to have the correct date. See Gerberding, *Rise*, pp. 143–4.
230 725. Fredegar, *Contin.*, ch. 12.
231 724. Fredegar, *Contin.*, ch. 11.

Bibliography

Primary sources

Individual sources

Acta Sancti Aunemundi alias Dalfini episcopi, P. Perrier (ed.), *AASS*, Sept. VII, Antwerp, 1760, 744–6.

Additamentum Nivialense de Fuilano, B. Krusch (ed.), *MGH, SSRM*, IV Hanover, 1902, 449–51.

Ado of Vienne, *Sancti Adonis Chronicon*, J. P. Migne (ed.), *PL.*, 123, Paris, 1879, 23–142.

Annales Alamannici, G. Pertz (ed.), *MGH, SS*, I, Hanover, 1826, 22–30.

Annales Francorum Mettenses, A. Duchesne (ed.), *Historia Francorum Scriptores coaetanei*, vol. III, Paris, 1641, 262–333.

Annales Laureshamenses, G. Pertz (ed.), *MGH, SS*, I, Hanover, 1826, 22–30.

Annales Marchianenses, L. Bethmann (ed.), *MGH, SS*, XVI, Hanover, 1859, 609–17.

Annales Mettenses Priores, B. de Simson (ed.), *MGH, SSRG*, Hanover and Leipzig, 1905.

Annales Nazariani, G. Pertz (ed.), *MGH, SS*, I, Hanover, 1826, 22–44.

Annales Petaviani, G. Pertz (ed.), *MGH, SS*, I, Hanover, 1826, 7–18.

Annales Sancti Amandi, G. Pertz (ed.), *MGH, SS*, I, Hanover, 1826, 6–14.

Annales Sancti Tiliani, G. Pertz (ed), *MGH, SS*, I, Hanover, 1825, 6–8 and 219–24.

Annalium veterum fragmenta partim ex Mettensibus desumpta, G. Waitz (ed.), *MGH, SS*, XIII, Hanover, 1881, 26–33.

Annals of Clonmacnoise, D. Murphy (ed.), Dublin, 1896.

Annals of Inisfallen, S. MacAirt (ed.), Dublin, 1951.

Annals of Ulster, W. Hennessey (ed.), Dublin, 1887.

Alcuin, *Vita Richarii Confessoris Centulensis auctore Alcuino*, B. Krusch (ed.), *MGH, SSRM*, IV, Hanover, 1902, 381–401.

Bede, *Historia Ecclesiastica Gentis Anglorum*, C. Plummer (ed.), *Venerabilis Baedae Opera Historica*, vol. I, Oxford, 1896.

Bede, *The Ecclesiastical History of the English People*, B. Colgrave and R. Mynors (eds. and trans.), Oxford, 1969.

Chronicon Ebersheimense, L. Weiland (ed.), *MGH, SS*, XXIII, Hanover, 1874, 431–53.

Chronicum Scotorum, W. Hennessey (ed.), London, 1866.

Clotharii Edictum, A. Boretius (ed.), *Capitularia Regum Francorum*, I, *MGH, Legum*, sectio II, vol. 1, Hanover, 1883, 20–3.

Concilium Leudegarii Episcopi Augustodunensis, C. de Clerq (ed.), *Concilia Galliae a 511– 695*, *Corpus Christianorum*, Series Latina, 148A, Turnhout, 1963, 319–20.

Concilium Modogarnomense seu Burdegalense, C de Clerq (ed.), *Concilia Galliae a 511–695*, *Corpus Christianorum*, Series Latina, 148A. Turnhout, 1963, 311–13.

Desiderius of Cahors, *Epistulae Sancti Desiderii*, D. Norberg (ed.), *Acta Universitatis Stockholmiensis*, Studia Latina Stockholmiensia, VI, Uppsala, 1961.

Divisio regnorum, A. Boretius (ed.), *Capitularia*, I, *MGH, Legum Sectio II*, vol. 1, Hanover, 1883, 126–30.

Einhardt, *Vita Karoli Magni*, L. Halphen (ed.), *Eginhard, Vie de Charlemagne*, Paris, 1967.

Formulae Senonenses Recentiores, K. Zeumer (ed.), *MGH, Legum*, sectio V, Hanover, 1886, 211–20.

Fredegar, *Chronicarum quae dicuntur Fredegarii Scholastici Libri IV Cum Continuationibus*, B. Krusch (ed.), *MGH, SSRM*, II, Hanover, 1888, 1–193; and J. M. Wallace-Hadrill (ed. and trans.), *The Fourth Book of Fredegar with its Continuations*, London, 1960. Reprinted, Westport, Connecticut, 1981.

Germanus of Paris, *Sancti Germani Parisiensis Episcopi Expositio brevis antiquae gallicanae in duas epistolas digesta. Epistola prima*, Migne, *PL*, 72, Paris, 1849, 89–94.

Gesta Dagoberti I. Regis Francorum, B. Krusch (ed.), *MGH, SSRM*, II, Hanover, 1888, 396–425.

Gesta Sanctorum Patrum Fontanellensis Coenobii, F. Lohier and J. Laporte (eds.), Rouen, 1936.

Gregory of Tours, *De virtutibus Sancti Juliani*, B. Krusch (ed.), *MGH, SSRM*, I, pt. 2, Hanover, 1885, 112–34.

Gregory of Tours, *De virtutibus Sancti Martini*, B. Krusch (ed.), *MGH, SSRM*, I, pt. 2, Hanover, 1885, 134–211.

Gregory of Tours, *Gregorii Episcopi Turonensis Historiarum Libri X*, B. Krusch and W. Levison (eds.), *MGH, SSRM*, I Med. alt., Hanover, 1951.

Gregory of Tours, *Liber in gloria martyrum*, B. Krusch (ed.), *MGH, SSRM*, I, pt. 2, Hanover, 1885, 34–111. Reprinted, 1969.

Gregory of Tours, *Liber Vitae Patrum*, B. Krusch (ed.), *MGH, SSRM*, I, pt. 2, Hanover, 1885, 211–94. Reprinted, 1969.

Historia S. Geretrudis, J. Gheldolf de Ryckel (ed.), Brussels, 1637.

Hugh of Flavigny, *Hugonis Chronicon I*, G. Pertz (ed.), *MGH, SS*, VIII, Hanover, 1848, 288–368.

Isidore of Seville, *Isidori Hispalensis episcopi Etymologiarum sive Originum Libri XX*, W. M. Lindsay (ed.), Oxford, 1911.

Jonas, *Vita Columbani Abbatis Discipulorumque eius*, B. Krusch (ed.), *MGH, SSRM*, IV, Hanover, 1902, 64–108.

Julian of Toledo, *Historia Wambae Regis*, W. Levison (ed.), *MGH, SSRM*, V, Hanover, 1910, 486–535.

Lex Salica, K. A. Eckhardt (ed.), *MGH, Legum*, sectio I, vol. IV, pt. 2, Hanover, 1969.

Liber Constitutionum, L. de Salis (ed.), *MGH, Legum*, sectio I, vol. 2, pt. 1, Hanover, 1892, 30–116.

Liber Historiae Francorum, B. Krusch (ed.), *MGH, SSRM*, II, Hanover, 1888, 215–328.

Liber Pontificalis, L. Duchesne (ed.), *Le Liber Pontificalis*, 2 vols., Paris, 1886–92.

Marculf, *Marculfi Formularum Libri Duo*, A. Uddholm (ed.), Uppsala, 1962.

Miracula Martialis, O. Holder-Egger (ed.), *MGH, SS*, XV, pt. 1, Hanover, 1887, 280–3.

Pactus Legis Salicae, K. A. Eckhardt (ed.), *MGH, Legum*, sectio I, vol. IV, pt. 1, Hanover, 1962.

Passio Praejecti Episcopi et Martyris Arverni, B. Krusch (ed.), *MGH, SSRM*, V, Hanover, 1910, 225–48.

Passio Ragneberti Martyris Bebronensis, B. Krusch (ed.), *MGH, SSRM*, V, Hanover, 1910, 207–11.

Passiones Leudegarii Episcopi et Martyris Augustodunensis, B. Krusch (ed.), *MGH, SSRM*, V, Hanover, 1910, 249–362.

Paul the Deacon, *Historia Langobardorum*, L. Bethmann and G. Waitz (eds.), *MGH, SSRL*, Hanover, 1878, 7–219.

Procopius, *History of the Wars*, H. B. Dewing (ed. and trans.), Cambridge, Massachusetts, 1928.

Sigibert of Gembloux, *Sigiberti Chronicon*, C. Bethmann (ed.), *MGH, SS*, VI, Hanover, 1844, 300–74.

Stephen of Ripon, *The life of Bishop Wilfrid by Eddius Stephanus*, B. Colgrave (ed. and trans.), Cambridge, 1927. Reprinted, New York, 1985.

Stephen of Ripon, *Vita Wilfridi I. Episcopi Eboracensis auctore Stephano*, W. Levison (ed.), *MGH, SSRM*, VI, Hanover, 1913, 163–263.

Sulpicius Severus, *Vita S. Martini*, J. Fontaine (ed.), *Suplice Sévère, Vie de saint Martin*, 3 vols, *Sources Chrétiennes*, 133–5, Paris, 1967–69.

Testamentum Aunemundi, A. Coville (ed.), *Recherches sur l'histoire de Lyon du Vme siècle (480–800)*, Paris, 1928, Appendix I, pp. 408–12.

The Theodosian Code, C. Pharr (trans.), Princeton, New Jersey, 1952.

Translatio S. Baltechildis, O. Holder-Egger (ed.), *MGH, SS*, XV, pt. 1, Hanover, 1887, 284–5.

Venantius Fortunatus, *Vita Germani Episcopi Parisiaci Auctore Venantio Fortunato*, B. Krusch (ed.), *MGH, SSRM*, VII, Hanover, 1920, 337–418.

Virtutes Beatae Geretrudis, B. Krusch (ed.), *MGH, SSRM*, II, Hanover, 1888, 464–71.

Virtutes Fursei Abbatis Latiniacensis, B. Krusch (ed.), *MGH, SSRM*, IV, Hanover, 1902, 440–9.

Vita Amandi Episcopi I, B. Krusch (ed.), *MGH, SSRM*, V, Hanover, 1910, 395–449.

Vita Ansberti Episcopi Rotomagensis, W. Levison (ed.), *MGH, SSRM*, V, Hanover, 1910, 613–41.

Vita Audoini Episcopi Rotomagensis, B. Krusch (ed.), *MGH, SSRM*, V, Hanover, 1910, 553–57.

Vita Audoini Episcopi Rotomagensis II, (Vita Altera S. Dadonis vel Audoeni Episcopi) J. Pinius (ed.), *AASS*, Aug IV, Antwerp, 1739, 810–19.

Vita Bertilae Abbatissae Calensis, W. Levison (ed.), *MGH, SSRM*, VI, Hanover, 1913, 95–109.

Vita Boniti Episcopi Arverni, B. Krusch (ed.), *MGH, SSRM*, VI Hanover, 1913, 110–39.

Vita Caesarii Episcopi Arelatensis, II, B. Krusch (ed.), *MGH, SSRM*, III, Hanover, 1896, 483–517.

Vita Condedi Anchoretae Belcinnacensis, W. Levison (ed.), *MGH, SSRM*, V, Hanover, 1910, 644–51.

Vita Desiderii Cadurcae Urbis Episcopi, B. Krusch (ed.), *MGH, SSRM*, IV, Hanover, 1902, 547–602.

Vita Eligii Episcopi Noviomagensis, B. Krusch (ed.), *MGH, SSRM*, IV, Hanover, 1902, 663–741.

Vita Eremberti Episcopi Tolosani, W. Levison (ed.), *MGH, SSRM*, V, Hanover, 1910, 652–6.

Vita Filiberti Abbatis Gemeticensis et Heriensis, W. Levison (ed.), *MGH, SSRM*, V, Hanover, 1910, 568–606.

Vita Fursei Abbatis Latiniacensis, B. Krusch (ed.), *MGH, SSRM*, IV, Hanover, 1902, 434–40.

Vita Germani Abbatis Grandivallensis, B. Krusch (ed.), *MGH, SSRM*, V, Hanover, 1910, 33–40.

Vita Geremari Abbatis Flaviacensis, B. Krusch (ed.), *MGH, SSRM*, IV, Hanover, 1902, 626–33.

Vita Hugberti Episcopi Traiectensis, W. Levison (ed.), *MGH, SSRM*, VI, Hanover, 1913, 482–96.

Vita Landiberti Episcopi Traeiectensis Vetustissima, B. Krusch (ed.), *MGH, SSRM*, VI, Hanover, 1913, 353–84.

Vita Lantberti Abbatis Fontanellensis et Episcopi Lugdunensis, W. Levison (ed.), *MGH, SSRM*, V, Hanover, 1910, 606–12.

Vita Leudegarii, C. Byeus (ed.), *AASS*, Oct., I, Antwerp, 1765, 463–81.

Vita Leudegarii metrica, J. Champollion-Figeac (ed.), *Vie et Passio de Saint Léger, Documents inédits tirés des collections manuscrites de la Bibliothèque Nationale et des Archives ou des Bibliothèques des départements*, vol. IV, Paris, 1848, 446–56.

Vita Leudegarii metrica, L. Traube (ed.), *MGH, Poetae Latini aevi carolini*, III, Berlin, 1896, 5–37.

Vita Odiliae Abbatissae Hohenburgensis, W. Levison (ed.), *MGH, SSRM*, VI, Hanover, 1913, 24–50.

Vita Sanctae Austrebertae Virginis et Abbatissae Pauliacensis in Caletis, J. Mabillon (ed.), *ASSOB*, saec. III, 1, Paris, 1672, 23–31.

Vita Sanctae Balthildis, B. Krusch (ed.), *MGH, SSRM*, II, Hanover, 1888, 447–74.

Vita Sanctae Geretrudis abbatisse Nivellensis, J. Gheldolf de Ryckel (ed.), Louvain, 1632.

Vita Sanctae Geretrudis, B. Krusch (ed.), *MGH, SSRM*, II, Hanover, 1888, 475–508.

Vita Sanctae Richtrudis, D. Paperbrochius (ed.), *AASS*, Mai, III, Antwerp, 1680, 81–9.

Vita Sancti Agilis Abbatis, J. Stiltingus (ed.), *AASS*, Aug., VI, Antwerp, 1743, 574–87.

Vita Sancti Waningi Confessoris, J. Mabillon (ed.), *AASSOB*, saec. III, Paris, 1669, 971–4.

Vita Trudonis Confessoris Hasbaniensis, W. Levison (ed.), *MGH, SSRM*, VI, Hanover, 1913, 264–98.

Vita Wandregiseli Abbatis Fontanellensis, B. Krusch (ed.), *MGH, SSRM*, V, Hanover, 1910, 1–24.

Vita Wandregisili Abbatis Fontanellensis II, J. Mabillon (ed.), *AASSOB*, saec. II, Paris, 1669, 534–46.

Collections of sources

Bruckner, A., R. Marichal (eds.), *Chartae Latinae Antiquiores*, vols, 13 and 14, ed. H. Atsma and J. Vezin, Dietikon and Zurich, 1981 and 1982.

Capitularia Regum Francorum, A. Boretius (ed.), *MGH, Legum*, sectio II, vol. 1, Hanover, 1883.

de Clercq, C. (ed.), *Concilia Galliae a 511–695, Corpus Christianorum, Series Latina* 148A, Turnhout, 1963.

Dümmler, E. (ed.), *MGH, Epistolae*, III, Berlin, 1882.

Dümmler, E. (ed.), *MGH, Epistolae*, IV, Berlin, 1895.

Guigue, M.-C. (ed.), *Cartulaire Lyonnais*, Lyons, 1885.

Halkin, J., and C. G. Roland (eds.), *Recueil des chartes de l'abbaye de Stavelot-Malmèdy*, Brussels, 1907.

Lauer, P., and C. Samaran (eds.)., *Les Diplômes Originaux des Mérovingiens*, Paris, 1908.

Norberg, D. (ed.), *Epistulae Sancti Desiderii, Acta Universitatis Stockholmiensis, Studia Latina Stockholmiensia*, VI, Uppsala, 1961.

Pardessus, J. (ed.), *Diplomata, Chartae Epistolae, Leges, Aliaque Instumenta ad res Gallo-Francicas Spectantia*, 2 vols, Paris, 1843, 1849. Reprinted, Aalen, 1969.

Pertz, K. A. (ed.), *MGH, Diplomata Imperii* I, Hanover, 1872. Reprinted, Stuttgart, 1963.

Tangl, M. (ed.), *Sancti Bonifatii et Lulli Epistolae, MGH, Epistolae Selectae*, vol. 1, Berlin, 1955.

Tardif, J. (ed.), *Archives de l'Empire – Inventaires et Documents, Monuments Historiques*, Paris, 1886.

Tardif, J. (ed.), Les Chartes mérovingiens de Noirmoutier, *Nouvelle Revue historique de droit français et étranger*, 22 (1899), 763–90.

Wampach, C. (ed.), *Geschichte der Grundherrschaft Echternach im Frühmittelalter, 1–2 Quellenband*, Luxembourg, 1930.

Secondary literature

Aigrain, R., *L'Hagiographie: ses sources, ses méthodes, son histoire*, Paris, 1953.

Amory, A., Names, ethnic identity and community in fifth- and sixth-century Burgundy, *Viator*, 25 (1994), 1–30.

Anton, H., *Studien zu den Klosterprivilegien der Päpste im frühen Mittelalter, Beiträge zur Geschichte und Quellenkunde des Mittelalters*, 4, Berlin, 1975.

Atsma, H, Les monastères urbains du nord de la Gaule, *Revue d'Histoire de l'Eglise de France*, 62 (1976), 163–87.

Atsma, H. (ed.), *La Neustrie. Le Pays au nord de la Loire de 650 à 850, Beihefte der Francia* 16, vols 1 and 2, Sigmaringen, 1989.

Baix, F., L'hagiographie à Stavelot-Malmèdy, *Revue Bénédictine*, 60 (1950), 120–62.

Balau, S. *Etude critique des sources de l'historie du pays de Liège au Moyen-âge*, Brussels, 1902–03.

Banniard, M., *Viva Voce. Communication écrite et communication orale du IVe au IXe siècle en Occident Latin*, Paris, 1992.

Bergengruen, A., *Adel und Grundherrschaft im Merowingerreich, Vierteljahrschrift für Sozial- und Wirtschaftsgeschichte*, Beiheft 41, Wiesbaden, 1958.

Berschin, W., *Biographie und Epochenstil im lateinischen Mittelalter*, Vol. 2, *Merowingische Biographie, Italien, Spanien und die Inseln im frühen Mittelalter, Quellen und Untersuchungen zur lateinischen Philologie des Mittelalters*, 9, Stuttgart, 1988.

Beumann, H., Nomen Imperatoris. Studien zur Kaiseridee Karls des Grossen, *Historische Zeitschrift*, 185 (1958), 515–49.

Bieler, L., *Ireland, Harbinger of the Middle Ages*, London, 1963.

Bleiber, W., *Naturalwirtschaft und Ware-Geld-Beziehungen zwischen Somme und Loire während des 7. Jahrhunderts*, Berlin, 1981.

Bloch, M., *Feudal Society*, trans. L. Manyon, London, 1965.

Böhmer, J. F., and E. Mühlbacher, *Regesta Imperii – Die Regesten des Kaiserreichs unter den Karolingern, 751–918*, second edition., Innsbruck, 1908.

Bonnell, H., *Die Anfänge des karolingischen Hauses*, Berlin, 1866.

Bosl, K., Die germanische Kontinuität im deutschen Mittelalter (Adel–König–Kirche), in his *Frühformen der Gesellschaft im mittelalterlichen Europa*, Munich, 1964, 80–105.

Bostock, J., *A Handbook on Old High German Literature*, second edition, revised by K. C. King and D. R. McLintock, Oxford, 1976.

Bresslau, H., *Handbuch der Urkundenlehre für Deutschland und Italien*, vol. 1, third edition, Berlin, 1958.

Brown, P., *The World of Late Antiquity*, New York, 1980.

Bullough, D., *The Age of Charlemagne*, London, 1965.

Cabrol, F., and H. Leclercq, *Dictionnaire d'archéologie chrétienne et de liturgie*, 15 vols., Paris, 1907–53.

Campbell, J., *The Anglo-Saxons*, Ithaca, New York, 1982.

Campbell, J., The First Century of Christianity in England, in his *Essays in Ango-Saxon History*, London, 1986, 49–67.

Chaume, M., *Les Origines du duché de Bourgogne*, Dijon, 1926.

Clarke, H. B., and M. Brennan (eds.), *Columbanus and Merovingian Monasticism. British Archaeological Reports*, International Series, 113, Oxford, 1981.

Classen, P., Kaiserreskript und Königsurkunde. Diplomatische Studien zum römisch-germanisch Kontinuitätsproblem, *Archiv für Diplomatik*, 1 (1955), 1–87, and 2 (1956), 1–115.

Classen, P., Karl der Grosse und die Thronfolge im Frankenreich, *Festschrift für Hermann Keimpel*, vol. III, Göttingen, 1972, 109–34.

Classen, P., Fortleben und Wandel des spätrömischen Urkundenwesens im frühen Mittelalter, in P. Classen (ed.), *Recht und Schrift im Mittelalter, Vorträge und Forschungen des Konstanzer Arbeitskreis für mittlelalterliche Geschichte*, 23, Sigmaringen, 1977, 13–54.

Claude, D., Die Bestellung der Bischöfe im merowingischen Reiche, *Zeitschrift der Savigny-Stiftung für Rechtsgeschichte*, LXXX, *Kanonistische Abteilung*, 49, (1963), 1–75.

Collins, Richard, Beobachtungen zu Form, Sprache und Publikum der Prosabiographien des Venantius Fortunatus in der Hagiographie des römischen Gallien, *Zeitschrift für Kirchengeschichte*, 92 (1981), 16–38.

Collins, Richard, Observations on the Form, Language, and Public of the Prose Biographies of Venantius Fortunatus in the Hagiography of Merovingian Gaul, in Clarke and Brennan (eds.), *Columbanus and Merovingian Monasticism*, 105–31.

Collins, Roger, Deception and Misrepresentation in Early Eighth-century Frankish Historiography: Two Case Studies, in J. Jarnut, U. Nonn and M. Richter (eds.) *Karl Martell in seiner Zeit*, Beihefte der *Francia* 37, Sigmaringen, 1994, 227–47.

Coquet, J., L'inscription tumulaire de Ligugué (fin du VIIe siècle), *Revue Mabillon*, 44 (1954), 97–104.

Courtois, C., L'avènement de Clovis II et les règles d'accession au trône chez les Mérovingiens, *Mélanges d'histoire de Moyen-âge dédiés à la mémoire de Louis Halphen*, Paris, 1951, 155–64.

Couturier, M.-J., *Sainte Bathilde Reine des Francs. Histoire politique et religieuse*, Paris, 1909.

Coville, A., *Recherches sur l'histoire de Lyon du Vme siècle au IXme siècle (480–800)*, Paris, 1928.

Davies, W., Suretyship in the Cartularie de Redon, in T. Charles-Edwards, M. Owen and D. Walters (eds.), *Lawyers and Laymen*, Cardiff, 1986, 72–91.

Davies, W., and P. Fouracre (eds.), *The Settlement of Disputes in Early Medieval Europe*, Cambridge, 1986.

Davies, W., and P. Fouracre (eds.), *Property and Power in the Early Middle Ages*, Cambridge, 1995.

Deansly, M., and P. Grosjean, The Canterbury Edition of the Answers of Pope Gregory I to St Augustine, *Journal of Ecclesiastical History*, 10 (1959), 1–49.

de Gaiffier, B., La lecture des actes des martyrs dans la prière liturgique en occident, *Annalecta Bollandiana*, 72 (1954), 134–66.

de Gaiffier, B., Hagiographie et historiographie: quelques aspects du problème, *Settimane di Studio*, 17 (1969), 139–66.

Delehaye, H., *The Legends of the Saints*, fourth edition, trans. D. Attwater, London, 1962.

Delehaye, H., *Les Passions des Martyrs et les genres littéraires*, Brussels, 1921, second edition, Brussels, 1966.

Demolon, P., *Le Village mérovingien de Brebières*, Arras, 1972.

De Poek, G., Le ms. Clermont-Ferrand 240 (anc. 189), les Scriptoria d'Auvergne et les origines spirituelles de la Vie Française de Saint Léger, *Scriptorium*, 18 (1964), 11–343.

Derouet, J.-L., Les possibilités d'interpretation sémiologique des textes hagiographiques, *Revue d'Histoire de l'Eglise de France*, 62 (1976), 153–62.

Deschamps, P., Critique de privilège épiscopal accordé par Emmon de Sens à l'abbaye de Sainte-Colombe (660, 20 août), *Le Moyen Age*, second series, 16 (1912), 144–64.

Dierkens, A., *Abbayes et chapitres entre Sambre et Meuse* (VII-XI siècles), Beihefte der *Francia* 14, Sigmaringen, 1985.

Dierkens, A., Prolégomène à une histoire des relations culturelles entre les îsles britanniques et le continent pendant le Haut Moyen-âge, in Atsma (ed.), *La Neustrie*, vol. 2, 371–94.

Doehaerd, R., *The Early Middle Ages in the West: Economy and Society*, Oxford, 1978.

Du Cange, C., *Glossarium mediae et infirmae Latinitatis*, ed. nova, 10 vols, 1883–87. Reprinted, Graz, 1954.

Duchesne, L., *Fastes épiscopaux de l'ancienne Gaule*, 3 vols., Paris, 1894–1915.

Dupraz, L., *Le Royaume des Francs. Contribution à l'histoire du Regnum Francorum pendant le troisième quart du VIIe siècle*, Fribourg-en-Suisse, 1948.

Durliat, J., Les attributions civiles des évêques mérovingiens: l'exemple de Didier, évêque de Cahors (630–655), *Annales du Midi*, 91 (1979), 237–54.

Durliat, J., *Les Finances Publiques de Diocletian aux Carolingiens (284–889)*, Beihefte der *Francia* 21, Sigmaringen, 1990.

Ebling, H., *Prosopographie der Amtsträger des Merowingerreiches*, Beihefte der *Francia* 2, Munich, 1974.

Eggers, H., Nachlese zur Frühgeschichte des Wortes Deutsch, in his *Der Volksname Deutsch*, Wege der Forschung, 156, Darmstadt, 1970, 374–91.

Ewig, E., Die fränkischen Teilreiche im 7. Jahrhundert (613–714), *Trierer Zeitschrift*, 22 (1953), 85–144. Reprinted, E. Ewig, *Spätantikes und fränkisches Gallien. Gasammelte Schriften (1952-1973)*, vol. 1, Beihefte der *Francia* 3/1, Munich, 1979, 172–230.

Ewig, E. *Trier im Merowingerreich. Civitas, Stadt, Bistum*, Trier, 1954.

Ewig, E., Milo et eiusmodi similes, *Sankt Bonifatius Gedenkgabe zum zwölfhundersten Geburtstag*, Fulda, 1954, 412–40. Reprinted, E. Ewig, *Spätantikes und fränkisches Gallien. Gesammelte Schriften (1952–1973)*. vol. 2, Beihefte der *Francia* 3/2. Munich, 1979, 189–212.

Ewig, E., Zum christlichen Königsgedanken im Frühmittelalter, in T. Mayer (ed.), *Das Königtum. Seine geistigen und rechtlichen Grundlagen, Vorträge und Forschungen*, 3 (1956), 7–73. Reprinted, *Gallien*, vol. 1, 3–71.

Ewig, E., Volkstum und Volksbewusstsein im Frankenreich des 7. Jahrhunderts, *Settimane di Studio*, 5 (1958), 587–648. Reprinted, *Gallien* vol. 1, 231–73.

Ewig, E., Beobachtungen zu den Klosterprivilegien des 7. und frühen 8. Jahrhunderts, in J. Fleckenstein and K. Schmid (eds.), *Adel und Kirche*, Freiburg-im-Breisgau, 1968, 52–65. Reprinted, *Gallien*, vol. 2, 411–26.

Ewig, E., Beobachtungen zu den Bischofsprivilegien für Saint-Maur-des-Fossés und Sainte-Colombe de Sens, *Festschrift, Ludwig Petry, Geschichtliche Landeskunde*, 5/2. Wiesbaden, 1969, 1–24. Reprinted, *Gallien*, vol. 2, 485–506.

Ewig, E., Das Formular von Rebais und die Bischofsprivilegien der Merowingerzeit, in *Aus Reichsgeschichte und nordischer Geschichte. Festschrift für Karl Jordan, Kieler Historische Studien*, 16 (1972), 11–42. Reprinted, *Gallien*, vol. 2, 456–84.

Ewig, E., Das Privileg des Bischofs Berthefrid von Amiens für Corbie von 664 und die Klosterpolitik der Königin Balthild, *Francia*, I (1973), 62–114. Reprinted, *Gallien*, vol. 2, 538–83.

Ewig, E., Studien zur merowingischen Dynastie, *Frühmittelalterliche Studien*, 8 (1974), 15–59.

Ewig, E., Das merowingische Frankenreich (561–687), in T. Schieder (general ed.), *Handbuch der europäischen Geschichte*, vol. 1 (T. Schieffer, ed.), *Europa im Wandel von der Antike zum Mittelalter*, Stuttgart, 1976.

Felten, F., *Äbte und Laienäbte im Frankenreich. Monographen zur Geschichte des Mittelalters*, 20, Stuttgart, 1980.

Fichtenau, H., *Das Karolingische Imperium. Soziale und Geistige Problematik eines Grossreiches*, Zurich, 1949.

Fichtenau, H., Byzanz und die Pfalz zu Aachen, *MIÖG*, 59 (1951), 1–54.

Fischer, J., Der Hausmeier Ebroin, dissertation, Bonn, 1954.

Flint, V., *The Rise of Magic in Early Medieval Europe*, Oxford, 1991.

Folz, R., *The Coronation of Charlemagne*, trans. J. E. Anderson, London, 1974.

Foltz, R., Tradition hagiographique et culte de sainte Bathilde, reine des Francs, *Comptes Rendus de l'Académie des Inscriptions et Belles-lettres*, (1975), 369–84.

Fontaine, J., *Sulpice Sévère, Vie de saint Martin*, 3 vols., *Sources chrétiens*, 133–35, Paris, 1967–69.

Fontaine, J., Hagiographie et politique, de Sulpice Sévère à Venance Fortunant, *Revue d'Histoire de l'Eglise de France*, 62 (1976), 113–40.

Fouracre, P., The Work of Audoenus of Rouen and Eligius of Noyon in extending Episcopal Influence from the Town to the Country in Seventh-century Neustria, *Studies in Church History*, 16 (1979), 77–91.

Fouracre, P., Merovingians, mayors of the palace and the notion of a 'low-born' Ebroin, *Bulletin of the Institute of Historical Research*, 57 (1984), 1-14.

Fouracre, P., Observations on the outgrowth of Pippinid influence in the 'Regnum Francorum' after the battle of Tertry (687–715), *Medieval Prosopography*, V, 2 (1984), 1–31.

Fouracre, P., 'Placita' and the settlement of disputes in later Merovingian Francia, in Davies and Fouracre (eds.), *The Settlement of Disputes*, 23–43.

Fouracre, P., Merovingian History and Merovingian Hagiography, *Past and Present*, 127 (1990), 3–38.

Fouracre, P., Cultural Conformity and Social Conservatism in Early Medieval Europe, *History Workshop Journal*, 33 (1992), 152–61.

Fouracre, P., Eternal light and earthly needs: practical aspects of the development of Frankish immunities, in Davies and Fouracre (eds.), *Property and Power*, 53-81.

Fustel de Coulanges, N., *La Monarchie franque*, Paris, 1888.

Frank, H., *Die Klosterbischöfe des Frankenreiches. Beiträge zur Geschichte des alten Mönchtums und des Benedictinerordens* 17, Münster, 1932.

Friedrich, J., Excurs über das Alter der Vita Geretrudis Nivellensis und die Genealogie des karolingischen Hauses, in his *Kirchengeschichte Deutschlands*, vol. 2, pt. 1, Bamberg, 1869, 667–70.

Friese, A., *Studien zur Herrschaftsgeschichte des fränkischen Adels. Der mainländisch-thüringische Raum vom 7, bis 11, Jahrhundert, Geschichte und Gesellschaft*, 18, Stuttgart, 1979.

Fuhrmann, J., Irish Medieval Monasteries on the Continent, dissertation, Catholic University of America. Washington, D.C., 1927.

Galinié, H., Fouilles archéologiques à Tours: rapports préliminaires, *Bulletin de la Société Archéologique de Touraine*, 39 (1978–81) 203–49, 607–49, 1041–84, and 40 (1982), 153–99.

Ganshof, F., *Feudalism*, trans. P. Grierson, London, 1964.

Ganshof, F. L., *Frankish Institutions under Charlemagne*, trans. B. and M. Lyon, Providence, Rhode Island, 1968.

Ganz, D., Bureaucratic shorthand and Merovingian learning, in P. Wormald (ed.), *Ideal and Reality in Frankish and Anglo-Saxon Society. Studies presented to J. M. Wallace-Hadrill*, Oxford, 1983, 58–75.

Ganz, D., *Corbie in the Carolingian Renaissance*, Beihefte der *Francia* 20, Sigmaringen, 1990.

Gasnault, P., Documents comptables du VIIe siècle provenant de Saint-Martin de Tours, *Francia*, 2 (1974), 1–18.

Geary, P., *Furta Sacra. The Thefts of Relics in the Central Middle Ages*, Princeton, New Jersey, 1978.

Geary, P., *Aristocracy in Provence. The Rhône basin at the dawn of the Carolingian Age*, Stuttgart, 1985.

Geary, P., Extrajudicial Means of Conflict Resolution, *Settimana di Studio*, 42, 1995, 569-601.

Gerberding, R., *The Rise of the Carolingians and the Liber Historiae Francorum*, Oxford, 1987.

Godman, P., *Poetry of the Carolingian Renaissance*, London, 1985.

Goffart, W., The Fredegar Problem Reconsidered, *Speculum*, 38 (1963), 206–41.

Goffart, W., From Roman Taxation to Medieval Seigneurie: Three Notes, Part 2, *Speculum*, 47 (1972), 373–94.

Goffart, W., Paul the Deacon's *Gesta Episcoporum Mettensium* and the early Design of Charlemagne's Succession, *Traditio*, 42 (1986), 59–93.

Goffart, W., *The Narrators of Barbarian History*, Princeton, New Jersey, 1988.

Goetz, H.-W., Karl Martell und die Heiligen. Kirchenpolitik und Maiordomat im Spiegel der spätmerowingischen Hagiographie, in J. Jarnut, U. Nonn and M. Richter (eds.), *Karl Martell in seiner Zeit*. Beihefte der *Francia*, 37, Sigmaringen, 1994, 108–18.

Graus, F., *Volk, Herrscher und Heiliger im Reich der Merowinger*, Prague, 1965.

Graus, F., Hagiographie und Dämonenglauben, *Settimane di Studio*, 36 (1989), 93–120.

Grierson, P., and M. Blackburn, *Medieval European Coinage. With a Catalogue of the Coins in the Fitzwilliam Museum, Cambridge*, vol. 1: *The Early Middle Ages (5th–10th Centuries)*, Cambridge, 1986.

Grosjean, P., Notes d'hagiographie celtique, *Annalecta Bollandiana*, 75 (1957), 372–420, and 78 (1960), 364–95.

Halphen, L., *Etudes critiques sur l'histoire de Charlemagne*, Paris, 1921.

Halsall, G., *Settlement and Social Organisation. The Merovingian Region of Metz*, Cambridge, 1995.

Haselbach, I., Aufstieg und Herrschaft der Karolinger in der Darstellung der sogenannten *Annalen Mettenses priores*, *Historische Studien*, 412 (1970), 1–208.

Havighurst, A. (ed.), *The Pirenne Thesis*, Boston, Massachusetts, 1976.

Heene, K., *Audire, legere, vulgo:* an attempt to define public use and comprehensibility of Carolingian hagiography, in Wright (ed.), *Latin and the Romance Languages*, 146–63.

Heidrich, I., Titular und Urkunden der arnulfingishchen Hausmeier, *Archiv für Diplomatik*, 11/12 (1965/66), 71–279.

Heinzelmann, M., Neue Aspekte der biographischen und hagiographischen Literatur in der lateinischen Welt (1.–6. Jahrhundert), *Francia*, I (1973), 27–44.

Heinzelmann, M., *Bishofsherrschaft in Gallien. Zur Kontinuität römischer Führungsschichten vom 4. bis zum 7. Jahrhundert. Soziale prosopographische und bildungsgeschichtliche Aspekte*, Beihefte der *Francia* 5, Zurich, 1976.

Heinzelmann, M., 'Sanctitas' und 'Tugengadel': zur Konzeptionen von 'Heiligkeit' in 5. und 10. Jahrhundert, *Francia*, 5 (1977), 741–52.

Heinzelmann, M., Studia Sanctorum. Education, milieux d'instruction et valeurs éducatives dans l'hagiographie en Gaule jusqu'à la fin de l'époque mérovingienne, in Sot (ed.), *Haut Moyen-âge*, 105–35.

Hempe, K., Reise nach England vom Juli 1895 bis Februar 1896, III, *NA*, 22 (1897), 607–99.

Herman, J., Spoken and written Latin in the last centuries of the Roman Empire: a contribution to the linguistic history of the western provinces, in Wright (ed.), *Latin and the Romance Languages*, 29–43.

Hlawitschka, E., Zur landschaftlichen Herkunft der Karolinger, *Rheinische Vierteljahrsblätter*, 27 (1962), 1–17.

Hlawitschka, E., Die Vorfahren Karls des Grossen, in W. Braunfels (ed.), *Karl der Grosse*, vol. I, Düsseldorf, 1965, 51–82.

Hlawitschka, E., Merowingerblut bei den Karolingern? in J. Fleckenstein and K. Schmidt (ed.), *Adel und Kirche*, Freiburg-im-Breisgau, 1968, 66–91.

Hodges, R., and D. Whitehouse, *Mohammed, Charlemagne and the Origins of Europe*, London, 1983.

Hoebanx, J. J., *L'Abbaye de Nivelles des origines au XIV*ᵉ *siècle*, Brussels, 1942.

Hoffmann, H., *Untersuchung zur karolingischen Annalistik*, *Bonner Forschungen* 10, 1958.

Hughes, K., (review of P. Grosjean, 'Notes d'hagiographie celtique'), *Irish Historical Studies*, 12 (1960–61), 64.

Hughes, K., *The Church in Early Irish Society*, Ithaca, New York, 1966.

James, E., Cemeteries and the problem of Frankish Settlement in Gaul, in P. Sawyer (ed.), *Names, Words and Graves. Early Medieval Settlement*, Leeds, 1978, 55–89.

James, E., Burial and Status in the Early Medieval West, *Transactions of the Royal Historical Society*, 5th series, 39 (1989), 23–40.

Jungmann, J., *The Early Liturgy to the Time of Gregory the Great*, trans. F. Brunner, London, 1959.

Kaiser, R., *Bischofsherrschaft zwischen Königtum und Fürstenmacht. Studien zur bischöflichen Stadtherrschaft im westfränkisch-französischen Reich im frühen und hohen Mittelalter*, *Pariser Historische Studien* 17, Bonn, 1981.

Kaiser, R., Royauté et pouvoir épiscopal au nord de la Gaule (VIIᵉ-IXᵉ siècles), in Atsma (ed.), *La Neustrie*, vol. 1, 143–60.

Kemp, E., *Canonisation and Authority in the Western Church*, Oxford, 1947. Reprinted 1979.

Knowles, D., *Great Historical Enterprises*, London, 1963.

Krüger, K. H., *Königsgrabkirchen der Franken, Angelsachsen und Langobarden bis zur Mitte des 8. Jahrhunderts*, *Münsterische Mittelalter-Schriften* 4, Munich, 1971.

Krusch, B., Zur Chronologie der merowingischen Könige, *Forschungen zur deutschen Geschichte*, 22 (1882), 473–7.

Krusch, B., Die älteste Vita Leudegarii, *NA*, 16 (1891), 563–96.

Krusch, B., Die älteste Vita Praejecti, *NA*, 18 (1893), 629–40.

Krusch, B., Die Urkunden von Corbie und Levillains letztes Wort, *NA*, 31 (1906), 335–75.

Krusch, B., Der Staatsstreich des fränkischen Hausmeiers Grimoald I, in *Festgabe für Karl Zeumer*, Weimar, 1910, 411–38.

Krusch, B., Chronologica Regum Francorum Stirpis Merovingicae, *MGH*, *SSRM*, VII, Hanover, 1920, 468–516.

Kurze, F., Ueber die Karolingischen Reichsannalen von 741–829 und ihre Ueberarbeitung. III Die zweite Hälfte und die Ueberarbeitung, *NA*, 21 (1896), 9–82.

Laporte, J.-P., *Le Trésor des saints de Chelles*, Chelles, 1988.

Latouche, R., *The Birth of the Western Economy*, London, 1967.

Le Bras, G., Notes pour servire à l'histoire des collections canoniques: sur la date et la patrie de la collection dite d'Angers, *Revue Historique de Droit Français et Etranger*, fourth series, 8 (1929), 775–80.

Leclercq, J., L'Ecriture Sainte dans l'hagiographie monastique du haut Moyen-âge, *Settimane di Studio*, 10, (1963), 103–28.

Lesne, E., *Histoire de la propriété ecclésiatique en France*, 6 vols., Lille, 1910–38.

Levillain, L., *Examen critique des chartes mérovingiennes et carolingiennes de l'abbaye de Corbie. Mémoires et documents publiés par la société de l'Ecole des Chartes*, Paris, 1902.

Levillain, L., Etude sur l'abbaye de Saint-Denis à l'epoque mérovingienne, *BEDC*, 82 (1921), 5–116; 86 (1925), 5–99; 87 (1926), 20–97 and 245–346; and 91 (1930), 1–65.

Levillain, L., Encore la succession d'Austrasie, *BEDC*, 106 (1945/46), 296–306.

Levison, W., *England and the Continent in the Seventh Century*, Oxford, 1946.

Levison, W., Die Iren und die Fränkische Kirche, in his *Aus Rheinischer und Fränkischer Frühzeit, Ausgewählte Aufsätze*, Dusseldorf, 1948, 247–63.

Levison, W., Zu den *Annales Mettenses*, in his *Aus Rheinischer und Fränkischer Frühzeit*, Dusseldorf, 1948, 474–83.

Lloyd, P. M., On the Names of Languages, in Wright (ed.), *Latin and the Romance Languages*, 9–18.

Lorren, C., Le village de Saint-Martin de Trainecourt à Mondeville (Calvedos) de l'antiquité au haut Moyen-âge, in Atsma (ed.), *La Neustrie*, 439–65.

Lot, F., *Etudes critiques sur l'Abbaye de Saint-Wandrille, Bibliothèque de l'école des hautes études* 204, Paris, 1913.

Lotter, F., Methodisches zur Gewinnung historischer Erkentnisse aus hagiographischen Quellen, *Historische Zeitschrift*, 229 (1979), 298–356.

Löwe, H. (ed.), *Die Iren und Europa im frühen Mittelalter*, vol. 2, Stuttgart, 1982.

Lynch, J., *Godparents and Kinship in Early Medieval Europe*, Princeton, New Jersey, 1986.

Mabillon, J., *De Re Diplomatica Libri VI*, Paris, 1681–1704.

McKitterick, R., *The Frankish Kingdoms under the Carolingians, 751–987*, London, 1983.

McKitterick, R., *The Carolingians and the Written Word*, Cambridge, 1989.

McKitterick, R., *The Uses of Literacy in Early Medieval Europe*, Cambridge, 1990.

McKitterick, R., Latin and Romance: an historian's perspective, in Wright (ed.), *Latin and the Romance Languages*, 130–45.

McNamara, J. A Legacy of Miracles: Hagiography and Nunneries in Merovingian Gaul, in J. Kirschner and S. Wemple (eds.), *Women of the Medieval World. Essays in Honour of John H. Mundy*, Oxford, 1985, 36–52.

McNamara, J., and J. Halborg, *Sainted Women of the Dark Ages*, London, 1992.

Magnou-Nortier, E., Etude sur le privilège d'immunité du IVᵉ au IXᵉ siècle, *Revue Mabillon*, 60 (1984), 465–512.

Magnou-Nortier, E., Les 'Pagenses' notables et fermiers du fisc durant le haut Moyen-âge, *Revue Belge de Philologie et d'Histoire*, 65, vol. 2 (1987), 237–56.

Magnou-Nortier, E., La gestion publique en Neustrie: les moyens et les hommes (VIIᵉ–IXᵉ siècles), in Atsma (ed.), *La Neustrie*, vol. 1, 271–320.

Manitius, M., *Geschichte der lateinischen Literatur des Mittelalters*, vol 1, Munich, 1911.

Mayer, T., (ed.), *Das Königtum. Seine geistigen und rechtlichen Grundlagen, Vorträge und Forschungen*, 3, Lindau and Konstanz, 1956.

Meyer, K., Verses from a chapel dedicated to St. Patrick at Péronne, *Ériu*, 5 (1911), 110–11.

Mitteis, H., Der Vertrag von Verdun im Rahmen der karolingischen Verfassungspolitik, in his *Die Rechtsidee in der Geschichte*, Weimar, 1957, 425–58.

Mohrmann, C., Les formes du latin dit 'vulgaire'. Essai de chronologie et de systématisation: de l'époque augustéenne aux langue romanes, in her *Etudes sur le latin des chrétiens*, vol. 2, Storia e Letteratura, 87 (1961), 135–153. Reprinted from *Actes du premier Congrès d'études classiques*, Paris, 1951, 207–20.

Mohrmann, C., Die Rolle des Lateins in der Kirche des Westens, in her *Etudes sur le latin des chrétiens*, vol. 2, Storia e Letteratura, 87 (1961), 35–62. Reprinted from *Theologische Revue*, 1956, 1–18.

Mohrmann, C., Le latin médiéval, in her *Etudes sur le latin des chrétiens*, vol. 2, *Storia e Letteratura*, 87 (1961), 181–232. Reprinted from *Cahiers de Civilisation Médiévale*, 1: 3 (1958), 265–94.

Montford, L., Civilization in Seventh-century Gaul as reflected in Saints' Vitae composed in the Period, Ph. D. dissertation, St Louis University, 1973.

Moyse, G., Monachisme et réglementation monastique en Gaule avant Benôit d'Aniane, *Hautes Etudes Médiévales et Modernes*, 47 (1982), 3–19.

Mühlbacher, E., *Deutsche Geschichte unter den Karolingern*, Stuttgart, 1896.

Müller, H., Die Kirche von Lyon in Karolingerreich, *Historisches Jahrbuch*, 107 (1987), 226–33.

Murray, A., Missionaries and Magic in Dark Age Europe, *Past and Present*, 136 (1992), 184–205.

Murray, A. C., Immunity, Nobility and the Edict of Paris, *Speculum*, 69 (1994), 18–39.

Musset, L., De saint Victrice à saint Ouen: la christianisation de la province de Rouen d'après l'hagiographie, *Revue d'Histoire de l'Eglise de France*, 62 (1976), 141–52.

Nelson, J. L., Inauguration rituals, in P. H. Sawyer and I. N. Wood (eds.), *Early Medieval Kingship*, Leeds, 1977, 50–71. Reprinted, J. L. Nelson, *Politics and Ritual*, 283–308.

Nelson, J. L., Queens as Jezabels: the Careers of Brunhild and Balthild in Merovingian History, *Studies in Church History*, Subsidia I (1978), 31–77. Reprinted, J. L. Nelson, *Politics and Ritual in Early Medieval Europe*, London, 1986, 1–48.

Nelson, J. L., The Wary Widow, in Davies and Fouracre (eds.), *Property and Power*, 82–113.

Norberg, D. *Syntaktische Forschung auf dem Gebiete des Spätlateins und des frühen Mittelalters*, *Upsala Universitets årsskrift* 9, 1943.

Norberg, D., *Beiträge zur spätlateinischen Syntax*, Uppsala, 1944.

Norberg, D., A quelle époque a-t-on cessé de parler latin?, *Annales*, 21 (1966), 346–56.

Norberg, D., *Manuel pratique de latin médiéval*, Paris, 1968.

Oexle, O., *Die Karolinger und die Stadt des heiligen Arnulf*, *Frühmittelalterliche Studien*, 1 (1967), 250–364.

Ogilvy, J., Mimmi, Scurrae, Histriones: Entertainers of the Early Middle Ages, *Speculum*, 38 (1963), 603–19.

O'Maille, T., *The Language of the Annals of Ulster*, Manchester, 1910.

Pei, M., The Language of Eighth-century Texts in Northern France, Ph.D. dissertation, Columbia University, New York, 1932.

Picard, J.-M., The Marvellous in Irish and Continental Saints' Lives of the Merovingian Period, in Clarke and Brennan (eds.), *Columbanus and Merovingian Monasticism*.

Picard, J.-M., Church and politics in the seventh century: the Irish exile of King Dagobert II, in *idem* (ed.), *Ireland and Northern France*, Dublin, 1991, 27–52.

Polheim, K., *Die lateinische Reimprosa*, second edition, Berlin, 1963.

Poly, J.-P., Agricola et eius modi similes: la Noblesse Romane et la fin des temps mérovingens, in Sot (ed.), *Culture, éducation et société*, Paris, 197–228.

Poly, J.-P., and E. Bournazel, La mutation féodale, Xᵉ–XIIᵉ siècles, *Nouvelle Clio*, 15 (1980), 315–35.

Pontal, O., *Die Synoden im Merowingerreich*, Munich, 1986.

Poulin, J. C., Saint Léger d'Autun et ses premiers biographes (fin VIIᵉ – milieu IXᵉ siècle), *Bulletin de la Société des Antiquaires de l'Ouest*, fourth series, 16 (1977), 167–200.

Prinz, F., *Frühes Mönchtum im Frankenreich*, Munich, 1965.

Prinz, F., Die bischöfliche Stadtherrschaft im Frankenreich vom 5. bis 7. Jahrhundert, *Historische Zeitschrift*, 217 (1974), 1–35.

Prinz, F., Columbanus, the Frankish Nobility, and the Territories East of the Rhine, in Clarke and Brennan (eds.), *Columbanus and Merovingian Monasticism*, 73–87.

Prinz, F., Der Heilige und seine Lebenswelt, *Settimane di Studio*, 36 (1989), 285–311.

Prou, M., *Les Monnaies mérovingiens*, Paris, 1896. Reprinted, Graz, 1969.

Quentin, H., *Les Martyrologes historiques du Moyen-àge*, Paris, 1908.

Reuter, T., Plunder and Tribute in the Carolingian Empire, *Transactions of the Royal Historical Society*, fifth series, 35 (1985), 75–94.

Reuter, T., The end of Carolingian military expansion, in P. Godman and R. Collins (eds.), *Charlemagne's Heir*, Oxford, 1990, 391–405.

Reuter, T., 'Kirchenreform' und 'Kirchenpolitik' im Zeitalter Karl Martells. Begriffe und Wirklichkeit, in J. Jarnut, U. Nonn and M. Richter (eds.), *Karl Martell in seiner Zeit*, Beihefte der *Francia* 37, Sigmaringen, 1994, 35–59.

Reynolds, S., Social mentalities and the case of medieval scepticism, *Transactions of the Royal Historical Society*, sixth series, I (1991), 21–41.

Riché, P., L'instruction des laïcs en Gaule mérovingienne au VIIᵉ siècle, in his *Instruction et vie religieuse dans le Haut Moyen-àge*, London, 1981,873–88. Reprinted from *Settimane di Studio*, 5 (1957), 873–88.

Riché, P., *Education et culture dans l'Occident barbare, VIᵉ–VIIIᵉ siècles*, Paris, 1962.

Riché, P., Centres of Culture in Frankish Gaul between the Sixth and the Ninth Centuries, in his *Instruction et vie religieuse dans le Haut Moyen-àge*, London, 1981, 211–236. Reprinted from S. L. Thrupp (ed.), *Early Medieval Society*, New York, 1967, 211–36.

Riché, P., L'enseignement et la culture des laïcs dans l'Occident pré-carolingien, in his *Instruction et vie religieuse dans le Haut Moyen-àge*, London, 1981, 231–53. Reprinted from *Settimane di Studio*, 19 (1972), 231–53.

Riché, P., Les representations du palais dans les textes littéraires du haut Moyen-àge, in his *Instruction et vie religieuse dans le Haut Moyen-àge*, London, 1981, 161–71. Reprinted from *Francia*, 4 (1976), 161–71.

Riché, P., La formation des scribes dans le monde mérovingien et carolingien, in his *Instruction et vie religieuse dans le Haut Moyen-àge*, London, 1981, 75–80. Reprinted from Paravicini, W. and K.-F. Werner (eds.), *Histoire comparée de l'administration (IVᵉ - XVIIIᵉ siècles), Actes du XIVᵉ colloque historique franco-allamand, Tours, 1977*, Beihefte der *Francia*, 9, Munich, 1980.

Riché, P., Columbanus, his followers and the Merovingian Church, in, Clarke and Brennan (eds.), *Columbanus and Merovingian Monasticism*, 59–72.

Rochais, M., Le 'Liber Scintillarum' attribué à Defensor di Ligugé, *Revue Bénédictine*, 58 (1948), 77–83.

Rollason, D., *The Mildrith Legend. A Study in Early Medieval Hagiography in England*, Leicester, 1982.

Rollason, D., The Miracles of St Benedict: a Window on Early Medieval France, in H. Mayr-Harting and R. Moore (eds.), *Studies in Medieval History Presented to R. H. C. Davis*, London, 1985, 72–90.

Rouche, M., L'Aquitaine des Wisigoths aux Arabes (418–781), thesis, Université de Lille III, 1977.

Rousseau, F., Le Meuse et le pays mosan en Belgique. Leur importance historique avant le XIIIᵉ siècle, Namur, 1930.

Sanders, G., Le remainiement carolingien de la Vita Balthildis mérovingienne, Analecta Bollandiana, 100 (1982), 411–28.

Sapin, C., Autun, archéologie d'un quartier épiscopal et canonial, Archéologia, 226 (1987), 30–5.

Sawyer, P. H., and I. N. Wood (eds.), Early Medieval Kingship, Leeds, 1971.

Scheibelreiter, G., Der Bischof in merowingischer Zeit. Veröffentlichungen des Instituts für Österreichische Geschichtsforschung 27, Vienna, 1983.

Schlessinger, W., Kaisertum und Reichsteilung. Zur Divisio regnorum von 806, in R. Dietrich and G. Oestreich (eds.), Forschung zu Staat und Verfassung, Festgabe für Fritz Hartung, Berlin, 1958, 9–51. Reprinted in W. Schlessinger, Beiträge zur deutschen Verfassungsgeschichte des Mittelalters, vol. 1, Göttingen, 1963, 193–232, with Nachtrag, 345.

Semmler, J., Episcopi potestas und karolingische Klosterpolitik, Vorträge und Forschungen, 20 (1974), 305–95.

Semmler, J., Zur Pippinidisch-Karolingischen Suzessionskrise, Deutsches Archiv, 33 (1977), 1–36.

Sharpe, R., Medieval Irish Saints' Lives. An Introduction to Vitae Sanctorum Hiberniae, Oxford, 1991.

Smith, J. M. H., Oral and written: saints, miracles, and relics in Brittany, c. 850–1250, Speculum, 65 (1990), 309–43.

Smith, J. M. H., Early medieval hagiography in the late twentieth century, Early Medieval Europe, I, pt. 1 (1992), 68–76.

Smith, J. M. H., Province and Empire. Brittany and the Carolingians, Cambridge, 1992.

Sot, M. (ed.) Haut Moyen-âge. Culture, éducation et sociétés. Etudes offertes à Pierre Riche, Paris, 1990.

Spiegel, G., History, Historicism and the Social Logic of the Text in the Middle Ages, Speculum, 65 (1990), 59–86.

Sprangel, R., Der merovingische Adel und die Gebiete östlich des Rheins, Forschungen zur oberrheinischen Landesgeschichte, 5, Freiburg-im-Breisgau, 1957.

Sprandel, R., Struktur und Geschichte des merowingischen Adels, Historische Zeitschrift, 193 (1961), 33–71.

Stenton, F. M., Anglo-Saxon England, third edition, Oxford, 1971.

Stroheker, K., Der sentatorische Adel im spätantiken Gallien, Tübingen, 1948. Reprinted, Darmstadt, 1970.

Stumpf, K., Über die Merovinger-Diplome, Historische Beischrift, 29 (1873), 343–407.

Tardieu, A., Histoire de la ville de Clermont-Ferrand, vol. 1, Moulins, 1879.

Taylor, P., The Latinity of the Liber Historiae Francorum, Ph.D dissertation, Columbia University, New York, 1924.

Tessier, G., Le Baptême de Clovis, Paris, 1964.

Van Uytfanghe, M., La Bible dans les vies de saints, mérovingiens, Revue d'Histoire de l'Eglise de France, 62 (1976), 103–11.

Van Uytfanghe, M., Le Latin des hagiographes mérovingiens et la protohistoire du français, Romanica gandensia, 16 (1976), 5–89.

Van Uytfanghe, M., Les Avatars contemporains de l'hagiologie, *Francia*, 5 (1977), 639–71.

Van Uytfanghe, M., *Stylisation biblique et condition humaine dans l'hagiographie mérovingienne (600–750)*, Verhandelingen van de Koninklijke Academie voor Wetenschappen, Letteren, en Schone Kunsten van België, Klasse der Letteren 49 nr. 120, Brussels, 1987.

Van Uytfanghe, M., Le culte des saints, *Settimane di Studio*, 36 (1989), 155–202.

Van Uytfanghe, M., A linguistic dichotomy in Carolingian Gaul, in Wright (ed.), *Latin and the Romance Languages*, 114–27.

Vacandard, E., *Vie de Saint Ouen, évêque de Rouen (641–684)*, Paris, 1902.

Van Dam, R., *Saints and their Miracles in Late Antique Gaul*, Princeton, New Jersey, 1993.

Van der Essen, L., *Etude critique et littéraire sur les vitae des saints mérovingiens de l'ancienne Belgique*, Paris and Louvain, 1907.

Vauchez, A., *La Sainteté en occident aux derniers siècles du Moyen-âge*, Paris, 1981.

Vince, R., *Ancient and Medieval Theatre*, London, 1984.

Viollet, P., *Histoire du droit civil français*, second edition, Paris, 1893.

Vollmer, F., Die Etichonen, in G. Tellenbach (ed.), *Studien und Vorarbeiten zur Geschichte des grossfränkischen und früdeutschen Adels*, Forschungen zur Oberrheinischen Landesgeschichte, 4, Freiburg im Breisgau, 1957.

Von Simson, B., Die wiederaufgefundene Vorlage der *Annales Mettenses*, *NA*, 24 (1899), 399–424.

Von Simson, B., Nachtrag, *NA*, 25 (1900), 177–83.

Waitz, G., Handschriften der Universitätsbibliothek zu Montpellier, *NA*, 7 (1879), 191–206.

Waitz, G., *Deutsche Verfassungsgeschichte*, third edition, Kiel, 1882.

Wallace-Hadrill, J. M., *The Long Haired Kings*, London, 1962. Reprinted, Boston, Massachusetts, 1982.

Wallace-Hadrill, J. M., *Early Germanic Kingship in England and on the Continent*, Oxford, 1971.

Wallace-Hadrill, J. M., *The Frankish Church*, Oxford, 1983.

Wattenbach-Levison, *Deutschlands Geschichtsquellen im Mittelalter, Vorzeit und Karolinger* pt. 1, *Die Vorzeit von den Anfängen bis zur Herrschaft der Karolinger*, Weimar, 1952.

Wemple, S. F., *Women in Frankish Society. Marriage and the Cloister 500 to 900*, Philadelphia, 1981.

Werner, K.-F., Bedeutende Adelsfamilien im Reich Karls des Grossen. Ein personengeschichtlicher Beitrag zum Verhältnis von Königtum und Adel im frühen Mittelalter, in W. Braunfels (ed.), *Karl der Grosse*, vol. I, Dusseldorf, 1965, 83–142., translated as Important Families in the Kingdom of Charlemagne: Prosopographical Study of the Relationship between King and Nobility in the Early Middle Ages, in T. Reuter (ed. and trans.), *The Medieval Nobility*, Amsterdam, 1978, 137–202.

Werner, K.-F., Les principautés périphériques dans le monde franque du VIIe siècle, *Settimane di Studio*, 20 (1972), 483–514.

Werner, K.-F., Le rôle de l'aristocratie dans la Christianisation du nord-est de la Gaule, *Revue d'Histoire de l'Eglise de France*, 62 (1976), 45–73.

Werner, K.-F., Les rouages de l'administration, in P. Perin and L.-C. Feffer (eds.), *La Neustrie*, Rouen, 1985, 41–6.

Werner, M., *Der Lütticher Raum in frühkarolingischer Zeit*, *Veröffentlichungen des Max-Planck-Instituts für Geschichte*, 62, Göttingen, 1980.

Werner, M., *Adelsfamilien im Umkreis der frühen Karolinger. Vorträge und Forschungen*, Sonderband 28, Sigmaringen, 1982.

Whitelock, D., The Pre-Viking Age Church in East Anglia, *Anglo-Saxon England*, 1 (1972), 1–22.

Wickham, C., La Chute de Rome n'aura pas lieu: à propos d'un livre récent, *Le Moyen Age*, 99 (1993), 107–26.

Wilson, S., Annotated Bibliography, in S. Wilson (ed.), *Saints and their Cults. Studies in Religious Sociology, Folklore and History*, Cambridge, 1983, 309–417.

Wolfram, H., *Intitulatio 1. Lateinische Königs-und Fürstentitel bis zum Ende des 8. Jahrhunderts*, MIOG, Ergänzungsband 21, Vienna, 1967.

Wood, I. N., A Prelude to Columbanus: the Monastic Achievement in the Burgundian Territories, in Clarke and Brennan (eds.), *Columbanus and Merovingian Monasticism*, 3–32.

Wood, I. N., The *Vita Columbani* and the Merovingian Hagiography, *Peritia*, I (1982), 63–80.

Wood, I. N., The Ecclesiastical Politics of Merovingian Clermont, in P. Wormald (ed.), *Ideal and Reality in Frankish and Anglo-Saxon Society. Studies Presented to J. M. Wallace-Hadrill*, Oxford, 1983, 34–57.

Wood, I. N., The Merovingian North Sea, *Occasional Papers on Medieval Topics*, 1, Alingås, 1983.

Wood, I. N., Pagans and Holy Men, 600–800, in P. Ní Chatháin and M. Richter (eds.), *Irland und die Christenheit*, Stuttgart, 1987, 347–61.

Wood, I. N., Forgery in Merovingian Hagiography, *MGH*, *Schriften*, 33 (1988), 369–85.

Wood, I. N., Administration, law and culture in Merovingian Gaul, in R. McKitterick (ed.), *The Uses of Literacy in Early Medieval Europe*, Cambridge, 1990, 63–81.

Wood, I. N., The Franks and Sutton Hoo, in I. N. Wood and N. Lund (eds.), *People and Places in Northern Europe 500–1600. Essays in Honour of Peter Sawyer*, Woodbridge, 1991, 1–14.

Wood, I. N., *The Merovingian Kingdoms 450–751*, London, 1994.

Wood, I. N., Teutsind, Witlaic and the history of Merovingian *precaria*, in Davies and Fouracre (eds.), *Property and Power*, 31–52.

Wormald, P., Bede and the Conversion of England. The Charter Evidence, Jarrow Lecture, 1984.

Wright, R., *Late Latin and Early Romance in Spain and Carolingian France*, Liverpool, 1982.

Wright, R. (ed.), *Latin and the Romance Languages in the Early Middle Ages*, London, 1991.

Wright, R., The conceptual distinction between Latin and Romance: invention or evolution? in Wright (ed.), *Latin and the Romance Languages*.

Zöllner, E., Die Herkunft der Agilulfinger, *MIÖG*, 59 (1951), 245–64.

Index

The persons and works which are the subjects of individual chapters are not generally indexed when they occur in the chapters dedicated to them. For the careers of such persons and for the structure and authorship of the works which concern them the reader should consult the appropriate chapters.